Experimental Psychology

THE CENTURY PSYCHOLOGY SERIES

Richard M. Elliott, Gardner Lindzey & Kenneth MacCorquodale
Editors

BENTON J. UNDERWOOD
Northwestern University

Experimental Psychology

SECOND EDITION

New York

APPLETON-CENTURY-CROFTS

Division of Meredith Corporation

PREFACE TO FIRST EDITION

In 1946 I was faced with the problem of teaching a course in undergraduate experimental psychology with no available text seeming suitable for background reading. Therefore, I started to bring together certain materials to be mimeographed and issued to the students as a substitute for a text. These materials were revised and expanded from quarter to quarter until the present final draft was written.

I am of the opinion that subject matter (content) and methodology should not be divorced in an experimental course; one without the other is deadening. However, since I have done no acceptable research on these problems, my opinion may be in error. And although I set up the objective of continuous unification of method and content, I must add quickly that I was unable to attain the objective completely. At some point in the writing it became apparent that to keep the text to a reasonable size some omissions would be necessary. The major omissions, as I see them, should be pointed out. (1) Factual data on the sensory (discriminal) processes. I found that I could not handle adequately the factual relationships which have stemmed from the great flow of research in this area and still give a comprehensible account of the methods. I chose methods. (2) Physiology of sense organs and nervous system. Because this material is not unique to psychology it was excluded. (3) Details of apparatus construction. I have eliminated nearly all engineering from the book; references to a piece of apparatus are in terms of how it is used, not how it is made.

In mimeographed form the text has been used in a two-quarter course for which Elementary Statistics was a prerequisite, and in a year course where statistics was taught as an integral part of the methodology. I believe that the factual subject matter can be comprehended readily without a statistical knowledge, but a full appreciation of experimental design problems requires some statistical thinking.

The experimental illustrations used throughout are, for the most part, recently published. In most areas I believe the temper of contemporary research is accurately reflected. In some instances I have attempted to guess the future trends of experimentation. It will also be noted that I have reported some experiments which in my opinion were poorly conceived, executed, or interpreted. I think it is clear that I have done this for pedagogical reasons and with no thought of malice.

The entire final draft was read critically by R. M. Elliott, Editor of the Series, and by Claude E. Buxton and Kenneth MacCorquodale. Parts of the final draft were read by R. W. Kleemeier and C. P. Duncan, who were also kind enough to use the mimeographed edition in their classes and gather student reaction as well as make suggestions of their own for revision. To realize fully my indebtedness to all these men I need only glance over the many pencilled notes which they made on the drafts. Louise Underwood has contributed toward the clarifying of expression and has helped with the proofs. Marion Cisar checked the references and was able also to type and "unsplit" infinitives simultaneously.

Permission has been granted by many publishers and editors to reproduce figures or passages, and I gratefully acknowledge these permissions: The American Psychological Association for its several journals; Prof. R. S. Woodworth for *Archives of Psychology*; Prof. K. M. Dallenbach for *American Journal of Psychology*; Dr. Carl Murchison for *Journal of Psychology, Journal of General Psychology*, and *Journal of Genetic Psychology*; the editors or publishers of *Journal of Educational Psychology; Journal of Comparative Psychology; Psychiatry;* and *British Journal of Psychology*, and the following publishing firms: University of Chicago Press, University of Iowa Press, Duke University Press, Columbia University Press, Yale University Press, National Society for Study of Education, Appleton-Century-Crofts, Holt, Rinehart and Winston, Inc., Longmans, Green & Co., Ronald Press Company, and Harper & Row, Publishers. The original source is given in each case.

Evanston, Illinois   B.J.U.

PREFACE TO SECOND EDITION

Essentially, this is a new book; otherwise it would be impossible to reflect to any extent the changes which have occurred in our discipline since 1949. At the same time, however, those familiar with the original book will find many similarities. The emphasis on methods of experimentation is retained, and the discussion of these methods occurs within a substantial body of content. The intended omissions are much the same. Perhaps the range of issues brought to the attention of the undergraduate is somewhat broader than was true in the first edition. Nevertheless, only one major change in approach was deliberately introduced, namely, that the content areas covered were to be such as to allow students in even the most ill-equipped undergraduate laboratory to do meaningful experiments. Choosing these content areas involved both a consideration of the research that could be done with a minimum of equipment and a consideration of the areas which are currently active (as judged by published reports).

It is a pleasure to acknowledge again the assistance given by Kenneth MacCorquodale. The typing was quickly and accurately done by Elizabeth Curtis and Elizabeth Cassell. Special appreciation must be expressed to the several hundred ingenious experimentalists whose works have been used to provide illustrative material. Reports in the several journals of the American Psychological Association have contributed heavily to the book. The editors of other journals, sometimes in conjunction with the authors, have kindly given permission to use certain materials. These journals include *American Journal of Psychology, Quarterly Journal of Experimental Psychology, Perceptual and Motor Skills, Psychological Reports, Journal of Psychology,* and *Journal of General Psychology.*

B.J.U.

CONTENTS

CHAPTER ONE

Introduction

Certain business organizations have as their major task the establishment of credit ratings. Individuals as well as businesses ordinarily need some minimum credit rating in order to borrow money or open charge accounts. This whole enterprise is based on the simple but critical assumption that there is consistency in man's behavior. If the history of the financial dealings of a man shows that he has regularly met his financial obligations, it is assumed that in the future he will continue to respond in the same manner. If, on the contrary, a man's history shows that he has frequently made late payments to his debtors, has often changed his place of residence to avoid being easily contacted, or has had merchandise repossessed, it is assumed that he will be a poor credit risk in the future. Both men have behaved in a consistent manner in the past, and it is presumed that each man's responses in the future will parallel to some extent those of the past: one man will continue to assume only the financial obligations he can handle, the other will not.

If two 25-year-old men have been driving automobiles for eight years and have driven approximately the same number of miles under roughly the same conditions, and if one has a record of 15 accidents and the other a record of no accidents, one would expect that in subsequent years the former (if he survives) will have more accidents than the latter. The accident actuarial tables of insurance companies leave these concerns no alternative but to charge the "accident-prone" driver higher rates than they do the average person. Perhaps they may even refuse to issue him a policy.

These two illustrations of the consistency or regularity of behavior are given in order to make two points which are fundamental to our background thinking. The first is that nature, even as exemplified in the rather complex behavior of a single man, is predictable with some accuracy from relatively crude observations made over time. Generally speaking, our behavior is not chaotic or capricious. A person is not a saint one moment and a sinner the next; he is not successively a genius and an idiot; he is not a grouch at one instant and a jokester the next. Careful observations made over time allow us to predict behavior. Furthermore, the more frequent our observations, the better will be our predictions.

The second point to be made from the above illustrations is that once we have said that behavior shows regularities or is predictable from even relatively crude observations, there is little more to be said. If we ask *why* certain people have become poor credit risks and others have not, we have no evidence, from the actuarial tables, which gives us an answer. Nor do such tables tell us why some people have many accidents and others but few. Obtaining answers to this question of "why" usually requires a different technique of research. To illustrate this technique, we may use a new illustration.

Let us assume that a careful survey by dental technicians shows that in one area of the country, Area A, the number of cavities found in the teeth of children of school age is far greater than in an otherwise equivalent group of children living in Area B. Furthermore, the record shows that this difference has existed for many years. If we were to issue insurance policies to cover the costs of filling the dental cavities, it is apparent that our rates would have to be higher for Area A than for Area B. We are predicting that, since the behavior of teeth in the two areas has differed in the past, it will continue to differ in the future. But when we ask the question *why* the behavior of the teeth differs between the two areas, we have no answer. We must approach this question in quite another way. For example, the hypothesis might be suggested that the mineral content of the water in the two areas differs and that this is in some way responsible for the difference in the number of dental cavities. The hypothesis might specify a particular chemical element that is assumed to be responsible. We might, then, examine the water supplies in the two areas and see if they do differ in the amount of that particular element. If they do, our hypothesis remains a reasonable one, but we have not answered the *why* question. To do this, we must introduce the element into the water (or perhaps into the toothpaste) for one group of children in the high-cavity area and not allow it to be present for an equivalent group of children in the same area. If these two groups now develop cavities at different rates, we have answered the *why* question. We would be able to conclude that this particular element is in some way involved in production of cavities. This single experiment leaves many questions unanswered, but it has answered one question definitively.

The experimental methods provide the most satisfactory ones known at the present time for approximating a level of understanding that is characterized by providing an answer of "why" about a phenomenon under study.

These methods are the best we have for allowing a conclusion that a particular behavior is caused by some particular event or events. However, drawing valid cause-effect conclusions is a difficult intellectual occupation, and it is this evaluative statement which will frequently be documented throughout this book. But, simply because it is difficult, we cannot shy away from attempts to devise experiments which will allow specific cause-effect conclusions. As the illustrations above are presumed to show, other research methods may fall short of the experimental methods as vehicles for establishing cause-effect relationships. Nevertheless, all methods of research in psychology are pointed toward the same end—the understanding of behavior—and they differ only in the levels of understanding produced. These levels are not differences akin to black and white, and if we subsequently speak as if they were, it is merely as a means of keeping ideas distinct. More of this later.

There are three research approaches which are used in psychology as well as in other areas dealing with living organisms (e.g., botany, zoology). We will discuss each of these approaches and, at the same time, try to gain a further understanding of the problems involved in drawing cause-effect conclusions.

THREE APPROACHES TO RESEARCH

Naturalistic Observation

Careful and prolonged observations of animals and plants in a natural setting may be used to give a precise description of the behavior of these plants and animals. Such descriptions will provide case histories from birth to death of a number of organisms of a given species; and when these histories are combined, we have normative data on the flow of behavioral events of the species over the entire life cycle. A new member of the species may be expected to approximate the behavior of those previously studied, and thus we are able to predict the behavior of the new member. In exactly the same manner we are able to predict a high probability of automobile accidents for a given man if his history approximates the histories of men studied earlier who have had accidents.

Books on ornithology for bird watchers represent an outcome of naturalistic observation. Such books not only describe the physical characteristics of the birds but also indicate when the birds will migrate, where they will nest, how many eggs the female will lay, what song is characteristic of each bird, and so on. Some of the so-called baby-care books reproduce tables which tell when (at what age) one may expect a child to take his first step, utter his first word-like sound, or respond positively to toilet training. They offer these and many other statistics which may be viewed with great enchantment by a new mother. Such data were obtained merely by observing scores of infants and recording at what ages these various events did in fact happen. The expectations concerning a new infant, therefore, are based on what has been recorded previously for other infants. Predictions are based on actuarial-like tables. Our knowledge concerning the natural behavior of some of our more exotic animals in the wild has come from naturalistic observation. Thus, an investigator may live for weeks on the edge of a colony of gorillas in the mountains of Africa, carefully recording all of the behavioral events he observes.

Naturalistic observation is the recording of behavior as it occurs in a more or less naturalistic setting with no attempt to intervene. Such observations provide a description of the behavior to be expected from the future members of the species. These observations exhibit the phenomenon of nature upon which further research, using different procedures, may be undertaken to arrive at a more fundamental understanding than that provided by the naturalistic observations. Just how these different procedures may lead to a different level of understanding, and why their use is so frequently demanded, requires further elaboration. Again, the issue reverts to an understanding of "why." This is not an easy issue to comprehend. Let us look at some common events as a means of illustrating the nature of the problem which confronts us when we want to make cause-effect statements.

Assume that you have a pin in your hand and that you suddenly stick it with some force into the arm of the person sitting next to you. The act of pin-sticking is likely to be followed immediately by other acts in which the stickee jerks his arm, jumps, and screams. Any observer would probably conclude that the immediate cause for the exhibition of startled behavior was the pin in the arm. Such an inference seems inescapable and not open to argument. But, as a means of posing the kinds of questions which inevitably arise when we wish to make cause-effect statements, let us examine several aspects of this situation.

One of the implications of the above illustration is that causal inferences require close temporal contiguity between two events; if the pin had been stuck in the arm at 10:00 A.M. and the jumping and screaming had occurred at 5:00 P.M., we would be unlikely to draw a cause-effect conclusion between the two events. Indeed, the absurdity of a lag between cause and effect is an old and honored means of creating humor. However, close temporal contiguity between two events is not a sufficient condition for inferring cause and effect. Assume the pin was plunged into the arm at exactly 10:00 A.M. Assume further that a jet plane touched down on the runway at the airport ten miles away at exactly the same moment. The landing of the plane and the scream occurred in the same contiguous relationship (temporally) as did the pin-sticking and the scream. Perhaps the plane's landing caused the scream. Of course we would say that such a notion is ridiculous; and it is ridiculous because we impose additional requirements, whether we know it or not, when we infer a causal relation between two events. We say that we *know* that a plane landing ten miles away could not possibly have caused a scream, and to say this means that we are drawing on our previous learning or knowledge. Among other things, we usually impose a physical contiguity requirement before drawing cause-effect conclusions. But we are really doing more than this. We are making a fundamental assumption which underlies all research attempts: namely, that all events in the world cannot influence all other events. If this were not so, research would be a hopeless affair. We have to assume that a given event has a limited number of possible causes. An enormous number of events took place at 10:00 A.M. just before the scream; all cannot be involved in a causal way. We must assume that there is a limited number of events which can influence other events, and, formally, we speak of this as the assumption of *limited or finite causality*.

To say that the landing of a plane ten miles away from the location of the scream has nothing to do with the scream seems eminently reasonable; our notions of what are and what are not reasonable causes, our experience with pins and their consequences, and our imposition of spatial contiguity as a further requirement for inferring causation all make it much more reasonable to conclude that the pin rather than the plane is the cause.We would say that the close temporal contiguity between the landing plane and the scream is entirely fortuitous and one has nothing to do with the other. Yet we must realize that temporal contiguity between events is both a source of useful hypotheses about causal relationships as well as a source of superstition. Rainmaking dances may have been followed by rain with sufficient frequency to merit a conclusion that the dance was responsible for the rains. An occasional evil event on Friday the 13th may lead to the belief that Friday the 13th as such is a diabolical cause. We have no infallible criteria to distinguish between a superstition (a false notion concerning cause and effect) and a "reasonable" hypothesis about cause-effect relationships prior to the time we put each to experimental test.

In still another way we need to look at the pin-scream sequence. It is possible that the scream might have occurred had the pin *not* been thrust into the arm. Screams may occur for reasons other than a pin-thrust; for example, a sudden stomach pain might cause an outcry. Admittedly, it would be quite a coincidence had the stomach pain occurred just after the thrust of the pin, but it is not impossible that such an event could have occurred. As a matter of dogma, one might also say that the scream did not have a cause at all. It might be said that it just suddenly occurred, or that it occurred, as the common phrase goes, for no reason at all. For most people, however, what this means is that the cause is not obvious.

This much ado about pins and screams may result in some impatience. It seems clear, however, that even from an obvious or stark illustration of naturalistic observation, completely logical conclusions concerning cause-effect are not easy to reach. We were forced to the conclusion that the pin initiated the sequence of events leading to the scream on other than strictly logical grounds; that is, we had to impose experiential knowledge. We may now summarize and extend what seem to be the principle issues we should keep in mind in thinking about cause-effect sequences.

1. Temporal contiguity between events is a compelling factor in drawing cause-effect conclusions. Indeed, for our purposes, we may say that it is a necessary condition. But temporal contiguity alone is an insufficient basis. Millions of events are temporally contiguous each moment without cause-effect being involved. Furthermore, because nature is what it is, many events which are causally related appear to be separated in time. They appear to be because we cannot always observe the chain of events in between the *apparent* events which we observe. Certain food allergies are very difficult to detect by simple observational techniques. Eating lobster today may have no apparent effect on the lobster-sensitive person until 48 hours later. The lack of contiguity between the eating and the effect makes it difficult to perceive the relationship.

2. Generally speaking, in naturalistic observations we perceive events which are not only temporally contiguous but also spatially contiguous. If we require both spatial and temporal contiguity as necessary conditions for drawing cause-effect conclusions, we will rule out scores of potentially causal events which are temporally contiguous but not spatially contiguous.

3. Within this fairly restricted range of potential causes for an event, we still have a serious problem in drawing cause-effect conclusions from naturalistic observations. Usually there remain a number of events which are both spatially and temporally contiguous to the event for which we seek a cause, and we need some way to eliminate some of these possible causal agents. If we are dealing with an event with which we have had considerable experience, we can often eliminate many of the possibilities, and sometimes (as in the case of the scream) we can eliminate all but one. When we deal with observations of relatively new natural events, however, we literally get logically stuck in trying to reach a decision; and, rather than wait for extended and prolonged experience to give us a likely answer, we effect an economy by trying to determine the cause by other methods, usually by experimental methods.

4. We are also aware of two other implicit assumptions which dominate our thinking as we attempt to analyze cause-effect relationships. The first of these is the assumption of finite, or limited, causality, in which we reject the notion that every event in the world can influence every other event. We rejected the notion that the plane landing at the local airport produced the scream. So also would we reject the notion that a rock tumbling down the side of Mount Hood or that a hen depositing an egg in a nest on a farm in Iowa or that the rain falling on the plain in Spain was responsible for the scream. The fact that we were sincerely seeking a cause for an event implies that we assume the event did have a cause—that the event did not happen for no reason at all. In short, we assume that every natural event has a cause

and that if we look diligently we will find that cause. This notion is generally known as the principle of *determinism*.

The seeming inevitability of a causal relationship between obvious events (pin-thrust and scream) becomes less inevitable when we consider naturalistic observations with which we have had much less experience. Suppose you are sitting in a park. At the far side two boys are playing. A large black dog comes out of the woods and trots toward the boys. You note that the boys suddenly run—apparently away from the dog. You idly speculate that the boys ran because of fear of the dog. The dog-run sequence takes on the same cause-effect relationship as the pin-scream incident. It is clear, however, that you are speculating, for there are many other possible causes for the running behavior. It may be a coincidence that the appearance of the dog and the running were contiguous. Perhaps one of the boys said, "Let's go down to the creek." Perhaps they knew they were breaking some rule by playing in the park and had seen a police car approach. Perhaps they remembered that they were due home at a particular time and suddenly discovered they were late Thus, the appearance of the dog is only one of several possible causes for the boys' behavior. Furthermore, even if the dog did prompt the running, it is not at all clear that running was fear-induced. Perhaps the dog is a stray that likes to follow small boys home to get a handout; and the boys, remembering that their father has warned them never to bring the dog home again, decide to get away from the animal so that he can't follow them.

Now, of course, many repeated observations of essentially the same naturalistic event may remove some of the alternative interpretations simply on the grounds that potential causal events would be eliminated by not being present. Thus, if the dog appeared the next day when the same two boys were present, and this time the boys did not run, one might conclude that the running of the boys on the previous day was not dog-inspired. Or, suppose you ascertained that there was no police car in sight but noted, too, that again the boys ran when the dog appeared; certainly, this makes the police car a much less likely cause than it was the day before. It is only by extended observations of natural events that many potential causal factors can be ruled out. But in nature many, many natural events may inevitably occur together so that no decision can be reached as to their specific causes. Birds fly north in the spring in a predictable fashion. There are many changes in the environment which constitute spring, and they will always be present together. Which one or ones are responsible for the birds leaving their winter residences?

We must conclude that the technique of naturalistic observation is a very inefficient way to determine cause-effect relationships. At its worst, in the hands of one who does not think through the dangers, it may lead to quite false conclusions. At best, careful naturalistic observations provide data which may be extraordinarily fertile sources of hypotheses about cause-effect relationships which may be tested explicitly by experimental methods. In between these two extremes, systematic observation clearly identifies phenomena which will have to be explained and indicates certain potential causal factors which may be eliminated, leaving fewer others to "check out."

Correlational Approach

This method represents a more formal way than does naturalistic observation of determining relationships between events. Sometimes called the psychometric approach, it is a widely used research method in psychology and is sometimes employed hand in hand with the experimental approach. Like naturalistic observation, it does not provide clear evidence for inferring cause-effect relationships. It does determine whether or not two events are related and provides a quantitative index of the degree of relationship if they are related.

Research in psychology using correlational techniques is most closely identified with use of standardized tests. It is a rare high-school senior today who is admitted to college without having taken at least one battery of tests given by national organizations set up to provide this service. The notion of these tests is basically simple; since there *is* a relationship between the performance exhibited on the tests and the academic performance in college, one can predict (with some margin of error) that good performance on tests will be followed by good performance in course work in college and that poor performance on the tests will be followed by poor performance in the course work in college. That there is a certain amount of error—the correlation between the two performances is far from perfect—indicates that the performances of two sets of skills do not completely overlap. It would seem that success in academic pursuits in college involves something in addition to the skills measured by the achievement tests. It is, perhaps, needless to say that there are many tests available—personality tests, tests of mechanical skills, sales skills, and so on. If it can be shown that the scores on these are related to other skills (e.g., if tests of finger dexterity predict the assembly skill of workers), we usually say that the tests are valid. It should be clear, however, that in our thinking we must not limit the term *correlation* to the testing approach only. Any relation is a correlation, and research endeavors to seek relationships by other methods as well. Yet, we must not lump everything together, for, as we shall see later, a more detailed examination of the different approaches provides some fairly fundamental differences. For the moment it is sufficient to note that, like the data derived from naturalistic observation, the correlation approach does not provide very good evidence for making cause-effect statements.

Let us take another example to show the relationship between the method of naturalistic observation and correlational approach. At the current time, certain data have provided a serious problem for public health authorities.

By systematic and careful naturalistic observation it has been determined beyond doubt that among men, at least, the greater the number of years that the individual has smoked cigarettes, the higher the probability that lung cancer will develop. Or, to cite another fact, if two individuals have smoked for the same number of years, the one who has smoked the greater number of cigarettes per day has a greater likelihood of developing lung cancer than the individual who has smoked a smaller number per day. These facts can be expressed in correlational terms: (1) the longer the period smoked, the greater the frequency of lung cancer; and (2) the greater the number of cigarettes smoked, the greater the number of lung cancers. These facts are clear; what, however, do we make of them with regard to cause-effect conclusions? Considering only these facts, cause and effect is in doubt. Perhaps those people who smoke the greatest amount would have developed more lung cancers than those who smoke a small amount even if none in either group had ever smoked. There *is* another difference between the two groups: namely, one group smoked a lot and the other didn't, and whatever the trait is that produced the difference in amount smoked may also be related to other characteristics or behaviors which are responsible for cancer.

The problem posed by these data has raised serious controversies, for, if indeed there is a clear causal relationship between smoking and lung cancer, consideration of the welfare of the public is of utmost importance. If, however, the relationship is a fortuitous one, then a large industry may be unjustly penalized. Just how these issues will be resolved is not clear at the present time. The only thing that is clear is that those concerned with the problem realize that other methods of research would be most helpful in determining the appropriate conclusion. In fact, these researchers are turning to the experimental approach via the use of lower animals. By introducing tobacco tars into the environment of one group of rats and not into that of another group, the experimenters can then make comparisons concerning the incidence of cancerous growths for the two groups. What we are saying, of course, is that at the present time we have no other procedures of research which so efficiently and quickly lead us to a position where cause-effect statements can be made as do the experimental methods. Again, however, let us not be misled; all research methods are valuable. Different methods give different levels of understanding. The experimental method is not a guarantee of the production of truth about nature as we seek it in cause-effect relationships. It is the most efficient and most nearly foolproof procedure we have, but in an absolute sense it is neither speedy nor foolproof.

The Experimental Method

Merely as a contrast with the other two methods discussed, we will give only the general notion of the experimental method here. The basic idea is that of controlling factors which may influence the phenomenon under study. More particularly, it is the not on that all factors are held constant except one, and this one is varied in soi ie manner to determine whether or not it influences the phenomenon. What it means to hold factors constant and what it means to vary one may be allowed to stand with no elaboration at the present time, although how in fact factors are held constant and how in fact one is manipulated requires much elaboration. In the abstract, the logic is straightforward. If nothing is allowed to change expect one factor and if behavior changes as this factor changes, it may be concluded that this factor is in some sense a cause for the noted change in behavior.

Does cigarette smoking cause cancer? If we were to use the experimental method to answer this question, we would get two groups of subjects prior to the usual beginning age of smoking. Then, at a certain point in time, one of the groups would be required to smoke a certain number of cigarettes each day over a period of years and the other would be prohibited from smoking. Periodic examinations of the subjects in each group would be made to determine the presence or absence of cancerous growths. If the smoking groups developed more such growths than the nonsmoking, it would probably be concluded that smoking is indeed one cause of cancer. It is clear why such an experiment has not been, and is not likely to be, carried out. People— the subjects—probably would not tolerate the necessary intrusion into their private lives; some would resist not being allowed to smoke and some would balk at being forced to smoke. Such a state of affairs will be found many times. That is, there are many instances in which the experimental method cannot be used, not because it would not give a clear answer to a question, but because our society is so constituted that it is impossible to impose the controls necessary for adequate application of the method. Nevertheless, such controls can be imposed under certain circumstances, as was true in the test of the Salk polio vaccine. Here, one group was given the vaccine, and another was not; differences in the incidence of polio for the two groups were tabulated during the months following.

To repeat: the basic idea of an experiment is simple but powerful. One group of subjects is treated in one fashion, another in a different fashion, and we determine if behavior differs as a consequence of the different treatments. If the idea of an experiment is so simple, why must we spend so much time in learning how to do experiments? The fact is that between the idea and its appropriate implementation by experimental procedures, there are many pitfalls.

Enough prologue. Let us get down to the business of establishing a common understanding of terminology.

BASIC CONCEPTS

We have been discussing cause-effect relationships; certain events are said to precede or antedate certain other events and are responsible for these latter events. When studying behavior, these antecedent or causal events are known as *stimulus events;* those which are caused and those which are said to constitute the behavior in which we are interested are called *response events.* Usually, we speak of them merely as stimuli and responses: what stimuli do produce changes in behavior (responses), what stimuli do not. Of course, it is clear that certain stimuli will be related to certain responses and not to others; and it is a part of the research process to evolve such distinctions, to classify them, and to determine the precise relationships between stimuli and responses which are related.

Stimulus and Response

Stimulus. A stimulus is always some form of physical energy, and as such may be measurable by instruments which other disciplines, notably physics, may provide us. Thus, the characteristics of sound, light, temperature, and so on may be measured precisely. So also may radio waves, gamma waves, and various forms of cosmic radiation. But not all such physical energy may be related to behavior; one of the tasks of research of psychology is to determine what physical energies *are* related to behavior. Radio waves acting directly on the organism are not known to influence behavior, but this may be because the behavior they influence has not been detected. Indeed, ionizing radiation has been found to influence motivation of animals, but it is not completely clear at this time what systems of the organism are involved.

While we must accept the premise that stimuli are always physical in nature, it would be quite misleading to insist that in our research we always specify the stimuli in terms of measuring scales provided us by the physical sciences. That is, we can by no means specify the relevant aspects of many stimuli by referring to inches, to millimicrons, or to pounds. We have to devise our own scales, and these scales may not at all reflect in any known way the physical differences of the events we are calling stimuli. Four other points should be made with regard to stimuli.

1. Certain stimuli are known to influence behavior; others are not known to do so. The former may be called *relevant stimuli.* Those that are not known to influence behavior fall into two classes. It may be that certain stimuli have been investigated and have been shown to have no influence on a certain response. These might well be called irrelevant stimuli for this particular behavior—this response—but at the same time they might be relevant for other responses. There are many other stimuli whose effects are unknown simply because they have not been introduced or varied in an experimental situation. These we will call *potential stimuli.*

2. We are most likely to think of stimuli as events originating outside the organism: a loud noise (causing a startle); a red light (producing a brake-depressing response). While it is true that many of our responses are initiated by external energy changes to which sense organs, in direct contact

with the external environment (exteroceptors) are sensitive, it must be recognized also that many stimuli are internal in origin, influencing sense organs not in direct contact with the external environment (interoceptors). A hunger pang is just as truly a stimulus as a sound wave.

3. Stimuli will often be referred to as stimulus variables, indicating that a given stimulus may in some sense be considered to vary (or be varied) in amount, degree, or kind. To include both kind and amount requires further discussion, but this matter is more conveniently elaborated at a later point. Finally, we may note, a stimulus variable is often referred to as the *independent variable*.

4. Some stimulus variables which we deal with are not easily thought of as representing either momentary events or forms of physical energy. Variables of this type might better be thought of as states of the organism and are illustrated by such factors as age, heredity, and birth order. We will speak of such variables as *subject variables*.

Response. A response is some observable change in behavior. To acquire a conception of what constitutes behavior, one must take a very broad view. A change in the amplitude of a brain wave is just as much a response as is the selection of a particular alternative on a multiple-choice test. A simple eyeblink is a response; so is a decision of an executive to invest 50 million dollars in plant expansion. An increase in the heart rate is a change in behavior, but so is the running of a rat in a maze. Under no circumstances should we restrict our thinking by the size or presumed importance of a response when we are thinking merely of what may constitute a response. Of course, all responses, to be useful, must be in some sense measurable. As we shall see, what constitutes measurement ranges all the way from simple counting of frequency of responses to making very precise measurements.

Paralleling the terminology for the stimulus, we will often speak of *response variable*—the behavior which is measured in an experiment. Furthermore, the response variable is commonly referred to as the *dependent variable*.

Experimental Framework

Using the diagram of Fig. 1-1, we may summarize one way of looking at the organism as a vehicle for attempting to understand experimentally the laws of nature as exhibited in the behavior of organisms. It is recognized that from within and from without, there is a multitude of stimuli impinging upon the organism. Responses may also become stimuli for subsequent responses. The experimental task is to hold all except one of these stimuli constant, and this one we manipulate or vary as our experiment demands. If we can show that the behavior changes in some fashion as the stimulus changes, we have established one causal variable involved in the particular behavior we are measuring.

Figure 1-1 also indicates that the organisms which we experiment on may produce many distinguishable different responses in a given situation. If a subject is learning a difficult list of words he may, in addition to attempting to recite the words, perspire, shuffle his feet, swear, blink his eyes, daydream, lick his lips, wring his hands, or bite his fingernails. Few investigators will attempt to measure all such responses exhibited by a subject in a given situation. Rather, they may select one or two particular responses for measure-

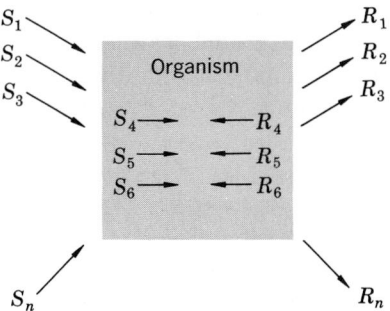

Fig. 1-1. The experimental framework of psychology. $S_1, S_2, \ldots S_n$ indicate stimulus events of an unknown number both in the environment and in the organism. $R_1, R_2, \ldots R_n$ indicate responses of the organism to the stimuli. Responses "turned back in" the organism (R_4, R_5, R_6) take note of the fact that responses may in turn become stimuli influencing later responses. Experimental psychology at the empirical level is concerned with the discovery of the laws which hold between the stimulus events and the response events. If this diagram seems lifeless, consider the square a torso and add legs, arms, and a head.

ment, the selection being made on many different grounds in different situations. But it is a fact, as research within an area develops, that the same responses may be used over and over by the same and by different investigators. We shall see that this may have both virtues and evils.

For some it is convenient to think of stimulus variables as inputs into the organism and of the responses as outputs. But by any conception in experimental work, we ask the straightforward empirical question, "What stimuli influence what responses?"

Classes of Stimulus Variables

We will find it useful to identify three different classes of stimulus variables. Problems of control and manipulation of these classes differ somewhat, and we will often find it worthwhile to identify the particular class to which a stimulus variable belongs in order to understand the problems we face in controlling or varying it.

Task variables. Nearly every experiment involves some sort of apparatus on which or with which the subject performs. Sometimes this performance involves only the use of pencil and paper; sometimes it involves the use of very complex apparatus, such as a simulated airport control tower. When we refer to task variables we mean the characteristics of the apparatus or of the problem involved in the performance. Even casual observation would support the notion that differences in task variables will reflect differences in behavior. The complexity of an algebra problem may determine whether or not it will be solved; the number of blind alleys in a maze will determine the rate at which an animal learns to traverse the maze; the characteristics of a baseball will determine how far it is batted.

Environmental variables. Any experiment is done in a context or setting. Characteristics of this setting, which are not a part of the task as such, are called environmental variables. The most literal translation of the word *environment* suggests such factors as temperature, humidity, or amount of light; and these are indeed classed as environmental variables. But we may range further. Passage of time, for example, is one of the most frequently manipulated environmental variables. In a social psychology experiment we might manipulate the number of people observing the subject as he attempts to perform a task. Any factor which is not identified as a physical part of the task would be considered an environmental variable.

Subject variables. Subjects on whom we experiment differ in many characteristics. Characteristics which may immediately occur to us are age, sex, height, intelligence, sense of humor, anxiety, and so on. Even the white rat, used a great deal in behavioral research, has been bred to produce different strains showing different emotional attributes. There is almost an unlimited number of characteristics on which the subjects, human or animal, may differ. Some of these are probably relevant variables for the behavior we are interested in.

The above-mentioned subject variables represent differences which the subject brings to the situation, but there are other types of subject variables which are induced by the experimenter. If one group of subjects is given a pep pill before performing a task and another is not, we are inducing a difference in subject variables. Or if we want to determine the influence of Task A on the learning of Task B, we give one group of subjects Task A before Task B, and to the other we give no task before Task B. Thus, as we are introducing experimentally a difference in the subjects, we ask if this influences subsequent behavior. Another type of experimenter-induced subject variable is often called an *instructional* variable. If, before attempting to do a task or solve a problem, one group of subjects is given one set of instructions and another is presented quite a different set, performance may be shown to differ. If one group of rats is "instructed" by pretraining on a given task and another is not, performance may differ as a consequence. We will find that to draw a distinction between natural subject variables and induced subject variables is of great importance when we start to draw cause-effect conclusions from manipulating subject variables.

Dimensions

As we pursue the task of getting some terminology problems settled, we must introduce the term *dimension*. At times, two phrases will be used, *stimulus dimension* and *response dimension*. When any given phenomenon or event can be demonstrated to vary reliably (consistently) with respect to some specific characteristic, we have a dimension. The characteristic may be one of many things. In the physical world, weight, length, and temperature are some of the scales used to describe phenomena; and the particular characteristic so described is said to be dimensionalized. As we have previously noted, many stimuli used in behavioral studies may be described along such physical scales and hence are said to be described by physical dimensions. However, in psychology, many stimuli and responses cannot be described meaningfully by such physical scales, at least not at the present time. Yet, it can be shown that these stimuli and responses do vary reliably in amount. Verbal units have a very obvious difference, which we call meaningfulness. The unit UQR has lower meaningfulness than CAT, yet we do not at the present time have any way to express this difference by using a physical scale. Therefore, we must speak of a psychological dimension which, in this case, is a psychological stimulus dimension. Such psychological stimulus dimensions can be established simply because different people respond to verbal units in much the same fashion, thus giving the required reliability.

Why use the term *dimension?* Isn't variable as a term sufficient? Not quite. This is most clearly seen with regard to stimulus variables. We have used the term *variable* to specify differences in stimulus conditions which differ in degree (or amount) and *kind*. Stimuli which differ in kind are those for which it is difficult to describe the differences on common scales, either physical or psychological scales. Yet, stimuli which differ in kind may be used in experimental work, if for no other reason than that the solutions to certain problems demand that they be used. Suppose, for example, we ask the question of whether learning occurs more rapidly by auditory presentation or by visual presentation of the material to be learned. We would readily admit that these are distinctly different stimulus conditions, but how, on what scales, do we describe the difference? Almost all we can say is that one is "through the eye" and the other "through the ear." Such differences are often spoken of as qualitative differences.

Unitary and complex dimensions. In defining a dimension, it was indicated that the phenomenon or event must be shown to vary reliably in amount with respect to some specific characteristic. Actually, this is an ideal; we may have dimensions of a certain level of usefulness which are made up of a complex of characteristics. For example, we might be able to obtain perfectly reliable judgments concerning the "degree of adjustment" of individuals. Such judgments may be based on some composite weighting of a number of different characteristics, such as anxiety shown, dreams had, fingernail biting, and many others. But, if such judgments can be reliably made—if different judges agree on the degrees for individuals—we have a reliable but complex dimension. In mentioning meaningfulness of verbal units as a dimension, we may seem to have implied that meaningfulness is a unitary dimension, whereas, in fact, it is now believed that several different highly related factors go together to make up this dimension.

Perfectly sound and systematic relationships can be determined between complex stimulus dimensions and behavior. We must be very careful, however, not to conclude that all characteristics making up the dimension are responsible for the relationship obtained; it is quite possible that only one characteristic, or a combination of several characteristics, is involved. This is a difficult analytical problem to which we must expose ourselves many times in order to get a clear picture of the issue, and this we will do at various points throughout the book. Unitary dimensions are an ideal, and undoubtedly one of the signs of progress in research is shown by our ability to break up a complex dimension into its more unitary characteristics.

Numbers and dimensions. Physical scales almost always involve numbers; hence, physical stimulus dimensions are described by reference to numbers reflecting differences in magnitude of the characteristic. So also may psychological dimensions be described along a scale in which numbers are used. Thus, we could have nine degrees of meaningfulness, represented successively by the numbers from 1 to 9. But we shall see that we must be careful about interpreting differences between successive numbers when assigned rather arbitrarily, indeed, often cavalierly, in such manner. But we do not have to assign numbers to our dimensionalized characteristics; words serve quite well. Meaningfulness groupings might be termed "high," "moderate," "low," "moderate-to-low," "moderate-to-high," and so on. Indeed, we are not required to have numbers for physical scales in order to describe differences reliably. We would get complete agreement among observers that the Empire State Building is taller than the Brooklyn Bridge, that the Brooklyn Bridge is taller than a particular tree on Madison Avenue, that the tree is taller than an advertising executive, and that the man is taller than his wife. This is not to avoid numbers for they give us a level of precision that words do not. Numbers, however, may also be misleading in that they may suggest properties of phenomena which may not in fact exist. We must be thoughtful about what numbers mean (or do not mean) whenever we see them applied to psychological dimensions.

As various experiments are reviewed in subsequent chapters, there will be ample opportunity for review of the concepts introduced above in a somewhat abstract fashion. We will find that the use of these concepts in our thinking will provide us a common basis for discussion.

TOPICAL COVERAGE

The range of topics or phenomena to which the experimental psychologist applies his method is immense. One may document this statement by examining the titles of experimental reports appearing in recent issues of journals published by the American Psychological Association. A

TABLE 1-1
TITLES OF SOME EXPERIMENTAL REPORTS APPEARING IN THE
AUGUST, 1965, ISSUES OF FIVE DIFFERENT JOURNALS PUBLISHED
BY THE AMERICAN PSYCHOLOGICAL ASSOCIATION

Journal of Experimental Psychology
  "Transfer of training across target sizes"
  "Relationship between static and dynamic visual acuity"
  "Effect of UCS strength on GSR conditioning: A within-subject design"
  "Short-term memory under work-load stress"
  "Tachistoscopic recognition thresholds, paired-associate learning, and free recall
    as a function of abstractness-concreteness and word frequency"
  "Relationship between latency and remoteness in preference judgments"
  "Discriminability and scaling of linear extent"
  "Reminiscence and forgetting in a runway"
  "Expected value and response uncertainty in multiple-choice decision behavior"
  "Graded contrast effects in the judgment of lifted weights"
Journal of Comparative and Physiological Psychology
  "Classical and instrumental conditioning with septal stimulation as reinforcement"
  "Decrements in avoidance behavior following mammillothalamic tractotomy in
    rats and subsequent recovery with d-amphetamine"
  "Auditory avoidance behavior after extensive and restricted neocortical lesions
    in the rat"
  "One-way and two-way learning and transfer of an active avoidance response in
    normal and cingulectomized cats"
  "Stimulus generalization along the dimension of angularity: A comparison of
    training procedures"
  "Probability learning in the T maze with noncorrection"
  "Readiness to eat: Effects of age, sex, and weight loss"
  "Effect of early environment upon later social preference in two species of mice"
  "Color vision in the Cebus monkey"
  "Detour learning and development in the domestic chick"

"Effects of water current on responses of planaria to light"
"Cue dominance in oddity discriminations by Rhesus monkeys"
"Sexual behavior of male rats after one to nine days without food"
"Spontaneous alternation and response to stimulus change in the ferret"
Journal of Applied Psychology
"Team-training effectiveness under various conditions"
"Radar target detection as a function of search area and viewing distance"
"Risk-taking set and target detection performance"
"Some effects of vibration upon visual performance"
"Effect of brand preference upon consumers' perceived taste of turkey meat"
Journal of Personality and Social Psychology
"Dream reporting following abrupt and gradual awakenings from different types of sleep"
"Studies in efficiency: Muscle-action patterns in reaction time as related to inhibition of eyelid conditioning"
"Effects of manipulated self-esteem on persuasibility depending on threat and complexity of communication"
"Ego involvement and the absolute judgment of attitude statements"
"Cognitive reorganization following disconfirmed expectancy"
Journal of Abnormal Psychology
"Mental activity at sleep onset"
"Rote learning in schizophrenic and normal subjects under positive and negative reinforcement conditions"
"Alcoholism and psychological differentiation: Effect of alcohol on field dependence"
" 'Defense' against traumatic concepts"
"Temporal effects of LSD-25 and epinephrine on verbal behavior"
"Commonality and stability of word association responses in good and poor premorbid schizophrenics"

sample of such titles is given in Table 1-1. It appears that the experimental psychologist can control everything except his curiosity. Consequently, he finds himself applying his methods to a most amazing diversity of phenomena and to an equally diverse number of organisms.

We will not deal with so wide a range of topics in this text as suggested in Table 1-1. Selection must occur. One criterion used in this selection has led to a choice of topics which present reasonable possibilities of doing meaningful new experiments in the undergraduate laboratory. The imposition of such a limitation eliminates certain areas of research with which you will become familiar in a factual or textbook manner in other courses. One of the most obvious omissions is the area known as physiological psychology. Research in all areas has increased in an astounding fashion since World War II, but none has made a more dramatic increase than physiological psychology. Let us examine briefly the nature of the work which may be pursued by a physiological psychologist.

Earlier, considerable time was spent in discussing the impediments to arriving at cause-effect statements. This discussion was limited to attempting to isolate a particular stimulus as it was "fed into" the organism. Obviously, the organism lies, in a manner of speaking, between this input and the behavior we measure. The physiological psychologist is often interested in pursuing this causal chain in an attempt to understand physiologically how "this" input results in "that" output. Understandably, therefore, much of his work is at the neurological level. Indeed, the responses he measures are often not what one thinks of when we say behavior. Measurements may be made of the electrical activity of the auditory cortex of the cat as a function of the intensity or frequency of a sound wave. Or, the investigator may study the changes in certain proteins in the cortex as a function of learning. By still another common method, he may induce physiological subject differences and determine the effect on gross behavior. What is the effect of lesions in different regions of the hypothalamus on the maze learning of the rat?

It is not to be concluded that there is a clear distinction between the work of the physiological psychologist and of other researchers in psychology. Measurements of physiological activity may be taken as supporting measures by an investigator who is not primarily interested in the physiological aspects as such. For example, an investigator may have a theory which states that the anxiety of the subject is related to rate of eyelid conditioning. While one measure of anxiety may be obtained by a paper and pencil test, it might be of some relevance to show that those subjects said by the test scores to have high anxiety differ on certain physiological measures from those who are said to have low anxiety. Thus, high-anxious subjects might have more rapid heart rate or higher palmar sweating.

Certain research reports appearing in journals normally thought of as carrying physiological studies might seem to be closely related to the area of social psychology. For example, an investigator may raise chickens in complete isolation from other chickens and then at a certain point in time determine what influence this isolation has on the social or flocking behavior. So, let us not conclude that we are dealing with a unique area of research when we speak of physiological psychology. Nevertheless, we must recognize that to do research of a strictly physiological nature requires special knowledge and often special skills; in the present study of experimental psychology, we must minimize discussion of such research.

A clear distinction must be made between an understanding of research methods and research *techniques*. This distinction may be seen initially in an illustration of the difference. A few years ago it was discovered that electrical stimulation delivered to certain areas of the brain of the rat produced approximately the same effect in learning as did a pellet of food fed to the animal. Thus, if a rat which has been given the task of learning a right turn in a maze is cortically stimulated following a right turn, the number of right turns on successive trials is increased. This discovery appeared to open up an entire new perspective on the processes by which rewards influence behavior. To perform an experiment on cortical stimulation requires certain techniques which are quite distinct from a knowledge of experimental design. Cortical stimulation of the animal is provided by inserting a microelectrode into the brain. To make these implantations of electrodes, which are relatively permanent fixtures, demands considerable surgical skill. Also required is a special knowledge in construction of the apparatus for producing the electrical stimulation through the electrode. To have the operative skills and the electronic skills does not at all insure that appropriate research designs will be used to determine the influence of cortical stimulation on whatever behavior the investigator is interested in. A good surgeon might have the operative technique to produce a beautiful implantation of the electrode but not have the faintest idea of how to design the experiment. An electrode engineer might devise a precise timing circuit to deliver the cortical stimulation at the appropriate moment but not know how to design the experiment to determine what effect the stimulation has on behavior.

The development of technical skill, as distinct from skill in the design of experiments, is not limited to the area of physiological psychology. We are told that it takes a special skill in working with schizophrenic patients to insure that they will cooperate in an experiment. The present author might be able to design an adequate experiment to test a given hypothesis about schizophrenic individuals but would be hopeless, initially, as the actual experimenter since he has had no experience in handling such patients. A person who understands the "personalities" of monkeys is a very valuable adjunct to a primate laboratory, but a person with this "technical" skill may not be the appropriate person to design the experiment in which the monkeys will be used.

The above discussion is relevant to a point made earlier: most of our time will be spent on topics or phenomena around which experiments can be done rather readily in the laboratory without having to spend much time or study in developing techniques of experimentation. Elaborate technical skills can be developed only through long experience, specialized training, or both. Since our emphasis is on research design rather than techniques, the major topical areas to be studied are those which minimize technique learning but still allow us to cover a wide range of problems associated with the design and interpretation of experiments for all classes of stimulus variables.

OBJECTIVES OF STUDY

There are three objectives for the material in this book and for the accompanying experiments to be performed in your laboratory.

1. The major purpose is to provide a wide variety of experiences in the

design of experiments and in the analysis of data derived from the experiments. The number of experiments which can be done in conjunction with your reading is far too few to provide firsthand experience with the variety of problems which arise in experimental work. For this reason much is to be gained by studying problems which other investigators have had to cope with and by learning how they handled them. Such study provides symbolic practice in handling many problems which occur in designing experiments. This is not to say that the experiments which you may do in the laboratory are of little importance for learning how the research process proceeds in psychology. Indeed, there is no substitute for "live" data; there is no substitute for following personally the progress of an experiment from the inception of the problem to the conclusions reached about the issue as a result of the data obtained. Usually this will involve a written report since this is the final and a critical part of the research process. As you will discover, there are special writing skills involved in reporting research, and, again, only by practice can such skills be developed. That you may be a writer of interesting letters or an aspiring novelist does not necessarily mean that you also possess the somewhat unique discipline and orderliness of thought which produces a research report. A report, although apparently impersonal, is as much a work of art as a fine poem. A systematic set of data has a beauty of its own, but this beauty is enhanced when placed in logical juxtaposition with a problem, a method, and an evaluation. So let us not conceive of experimental research methods in a narrrow way; research is a series of steps, and all must be viewed together if we are to experience them in a manner which leads to maximum understanding.

2. In the process of learning experimental methods, we will deal with many facts of behavior. Often the understanding of why a particular experiment was done depends upon a knowledge of what has been found by previous investigators. We will not attempt to learn experimental methods in a vacuum; we will want to learn some of the laws which govern the appearance of, or the magnitude of, a given phenomenon. It is a truism of research that the more advanced our factual knowledge of a given phenomenon becomes, the more refined the experimental designs become when used to investigate that phenomenon further. Various illustrations of this relationship between knowledge and experimental designs will be pointed out in the subsequent chapters. Often your instructor will supplement the facts of behavior given here with other facts, particularly those in his own area of research interest.

So we must learn *some* facts of behavior; we must learn concepts; we must learn names of apparatuses and what they are used for, although we need not necessarily know about the "internal workings" of such devices in order to use them in research. A thorough understanding of a given topic of research will involve a historical perspective on the topic. To ignore the work done on a given phenomenon over the years results not only in a form of scholarly bigotry but also in a lack of comprehension of how the current problem about the phenomenon evolved. We cannot, of course, provide this historical perspective for the many topics to be covered. However, as illustrative of the evolution of a topic, we will provide the historical perspective for some. Sometimes, although the entire history of a phenomenon may extend back only a few years, the work on it may have been so intensive that it might be used to illustrate the evolution of research on a topic over many decades when the research proceeded at a slower pace.

3. The third objective of our study is concerned with the thought processes by which an investigator comes to study the effect of a particular variable in a particular experiment. "How did this investigator come to do this particular experiment?" There is no set answer to this question. An experiment may be done simply to find out what will happen. These I-wonder-what-will-happen experiments are essentially the translation of a quizzical expression into a set of experimental operations. This does not necessarily mean that the investigator does not at least have a hunch about what may happen, although he has not formalized this hunch in any sense. Sometimes a hypothesis about how a variable will influence behavior may arise from naturalistic observation, systematic or unsystematic. Sometimes a variable shown to be effective in influencing the behavior of a rat may be tried on a human subject to test the generality of the variable. Sometimes a more or less formal theory is involved from which the investigator deduces that a given phenomenon should occur if a given variable is manipulated.

We must realize that there is no one way of getting to an experimental problem; there is no one way of arriving at a decision to investigate the influence of a particular variable. There are many ways, and we will illustrate these many ways. Furthermore, we may sometimes go beyond the apparent bases by which an experiment is introduced and speculate a little about the thought processes of the investigator which led him to the investigation. This prying into the mind may give some insights into the research process which are not entirely apparent in the written report.

SUMMARY

Three types of research approaches were described: (1) naturalistic observation, (2) the correlational or psychometric approach, and (3) the experimental method. The application of these different approaches results in somewhat different levels of understanding of behavior. The purpose of the experimental approach is to reach as quickly as possible the level of understanding which allows a specification of cause-effect relationships.

An experiment requires a minimum of two different treatments. That is, one group of subjects is treated in one way and a second, in another way. If the behavior of the two groups differs, we say that the differences in the behavior are in some sense caused by the differences in the treatments. Treatments are commonly spoken of as stimulus events or independent variables or stimulus variables; behavior is spoken of as response events or dependent variables or response variables. When either of these classes of variables is shown to vary reliably in amount with respect to some specific characteristic, we speak of stimulus dimensions and response dimensions. Either numbers or words may be used to indicate differences in quantity, and the dimensions may be unitary or complex.

Three classes of stimulus variables were identified: (1) environmental variables, (2) task variables, and (3) subject variables. The latter class consists of two subclasses. There are subject variables which are a property of the subject as such, and he carries them with him and brings them to the laboratory (e.g., age or sex). Other differences among subjects may be induced by the investigator in the laboratory.

After limiting the scope of the topics to be covered, three objectives were stated: (1) designing sound experiments, (2) learning some facts of behavior, and (3) acquiring a knowledge of the various ways by which investigators have come to perform particular experiments.

CHAPTER TWO

Time Perception

We are able to respond in a selective or discriminative fashion to the enormous complex of stimuli which impinge upon us at all times. We tend to take it for granted that, because we are what we are, certain stimuli will cause us to respond in one way, other stimuli will bring about quite a different response, and some apparent stimuli will elicit no noticeable response. The selective capacity of the organism, that is, the ability to respond in different ways to different stimuli, presupposes what we shall call the *discriminal processes*. We are constantly exercising these processes, as shown by such discriminating reports as "It is raining" or "It isn't raining"; "This coat is a darker brown than that one"; "That mountain peak must be about thirty miles away"; "These fence posts are out of line"; "This type is more difficult to read than that type"; "She has changed the color of her hair." The study of the discriminal processes represents one of the oldest areas in which the experimental methods have been applied in psychology. In the initial chapters the topics, or subject matter, represent samples of phenomena associated with the discriminal processes.

We will initiate our study of experimental design by examining some of the procedures which have been used to study phenomena associated with the perception or judgment of temporal duration. When we say that we will study phenomena associated with judgments of time, we mean that we will examine the variations of judgments of temporal duration as a function of certain independent variables. It should be emphasized that time perception as an area of study should be given no special significance. Time perception is used here primarily as a vehicle for examining problems in experimental design, but any one of several other areas of study could have been used equally well to achieve this end. However, having chosen it as a vehicle, we will treat it with the respect we owe any area of study.

That certain situations or conditions will influence our judgments of elapsed time can probably be supported by incidental experiences all of us have had. Fifteen minutes in a waiting room, in a boring class, or under intense pain may seem like an eternity; fifteen minutes dancing at a gay party, reading an exciting novel, or viewing a gripping movie may seem but moments. Such observations—unsystematic naturalistic observations—may lead to precise experimental tests of judgments of length of time intervals as a function of the nature of the activity we engage in during those intervals. The investigator may "feed in" different kinds of activities during intervals and obtain from the subjects judgments or estimates of the length of the intervals. Thus, the nature of the activity is said to be one of many potential stimulus variables which may influence the accuracy of judgments of temporal durations.

Before considering specifically the manner in which we may design an experiment to study the influence of an independent variable on time perception, some preliminary discussion is needed concerning the minimum requirements which must be met before we have an experiment and, also, some of the initial decisions which must be made in designing an experiment.

EXPERIMENT VS. DEMONSTRATION

We will insist that an experiment has been performed only if the effects of at least two different conditions have been determined. By different conditions we mean different treatments or different values of an independent variable. This is to be contrasted with procedures which result in a *demonstration*. A demonstration usually means a procedure in which a single condition is present or one treatment is applied. If thirty seconds elapse between two discrete events and each of a group of students is asked to judge how long the interval was, we have a demonstration of time judgments. We may find that on the average the students estimated the interval to be 27.5 seconds, thus allowing us to say that for this interval there is an underestimation of true duration. But we have not, in this demonstration, determined the *differential* effects of two (or more) conditions or treatments; and such is necessary before we have a true experiment. Therefore, in our thinking, we must always start with the idea that at least two different treatments must be applied before we may talk about an experiment. Given measurements of behavior under these two treatments, we are able to compare these measurements to determine if the treatments produced a difference in behavior.

INITIAL DECISIONS

The process of designing an experiment is a series of decisions. Of course, the first decision concerns the area of study and the particular variable to be manipulated. For the moment, however, our interest centers in the initial decisions of experimental design to be made after the independent variable has been chosen.

In our discussions of experimental design we will find it economical to use certain conventional abbreviations. The word *subject* will be abbreviated to S, and its plural to Ss. *Experimenter* will be designated by *E* and its plural, *Es*.

First decision. The first decision which must be made is in answer to the question, "Shall I use a different group of Ss for each condition, or shall I put each S through all conditions?" Thus, if we are going to obtain time judgments following the administration of a certain drug and compare these judgments with those obtained when no drug is administered, a first decision is required. A decision must be made as to whether to use two *independent groups* of Ss, one group being given the drug and the other not, or to use a *single group* of Ss who give time judgments on one occasion following administration of the drug and judgments on another occasion when the drug has not been administered.

There are many different matters which must be weighed in reaching this decision. The use of either method raises certain additional problems which must be handled appropriately. Actually, there is no simple set of principles which can be applied universally so that an automatic decision can be made. Furthermore, many practical or mechanical problems may be involved in the decision. For example, suppose we need to run an experiment with five different conditions but have only eight Ss available. An attempt to use independent groups might be a little ludicrous in this situation since we would have two Ss in three of the conditions and one in each of the other two. Very likely *E* would quickly reach a decision that he would use all eight Ss in all five conditions.

There are many situations in which neither evidence nor logical considerations lead to a preference of one method over the other. Either could be used with equal effectiveness. Matters of mere convenience may then dictate the choice. We must realize, however, that many implications follow the choice of a method, implications which will be pointed out from time to time as various experiments are discussed. By such means we shall expect to accumulate the wisdom necessary to make the appropriate decisions in new situations.

We must not overlook the fact that traditions in method develop over the years in a given area of research. In the general areas of perception, judgment, and the study of sensory attributes (e.g., pitch and brightness), tradition shows that the bulk of the investigations use the same Ss in all conditions. Blindly following a tradition, however, can never be recommended. A traditional method may represent the distillation of certain knowledge which has occurred over the years, and by following tradition we may avoid the pitfalls which have been experienced with other methods. Yet, at the same time, the history of experimental psychology shows instances in which the use of traditional methods has prevented discoveries of high importance. So, in fact, tradition may present a dilemma; to follow it is comforting, but to break away from it may produce new avenues for the understanding of nature. Thoughtful evaluation of the possible implications of methods, both new and old, seems to be a level of planning for which most research workers strive.

A possible second major decision. Let us assume that we have chosen to run our experiment by using the same Ss in all conditions of the experiment. Having made this decision, another immediate decision is required. The experiment may be designed so that each S will serve in all conditions in such a manner that no experimental bias will occur for his measurements under the various conditions and, therefore, the results for each S will provide sound information of the effects of the variable being manipulated. Again, traditionally, this has been the method frequently used in the area of perception. There is, however, a second alternative which may be followed. This method also requires that all Ss serve in all conditions, but the data for any given S are biased. Unbiased results are obtained only by adding the results for all Ss together. The detailed working out of both of these alternatives so that an understanding of how they do what they are said to do requires much elaboration. We will shortly discuss in detail the logic of the first alternative (wherein each S provides unbiased data) but delay the discussion of the second alternative until a later chapter.

Third set of decisions. The third set of decisions concerns the detailed working out of the procedure. Certain of these details may be "set" by earlier decisions; indeed, this may work in reverse. That is, certain procedural details which are judged absolutely essential for a given study may in turn form the major basis for a conclusion on the earlier questions we have discussed. There is not always an inevitable march of decisions from the general to the specific in designing an experiment.

The detailed planning will, of course, differ with each experiment. Many decisions, it will be seen, are quite arbitrary. For an understanding of the decisions regarding these detailed procedures we must refer to actual experiments.

TIME JUDGMENTS AS A FUNCTION OF LENGTH OF INTERVAL

One of the most obvious variables to study concerning the judgments of passage of time is the length of the interval to be judged. More particularly, we may ask about the accuracy of the time judgments as a function of length of interval being judged. Length of interval is the independent variable—the stimulus variable. In this particular case, time is a task variable since we are varying the duration of time and requesting judgments about these durations. The response variable—the dependent variable—is, of course, the judgments Ss make as to elapsed time.

We will examine an experiment conducted by the author in conjunction with his class in experimental psychology. It is a simple experiment, one that can be done quickly, and yet it yields considerable information. The procedure and results will be presented without much analytical comment. Then we will return and consider in detail the implication of some of the steps.

Procedure. Intervals of four "lengths" were chosen, namely, 8, 12, 19, and 32 sec. Thus, the independent variable was being sampled at four levels—four durations. The experiment was conducted as a group experiment, and each interval was given to all Ss. Furthermore, each S made three judgments at each interval, for a total of 12 judgments.

The Ss were told that they were to judge the length of various time intervals, and a prepared data sheet with 12 blank spaces in a column was provided. They were further instructed that in judging the length of the interval they should not count or tap and, of course, must not refer to their timepieces. In presenting an interval E said, "Get ready," and approximately 1 sec. later said, "Start," at the same time starting a stopwatch. At the end of the specified interval E said, "Stop," and S recorded his judgment of the length of the interval between Start and Stop. The judgments were recorded in whole seconds. Two practice trials using 10 and 23 sec. were given prior to presenting the experimental series.

The order in which the intervals were presented was 12, 8, 31, 20, 8, 31, 20, 12, 12, 20, 31, and 8 sec. Approximately 5 sec. elapsed between the termination of one interval and the start of the next one, which was sufficient time for S to record his judgment and prepare for the next presentation.

As can be seen, the experiment took only a few minutes. It was done at 9:00 A.M. on Tuesday morning during a regular meeting of the class and was repeated at 9:00 A.M. the following Thursday morning. There were 23 Ss taking both series of trials.

Results

The basic purpose of the study was to determine the relationship between length of interval and accuracy of judgments of the interval. For each session S gave three judgments at each interval. The mean of these three judgments was determined for each S, and then the mean of the 23 means was calculated. The results are presented in Fig. 2-1.

Certain of the mechanical features of Fig. 2-1 may be pointed out first. Note that the scale is identical on both axes of the graph, namely, seconds. This is not a common occurrence in psychology; that is, it is not often that the independent variable and the dependent variable are measured along the same scale. Note also that the independent variable is plotted along the

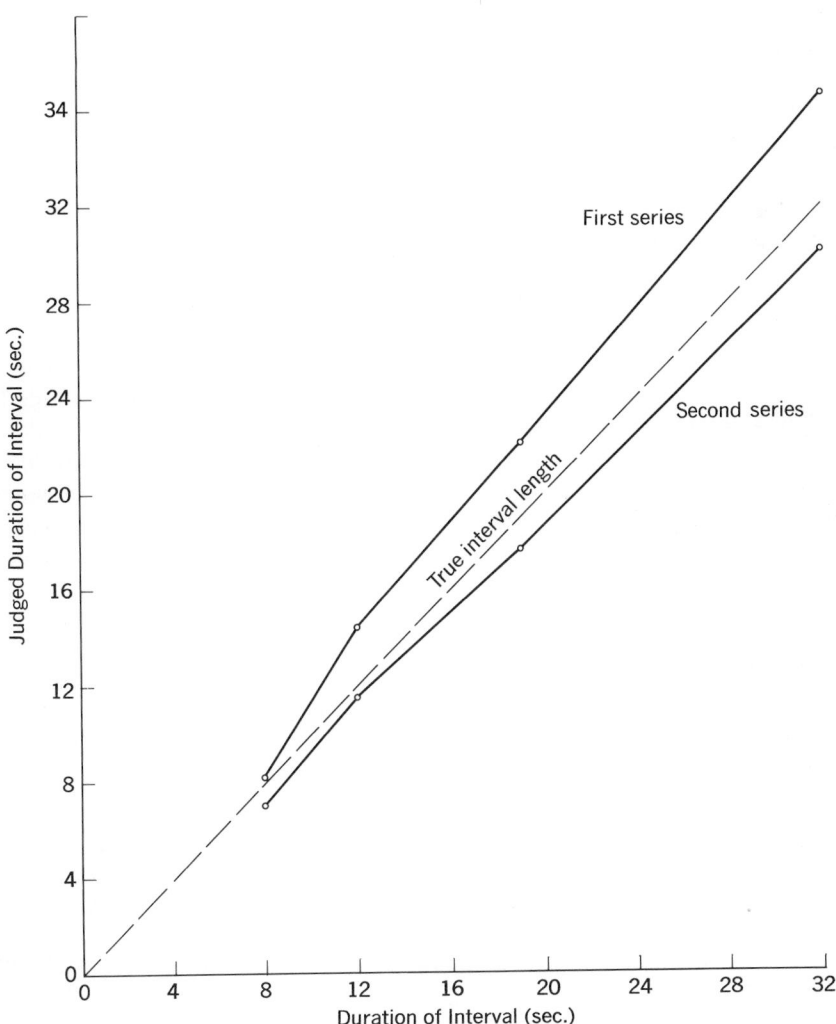

Fig. 2-1. Judgment of duration of time intervals as a function of the duration of the intervals presented. Both series were identical except that they were separated by two days.

X axis, the abscissa. This is a general rule with only a rare exception toler-
ated for special circumstances. The dependent variable—the behavior one is
measuring—is always plotted along the Y axis (ordinate). That the ordinate
should be about two-thirds as long as the abscissa is a rule of thumb based
entirely on aesthetic considerations and is often violated, as it is in Fig. 2-1
where there was reason for keeping the length of the two scales equal since
the units are the same.

Now let us see what is indicated by the graph concerning the relationship between the length of interval and the judged length. First, it is
clear that the longer the interval, the longer the judged interval. But it is
also clear that on the first series there is a tendency to overestimate the length
of the intervals; the Ss judge the length of the intervals to be longer than in
fact they are. On the second series, taken two days later, there is an underestimation at all intervals. Indeed, by conventional statistical standards, the
difference between the mean judgments on the first series and the mean judgments on the second series at each interval is significant. We will return to
these differences shortly. Having seen the basic results, let us analyze the
procedure.

ANALYSIS OF PROCEDURE

Why were the particular four intervals chosen? The choices
were arbitrary only in part. Very short intervals, such as 2 or 3 sec., might
be affected by an error in measurement through the use of a stopwatch; that
is, slight errors in starting and stopping the watch might occur at the moments "Start" and "Stop" were said. This same error might be present with
longer intervals, but the error magnitude would be of little consequence.
More precise timing mechanisms should be used to explore very short intervals. A limit was placed on the length of the longest interval used, simply to
avoid having the experiment stretch out over too long a period of time. For
the purposes intended, there was no reason to explore intervals of several
minutes. The intervals actually used were not spaced evenly along the dimension (such as 5, 10, 15, and 20 sec.). This was done in order to accommodate a basic fact of discrimination of magnitudes, namely, that the less
the magnitude of a stimulus (within limits), the better the discrimination.
Therefore, phenomenally speaking, the intervals used were intended to represent a scale in which the differences between the durations actually used
had some equality. We will return several times to this fact that accuracy of
discriminations varies as a function of the magnitude (duration, in this case)
of the stimulus.

Why use the two practice judgments? This was a compromise procedure.
Suppose E had told the Ss nothing about the intervals to be used. This might
be satisfactory. However, because one S might anticipate being given intervals of several minutes and another S, of only a few seconds, it is, perhaps, a
little better to provide some idea of what the interval lengths will be with-

out placing any limitations on them. If E had told the Ss that the intervals would range between, say, 5 and 50 sec., he would have been placing a restriction on the judgments, for certainly no S will record an interval as being over 50 sec. or under 5 sec. following such instructions. As it was, some Ss judged the 32-sec. interval to be as long as 60 sec. and the 8-sec. interval as short as 3 sec. The two practice trials, therefore, gave the Ss a gross idea of the range of intervals involved (although, of course, they were not told the true length of the two practice intervals). Even so, the fact that the two practice intervals were neither as short as the shortest nor as long as the longest, may have resulted in some restriction on Ss' judgments, at least early in the series.

The instruction disallowed the use of a timepiece by S; this seems eminently reasonable. The use of a timepiece would change the purpose of the study from one of time estimation to one of accuracy in reading dials. Instructing the Ss not to count is a common procedure (although some investigators have studied time judgments with counting required). In this experiment, as well as in most experiments of all kinds, E will ask if there are any questions about the procedure which the instructions have left unclear. In the present experiment two different questions were asked at this juncture. One S asked how he could be expected to judge the length of the intervals if he couldn't count. To this question E replied that S *would* find it possible to make the judgments with some accuracy and that in any event, he was to do the best he could. A second S asked if he could judge the length of the intervals by holding his breath. As a result of considerable experience in swimming underwater, this S had developed a correlation between the passage of time and the changes in the subjective feelings which occur as the breath continues to be held. To this question E answered in two parts: first, it was noted that this technique for judging the passage of time was allowable by the instructions; secondly, it was pointed out that the nearest first-aid station was three blocks away.

Why were three trials given on each interval? Why not one? Or ten? Again, this was quite arbitrary. The purpose for giving more than one trial is to increase the stability of the judgments. If only a single trial on a specific interval is given, a momentary distraction might distort the judgment. However, unless the same momentary factor influenced all Ss, there would be no reason to believe that the mean judgment of all Ss for a specific interval presented only once would be unstable or invalid as an estimate of the judgment for the group. Nevertheless, since several judgments could be obtained without difficulty, this was done.

Balancing of Progressive Errors

We now come to a matter of universal importance in the design of experiments where the same S serves in all conditions of an experiment. We ask the question, "Why were the intervals given in this particular order?" The answer requires a rather extended discussion, and this discussion demands some digression from the specifics of the present experiment. Let us digress.

Progressive error means any change in behavior which occurs as a consequence of continued experience or successive trials with a given task. In certain tasks the S may perform better with each successive trial, and this is usually identified as a *practice effect*. But it is also true that performance may deteriorate over an extended series of trials; S may get tired or bored, or he may not "try as hard," and the result could be poorer performance. Generally speaking, E will attempt to avoid a series of trials of such length that S may actually become fatigued. Nevertheless, fatigue or boredom may be involved in any experiment, and progressive error may be thought of as a summation of positive (practice) and negative (fatigue) factors on performance over a series of trials. And let it be said that progressive errors are not the product of someone's imagination. They are real and can be measured in many different situations. Indeed, a little later we will return to the interval judgment experiment to look at the progressive error which did occur.

What are the implications of progressive error? Unless the experiment is designed properly the progressive error may bias the results so that a partially or wholly false conclusion may be reached. That is, the results may be attributed to the independent variable when in fact they were due to progressive error. When such ambiguity prevails, we speak of a *confounded* experiment or confounded results. While "confounded" is a technical term as used here, its literary affective tone is perfectly appropriate for the situation. Thus, a confounding means that two or more stimulus variables have changed concurrently so that the results cannot be said to be attributable to a single stimulus variable. A confounded experiment is one in which the rule of allowing one and only one variable to change is broken. The result is ambiguity in stating a cause-effect relationship.

Now let us back up a little. A progressive error—a change in behavior as a result of successive trials—is not a stimulus variable. It is a response variable which can be measured if we wish. The stimulus variable to which progressive error is related is commonly called *stage of practice*. This in turn would be identified with number of trials, number of judgments, time spent, or some other measure reflecting different stages of practice. Therefore, a confounding may result if the stage of practice varies in some systematic fashion with our independent variable—the variable whose effect we are studying. For example, in the experiment in which time judgments were made, suppose we had given the 12 judgments in the following order: 8, 8, 8, 12, 12, 12, 20, 20, 20, 32, 32, 32. Now, presume also that S became more and more accurate in his judgments merely as a function of practice so that on the twelfth trial he was much more accurate than he was on the first. Since all of the three judgments of the 8-sec. interval came first and the three judgments on the 32-sec. interval came last, we might well obtain results leading us to a conclusion that the longer the interval, the more accurate the judgments. But, in fact, it can be seen that the length of the interval and stage of practice vary together in such a design; hence, the results would be confounded. The greater accuracy might be due entirely to stage of practice, to length of interval, or to some combination of the two. We would be quite incapable of reaching a decision on this matter when such a design is used. We need to consider how to avoid such confounding, and there are several possibilities.

First, of course, we might make an early decision to use different groups of Ss for each condition. Thus, in the interval judging experiment, one group would get the 8 sec. interval, another the 12-sec. interval, and so on. In some respects this may be the best solution in spite of certain inconveniences of assembling different groups for very short experimental periods. However, as we shall see, there is every reason to believe that we can use the same Ss in all conditions and still avoid confounding.

A second solution might be to eliminate progressive errors in some manner. Thus, we might practice and practice S until we know that his judgments are not changing with additional trials. Clearly, the change in behavior must have a limit, and it is only after finding this limit that we would measure the judgments "for keeps." In actual fact, this method has sometimes been used; but, except in special circumstances, there is little basis to justify the extended work necessary in the method.

The third solution is to accept the fact that progressive errors will occur in experiments and to design the experiment so that the effects of different stages of practice will not *differentially* influence the results (the behavior) which we wish to attribute to differences in our independent variable. Note that we do not *eliminate* the progressive change in behavior related to stage of practice. We are, in effect, adding (or subtracting) a constant to the measurements of behavior associated with each level of the independent variable. Sometimes it is possible to "subtract out" this constant from the results for all conditions if there is an interest in the absolute level of behavior produced by the independent variable. However, we will not consider how this is possible at this point, as we wish to turn to the techniques for balancing the effects of progressive error in an experiment. Three techniques will be discussed: *counterbalancing, complete randomization,* and *block randomization.*

Counterbalancing. For purposes of discussion, let us say that we are going to do a simple two-condition experiment in which two different time intervals will be judged, namely, 10 and 20 sec. Each S is to make 12 judgments for each interval, and we wish to have no bias in the results of each S due to progressive error. To repeat a point made earlier, it is quite clear that we cannot give all 12 trials on the 10-sec. interval followed by all 12 trials on the 20-sec. interval. If there is a progressive error, its effects will fall more heavily on the judgments for the 20-sec. interval, thus biasing the results. Counterbalancing is a classic solution to this problem. The purpose of counterbalancing is to present the two conditions in such a fashion that the effects of the progressive error will fall equally on both conditions. For the two conditions under discussion here, this would be handled by presenting the intervals in the following order:

> 10 sec. (6 trials)
> 20 sec. (6 trials)
> 20 sec. (6 trials)
> 10 sec. (6 trials)

One may also present the order 20-10-10-20, since there is nothing magical about which condition comes first. Indeed, we may have half the Ss use the 10-20-20-10 sequence and the other half, the 20-10-10-20 sequence. Counterbalancing, when expressed in general terms for any two conditions, is spoken of as *abba*, where *a* and *b* symbolize the two conditions of the experiment.

Let us examine the logic of counterbalancing as a technique for distributing the effects of progressive error equally over the measurements made for each condition. Assume that the relationship between the magnitude of progressive error and stage of practice is a linear one, that is, each additional stage of practice of equal size (same number of trials) adds an equal amount of progressive error. Such a relationship is shown in Fig. 2-2. Aligning this

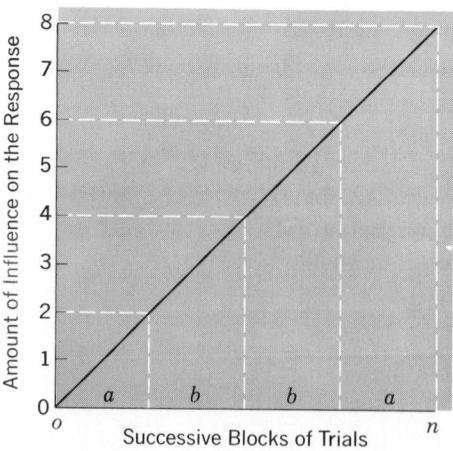

Fig. 2-2. How the influence of progressive errors on response can be equalized for all conditions by using the *abba* order of presentation. See text for complete explanation.

illustration with the two-condition experiment outlined, we see that each block consists of 6 trials (6 trials with 10 sec., 6 with 20 sec., 6 with 20 sec., and finally, 6 more with 10 sec.). Thus, each *a* and *b* block consists of 6 trials. The ordinate is in quite arbitrary units. The graph shows that as successive trials are given, there is a linear change in the magnitude of the progressive error.

It was stated that the *abba* sequence distributes the progressive error equally over both conditions. Let us see in a quantitative fashion how this can be proven by examining the implications of Fig. 2-2. In the first block (the first *a*) the average influence of the progressive error on the response is 1. To obtain this we assume that on the very first judgment—the first trial in the *a* block—there is *zero* influence of a progressive error. This is simply to say that S has to have a trial before anything can produce a progressive error. On the sixth or last trial of this *a* block, the progressive error had 2 units of influence on the response. Consequently, the average influence of the progressive error on the six trials in the block would be 1. Similarly, the influence in the first block of the *b* trials varies from 2 to 4 units, with an average of 3. Computing the values for the second *b* and second *a* block in a like fashion yields values of 5 and 7, respectively. Across the four successive blocks, then, the progressive error influence is 1, 3, 5, and 7. The amount of influence on the *a* condition is 1 plus 7, or 8 units; the amount of influence on the *b* condition is 3 plus 5, or also 8 units. Thus, it does appear that counterbalancing will distribute the effects of progressive error equally over both conditions.

It can also be seen from Fig. 2-2 that if we had not used the *abba* sequence, but had used *aabb* instead, the influence of progressive error under the *a* conditions would be 1 plus 3, or 4 units, while under the *b* conditions it would be 5 plus 7, or 12 units. Thus, the responses under the two conditions would have been differentially influenced by the progressive error and a clear confounding would exist.

The thoughtful student, having assimilated the simple beauty of the counterbalancing procedure, may be skeptical of the fact that the world can be so simply organized. Such a skepticism may lead to an important question. "What happens if the relationship between stage of practice and change in progressive error is not linear but is curvilinear, whereby with each successive block there is a smaller and smaller change in the progressive error?" Such a situation is depicted in Fig. 2-3. This relationship, commonly known as a negatively accelerated relationship, is quite usual in psychology. Many learning curves show this form; and if progressive errors may be in part a function of practice or learning, then to suppose that the relationship is negatively accelerated is not at all out of line. Furthermore, it can be seen (Fig. 2-3) that if we calculate the influence of the progressive error it will be seen to fall more heavily on the *b* condition than on the *a* condition (roughly, 11.50 for *a*; 13.75 for *b*). Although this difference is not large, if we are manipulating an independent variable whose influence is also not large, the counterbalancing by blocks of trials as in Fig. 2-3 could give us misleading results.

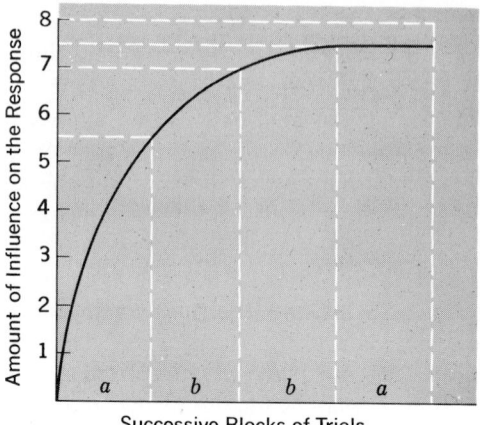

Fig. 2-3. **The failure of counterbalancing by blocks of trials to equalize progressive error for a curvilinear relationship between practice and progressive error. See text for full explanation.**

All is not lost, however. If we do not counterbalance in *blocks* of trials but rather counterbalance with a *single* trial as a unit, the bias will be eliminated even with extreme curvilinear relationships. Thus, in our hypothetical two-condition experiment, we would have six successive *abba* sequences, producing the 12 trials on each interval. Under such circumstances, the amount of change for each *abba* sequence will be relatively small (since each sequence consists of only four trials). Even with an overall curvilinear relationship, the change in progressive error is essentially linear with each successive small segment of practice.

The above discussion suggests that as a general rule we should counterbalance in as small units as possible (namely, one-trial units), unless we know that the shape of the progressive error curve is essentially linear.

It should be clear that *abba* is used to symbolize the counterbalancing notion in the minimum experiment. If there are four conditions we would have *abcddcba*, eight conditions, *abcdefghhgfedcba*, but for 27 conditions we would go to a different symbol system. The notion of counterbalancing is a fundamental one to which we will refer many times.

Complete randomization. This is a second method for balancing the effects of progressive error so that the behavior under different values of the independent variable is not biased by the error. The logic by which randomization is supported is essentially the same as that for counterbalancing, namely, that with randomization the effects of the progressive error will influence all conditions an equal amount.

It is customary, in randomizing conditions, to place one restriction on the sequence: that each condition will occur equally often. Thus, we might decide that *a* must occur 12 times (12 trials) and that *b* must occur 12 times. How do we get the randomized sequence? In the appendix there are 1000 instances of randomized sequences of the numbers 1 through 8. We wish to develop a randomized sequence consisting of 24 trials in which *a* occurs 12 times and *b* occurs 12 times, but the order in which they occur is random. There are several ways we could generate a random sequence using the sequences in the appendix. Let us follow one plan which is fairly efficient. The first number in each of the 1000 sequences may be an odd number or an even number. We may associate the odd numbers with *a* and the even numbers with *b*. The first numbers of the initial six sequences are:

$$5 \quad 4 \quad 8 \quad 2 \quad 3 \quad 4$$

or

$$a \quad b \quad b \quad b \quad a \quad b$$

If successive numbers beyond the first six are listed, and associated with *a* and *b*, it will be found that we obtain 12 *b* entries at a point where we have only 9 *a* entries. Since we have ruled that there must be 12 of each, we must arbitrarily add the three missing *a* entries to the end of the sequence, thus giving us an order for the 24 entries as follows:

$$a\,b\,b\,b\,a\,b\,a\,b\,b\,a\,b\,a\,a\,a\,a\,b\,a\,b\,b\,b\,b\,a\,a\,a$$

Given such a sequence, it appears quite unlikely that even with a fairly drastic curvilinear relationship between trials and progressive error that the error would fall more heavily on one condition than the other. Furthermore, if we are going to combine data from different Ss as we normally do, we could produce a different random sequence for each S.

Let us consider another illustration of how to produce a random sequence. Assume we are going to give each S four different conditions six times. Let the numbers 1, 2, 3, and 4 stand for *a, b, c,* and *d,* respectively. Again, we take successive first numbers in each sequence, ignoring those sequences which have 5, 6, 7, and 8 as the initial number. The initial numbers are:

$$4 \quad 2 \quad 3 \quad 4 \quad 3 \quad 2 \quad 3 \quad 1 \quad 4$$

or

$$d \quad b \quad c \quad d \quad c \quad b \quad c \quad a \quad d$$

We continue, dropping out a number when six entries for it have occurred, and the following sequence is obtained:

$$d\,b\,c\,d\,c\,b\,c\,a\,d\,b\,d\,a\,b\,b\,b\,a\,c\,a\,a\,d\,d\,a\,c\,c$$

In using tables of random numbers or random sequences, it is customary to determine ahead of time just where the starting point in the tables will be. Obviously, we should not always start with sequence number one, for we would not be making the best use of the tables; in a sense, we would not be randomly sampling randomness. In determining the starting point for developing any one sequence, one should, perhaps, use a random procedure. Thus, some number between 1 and 1000, which might be ascertained on some random basis, determines the starting point. But, having determined the starting point, one need not move forward only. One might move backward, or one might move either backward or forward using every other sequence. The point is, we should not always use the same starting location or the same system.

Block randomization. In block randomization each condition occurs once in each successive block of trials, but the order of the conditions within the blocks is random, and a different random order is used for each block. Obviously, in following this procedure, all conditions must necessarily occur an equal number of times, and the number of times they occur is determined by the number of blocks.

In making up a schedule of conditions representing block randomization, we may use the random sequences in the appendix. First, to illustrate a two-condition sequence again, we may let the numbers 1 and 2 correspond to conditions *a* and *b*. In the first sequence, 1 precedes 2, in the second, the order is reversed, and so on. If we wish to give 12 trials on each of the two conditions, we would use the first 12 sequences:

```
1 2 2 1 1 2 2 1 1 2 1 2 1 2 2 1 2 1 1 2 1 2 2 1
a b b a a b b a a b a b a b b a b a a b a b b a
```

It is worth noting that for the first eight trials we have two *abba* sequences, a happening that will not be too unusual when only two conditions are involved.

As a second illustration, assume we have four conditions, each to be presented six times. In randomizing these four conditions we may use the first six sequences, each sequence contributing one block. The following occurs:

```
4 1 3 2 4 3 2 1 3 4 1 2 2 1 4 3 3 4 1 2 4 3 1 2
d a c b d c b a c d a b b a d c c d a b d c a b
```

Note that each block, consisting of four trials, contains each condition once. Again, if we wish, we may use a different order for each S.

In these illustrations we have translated the numbers into letters. This would not, of course, have to be done if we wished to label our conditions with numbers instead of letters. We have made the translation here merely to keep the symbol system for the randomization procedures the same as that commonly used in counterbalancing.

In the time estimation experiment which introduced the present discussion, each of four intervals was presented three times, the series being 12, 8, 31, 20, 8, 31, 20, 12 ,12, 20, 31, 8. An examination of this series shows that it is a block randomization series; and since the experiment was done as a group experiment, all Ss had the same series.

Choice of method. Which of the three techniques for balancing of progressive errors is to be preferred? It does not seem that any general answer to this question can be given. In many experiments, all three methods would be judged to be equally effective in balancing the progressive error. Nevertheless, we must be thoughtful about the choice of a particular method in a particular experiment. None should be used blindly. Here are some points which may be of value in selecting a method for a particular experiment, although no pretense is made that these points exhaust everything about which one must be thoughtful.

1. Sometimes simple mechanical matters may dictate a decision concerning the choice of method. It may be experimentally easier to manipulate the apparatus or material for the same condition over two or more trials than to change from one condition to another. Thus, counterbalancing might be used since at least two trials on the same condition occur in succession (and more under some circumstances).

2. There are some situations in which all considerations would recommend that counterbalancing *not* be used. In a general sense, counterbalancing should not be used in a procedure in which S can obtain cues from a sequence which will affect his judgment. For illustration, we may turn to the time estimation study in which four intervals were used, each presented three times. Suppose that these had been presented in counterbalanced order as follows: 8, 12, 19, 32, 32, 19, 12, 8, and so on. It is not unreasonable to expect that over a series of trials S would detect the up and down sequence, and his judgment on a particular trial might be influenced by this. The judgments might not be "pure" phenomenal judgments, for if the sequence has led him to expect a shorter interval than presented on the preceding trial, his judgment will undoubtedly be shorter than it had been the preceding trial. Of course, one might minimize such possibilities by not making the counterbalancing sequence systematic with respect to the length of the interval, giving instead, let us say, 12, 8, 32, 19, 19, 32, 8, 12, and so on. When only a few such blocks are used, it is unlikely that S would "catch on" to the order; but over an extended series of blocks, he might learn the sequence and thereby have his judgments influenced.

3. If only a few trials are to be given and if all Ss are to receive the same sequence of trials (as in a group experiment), it could be argued that complete randomization is not as appropriate as either counterbalancing or block randomization. Suppose each of two conditions, *a* and *b*, are to be given for four trials each. With complete randomization it is not too improbable that

we could get a random sequence, *aaaabbbb*. If this occurs, we clearly would not have a balancing of progressive error. How probable is such a sequence? It would have the same probability of occurring as would four heads in a row on four successive flips of a coin, namely, one chance in sixteen. Still higher would be the probability of getting a sequence such as *aaababbb*, and we would not judge this to be very adequate for the balancing of progressive error. In counterbalancing, on the other hand, we do not take this chance; we make the sequence *abbaabba*. In block randomization the worst possible sequence we could get would be *abababab* (or *babababa*).

We will insist from time to time throughout the book, just as we are insisting now, that we must be thoughtful about choice of methods when there are alternatives. The above points may guide our thinking somewhat. But we must not be bound by any method; we may have to devise our own in certain situations. We have discussed three ways to balance progressive error, but it is possible that in some experiments none of these would be appropriate.

The digression on the problems involved in balancing progressive error is now complete, and we may return to the results of the time judging experiment.

CONSTANT AND VARIABLE ERRORS

Constant Error

In our discussion of Fig. 2-1 we noted that on the first series of judgments the Ss, on the average, overestimated the length of all four intervals, whereas on the second series, they underestimated the intervals. Such consistent over- or underestimations are called *constant errors*. Generally speaking, we note the presence of a constant error when judgments or discriminations differ significantly from some standard stimulus. More specifically, the magnitude of the constant error is the difference between some standard and the mean of the judgments made while attempting to match or identify in some way the magnitude of the standard. If the mean represents an underjudgment, we say the constant error is *negative;* if an overjudgment is found, it is called a *positive* constant error.

The word *constant* cannot be taken literally, and there are several reasons for this. The direction of the error need not be constant. This is quite apparent in Fig. 2-1 where the first series showed a positive constant error, the second series, a negative constant error. Furthermore, not all Ss in a given series showed the same direction of error; even in the first series some showed a negative constant error. So, one must distinguish between the mean constant error for a group of Ss and the mean constant error for several judgments for a single S. It is true that in certain situations the direction of

red	black	red	yellow	green	green
brown	brown	black	yellow	green	yellow
brown	blue	blue	green	red	yellow
green	green	blue	brown	black	blue
red	red	green	yellow	green	brown
yellow	black	blue	black	blue	brown
red	blue	black	yellow	green	blue
brown	red	blue	brown	black	red
black	brown	green	black	blue	red
brown	yellow	black	red	yellow	yellow

Fig. 12-10. An illustration of interference produced by highly developed habits. The task is to name the color of the ink in which each word is printed, naming them as rapidly as possible row by row.

the constant error is almost universal. For example, in the next chapter where we consider some illusions, it will be seen that the illusory effect, which is a constant error, is in the same direction for nearly all Ss.

The word constant should not be understood to mean that the direction of error (positive or negative) is consistent for a given S on successive trials nor that the magnitude of the error is equivalent on each trial. Indeed, we are forced to say that the magnitude of a constant error for a given S on successive trials is variable, a language which may be a little confusing at first. But if the mean of the series of trials for a given S, or for a group of Ss, differs significantly from the standard stimulus, we speak of a constant error.

Again referring back to Fig. 2-1, it is quite clear that a puzzle is present. Why did a positive constant error occur on the first series and a negative constant error on the second series two days later? As a matter of fact, why were the two series run in the first place? The problem as stated did not require two such series. Now, in fact, the second series was run for a specific purpose, which will not be considered here, but the purpose was quite un-related to the fact that the constant error differs for the two series. That we have this shift in the constant error is a bonus from the experiment; we were not looking for it, had no notion that it would occur, and are intrigued by what may be producing it. Some experiments will turn up phenomena quite unexpectedly if one gives the data "half a chance" to do so. For example, the data from both series might have been combined initially, in which case we would have obtained mean judgments that would essentially be on top of the line showing the true length of the interval. Generally speaking, it is quite worthwhile to chop the data up in several different ways. In the process of running an experiment or in working over the data, it may be discovered that the data are quite suitable for answering questions which had not occurred to E in the process of designing the experiment. If an experiment can answer more than one question about nature, so much the better. We must make any set of data work for us by analyzing it in as many different ways as possible. Even if the new bonus questions we ask cannot be answered in a definitive way by the data, these data may at least suggest that a new experiment to maximize the effect of the "new" variable presumed to be operating would have a strong chance of success, that is, of showing that a hitherto unexplored variable was indeed involved.

The unexpected fact shown in Fig. 2-1 is that the constant error shifts from one series to the next. What are we to make of this? We note several differences obtaining at the time the two series were given. The first was given on Tuesday, the second on Thursday. It does not seem very reasonable to think that the day of the week is responsible, although it is possible that mood changes as a function of the day of the week could be involved. Per-haps the "mental atmosphere" of the Ss differed on the two occasions, and this is responsible. It is true that prior to the first series the Ss were given a quiz over course material, and prior to the second series the results of the quiz, on which the grades were not very good, were discussed. Other possibilities may also be suggested.

Do we have any way of narrowing the number of possible causes for the difference in judgments for the two series? In fact we do. The evidence as given in Fig. 2-1 suggests that the judgments "jumped" downward from the first series to the second. However, this impression may be false. Suppose the possibility is suggested that the first and second series may be considered continuous and that rather than the existence of a jump between series there is a gradual reduction in the mean judgments from trial to trial. This is to say that there may be a progressive error as a function of stage of practice. Of

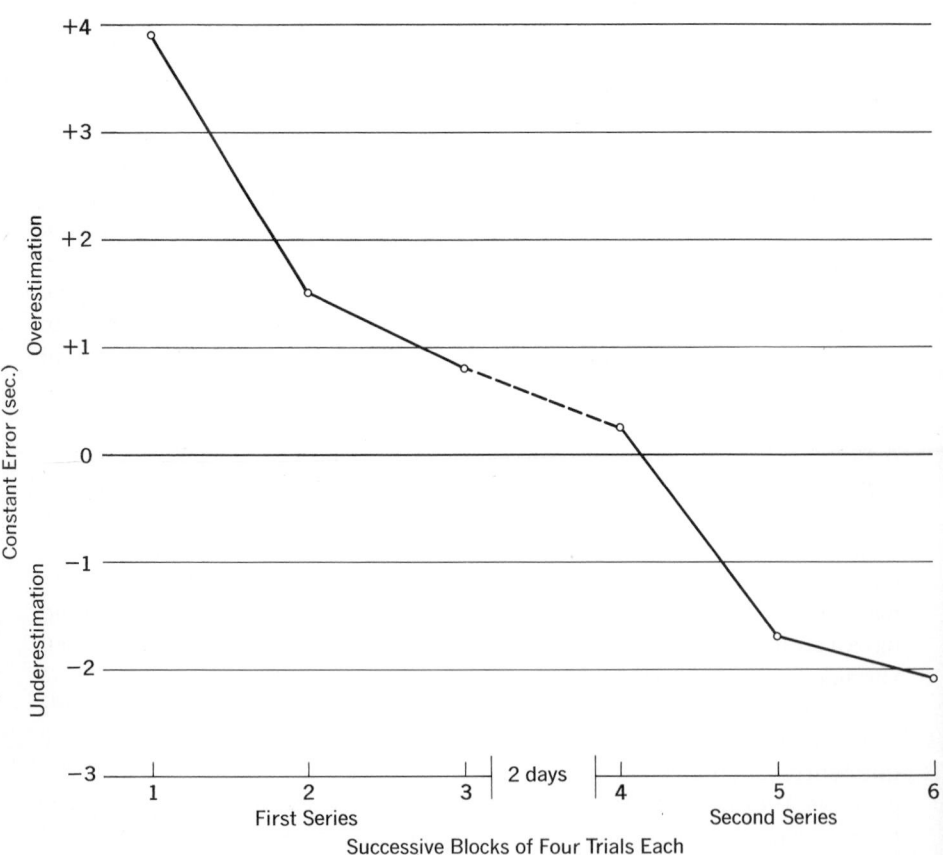

Fig. 2-4. Constant error in judging temporal duration as a function of stage of practice.

course we balanced such errors, making them fall equally on all intervals, by randomizing the four intervals within each successive block of four trials. If this balancing was successful, there should not be a distinct jump downward between the first and second series if there is a progressive error leading to shorter and shorter judgments for all intervals as trials proceed and if this progression continues across the two series. Obviously, therefore, we need to know if there was a progressive error.

Each successive block of four trials contained each of the intervals. We may, therefore, ask about the judgments on each of these blocks of four trials, combining the judgments within each of the blocks. To bring these data together, we have determined the constant error (combining all Ss) for each judgment within a block and then have taken the mean for these four judgments. There were three blocks of four trials each on the first series and a like number on the second. Now we may plot the constant error for each block so that six points on the curve are available.

The result of this plot is shown in Fig. 2-4. At the start of the first series the positive constant error is maximal, and there is a consistent decrease across successive blocks. Indeed, it would seem reasonable to conclude that the constant errors on the second series represent a reasonable continuation of the trends noted on the first series. Clearly, there is no sudden jump between the two days. The curve for the second series seems to be what might be expected had the second series immediately followed the first. At least, this would be a more reasonable hypothesis than to suggest something intrinsic to Thursday that is responsible for the differences between the two series. If, experimentally, we were to pursue this matter further, we would, as a first test, probably run both series during the same experimental period. If the progressive error curve for the second series in Fig. 2-4 is indeed a reasonable extension of the first, we would expect an essential duplication of Fig. 2-4 when the two series are given during the same period.

We did in fact carry out such an experiment. The 24 judgments were obtained in exactly the same manner as in the first experiment except that all were given within a single experimental period. There were 28 Ss who participated. These were less advanced students than those who had given the first set of data. The results concerning stage of practice were determined in exactly the same manner as for the first experiment and are plotted in Fig. 2-5.

The results shown in Fig. 2-5 give fairly conclusive evidence on one question, but they raise another. It can be seen that there is a fairly consistent decrease in estimated length of intervals (an increase in size of negative constant error) across successive blocks of trials, comparable to that shown in Fig. 2-4. However, as seen in Fig. 2-5, these Ss as a group show a slight underestimation (negative constant error) on the first block, whereas the Ss in the earlier experiment had shown overestimation. One consequence of this is that the slope of the curve in Fig. 2-5 is less than that in Fig. 2-4. We

cannot expect these curves to decrease forever, for this would imply that
sooner or later Ss would be estimating all intervals to be zero seconds in
length; sooner or later they must become horizontal. The Ss in the second
experiment do not have to go as far to reach this point as do those in the
first. This does not mean, necessarily, that both groups would level off at the
same point, but it would be expected that the difference at the leveling-off
point would be less than the initial difference—the difference on the first

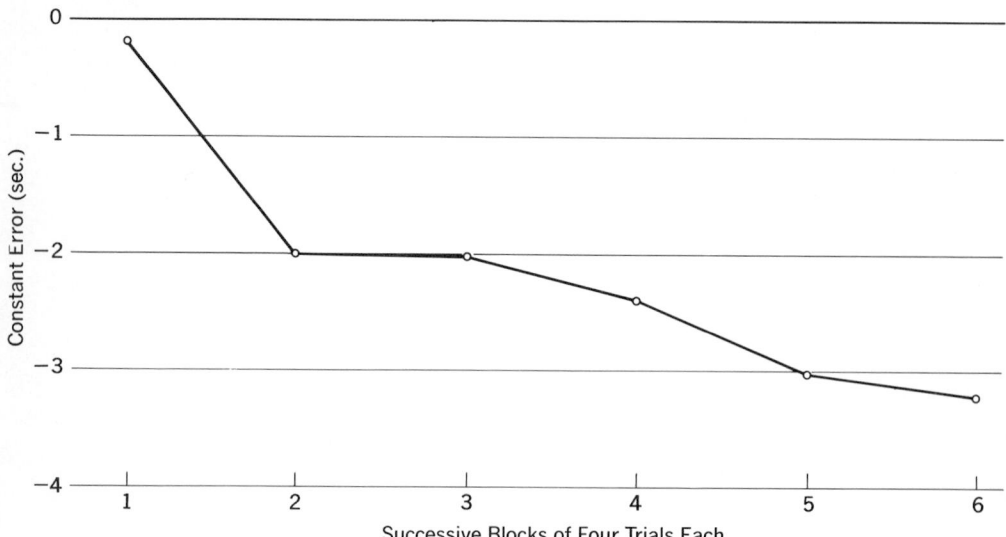

**Fig. 2-5. Further evidence on changes in the constant error in
time estimation as a function of stage of practice.**

block. In any event, we may expect judgments to change with practice, and
that is the major point to be made. Such changes have also been found by
other investigators using different methods (e.g., Falk & Bindra, 1954).

The new question raised by Fig. 2-5 comes from the evidence that this
second group of Ss were, on the average, underestimating the intervals
initially whereas the earlier group initially overestimated. Since the methods
of measurement were the same, there is only one possible conclusion—the Ss
represent different populations.

Figures 2-4 and 2-5 raise a further question. These curves indicate that
as judgments proceed, the intervals appear shorter and shorter. Why should

this be? We might suspect the opposite; that is, we might suspect that with successive trials S would get bored, and the intervals would appear longer and longer. Obviously, this is not the case. Perhaps testable notions can be derived to explore further this change in judgments with practice.

Variable Error

We noted earlier that the constant error for a group of Ss is based on the mean judgments of the Ss. All Ss may not show, indeed will probably not show, the same magnitude of constant error. The mean constant error for the group may be negative, yet some Ss in the group may show a positive constant error. We have long ago accepted as a fact of life that there will be individual differences on almost any trait, capacity, skill, or whatnot that we care to measure. Too often, however, we look at this fact of individual differences merely as an irritating state of affairs since we usually have to insert some measure of individual differences in our statistical tests when we are interested in determining whether or not two means differ significantly. This measure, the standard deviation or derivatives therefrom, is often used as a measure of what is called *variable error* in studies of judgments and discriminations.

Classically conceived, the variable error refers to the variability shown in a series of judgments or discriminations by an individual. Thus, it refers to intraindividual variability. Just as we accept differences among Ss as a basic fact, so also must we accept differences in performance for a given S from moment to moment. While we assume these changes from moment to moment have causes, we are usually quite unable to identify them. It is not quite correct to insist that these fluctuations from trial to trial are to be attributed entirely to momentary changes in S's state. The differences in a series of measurement on a given S may also represent some variability in E's presentation of the successive trials, or some variation in the recording of response, or some error in any mechanical device used. Of course, it is an aim of an experiment to reduce these variations produced by sources outside the S, but perfect constancy is rarely if ever achieved.

We may broaden the use of the term *variable error* to include interindividual variability and also measure this by the standard deviation. We derive a single score for each S, perhaps the mean of a series of judgments if more than one judgment was given, and determine the standard deviation of the distribution of scores for all Ss. The important consideration, however, whether we are dealing with inter- or intraindividual variability, is that the variable error is a response measure, just as a mean is, and may vary in magnitude in a predictable manner as the independent variable changes. In later chapters we will see how certain considerations may lead to an expectation of changes in variability of behavior without, perhaps, any change in the mean performance. Generally speaking, we probably do not use variability, particularly variability among Ss, as a significant indicator of behavior as frequently as we should. Too often we use a measure of variability in our statistical formulas without carefully considering implications of differences in magnitude of the measure of variability.

In the general area of the discriminal processes, however, which we shall be concerned with for several chapters, the variable error has been examined carefully with regard to possible changes in magnitude as a function of stimulus variables. Laws of behavior are clearly reflected. An illustration of such a law is shown in Table 2-1. These data are from the time estimation experiment. A mean judgment was determined for each S for each interval

TABLE 2–1

VARIABILITY AMONG Ss (STANDARD DEVIATIONS) IN TIME JUDGMENTS AS A FUNCTION OF LENGTH OF INTERVAL FOR TWO SERIES

INTERVAL	FIRST SERIES	SECOND SERIES
8 sec.	2.21	2.38
12 sec.	3.83	3.42
19 sec.	7.09	4.80
32 sec.	10.85	8.34

for each series. For example, in the first series the judgments given by each S for the three trials on which the 8-sec. interval was presented were averaged. The standard deviation was determined for these 23 means (there were 23 Ss) for each interval.

The first fact clearly apparent in Table 2-1 is that the standard deviation increases as the duration of the interval judged increases. This is a general fact which occurs almost without exception in studies of the discriminal processes. It occurs also for variability for a given S, although we have not derived such a measure from the present data. What this indicates is that as the magnitude of the stimulus being judged or discriminated increases, the sensitivity to differences decreases. Thus, an interval of 45 sec. would more likely be judged equivalent to a 50-sec. interval than a 5-sec. interval would be to a 10-sec. interval, in spite of the fact that the difference between the two in each case is equal. That S is less sensitive to equal differences as the magnitude of the stimulus increases will be reflected in the variable error. An 8-sec. interval might occasionally be judged as low as 3 sec., occasionally as high as 12 or 13 sec. on successive trials. But a 32-sec. interval may be judged as high as 45 sec. or as low as perhaps 20 sec. Thus, the range of responses elicited by a given stimulus is greater the greater the magnitude of that stimulus; and this greater range will, of course, be reflected in the standard deviation.

The fact that interindividual variability increases as the magnitude of the stimulus being judged increases (as in Table 2-1) would also be expected. One S may have a true bias toward overestimation—a positive constant error. With a short interval this may be only 1 sec. But at a long interval it will be magnified, perhaps to 5 sec., because sensitivity to changes decreases with increases in the magnitude of the stimulus. Another S, with a negative constant error, will produce an increase in the magnitude of the negative error as the stimulus magnitude increases. Thus, the range of scores for a group of Ss should increase as the magnitude of the stimulus increases, which is exactly what is implied in Table 2-1.

We have seen that as the mean judgments increase (as a function of the interval presented) the variability increases. This implies that there is a direct relationship between the magnitude of the mean judgments and the variability. Indeed, there is rough constancy in the proportionality between the magnitude of the mean judgments and the variability. The percentage that the standard deviation is of the mean ($100 \times SD/M$), called the *coefficient of variation*, varies only from 27 percent to 32 percent in the first series, and from 28 percent to 34 percent in the second series.

Two major points have been made about the variability within a given S and between Ss. The first is that the variability shown in a set of data may give us knowledge about behavior—about relationships between independent variables and variability in behavior—which is not given by mean performance. We must not overlook this source of information. The second point is that in the study of the discriminal processes, we inevitably find that the sensitivity or precision of discriminations decreases as the magnitude of the stimuli involved increases, and this is reflected in the measure of variability. This fact, that sensitivity decreases as magnitude increases, is the basic notion of Weber's Law, to which we will return in a later chapter.

Reliability of Response Measures

In the previous section it was argued that inter-S variability should increase as the duration of the interval being judged increased. It was said that if S had a true (reliable) tendency to overestimate (or underestimate), the magnitude of the overestimation would increase as the magnitude of the stimulus presented increased. This reasoning implies that there is consistency in S's behavior from moment to moment. It implies that if he is an overestimator one moment, he will be an overestimator a few minutes later. Is this in fact true?

The usual method of estimating consistency of behavior is by determining the correlation between successive measurements. In the present study, we may ask about the correlation between the judgments for the intervals of different lengths. Thus, we correlate the judgments at 8 sec. with those at 12, 19, and 32; those at 12 with 19 and 32; and those at 19 with 32. The result of this is often termed a correlation matrix. The matrix for the first series, and for the second series, is shown in Table 2-2.

TABLE 2–2

WITHIN-DAY PRODUCT-MOMENT CORRELATIONS FOR JUDG-MENTS AT DIFFERENT INTERVALS FOR SERIES 1 AND SERIES 2 (IN PARENTHESES)

		INTERVALS (SEC.)		
		12	19	32
	8	.81 (.76)	.63 (.45)	.75 (.44)
INTERVALS (SEC.)	12		.83 (.82)	.86 (.75)
	19			.87 (.85)

All correlations are positive and would be judged significantly different from zero, which is to say that there is some stability in behavior within each session. Although not entirely consistent throughout the matrix, there is a tendency for the correlations to be higher for adjacent intervals than for intervals of maximum difference in length. For example, in both series, the judgments at 8 sec. correlate more highly with those at 12 sec. than with those at 19 and 32 sec. If this is true in general, it might lead to the hypothesis that as intervals get longer, different cues are used in the judgments or different processes of some sort are involved in the judgments.

Do the data of Table 2-2 indicate that the judgments are reliable? There is no "yes" or "no" answer to this question. Reliability, as measured by the correlation, is a quantitative matter; the important point is what to make of correlations varying in size. Actually, in view of the fact that an entry for a given S is based on only three judgments, the correlations might be considered quite high. If we had had, let us say, 20 judgments on each interval and we divided these into two scores based on 10 judgments each so that we compare judgments to the *same* interval (which is a customary procedure for determining reliability), we probably would get correlations in the .90's. Generally speaking, within-day correlations of various performances in various areas of research may be expected to be in the .80's and .90's.

Let us suppose that the correlations in Table 2-2 were so low that we could not reject the hypothesis that there is no consistency from moment to moment in the magnitude or direction of constant error for a subject. Would this fact deny our studying time judgments experimentally? While such a state of affairs would be unusual, it would not prohibit the discovery of reliable laws or relationships between independent variables and time judgments. For example, suppose we had used only the 8-sec. interval and the 32-sec. interval, and the correlation of the scores in the two distributions was zero. This could obtain, and yet, at the same time, the mean judgments of the group could be significantly higher for the 32-sec. interval than for the 8-sec. interval. Thus, while the position (rank) of a given S in one distribution of scores bears no consistent relationship to his position in the other, the distributions as a whole may have quite different levels. So even if we have a response measure which shows no consistency from moment to moment, this does not prohibit us from discovering general laws which hold for the group.

METHODS OF ATTACK

In an experiment to ask a question about the influence of a particular stimulus variable, we often have to make a choice among various *methods of attack*. The decision to present an interval to S and to ask for an estimate of the length of the interval represents a decision concerning a method of attack. The experiment may be instigated by a simple question: "What is the relationship between the length of a temporal interval and the accuracy of estimation of the interval?" The particular method of attack used was only one of several which might have been used in attempting to obtain an experimental answer to the question. Indeed, for almost any question we ask about judgments of time, or any other judgments, there will be various alternative methods of attack. We may now consider three such methods which have been used to study temporal judgments, and we will relate these to the more general methods used in the study of a great number of different discriminal processes. (Some of the terminology to be employed is taken from Bindra and Waksberg [1956].)

Verbal estimation. Verbal estimation is the method used in the experiment discussed above. The S was presented with an interval, delimited by "Start" and "Stop," and then was asked to give a verbal estimate of the time which elapsed between "Start" and "Stop." The generalized name for any procedure in which a single stimulus is presented to S with a request for a judgment about some characteristic of the stimulus is the *method of absolute judgment,* or the *method of single stimuli.* The judgments are said to be absolute in the sense that no other stimulus is presented for comparison; S must make his judgment by referring to some "internal" measuring stick which, presumably, he has built up by his past experiences. There is an enormous number of situations to which the method is applicable. We could ask for judgments in miles per hour of the speed of automobiles, for lengths of lines or objects in feet or inches, or for frequency (cycles per second) of a tone, the last a difficult task for most people since very few have absolute pitch. But we may also use scales for judgment which are not physical scales but, rather, psychological scales. Thus we might use a *rating scale* and ask for judgments concerning the energy level of people from low to high, with low given a value of 1 and high, a value of 7. We might request aesthetic judgments on a group of art works, using a scale defined as "great" at one end and "phooey" at the other. The method of single stimuli or absolute judgment is widely applied in psychological research, and in later chapters we will have ample opportunity to evaluate its use in other areas. The choice of the method for studying estimation of time intervals in the experiment discussed was, therefore, merely following the method used by many investigators.

Production. In this method, E verbally gives S a number representing a time interval and asks him to produce it. Thus, E says, "10 sec.," and S signifies, by some signal (e.g., "Start"), the beginning of the interval. After S thinks the requested interval has elapsed, he signals a stop. This method must also be classed as· a variant on absolute judgment. Rather than asking how fast a vehicle is traveling, S is required to point out a vehicle that is traveling at the speed indicated by E. Rather than asking for the frequency of a tone, E asks S to find a tone with such-and-such frequency. If the act of production itself does not change the judgmental processes, there would appear to be no reason to believe that the two methods (verbal estimation and production) would yield different results. In fact, two different studies have shown moderately high correlations of scores from the same Ss tested under the two different methods of attack (Clausen, 1950; Siegman, 1962).

Reproduction. This method combines aspects of the first two methods. By appropriate signals, E delimits a given interval; immediately afterward, S attempts to reproduce the length of the interval by his appropriate signals. Thus, E may say "Start," at the same moment starting a stopwatch, and after 10 sec., may stop the watch as he says "Stop." Then S says "Start," and after the interval has transpired which he thinks is equal to the interval marked off by E, says "Stop." E, of course, measures the length of the interval designated by S. Or S might himself have a stopwatch and attempt to match E's interval by starting and stopping the watch appropriately without, of course, looking at the dial. If he were allowed to look at the dial, the method would, in effect, become the method of production since S would undoubtedly estimate to himself the length marked off for E and then simply allow his watch to run for that interval.

The generalized name for this method is the *method of average error*, sometimes called the *method of adjustment*. This method consists of presenting some standard stimulus to S and asking him to match or reproduce that stimulus in some manner. The method has wide applicability. We might present S a three-inch line, and ask him to draw a line of the same length, and then study the variable and constant errors as a function of the line length. We could present S a certain velocity, as a dot moving across a screen, and then ask him to make a dot move at the same speed as the one shown.

From the illustrations, however, it can be seen that two distinctly different situations may be involved when the method of average error is used. By the nature of certain stimulus events, the standard cannot be present while S is trying to make a match or reproduce the standard. This is true for time judgments. It does not appear that there could be any operations by which S could reproduce the length of an interval while that interval— the standard interval—is being shown to him (but see later). On the other hand, S could attempt to reproduce the length of a line while the standard line is physically present. This difference in procedure, a difference which may be determined by the nature of the phenomenon which E is investigating, may produce different results. For, if the matching or the reproduction must follow the presentation of the standard, with the standard no longer present, memory of S for the characteristics of the standard is involved. Insofar as memory is more fallible than immediate perception, differences in results may be expected.

These three methods of studying time perception are the most frequently used ones, but they are not the only ones. Almost any method may have variants. For example, Doehring (1961) devised four different variants on the method of reproduction and tested a small group under all four methods. While he found no difference in the accuracy of the judgments made under the four procedures, he did find some differences in the variability of the judgments within Ss. Other methods of attack have been used, particularly in judging very short intervals, such as 1 sec. (e.g., Goldstone, Boardman, & Lhamon, 1959), but since these methods will be reviewed in a later chapter in relation to other phenomena, they need not be considered here.

Implications of Different Methods of Attack

Let us suppose we wish to determine the influence of some variable on accuracy of time estimations. Which of the methods of attack should we use? Is there a best method? A fundamental truth which we must recognize at the outset is that the methods of attack in any area must be considered potential variables in the same sense that a change in the environment, a change in the type of S, or any other change is a potential variable. Whether or not the method of attack is a relevant variable is an empirical matter; it is a matter that can be settled only by discovering experimentally whether the methods produce different results. We will discuss two studies as samples of attempts to determine whether or not method of attack is a relevant variable.

Present time versus past time. In discussing the method of reproduction as an illustration of the more general method of average error, we noted that in reproducing the time intervals, the reproduction of the standard follows the termination of the standard interval. If memory is of any consequence in this situation, the measurements should be affected. In an attempt to circumvent this problem, Frankenhaeuser (1959) devised a new method whereby she could measure perception of the passage of time during the passage. This method was developed because the investigator had developed a theory which required such a technique for testing. Without giving the details of her theoretical thinking, we may say that the theory led her to the hypothesis that the nature of the memory for a time interval just terminated (past-time estimate) would result in underestimations of the interval relative to judgments of time made during the passage of time (present-time estimate). Her ingenious methods for testing the hypothesis provide us with a new method of attack.

In the usual instructions for time estimations *E* asks *S* *not* to count. Frankenhaeuser wanted to get a measure of present-time by having *S* count at what *S* thought to be a 1-sec. rate but at the same time wanted to prevent *S* from knowing how many "counts" had been made. Obviously, if *S* counted serially (1, 2, 3 etc.), at the termination of the interval he would naturally report the last number counted. To prevent this, *E* used a simple device whereby *S* pulled a paper tape in front of a small window. The *S* was instructed to advance the tape once each second, at the same time reading the single number which appeared on the tape in the window. However, the order of the numbers was random, so that on successive pulls *S* may have seen a series like 9, 4, 7, 9, 3, 6, 0, 8, 4. This, it was reasoned, would prevent *S* from knowing with any precision how many numbers had been pulled through the window. But since *S* was instructed to pull at a 1-sec. rate, the number of numerals he pulled during a given interval would give a measure of present-time estimate—estimation of time as time is passing. If, in addition, following the termination of the interval, *S* is asked to state how long the interval was (verbal estimation), a measure of past-time would also be available for the same interval for which present-time estimate was given. In this particular experiment, *S* probably estimated this past time by trying to remember the number of numbers he had pulled through the window.

Twenty-five Ss were used with estimates of both kinds being obtained for 12, 21, 32, 42, and 53 sec. Each interval was presented several times, the order of presentation being random. The results are shown in Fig. 2-6. The present-time judgments are almost identical to the intervals presented, only a very slight overestimation being present. This means that the Ss were able, on the average, to pull the tape at about a 1-sec. rate as instructed. The past-time estimates, however, show a clear underestimation of the intervals. This result is quite in line with *E*'s hypothesis concerning memory loss, although, as we shall see many times, we do not speak of this as "proving" the hypothesis. Other hypotheses may give an equally good accounting for the result. However, the two methods of attack on time estimations yield different results concerning accuracy of judgments as a function of length of the interval judged, and this is the major point we wish to make.

Verbal estimation versus reproduction. This study was conducted by the writer. The basic idea was to obtain both a verbal estimate
of the duration of an interval and a reproduction of that interval. Thus, an
interval was presented, and S immediately gave a verbal estimate of the
length of the interval which was followed immediately by a reproduction of
the interval. The major question to be asked of the data was how do the two
kinds of measurements change as a function of stage of practice.

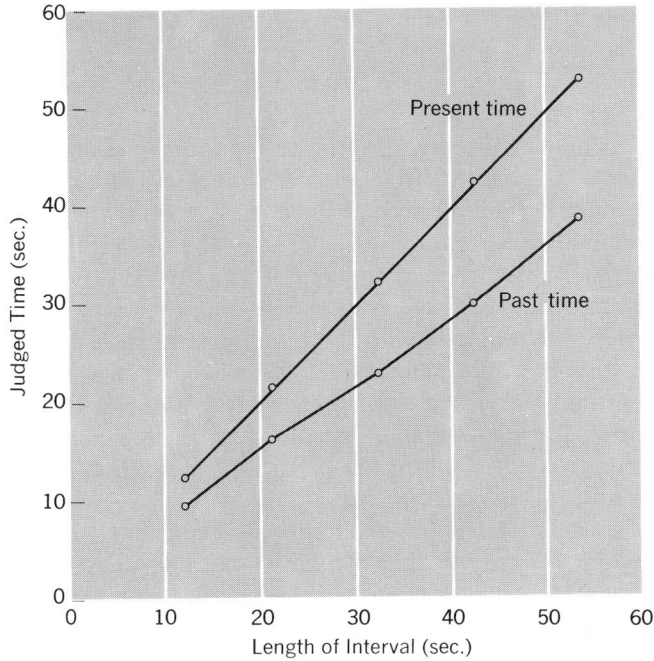

**Fig. 2-6. Estimates of present time (time as it is passing) and
past time (interval that has passed) as a function of the duration
of the interval. Data from Frankenhaeuser (1959), by permission
of the author.**

The S faced a panel into which two small blue light bulbs were inserted
24 inches apart. In presenting an interval, *E*, seated behind the panel, lighted
the bulb to S's left and let it remain on for the specified interval. Immediately, S made a judgment as to the number of seconds the light was on, and
then, with a switch placed below the right bulb, lighted this light allowing
it to remain on for a period of time judged to be equal to the interval the
left light had been on. The *E* could record the length of time the light was
on by a clock in circuit with the right-hand bulb—when the bulb lighted, the
clock started, and when the light went out, the clock stopped.

Four different intervals were used, namely, 8, 12, 19, and 32 sec. Each was presented six times, with block randomization being used to determine the ordering. A total of 60 Ss (college students) served individually, and all were given the same ordering of the intervals. Since each interval was presented six times, once in each of the successive six blocks, we could determine the effects of six stages of practice on the verbal estimates and the reproductions for each of the four intervals. For each stage of practice for each interval, 60 Ss contributed one judgment for each method. The constant error was determined for each S for each interval at each stage of practice and the means determined for the 60 Ss. The results are plotted in Fig. 2-7. The figure consists of four panels, each representing one of the four intervals.

Looking at the curves for the verbal estimation measure, we see clearly that for all intervals there is a sharp drop from the first stage of practice to the second. Beyond the second stage of practice, there is some inconsistency for the intervals. For the 8-sec. and 32-sec. intervals, the estimates continue to be shorter and shorter as stage of practice increases, but this is not so apparent with the 12-sec. and the 19-sec. intervals. Nevertheless, a comparison of the estimates with the reproductions shows that, relatively, stage of practice has little influence on the reproductions—the reproductions remain essentially constant across all six stages of practice. For this variable, therefore, the two methods of attack produce different results. For one method we reach a conclusion that stage of practice is a relevant variable, but for the other, that it is not.

Two other facts derived from this experiment are worth mentioning briefly. First is the fact that the individual differences, as indexed by standard deviations, are far greater for the verbal estimates than for the reproduction measure. Second is the fact that there is essentially a zero correlation between the verbal estimate and the reproduction, a fact also reported by other investigators. The usual college student appears to have no very good notion of the passage of time in an absolute sense. In the present data this is seen somewhat dramatically in a final task given S. After the completion of the 24 trials, S was asked to estimate the average length of all the intervals presented. These estimates varied from 5 sec. to 60 sec., with an average of 15.53 sec. (The actual average was 17.75 sec.) After S had made this estimate, he was requested to *produce* it. The correlation between the estimate and the production for the 60 Ss was .04. One S who had estimated the average interval to be 5 sec. produced an interval of 18 sec. The S who had estimated the average length to be 60 sec. produced an interval of 14 sec. Yet the average production was 15.58 sec., almost exactly the average estimate. The standard deviation for the estimates was 8.21 sec., for the productions, 4.25 sec.

Earlier, in discussing the production method, it was noted that there was a moderately high correlation between production and verbal estimation.

The careful reader will have noted that the data given in the paragraph above do not support the existence of such a correlation. The average length of interval as estimated by S showed no relationship with his ability to produce that interval. The reason for the discrepancy is not clear. Of course, the procedures are somewhat different. In the usual production method, E

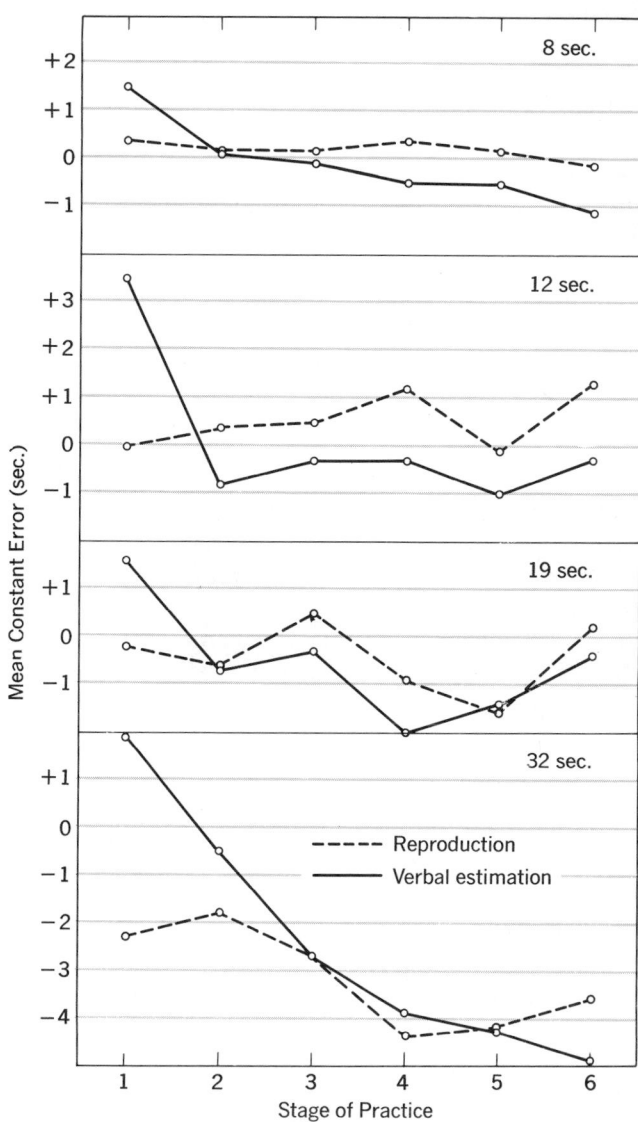

Fig. 2-7. Changes in time judgments as a function of stage of practice for two methods and four different intervals.

specifies to S the length of the interval he should produce. In the above situation, S, in a manner of speaking, specified his own interval. It is possible also that the single estimate and the single production resulted in unreliable scores for an S, in which case the correlation would be expected to be low. The single verbal estimate can be shown to be reliable, however. The correlation between this single verbal estimate and the average of the 24 verbal estimates given during the main part of the experiment is .86. This tells us that the S who, during the 24 trials, underestimated the length of the interval in the verbal estimates also underestimated the average length in the final estimate, and that the S who overestimated during the 24 trials also overestimated on the final. A correlation this high cannot be obtained with an unreliable measure. However, it is possible that the single production measure is unreliable since it has not been found to correlate significantly with any other measure obtained in the experiment. In any event, we note the lack of agreement between the present findings and those reported by other investigators, but we do not have evidence to resolve the contradiction.

A SAMPLING OF EXPERIMENTS

We are acquainted now with some of the methods used to study an apparently simple judgment, the judgment of the passage of time. We may repeat that these methods are not limited to experiments in which time perception is of interest. In one form or another they are used to study the perception of many different objects or events, some of which we will discuss in later chapters. For the moment, we are concerned with the application of these methods to the study of the judgments of temporal durations. Of course, we might always ask why anyone would *want* to study the perception of temporal durations. We might get as many different answers to this question as the number of people we asked. Some might start their study out of simple curiosity as to the accuracy of temporal judgments. Others might see the study of time judgments as a means by which many different forms of perception might be understood. Some might conduct experiments in order to test hypotheses or theories about "internal clocks." Some might study the factors influencing temporal judgments because of observations which indicate that some symptoms of certain mental illnesses indicate a temporal disorganization. Others might undertake the study of the development of the comprehension of time as a function of age with a commercial objective in mind, namely, the age when the usual child might be expected to use a watch in a meaningful fashion.

The fact is that studies of time perception have a long history. A recent book by a French psychologist (Fraisse, 1963), *The Psychology of Time*, lists 566 references. Of course, not all of these are experiments, and all do not deal directly with the perception of time; but all are judged relevant to attempts to understand the perception of time. Scores of experiments on judgments of time have occurred since this book was published. So, for a great variety of reasons, investigators have shown a persistent interest over many years in the perception of time.

An experiment, of course, involves the manipulation of some independent variable, and the particular variable to which the E's interest, or theory, or hunch led him will be the chosen one. However, in nearly all experiments on time perception, particularly those done in recent years, there is one primary objective: an attempt to identify the cues or events to which S correlates his judgments. Most investigators do not proceed on the assumption that there is a time sense per se; most assume that time perception is a by-product of the perception of events which occur in time. If this is true, it immediately follows that time perception can be made to vary by introducing different kinds and numbers of events in a given time interval and by examining how the judgments vary as a function of these events.

At one time in the study of time perception there was some interest in advancing a general law concerning whether S overestimates or underestimates time intervals. Although many investigators had noted exceptions, one of the "laws" handed down over the years is that Ss overestimate short intervals (1 to 2 sec.) and underestimate longer intervals. At the present time there is little evidence in the literature that Es have any interest in the validity or invalidity of this law. The critical question is not how accurate S is in an absolute sense; the critical question concerns the variables that may be introduced experimentally which will influence S's judgments, with little or no attention paid to the absolute accuracy of the judgments. Indeed, the usual instructions which disallow counting or tapping is an effort to rule out a particular variable which is known to allow more accurate judgments in an absolute sense. The more critical question concerns the cues or events used to mark the passage of time when the obvious event markers (such as counting) are eliminated. We have seen that counting is not the only event which allows perception of the passage of time. When Ss are not allowed to count they still have considerable discrimination of differences in duration; they do not often report that a 20-sec. interval is of the same length as a 40-sec. interval. And so the primary interest of most modern experimental work is the attempt to determine what cues or events are used by S to measure temporal duration when the obvious mechanism (counting or tapping) is eliminated. Thus, we would say that the analytical problem being given to experiments is concerned with relevant and irrelevant cues which form the basis for estimating passage of time. Our intent is to sample some of these experiments.

Judgment as a Skill

Some experiments have asked whether or not S can be trained to be accurate in his judgments. If S can be so trained, it must mean that learning consists of attending to appropriate cues or events which accurately mark the interval. The fact is that, at least within limits, one can train S to be accurate or to be inaccurate; he can learn to adjust his judgments to what E tells him is appropriate. We will consider two studies.

Robinson (1963) used the production method. The E would specify a particular interval that S was to produce, and S would attempt to produce it by closing a switch (which started a timer) and opening it (which stopped the timer) when he judged that the appropriate time had elapsed. In this experiment there were nine different conditions which were defined by the length of the interval to be judged (5 sec., 10 sec., or 15 sec.) and by the nature of the information given after each production. There were three levels of information. In one, a control, S was told nothing. In a second, S was told "that was too much" or "that was not enough," referring to the production S had just completed. In the third, S was told to the nearest .01 sec. just what the production was. These instructions are commonly said to provide knowledge of results; they give S knowledge concerning the adequacy of his performance after each trial. The second condition is said to give less precise knowledge than the third, but both give knowledge of results when compared with the first (control).

A different group of Ss was used in each condition of length of interval and instructions. That is, for the 5-sec. interval, three different groups of Ss were used, these three groups differing only in terms of the knowledge-of-results variable. Three more groups were used for the 10-sec. interval, and the final three, for the 15-sec. interval. It can be seen, therefore, that there are two independent variables in this experiment, namely, length of interval and the nature of the knowledge of results. This, superficially at least, seems to violate the rule that only one factor should be allowed to vary in an experiment. For the present, however, we may consider the overall experiment as consisting of three experiments done simultaneously, one experiment being concerned with the effect of knowledge of results on judging a 5-sec. interval, another concerned with the same variable on judging a 10-sec. interval, and the third, on judging a 15-sec. interval. In a later chapter we will return to this matter in somewhat more detail.

However, it is clear that this design, in using independent groups of Ss, deviates from those considered earlier. In the earlier experiments, each S served in all conditions, and these conditions were balanced for progressive-error effects so that each S's data actually constituted an experiment unto itself. Now, in the present experiment, Robinson has chosen to use the other type of design where S serves in only one condition and different groups of Ss are required for each condition. Several problems concerned with assigning Ss to the conditions in such an experiment will be reserved for Chapter Four. For the moment, we must ask why Robinson did not use a design in which each S served in all conditions. Why did she choose the present design? We suspect you can answer this question yourself given the appropriate "set." Let us reduce the experiment to a two-condition experiment, in which the interval is always 5 sec. Over a series of trials S is to be given either Cond. *a* or Cond. *b*. Condition *a* consists of being told nothing after a given trial, and Cond. *b* consists of being given complete knowledge of performance on that trial. Assume further that we randomize 30 trials, 15 on *a* and 15 on *b*, so that the sequence starts out as *ababbaabab*. Assume that you are the S in this experiment. Do you think your performance on Cond. *a* would be uninfluenced by the information you get after each trial under Cond. *b*? If you think this over carefully, remembering that E wants to get a relatively pure case of the effect of no knowledge of results versus knowledge of results, you will probably conclude that the design was appropriate for the problem and that if a given S had been used in both conditions, the variable might be shown to be ineffective. As a general point, in thinking about the adequacy of any design, it is often wise to put yourself in S's position and imagine how you might be influenced by the different conditions.

Robinson gave each S 30 trials under the particular condition to which that S was assigned. Therefore, we may trace the course of the judgments as a function of practice. The results for the three intervals were essentially equivalent so we may omit this variable from further discussion. Let us first examine the control condition—the condition where S was told nothing after each production. On the initial trials, the mean production of the 16 Ss given this condition was short—S produced an interval that was a second or two short of the true interval. By the end of 30 trials, however, S was producing intervals that were from 2 to 3 sec. too long. This is to say, there were clear changes with practice over the 30 trials. Now, there is a rather tricky point involved in the response measures when considering the production method and the method of verbal estimation. We have seen that with verbal estimation S's estimates are initially higher than the true interval but they change to an underestimation. On the surface, it appears that the present results with the control group are just the opposite: S produces an interval that is too short initially and subsequently switches over, producing an interval that is too long (when compared with the requested interval). However, phenomenally speaking, these two sets of results indicate the same change. If I initially present S with a 10-sec. interval and ask for a verbal estimate and if this verbal estimate is 12 sec., it implies that S's conception of the passage of time is faster than it should be for absolute accuracy. Now, if I ask S to produce a 10-sec. interval and if he conceives of time passing faster than it does, in fact, pass, he will produce an interval shorter than 10 sec.—the 10 sec. will seem to have passed before, in fact, it did. Thus, the present results with production show exactly the same trend over trials as have the previous data on verbal estimation.

The above discussion related to the control group. The two groups, given knowledge of results, did not differ in their judgments over trials. Roughly speaking, both groups began to be quite accurate by the tenth trial and remained quite close to the true length of the interval for the remaining 20 trials. There was some small tendency toward underestimation (setting the interval too long) on the later trials, suggesting that they were still somewhat influenced by the same "force" which produced the rather severe underestimation in later trials for the control group.

This study indicates that S can learn to make judgments of temporal duration which correspond well to true durations. Just what cues or events are critical or just what reevaluation of cues and events is made is not known from this study. The following study also indicates that S can adjust his estimates to the information given in spite of the fact that the information is quite incorrect.

Craik and Sarbin (1963) wired a large wall clock in such a way that it could be made to go either twice as fast or half as fast as it normally would. The method of verbal estimation was used for five trials without any information concerning the accuracy of the judgments. Then one group of Ss made nine verbal estimates, and after each estimate Ss were allowed to turn around and look at the clock to see how accurate they were. The clock in this case had been set to the twice-as-fast level. Another group went through the same procedure but observed the accuracy of their estimates on the half-as-fast clock. Over the nine trials the Ss in the first group gradually increased the magnitude of their estimates; those in the second group gradually decreased theirs. The Ss were in some way adjusting their judgments to correspond to the information being given them by E. Judgment of duration can be conceived of as a skill and, like any skill, will be subject to modification by various training procedures. Since the training procedure requires S either to attend to new events or to reevaluate the temporal implications of old events, or both, a search for the relevant events seems to be a reasonable undertaking.

Variation of Events

At this point we will consider three studies in which the nature of the events correlated with the passage of time is varied. If we consider the three methods used in studying time perception, we see that in verbal estimation E may vary the nature of the activity while S is "waiting out" the interval. In the production method, on the other hand, the activity may be varied only while S is producing the interval. Only the reproduction method allows E to vary the activity both during the presentation of the interval and during S's attempted reproduction.

Variations in tapping rate. In a study by Denner, Wapner, McFarland, and Werner (1963), the reproduction method was used, and a specified rate of tapping was inserted both during the presentation and during the reproduction. These Es determined first what may be called a natural or preferred tapping rate for a large group of Ss. A simple telegraph key was wired to a counter, and S was asked to tap on the key at a rate which seemed comfortable to him. He did this for 60 sec. The range of preferred rates fell between .8 taps per sec. and 4.8 taps per sec. It is worth noting that this characteristic for a given S is highly stable. When Ss were tested at two different times, the correlation between the two distributions of tapping rates was .93.

For this particular study the Es wanted Ss who were very homogeneous in their preferred tapping rate, so from the large group of Ss tested, 18 were chosen, all of whose rates fell between 1.8 and 2.4 taps per sec. Two additional rates were set for the experiment. One of these was called a fast rate at 1.3 taps per sec. above a given S's preferred or natural rate. The slow rate was 1.3 taps below the natural rate. Now, as noted above, the activity may be introduced during the presentation of the interval or during the reproduction of the interval, or both. In this experiment a given rate of tapping was always imposed during both the presentation and the reproduction, and all possible combinations of the three rates were used. Thus, the rate could be either slow during the presentation and natural during the reproduction or slow during the presentation and fast during the reproduction, and so on, with all possible combinations representing nine different conditions.

The rate of tapping was enforced by a simple technique. A light flashed at the specified rate, and S was required to synchronize the key taps with the flashing light. The presentation of the interval was marked by quite a different light which flashed on and off for the specified interval of time. Then, after a 10-sec. pause, the light would start flashing again; and after S thought the equivalent interval had passed, he signaled E. The interval judged in this experiment was always 70 sec. Each of the 18 Ss was given all nine conditions, one trial on each.

The results of this experiment are shown in Fig. 2-8. In examining this figure we may think of the results as representing three separate experiments. In each experiment there was variation of the tapping rate during presentation, but in one experiment the rate was slow during reproduction, in another it was the natural rate, and in the third it was fast. In general, all three experiments show the same trends: with a slow tapping rate during presentation, the reproduced intervals are longer than with a fast tapping rate during presentation, with the natural rate falling in between. Judgments are not influenced by the tapping rate as such, but they are influenced by a discrepancy between the rate during presentation and the rate during reproduction. That is, when the tapping rate is the same during the reproduction as it is during the presentation (slow-slow, natural-natural, fast-fast), the intervals reproduced are almost identical (75.5, 74.3, 74.0). Differences occur when the rate changes from the presentation to the reproduction. Thus, it seems clear that the perception of the duration of an interval is somehow tied to the rate of occurrence of events in that interval, and when that rate changes during the reproduction, the correlation is disturbed. This same law occurs in the following study where the nature of the activities during the intervals was quite different from those just discussed.

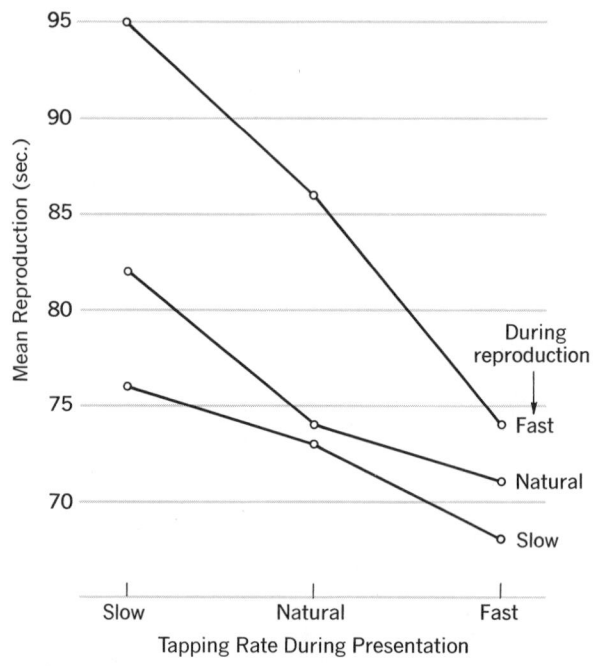

Fig. 2-8. Reproductions of a 70-sec. interval as a function of tapping rate during presentation of the interval and tapping rate during reproduction. Data from Denner, Wapner, McFarland, and Werner (1963).

Active versus passive activities. In an experiment by DeWolfe and Duncan (1959) a 26-sec. interval was used with the judgments being made by the reproduction method. In the passive condition, S merely leaned back in the chair and relaxed; in the active condition he tried to solve anagrams (rearranging jumbled letters to form a word). Each activity could be introduced during the presentation of the interval or during the reproduction of the interval (active-active, active-passive, passive-active, passive-passive). The active-active and the passive-passive conditions gave almost identical mean reproductions. Only when there was a discrepancy between the activity of the presentation and of the reproduction periods did the judgments change.

Word recognition and temporal judgments. An indirect way of varying the duration of an activity and correlating this with perception of time was used by Warm, Greenberg, and Dube (1964). The S was told that a word would appear on a screen for a short interval and that when it disappeared S was to estimate how long it had appeared. In fact, all words were flashed on the screen for a period of only 1 sec. There were 24 words, 12 of which were common words (e.g., *scientific, physics, automobile*) and 12 quite uncommon (e.g., *percipience, statics, frugality*). The two types of words were randomized in a series so that any progressive error would affect each equally. The question asked of this experiment is whether or not perceived duration would vary as a function of the common-uncommon dimension. It did. The 45 Ss gave an average estimate of .93 sec. for the common words and .83 sec. for the uncommon. Why should this be? If we assume that S could identify the common words more quickly than the uncommon, there would be a longer period for a common word than for an uncommon word between the point of identification and the disappearance of the word from the screen. In a manner of speaking, the process of identification of the uncommon word filled more of the 1-sec. interval than did the identification of the common word. If S used the duration of the unfilled portion of the interval as a cue for his judgment, the common words had, in fact, a longer unfilled portion than did the uncommon words. Thus, S may have been led to estimate the overall interval as being longer for the common than for the uncommon words.

Physiological Factors

We have noted that in the usual study on time perception the Ss are instructed not to count or tap. We cannot, however, eliminate all rhythmic activities, for S must continue to breathe and his heart must continue to beat. One might ask, therefore, if differences in time estimations from individual to individual are in any way related to differences in the rate of such rhythmic physiological factors. The findings appear to be inconclusive on this matter (Dimond, 1964). There have been some reports that time perception varies as a function of body temperature. For example, it has been said that a person with a high fever during an illness has a different perception of time from his perception when he is without a fever. Such scattered observations have led to the possibility that time perception is in some way correlated with action of chemical processes, these processes differing as body temperature changes. We will examine one study in the interest of examining not only the results, but also the method.

When body temperature changes as a function of illness, we have a confounding of variables that might be involved in changes in time perception. As compared with a normal state, an illness involves changes in addition to temperature changes. If an infected throat raises the temperature, we have, as compared with a normal state, both a change in the soreness of the throat as well as an increase in the temperature. Time estimations might be changed by alterations in either of these factors. But, like any study of this naturalistic observation type, one might state a hypothesis that temperature changes are associated with changes in time estimations. The experimental problem is to test this hypothesis by experimentally allowing only one factor—temperature—to vary. Such an attempt was made by Bell and Provins (1963).

They performed three experiments and used three different methods of measuring time perception, namely, counting, verbal estimation, and production. Each S made judgments under normal environmental temperatures (68 to 70 degrees F.) and under raised temperature conditions. The body temperature was raised in a very simple manner: the S was placed in a room in which the temperature of the air was raised. Roughly speaking, the temperature in the room varied in the different experiments from 120 degrees to 145 degrees. The critical fact, however, is that body temperature, measured orally, was raised significantly. However, no consistent effect of temperature on time perception was discovered in the experiments; the conclusion must be that changes in body temperature produced in the manner described are not related to time perception.

Of course, there are many other approaches which may be taken to relate time perception to physiological changes. Some of these approaches may be mentioned briefly. Time perception might vary following administration of certain drugs (e.g., Frankenhaeuser, 1959). Time perception may be related to level of metabolic activity. It is known that metabolic activity changes throughout the course of a day; therefore, time perception could vary as a function of time of day. Some evidence in support of this notion is available (e.g., Thor, 1962). Finally, time perception has been shown to differ before and after certain brain operations (e.g., Clausen, 1950).

Use of Lower Animals

Can animals tell time? Or, can they be taught to tell time? A time sense of sorts does seem to be present in certain animals. That birds migrate at certain times and not at others is one illustration. That bears hibernate at a given time is another. We would also suspect from casual observation that animals can, in a manner of speaking, be taught to respond to cues which indicate some sort of a time-keeping mechanism. Cows that are consistently brought into the barn at 6 P.M. for milking will often appear at the barn door just before 6 P.M. We can formalize such observations in the laboratory.

We may use the white rat as the subject. Initially this rat is taught to press a lever in a small box. Each time the lever is pressed a small pellet of food is released. After the association between pressing the lever and appearance of food is well established, we fix the mechanism of the pellet dispenser so that pellets will be released for only five seconds at a time, with 5-min. periods between each 5-sec. period during which time no pellets will be released. Thus, only for a 5-sec. period out of each 5 min. will the rat receive food for pressing the lever. What is eventually observed are peaks of lever-pressing activity occurring at 5-min. intervals. The animal will press furiously during the 5-sec. interval, but when pellets stop being released the animal will stop pressing and will make relatively few presses for nearly 5 min. Then the pressing activity builds up rapidly to the same furious pace noted 5 min. earlier. It seems reasonable to conclude from such behavior that the animal has learned in some manner to judge the passage of an interval of 5 min. duration.

Individual Differences

Earlier in the chapter we have seen that there are consistent individual differences among Ss in their time estimations. One S may consistently overestimate a temporal interval, and another may consistently underestimate the same interval. It is reasonable to ask questions about other differences between these two Ss which may be related to (correlated with) time perception. In the general sense this means we will manipulate S variables. We may study time perception as a function of age, of sex, of certain personality characteristics such as introversion-extroversion, of diagnostic category of mental illness, of juvenile delinquents versus nondelinquents, and so on. Indeed, scores of such studies have been performed. We will not be concerned here with the results of such studies but rather with the nature of the conclusions which may be reached from them.

Let us assume that we have done an experiment in which we found that schizophrenic patients produced a different distribution of time estimations from the distribution produced by normals. Does this mean that schizophrenia is responsible for (caused) the difference in time perception? It might be, but this experiment would provide no evidence to allow such a statement. We know there are wide individual differences among normals in the accuracy of time estimations; perhaps these schizophrenics would have given the same deviant judgments before they became ill. Or we might view this another way. Suppose it was within our power to do an experiment in which we experimentally induced schizophrenia. We have two groups of normal Ss, both known to be equally accurate in estimating time. Then we experimentally make schizophrenics of all of the members of one group, leaving the other group normal. Again we obtain measures of time perception on both groups. If the two groups differ under these circumstances, we would clearly be in a position to say that the experimental manipulations we used in producing schizophrenia also produced differences in time perception.

It should be evident that this experimental situation is not the one we have when we measure time estimation of a group of Ss who had become schizophrenic naturally and compare these measures with those obtained from normals. The schizophrenics and the normals may differ on a multitude of factors other than those which led to the diagnosis of schizophrenia in one case and not in the other, and any one or a group of these other factors may be responsible for the difference. Of course, if in fact it were shown that schizophrenics and normals differ consistently in time perception, a test of time perception could be used as one of the diagnostic tools for determining whether or not a person is schizophrenic. That is, in making a diagnosis of a troubled person, time perception scores might be used as one of several indexes to be weighed in reaching a decision concerning the class of illness involved if classes other than schizophrenia do not have distortions in their time perception. In such a case we are using time perception scores in a predictive manner without attempting to state a causal relationship between schizophrenia and time perception.

SUMMARY

Experimental studies of time perception were used to initiate the discussion of the design of experiments and the handling and interpretation of data derived therefrom. The discussion was built around the following topics:

1. In designing an experiment a decision must always be made whether to use independent groups of Ss (a different group for each condition of the experiment) or to use a single group of Ss with all Ss of the group serving in all conditions. There are no general rules which may be used to generate this decision; in the study of the discriminal processes, the single-group technique has been used traditionally.

2. The use of a single group of Ss requires that particular attention be paid to the ordering of the conditions so as to balance the progressive error (changes in performance with successive trials) over conditions and thus avoid a confounding. A confounding exists when there is ambiguity as to what role the independent variable plays in producing the obtained results. Three methods for balancing progressive-error effects were detailed: namely, counterbalancing, complete randomization, and block randomization.

3. Constant errors may occur in the measurements of time perception. A constant error is some consistent overestimation of a standard stimulus (e.g., reporting a 30-sec. interval to be 35 sec.), in which case it is called a positive constant error; or it is some consistent underestimation of a standard stimulus, in which case it is called a negative constant error. Constant errors are not constant. They may show changes in magnitude as a function of certain independent variables, but even if no such systematic changes

occur, there will be variability of the judgments around a central or mean point defining the magnitude of the constant error. This variability, the variable error, may also change systematically as a function of independent variables.

4. The reliability of response measures was discussed. While consistency (reliability) within S is normally found with time estimations (as with most behaviors), the reliability may be zero and still lawful relationships between independent and dependent variables may be found for groups of Ss.

5. The phrase *methods of attack* was used to refer to particular methods used in studying a given area of behavior. Although many variants have been used, these have revolved around three basic methods of attack, methods which are used to study not only time perception, but other discriminal processes as well. The three methods are:

(a) Verbal estimation, in which S is asked to give a verbal estimate of the duration of an interval. This is a special case of the more general method of absolute judgment or single stimuli.

(b) Production method, in which S attempts to "mark off" an interval of a duration specified verbally by E.

(c) Reproduction method, in which E marks off an interval and then S tries to mark off an interval of the same duration. This is a special case of the more general method of average error or method of adjustment.

6. Most contemporary experiments on time perception are concerned with identifying the events or cues which form the bases for time perception. A sampling of studies was presented to illustrate the wide variety of approaches being taken.

CHAPTER THREE

Illusions

In this chapter we will expand our knowledge of the experimental techniques used by psychologists. At the same time, more practice will be given in handling data and in making inferences from the data. The vehicle for this discussion will be visual illusions. Many of the figures which induce illusory experiences are very simple; even the most ill-equipped laboratory can do perfectly satisfactory studies. Furthermore, even a cursory consideration of the materials used to produce a given illusion suggests many potential variables which may cause the magnitude of the illusion to vary.

First, we should get some notion of what we are looking for when we study illusions. A very simple example, known as the horizontal-vertical illusion, is demonstrated in Fig. 3-1. Both lines are of equal length, but to most people the vertical line appears longer. That is, there is a consistent

Fig. 3-1. The horizontal-vertical illusion. Both lines are of equal length, although most observers will conclude that the vertical line is longer.

discrepancy between the phenomenal length of the two lines. It is sometimes said that an illusion represents a discrepancy between the real world
and the phenomenal world—the world as the observer perceives it. This is
not quite accurate, however, since it implies that a real world exists independent of an observer and therefore raises a philosophical question that is
best left to the philosophers. What we usually mean by an illusion, unen-
cumbered by the philosophical overlay, is that there is a consistent discrepancy between two ways of observing an object or an event. One of
these methods of observation is unaided by any instruments of measurement; these are the phenomenal "measurements" you make when you judge
the relative lengths of the two lines in Fig. 3-1. The other method is accomplished by the use of instruments which are used to measure the objects or
events, and these instruments measure along a physical scale. In order to
speak of an illusion, we must have a consistent difference in judgments between these two kinds of observation. A ruler shows that the two lines in
Fig. 3-1 are equal in length; unaided by a ruler, most people say they are
not equal. As a matter of fact, even the person who measures the line and
assures himself they are equal will, if he respects his phenomenology, continue to report that they "look different." We have said that an observation
made by the use of an instrument expressed in physical measuring units is
the base for determining whether or not an illusion exists. This means, therefore, that we never speak of an illusion when there is a discrepancy in results
between two different ways of measuring phenomenal appearance. For example, if we had Ss in one case estimate the absolute length of the lines in
Fig. 3-1 and, in another case, draw lines which they believed were the same
length as those in Fig. 3-1, and if there is a discrepancy in the results from
these two modes of attack, we would never speak of this discrepancy as
representing an illusion. To use the term *illusion*, we must refer back to
measurements along a physical scale.

An illusion, in the terminology with which we are already acquainted,
is a constant error. But, in common usage of the term, illusion is applied to
a constant error only when the direction (negative or positive) of the error
is fairly universal, that is, when most people are subject to the illusion. Obviously, this is not a satisfactory criterion since the word *most* is a little
indefinite. Thus, although we might be better off not using the word *illusion*
at all, in deference to tradition we will do so. Before getting involved in an
examination of methods used to study some of the classical illusions, we
need to look at some preliminary data by way of leading up to the central
problems.

Reproduction of Length

We will follow through a simple procedure which may be
used to evaluate accuracy in *reproducing* lines of different lengths. The procedure as described was given to only one S, but it could, of course, be

applied to groups. The stimulus materials consisted of three 5 by 8-in. cards. On one card a straight black line 1 in. long was drawn; on another the line was 2 in.; and on the third, 3 in. These, in conformance with our previous usage of words, are called the standard stimuli. The S was given one card at a time under instructions to place it upright—with the line horizontal— at the top of a sheet of unruled 8½ by 11-in. paper. The simple task for S was attempting to reproduce the length of this standard by drawing a line on the unruled sheet. A single excursion of the pencil was used, and no special sighting was allowed in making the reproductions. A number of lines were drawn on each sheet, but each preceding line drawn was covered

TABLE 3–1

RELATIONSHIP BETWEEN LENGTH OF LINE AND CONSTANT AND
VARIABLE ERRORS IN THE LINE-DRAWING EXPERIMENT

DEVIATION FROM STANDARD	LENGTH OF STANDARD LINE		
	16/16 in.	32/16 in.	48/16 in.
−3	0	0	2
−2	6	1	5
−1	14	5	6
0	56	9	11
1	110	18	16
2	126	46	38
3	87	76	65
4	33	87	74
5	8	76	60
6		66	64
7		36	45
8		15	31
9		5	13
10			8
11			2
Mean length of reproductions	17.747	36.254	52.606
Standard	16.000	32.000	48.000
Constant Error	+ 1.747	+ 4.254	+ 4.606
Standard Deviation	1.37	1.99	2.49

so that each new line was drawn on a homogeneous field. No knowledge of results was given, that is, S was never told how accurate the reproductions were.

A total of 440 reproductions of each of the three standards was made by this patient S; thus, a total of 1320 lines was drawn. The drawing extended over 12 experimental sessions so that, on the average, 110 lines were drawn each session. An equal number of the standard lines was reproduced on each session, and a random order of presenting the standard lines was followed within each session.

The first step in analyzing the reproductions consisted of measuring each and recording how much it deviated from the standard. If the reproduction was less than the standard, it was assigned a minus value, and, if greater, a plus value. The unit of measurement was 1/16 in. With such a large number of trials for a given condition (for each standard) it is economical to bring the data together in a frequency distribution. The resulting distributions for each standard are shown in Table 3-1. A quick visual inspection shows that this S's reproductions were *not* distributed randomly around the standard lines. This is shown by the fact that the mode (greatest number of responses in a given category) for the 1-in. standard is at +2/16 in., that for the 2-in. standard, +4/16 in., and that for the 3-in. standard, also +4/16 in. Of course, as will be remembered from a study of distributions in statistics courses, the modal value does not necessarily imply that the *mean* constant error can be inferred from the mode. This is only true if the distribution of scores is fairly symmetrical. But these distributions (Fig. 3-2) are fairly symmetrical; and as can be seen at the bottom of Table 3-1, there is a positive constant error for each standard, the size of the constant error being greater for the 2- and 3-in. standards than for the 1-in. standard. It is also to be noted that the standard deviation of the reproductions increases directly as the length of the standard increases, a relationship also noted in the time estimation data. This relationship is reflected in Fig. 3-2 in the flattening of the distributions as the standard increases.

Very often in experimental work in psychology too few measurements are taken on a given S (or too few Ss are measured) to produce the types of curves shown in Fig. 3-2. Not only is there a simple beauty in the symmetry of the distributions of a large number of response measurements, but there is also some provision of comfort when we realize that many of our statistical tests make assumptions about the normality, or at least symmetry, of the measurements.

What variables might influence the line-drawing behavior? One which will produce marked differences in the constant error is knowledge of results. If after each reproduction we measure the line and tell S how much he overshot or undershot the standard, he will rather quickly "zero in" on the standard length and achieve a constant error of essentially zero. However, suppose we told him only that he overshot or undershot, not telling him how much. It is likely that when such gross information is given, the variability will increase (at least on the initial reproductions) if S had an initial constant error of some size. This might be expected because his reproductions may start bracketing the standard length, first being longer and then shorter, then longer, and so on, as he gradually zeros in on the standard length. An S not given such knowledge of results over a comparable number of trials may continue to have a constant error but may at the same time be quite consistent in the reproductions.

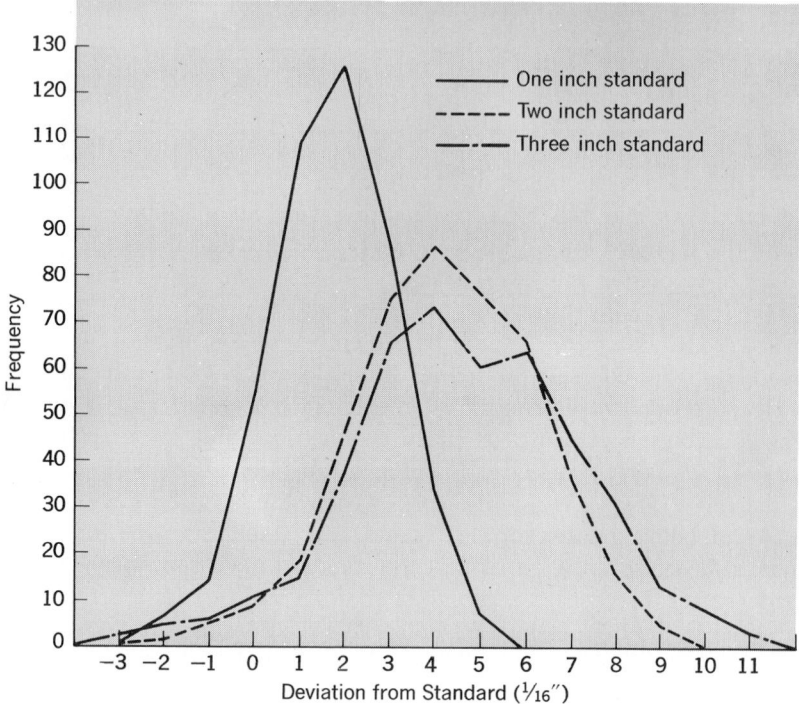

Fig. 3-2. Results of line drawing experiment. Three standards were used as indicated and S made 440 reproductions of each. Deviation from standard is plotted against the frequency with which that deviation occurred.

Another set of variables could deal with the method of attack. In the above procedure S reproduced the line length; thus, this is the method of average error. But we could also ask S to estimate the length of lines to the nearest 1/16 in., thereby using the method of absolute judgment. In the method of average error it is clear that two different processes are involved. First, S must perceive the line and, then, must make an instrumental response of drawing what he perceived. Are we to attribute the constant error of the S to faulty perception or to the inability to translate what he saw into a line of the perceived length, or are both involved? Having S make absolute judgments removes the instrumental response of drawing but introduces another process which certainly may be expected to influence the constant error, namely, the conception S has of "how long is an inch" or "how long is 1/16 of an inch."

A series of experiments could be devised in an effort to "analyze out" the effects of the various factors. For example, we might find out just how long are the lines drawn under instructions to draw lines of specified lengths. To remove variation of or influence on the constant error in actually drawing a line, we might have a series of straight lines on a sheet of paper all of which are much longer than any standard to be shown S. Then, rather than asking S to draw the line, we could have him simply mark a point on the prepared line. A direct comparison of several methods of attack is an excellent way to obtain an initial understanding of the factors that go into the constant and variable errors, such as are exhibited in the data presented earlier on a single S.

It might seem that it would be difficult to make an error in experimental procedure or design for such a simple task as line drawing. However, let us consider a simple extension of the procedure used to derive the data in Table 3-1 and Fig. 3-2. The only change made is that the lengths of the standard lines will be 1, 4, and 7 in.; all other aspects of the procedure remain exactly the same. It is a reasonable prediction that data from such an experiment would show that the variability of the reproductions first increases and then decreases as the length of the standard increases. Clearly, a prediction would be made that the variability of the reproductions of the 7-in. standard would be less than those for the 4-in. standard. Such a finding would contradict the general principle noted earlier that as the magnitude of a standard increases, the variability of judgments around the standard increases. Would we take the expected results as a contradiction to the principle, or have we confounded our measurements in some way? There is reason to believe there is a confounding. Perhaps you can figure it out before reading the footnote.*

THE H-V ILLUSION AND THE METHOD OF AVERAGE ERROR

We will examine three studies which were concerned more or less directly with the horizontal-vertical (H-V) illusion and used the method of average error in its measurement. There is a simple lesson to be

---

*Drawing a 7-in. line on paper 8½ in. wide would probably result in S's drawing a line so that it ended a short distance, an inch perhaps, from the right edge of the paper. On successive trials S would probably always try to end the line the same distance from the edge of the paper; hence the variability would be very low. In effect, then, S is "reproducing" a 1-in. line rather than a 7-in. line. In attempting to detect such flaws in an experiment, look first at the most sensitive point. The fact that the 7-in. reproductions are the ones which deny the general principle suggests strongly that one should examine the situation for the 7-in. line from the S's point of view. That is, what would you do if you were the S?

learned from the results of these experiments over and above a fuller comprehension of the method of average error: most phenomena are not dependent for their appearance upon a highly specific set of conditions. They may occur with optimal magnitude under a highly specific set of conditions, but they are usually not all-or-none affairs; some variations from these conditions will not destroy them. The H-V illusion is so named because in the standard procedures S compares the lengths of horizontal and vertical lines. But do these lines have to be precisely vertical and precisely horizontal?

Line orientation. Imagine that you are an S in the following experiment performed by Pollock and Chapanis (1952). You are seated 15 ft. from a square white screen that is 6 ft. on a side. A little to the center-right of the screen is a black horizontal line 6 in. long and ½ in. wide. This is the standard line. To the left of center is another identical line. However, this line (the variable line) can be rotated around a midpoint axis so that it can be given any angular orientation desired. Furthermore, as an S, you can lengthen or shorten this line by pulling on a string which is attached to the line by a pulley arrangement. Your task is to adjust the length of this variable line so that it appears to you to be of the same length as the standard 6-in. line to your right, which remains fixed in length and orientation (horizontal). The independent variable is the orientation of the left line—the variable line.

The orientation of the variable line was varied in 10-degree steps. Let the upper point of this line at 9 o'clock position represent 0 degrees; then, proceeding clockwise, vertical (noon) will be 90 degrees, and 3 o'clock, 180 degrees. Of course, both the 9- and 3-o'clock positions represent a horizontal line and, hence, in orientation are the same as the standard.

These Es used 20 Ss. Each S was given two trials for each orientation of the variable line, the order of the orientations being random. On each trial the S was given a particular orientation of the variable line and was requested to adjust this line until it appeared to be the same length as the standard. One half of the trials in which the variable line was set to be obviously longer than the standard was alternated with the other half in which the variable line was set to be obviously shorter than the standard. The S was given as much time as he wanted to make the match. It is apparent that the outlines of the procedure fit the method of average error.

Obviously, the apparatus permitted measurement of the length of the variable line for each trial. The data, given in Fig. 3-3, are means for the 40 trials involved (two for each S). The dependent variable used here is the actual length of the variable line which appeared to be equal to the length of the standard. It is seen that as the orientation goes from zero degrees toward the vertical, the length judged equal to the standard decreases; this is to say that there is a negative constant error. Since a vertical line appears longer than a horizontal line of the same length, the S tends to set a variable line shorter than the standard to make it appear equal to the standard.

Essentially, Fig. 3-3 shows that any slanted line appears longer than a horizontal line. But one interesting aspect of the data emphasized by Pollock and Chapanis is the lack of symmetry in the perceptions. The line slanted or tilted left, about 30 degrees from vertical, apparently appears longer than a line slanted or oriented 20 to 30 degrees right of vertical. The

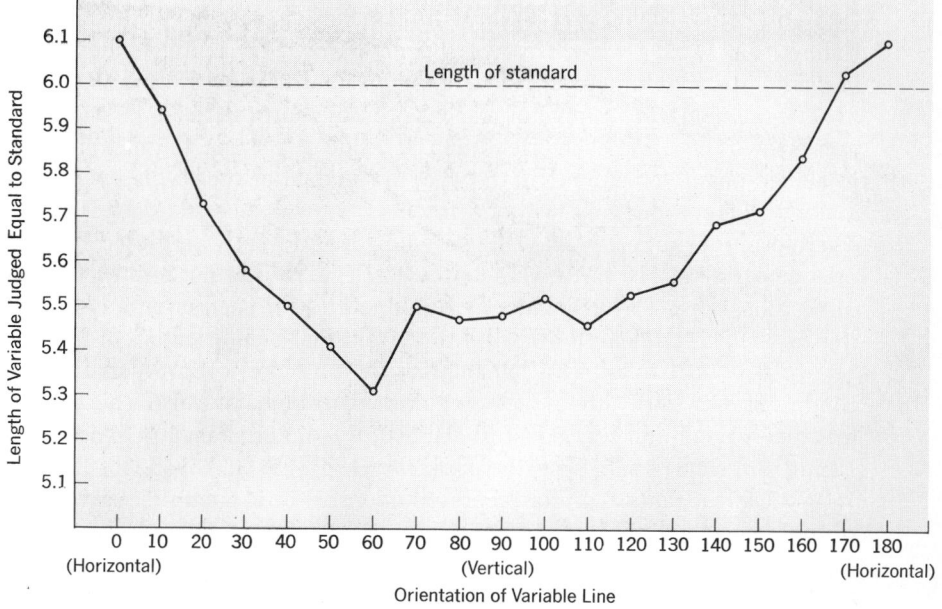

Fig. 3-3. Mean lengths of lines of various orientations judged equal in length to a standard horizontal line of 6 in. Data from Pollock and Chapanis (1952).

line oriented to left of vertical actually appears longer than the vertical, although both appear longer than the horizontal. It might be suggested that the asymmetry around the vertical represents some chance factor and that the same effect would not appear with additional studies. This is not true. These investigators have several experiments or sets of conditions in addition to those given here, and the effect cropped up rather persistently. Pollock and Chapanis conclude that it is a reliable phenomenon; lines tilted to the left of vertical appear longer than those tilted to the right. Let us examine this same phenomenon using a different method of attack.

Orientation with reproduction. This experiment was performed by the students in the author's class. The S was shown a line of a given orientation, and its length was then reproduced by S who drew a *horizontal* line; regardless of the orientation of the line shown, the reproduction was always drawn horizontally. Four orientations were used, namely, 45 degrees left of vertical (10:30 o'clock), vertical, 45 degrees right of vertical (1:30 o'clock), and horizontal. To correspond to the above study these may be referred to as 45, 90, 135, and 180 degrees.

The standard lines were drawn on 5 by 5-in. cards. With only four different lines, only four cards were needed. However, another independent variable was manipulated, not because of interest in the variable but to avoid a possible stereotyping of responses on the part of the S. We wanted to give S several trials at each orientation. If a line of a single length were used, it seemed possible that S might discover this and, after such a discovery, start making his reproductions without, in effect, viewing the standard stimulus. Therefore, four different line lengths (1, 2, 3, and 4 in.) were used for each orientation so that 16 cards were employed. The Ss were not told the lengths of the lines used. Each S made 12 reproductions for each orientation of the line, and each line length occurred three times at each orientation.

Just as in the Pollock-Chapanis study, therefore, each S served in all conditions. Obviously, the progressive error must be balanced. To accomplish this, line orientation was counterbalanced, a counterbalancing "block" consisting of a single trial. Thus, the order was 180, 135, 90, 45, 45, 90, 135, 180, 180, 135, 90, 45, and so on for 48 presentations. Within each successive block of four trials the line lengths were randomized, subject to the restriction that each line length occur with each orientation three times.

The E presented each standard stimulus to S's view for 3 sec., after which S drew a line in an attempt to approximate the same length as the line shown. All previous lines were covered before drawing a given line, and 16 reproductions were made on a standard size sheet of paper.

The reproductions were assessed in terms of the constant error. Each reproduction was measured to the nearest $\frac{1}{16}$ in., and E recorded the constant error (reproduced length minus standard length). Length of line was ignored in bringing these data together so that the constant error for each S was based on 12 reproductions of each line orientation. There were 16 Ss so that for each orientation there were 192 observations.

The data are plotted in Fig. 3-4. To understand these data in conjunction with the Pollock-Chapanis data we have to rearrange our thinking. The constant error is plotted in Fig. 3-4, whereas the lengths of lines judged equal to the standard were plotted in Fig. 3-3. We also have differences produced by the two variations on the method of average error. In Fig. 3-3 the data show that when the orientation was horizontal, the adjustment of the variable line was almost perfectly accurate. This is patently not true in the present experiment where Ss reproduced the horizontal line by drawing horizontally. Here there is a constant error showing that the line drawn is appreciably shorter than the line shown (the standard line). However, the reproduction of the horizontal line serves as a base for evaluating the influence of the other orientations. Looking at the results for the vertical line (90 degrees), we see that, on the average, the reproductions are slightly longer than the standard. Since the lines drawn for this orientation are much longer than those drawn when the standard was horizontal, we conclude that the vertical line must appear longer to S.

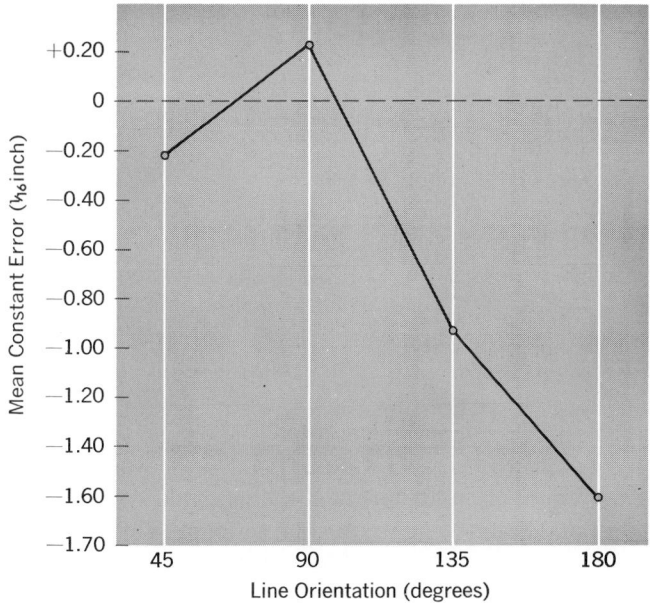

Fig. 3-4. The constant error in drawing a horizontal line to reproduce the length of lines shown in four different orientations.

We may also note the asymmetry between the line tilted left and that tilted right: the line tilted left must have appeared longer to S than the line tilted right. Statistically, the mean constant error under the two conditions differs significantly. So, in this respect, we confirm the Pollock-Chapanis study. The asymmetry occurs with the method of reproduction as well as with the method of adjustment. Indeed, the correspondence between the two studies is quite remarkable in view of the fact that in the present study the Es were inexperienced, the constancy of conditions probably varied somewhat from S to S, each student served as both S and E, and so on. So it appears that two facts emerge: horizontal lines appear shorter than vertical lines, and lines tilted to the left are likely to appear longer than those tilted to the right.

Comparison necessary? Vertical lines appear longer than horizontal lines of the same length. But, in the studies examined thus far, S is always making a comparative judgment; both the horizontal and vertical lines are present. Even when S is shown a vertical line and is asked to reproduce it horizontally, the comparison is present; S draws a horizontal line in the presence of a vertical one. Even if the vertical line were removed before S attempted the reproduction we could say that he is holding the vertical line in his memory and is comparing the length of the horizontal line he is drawing with the length of the vertical line held in his memory. What we need to do is expose one group of Ss to a horizontal line and get a judgment or reproduction, or match of its length, and expose another group to a vertical line of the same length and get a judgment of its length. If the "illusion" appears under such circumstances, we would be forced to say that in some absolute sense vertical lines appear longer than horizontal lines. Such a possibility seems a little eerie, but perhaps it should be tested experimentally just to make sure we are dealing with a phenomenon that is based on comparative judgments.

The 27 students in the writer's class served as Es in performing the experiment. There were four conditions to the experiment, each condition represented by a different group of 54 Ss. Thus, each student ran eight Ss, two in each of the four conditions. A 2½-in. line on a square card was used as the standard stimulus for all conditions and was shown either in a horizontal orientation or in a vertical orientation. The S reproduced the length either by drawing a horizontal line or by drawing a vertical line. Thus, the four conditions emerge as follows:

PRESENTED	DRAWN
Horizontally	Horizontally
Horizontally	Vertically
Vertically	Horizontally
Vertically	Vertically

Consider the logic behind these four conditions. If vertical lines appear longer than horizontal lines in some absolute sense, the reproductions under the vertical-vertical condition should, on the average, be longer than those reproduced under the horizontal-horizontal condition. However, if a comparison between horizontal and vertical lines is necessary for the illusion to be demonstrated, the illusion should be present only in the vertical-horizontal and the horizontal-vertical conditions, for in these two conditions there is a difference between the standard orientation and the orientation of the reproduction, a difference which allows S to make a comparison between the standard and his drawing.

Each S drew four lines to increase the stability of the data. It should be clear that these four reproductions were under exactly the same condition. That is, if S was in a vertical-vertical condition, he drew vertical lines to match a vertical line, but he did this four times. The score for a given S was the mean length of the four lines drawn. (Just how the Ss were assigned to particular conditions will not be discussed here since it is the topic for the next chapter.)

The reproduced lines were measured to the nearest $\frac{1}{16}$ in. Since the standard was 2½ in., it consisted of 40 sixteenths. If the reproductions were accurate, the means should be about 40. The means in Table 3-2 show that with the vertical-vertical condition (39.86) and the horizontal-horizontal condition (40.04), the means are indeed almost exactly 40. Since the vertical

TABLE 3–2

MEAN REPRODUCTIONS OF LINE LENGTHS AS A FUNCTION OF THE ORIENTATION OF THE PRESENTED AND REPRODUCED LINES

PRESENTED	REPRODUCED	MEAN LENGTH (1/16 INCH)	STANDARD DEVIATION
Horizontally	Horizontally	39.86	4.75
Horizontally	Vertically	37.51	4.32
Vertically	Horizontally	43.58	7.14
Vertically	Vertically	40.04	4.01

should have been significantly longer than the horizontal in these two conditions in order to support the notion of absoluteness in the illusion, we must conclude that no support for the notion is present. At the same time, there is support for the necessity of making comparisons between vertical and horizontal lines before the illusion is experienced. When the line is presented horizontally and the reproduction is drawn vertically, the reproduction is appreciably shorter than the standard (the horizontal line), indicating that a vertical line of the same length as the horizontal line would appear longer. Too, when the line is presented vertically, S draws an appreciably longer line when drawing horizontally, in order to "compensate" for the illusory effect. Just why the variability in this condition is greater than in the others is now known.

THE METHOD OF CONSTANT STIMULI

We must now introduce a new method of attack, the method of constant stimuli. This has long been used to study the discriminal processes, and in its various forms allows the derivation of several different response measures, reflecting different discriminal processes. For the present, we will emphasize only one of the two major forms the method takes, and we will be concerned with deriving only one major measure.

The procedures involved in the method of constant stimuli may be explained by contrasting them with those constituting the method of average error. In the method of average error S is presented a standard stimulus and is asked to adjust a variable stimulus until it appears equal to the standard. The term *adjust* is used loosely since we have applied it to the case where S attempted to draw a line which had the same length as a standard. In the method of constant stimuli S is also presented a standard stimulus. However, simultaneously or immediately after presenting the standard, S is presented another stimulus (variable stimulus) and is asked to judge whether the magnitude of the variable stimulus is greater or less than that of the standard. More than one variable stimulus is used. A series of variable stimuli is arranged so that their magnitudes increase systematically from a point well below the magnitude of the standard to a point well above the magnitude of the standard. Usually, but not necessarily, the variable stimulus of lowest magnitude is chosen so that S will always, or nearly always, judge its magnitude to be less than the standard, and the variable of greatest magnitude is chosen so that he will nearly always judge it to be of greater magnitude than the standard. The S will make a series of judgments; each variable stimulus will be presented with the standard stimulus for a judgment. Indeed, many such judgments are usually required. However, in presenting the variable stimuli for comparison with the standard, the order is not systematic with respect to the magnitude of the variable stimuli. Rather, the order in which the variable stimuli are chosen is essentially random with respect to their magnitude. Thus, S might first be presented with a variable stimulus that is of greater magnitude than the standard, then one that is smaller, then larger, again larger, and so on. The E does *not* present the variable stimuli in succession of either decreasing or increasing magnitude. Therefore, S cannot build up any expectations concerning the size of the variable stimuli to be presented on successive trials.

The method of constant stimuli can be applied to many problems. For example, it could be applied to the study of time estimations. Suppose we wished to study the accuracy in judging a 10-sec. interval. We might choose variable intervals of 6, 7, 8, 9, 10, 11, 12, 13, and 14 sec. We would present the 10-sec. interval to S, followed immediately by a variable interval of, perhaps, 7 sec., and request S to judge whether the second interval was longer or shorter than the first. On successive trials the order of the variable stimuli would be random, probably with the restriction that each be presented with the standard an equal number of times.

The accuracy in judging length of horizontal lines could also be attacked by the method of constant stimuli. In this way the standard might be a 2-in. line and variable stimuli of lengths systematically shorter and longer. We will return to this possibility in a moment.

The nature of the phenomenon being studied may produce a variation on the method of constant stimuli. The standard and variable stimulus may, theoretically, be presented for comparison simultaneously or they may be presented successively. But with certain types of stimuli simultaneous presentation has little meaning. How would we present a standard and variable time interval simultaneously and expect S to err? If a buzzer were used to mark off the standard and a light to mark off the variable, and if both were initiated simultaneously, S's judgment would surely be based on whether the buzzer or the light "went out" first. Such a judgment is not of the type that E is interested in, so the standard and variable stimuli must be presented successively. Other types of stimuli may be presented simultaneously or successively; lengths of lines could be presented in either manner. But it must be realized that the method of presentation (simultaneously versus successively) could well be an independent variable related to the accuracy and variability of the judgments. As a matter of fact, variation in the length of time between presenting the standard and the variable stimulus has been a variable of some importance in many studies, since the judgments may vary systematically as a function of the length of this interval. If indeed the judgments do vary systematically, it is known as a *time error,* and this constant error has been a phenomenon of considerable study in its own right. We will not consider this literature; it is enough for us to realize at the moment that successive presentation of standard and variable stimuli may produce different results from simultaneous presentation but simultaneous presentation for some types of stimuli does not have any but trivial psychological implications.

Handling data. For the present we will aim to derive only one basic measure from the method of constant stimuli. The measure is the *point of subjective equality,* often abbreviated, PSE, which is the value along the scale of the variable stimuli which is judged equal in magnitude to the standard stimulus. If the task involved does not produce a constant error in the judgments, the PSE will not differ statistically from the standard stimulus. If there is a constant error, such as is produced by an illusion, the PSE *will* differ from the standard stimulus. Therefore, when using the method of constant stimuli, we are asking what variables influence the discriminal processes so as to produce a discrepancy between the PSE and the standard stimulus. The immediate need is to determine how the PSE may be calculated from the data obtained by the method of constant stimuli.

The procedure may be illustrated by a hypothetical experiment in judging lengths of lines. The standard line is 5 in. We choose 10 variable lines, five of these deviating successively below 5 in. by ⅛-in. steps and five deviating above by similarly sized steps. For ease of handling, we may translate all lengths into eighths of inches so that the standard line is 40 and the variable lines, 35, 36, 37, 38, 39, 41, 42, 43, 44, and 45. We shall use successive presentation of the standard and variable stimuli. On half the trials the standard will be presented first, followed by the variable; and on the other half the order will be reversed. This balancing procedure will prevent any bias in the data due to the *time error*. Note that we do not eliminate the condition which may produce the time error (successive presentation); rather, we distribute the effect of this condition so that the judgments made when the standard follows the variable will be affected in the same manner as the judgments made when the variable follows the standard. By this procedure any time-order effect should be canceled if we ask, as we will, how frequently each variable stimulus is judged greater than the standard. If we want to determine whether or not there was a time-order effect, we would compare the judgments made when the variable stimuli were presented first with the judgments made when these stimuli were presented after the standard.

Let us say a single S was used. Each variable stimulus was presented with the standard 100 times. For each judgment we record whether the variable stimulus was judged shorter or longer than the standard stimulus. No equal judgments were allowed; S always had to make a decision of "longer" or "shorter." In transcribing these we may simply record for each variable stimulus the number of times it was judged longer than the standard. The hypothetical data are shown in Table 3-3. Since there were 100 judgments

TABLE 3–3
BASIC DATA FROM THE METHOD OF CONSTANT STIMULI AP-
PLIED TO THE JUDGMENT OF RELATIVE LINE LENGTHS
**The standard stimulus was 40 and the variable stimuli ranged from
35 to 45. The data are hypothetical.**

VARIABLE STIMULI	PERCENTAGE OF TIMES VARIABLE WAS JUDGED LONGER THAN STANDARD
35	3
36	7
37	14
38	23
39	35
41	67
42	77
43	85
44	92
45	96

for each variable stimulus, the number of times the variable was judged longer and the percentage of times judged longer are identical. These percentages are plotted in Fig. 3-5, and a smooth curve is drawn through the points. The ogive or sigmoid curve is commonly found from data plotted in this manner.

There is a long history behind the variety of methods which are used to find the PSE (and other measures which we will discuss in a later chapter) from data such as shown in Table 3-3. To a large extent we shall gloss over the history and present here simple techniques which will be found quite adequate for most work. The interested student can turn to Guilford (1954) for a careful evaluation and exposition of all the various techniques developed over the years.

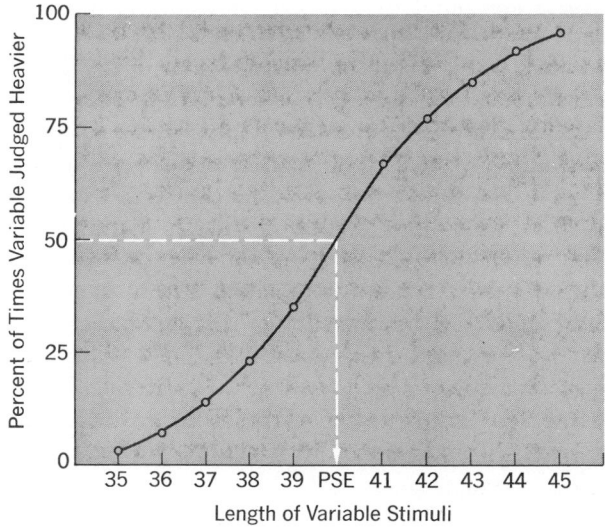

Fig. 3-5. Determination of the point of subjective equality by the graphical method from data derived by the method of constant stimuli.

A rough method of determining the PSE is the *graphical method*. The PSE is that value along the variable-stimulus continuum which is phenomenally equal to the standard stimulus. This means, in turn, that we must calculate a value for a variable stimulus which, if presented directly to S for comparison with the standard, would be judged longer 50 percent of the time and shorter 50 percent of the time. What value would be judged in such a fashion? Graphically, it is a variable stimulus value which lies directly below the point where the curve crosses the 50 percent ordinate value. Therefore, as shown by the dotted line in Fig. 3-5, we can go from the 50 percent point on the ordinate across to the curve and then down to the baseline. At the point where this curve hits the baseline we identify the PSE—the variable stimulus which is judged equal to the standard. In Fig. 3-5 the value is not clearly distinguishable from 40, which is the value of the standard stimulus. There is no evidence, therefore, for a constant error.

A second method, somewhat more precise, is that of calculating the median of the distribution of judgments. You will remember that a median cuts a distribution in half so that half the scores lie above it and half lie below. The logic of the median can be applied to the data of Table 3-3. We want to know what variable stimulus value will cut the distribution in half so that above the point we will get increasing frequencies of longer judgments and below the point, decreasing frequencies of longer judgments. We know that this point is above the variable value of 39 (35 percent) and below 42 (67 percent). The difference between 35 and 67 is 32; we want to go 15 points along this distance since 35 plus 15 will give us 50 percent. Accordingly, we calculate $^{15}\!/_{32} \times 2$, since there are two step intervals between 39 and 41. This value, .94, is added, then, to 39 (our base) with the resulting value of 39.94. This is the PSE and is seen to be only slightly less than the standard value. The use of the method assumes a straight line relationship between the two values used in the interpolation and is therefore often called the *linear interpolation* method.

Actually, one may use the arithmetic mean as a measure of the PSE without doing serious violence to the data if the distributions are fairly symmetrical. For example, we might make a distribution of scores from those in Table 3-3 to show the frequency of times for each variable that S was "wrong," wrong in the sense that he said the variable stimulus was longer (or shorter) than the standard when in fact it was not. The mean of this distribution would represent the value of a variable stimulus at which S could be said to be most wrong or the value which, if presented to S along with the standard, would be judged longer about 50 percent of the time. Such a mean from the data of Table 3-3 is 39.99. Obviously, the median of this distribution will give the same value as calculated above. Whether or not one should be overly concerned about the precise value of the PSE depends to a large extent upon the use one wishes to make of the obtained value. If it is to be used as a value representing a fundamental or absolute property of the discriminal processes, then the use of the most precise methods available is mandatory. If, however, one is asking about changes in a response measure such as the PSE as a function of certain independent variables, then the concern with absolute values becomes much less important. Generally speaking, we may use the median as quite a satisfactory measure for most elementary laboratory experiments.

A few other remarks about the method of constant stimuli seem appropriate before proceeding with its application to the study of illusions.

1. In the hypothetical experiment above, a variable stimulus of the same magnitude as the standard could have been used. Thus, on certain trials S would be asked to judge whether the second of two lines, both of the same

length, was longer or shorter than the first. The percentage of times this judgment was made could then be plotted along with the other points. Obviously, if there is no time-order error or any other biasing factor, this value will be 50 percent, or at least not significantly different from 50 percent. If it does not differ significantly, the PSE is equal to the standard stimulus value. If it does differ significantly, then we need to utilize the other points in determining the PSE.

2. Should E allow S to make equal judgments? Many Es have. It might be said that if S perceives two stimuli as equal, he should be allowed to say so. On the other hand, some Ss might use an equal judgment as an "out"— as a means of not trying to discriminate small differences. It is known, furthermore, that even when S is required to guess in situations in which he insists he cannot detect a difference, he is more likely to be right than wrong. But it is also true that if two stimuli do appear equal, irrelevant matters might determine the judgment. By way of example, for some unexplained reason S might prefer saying "longer" to "shorter"; consequently, when the stimuli *are* equal phenomenally, he may produce more "longer" than "shorter" judgments. If one does allow equal judgments (some Es prefer "doubtful" rather than "equal"), the PSE can be obtained by calculating the median of the distribution of equal judgments.

3. In the method of constant stimuli (as well as any other method where differences in magnitude between stimuli are being varied), other response measures are usually found to reflect the same basic relationship exhibited in Fig. 3-5. For example, if one measures the latency, or time required for S to make judgments, it will be found that these latencies increase directly as the magnitude of the stimulus difference decreases; that is, the smaller the difference between two stimuli, the longer the time required for a decision. Likewise, the less the difference in magnitude of stimuli to be judged, the less confident S is of the correctness of his judgments. Both sets of facts have been demonstrated in judging line lengths by the method of constant stimuli (Festinger, 1943).

The PSE and Constant Errors

The H-V Illusion. The PSE as derived from the method of constant stimuli may be used to measure the extent of the H-V illusion. But we must be careful to anticipate the direction the PSE must deviate from the standard stimulus in order for the H-V illusion to be demonstrated. Suppose the standard stimulus is a horizontal line of a given length. A number of variable stimuli are brought together, with lengths both less than and greater than the standard. However, the variable lines are always presented in a vertical orientation and judged as being longer or shorter than the standard line (which is shown horizontally). If the H-V illusion is operative, the PSE will be *less* than the standard length. This means that in order for a vertical line to appear equal to a horizontal line of a given length, the vertical line must be shorter than the horizontal line. But, now, if the standard is a vertical line and the variable stimuli horizontally oriented, the PSE will be greater than the standard; for a given length vertical line, some longer horizontal line is required to be judged equivalent in length.

The time error. We have noted the possibility of a constant error which may result from successive presentation of stimuli in the method of constant stimuli. In order to study the time error, we always present the standard stimulus followed by the variable stimulus. The error will then appear as a significant deviation of the PSE from the standard stimulus. If the PSE is greater than the standard, a *positive* time error is said to occur; if less than the standard, a *negative* time error has been measured. The time error does not seem to be in any sense universal or of great magnitude when it does occur. The present writer has had no luck in attempting to produce this error, either in a positive or negative direction, in class laboratory experiments. This is true in spite of the fact that several different types of judgments have been explored (weight lifting, line-length judgments, density-of-dots judgments) and intervals of as long as 20 sec. interposed between the standard and variable stimuli. It is, therefore, perhaps of small magnitude and occurs only with many, many judgments by well-practiced Ss.

TWO COMPONENTS IN THE HORIZONTAL-VERTICAL ILLUSION

We are now prepared to examine some analytical studies dealing with the H-V illusion. It is quite likely that some Ss may not experience an illusory effect from the two lines that are shown in Fig. 3-1. Actually, this is a "pure" form of the H-V illusion. The illusion has often been demonstrated by the use of an inverted-T as shown in the left section of Fig. 3-6. The figure on the right is a T on its side. Cover one figure with your hand and make a judgment of whether the vertical line in the other figure is longer or shorter than the horizontal line. Then cover the other figure and do the same with the remaining one. In which of the two figures does the illusion appear to be greater? If your judgments reflect those obtained from careful experimentation, the illusion will be greater for the inverted-T than for the T on its side. Indeeed, for the T on its side some will say there is no difference in the length of the two lines or that the horizontal line is actually longer than the vertical. These observations suggest the possibility that the use of T-figures does not allow a "pure" exhibit of the H-V illusion; some other factor must be involved. Otherwise, the two T's in Fig. 3-6 should give about the same illusory effect.

The above observations have led investigators to suggest that the T-figure involves two components: the pure H-V illusion in which vertical lines appear longer than horizontal lines of the same length and another illusory effect which may result from what we will call division of a line by another. More specifically, it would appear that a line which intersects another, thus dividing the latter, will appear longer than the latter. That is, a dividing line

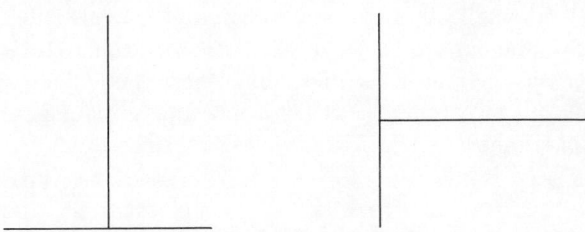

Fig. 3-6. Two forms of the T-figure in illustrating the horizontal-vertical illusion. Cover one figure while viewing the other and observe whether or not the vertical line appears longer than the horizontal. This is more likely to happen in the left figure than in the right. All lines are the same length.

will appear longer than the divided line. If this is true, then we find in the left-hand figure of Fig. 3-6 that both the H-V illusion and the divided-line illusion would be operating in the same direction, thus combining to produce a maximum effect. In the right-hand figure, however, the H-V illusion and the divided-line illusion are opposed; the H-V illusion should make the vertical line look longer than the horzontal and the divided-line illusion should make it look shorter. If these were of equal magnitude in their effects, they might cancel each other and give the phenomenal appearance of equality. Results tend to support these expectations (e.g., Finger & Spelt, 1947). Furthermore, it would be expected that if illusory effects were measured on the inverted T versus the separated lines as shown in Fig. 3-1, the total illusory effect would be greater for the former. This prediction has been supported by Fraisee and Vautrey (1956). Their Ss varied from six years of age to adulthood, and their adults consisted of widely different educational backgrounds. For all groups the magnitude of the illusion for the inverted T was about twice as great as for the separated lines. Yet, the illusion was still present with the separated lines, so we still have a phenomenon that can be called the pure H-V illusion.

Recently, one other fact has been reported concerning the H-V illusion when studied by the method of average error. The magnitude of the illusion varies depending upon whether the vertical line is the standard, with S adjusting the length of the horizontal, or whether the roles are reversed. The facts indicate that the standard line (whichever line it is) appears longer than the variable (Gardner & Long, 1960a; Gardner & Long, 1960b). It is as if when attention is directed to a given line by designating it a standard, it appears longer. Thus, in the inverted-T figure, the magnitude of the H-V illusion is much greater when the vertical line is the standard than when the horizontal line is the standard. Even with the disconnected lines, as in Fig. 3-1, there is a small difference in the magnitude of the illusion as a function of which of the lines is the standard stimulus when using the method of average error. The reason for these differences is not clear; nor is it clear that they will occur with other methods of investigation, for example, the method of constant stimuli.

EXPLANATIONS OF THE H-V ILLUSION

The major concern in this section will be to illustrate how one man tested a hypothesis he developed concerning the cause for the H-V illusion. However, certain comments about the use of theory or hypothesis should precede an examination of this man's work.

It was noted earlier that one of the purposes of hypotheses about the cause of a given phenomenon is to direct the E toward the manipulation of certain independent variables. We also noted that there are other means of choosing independent variables for manipulation in an experiment. At the simplest level, one can merely examine a situation and ask direct questions about the constituents of the situation. For example, with no theory at all one might ask about the influence of the length of lines on the magnitude of the H-V illusion, about the viewing distance of the S, about the width of the lines, about the characteristics of the Ss, and so on. The research results stemming from such questions would be just as sound and, perhaps in the long run, just as valuable as those results obtained when the choice of independent variables is directed by some hypothesis. Over the years, however, the results of experiments cannot remain a mere assortment of facts, unrelated by some unifying theme or general principle. Sooner or later someone must make out of research results something that is more than an isolated collection of facts. But as we shall have occasion to see throughout this book, there are many ways of going about this.

The choice of independent variables directed by the use of a working hypothesis may, perhaps, be a little more exciting than the choice directed by a straightforward examination of various potential variables in the experimental situation. One may get ego-involved in his supposed insights as reflected by a theory so that an evaluation of the results may have an affective component that is not always present when the variables are chosen somewhat blindly. Yet, blind dates can be exciting. Probably no investigator ever *really* enters into an experiment of his own devising without some notion of how he expects the results to come out. And, certainly, as he collects results from an experiment or two, he will find himself developing hypotheses which lead him in certain directions in future research. Probably no persistent investigator can remain a completely crass empiricist; his data will not allow it, regardless of his attitude initially. Hypotheses and theory are bound to get imbedded in his work.

It was mentioned earlier that the nature of the hypotheses developed by different investigators will vary as a function of particular interests, particular skills, and overall orientation toward the subject matter of psychology. Let us speculate about the various forms that theory about the H-V illusion may take and how the independent variables suggested by the various theories may differ.

The physiological psychologist may be led up several paths. He might assume first that the H-V illusion is strictly due to the nature of the visual mechanisms. Differences in eye movements on a vertical plane versus the horizontal have been suggested as a possible cause for the illusion. Vertical movements may require a little more strain in traveling a given distance than do horizontal movements. Therefore, for the same distance of eye-travel, the feelings of strain would be greater for the vertical than for the horizontal with the conclusion by S that the vertical is longer. One implication of such a hypothesis is that the illusion would not be present under very rapid speeds of presentation since eye movements could not occur. However, some evidence indicates that the more rapid the presentation, the greater the illusion (e.g., Fraisse & Vautrey, 1956.) So, if one tried to hold to this hypothesis, some additional notions would have to be considered.

One might look to the visual mechanisms, noting that in the H-V illusion different portions of the retina must necessarily be stimulated. Perhaps there is a greater spread of excitation in the vertical direction than in the horizontal. Or, perhaps the projection areas for vertical and horizontal lines in the occipital cortex differ in some way that could be related to the differences in judgments. Such notions might lead to controlling the locus of stimulation of the lines; by appropriate devices the lines could be projected on different areas of the retina—the periphery versus the fovea or center.

An investigator might not have a specific hypothesis concerning the cause for the illusion but still might maintain that it is not due to the experience of S. That is, the illusion is intrinsic to the viewing mechanisms of living organisms and is little influenced, if at all, by experience. Such a hypothesis might lead to research on human Ss of different ages in an attempt to demonstrate that the illusion is present in the very early years. Or, it might lead to an attempt to determine whether or not lower animals are influenced by the H-V illusion. This would, as you can see, provide a very fascinating problem in experimental technique. How is an investigator going to tell whether the animal has an illusion? It is, in fact, possible, as seen in the report of one investigator (see Dember, 1961, p. 207) who worked with an illusion influencing chickens.

Another investigator might take quite the opposite view of the nativist in the above paragraph. He might say that the H-V illusion is due entirely to differential experience with horizontal and vertical lines. The experience of a citizen in a large city, where the vertical is predominant, would be different from the experience of an African native living in the bush. This point of view is elaborated by Segall, Campbell, and Herskovits (1963) as a consequence of their tests made in many different localities, including the villages of many different tribes of natives in Africa.

One more. An investigator may be very clinically oriented. He notes the fact that a father is a powerful, omnipotent object in the life of his small child. Furthermore, the child usually views the father in a vertical position, generalizing power and omnipotence so that the vertical lines of the father take on a longer or taller appearance than do corresponding horizontal lines. Such a hypothesis may be perfectly silly; furthermore, it may not lead easily to independent variables which can be manipulated to test the hypothesis, which, certainly, must be a requirement of any theory. On the other hand, perhaps it can be tested.

So much for a certain amount of fantasy. The point being made is that even a phenomenon produced by two lines shown to the S can lead investigators into certain lines of thinking which in turn lead to very divergent lines of research in an attempt to explain the phenomenon. Furthermore, even if an explanation is generally confirmed and accepted, it is just the beginning of the explanatory problem. For such an explanation cannot be isolated any more than facts can be isolated. This explanation must be related to those given for other illusions, for other perceptual phenomena, and so on.

The Künnapas Series

We will examine certain works in a series of studies by a Swedish investigator, Künnapas, in order to illustrate how a particular hypothesis about the H-V illusion led to experiments determining the effects of certain variables. The series is particularly enlightening in view of the fact that the source of the hypothesis is made quite explicit.

Source of the hypothesis. In this experiment (Künnapas, 1955) the method of constant stimuli was used. The standard stimulus was always a white square cardboard, 7 cm. (approximately 2¾ in.) on a side, upon which a horizontal black line 50 mm. (approximately 2 in.) was drawn. The independent variable was the size of the square cards of the variable stimuli. Four such sets were constructed, the sizes being 9, 12, 16, and 21 cm. on a side. On the cards within each set, lines of varying length around 50 mm. were drawn. Therefore, each set, consisting of cards of the same size but on which the length of the horizontal lines differed systematically, could be used to compare with the standard stimulus by the method of constant stimuli. The purpose was to determine the PSE for line lengths as a function of the size of the cards on which the variable lines were drawn.

On a given trial the standard card and one of the variable cards were presented about 3½ ft. from S in such a way that the two horizontal lines were always at the same level. For each presentation S was asked to judge which of the two lines was longer.

There were 10 Ss; all conditions were given to each one. In a given session all of the cards within a set (all having the same size) were judged against the standard before moving on to the next set. However, for different Ss the order in which the sets were given was varied so that across all Ss combined, any progressive error should fall equally on all of the sets. This particular method of balancing progressive error across Ss has not been discussed; we will defer such discussion to a later chapter. For the time being, it may be accepted that progressive error would fall equally on all conditions. The report does not tell the number of variable cards used within each set, hence we do not know the number of different variable lines employed around the standard. However, the order in which these variable lines were shown to S (for comparison with the standard) was random. A total of 40 judgments was made by each S for each set.

For each S for each size card, the PSE was determined and the mean PSE for all 10 Ss calculated. These mean PSEs are plotted (Fig. 3-7) as a function of the size of the cards on which the variable lines were presented. The magnitude of the PSE increases directly as the size of the card increases. We need, perhaps, to point out the psychological implications of Fig. 3-7. The standard line was always 50 mm. Therefore, as the size of the squares on which the variable lines were drawn increased, a longer and longer line was required in order for it to appear phenomenally equal to the standard. Or, to say this in another way, if a 50-mm. line appears on the cards, as these cards get larger and larger, the apparent length of the line tends to decrease. It is as if the larger the card becomes the more the line tends to shrink. In fact, Künnapas reports that some Ss spontaneously reported that the width of the lines also appeared to become less and less as the size of the cards increased. In order that your thinking about the PSE as derived from the method of constant stimuli is clear, it might be wise to sketch out a graph on which four ogives are plotted, one for each size of square, so that you can assure yourself that you understand just how the PSEs increase and how Fig. 3-7 could be derived from such plots.

The Künnapas effect shown in Fig. 3-7 does not necessarily demonstrate a new principle. The effect falls within the general statement that judgments of stimuli may be influenced by the context (other stimuli) which appear in the same visual field. The context or background stimuli may give rise to two diverse phenomena. One of these is called, as a general descriptive term, *contrast.* If variation of background stimuli along a specified dimension or characteristic occurs in a given direction, and if this influences the judgment of the focal or central stimulus in the opposite direction, we may speak of a contrast effect. On the other hand, if variation of the background stimuli in a given direction produces judgments concerning the central stimulus which follow the same direction, the term *assimilation* may be applied. For

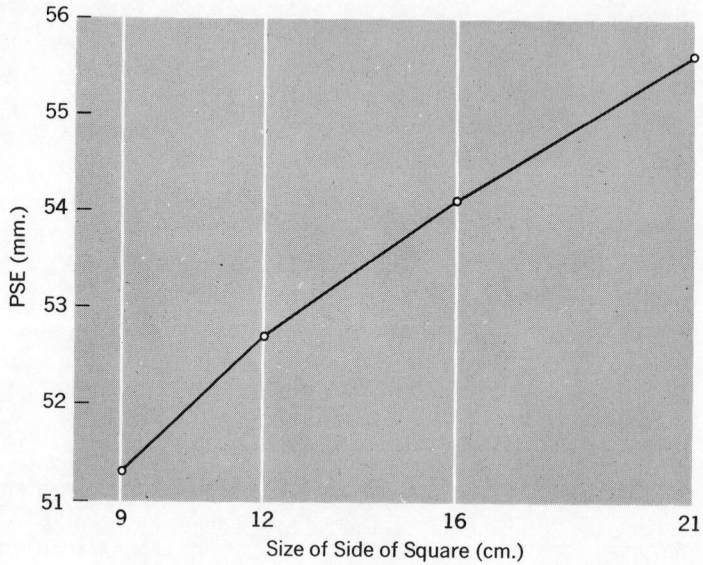

Fig. 3-7. **Apparent length (measured by PSE) of a horizontal line as a function of the size of the square card on which it is drawn. The variable-length lines on the different cards were always compared with a standard line of 50 mm. on a 7 by 7-cm. card. Data from Künnapas (1955).**

the time being we should keep these two terms as merely descriptive of what may happen; as technical terms describing the mechanisms involved, they fall short of being satisfactory. But they do allow us to talk in shorthand form about phenomena. It is clear that the findings of Künnapas in Fig. 3-7 may be described as a contrast effect; as the squares become larger, the lines on them appear shorter.

The next step is to examine what Künnapas did with the relationship shown in Fig. 3-7. Note that because S never judged vertical lines, the H-V illusion is not directly involved, although we might say that the contrast effect is merely an illusion of a different kind. In any case, Künnapas was led to the hypothesis that the H-V illusion was simply another illustration of the fact demonstrated in Fig. 3-7. Let's see how he managed this. He assumes that the visual field is a horizontal ellipse. That is, the horizontal field is wider than the vertical field is tall, so that the field of vision is shaped somewhat like an egg. This is depicted in Fig. 3-8. Within this field are drawn a horizontal and a vertical line as one might view them in an experiment.

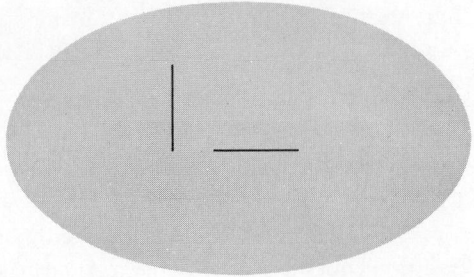

Fig. 3-8. Schematic field of vision showing the H-V figure. This conception led to a hypothesis by Künnapas (1957) about the cause of the H-V illusion. See text.

Künnapas then points out that a greater extension of the horizontal line (in either direction) is required to reach the edge of the field of vision than is true for an extension of the vertical line in either direction. Thus, the horizontal line is comparable to a line on a big card, and the vertical line, to a line on a smaller card. Applying the fact demonstrated in Fig. 3-7, therefore, we can see not only that the vertical line should appear longer than the horizontal line, but also that the H-V illusion is not due to something intrinsic to vertical or horizontal lines as such; it just happens that a vertical line of a given length more fully crosses the visual field then does a horizontal line of the same length.

This form of theorizing is fairly widespread in psychology, and in many ways it is the most effective. It is a form of *empirical extension*. A fact or phenomenon discovered or shown in one situation is hypothesized to be operating in a superficially different situation. Phenomena discovered in each situation may seem diverse and unrelated because the nature of the situation may somewhat disguise the similarities. Only by careful analyses can we detect the possible relationships. Suffice it to say, this was the form of theorizing used by Künnapas; the H-V illusion is asserted to be only a special case of the contrast phenomenon demonstrated in his earlier experiment. Let us be sure we understand what the possible implications of the hypothesis are. If subsequent research supports his idea, then we may indeed conclude that both situations are demonstrating the same contrast effect. Of course, in a manner of speaking, we haven't explained anything; what we have done is to show that when an explanation for a contrast effect is found, it will also explain the H-V illusion. This sort of theorizing, therefore, reduces the number of independent phenomena which require explanation; and if it indeed can do this, it is a very sizable contribution.

The next step in Künnapas' thinking was to design some experiments to test his hypothesis. He asks himself the questions: "To what independent variables does my hypothesis lead me and what must happen when these variables are manipulated to lend support to my identification of the H-V illusion with a contrast effect?"

The first test. The first deduction at which Künnapas arrived is stated as follows: "If the overestimation of the vertical direction is due to the elliptical form of the visual field with its greater horizontal axis, it must disappear in complete darkness where the visual field has no distinct boundary." (1957, p. 405) Thus, the first independent variable to which he is drawn is darkness versus light; the illusion must be greater in light than in darkness to sustain his hypothesis. This is how he worked out the experiment to make the test.

The L-shaped form of the illusion was used. A white circular background surface, 600 mm. in diameter, provided the viewing field. Near the center of the surface were two narrow slits, one horizontal, the other vertical. The slits per se were not visible, but each appeared to be two luminous lines when a light was projected on them from the rear. For this experiment the method of average error was employed. The horizontal line was the standard stimulus and was always 50 mm. in length. The vertical line was variable by virtue of a small knob which when turned made the vertical line appear shorter or longer as desired. So, the S's task was to adjust the variable vertical stimulus on a given trial until it appeared equal in length to the fixed standard horizontal stimulus. The S sat 400 mm. from the white circle, and his head was held in a constant position by a chin support. Before a given trial, the variable was set noticeably longer (or noticeably shorter) than the standard, and S was to adjust to equality. Between trials the lights were turned out behind the white surface so that the two lines were not visible.

In the Light Condition the room was lighted by a 150-watt bulb suspended from the ceiling behind S. In the Dark Condition the room was completely dark except for the slight light produced by the stimuli. The room light, however, was always turned on between trials in the Dark Condition so that the effect of the stimuli in lighting the room was negligible.

Each of the 20 Ss made 32 adjustments or matches under each of the two conditions. For half the Ss the conditions were counterbalanced Light-Dark-Dark-Light, and for the other half, Dark-Light-Light-Dark. In each case, 16 trials were given in each block.

In the Light Condition the mean length of the variable vertical line judged equal to the standard horizontal line of 50 mm. was 46.46 mm. Thus, on the average, the variable vertical stimulus was set about 3.5 mm. less than the standard stimulus. Although this may not seem great in an absolute sense, it is highly significant statistically. Hence, the H-V illusion was shown to be operating in the Light Condition as would be expected. For the Dark Condition the mean setting was 47.61 mm. This is about 2.4 mm. less than the standard, and again statistically differed not only from the standard but also from the mean for the Light Condition. The amount of the illusion was less in the Dark Condition than in the Light Condition. This finding is in line with the hypothesis. But doesn't the hypothesis predict that the illusion should disappear in the dark? In fact, it does predict the disappearance; but it is possible that a complete elimination of the elliptical visual field was not achieved by the procedure; the stimuli would have had to emit some light or S could not have seen them. Künnapas clearly felt the results were encouraging enough to make further tests.

A second test. Particular hypotheses about a given phenomenon often lead to the manipulation of variables which might never have occurred otherwise. The variable manipulated in the next experiment by Künnapas (1958) may be of this nature. If S views the H-V figure with his head tilted 90 degrees to the right or to the left, the visual field changes from a horizontal ellipse to a vertical ellipse. Under such viewing conditions the ends of the vertical line are now at a greater distance from the edge of the visual field than are the ends of the horizontal line. If the contrast effect is responsible for the H-V illusion, it should be reversed under the head-tilted viewing conditions; now, the horizontal line should appear longer than the vertical. Testing of the illusion under normal upright head conditions versus the tilted condition of the head constituted the purpose of this experiment.

The apparatus was exactly the same as that used in the previous experiment, although all tests were made in a lighted room. In the Upright Condition the head position was normal. In the Tilted Condition the head was inclined to the right about 85 degrees. In both conditions the head was held in a fixed condition. Each of 20 Ss was given 32 trials under each condition using a counterbalanced order. On each trial the horizontal line of 50 mm. was the standard, and S adjusted the vertical line to appear equal in length to the standard.

The results show that under the normal or Upright Condition, the mean length of the vertical line judged equal to the horizontal was 48.13. Although the magnitude of the illusion is less than in the previous study, it is clearly present. In the Tilted Condition the mean length of the variable judged equivalent to the standard was 51.60. This is to say that the horizontal line appears longer than the vertical line. Of the 20 Ss, only two failed to show the effect. The difference between the two means is highly significant. Künnapas continued to be encouraged and undoubtedly began to feel considerable affection for his hypothesis.

A third test. In this experiment Künnapas artificially varied the shape of the visual field by using specially constructed spectacles (1959). The glasses were opaque except for two tiny openings so situated in front of each eye that normal fused vision of the two eyes occurred. The independent variable was the shape of these openings, and there were five different shapes. At one extreme the openings were a flat horizontal ellipse in which the vertical axis was 2 mm. and the horizontal, 4 mm. Thus, the ratio of the horizontal axis to the vertical axis was .50. At the next step the ratio was .75, which approximates the normal visual field. At the third step the ratio was 1.00, which means the openings were circular. At the fourth it was 1.33, and at the fifth, 2.00. This fifth set of openings represents the same ellipse as the first one described (ratio of .50), but at this extreme it is oriented in the vertical direction.

The apparatus and general procedure were the same as in the earlier experiments. The distance of S from the test apparatus was such that he could see nothing through the tiny openings in the spectacles except the white surface. Each of the 16 Ss received trials under all five conditions via a counterbalanced order. As before, the 50-mm. horizontal line was the standard, with S adjusting the vertical line on each trial until it appeared equal in length to the standard.

The results of the experiment are plotted in Fig. 3-9. The response measure used is percentage illusion. Thus, if the mean length of the variable stimulus judged equal to the standard was 48 mm., the mean illusion is 2 mm., or $2/50 \times 100$ is 4 percent. The independent variable is designated as the ratio of the vertical axis to the horizontal axis. The first point represents the flattest horizontal ellipse; the middle point, the circle; and the fifth point, the flat vertical ellipse. It is apparent that there is a continuous relationship between the percent illusion and the shape of the visual field. The greatest amount of illusion, occurring as it does with the flattest horizontal ellipse, would be in line with the Künnapas hypothesis since the visual field is flatter than normal, perhaps roughly resembling the field when one squints. At the other extreme, with the upright narrow ellipse, the magnitude of the illusion is least. Still, even with this field there is present an H-V illusion; the vertical line still appears longer than the horizontal since it is set shorter to produce equality. If the shape of the visual field is the only factor involved, we would expect a reversal of the illusion in this condition

—the horizontal line should look longer than the vertical, a reversal similar to the one found in the previous experiment.

We will leave the Künnapas hypothesis at this point. Has he proved his hypothesis? This is not the language that is appropriate; as pointed out earlier, we do not speak of proving a hypothesis. Rather, we say that the data "are in line with," "are consonant with," "support," and so on. To speak

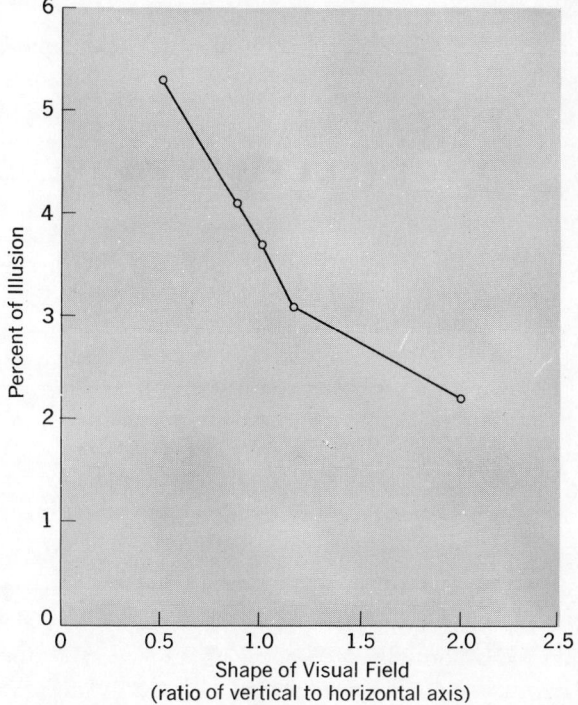

Fig. 3-9. Percent H-V illusion as a function of the shape of the visual field. The left point represents a field like a flat horizontal ellipse, the right point, an upright ellipse of the same shape, and the middle point, a circle. Data from Künnapas (1959).

of proving a hypothesis implies that this hypothesis is right and all other possible hypotheses are wrong. Yet, there may be a dozen other hypotheses that one could dream up which would be shown congenial with available data. Künnapas himself concludes that his hypothesis, which states that the H-V illusion is produced by the shape of the visual field, has been supported by his experiments. At the same time, however, as he points out, his results have not consistently shown that the entire H-V effect could be attributed to the shape of the visual field. Therefore, he suggests that one or more other factors must be involved. Subsequent hypotheses about these other factors may then lead to another series of pointed experiments, pointed by the nature of the hypothesis toward the manipulation of particular independent variables.

In leaving Künnapas we will also leave the H-V illusion. A careful consideration of the H-V illusion in conjunction with other illusions (some to be discussed shortly) may show how transition experiments could be performed, experiments which attempt to show how two or more illusions are based on the same principle. Certainly, each illusion cannot remain as an isolated phenomenon; there must be some general laws which underlie them all.

THE MÜLLER-LYER ILLUSION

A common figure for producing the Müller-Lyer illusion is shown in Fig. 3-10. The horizontal line bounded by the "wings" turned in-

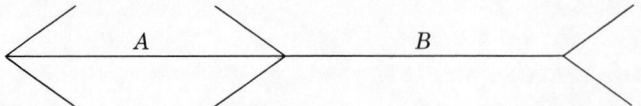

Fig. 3-10. The Müller-Lyer illusion. Line *A* appears to be shorter than Line *B* though both are 1½ in. long.

ward (Line A) is normally seen as being appreciably shorter than the line bounded by wings which turn outward (Line B). The illusory effect of this figure is far more powerful and universal than is the effect produced by the H-V figure. Errors in judgment of as much as 25 percent are not at all uncommon, and the naive S will be quite unaware of the constant error he is showing by his judgments of length. The author at one time constructed some of these illusion figures for laboratory use. To say the least, the construction was very crude, and the students were rather skeptical of working with the devices since they did not see how reliable data could be obtained from them. One S, for example, after having been given several trials, said, "These things aren't any good—I don't get an illusion." Yet an examination of his judgments showed that the constant error—the illusory effect—was about 30 percent. This incident is not reported to justify the use of shoddy apparatus; rather, it is reported only to emphasize the strong illusory effect which may be produced by the Müller-Lyer figure even under adverse circumstances.

Methods of Attack

Average error. The method-of-adjustment version of the method of average error is commonly used in experiments studying the Müller-Lyer illusion. Normally, Line B (Fig. 3-10) is the variable stimulus, and Line A, the fixed or standard stimulus. By overlapping cards in a frame, one can move the card containing Line B in and out, thus decreasing and increasing the length of Line B. The Ss' task is to adjust the length of Line B so that it appears phenomenally equal to the length of Line A.

As in most of the studies discussed thus far, the common procedure is to have the same S serve in all conditions. Thus, if the angle of the wings is the independent variable, each S would make judgments for all angles. Obviously, counterbalancing or one of the two forms of randomization of the order of the conditions would be employed to balance progressive error.

Associated with experimental work on the Müller-Lyer illusion are two potential sources of constant error other than the illusion itself. By the nature of the figure, the standard stimulus and the variable stimulus cannot be in exactly the same visual field; one is to the left, the other to the right. It is possible, therefore, that the magnitude of the illusion when the variable is on the left will differ from the magnitude when the variable is on the right. If it does it is called a *space error*. Such a phenomenon may occur in any experiment where two stimuli are present simultaneously in space and a judgment is to be made concerning them. Another potential constant error is called the *movement error*. By the method of adjustment, it will be remembered, E sets the variable stimulus on a given trial so that it is noticeably different from the standard (longer or shorter in the case of the Müller-Lyer figure). The S then adjusts the variable stimulus until it appears phenomenally equal to the standard. It will be noted that E can, initially, make the variable noticeably different from the standard by setting it in either one of two ways: by giving it greater magnitude or less magnitude than the standard. In the case of the Müller-Lyer, he may set the variable longer or he may set it shorter than the standard. If he sets it longer, S must move it in to attain a match; if he sets it shorter, he must move it outward. It is conceivable that the final settings of the variable stimulus may differ depending upon whether Ss move it in or out; if they do, a movement error is said to be present.

In some experiments using the method of adjustment, E may allow S to take as much time as he needs to make the match on each trial. In the process, S may move the variable stimulus in, then out, then back again, and so on, until phenomenal equality is attained. If E allows this back-and-forth adjustment on a given trial, the original direction of movement loses its meaning, and it is quite unlikely that a movement error would occur. If S is not allowed to change the direction of initial movement, however, a movement error may occur. Although it was not mentioned in the earlier discussion, Künnapas reported a movement error in the Light-Dark experiment. The magnitude of the illusion was greater when the variable line was lengthened than when it was shortened.

Names applied to phenomena can sometimes distort their importance, so let us be sure we have the proper perspective on the space and movement errors. If there is a space error, it means that location of the variable and standard stimuli in the visual field is a relevant independent variable; in this particular case, a space error means only that the location of the standard and variable stimuli influences the magnitude of the Müller-Lyer illusion. Likewise, if a reliable movement error is demonstrated, it merely means that direction of adjustment of the variable stimulus is a relevant independent variable. But we realize that there are countless other potential independent variables which may influence the magnitude of the phenomenon with which we are dealing. To cull out these two variables for special attention may be misleading. However, in the usual experiment E often does pay special attention to them, apparently as a result of some tradition that has been built up over the years. By paying attention we mean that he balances his conditions so that if he wishes, he can determine whether or not space or movement errors are present. Let us illustrate how this might be done with the Müller-Lyer illusion.

Suppose E is interested in the magnitude of the illusion for schizophrenics versus normals. (A number of such studies have been done.) He gives a large number of trials to each S in each group. For our purposes, however, we may restrict the illustration to 16 trials to see how a form of double counterbalancing may be used. Let L stand for the position of the variable stimulus in the Left portion of the visual field, and let R indicate a position in the Right visual field. Let O stand for Out when the variable is set shorter than the standard (S then moves it Out), and I for In when the setting for the variable is longer (S then moves it In). The 16 settings or trials could be distributed as follows:

L(4 trials)	R(4 trials)	R(4 trials)	L(4 trials)
O I I O	O I I O	O I I O	O I I O

If E uses such sequences, he is, in effect, manipulating two variables in addition to type of S. He can, if he wishes, determine if there is a space error by comparing the settings for all trials under the L condition with those under all trials of the R condition. And if there is a movement error, this can be determined by comparing O's with I's. By virtue of the counterbalancing, no progressive error should bias the results for these two variables.

Now let us suppose that E did not wish to balance the spatial position and direction of movement of the variable. Suppose that for all Ss in both groups the variable stimulus was on the right on all trials, and suppose further that the variable stimulus was always set longer than the standard so that S had to move it in. Do we now have a confounding of variables? Of course not. All Ss in both groups were tested under identical conditions; there can be no confounding as a consequence of not having collected judgments under both L and R conditions and under both O and I conditions. But, some may protest, perhaps the magnitude of the illusion would have differed had conditions been arranged to use both L and R settings and I and O settings. It is indeed quite possible that the overall illusion might have been different had this been done. But the illusion might also have differed in magnitude had all Ss been measured at midnight, had the angle of the wings been different, had the length of the standard line been different, and so on. Failure to manipulate a second or third or fourth variable in a given experiment cannot lead to a confounding—a biasing of the results for one group as compared with the other. Rather, it only restricts the generality of the conclusion; but this is a very minor restriction since, as was noted, there were many, many other possible independent variables which were not manipulated in the experiment. The fact is that in many studies it is relatively easy to measure the effects of such variables as those that produce the space and movement error at the same time that the independent variable of major interest is being investigated, and so it seems to have become a habit. But the worth of an experiment does not at all depend upon the variation of such factors at the same time as the variable of interest is being manipulated. This is what was meant, therefore, when it was mentioned earlier that we should not let the implications of such named phenomena as space and movement error get out of hand. Of course, it is quite another matter if these errors are in themselves the object of study—if they are the fundamental interest in an investigation.

Other versions of the method of average error could also be used to study the Müller-Lyer illusion. There is no reason why the reproduction method could not be used. The E might present a series of cards in which the lengths of the two horizontal lines are equal on each card but the lengths from card to card vary. For each card S would be requested to draw two lines which to him are of the same length as the two lines on each card. Or the horizontal lines might be omitted from the cards and with S being asked to draw lines just long enough to fill each space between the wings. Or S could be given a set of horizontal lines gradually increasing in length (one to a card) and asked to go through the pack of cards until he finds the two that he thinks will just fill the gaps.

Constant stimuli. This method could be adapted to study the influence of certain variables on the Müller-Lyer illusion. For example, suppose we want to study the magnitude of the illusion as a function of the angle of the wings. We choose three angles for study, and a standard card is constructed for each with the wings pointed in. Then a series of cards for each angle is made up on which the wings point out—all at the same angle for a given set and all the same as on the standard card except that the

horizontal line varies systematically, being appreciably shorter
dard at one extreme and appreciably longer at the other. Then
l with the standard and one variable card and is asked to de-
the horizontal line of the variable card is longer or shorter
~. ue standard. The order of the variable cards within a set would
be random. From such data we can construct ogive functions for each angle
of the wings and determine the PSE, the PSE identifying the length of the
horizontal line with wings turned out which is judged equal to the horizontal line with wings turned in. If the PSE varies significantly as a function of the angle of the wings it is clear that this is a relevant variable (which
it is, as any careful consideration of the illusion would show).

Absolute judgment. This method could also be used in various forms. The essential procedure is to require S to make an absolute judgment of the length of the two horizontal lines. This might be done with each
section presented singly or in standard form. The lengths of the horizontal
lines would be varied to avoid stereotyping of responses, an event which
might occur if the same lengths were presented on several successive trials.
If the illusion operates, the horizontal lines associated with the tails out
must be estimated to be longer than the equivalent length lines with the
tails in.

Practice Effects

We have noted that an accounting of a given illusion should
not merely explain the particular illusion but should, if possible, be related
to more general perceptual processes. A good theory will be stated in terms
of basic processes, whether these be conceived of as psychological processes
or physiological processes. Probably more than any other illusion, the Müller-
Lyer has been a vehicle to study what are considered general perceptual
processes mediated through the visual system. We will make no attempt
here to detail such explanatory attempts, but, as an example, we will consider briefly an implication of one of the theories. This theory assumes a
form of inhibition which develops as S views an illusion, and one of the implications of it is that with continued trials the magnitude of the illusion
will decrease. In short, the theory predicts a change in performance with
successive trials.

Our concern with practice effects thus far has been largely restricted
to the design problems they present. Practice effects, in our terminology,
are a major component in progressive error; and progressive error is a pesky
change in behavior which we balance out to avoid its biasing our measurements under the various conditions of an experiment. But, now, in conjunction with measurements on the Müller-Lyer illusion, change in performance
as a consequence of successive trials becomes theoretically relevant and is

to be studied as a phenomenon in its own right. The independent variable in such experiments is stage of practice.

What do the results of investigations show with regard to changes in magnitude of the Müller-Lyer illusion as a function of stage of practice? The data leave no conclusion except that the magnitude of the changes are a function of variables other than stage of practice. This is to say that the changes appear to be a joint effect of stage of practice and one or more other variables. A good summary of studies is found in a monograph by an Australian investigator (Day, 1962). It is his conclusion that the illusion will reduce with practice when S is given visual freedom to compare actively the portions of the Müller-Lyer figure. If S is required to consistently fixate a particular point in the visual field while making judgments, little change occurs. Furthermore, changes with practice are more likely to occur if S is instructed to compare physical equality rather than apparent equality. These two types of instructions *are* different. The S can be told to adjust the variable stimulus until its physical length *is* equivalent to the standard, or he can be told to adjust the variable until its length *appears* to be equivalent to the standard. Mountjoy (1965) has shown the critical role which instructions play in the changes with practice. If S is misinformed about the nature of the illusion, very little change is shown over trials; if he is correctly informed, rather dramatic changes occur.

The change (when shown) in the magnitude of the illusion over trials is not permanent. Mountjoy (1958; 1961) shows that after a decrement in the magnitude of the illusion is produced on one day, a test on the following day will show a greater magnitude than was present on the last trials of the preceding day. Furthermore, the greater the amount of decrement on one day, the greater will be the magnitude of the recovery on the following day.

SOME OTHER ILLUSIONS

Visual figural aftereffects. Look at Fig. 3-11. To the left is a curved line with a small cross slightly to the left. Fixate this cross for 10 to 15 sec. Then, move the book so that the right figure occupies essentially the same position as the left figure occupied as you viewed it, and fixate the cross by the right figure. Observe the straight line as you fixate the cross. Very likely the straight line will appear somewhat curved in the opposite direction from the curve of the left-hand figure. If so, this would be a demonstration of a visual figural aftereffect. The left figure is commonly called the inspection figure, and the right, the test figure. Many different types of inspection and test figures have been used in studying these aftereffects, and the aftereffects as such may take many forms depending upon the test figure used.

Two points of procedure must not be overlooked in conducting experiments on figural aftereffects. First, a control condition must be used in which the appearance of the test figure is measured without having first fixated the inspection figure. Second, as implied by the word *measure* in the above sentence, some technique for measuring the distortions must be evolved. Two facts are relevant to the derivation of a method of measurement. First, the distortions will last for several seconds, so that time is available for making measurements. Second, the distortions are very local-

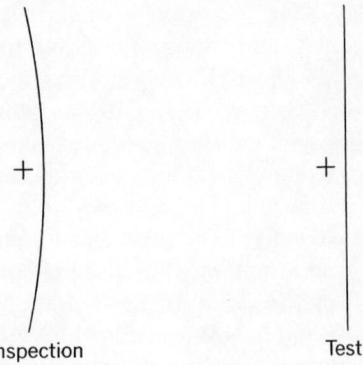

Inspection   Test

Fig. 3-11. A demonstration of a visual figural aftereffect. Fixate the cross near the left figure for several seconds, then shift the book so that the right figure is in the same visual field as the left had been. Fixating the cross by the right figure, observe the apparent curvature of the straight line.

ized with respect to the part of the visual field stimulated by the inspection figure. Thus, on a test, a comparison figure could be presented in a different part of the visual field, and S could compare this figure with the distortions of the test figure. For the curved effect produced by the inspection figure of Fig. 3-11, we might have comparison figures of different curvature on different trials with S indicating whether the curvature of the test figure was greater or less than that of the comparison figure. Or better still, we might provide a means whereby the comparison figure is adjustable in curvature so that S could match the curvature of the test figure. Other inspection figures may produce a horizontal displacement of the test figure—it moves away from the fixation point. Such a displacement could be measured by having a movable comparison figure in the lower (or upper) part of the visual field which could be set by S to the horizontal position occupied by the test figure.

Kinesthetic figural aftereffects. A phenomenon analogous to visual figural aftereffects can be produced by kinesthetic stimulation. The procedure might be as follows. A smooth wooden block, perhaps an inch wide, is used as the inspection stimulus. The blindfolded S lightly squeezes this block between thumb and forefinger, perhaps rubbing it back and forth, for several seconds. The test stimulus is wedge-shaped, extending from a width appreciably less than the inspection block to a width appreciably wider. After the inspection period S places his thumb and forefinger on the test block in the same manner as on the inspection block and moves along the test block until he reaches a point which to him is of the same width as the inspection block. Note that the response measurement is simple in this case; S indicates where along the test block the width is equivalent to the inspection block; that width defines the width of subjective equality (the PSE) for that trial. Of course, several trials would normally be given and the mean PSE used as the measure of the magnitude of effect.

The basic aftereffect measured by such procedures shows that the PSE is greater than the width of the inspection block. Exposure to the inspection stimulus tends to expand the width judged equal when measured on the test block. The effect may be related to another phenomenon which most of us have experienced. If one stands in a doorway and presses outward for a few seconds on the frame with the backs of both hands (arms downward) and then steps away, his arms will actually remain extended from his body as if being pulled out. Incidentally, this latter phenomenon does not seem to have been investigated very systematically. Suppose you were charged with the responsibility for deriving a means of measuring the effect. How would you go about it?

Autokinetic illusion. One of the most dramatic illusions is that called the autokinetic effect. It may be produced by introducing to S a pinpoint of light in an otherwise dark room. Although the light in fact remains stationary, S after a few moments of fixation will report that it moves. He will also make judgments as to how far and in what direction it moves. If a naive S makes judgments as to the distance and direction of movement *after* hearing those made by another S who is a confederate of E, it is shown that the judgments made by the naive S will correspond closely to those made by the confederate. The illusion appears to be quite useful in studying such conformity behavior.

Suggestibility may be used to study somewhat more dramatic instances of the autokinetic illusion. If the S is instructed that the pinpoint of light is hooked up to an apparatus in such a manner that the light will "write" a word, the S may indeed report what the word is that was written (Rechtschaffen & Mednick, 1955). Of course, since the light does not move, it means that the word reported by S is somehow "dreamed up" by him. The particular word reported may have clinical significance in the same sense that what S sees in an inkblot may have clinical significance. The average S will not always report a word; indeed, he may not always report that the light moves. But, given the appropriate in truction, most Ss will at one time or another report the movement; and it is known that the frequency of reports of seeing words and individual letters increases with continued exposure to the situation (Rethlingshafer & Sherrer, 1961).

The question may be raised as to how it is known that the pinpoint of light is responsible for the illusion. Perhaps if S were put into the same situation without a pinpoint of light and told that a light would appear and seem to move, he would report in the same manner as have those Ss when the light is present. This necessary control has been run (Rethlingshafer & Sherrer, 1961), and no movement of a light was reported.

Just why the apparent movement occurs is not clear, although the conditions necessary for it to occur are fairly obvious. In the dark room there are no other objects or stimuli which may serve as reference points. Judgments of movement are normally made by such reference points. If the lack of reference objects is critical, then the illusion should be produced in a completely lighted environment in which there are no reference objects. Cohen (1958) has shown that this does occur. If the viewing field is a completely lighted homogeneous one, a small black fixed dot in this field may also appear to move.

Size-weight illusion. Given two objects which are of the same weight, and also alike on all other characteristics except size, the S in judging the weights (by lifting) will usually judge the smaller to be the heavier. The illusion must disappear if the S is blindfolded. Because we will have reason to return to an experiment in a later chapter where this illusion is used, we will say no more about it at the moment. Some of the theories that have been advanced to account for this illusion, as well as some of the basic experimental facts about it, may be found in Werber and King (1962).

Part-whole proportion illusion. Assume that we have a series of cards, each about the size of the pages in this book. In the middle of one we place a small black rectangle, in another, a somewhat larger rectangle, and so on, so that our series could be identified as the proportion of the total card occupied by the black rectangle. These cards are presented to S in a random order, and he is requested to make an absolute judgment on the proportion of the total space occupied by the rectangle. The results of such an experiment will show that S rather consistently overestimates the proportions. Maximum overestimation occurs near the middle (40 to 50 percent of the card occupied by the black rectangle) with the minimum at the extremes. Obviously, if the entire card is black, or if the rectangle is so small it cannot be seen, the judgments will be accurate at 0 and 100 percent. The amount of overestimation will sometimes be as high as 25 percent (Helson & Bevan, 1964).

The moon illusion. Most of us have noted that the moon appears larger when it first "comes up" just above the horizon than when it is viewed at its zenith (overhead). This illusion has intrigued men for centuries, and speculation about the cause has accompanied the intrigue. The fact is that the distance to the moon at the horizon is a little greater than the distance at the zenith so that the retinal image of the former is minutely smaller than that of the latter. Essentially, however, we can consider the two distances the same. There are other apparent differences in the two moons. The moon at the horizon has a reddish color when compared with the moon overhead, and the moon overhead appears brighter than the horizon moon. The moon on the horizon is viewed in a context of the terrain—trees and buildings; the moon overhead is essentially without context, unless clouds are present.

Given these differences between the horizon moon and the zenith moon, we can see that any attempt to hold all factors constant except one is going to be a little troublesome, to say the least. Nevertheless, it is possible through combined laboratory experiments and direct observation of the moon to eliminate gradually the role which may be played by the various factors. Such a series of experiments has been completed (Kaufman & Rock, 1962; Rock & Kaufman, 1962). We cannot devote the space necessary to detail the many observations made, but it would be quite worthwhile for anyone to follow through the experiments, the reasoning which led to them, and the inferences made from the results. We will do no more than note here that according to these investigators the critical factor is the terrain, which is present for the horizon moon and not for the zenith moon.

OTHER PERCEPTUAL PHENOMENA

The study of illusions is but one small part of the study of perception, although the causes of illusions are often related to more general principles of perception (particularly visual perception) derived from investigations of nonillusory phenomena. But it would be misleading to leave an impression that investigators studying perception are primarily concerned with illusions. We have built our discussion of methods of study around illusions; they served this purpose and are in themselves somewhat fascinating phenomena. But the same discussion of methods could have been accomplished by choosing one of several other areas of study in perception. Had this been done there would have been little change in the methods discussed.

A presentation of other perceptual phenomena may be found in specialized books on perception (e.g., Dember, 1961) or in more advanced books in general experimental psychology (e.g., Woodworth & Schlosberg, 1954). These sources offer discussions of depth perception and the factors that determine it; variables involved in the perception of form; the various constancies (e.g., size constancy, in which familiar objects viewed at a distance do not appear smaller than when viewed nearby, in spite of the fact that the retinal image differs in size); the variable influencing localization of sound in space; and many others. An examination of the issues of the *Psychological Bulletin* for the past few years will show that many summary articles on various perceptual phenomena are available. These summaries commonly provide a synthesis of empirical findings and in addition often state the various theoretical approaches taken.

SUMMARY

An illusion is a particular type of constant error; it is a discrepancy between the measurements of objects by a physical scale and their measurements by a phenomenal scale (the judgment of S). If the direction of this discrepancy is the same for most Ss, it may be called an illusion. The discussion of methods of experimentation, applicable to many perceptual phenomena beyond illusions, was primarily built around the horizontal-vertical illusion and the Müller-Lyer illusion. Variants on the method of average error are frequently used to assess the influence of independent variables on the magnitude of these illusions.

The new method of attack discussed was the method of constant stimuli. By this method the magnitude of a standard stimulus is judged against the magnitude of several variable stimuli presented one at a time in random order. The data obtained by this procedure specify the percentage of time each variable stimulus magnitude is judged to be greater than the magnitude of the standard. From these data, in turn, it is possible to calculate a point of subjective equality (PSE), this value representing the magnitude of the stimulus in the variable-stimulus series judged equivalent to the magnitude of the standard stimulus. If these two values differ, an illusion may be present. One particular constant error which may occur in using this method, an error that is not said to represent an illusion, is called the time error. If the standard and variable stimuli are presented in succession, rather than simultaneously, and if the length of time between the two stimuli influences the judgments, a time error is said to be present.

By way of illustrating how theory and research become intertwined, a hypothesis specifying the cause of the horizontal-vertical illusion was stated. Three experiments testing the implications of the hypothesis were then examined. The hypothesis survived.

Various methods of attack used to study the effects of independent variables on the magnitude of the Müller-Lyer illusion were presented. These methods included a particular form of double counterbalancing often used to eliminate differential effects of two special sources of constant errors. One of these sources may produce a space error, the other may produce a movement error. However, it was emphasized that we must treat the sources of these two constant errors in the same manner that we treat any other independent variable.

Finally, certain other illusions (figural aftereffects, autokinetic illusion, size-weight illusion, part-whole proportion illusion, moon illusion) were identified and discussed briefly.

CHAPTER FOUR

Experimental Designs Using Independent Groups

It was pointed out in Chapter Two that one of the initial decisions which E must make in designing an experiment is whether to use a single group of Ss (giving each S trials under all conditions) or whether to use a different group of Ss for each condition. In experiments in which some aspect of the discriminal processes is being studied, it has been traditional to use a single group of Ss. Many of the studies reviewed in the previous two chapters have conformed to this tradition. But some have not; some have used several groups of Ss, each group being given a different experimental condition. In presenting these studies we skirted or ignored certain problems of design. It is the purpose of the present chapter to correct these deficiencies by presenting in some detail the problems that arise in designing experiments in which independent groups of Ss are used, with each group being assigned a different condition—a different value of the independent variable.

The design technique wherein each S serves in all conditions may be designated the *within-S design*. By appropriate balancing of the order of the various conditions, differential effects of progressive error are eliminated. Thus, the data from a single S may be used to represent the effect of the independent variable. That more than one S is commonly used in such designs (with the data being averaged across Ss) is in the interest of stability and generality.

Two types of designs are appropriate when independent groups of Ss are used. One of these is designated the *random-groups design,* the other, the *matched-groups design.* In evaluating them we should remember a distinction we have drawn between designs of experiments and methods of attack. Methods of attack are at a more specific level of discourse than are types of designs. The method of average error, the method of constant stimuli, and the method of absolute judgment are methods of attack. Generally speaking, these methods of attack could be employed in conjunction with any of the three types of designs (within-S, random groups, matched groups).

RANDOM-GROUPS DESIGN

For reasons which will become apparent as the discussion proceeds, it would seem more accurate to label this design the unbiased-groups design. However, because it has become rather standard practice to refer to it as the random-groups design, we will continue the terminology here.

The Logic of the Random-Groups Design

In a random-groups design Ss are placed in the different groups (to receive different treatments) in an unbiased manner. If Ss are assigned to the groups in an unbiased way, the groups should be statistically equivalent on subject variables which may influence the performance being studied. This is to say that if all groups are measured on the same task, under the same conditions, the mean performances for the groups will not differ statistically. Therefore, if the groups are treated differently during (or before) the performance on the critical task, and if mean performances differ significantly, we must conclude that the differences must have been produced by the differences in the treatments. Let's go through that again. When we place Ss in different groups (groups which will *subsequently* be treated differently by being given different values of the independent variable), we would expect the mean performance of the groups on a task given under the *same* conditions to be equivalent. Therefore, if we give *different* experimental treatments to the groups and differences in performance *do* occur, we conclude that it was due to the different treatments.

As will be realized, the tender point in the above reasoning is the assumption that groups formed in an unbiased manner will in fact be statistically equivalent on subject variables (capacities, skills, attitudes) which may influence the performance on the task used in the experiment. Would the groups have been equivalent if we had tested them on the same task under the same conditions? The support of the design must rest on two points. First, the statistical reasoning appears sound. Second, there have been many, many instances in which different groups of Ss have been formed in an unbiased manner and when tested on the same task *were* found to be statistically equivalent. At the same time we must recognize that occasionally groups, apparently formed in an unbiased manner, do differ when measured on the same task. Such occurrences are to be expected by statistical theory. Let us pursue this further.

Sampling theory starts with the notion of a specified population, for example, all full-time students at a given university. If on a random basis we draw a single sample of 10 Ss from this population, the drawing being made on a random basis, we expect this sample to be representative. If we measure each S in the sample on some attribute (such as weight), we expect the mean for the 10 Ss to approximate the mean of the population. Now assume we draw successive samples of 10 Ss each and determine the mean for each successive sample. Statistical theory tells us that we will occasionally draw a sample whose mean differs significantly from the mean of the population. (The word "occasionally" is used to avoid getting entangled in the problem of what will be called significant statistically.) Such sampling deviations are to be expected, but only infrequently. However, if this infrequent event had occurred in drawing a single sample, we would have been in error had we generalized from the sample mean to the population.

Now, for the moment, our concern is not with generalizing to a population from a sample. In fact, in doing an experiment, we often have a specified number of Ss available, all of whom are to be used in the experiment. We usually do not know in any precise way what population these Ss might represent. For our purposes, we consider the population to be the group of people who are going to serve in the experiment. Our problem is to divide the group into subgroups so that (if all Ss were measured on the same characteristic) the mean of any subgroup would not differ significantly from the means of the other groups. Placing Ss into the subgroups in an unbiased manner is the way in which this is accomplished. However, as in sampling from a population, we will occasionally get a subgroup whose mean does differ from the means of the other subgroups. What do we do about this?

We, in fact, do nothing systematically about it. We assume that if our groups were formed in an unbiased manner, the means would have been statistically equivalent if we had measured all Ss on the same task under the same conditions. Therefore, if we get a difference in mean performance, we conclude that this is due to the differences in the experimental conditions. Obviously, we will occasionally be wrong in reaching such a conclusion, for the groups may have differed initially. In the long run of research, such erroneous conclusions will be corrected. The E may repeat a part or all of the experiment in doing further work, or another investigator may repeat it. If the same results are not obtained, it is a reasonable hypothesis— but by no means the only one—that the original result might have been due to chance factors in assigning the Ss to groups. When direct conflicts of this nature do arise, *E* may go back and repeat as exactly as possible his original experiment. If the original result was due to chance factors, it is highly unlikely that these factors would "throw" the results in the same direction twice in a row.

We have been discussing the infrequent instance in which the use of the random-groups design led to a conclusion that an independent variable is a relevant one when in fact it is not. By the same reasoning it can be shown that we might do an experiment using the random-groups design leading to a conclusion that the variable is not relevant when in fact it is. Suppose we are going to examine the effects of Condition A and Condition B on the magnitude of an illusion. Assume that Condition A decreases the illusion and Condition B has no influence. Assume further that one of those infrequent events occurs whereby the Ss assigned Condition B have a "naturally" smaller mean illusion than those assigned Condition A. In the experiment, Condition A causes the magnitude of the illusion to decrease, but the amount of the decrease is such that the mean for the Ss in this condition is equivalent to the mean for the Ss in Condition B. The conclusion would be that Condition A does not influence the magnitude of the illusion, when in fact it does. Of course, this is quite an unlikely set of circumstances.

The dangers of the random-groups design as pointed out above should not be overemphasized. We *must* accept the fact that occasionally we will reach a wrong conclusion. Indeed, we must be a little fatalistic about this matter since there is nothing we can do about it unless we want to repeat every experiment we do, which is not an exciting prospect. There are many other more frequent ways we can reach wrong conclusions; and we can do something about them, that is, we can learn to avoid wrong conclusions due to the other matters which *are* under our control. One of these important matters is to understand how to form groups in an unbiased manner.

Forming Unbiased Groups

In forming unbiased groups, we adhere to the following criterion: Ss are to be assigned to groups in such a way that there will not be a systematic relationship between any characteristic of the Ss and the particular group to which they are assigned. The best way to see how this criterion is met is by examining a number of different ways of placing Ss in groups. The illustrations will be centered around two somewhat different situations with which we are often faced in doing research.

Captive assignment. In this situation all Ss who are to serve in the experiment are known by name, and all are present at one time. Of course, this is the situation that prevails when all the students in a class are to serve in an experiment. Let us assume we have 30 students and that we are going to do a three-condition experiment. We wish to assign the students to three groups of 10 Ss each in such a way as to make it very unlikely that the groups will differ on subject variables relevant to performance on the experimental task to be used. It should be noted that we do not *have* to have an equal number of Ss in each group, although for certain statistical analyses it is a great convenience, and throughout the discussion we will work toward that end.

1. Each of the 30 students is assigned a number from 1 to 30. It doesn't make any difference how this is done. On 30 equal-size slips of paper, or in 30 capsules, we have put the numbers from 1 to 30. The slips or capsules are placed in a receptacle and stirred; then one capsule at a time is drawn out haphazardly. The students whose numbers correspond to the first 10 numbers drawn form one group; those representing the second set of 10 numbers drawn, a second group, and the remainder, the third. We have three conditions in our experiment: A, B, and C. Some *E*s, at this point, may proceed to pair a group and a condition on a random basis, but this seems quite unnecessary; our groups are formed and the critical matter is not that the groups are assigned to particular conditions but that they are formed in an unbiased manner. The first group drawn may be paired with Condition A, the second with B, and the third with C.

Have we met the criterion that there be no systematic relationship between any characteristic of the Ss and the particular group to which it is assigned? It would seem so. There is little likelihood that one group contains preponderantly bright students, another preponderantly dull. There is little likelihood that one group contains mostly women and another mostly men. There is little likelihood that tall students fall in one group, short students in another, and so on. We would probably agree that there is only a remote possibility that our method of placing Ss in groups resulted in a systematic relationship between some characteristic of the Ss and the particular grouping.

2. Another common method of assigning Ss to groups is by using tables of random numbers. The random sequences given in the appendix (and discussed in Chapter Two) may be adapted for this purpose when assigning a particular S to a condition. In the present case, we wish to assign a given S to one of three groups. The first number in each sequence (of eight random numbers) will be used. The names of the 30 students are listed alphabetically. We choose a given starting position in the table and then attend to only the first number in successive series and then only if it is either a 1, 2, or 3. For example, starting with sequence number 145, we obtain a series as follows: 3, 2, 3, 1, 3, 3, and so on. The first student in the alphabetical listing is assigned to Group 3, the second to Group 2, the third to Group 3, the fourth to Group 1, and so on. Once a given number has been assigned 10 times, it is ignored in further sequences so that our three groups will contain 10 Ss each.

3. Still working with the 30 students in the class, we may consider another method of assignment. Assume that as the students enter the classroom, they are allowed to take any seats they wish. We start at the left end of the first row, counting students along this row, then go to the next row (if necessary) until we have counted off 10 students to form the first group. Still continuing, we count off 10 more, allowing the remaining 10 to form the third group. We have formed three groups of 10 Ss each. Was the method biased? Probably. The procedure results in a systematic relationship (correlation) between "where students sit" and the group into which they are placed. Could the subject characteristic, "where sit," be related to performance on whatever experimental task we are using? It could, but even if we could not see such a possible relationship, we would still not use the procedure because we avoid basing a judgment of biased or unbiased assignment on psychological insight. If we see a relationship between a subject characteristic and the particular group to which Ss have been assigned, we deny that Ss have been assigned in an unbiased manner. In this particular illustration, students who sit near the front of the class may be more eager than those who sit in the rear, and eagerness may be related to performance on the experimental task. Students who arrive late for class may be forced to take seats in the back, or in the front, depending upon the sociology of the class structure; and lateness could conceivably reflect a skill or capacity which might influence performance on the experimental task. In almost every instance in which there is a relationship between a subject characteristic and assignment to particular groups, we can suggest a potential relationship between that characteristic and the performance to be measured in the experiment. But, to repeat, it is not necessary that such a relationship be perceived. If the method of assignment has produced a relationship between a subject variable and successive groups, the procedure is inadmissible.

4. Let us somewhat modify the above procedure. If we start with the students in the front row and ask them to count off by threes (1, 2, 3, 1, 2, 3) up and down each successive row until all students have been "assigned" a number 1, 2, or 3, those assigned 1 become members of one group, those assigned 2 become members of the second group, and those assigned 3 form the third group. Does this procedure result in unbiased groups? Unless some extraordinary situation prevails in a given classroom, it is difficult to see how a bias could exist by this method. Can you see how a particular subject characteristic would be involved so that those Ss with the greatest amount of this characteristic would be placed in one group and those with the least amount in another? It seems doubtful.

5. We may return to the use of the alphabetical listing. Suppose we assigned the first student in the list to Group 1, the second to Group 2, the third to Group 3, the fourth to Group 1 and so on. Would this result in unbiased assignment? It probably would. On the other hand, if we took

the first 10 names in the list to form one group, the second 10 to form the second, and the remainder to form the third, we might have biased assignment since certain names are associated with national origins which may in turn be related to performance on certain tasks.

6. Sometimes the captive students to be used as Ss consist of intact subgroups. For example, an instructor may have two sections of a course which meet at different times. With a two-condition experiment, perhaps done by a group procedure, it would be convenient to give one section one condition and the other section the other condition. However, you can see at once that such a procedure is biased; it results in a relationship between a subject variable ("section chosen") and the particular experimental condition to which assigned. Reasons for choosing a particular section may be related indirectly to the performance required in the experimental task. It is necessary to consider all students in both sections as a pool and then follow one of the procedures discussed earlier.

The above illustrations should be sufficient for the time being. However, it is a worthwhile exercise to try other procedures (symbolically, of course) and examine each for possibility of bias. The following exercise may also be instructive. Suppose all members of a class are measured on some simple task that takes only a few minutes to administer. For example, a half a dozen time estimations could be obtained quickly from all students in a group and the mean for each student used as the estimate of his time-judging ability. Now, using the various procedures discussed above, and perhaps others, sort all students into two (or three or more) groups. In other words, use two procedures for sorting which appear unbiased and two which may be drastically biased. After each sort, determine the means and the significance of the difference between the means on the time judgments as a way of determining whether or not the biased and unbiased procedures are reflected in differences in the ability level of the groups. Of course, even with what appears to be a very biased sorting procedure, no difference in performance may occur simply because the subject variable upon which the sorting is biased may not be related (may be irrelevant) to performance on the task (e.g., time judgments). However, if a task is chosen which is believed to be related to a given subject variable and if the groups are biased on this variable, differences will probably be evident. If they *are* evident, not only have you demonstrated how biased groups may lead to false experimental conclusions, but you have also demonstrated the relevancy of a subject variable for the task. In an obvious case, if the task requires muscular strength, and if a bias occurs in forming groups so that one group consists preponderantly of girls and the other preponderantly of boys, you are apt to get extreme differences in performance on the task. At the same time, you will have rediscovered the fact that, generally speaking, boys have stronger muscles than girls.

Sequential assignment. Much research is done without captive Ss. The E knows only that there is a pool of Ss available; he does not know which particular Ss will eventually serve in his experiment. In the usual circumstances, the experiments may extend over many days or weeks. The E may run two Ss one day, three the next, two the next, five the next. When any given S appears at the laboratory he must be assigned to one of the two or more conditions of the experiment. The E faces the problem of assigning the Ss to the conditions in such a manner that when the experiment is completed he can conclude that overall the Ss were assigned to the groups in an unbiased manner. We must remember that collection of the data may extend over a period of weeks or months, and usually we have no assurance that those Ss who come early in the period have the same ability level (as far as the particular experimental task is concerned) as those who come late in the period. Sequential assignment must be such that it will accommodate possible changes and still not allow bias in the assignment of Ss. Let us examine some possibilities.

1. Consider a two-condition experiment that is expected to require two months to complete. It is immediately apparent that E should not put all Ss appearing the first month into one condition and all those appearing the second month into the other condition. This would be comparable to using one class section for one condition and another for a second, as discussed above with captive Ss.

2. Random procedures may be used. Let us adjust the slip or capsule method used with captive Ss to make it applicable to the present situation. Again, let us assume that we are going to run 30 Ss in our experiment, placing 10 in each of the three conditions A, B, and C. Into a receptacle we put 30 slips of paper, 10 with A printed on them, 10 with B, and 10 with C. After stirring, we draw them out haphazardly and list them in the order drawn out of the receptacle. Then, the first S coming to the laboratory is assigned the condition on the first slip drawn, the second S, the condition on the second slip, and so on. We would hope that this method would result in each of the three conditions occurring almost equally frequently for the Ss that come first to the laboratory and for those who come last. In other words, we are trying to avoid a correlation between the particular conditions assigned and the times within the period of running the experiment when the Ss appear at the laboratory.

The sequences in the appendix may be used in much the same manner as described earlier for captive assignment. The E makes up a schedule of 30 entries with A, B, and C each occurring 10 times. Each letter is associated with a number, and the order of these numbers is determined from the order of the initial numbers in successive sequences. The first S coming to the laboratory is assigned the condition entered first on the schedule sheet, the second S, the second entry, and so on.

Here is a series prepared in the above manner by the writer: C, C, B, C, B, B, C, C, C, B, B, A, B, A, B, C, B, C, A, A, A, B, B, C, A, A, C, A, A, A. This has some undesirable characteristics. Note that the A condition is not administered at all for the first 11 Ss; it is first given to the twelfth S appearing at the laboratory. Since a total of 10 Ss is reached for both B and C earlier than for A, the A entries are very frequent near the end of the series. This is to say that there is some correlation between the succussive points in time and particular conditions. Of course, if we ran a larger number of Ss in each condition, this minor imbalance would probably disappear. As it stands, however, if there is a correlation between the point in time at which Ss arrive for the experiment and performance on the task used in the experiment, our performance scores would be somewhat affected. The series is undoubtedly a little atypical, but it is the series drawn on the "first try." To avoid such series, particularly when a small number of Ss are to be run, many Es prefer to use *block randomization*.

3. In block randomization, a block consists of each condition occurring once but with the order of conditions within each block randomly determined. Obviously, this procedure produces an equal number of Ss for each group, and if there is a correlation between the order in which Ss appear at the laboratory and ability on the experimental task, no bias should result. In the illustrative experiment (30 Ss sorted into three conditions), we will have 10 blocks, with each condition being represented once, and only once, within each block. The order of conditions within each block is random. Here is the series resulting from this method when using random numbers to order the conditions within the blocks: C, A, B; A, C, B; C, A, B; B, C, A; B, A, C; C, A, B; B, C, A; A, C, B; C, B, A; C, B, A.

We may note that this method is not entirely new to us. It will be remembered that in discussing ways of balancing propressive error in the within-S design, we indicated that we might use counterbalancing, complete randomization, or block randomization. In block randomization in the within-S design, each condition occurs once within each block with the order random. Exactly the same situation prevails for block randomization in the random-groups design. However, in the former design, the order within a block specifies the sequence in which the conditions are to be administered to a given S; in the latter design, the order specifies the pairing of conditions with successively appearing Ss.

4. Let us consider another possibility of sequential assignment. Suppose that we do not want to fuss with random numbers. Instead, we decide to use the block idea, but we will have the order of conditions within each block A, B, C—simply repeating this 10 times. This would be comparable to having Ss count off by threes in the captive-assignment procedure and might possibly be quite satisfactory. However, we would need to know a little more about details of the experiment before making a decision as to whether the assignment would or would not be biased. Let us show how a

bias could exist with this method. Suppose E decided he would run three Ss a day, one at 2 P.M., one at 3 P.M., and one at 4 P.M. Those Ss who can come at 2 P.M. may represent a somewhat different "breed" from those who can come at 3 P.M. (or 4 P.M.). If the Ss are always assigned in the order A, B, C on a given day, it means that we are producing a correlation between the time at which the S can serve and the particular condition to which he is assigned. Obviously we are getting a correlation between a subject variable (when he can appear at the laboratory) and the particular condition to which he is assigned. Such regularities should be broken up, which can be done by random ordering of the conditions within each block.

We will have opportunity to examine the application of sequential assignment in later chapters, so we will leave it at this point for the time being. We will turn next to another problem we often face, namely, that of retaining unbiased groups once we get them.

Loss of Subjects

In the course of running an experiment it is not unusual to lose Ss. They do not literally drop out of sight, although sometimes this seems to happen if E is running a particular type of an experiment, such as a retention experiment, where S must return to the laboratory a second time and fails to do so. The more usual circumstances by which Ss are lost will appear in subsequent illustrations. The problem posed by a loss of Ss after they were assigned originally in an unbiased manner, is whether or not the remaining Ss are representative of the original groups. Is the number of Ss lost in the various conditions systematically related to the effects of the independent variable? Illustrations are in order.

1. An E is interested in the change in magnitude of the Müller-Lyer illusion from day to day as a function of number of trials on each day. There are only two conditions in the experiment, namely, 10 trials a day for five days, and 100 trials a day for five days. By sequential assignment a schedule is made so that the two groups initially will be unbiased. However, by the end of the experiment, 10 of the original 30 Ss assigned to the 100-per-day condition have failed to show up for the later days, so that the number is reduced to 20. All Ss in the 10-per-day condition have come for all five days. The performance of the two groups could be compared despite unequal numbers. However, we must ask why 10 Ss failed to complete their series in the one group. It is obvious that this task can become boring, exceedingly so, if a total of 500 trials is given. These 10 Ss who failed to complete their series may have found it convenient to become "sick" or to attend a grandmother's funeral. If these Ss are not representative of the original unbiased group, if they have less or more illusion effect than the original intact group, it is clear that the equivalent groups (resulting from unbiased assignment) may no longer be equivalent.

2. We will discover later that certain task variables produce very large differences in rate of learning. Let us say one of these variables is X. We design an experiment to study changes in learning rate as a function of X. We require the Ss to learn the task to a criterion of perfection. However, increases in amount of X make the task more and more difficult. All the Ss in the task with small amounts of X learn quite readily; those with large amounts find it very difficult. Some Ss in the latter condition may give up; some may have to stop trying to complete the learning because they have another engagement. The greater the difficulty of the task, the greater the loss of Ss for failure to learn. The Ss remaining in the most difficult condition will be the better learners assigned to that condition; those in the easy condition will represent the full range of learning ability as determined by the original assignment. Therefore, the mean performances as a function of X will not be based on unbiased groups, and we would underestimate the magnitude of the effects of X. A simple solution to this problem is to give all groups a constant number of trials or a constant period of time for study and use as the response measure the total learning occurring in the constant number of trials or study time. In this fashion Ss will not be lost for failure to learn.

3. In many experiments Ss may be lost for apparatus failure, an error by E, or for other mechanical reasons not related to the ability of S. If the number lost for such reason is approximately the same for all conditions, we normally believe that our original unbiased groups remain unbiased. If we want to finish the experiment with the same number in each group as originally intended, we would replace a lost S with the next S appearing at the laboratory. Only if we can see some relationship between the performance of S (as related to the variable under experimentation) and loss for mechanical reasons would we feel that we were destroying our unbiased groups.

4. Animal experimentation is commonly done by captive assignment. All Ss for an experiment are available in the colony room. In performing the experiment we have to watch for any differential subject loss just as much as we do when using human Ss. If the conditions imposed by the experiment produce differential losses, the experiment is in trouble. Deprivation experiments (withholding food or water for varying intervals of time) may produce a relationship between degree of deprivation and susceptibility to sickness and death.

5. Any experimental discipline dealing with living organisms as Ss must face the implication of loss of Ss. As an example of the problem, we cite work done by a medical research center in England which has devoted much energy to experiments designed to aid the understanding of simple respiratory virus infections. For our purposes we may lump these together as representing the common cold. Colds occur more frequently in the winter months than in the summer months. One of many possible reasons for this relationship is that people are more susceptible (less resistant) to the cold

virus in the winter than in the summer. The basic features of the design used to test this hypothesis may be reconstructed from a report by Andrewes (1964). The method of attack was to use volunteers who were willing to be inoculated in the laboratory with an appropriate virus and then to follow the inoculation with a period of observation in order to determine whether the person did or did not catch cold. The volunteers were divided randomly into two groups: those who would be inoculated in the winter and those who would receive the virus in the summer. If there are differences in the frequency with which colds ensue, the hypothesis that there are differences between susceptibility in winter and susceptibility in summer would seem reasonable. The experiment was carried out, and the results showed no difference in frequency of colds for the two groups.

Andrewes, however, is quick to point out that this finding is not very conclusive because of a differential loss of Ss. Volunteers assigned to the winter group were forced to cancel their appearance more frequently than those in the summer group because they more frequently had a cold on the day they were supposed to arrive at the unit. Furthermore, more members of the winter group developed colds during the quarantine period in the laboratory which was imposed on all Ss *prior* to the inoculation, and all who did were not included in the test. So there was a greater loss of Ss from the winter group than from the summer group, and those lost were very likely to be those who were most susceptible to colds—since that is why they were lost. Had no S been lost the results might have shown a greater susceptibility in winter than in summer.

Let us summarize. It is of little use to take great care in working out a plan of forming unbiased groups in the first place if we ignore the possibilities that loss of Ss while performing the experiment may destroy the equality. Therefore, a careful record must be kept of Ss lost and the reasons for loss, so that whether or not a biasing factor has entered can be determined.

WITHIN-S DESIGN OR RANDOM-GROUPS DESIGN?

We now have some knowledge of the random-groups design (in the abstract, at least), and we are fairly familiar with the within-S design. We have said that one of the early decisions an E must make in preparing an experiment is to decide which of the two designs to use. Let us set down some of the considerations which may be relevant to the decision.

1. The within-S design avoids any problem related to loss of Ss. Since each S serves in all conditions, the data for Ss completing the experiment are perfectly valid. Of course, as a reminder, the question as to what population the Ss represent is a different issue. If an experiment is done using the within-S design with the intent of getting an estimate of a population mean

(or some other value), and if Ss are initially drawn randomly from this population, loss of Ss may destroy the representativeness of the sample. But, if we have a certain number of available Ss for an experiment and are not concerned about the population they represent, the within-S design avoids the pitfalls of differential loss of Ss which we may face when using the random-groups design.

2. As noted in a previous chapter, there are certain types of experiments in which it is not advisable to use the within-S design. Suppose we are going to study the effects of knowledge of results (KR) on the Müller-Lyer illusion. Under the KR Condition we tell S after each trial just how large his constant error was. It is a fact that over a series of trials the illusion will rapidly decrease to near zero. The other condition will be a Control in which no KR is given. In the within-S design we give both conditions to each S. Let us say we use counterbalancing, giving 10 trials KR, 20 C, and 10 KR. Ostensibly, this should balance progressive error. However, in the first 10 trials S may essentially learn how to adjust his response to make the constant error zero. Perhaps this skill will carry over to the 20 C trials so that on these trials, as well as on the last 10 KR trials, the constant error remains zero. In effect, we would reach a conclusion that KR has no influence on the illusion, or we might even conclude that under KR the illusion is greater (since on the initial KR trials a large constant error may be present). Clearly, this is not an appropriate estimate of the influence of KR. If we used the random-groups design, one group getting KR and the other not, we would show large differences in the constant error as a function of the different treatments.

The general principle we try to follow is that if conditions are such that we expect differential transfer effects from one condition to another, we do not use the within-S, design. By differential transfer we mean that in moving from the A condition to the B condition the effects are different from those in moving from the B condition to the A condition. Thus, in the above illustration, if we give one group KR followed by C, and another, C followed by KR, the performance under the two C conditions would probably differ drastically. Furthermore, influence on performance is much greater on C when preceded by KR than on KR when preceded by C.

3. The within-S design may be preferred for certain statistical and mechanical reasons. We know, for example, that, statistically, there are advantages in using the same S in all conditions. If performance is correlated across conditions, a smaller mean difference is required for statistical significance than if the random-groups design is employed. In the study of the discriminal processes a single condition may require only a minute or two for completion (even for several trials), and it seems very wasteful of time not to use the S in a number of other conditions while he is in the laboratory. This, therefore, might be used as a consideration in determining whether to use one design or the other.

4. There seems to be only one independent variable for which an unqualified assertion may be made about the choice of design. If the independent variable is stage of practice, we should use the within-S design. It would not be wrong to use a random-groups design, but it would certainly be silly. Assume that we wish to study the magnitude of the progressive error after 5, 10, 20, and 50 trials on a given task. We *could* use a different group for each of these four conditions (one group having 5 trials, another 10, another 20, and another 50), but, obviously, a single group given all 50 trials is a far more economical way to proceed.

While the above general points might help in making a decision concerning choice of design, finer points may be thoroughly understood only by the expert in a given field. For example, it is not easy to assess a new situation and make a decision as to whether or not differential transfer will occur. The expert in the field could probably tell us. However, the expert may be founding his decisions on tradition, which, as we have mentioned before, should not always be an automatic basis for using a particular method. A dispassionate outsider may sometimes detect possibilities that one close to the research cannot see.

MATCHED-GROUPS DESIGN

We come now to another technique for forming independent groups. In the matched-groups design, all Ss are measured on a common task and then are formed into groups which are equivalent in performance on the task. Then different conditions are introduced to each group. Superficially, at least, it might seem that such a design would eliminate those infrequent instances where the random-groups design may result in groups which are not initially equivalent. However, we should examine the details of the method before reaching any final conclusion concerning its virtues. Two matters need to be considered, namely, the requirements of the matching task and the method of matching.

Matching Tasks

With the matched-groups design we measure all Ss on a common task prior to the introduction of the experimental variable. The common task, often called the pretest, may be either of two kinds.

Different but highly correlated task. If we have a pretest task on which the performance scores are highly correlated with scores on the task to be used in the experiment, the pretest task may be used as a source of matching data. The essential requirement is that performance on the two tasks be correlated. Breakdowns in the application of the matched-groups design often occur because the *E assumes*, without ever making a statistical determination, that the pretest and the experimental task yield correlated performance scores. Too often an intelligence test is used as a pretest when, in fact, such a test may have little if any predictive value for performance on the experimental task. In many cases a pretest which is known to yield scores correlating with those to be obtained from the experimental task is not available, and this fact has led to the second kind of matching procedure.

Initial performance on experimental task. It is often convenient and feasible to give all Ss a few trials or a short period of practice on the task to be used in the experiment. All Ss are given these trials as a pretest, and then the two or more groups of Ss are formed from these initial performance scores. It would seem that if ever we would expect a high correlation between two sets of scores it would be between two sets of measurements on the same task. Generally, this expectation is borne out.

Ways of Matching

There are two ways by which the actual matching of groups, based on pretest scores, may be carried out.

Matched on means and variability. By this method, E does no more than form groups (as many as needed for the experiment) so that the means and variabilities of the distributions of scores are statistically equivalent. Let us assume we are going to form three groups from 30 Ss, all given a pretest, and these groups are then to be given Conditions A, B, or C. The pretest scores should be rank ordered. Starting at the top (or bottom) of the distribution, we apply the procedure used in forming the random blocks for sequential assignment. That is, the first three Ss, represented by the first three scores, would be assigned A, B, and C on a random basis, with one S to each of the three conditions. The remaining Ss would be treated in like fashion, sequentially blocking them into groups of three and giving them random assignments to groups.

As an alternative, assume that from our ranking of pretest scores we assigned the S with the highest score to Condition A, the S with the next highest to B, and so on, in an A, B, C, A, B, C, A, B, C order until all 30 scores are sorted into three groups. It can be seen that while the variabilities of the three resulting distributions would be quite comparable (if the distribution of pretest scores was symmetrical), the means of the three distributions would differ systematically. That is, the Ss placed in Condition A would have the highest mean, those in Condition B, one slightly lower, and those in Condition C, a still lower mean. If we assigned Ss by using a counterbalanced order (A, B, C, C, B, A) the means of the three distributions should be essentially equal, but the variability of the scores of Ss in the A Condition would be greater than B and B greater than C. While neither of these methods would produce serious distortion, we are probably a little better advised to use the random-blocks procedure.

Matched Pairs. By this method *E* also gives all Ss the pre-test. On the basis of the pretest scores, *E* matches Ss. That is, *E* would find three scores which are equal, or nearly so, and place one S from the three obtaining this score into each group. What he attempts to do is to make identical triplets of each set of three Ss in terms of performance on the pre-test. How much tolerance is allowed in the scores in defining equality is quite an arbitrary matter. If *E* insists on precise matching, some Ss in the original group, such as an S with a deviant pretest score, may have to be eliminated. The number of Ss in each group may, therefore, be less than one-third of the size of the original group given the pretest. There is, of course, nothing wrong with this unless the results are to be used to generalize back to a population of which the original group was a representative sample.

An Illustration

A set of "live" data may now be examined to provide con-crete illustrations of matching procedures. Assume that we are going to do a study on time estimation using three conditions. It is not important what these are, so we will continue to call them A, B, and C. We have already seen that there is some degree of stability within S in time perception as obtained by the method of verbal estimation. This is to say that judgments from a person at one time correlate quite highly with his judgments at an-other time. Therefore, we will use the same task as a pretest. In this case 30

Table 4–1
Pretest Scores for 30 Ss Rank Ordered

S#	Score	S#	Score	S#	Score
1	75	11	40	21	27
2	65	12	39	22	25
3	64	13	37	23	21
4	63	14	37	24	19
5	60	15	34	25	19
6	45	16	32	26	16
7	45	17	31	27	15
8	42	18	30	28	13
9	41	19	30	29	10
10	41	20	30	30	2

Ss made three judgments each. The intervals were 20, 10, and 35 sec., and all Ss made the judgments in the order listed. For each S a sum of the constant errors for the three intervals was calculated and used as the pretest score. To avoid dealing with negative constant errors, a value of 40 was added to each score. These scores are listed in rank in Table 4-1, with the Ss numbered from 1 through 30. It is apparent that a broad range of scores is involved and that there are gaps in the distribution. Nevertheless, this is probably not an atypical distribution for many kinds of scores for this many Ss.

The results of the three different procedures for matching on means and variability as discussed earlier are presented in Table 4-2. The conditions A, B, and C were associated with the numbers 1, 2, and 3, respectively (as previously discussed), in assigning Ss to conditions by the random-block method. Thus, the first random order of the three numbers was 3-1-2, S #1 being assigned to C, S #2, to A, and S #3, to B. A new random order was determined to assign the next three Ss, and this procedure was continued for 10 blocks.

TABLE 4–2

RESULTS OF THREE MATCHING PROCEDURES FOR THE DATA OF TABLE 4–1

Three groups, A, B, and C, are matched by three different procedures.

	RANDOM BLOCKS			A,B,C,A,B,C, ETC.			A,B,C,C,B,A, ETC.		
	A	B	C	A	B	C	A	B	C
	65	64	75	75	65	64	75	65	64
	63	60	45	63	60	45	45	60	63
	42	41	45	45	42	41	45	42	41
	41	39	40	41	40	39	39	40	41
	34	37	37	37	37	34	37	37	34
	31	32	30	32	31	30	30	31	32
	30	27	30	30	30	27	30	30	27
	19	25	21	25	21	19	19	21	25
	19	15	16	19	16	15	19	16	15
	2	10	13	13	10	2	2	10	13
Mean	34.6	35.0	35.2	38.0	35.2	31.6	34.1	35.2	35.5
SD	18.5	16.5	17.1	18.2	16.8	16.5	18.6	16.8	16.6

For the second procedure, labeled in Table 4-2 as A, B, C, A, B, C, etc., the score for the first S went into Condition A, the second in B, the third in C, the fourth in A, and so on. For the third procedure, labeled A, B, C, C, B, A, etc., the score for the first S was placed in Condition A, the score for the second S in B, the third in C, the fourth in C, and so on.

The means and SDs (standard deviations) for each column are also shown in Table 4-2. As expected, only the middle procedure (A, B, C, A, B, C) produces fairly large differences in the means and so cannot be recommended for matching purposes. As discussed earlier, the third procedure might be expected to produce decreasing variability from A to B to C. While this is literally true, the differences are small and certainly no greater than those present in the random-block method. Nevertheless, it would appear that the soundest matching procedure is the random-blocks method.

Now let us consider the problems that arise if we attempt to match S for S. The purpose is to get successive blocks of three Ss each, in which the Ss within each block had the same or nearly the same pretest score. These three Ss are then assigned randomly to the three conditions. Obviously, for the data of Table 4-1, we cannot require identical scores, but how much tolerance shall we allow and still treat the Ss as identical? A difference of 1? Of 2? Of 5? If the tolerance gets too great, we might just as well match on means and variability using random blocks. Suppose we allowed a tolerance range of 5 score points. The Ss numbered 2, 3, and 4 in Table 4-1 could be used as one block; Ss 6, 7, and 8 as another, and so on. But, if you follow through, you will discover that it is possible to match only eight blocks of three Ss each; 6 Ss will have to be eliminated. Thus, our experimental groups would consist of 8 Ss each instead of 10. This is not particularly serious, however, if we are not concerned about the population the Ss represent (as noted earlier). Perhaps the increase in statistical precision gained by dropping the more deviant Ss will more than compensate for the reduction in number of Ss in each group. Of course, if we had a much larger pool of Ss at the outset, we could not only achieve a closer match for our so-called identical triplets, but we could also have more than eight Ss in a group.

Further Evaluation

The inevitable question arises, "Which method should we use? Should we match on means and variability or should we match S for S?" There is no pat answer to this question. Each method has certain drawbacks and assets as noted; we make a decision on the particular features we want to emphasize—precision or greater range of ability levels.

Should our pretest be an independent task or should it be the same task? Recommendations can be a bit more firm here. If no independent task is known which will predict performance on the experimental task, one is taking a risk that a pretest on a task which *appears* that it should correlate with the experimental task may not in fact do so. And even if we find a significant correlation between the pretest scores and the scores on the experimental task, we must remember that significant correlations can occasionally occur by chance in exactly the same way that groups formed randomly will occasionally differ significantly. Generally speaking, if we use an independent task for the pretest, the relationship between the scores on this task and the experimental task should have been established in a previous investigation as well as being demonstrated again in the particular experiment being performed at the moment. If this situation does not prevail, one should, if at all possible, use initial trials on the experimental task as the pretest. For many different tasks it has been shown that there is a substantial correlation between initial and later trials. The correlation is likely to be far beyond the level that makes it reasonable to interpret as a chance correlation. All in all, the use of the initial trials as a pretest is recommended over the use of an independent task as a pretest. However, there may be experiments in which E does not want to use the initial trials as a pretest simply because he wants to study the influence of his independent variable on the initial trials. In such cases, if an independent task of known predictive value is not available for matching, one should use the random-groups design.

And this brings us to the final question to be weighed in making design decisions, namely, if we have decided to use independent groups, should we use the random-groups design or the matched-groups design? Different investigators will give different answers to this question, which suggests that there is no strong or compelling reason for choosing one over the other. If we "read" the last decade of research correctly, there is a clear trend toward more frequent use of the random-groups design and less frequent use of the matched-groups design. These trends may reflect only matters of convenience since it is troublesome to obtain pretest scores and match the Ss. Furthermore, many of the advanced statistical procedures are more simply applied to the results of a random-groups design than to those from a matched-groups design. Yet, it appears that if we rule out chance correlations between pretest and experimental test (which, it was argued, are very likely ruled out when we match on initial trials of the experimental task), the matched-groups design may provide slightly more protection against infrequent but real chance factors than the random-groups design provides. Both methods are equally susceptible to bias resulting from differential loss of Ss.

At the same time, if one studies the random-groups design with assignment by block randomization and compares it to the matched-groups design in which matching occurs on the basis of means and variability and assignment is made by block randomization, he will find the two methods to be very much the same. However, the expert on correlations may point out subtle regression effects which might occur (effects which we will not attempt to discuss) as an argument against the use of the matched-groups design, particularly if matching occurs by matched pairs. Let us conclude by saying that either method can be used successfully to do experimental work and that perhaps the critical issue is not the choice of one over the other but rather the rigor in which the experiment is carried out once the design is chosen.

HOLDING FACTORS CONSTANT

Let us conclude this chapter by considering an issue which should increase our understanding of the implications of various designs regardless of the one chosen. We often hear the following admonition: "In an experiment we must hold all factors constant except one, and that one we vary to determine its effect on behavior." We wish to make clear that the phrase "hold all factors constant" is merely a manner of speaking and that in fact we do *not* hold all factors constant. Indeed, we hold very few factors constant even in the most rigorously performed experiment.

Consider the procedure for a typical experiment. The experiment extends over days. Two different Es may be involved in running the Ss. Different Ss may be run at different hours. Are all factors held constant except the independent variable? Of course not. Is the temperature of the room identical (constant) for all Ss? Is the humidity? Do Ss respond to the two Es in exactly the same way? Probably not. Apparatus calibrations may change slightly during the course of the experiment. An illusion figure may get a slight smudge on it. A watch may run one one-thousandth of a second slower per minute at the end of an experiment than at the start. What, then, is the meaning of the exhortation to hold all conditions constant?

What we mean when we say we hold all conditions constant is that we do not let other factors (other potential or known variables) operate differentially so as to bias the measurements for one condition more than for another. Our conditions—our different treatments—are so arranged that the variations in the many factors we say are constant (but really aren't) will not influence behavior more under one condition than under the other. We often speak of these as random variables; this means that they are not controlled but that their influence is randomly distributed over all conditions. If there are two Es, each must run Ss under all conditions of the experiment. If Ss are run at different hours, each hour will be equally represented for each variation in the independent variable. If the accuracy of the watch gradually changes as the experiment proceeds, we have the various conditions represented at all points in time when running the experiment in order to avoid a bias. Many factors are not held constant, but our experiment is so designed that if these either vary randomly or change systematically over the course of time, the measurements will not be biased in favor of one condition over another. We expect variations in uncontrolled factors to add variability to our scores but not to introduce a bias.

Strangely enough, in group experiments we probably come nearest to having true constancy of factors. Thus, if we could run all Ss at the same time in a given room with a single E for one trial only, we would probably come fairly close to attaining constancy, hence reduction in variability of the scores over that which occurs when our experiment involves Ss being run singly and when the experiment takes weeks or months to complete.

It should be noted that in the listing of various factors which may change randomly or systematically during the course of an experiment, no attempt was made to be exhaustive. One could list many more. But even if we drew up what we think is an exhaustive list, another person could probably add to it. Consequently, you may say to yourself, if we do not know what all these factors are which may influence behavior, how are we going to design an experiment so that we know they are not going to bias our measurements of the effects of the independent variable—so that the measurements under one treatment will not be influenced more or less than those under another.

The first thing we must *not* say is that many of the factors are probably irrelevant, therefore we do not have to worry about them. We cannot make a judgment like this. Unless a factor has been investigated thoroughly and has been shown not to influence the measurements to be taken in a particular experiment, we cannot judge it a priori and conclude that it will not influence behavior. If a five-degree variation in the temperature of the room occurs, and if it is not known whether or not temperature has an effect on the task we are using, we cannot assume that it is irrelevant for the situation even though it *seems* quite unlikely that it is. Our first impulse might be to have a temperature-controlled room to avoid this problem. This would indeed be fine, but much research would stop if this were a prerequisite. Furthermore, if we went through our list of all potential factors which may influence the behavior we are interested in and tried indeed to hold them constant, as we might the temperature, we would never get an experiment done. Although holding factors truly constant, particularly those factors known to influence the behavior, is an ideal as a means of increasing precision, we usually are quite unable to accomplish it. We must look to other devices, always keeping in mind that while we cannot control all variables, we can prevent them from biasing our results. When we said that after the choice of a given design the experimental procedure must be carried through with rigor, and that this is probably more important than the particular design chosen, it was this problem of bias to which we were referring. We lay out the schedule and ask ourselves if there is any known factor which is systematically related to the occurrence of one of our treatments more than to another. Will each treatment be given about equally often at each hour of the day that the experiment is to be run? Will each E, if there is more than one, be given an equal number of Ss to be run under each condition? If E gets more proficient in performing his duties as the experiment proceeds, will this increased proficiency fall equally on each treatment? Will the Ss under each treatment be run equally often on each day of the week? A few basic questions such as these will lead one to the position that an immense number of potential variables—variables which might or might not influence the behavior we are interested in—will not bias the results even if they are not held constant. We see that many of these variables are correlated; if each treatment is given with equal frequency at a given hour of the day, temperature, humidity, and probably several other factors which might bias the results will not in fact do so. If each treatment is given with equal frequency on each day of the week, factors related to day of the week (the Monday Blues, the Thank-God-It's-Friday syndrome) will not bias the results. Even if the "dark of the moon" or cosmic rays influence behavior, they should influence it equally under all treatments.

Of course, we cannot say with absolute certainty after any experiment that these other factors have not biased the results. But if we, or others, repeat the procedure with variations in design and the same results are found, we become fairly confident. The fact is that we can get repeatable results when many, many factors are not held constant. This means either that these factors are not relevant for the behavior being measured or that if they are, they have not biased the results. This is not to say that we should not strive for situations in which we do indeed hold factors constant, hold them at a given fixed level, for we should. But, practically, we can only approach the ideal.

SUMMARY

Two design techniques, both using independent groups of Ss, were outlined. These designs were contrasted with the within-S design, presented in the previous chapters, wherein each S serves in all conditions of the experiment. In the random-groups design, independent groups are formed by assigning Ss to different groups (to serve under different conditions) in an unbiased manner. In the matched-groups design, Ss are given a pretest and on the basis of scores on this pretest are assigned to various groups so that the groups are known not to differ prior to the introduction of the different experimental conditions.

Various procedures for assigning Ss to groups in an unbiased manner in the random-groups design were discussed, and these procedures were contrasted with those which were biased. Implications of the differential loss of Ss from the groups were pursued.

The matched-groups design depends for its effectiveness upon the correlation between the pretest scores and scores on the experimental task. Scores on an independent task or scores on the initial trials of the experimental task may be used for matching purposes. Groups may be matched on the basis of means and variability or may be matched S for S.

A comparison of the features of the random-groups design with those of the matched-groups design led to a conclusion that only the convenience of the random-groups design provided a preference.

What it means to "hold all factors constant except the independent variable" was interpreted to imply that all relevant factors (variables) are not and cannot be held constant in an experiment. The experiment, however, is devised so that the effect of these nonconstant factors is not allowed to fall differentially on the scores obtained under the different conditions of the experiment.

CHAPTER FIVE

Thresholds

The study of the discriminal capacities of an organism is closely identified with the study of thresholds. Two basic questions are asked about these capacities: "What is the range of the impinging energy to which the organism's sensory equipment is sensitive?" and "How sensitive is the organism to changes in impinging energy?" The first question is asking about *absolute thresholds,* the second, about *difference thresholds.*

The sensory equipment consists of the eyes, the ears, receptors associated with smell, with taste, with pain, with pressure, and so on, plus all of the neuro-cortical systems involved in each. We know that the eye is sensitive to certain forms of impinging energy and not to others and that the ear is sensitive to certain other forms but not to the energy to which the eye responds. Unfortunately, we do not have sensory equipment which is immediately sensitive to all forms of impinging energy. Carbon monoxide gas is not detectable, and certain forms of deadly radiation have no immediate sensory consequences. Yet, the organism moves about, adapts, and survives only because of the sensory equipment which *is* sensitive to various energy changes.

If the phrase "raw experience" can be given meaning, it would be "uninterpreted sensations produced by energy appropriate to sensory systems." But because we so readily assign words to these experiences, raw experience is fleeting. Radiant energy falling on the retina becomes a bright or dim light; a series of auditory stimuli becomes melodious or cacophonous; an odor is rancid, musty, or spicy. The skilled writer, by the right choice of words, reverses the process for a reader by making him "experience" the sensations, either in isolation or as a complex of associated sensations:

Eugene was loose now in the limitless meadows of sensation: his sensory equipment was so complete that at the moment of perception of a single thing, the whole background of color, warmth, odor, sound, taste established itself, so that later, the breath of hot dandelion brought back the grass-warm banks of Spring, a day, a place, the rustling of young leaves, or the page of a book, the thin exotic smell of tangerine, the wintry bite of great apples; or, as with *Gulliver's Travels,* a bright windy day in March, the spurting moments of warmth, the drip and reek of the earth-thaw, the feel of the fire.*

Returning to the world of the experimental psychologist, we may note that, as usual, our emphasis will be on the methods used for determining thresholds. Nevertheless, we will try not to let this emphasis obscure the basic fact that the concept of thresholds has a widespread application in seemingly quite diverse situations. Because the beginnings of experimental psychology are closely associated with this area of research, an appropriate historical perspective would be of great benefit. But a short course of a long history would be quite inappropriate, and so the reader is referred to Guilford (1954) for a perspective on the development of the methods of research and to Boring (1942) for the full sweep of history.

The Thresholds

Let us illustrate the absolute and the difference thresholds before we specify them precisely in terms of the methods used for measurement.

The absolute threshold is sometimes called a stimulus threshold, but it might better be called a threshold of response. Any energy to which the organism is sensitive must exist in a certain amount before it will arouse a response—before S will report the presence of a stimulus. The lowest stimulus value which will elicit a response is said to lie at the lower absolute threshold. For most people, 16 to 20 cycles per second (cps) of the sound wave represents the lower threshold for pitch. Frequencies below this are not heard, although they may be experienced as a vibration if the intensity is great enough. At approximately 20,000 cps, sound disappears so that we can determine an upper absolute, or terminal, threshold.

After S has heard a tone of known frequency, how large an increase or decrease in frequency will be necessary before he signifies the pitch has changed? The amount of change in the frequency necessary to bring this about is called the difference threshold and is sometimes referred to as a *just noticeable difference,* abbreviated JND. Given a standard weight of 100 grams, how many grams will have to be added to the standard before S will

*Reprinted with the permission of Charles Scribner's Sons from *Look Homeward, Angel,* p. 66, by Thomas Wolfe. Copyright 1929 Charles Scribner's Sons; renewal copyright © 1957 Edward C. Aswell.

indicate, upon lifting it, a change in weight? How much weight must a 100-pound woman gain before it becomes visibly noticeable to her friends? Thresholds are sometimes called limens, and the difference limen—difference threshold—is abbreviated as DL.

Let us now be a little more precise.

Absolute threshold: the minimal physical stimulus value (or maximal for upper thresholds) which will produce a response 50 percent of the time.

Difference threshold: the value of the physical stimulus change that is noticeable 50 percent of the time.

As the above definitions indicate, we shall have to use statistics to obtain an adequate value for a threshold in any given situation. Thresholds will vary with individuals, and they will also vary from moment to moment for an individual. The measured threshold obtained on one trial will probably differ somewhat from the value obtained on the following trial. The best measure we can provide of a threshold is a statistical abstraction—the mean or median of many threshold measurements. These may be taken on a single S if we wish to specify *his* threshold, or we may take measurements on many Ss if we wish to specify a generalized threshold. These latter types of measurements provide the basis for detecting sensory deficits. A hearing test compares the patient's absolute threshold against a generalized threshold; a visual acuity test compares the patient's absolute threshold against a generalized threshold.

One word of caution should be given concerning statistical abstractions, one of which is the threshold. In considering the mean or median value of a series of measurements as a threshold, we may sometimes fall into the error of wondering what the "real" threshold is. This, of course, is an unanswerable question. The threshold, as inferred from our measurements, varies from moment to moment. It will change as a function of methods of measurement and of other factors. We can know phenomena only by the ways we measure or observe them, and for experimental purposes, the statistical threshold is the "real" threshold. Johnson (1939) tells of a study in which a group of speech experts judged the number of times a so-called stutterer stuttered. There was a wide divergence among these experts in their tabulations. Johnson indicates that after reporting this study to a class, he will occasionally hear the query, "But, how many times *did* the person stutter?"

Most of us do not have difficulty in conceptualizing a threshold, whether it be a stimulus threshold or a difference threshold. Furthermore, our experiences tell us that the threshold should *not* have an immutable, fixed value. A ticking watch held at a certain distance from the ear will alternately be heard and then not heard; the ticking appears to wax and wane. At one moment you may think you can distinguish a difference between two very similar colors, but at the next moment you cannot. Around the statistical absolute threshold there is truly a range of uncertainty; the statistical threshold is like a person standing in a doorway—he is neither in nor out, and he must move one way or another before he gets all the way in or all the way out. So let us not be too concerned about the "real" threshold. The concept of a threshold, a statistical concept, has enormous usefulness in understanding the processes involved in the various sense modalities.

Two methods, and variants thereof, have been used to measure thresholds. One of these is the *method of constant stimuli*, a method which we already know something about, and the other is the *method of limits*. We may examine each procedure in turn to determine how the two kinds of thresholds are measured.

THE METHOD OF CONSTANT STIMULI

Determination of absolute thresholds. By preliminary work E delimits the range of stimuli to be employed. At one extreme the stimulus will be so weak that rarely if ever will S report its presence; at the other extreme the stimulus will be of sufficient magnitude that S will almost always report its presence. Somewhere between these two extremes lies the threshold. Between these two end stimuli E will add several others spaced in equal steps along the physical scale used to measure the attribute of the particular stimulus energy being employed. The total number of stimuli used may vary from 4 to 10, rarely less and rarely more. A random order is used in presenting the stimuli; they are not presented as a series of increasing or decreasing magnitudes. Each stimulus is usually presented an equal number of times, although this is clearly not a requirement.

Let us say that we are going to determine the lower absolute threshold for light intensity of a given wave length. Six intensities are chosen with one unit along a physical scale separating each successive intensity. The lowest stimulus magnitude has a value of 7, and the highest, a value of 12. These are presented to S in random order 100 times each, with instructions to report on each trial if a stimulus is "present" or "not present." The experiment would normally be carried out in a dark room, with S well habituated to the situation and watching a fixation point so that he knows where to expect the stimulus. Of course, we could determine the threshold in a well lighted room, but it would certainly be expected to vary from that found in a dark room. After the presentation of each stimulus, E records whether S responded positively or negatively. For each stimulus value a percentage is obtained indicating the relative frequency with which S reported the stimulus present for each intensity. In this hypothetical experiment the following data on one hypothetical S were obtained:

Stimulus value:	7	8	9	10	11	12
Percentage of times reported present:	3	11	35	68	87	99

The absolute threshold, it will be remembered, is the lowest stimulus value which is noticeable 50 percent of the time. In the data above we note that a stimulus value of 9 was percieved 35 percent of the time and a stimulus value of 10, 68 percent of the time. The threshold must lie somewhere between these two values since, presumably, some value between 9 and 10 would, if actually presented a number of times, be judged present half the time and absent half the time.

From such data there are two relatively simple ways in which a close approximation of the threshold can be obtained. Both techniques have been discussed in an earlier chapter when determining the PSE (point of subjective equality). One, the graphical method, consists first in plotting the data with the stimulus values along the abscissa and the percentage values along the ordinate as in Fig. 5-1. A smooth curve has been drawn through the

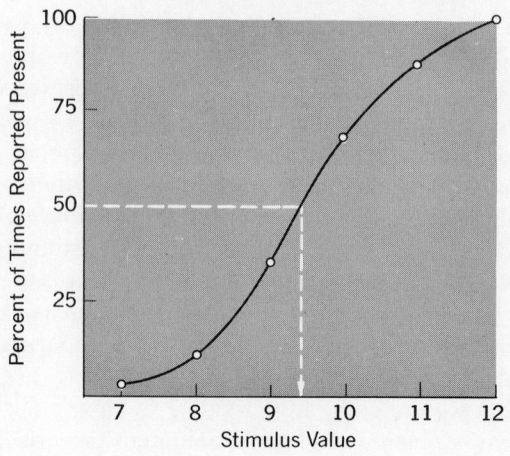

Fig. 5-1. Graphical determination of the absolute threshold. The threshold value is approximately 9.4.

points, and a vertical line is dropped to the abscissa from the 50 percent point on the curve. This point, 9.4, is the absolute threshold; above this point we expect more than 50 percent "present" responses, and below the point we expect fewer than 50 percent "present" responses.

The second method, the linear interpolation method, involves finding the median of the distribution. For the present data, we obtain a median of 9.46, which is very close to that found graphically.

Determination of difference threshold, or DL. This method of collecting data has been described in an earlier chapter. However, it will be worth repeating the procedures; furthermore, we will need to "get more out of the data" than we did previously. As an illustration, the classic laboratory exercise of judging weight differences will be used.

Each judgment is made on the basis of two stimuli, one a standard stimulus and the other a variable stimulus. For this illustration the standard weight against which all other weights are judged is 100 grams. A series of comparison weights is constructed, these weights varying from the standard only in weight; that is, they are of the same size, same texture, and so forth. Small aluminum cans of identical size, with lead shot determining the weight, have often been used. The shot is held in fixed position by stuffing cotton in the cans. Thus, the blindfolded S can get no cues for making his judgments other than those supplied by the independent variable—the weight. In choosing the weights it is customary (although not necessary) to make the extremes of the series clearly different from the standard so that the lightest will be judged lighter than the standard nearly 100 percent of the time and the heaviest judged heavier with equal frequency. In the present series the lightest weight is 90 grams, and the heaviest, 110 grams, with step intervals of 2 grams so that the comparison series is as follows: 90, 92, 94, 96, 98, 102, 104, 106, 108, and 110. Each variable or comparison weight is judged against the standard many times. The order in which the comparison weights are presented with the standard is random.

The two stimuli (standard and variable) are presented to S *in succession,* S "hefting" them one at a time with one hand—never lifting them simultaneously with one in each hand. If the standard weight were always lifted first and the variable, second, a constant error (time error) might be introduced. Therefore, for half the trials the standard is lifted first and the variable second; in the other half the reverse order holds. On each trial S must judge whether the second weight lifted is heavier or lighter than the first. The basic data consist of the percentage of times each comparison weight is judged heavier than the standard.

Figure 5-2 is a graphical representation of the results of this hypothetical experiment for a single S. Since we have balanced the order of presentation of the variable and standard weights, no constant error should be present. Hence, the PSE should not differ appreciably from the standard weight; the place where the curve crosses the 50 percent level should be directly above the standard weight of 100 grams as indicated on the abscissa. Of course, we could also determine the PSE by finding the median.

The data plotted in Fig. 5-2 produce two different thresholds—two DLs. The PSE represents phenomenal equality. Therefore, we may ask how much *increase* in weight above the PSE is necessary before S detects an increase, and we may also ask how much *decrease* in weight below the PSE is necessary before S detects a difference. The former is called the upper DL, the latter, the lower DL. The upper DL would be the "distance" from the PSE to the point at which the judgments become 50 percent or more above chance. In terms of the graph, this would actually be at the 75 percent level.

The lower DL would be the distance between the PSE and the point of the lower stimulus value at which the judgments also become 50 percent or more better than chance. This is the 25 percent point on the graph.

This determination of DLs may seem a little confusing at first, but if you will recheck the definition of a DL and study the graph, it should become clear. Note, for example, how the curve would look if we assumed a small DL—much smaller than that shown on the graph. The smaller the DL, the sharper the rate of rise of the curve, for it means that S is getting more judgments correct for comparison weights which are close to the standard. If verticals are dropped at the 25, 50, and 75 percent points on such a curve, it can be seen that they would be more closely bunched than in Fig. 5-2, thus indicating smaller DLs. On the other hand, if the curve is flattened more than in Fig. 5-2, it would imply poorer discriminability, hence larger

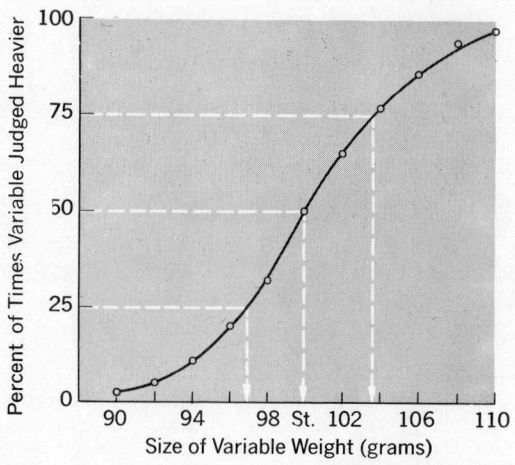

Fig. 5-2. Representation of the results of the weight-lifting experiment using the method of constant stimuli. A standard weight of 100 gm. was used and compared with each variable weight. The points for the curve are determined by the percentage of times each weight was judged "heavier than" the standard. As depicted here, the point of subjective equality is 100 gm., the lower difference threshold is slightly over 3 gm., and the upper difference threshold, slightly less than 4 gm.

DLs. The DL is the amount of change in magnitude which can be detected 50 percent of the time. If the standard is compared with the standard, a "change" in magnitude is detected zero percent of the time, although this point (the PSE) is given as the 50 percent point on the graph. The "distance" from this 50 percent point to the 75 percent point (or 25 percent point) is 50 percent of the distance from the 50 percent point to the 100 percent point (or zero percent point).

An absolute threshold is a point—a point along a physical scale representing a stimulus value which will be detected 50 percent of the time. The difference threshold—the DL—is *not* a point; it is a span or distance, or it is the magnitude of the change which must occur before a phenomenal change will be detected 50 percent of the time.

THE METHOD OF LIMITS

Determination of absolute thresholds. We may parallel the illustration used for the method of constant stimuli, and by using the method of limits, determine the lower absolute threshold for light intensity. Our apparatus allows us to increase and decrease the intensity of a light source continuously. Thus, we may gradually make the light less and less intense until it is no longer visible, and then we may gradually increase the intensity until it becomes clearly visible again. In fact, this is essentially what we do. For half the trials the light is initially clearly visible and then is decreased gradually until S reports "not visible." For the other trials, we start with an intensity that is not visible and gradually increase the intensity until it is "visible." For each trial a threshold measurement is obtained, momentary as it may be. But an average of a series of trials would give a fair estimate of the value which is detected 50 percent of the time.

Table 5-1 is a representation of 10 measurements, five in the ascending direction, five in the descending. The intensity scale is in quite arbitrary units. A *plus* indicates that the light source was visible, a *minus* that it was reported not visible. Thus, on the first trial, E started the series at a stimulus value of 3, invisible to S who continued to report not seeing the light for the values 4, 5, 6, 7, 8, 9, and 10, but when the intensity reached 11, reported it visible.

The transition point for an ascending trial in Table 5-1 is in the step interval where S last reports that he does not see the light and the interval where he first reports seeing it. Therefore, on the first trial the transition point is between 10 and 11 units. For the descending series the transition point is in the interval bounded by the last plus and the first (and only) minus. For the second trial, this transition point is between 10 and 9. Where is the threshold of each trial? Certainly it is not at the point where S still sees the stimulus, and just as certainly it is not at the point where he no longer sees it. For each trial the best estimate of the threshold is some value between the points "see" and "don't see"—it is some value within the transition zone. In each case, the best guess we can make is that it is halfway between the plus and the minus—halfway within the transition zone. On the first trial it would be 10.5, on the second, 9.5, and so on. What we are saying is that if we had data from only one trial, the best guess we could make concerning a stimulus value which would be reported "seen" half the time and "not seen" the other half the time, would be a value in the middle of the transition zone. A series of trials should produce a more stable estimate, and so we get a mean of the thresholds for all trials, which, for the data of Table 5-1, is 10.8.

TABLE 5–1

ILLUSTRATION OF A SERIES OF MEASUREMENTS TO DETERMINE THE LOWER ABSOLUTE THRESHOLD TO LIGHT

STIMULUS VALUE	ASC.	DES.	ASC.	DES.	ASC.	DES.	ASC.	DES.	ASC.	DES.	STIMULUS VALUE
20								+			20
19								+			19
18		+						+		+	18
17		+				+		+		+	17
16		+				+		+		+	16
15		+		+		+		+		+	15
14		+		+		+		+		+	14
13		+		+		+		+		+	13
12		+		+	+	−		−		+	12
11	+	+		−	−				+	−	11
10	−	+	+		−					−	10
9	−	−	−		−		+			−	9
8	−	−	−			−		−		−	8
7	−	−	−			−		−		−	7
6	−	−	−			−		−		−	6
5	−			−		−		−			5
4	−							−			4
3	−										3

Individual Thresholds   10.5   9.5   9.5   11.5   11.5   12.5   8.5   12.5   10.5   11.5

Mean Threshold Value: 10.8   Standard Deviation: 1.27

If we expect that the particular independent variable being manipulated may produce differences in variability of thresholds, a standard deviation may be used to measure this variability and may be referred to as the variable error.

Are there factors involved in the method of limits which may produce a constant error? There are, of course, the ever-present changes which may occur with practice and fatigue. In addition, the particular techniques used in the method of limits may produce two other constant errors. One of these is called the *error of habituation*. Let us suppose that in a descending series the light is initially well above threshold and then is gradually reduced in intensity. The error of habituation supposes that S will fall into a habit, or set, of giving the response "see" and may, therefore, continue reporting this past the point where in fact the light is no longer visible. If this error is operative, it would tend to make the threshold for the descending series lower than in fact it really is and make the threshold for the ascending series higher than it really is.

The other constant error which may occur is called the *error of expectation*. It may occur because S, expecting a change will report such before in fact it occurs phenomenally. After several trials S knows that on a descending series the light will reach a point where he no longer can see it; if he reports this before in fact that point is reached, it would be an error of expectation. The error of expectation would tend to make the descending thresholds higher than they really are and the thresholds for the ascending series lower than they really are. Upon reflection, it will be seen that the influence of the two errors is directly opposed. If the magnitude of the two opposed tendencies is equivalent, therefore, their effects should cancel, and no bias would be present.

How can we measure the magnitude of the effects of such tendencies? We can't. We can tell only whether one tendency is operating more strongly than the other. We do this by comparing the mean thresholds for the ascending and descending series. Suppose the mean of the descending series is higher than the mean of the ascending. This suggests that expectation is operating more strongly than habituation; for either the ascending series or the descending series, or both, expectation tends to cause the S to report a change too soon. On the other hand, if the descending threshold is lower than the ascending, it suggests that habituation is operating more strongly than expectation; the S goes beyond the "true" threshold.

Now we may see somewhat more clearly that it is rather silly to talk seriously about a "true" threshold. Threshold values are a product of the measuring techniques and will vary as a function of these techniques. Suppose we used all ascending series in our measurement. Have we measured the threshold? Of course we have; we have measured and defined a threshold for those particular techniques. True, it may differ from the value obtained by other techniques (such as using all descending series or using the method of constant stimuli), but if any given technique produces consistent or reliable measurements, that is all we can ask. However, there is another issue here which *should* concern us. Suppose we did an experiment to determine the influence of a certain barbiturate on an absolute threshold. We run two parallel experiments, which are exactly the same except that for one we use the method of limits and for the other we use the method of constant stimuli. Now, suppose further that one of these experiments showed a direct and striking relationship between the amount of the barbiturate and the threshold and that the other showed no relationship at all. At this point we would indeed be concerned, for it would appear that the two techniques are not measuring the same thing; one is measuring a "threshold" that is heavily influenced by the barbiturate, and the other is measuring a "threshold" that is not. Still, if each experiment has been done properly, one set of results is as valid as the other. We would, of course, immediately attempt by further research to discover why the two techniques produce different results.

One of the variants on the method of limits is known as the staircase method. The E initially determines a particular starting point, presents the stimulus, and asks S to report presence or absence. If absence is reported, E increases the magnitude by a step (the step unit determined in advance) and asks for another judgment. Eventually, of course, S will report the presence of the stimulus if the magnitude is increased on successive trials. At the point where it is first reported it would appear that the threshold has just been crossed. Furthermore, when this point is reached, E reverses the procedure by reducing the magnitude of the stimulus by one step prior to the next judgment. If S reports the stimulus is present, the magnitude is reduced another step. When S fails to report its presence, the direction of change is reversed again. It can be seen that E reverses the direction of the change in magnitude when S's judgment on a given trial differs from the one made on the immediately preceding trial. This procedure is continued over a predetermined number of trials where a trial is defined by each successive change in the magnitude of the stimulus. In effect, by this staircase method, the magnitude of the stimulus presented to S "sticks close" to the threshold. The area between the points (trials) where S detected the stimulus and those where he did not represents an area of uncertainty.

A detailed discussion of the staircase method has been provided by Cornsweet (1962), and he suggests a further variant called the double staircase method. For our purposes, a knowledge of the single staircase method is quite satisfactory since it works well with a serious and honest S. In examining the method in a little more detail, we may adapt one of Cornsweet's illustrations. Assume that we are going to use the staircase method to determine the threshold for the light stimulus with which we have been working. A simple way to proceed is to obtain a rough notion of the location of the threshold prior to the initiation of the experimental trials. In the present hypothetical experiment this was "found" to have a value of 8, and this is the value of the stimulus presented S on Trial 1. The reports by this S on successive trials are given graphically in Fig. 5-3. On Trial 1, S reported "no"; he did not detect the light. The intensity was increased by one unit so that the value was 9 on Trial 2. Still S reported no light, and the response was also "no" on Trial 3. (These reports suggest that our preliminary work, intended to provide a rough notion of the threshold, gave us only that—a rough notion.) On Trial 4, however, S reported "yes." On Trial 5, therefore, the stimulus magnitude was set one unit lower than it had been on Trial 4. On Trial 6 a "no" report was received, and the direction of the change in magnitude of the stimulus was again reversed. This procedure continued for 20 trials.

How do we determine a threshold from such data? It can be determined quite simply by calculating a mean value for all the stimuli presented. This value will be between the values for those stimuli to which S responded "yes" and those to which he responded "no." It will be in the middle of the range of uncertainty. For the present data the threshold is 10.20. This method is quite satisfactory for determining the threshold, particularly if we have been reasonably successful in determining a near-threshold value by the preliminary work.

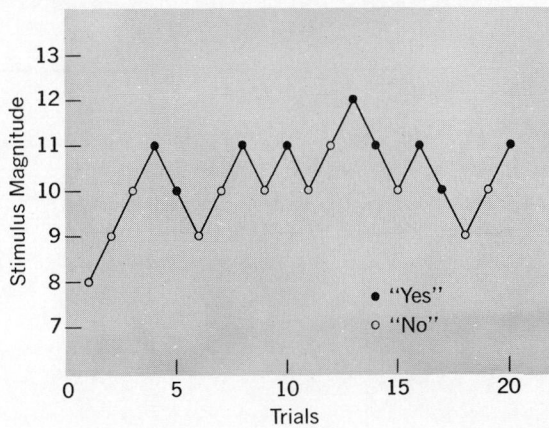

Fig. 5-3. Results of an experiment used to determine the absolute threshold by the staircase method. See text for an explanation of this hypothetical experiment.

Determination of difference thresholds. Next we will consider the application of the method of limits to the measurement of difference thresholds. We will continue with the light-intensity problem, but this time we add another light source to our apparatus. This new light source serves as the standard stimulus, and its intensity will not be varied. We set this standard at a fixed intensity and then proceed to find out how much the variable stimulus must differ from the standard before S reports a just noticeable difference. Again we would use the alternate ascending and descending series. We start the variable light at an intensity value that is clearly brighter than the standard (for a descending trial) or at a point that is clearly less bright than the standard (for an ascending trial) and then gradually decrease or increase the intensity. As the intensity is gradually decreased, a point is reached at which S reports that the two lights are of equal brightness. We normally do not stop here; instead, we continue decreasing the intensity of the variable stimulus until S reports that the variable stimulus is now less bright than the standard. We have taken S through successive experiences of "brighter," "equal," and "less bright." The procedure would then be reversed, using an ascending series.

Data from such an experiment may appear as in Table 5-2. The standard stimulus was set at an intensity value of 50. First there is an ascending series in which the variable is set so that its brightness is clearly less than the

TABLE 5–2

AN ILLUSTRATION OF THE MEASUREMENT OF DIFFERENCE THRESHOLDS BY THE METHOD OF LIMITS

STIMULUS VALUE	ASC.	DES.	ASC.	DES.	ASC.	DES.	ASC.	DES.	ASC.	DES.	STIMULUS VALUE
58				+						+	58
57		+		+				+		+	57
56		+		+		+		+		+	56
55		+		+		+		+		+	55
54		+	+	+		+		+	+	+	54
53	+	+	=	+	+	=		+	=	+	53
52	=	+	=	+	=	=		=	=	+	52
51	=	=	=	+	=	=	+	=	=	+	51
50	=	=	=	=	=	=	=	=	=	=	50
49	=	=	=	=	=	=	−	=	=	=	49
48	−	=	−	=	−	=	−	−	=	−	48
47	−	−	−	=	−	−	−	−	−	−	47
46	−		−		−		−				46
45	−		−		−		−				45
44	−		−		−		−				44
43	−			−							43
42				−							42

Upper
Threshold 52.5 51.5 53.5 50.5 52.5 53.5 50.5 52.5 53.5 50.5
Lower
Threshold 48.5 47.5 48.5 46.5 48.5 47.5 49.5 48.5 47.5 48.5

Mean Upper Threshold: 52.1   Upper difference Threshold: $52.1 - 50 = 2.1$
Mean Lower Threshold: 48.1   Lower difference Threshold: $50 - 48.1 = 1.9$

standard, and then the intensity is gradually increased. As the intensity increases, S eventually reports that the brightness is equal to the standard and, subsequently, that it is brighter than the standard.

For each trial it is evident that there are two transition points, points which may be termed thresholds of change. First, in the ascending series, there is a change from "less than" to "equal." This is the lower threshold of change. Second, there is a change from "equal to" to "greater than" the standard. We have two DLs based on the two thresholds of change. In computing the DLs, we take the difference between the value of the standard stimulus and the value at the threshold of change. Just as in the method for determining absolute thresholds, the threshold of change is taken as that value which lies midway between the two values at which the change occurred. For example, in the first trial, the last *minus* is at 48 and the first *equal,* at 49. Our best guess is that the threshold of change is halfway between these two values, namely, 48.5. The last *equal* is at 52, and the first *plus* is at 53, so the upper threshold of change is 52.5. Taking the difference between the value of the standard stimulus and the upper threshold of change gives us the upper DL, 2.5. The lower DL is 1.5. Thus, for each trial, we have an upper DL and a lower DL.

If there is a constant error produced by the method of limits so that the PSE is not equivalent to the standard stimulus, we would not be justified in using the value of the standard stimulus to determine the thresholds. Instead, we should use the PSE, which is determined by taking the mean of the *equal* judgments. For example, on the first trial, the PSE is 50.5—midway in the band of equal judgments. For the second series, it is 49.5. The mean of these points for all trials would provide the most stable measure of the PSE. If this value differs appreciably from the standard-stimulus value, we should use the PSE in determining the DLs. As a matter of fact, we can never be wrong by using it at all times. If it is equal to the standard, we are in good shape; if it is different from the standard, we are using the most appropriate point of phenomenal equality for calculating the DLs. In the present data, the PSE is 50.1, so it matters little which is used.

So much for the method of limits as viewed in a rather ideal manner. We must now see how both the method of limits and the method of constant stimuli are applied in practice. In so doing, we will expect to obtain a notion of just how broad and how firmly the threshold concept is entrenched in psychology.

SOME VISUAL THRESHOLDS

The effective stimulus for vision is electromagnetic radiation. However, the visual system is responsive to only a very narrow band of radiation, specified in terms of the wave length, for the radiation may be conceived of as traveling through space in wave form. Waves which are longer than those to which the eye responds include radio waves, television waves, and those commonly called radar. Radiation waves of shorter length than those to which the eye normally responds include X rays and ultraviolet rays. Within the narrow band of energy—the light waves—to which the eye is responsive, different wave lengths are associated with different colors, the shorter ones with violets, the longer ones with reds.

From previous courses you will remember that the immediate receptor cells in the retina are constituted of at least two somewhat different types of cells, the rods and the cones. Furthermore, you may remember that the cones are concentrated in the center of the eye, the fovea, and diminish in frequency as they extend outward toward the periphery of the retina. Contrariwise, the rods occur with increasing frequency as they extend outward from the fovea toward the periphery. The rods are more sensitive than the cones. This is to say that a very weak source of light which may not be perceived in foveal fixation can be seen out of the "corner of the eye." But only the cones can mediate color vision. One of the classical laboratory exercises for elementary students is that of mapping the color zones. The S fixates a given point directly in front of him. A small circular patch of color, perhaps a quarter of an inch in diameter, is pasted on the end of a slender wand. The E gradually moves this small patch of color from outside the field of vision toward the line of regard being maintained by S and perhaps 12 in. in front of S. As this color stimulus first appears in the visual field, the image must necessarily fall on the periphery of the retina. At this point S can clearly report the presence of a stimulus, but it appears achromatic, that is, it appears to have no color. As the patch continues to move closer and closer to S's line of regard, it will eventually stimulate the cones, and S will report the color of the patch. Then E may start the patch directly in the line of regard and move outward until S reports that color is no longer perceived. It is apparent that the method of limits is involved. The point at which color is no longer perceived (when moving outward) or first perceived (when moving inward) is the best estimate of threshold or edge of the color zone for that particular color. The point can be expressed in terms of degrees, using S's line of regard as zero degrees. Now, if these procedures are repeated at various points around the field of vision (from above, from below, from left, from right, and perhaps at intermediate points), it is possible to plot the boundaries of the sensitivity zones for each color. These are often plotted on a circular matrix, representing the visual field, in which the center is zero degrees. A series of concentric circles of increasing diameter are used to represent increasing degrees from the zero fixation point.

An essentially unique vocabulary is developed in any highly specialized research area. It is built up not only with regard to the phenomena investigated but also with regard to the units of measurement of stimulus characteristics and measuring scales of the instruments used. To an outsider, at least, it would appear that the specialization of vocabulary has reached its peak among those actively doing research on visual problems. Let us assume we overhear an informal discussion among a group of experts in visual research. We will make no attempt to insert continuity in this discussion.

First remark. "Assuming the scotopic visibility curve is maximal at about 500 mews, and the photopic curve at 550 mews, then it seems to me that . . ."

Translation aids. What is a mew? It turns out that the measurement of the length of the waves of radiant energy to which the eye is sensitive is expressed in units known as millimicrons. A millimicron is one-millionth of a millimeter and is abbreviated $m\mu$. For conversational purposes, and perhaps in conformance with the law of least energy in use of words, the spoken abbreviation has become "mew." A scotopic visibility curve shows that in low illumination, such as at twilight, maximal sensitivity to a light source of a given radiance is about 500 mews. This reflects the fact that cones (which respond in dim light) are more sensitive than rods. The photopic curve is derived under daylight conditions and shows that maximal sensitivity is at a longer wave length—550 mews; in daylight the cones are playing a larger role than they do in twilight.

Second remark. "It might be that whatever substance mediates cone vision, comparable to the rhodopsin of the rods, is in an impure state in the anomalous trichromat."

Translation aids. Anomalous trichromacy is a particular deficiency in color vision, or roughly, a form of color blindness. Use of people with various forms of color blindness has played an important role in attempts to understand the way in which color vision is mediated. Rhodopsin is a chemical substance in the rods which is quite definitely known to be involved in the reactions of the rods to the light wave. A comparable substance for the cones has not been identified.

Third remark. "Recording from single fibers of the Limulus . . ."

Translation aids. We discover that the Limulus is a horseshoe crab, the neural arrangements of which make recordings of nerve impulses from the receptor cells fairly convenient. It has, therefore, been extensively used to study visual mechanisms.

This is enough, even though we have just scratched the surface. It is obvious that fundamental work on psychology and physiology of vision is a highly technical and specialized field. Nevertheless, there are certain visual threshold phenomena which can be investigated without extensive equipment, and it is to these that we will turn for some illustrations of application of various methods in the measurement of thresholds.

Critical Fusion Frequency

Consider the situation in which successive light flashes are produced from a stationary source. If these light flashes occur with, let us say, a second between each flash, S will report only a series of flashes. But if the interval between successive flashes is gradually reduced in length, an interval will be reached at which S reports a steady light source; no longer will he report flashes. The length of the interval between successive flashes at which S first reports a steady light source is called the *critical fusion frequency,* commonly abbreviated CFF. Frequency, in this instance, indicates frequency of periodic flashes per given unit of time; obviously, the more frequent the flashes, the less the interval between successive flashes.

The CFF is not a mere curiosity. It is a threshold that is used to help understand the visual processes. It is known to change under a variety of S conditions, such as reduced food intake, neuroses, and brain injury. And, of course, it will be a function of the particular stimulating conditions used to measure it. It is to two such variables that we turn our attention, using a study by Lloyd (1952). The two variables were the intensity of the flashing light and the retinal location stimulated.

The production of an interrupted light source is usually accomplished by a device called an *episcotister*. In its simple form an episcotister consists of a revolving disc in which two 90-degree segments, directly opposite each other, have been removed. That is, the "pie" is cut into four pieces, and two pieces in opposition have been removed. Thus, the amount removed is the same as the amount remaining. If this disc is rotated slowly in front of a light source, S will see light and dark flashes of equal duration. As the speed of revolution is increased, a point will be reached at which S reports continuous light—the CFF.

By the use of a device placed between the light source and the episcotister, a very small amount of retina could be stimulated. For the particular conditions we will consider, the amount is spoken of as 2 degrees of visual angle. To understand visual angle, assume that the light enters the lens of the eye as a point source but then is projected to the retina at the back of the eye, once again assuming extension (although the image is inverted). The angle determined by the boundaries of the image converging on the lens is the visual angle. Since opposite angles formed by the crossing of two straight lines are equal, the angle formed by the boundaries of the object converging on the lens of the eye determines the size of the image on the retina—the visual angle. Obviously, the size of the visual angle is determined not only by the size of the stimulus object but also by its distance from the eye. A very small object close to the eye would subtend a large visual angle; a large object at a great distance will subtend a very small visual angle. In the present study, a circular patch of light subtended 2 degrees of visual angle.

In one set of conditions, the stimulus was projected on the fovea of the retina, and in another set, in the peripheral part of the retina, 20 degrees from the center of the fovea. A total of 18 different intensities was used. It is common to report intensity of light sources in millilamberts, and, in this particular study, the logarithms of the millilambert scale (log I) was used for reporting.

We have noted several times that any threshold may change as a function of the conditions under which it is determined. In the present study, Lloyd wanted CFFs obtained in a darkened room and with the S well dark-adapted. All of us have had the experience of going from sunlight into a darkened room, such as a theatre, and we know that for a number of minutes we have difficulty seeing. But as we remain in the darkened room, we become "adjusted" and can soon distinguish objects which we could not distinguish earlier. It is known that dark adaptation is essentially complete within 30 min., and that is the period which Lloyd allowed in the darkened experimental room prior to making CFF measurements.

For each of 18 intensity levels, six determinations of the CFF were made for each locus of stimulation. Three of these were "ascending series," in which the order was from flicker to fusion, and three were "descending," in which the order was from fusion to flicker. The mean of these six thresholds, expressed in terms of revolutions per second of the episcotister, provides the basic response measure. Three Ss were used in a within-S design, and for presentation here we have combined the results for all Ss. Figure 5-4 gives a visual picture of the results. It shows that as intensity of stimulation

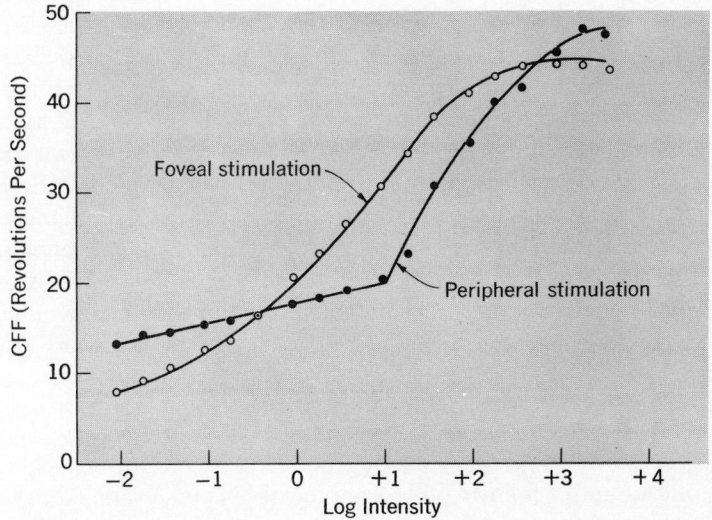

Fig. 5-4. CFF as a function of intensity of stimulation and locus (fovea or periphery) of stimulation. Data from Lloyd (1952).

of the fovea increases, there is a quite regular increase in CFF up to about 45 revolutions per sec., where it appears that a leveling off is occurring. To say this another way, the brighter the intensity of the light, the smaller the interval between successive flashes must be before fusion will occur. The "curve" for peripheral stimulation presents a somewhat different picture.

With lower intensities, there is only a small (but consistent) increase in CFF up to an intensity of 1. At this point there is a radical change in the slope of the curve, and with the higher intensities, CFF is higher than with foveal stimulation.

What is one to make of this disjointed curve for peripheral stimulation? Let it be said first that the finding of such a curve is not usual in psychology. However, when such a relationship is turned up, it is a most provocative event, for it is usually taken to indicate that some new process enters dramatically at the point where the slope of the curve suddenly changes. An imaginative theoretician will do much with such a finding. For example, he might assume that two processes change as a function of increases in intensity, but the rate at which they change differs appreciably. Then he may try to construct two curves which, when summated, will produce the empirical curve. His two imaginary curves may be identified with a known process, or they might be used to suggest the nature of two hypothetical processes which subsequent research might then in fact discover. In this particular case, however, the effects may be quite closely tied to the functioning of rods and cones. With low intensities, rods are primarily responsible for the CFF since they are more sensitive at low levels of intensity than are the cones. As intensity increases, more and more cones are stimulated. It is possible, therefore, that the point of sudden change in the curve represents a sudden increase in number of cones stimulated. Or it is possible that a particular interaction may occur when both rods and cones are stimulated at a certain intensity. Or it may be that cones of the fovea have different characteristics from those scattered in the periphery. Lloyd comes to no final conclusion on these matters. The major point to be made is that E should always be alert to such sharp switches in a relationship between a dependent and an independent variable; they are extraordinarily fruitful bases for explanatory attempts.

Word-Recognition Thresholds

When a new phenomenon is discovered, subsequent research built around it follows quite a predictable course. The course of this research is toward finer and finer analysis in an effort to pinpoint the precise conditions under which it will occur, or, in other words, what is responsible for its occurrence. Of course, the speed with which such analysis occurs will be in large part determined by the number of research workers who become interested in the problems of analysis. And the number who become interested in the problem may often be a result of the original interpretation placed on the phenomenon. If the interpretation is one which seems to strike at cherished beliefs, it is likely to provoke other researchers, hence, other research. If the interpretation is one which seems to open up a whole new area of behavior theory, it is likely to attract workers who may not believe the theory or who do believe it and want to advance it. If the phenomenon is judged to be of great importance, by any of many criteria, it may attract many new workers regardless of the interpretation placed upon it. It would appear that some findings concerning thresholds for word recognition and the interpretation placed upon the findings had all of the characteristics noted above to attract suddenly many researchers bent upon analysis of the situation to support or refute the initial findings or to question the interpretation. It would require a book to document and evaluate in detail the history of the work on word-recognition thresholds, in spite of the fact that it covers a relatively short period of time. We cannot, of course, do this, but we will attempt to pick up a few of the highlights as a fundamental lesson in analytical experiment work.

In the middle 1930's some new interpretive notions began to appear in accounts of perceptual phenomena. These notions emphasized the importance of subject variables. More particularly, they were concerned primarily with "dynamic" subject variables such as motivation, as opposed to more static subject variables such as sex and IQ. They made no attempt to deny the influence of task and environmental variables on perception. Rather, they pointed out that experiments which manipulated only variables in these classes could not provide a complete account of perception. Dynamic subject variables must be included, it was asserted, in explanatory equations of perception. To support these assertions certain studies were undertaken. For example, experiments were reported in which the results were interpreted as demonstrating that a hungry S perceived differently from one not hungry. And in addition, data were reported which purported to demonstrate that a poor boy would judge the size of a coin to be larger than would a boy from a wealthy family. Some of the work on word thresholds was clearly an extension of this direction of thinking. Our exercise in analysis may begin with a study reported by McGinnies in 1949.

The McGinnies study. Word-recognition thresholds are usually determined by use of the method of limits with an ascending series only. A word is presented initially for a very short interval of time, perhaps .01 sec. This is done by a *tachistoscope* consisting of some form of shutter mechanism which must, of course, be capable of opening and closing very rapidly to expose material for so short an interval. The S is instructed that a word will be exposed initially at too short an interval for him to recognize what the word is, but on successive trials when the length of exposure will increase, he is to call out the word as soon as he thinks he recognizes it. As per the instructions, E gradually increases the length of time the word is presented, and the interval at which S correctly responds is said to be the threshold—the word-recognition threshold.

McGinnies' Ss were 16 college students, 8 men and 8 women. Using the within-S design, Ss were presented a series of words (one at a time), some of which were called neutral or nonemotional words (e.g., *apple, glass, trade*) and some of which were emotional or taboo words (e.g., *raped, whore, bitch*). He found that the thresholds for the taboo words were significantly higher than for the neutral words. This is to say that on the average the taboo words had to be exposed a longer period of time before S correctly named them than did the neutral words. Now, when it is said that the taboo words have to be exposed a longer period of time, we should realize that in an absolute sense the interval is very short. For the neutral words, the average was .053 sec., for the taboo words, .098. Thus, the taboo words had to be exposed about one-tenth of a second before being recognized correctly.

The difference in the threshold for two types of words led McGinnies to suggest that the taboo words, prior to being recognized as seen correctly, elicit anxiety which in turn arouses a form of perceptual defense; the S is protected against or delayed in experiencing further anxiety by "refusing" to recognize the word. Of course, this is all presumed to occur at an unconscious level. Such notions may be expressed in other terms, but the basic idea is that anxiety-provoking words can elicit the anxiety before the word per se can be correctly recognized, and, as a consequence, mechanisms are set into action which raise the threshold for the word. Of course, it is puzzling how such mechanisms can be elicited before the word is correctly recognized, but, if it is possible, the implications are exciting; ways may be provided to investigate experimentally the role of unconscious factors in behavior.

As might be expected, however, other investigators immediately viewed McGinnies' procedures and interpretation skeptically with one eye and analytically with the other. We may consider two points raised by Howes and Solomon (1950). First, they noted that in McGinnies' experimental room both a male and a female E were present and that both male and female Ss were used. Under such conditions, an S of either sex might be a little reluctant to report a taboo word; Ss would want to be very sure the word being flashed in the tachistoscope was indeed *raped*, before they reported they saw *raped*. If this were true, we might expect the thresholds for the taboo words to be higher than those for the neutral words and would need no recourse to unconscious defense factors. Second, it was pointed out, there may be a confounding variable. The taboo words may differ from the neutral words on some variable other than "emotion-evoking characteristics." If this is true, the difference in the thresholds might be attributed to this other variable.

The particular "other variable" which Howes and Solomon had in mind was word frequency. It was reasoned that Ss in McGinnies' experiment had probably seen the neutral words much more frequently in print than they had seen the taboo words. If, then, recognition threshold was a function of word frequency, the differences obtained might have been due to this alone. Howes and Solomon then show that the neutral words *do* occur more frequently in printed discourse than do the taboo words. It appeared not unreasonable, therefore, to suggest that word frequency may have been responsible for McGinnies' results.

We will not pursue further the experiments dealing with tests of the notion that something intrinsic to taboo words (e.g., their anxiety-provoking characteristic) may be involved in recognition thresholds. This issue seems not to have been completely settled at this time (e.g., Minard, 1965). The line of research to be explored here concerns the relationship between word frequency and recognition thresholds.

The Howes-Solomon study. When Howes and Solomon suggested that word frequency might have been critically involved in McGinnies' results, they were not merely guessing that a relationship existed; they had, in fact, performed two studies exploring the effect of frequency (1951). We may examine the procedure and materials used in one of these studies.

Fifteen words were used, varying widely in frequency. Among the very frequent words were *country, promise,* and *example,* and among the infrequent ones, *titular, figment,* and *machete.* The source of information on word frequency is tables prepared by Thorndike and Lorge (1944), who tabulated several million words from texts of widely varying kinds. Their tables show the frequency per million words with which 30,000 of the most frequently used words occur.

For each of the 20 Ss in the Howes-Solomon experiment (within-S design), a different random order of presenting the words was used. Thus, differences in thresholds that might be due to progressive error would not bias the thresholds for any given frequency level. Is such a precaution necessary? Is there a change in thresholds for word recognition as a function of number of words tested? There is indeed. In another experiment in this same report, Howes and Solomon measured thresholds for 60 words—all Ss having all 60 words. On the initial words the mean threshold was approximately .25 sec., whereas on the words given near the end of the series, it was approximately .12—half the initial threshold. This is just one more illustration of the fact that thresholds are not fixed and static; as with all phenomena, they are a function of the conditions under which we measure them.

Here is what E told each S at the start of the experiment:

'This is an experiment to see how keen your vision is when a word is briefly flashed before your eyes. You will be given words to identify. A number of increasingly long flashes will be presented for each word. I will notify you before I change the word that is being flashed.

'The first flashes will be very brief, and you probably will be unable to recognize the word. I will then gradually increase the duration of the flash for the successive trials of that word. After each flash, please state clearly and distinctly whatever you think you saw. There is no objection to guessing; but, if you have no idea what it is, say so.

'Before I present each flash, I will say, "Ready." You will then look into the eyepiece and focus on the area between the two orange lines. After the ready signal, do not say anything until you have made your response to the flash. After you have made your response, sit back and relax until I give the ready signal for the next presentation.' (p. 402)

A mean threshold was determined for each word. The relationship between thresholds and word frequency is expressed as a correlation between the two variables. The correlations varied from —.71 to —.79, the variations within this range depending upon which one of the several frequency measures given by Thorndike and Lorge was used. Thus, the higher the frequency with which a word occurs in printed discourse, the lower the visual recognition threshold. Clearly, there is a strong association between the two variables.

The Solomon-Postman study. The correlations found by Howes and Solomon provide strong evidence for suggesting that word frequency per se is a powerful causal mechanism in determining the word thresholds. But most experimentalists are always just a little uneasy about such conclusions from correlational data when different quantities of the independent variable (word frequency, in this case) are not actually produced in the laboratory. Perhaps some other characteristic of words differs as a function of frequency differences. We know that, on the average, less frequently used words have more letters than those more frequently used. Of course, such differences can be controlled by using words of equivalent lengths but having different frequencies. Perhaps low-frequency words have more peculiar letter combinations or syllable combinations than high-frequency words and these peculiarities make the low-frequency words more difficult to perceive. If this is true, we might be able to find high-frequency words which have these same peculiarities. Would the thresholds for such words still differ from those obtained on low-frequency words? Obviously, we cannot make a low-frequency word and a high-frequency word identical in all respects, for this would mean they would have to be the same word. But we *can* do this in the laboratory; we can produce frequency differences for a single verbal unit and determine if thresholds are affected. If the relationship between frequency and threshold level is maintained under these circumstances, we could conclude that there is a causal relationship between frequency and recognition thresholds. This is the approach taken by Solomon and Postman (1952).

Pronounceable nonsense words, such as *jandara, zabulon,* and *lokanta,* were used. The words were first given to the Ss on a deck of cards. In the total deck, some of the words occurred 25 times, some 10, some 5, some 2, and some only once. The S was instructed to go through the deck, studying and pronouncing each nonsense word. For different Ss, a given word was given different frequencies. For one S, *jandara* may have occurred 25 times in the deck and for another S, only once, thereby allowing E to produce different frequencies for the same word.

Following the experimental induction of frequency differences, thresholds were obtained. The results are shown in Fig. 5-5. The greater the frequency, the lower the threshold. Such data make it clear beyond reasonable doubt that frequency is directly involved in word thresholds. The ultimate in the induced-frequency experiment was performed by Goldiamond and Hawkins (1958). After inducing different frequencies for 10 three-letter nonsense words (e.g., WUX) by much the same method as that used by

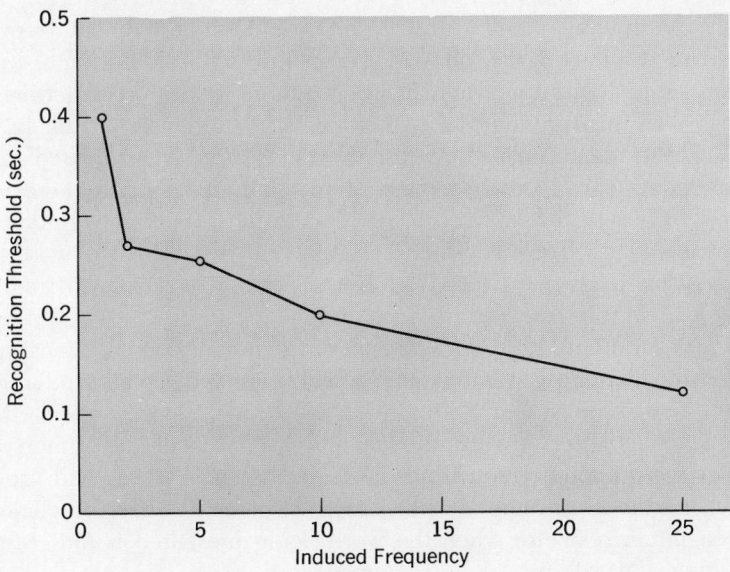

Fig. 5-5. Word-recognition thresholds as a function of induced word frequency. Data from Solomon and Postman (1952).

Solomon and Postman, E led S to believe that the words were being flashed on a screen when, in fact, nothing was flashed but a flash. The Ss were instructed that whether or not they were sure of what they saw, they were to respond with one of the words and to respond with a word to each flash until they got it "correct." They were told further that after they correctly reported the first word, another word, chosen randomly from the pool of 10, would be shown so that they could once again respond until they were correct.

Without providing details of the results, it can be said that the more frequently the item had been seen in the pretraining, the higher the probability that it was given in the initial responses to the flash. It was as if these words had lower visual recognition thresholds. Such evidence can be taken to mean that frequuency produces a response bias; the more frequently a word has been experienced, the earlier it will be emitted in a situation in which all words are equally appropriate. But this does not mean that the stimulus word being shown in the tachistoscope is irrelevant to the responses produced by S in the usual word-threshold experiment—that the frequency-threshold relationship is dependent only upon response bias.

The Havens and Foote study. These investigators addressed themselves to the problem of trying to explain how word frequency could influence thresholds. Solomon and Postman had suggested that frequency may mediate its effect in the following manner. The S, as duration of presentation increases, "picks up" fragments of words—a letter, or two letters, or a syllable. Given this fragment as a stimulus, word responses are likely to be elicited. The fragment will, however, be most strongly associated with a high-frequency word. Therefore, the prerecognition responses (the words which might be elicited or thought of prior to the correct recognition) are more apt to be high-frequency than low-frequency words. If the word being shown is a low-frequency word, the prerecognition responses to fragments of the word will interfere with its recognition.

Havens and Foote (1963), as a result of preliminary observations, speculated that the first and last letters are critical fragments in the production of prerecognition responses. If a low-frequency word is being presented, and if its first and last letters are also the first and last letters of one or more high-frequency words, competition from the high-frequency words will probably occur during the prerecognition phase. For instance, *list* may be elicited as a prerecognition response when the word being presented is *lint. List* is a high-frequency word, *lint,* a low-frequency word.

Sixteen four-letter words were selected, eight of which were expected to produce strong competitive responses and eight of which were expected to elicit few if any competitors. Within each set of eight, four words had high frequency, four had low. Therefore, there were two independent variables, competition probability and word frequency. A word from each of the four categories may be used to illustrate the four conditions. *Desk* is a high-frequency word and elicits competitors (e.g., *deck, duck*). *Mare* is a low-frequency word but also elicits competitors (e.g., *more, mere*). *Book* is a high-frequency word with little competition, and *wren* is a low-frequency word with little competition. All Ss were given all 16 words by a within-S design.

The results show that the words expected to elicit competitors in prerecognition responses had significantly higher thresholds than did those words expected not to elicit competitors. That this difference was probably due to differences in competition was shown by a study of the prerecognition responses (errors). The errors produced by the competition-eliciting words had structures that were more similar to the correct word than did the errors produced by the other class of words. The differences in the thresholds as a function of word frequency were not significant statistically but fell in the direction found in previous studies. Havens and Foote conclude that competitional differences between high- and low-frequency words is probably largely responsible for the word frequency-threshold relationship. There is no implication, however, that this principle is responsible for the effects of frequency when differential frequency of nonsense words is established in the laboratory; but it may be.

We have seen that recognition thresholds are lower for high-frequency words than for low-frequency words. Prerecognition responses to low-frequency words are likely to be high-frequency words, thus producing interference in attempts to recognize the low-frequency word. The S has a bias or set toward giving high-frequency words to fragments of words. If we could eliminate this bias, and if there is no other factor involved, the recognition thresholds of high- and low-frequency words should be equivalent. But how may we eliminate the bias? It can be done in a very straightforward manner. We give S the list of words which will be shown to him; therefore, his prerecognition responses will be drawn only from this small pool of words. For determining the thresholds for low-frequency words, we give him a list of the low-frequency words which will be shown to him. We do the same for the high-frequency words. When such procedures are used to eliminate the bias of producing high-frequency words in prerecognition responses, word frequency is shown to have no effect on recognition thresholds (Pierce, 1963).

The analysis of the role of word frequency on word-recognition thresholds seems to be complete.

An Interaction

One final study on word-recognition thresholds will be presented, primarily as a vehicle for a discussion of certain types of experimental designs and the interpretation of the data obtained from the use of such designs. The studies reviewed above have used within-S designs. In the present experiment (Glucksberg, 1962) a random-groups design was used, and two independent variables were manipulated. We have already reviewed experiments in which two independent variables were manipulated (e.g., Havens & Foote, 1963), but we did not give them the careful scrutiny which we will give to the Glucksberg experiment. Instead of presenting only one word at a time in the tachistoscope, Glucksberg presented two: a high-frequency word printed in black uppercase letters, and a low-frequency word printed in pale-red lowercase letters. *LAWYER* and *mundane* is representative of one of his pairs. Both the frequency and the print would make the former much easier to recognize than the latter. Therefore, one of the variables was *high dominance* of one member of each pair versus *low dominance* of the other member of the pair.

The other variable was reward offered for quick recognition. One group, the low-reward group, was told that E was doing some pilot work in order to decide how best to carry out the procedures of an experiment to be done later. The high-reward group was told that the top 25 percent of the Ss in the task would receive $5 each and that the one person with the very best performance would receive $20. The reward variable was not just pulled out of the hat by Glucksberg as a result of a sudden attack of curiosity. The offering of high and low rewards was assumed to influence the drive or motivational level of the Ss, and a theory was outlined concerning the influence of drive in situations in which there is response competition (assumed to be produced by the presence of high- and low-dominant words).

The design used is commonly known as a 2 by 2 random-groups design. This means that the influence of two levels of each of two variables is explored. Each variable is said to be orthogonal to the other, that is, for any given level of one variable, the two levels of the others appear as independent conditions. Thus, there must be a total of four different combinations of the two variables. If each variable were manipulated at three different levels, it would be termed a 3 by 3 design, and there would be nine unique conditions. Or, we might have two levels of one variable and three of another (2 by 3) for a total of six unique conditions. It is common to picture these as a plane surface broken into squares, the total squares representing the number of unique conditions. We may speak of this as the experimental matrix. In Glucksberg's experiment, half the Ss were instructed that they were to recognize the word printed in uppercase or black letters and to ignore the other word. The other half were told that they had to recognize the word in red letters and to ignore the black. Thus, we may speak of the dominance variable as High and Low, recognizing that it refers to which member of the pair S was instructed to recognize. The other variable, the reward variable, may also be spoken of as High and Low, referring to differences in amount offered S for good performance. For this experiment, the matrix is shown below:

		DOMINANCE	
		High	Low
REWARD	High	16 Ss	16 Ss
	Low	16 Ss	16 Ss

It is conventional to enter the number of Ss serving in each unique condition of the matrix. In the above, 16 Ss were assigned to each condition or cell, and they served only in those conditions.

The usual ascending method of limits was employed in obtaining the thresholds. The mean thresholds for the Ss in each cell are shown in Table 5-3. First, we will consider the influence of each variable separately. We actually have two independent tests of the role of dominance; that is, both high and low dominance have occurred with each level of the other variable. Therefore, the way to obtain the best estimate of the role of dominance for all conditions of the experiment is to find the mean for all Ss having high dominance and the mean for all Ss having low dominance. Obviously, these would be the means obtained by combining "across" rewards, which is ignoring reward as a separate variable. These are given as the combined means at the bottom of each of the columns. There was a large

TABLE 5–3
MEAN WORD-RECOGNITION THRESHOLDS AS A FUNCTION OF RE-
WARD AND DOMINANCE OF THE WORD IN THE PAIR OF WORDS.
DATA FROM GLUCKSBERG (1962).

		DOMINANCE		
		Low	High	Combined
	Low	.152	.047	.100
REWARD	High	.200	.034	.117
	Combined	.176	.041	

difference in the thresholds when Ss had to recognize the black high-frequency words in one case and the red low-frequency words in the other. The threshold for the former is just over .04 sec., and that for the latter, .176 sec.

By the same reasoning as above, we have two independent experiments on the influence of reward, one with high-dominance words and one with low-dominance. These means are given to the right of the table and appear to be nearly identical, which they are, statistically. We would conclude at this point, then, that dominance heavily influenced recognition thresholds, but amount of reward did not. Yet, this is not quite the total picture, as a careful inspection of the cell means will show. This may be seen more quickly by plotting the four means, as in Fig. 5-6. Here we may note that if the experiment had manipulated *only* reward, the conclusion reached about the effect of reward would have been different depending upon the dominance level chosen. When recognition of the high-dominant words is required, recognition times become shorter as we go from low to high reward. When recognition of the low-dominant words is required, recognition times become longer as we go from low to high reward. Clearly, any statement about the influence of reward is conditioned by the dominance level used. This is what is meant when we say there is an *interaction* between two variables. To formalize this for any two variables, we say that *interaction occurs when the relationship between the dependent variable (behavior) and a given independent variable varies as a function of the setting or level of another independent variable.*

We have already seen interactions in data presented earlier. Figure 5-4 shows an interaction, an interaction between intensity of the light stimulus and the location of the area stimulated. The CFF changes *differentially* for foveal and peripheral stimulation as intensity increases.

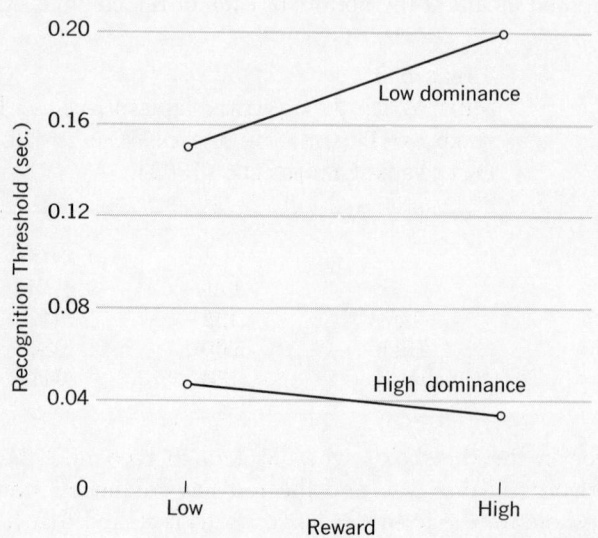

Fig. 5-6. The influence of reward and dominance of the word on word-recognition thresholds. Data from Glucksberg (1962).

The interaction between two variables can be "picked up" by examining a matrix of results such as that given in Table 5-2. The graph, however, is probably a superior device for exhibiting interactions, particularly if the matrix, like a 3 by 4 matrix, is a complex one. In Fig. 5-7, two sets of graphs are shown, one set demonstrating interactions between the two variables and the other set demonstrating the results when no interaction has occurred. In these graphs one variable is called A and is identified along the abscissa. The other is called B; two levels of B have been used, B1 and B2. The B variable is identified within the body of the graph in the same manner as the dominance variable was identified in Fig. 5-6. Of course, B could be noted on the abscissa, with A identified in the body. For simplicity, all relationships are drawn as linear relationships in Fig. 5-7.

A study of Fig. 5-7 will show that whenever we have parallel curves from a two-variable experiment, we do *not* have an interaction. Conversely, whenever there is divergence or convergence of the curves, we *do* have an interaction. It goes without saying that we do not reach a decision concerning an interaction, or the lack of such, merely by inspecting curves. There are statistical tests to determine whether a supposed interaction is due to chance fluctuations. Essentially, they tell us whether or not the slopes of the curves differ.

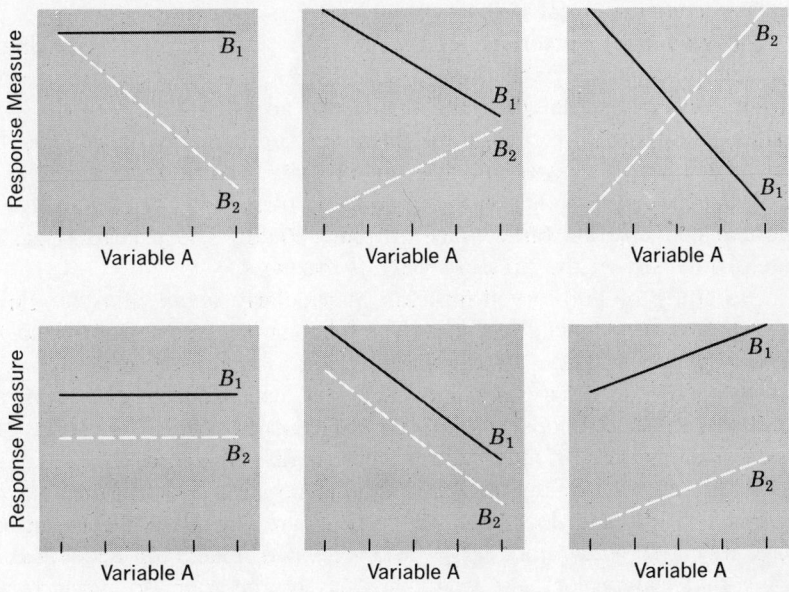

Fig. 5-7. Interactions (top graphs) and lack of interactions (bottom graphs) between the effects of two independent variables.

AUDITORY THRESHOLDS

We have seen how the development of research in vision has led to high specialization and unique vocabularies, and why it is not the province of any one discipline. The same situation exists in research on audition. While psychologists are firmly entrenched in the research efforts, so too are physicists, physiologists, acoustical engineers, and neurologists. Medical men are involved if for no other reason than the fact that the ear includes the mechanisms which are critically involved in seasickness, airsickness, and more recently, spacesickness.

The effective stimulus for hearing is a change in pressure. A vibrating body sets up these wavelike pressure variations which, in a manner of speaking, travel through the air. Of course, if the changes in pressure are too slight, we hear nothing; the pressure changes must be of a certain magnitude before the sensory apparatus will be so effectively stimulated that we say we hear something. The pressure wave has two characteristics. One is the frequency of the wave, measured in cycles per second (cps). The basic psychological correlate of the frequency of the wave is *pitch;* the greater the frequency, the higher the pitch. This, however, is not without limit, for we have an absolute upper threshold, which is the point at which the frequency becomes so great that it will no longer be heard.

The second characteristic of the pressure wave is intensity, which is measured physically by the *decibel* (db.) scale, the exact nature of which will not concern us. Roughly, the scale is so adjusted that zero db. is approximately at the lower absolute threshold for intensity. The scale then "runs up" to reflect greater and greater intensity, and at approximately 130 to 140 db., the intensity is great enough to be painful to the human listener. A normal conversation takes place at about 60 db. The psychological correlate of intensity of the pressure wave is *loudness*.

The study of auditory thresholds, particularly lower absolute thresholds, requires very special facilities. The basic unit is known as an *anechoic chamber,* which is often a room within a room, soundproof, vibration-proof, and echo-proof, as nearly as engineering skill can make it. The room may be set on rubber cushions, minimizing the transmission of vibrations from outside sources, and it may have several walls separated by "dead air." Within the room itself, one may have the impression of being in a cave in which the walls, the floor, and the ceiling are completely covered with stalagmites and stalactites: large wedge-shaped pieces of acoustical absorbing material project out from all areas of the room in order to trap sound so that no echo occurs. Of course, if wedges are on the floor, there must be some way of "using" the room, and this may be handled by a suspended platform.

The S in an experiment conducted in an anechoic chamber is provided with an experience that would rarely if ever be duplicated in real life. Alone in the closed chamber, one experiences a stillness that at first seems complete. But, then, one becomes aware of sounds emanating from the body, some of which have never been sensed before. What would be a mild stomach rumble in a normal environment becomes thunder in the chamber. One hears circulatory noises of the heart pumping and the coursing of the blood, and some have reported "brain squeaks." Such noises are of more than passing interest if, for example, lower absolute thresholds are being measured, for it is clear that S must discriminate between the barely perceptible tone being fed to him through earphones and the "tones" emanating from the body. We see at once why well-practiced Ss may be necessary in such studies, because a part of the practice involved is that of distinguishing between body noise and the signal to be detected.

Let us look briefly at a set of lower absolute thresholds obtained from a group of 38 college-student Ss with normal hearing. In this study (Corso & Cohen, 1958) lower absolute thresholds for intensity were measured at nine different frequencies, varying from 250 cps to 8000 cps. The method of limits was employed with two ascending and two descending series for each S for each frequency, using a within-S design.

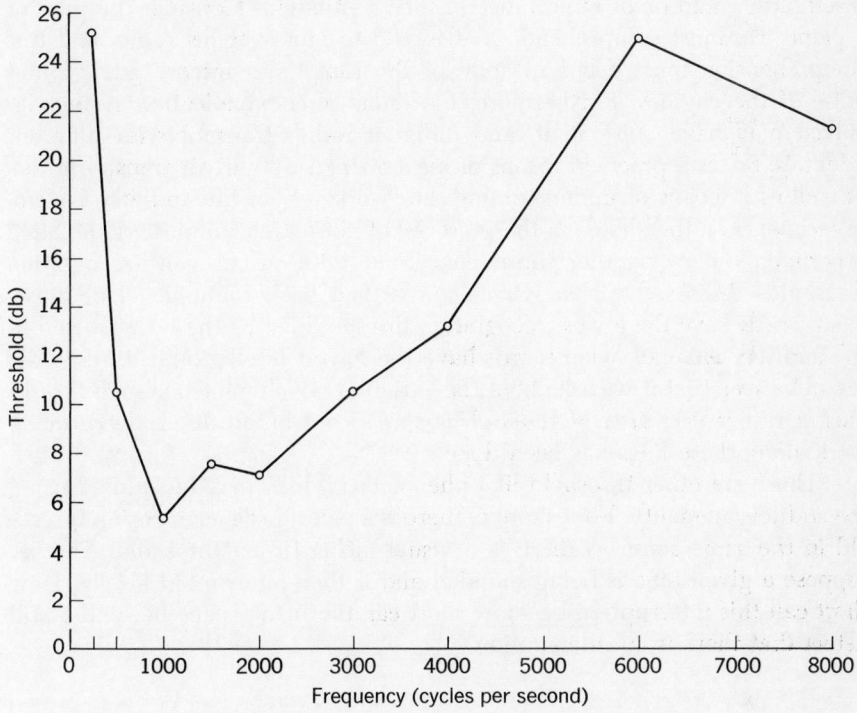

Fig. 5-8. Lower absolute intensity thresholds as a function of frequency of the sound wave. Data from Corso and Cohen (1958).

The threshold measurements for the right ears of these Ss are plotted in Fig. 5-8. We note a sharp drop from the lowest frequency level measured (250 cps) to maximum sensitivity (lowest threshold) at 1000 cps. Beyond this frequency, the thresholds become higher again—it takes a more intense tone for the S to be just able to detect it.

Most undergraduate laboratories do not have facilities for making absolute lower threshold measurements. But there are other auditory thresholds which can be measured without the need of anechoic chambers. We noted that even in the anechoic chamber there is still "noise," so that in effect, it is impossible to measure absolute thresholds in the complete absence of noise. We might, therefore, put a constant noise into the "system" and measure thresholds above the noise. This can be done in nearly any room as long as the noise we put in effectively masks outside noise. Thus, by the use of a sound generator, we might introduce *white noise,* which consists of the whole spectrum of frequencies produced simultaneously. But what thresholds would be of importance in such a situation? Consider the pilot of a plane. He must comprehend what is said to him over his radio, and this comprehension must occur in spite of the sometimes intense background noise of the engines. Furthermore, the radio or communication system involved may have noise in it, and different radios transmit with different fidelities. So, as a practical means of maximizing safety in air transportation, as well as a means of understanding the "workings" of the auditory system, experiments on thresholds in the presence of noise are of utmost value. Such experiments may parallel those concerned with visual word-recognition thresholds discussed earlier. Given a specified background level of noise, what words have the lowest recognition threshold; or, as the term is used in the auditory channel, what words have the lowest intelligibility thresholds? It can be seen that if we ask about the variables which influence such thresholds, a rather vast area of research is spread out before us. Indeed, much work along these lines has been done.

There are other threshold-like phenomena which may be studied using the auditory modality. For example, there is an auditory flicker-fusion threshold in the same sense as there is a visual flicker-fusion threshold. That is, suppose a given tone is being sounded and is then interrupted briefly. How short can this interruption be—how short can the blank space be—and S still detect that there is an interruption?

DIFFERENCE THRESHOLDS AND WEBER'S LAW

Let us examine some common observations about phenomenal changes which accompany environmental changes. In our homes most of us have what are called three-way lamps. Turning the switch to the first position produces 100 watts of light; the next position adds another 100 watts, making the total 200; and the third brings the total wattage to 300. What are the phenomenal experiences of changes in brightness which accompany the changes in wattage? If you will remember your experiences with such a lamp, you will recall that the amount of change in apparent brightness in "going from" darkness to 100 watts is much greater than the change produced in going from 100 to 200. Furthermore, the apparent increase in brightness in going from 100 to 200 is greater than in going from 200 to 300. Indeed, in going from 200 to 300, it is sometimes difficult to determine whether or not any change in brightness of the illumination of the room has occurred. Thus, we see that the same amount of change in the physical stimulus is not accompanied by a corresponding change in phenomenal brightness.

Pouring a pint of water into a small pail which has only a small amount of water in it will produce a very noticeable difference in the amount of water in the pail. Pouring a pint of water into Lake Michigan will probably not result in a noticeable increase in the water level of the lake. If we add five students to a class of 10, the increase is very noticeable to the instructor but the addition of five students to a class of 500 students would probably not be detectable by him. At a more gross level, mothers of large families sometimes report that when the first baby arrived, the household routine was seriously disrupted, but that when the eleventh baby became a member of the household, its influence was hardly noticeable.

These observations suggest that the amount of change in a stimulus necessary to produce a noticeable difference is tied in some way to the value of the stimulus in the first place. Adding 100 watts to 100 watts produces a greater change in apparent brightness than adding 100 watts to 200. This must mean, therefore, that the amount of wattage necessary to produce a perceived difference is greater when the base or standard stimulus is 200 watts than when it is 100 watts. As a generalization we can say for all of the above observations that the amount of change necessary to produce a given phenomenal change is greater the greater the magnitude of the base or standard stimulus. In research on this matter, the phenomenal change with which we usually deal is the difference threshold (DL); therefore, the suggested law is that the greater the magnitude of the standard stimulus, the greater the size of the DL.

The above law has very great generality; there are no cases known to the writer for which the law does not hold when stated in this general way. Many relationships between dependent and independent variables in psychology are given in much the same way as this law is given, namely, that as X increases, Y increases (or decreases). However, few are content to allow a general relationship to remain in this form. Rather, we ask, "What is the mathematical relationship?" "At what rate does the DL increase as the standard stimulus increases?"

One such statement of the specific relationships between the standard stimulus and the DL is Weber's Law. The law states that for a given stimulus dimension, *the DL bears a constant ratio to the point on the dimension (standard stimulus) at which the DL was measured.* The ratio, of course, varies with different observers, with difference sense modalities, and with different characteristics of the stimulus which may be varied within a given modality. The ratio would be expressed as follows:

$$\frac{DL}{\text{Standard Value}} = \text{Constant}$$

For example, as the only source of light, suppose that we have 100 candles burning in a room. We find that it takes an addition of exactly 10 candles to produce a DL of brightness. The Weber fraction becomes 10/100, or 1/10. If the law holds for all brightness levels, it means that with 1000 candles burning, we would expect the DL to be 100 candles; it must be this if we are to maintain the constant ratio of 1/10 between the standard stimulus and the DL. Moreover, according to Weber's Law, if we have 10,000 candles initially, we would expect to have to add 1000 to produce a just noticeable difference.

Does Weber's Law hold? At best we can say it does hold approximately, with the precision being best in the middle range of a dimension, with a breakdown at the extremes, where the standard is very weak or very strong. Now we may examine some sets of data to see how a test of Weber's Law works out in practice.

Time Judgments

This experiment was designed to determine the DLs for passage of time. The method of constant stimuli was used, with five different standards, 5, 10, 15, 20, and 25 sec. As may be seen in Table 5-4, eight variable stimuli were used for each standard.

With five standard stimuli and eight variable stimuli for each standard, a total of 40 trials would produce a single comparison of each standard with each of its variable stimuli. As we have seen, such experiments are usually done within the framework of a within-S design. That is, each S serves in all conditions, and the order of conditions is balanced so that progressive errors will not bias the results. However, in the present experiment, to make each of the 40 comparisons several times would require a very extended period of testing, and only by presenting each of the 40 comparisons several times could an adequate balancing of progressive errors be achieved. We did have available, however, a rather large number of Ss who could be used for a single session. Therefore, a different rationale was used to balance possible effects of progressive error.

A total of 105 Ss was run. Each S was given each of the 40 comparisons once. The 105 Ss were run in six subgroups with approximately an equal number in each subgroup. Using a table of random numbers, we made up six different random orders of the 40 comparisons. The order of the 40 comparisons or trials was thus different for each of the subgroups. The notion is that the effects of progressive error, if such are present, will balance out (will fall equally on all comparisons) when the data from all Ss are averaged. For example, take any given comparison: the comparison of the 20-sec. standard with its 23-sec. variable stimuli will do. For the six different random orders, this comparison occurred on Trials 2, 4, 14, 19, 36, and 40. Since it occurred at various stages, merging the data for the six subgroups should

TABLE 5-4

PERCENTAGES OF TIMES THAT THE VARIABLE STIMULI WERE JUDGED LONGER IN DURATION THAN THE STANDARD STIMULI IN AN EXPERIMENT TO DETERMINE DLs FOR PASSAGE OF TIME

The Five Standards are Italicized

VARIABLE STIMULI	PERCENT LONGER	VARIABLE STIMULI	PERCENT LONGER	VARIABLE STIMULI	PERCENT LONGER	VARIABLE STIMULI	PERCENT LONGER	VARIABLE STIMULI	PERCENT LONGER
1	0	2	0	4	0	5	0	6	0
2	4.8	4	1.0	8	1.9	10	1.0	13	2.9
3	6.7	6	3.8	11	21.0	14	12.4	18	15.2
4	24.8	8	21.0	13	27.6	17	27.6	22	29.5
5		*10*		*15*		*20*		25	
6	75.2	12	82.9	17	69.5	23	69.5	28	66.7
7	75.2	14	90.5	19	83.8	26	78.1	32	75.2
8	95.2	16	90.5	22	89.5	30	94.3	37	82.9
9	97.1	18	98.1	26	96.2	35	97.1	44	97.1

make the effects of progressive error for this comparison almost equal to those of any other comparison, since the other comparisons also occurred at various stages of practice when the data for all Ss are considered as a whole. There is one other matter with regard to presentation: for three of the six random orders the standard stimulus always preceded the variable stimulus in presenting the two, and for the other three random orders, the variable stimuli were always presented first.

The stimuli used to designate passage of time were two dim red lights, each in circuit with a timer and a mercury switch. Turning on a light started the timer. At the end of the specified interval, the switch was opened, shutting off the light. As the first light was turned off, the second was turned on, and after the specified interval, turned off. The S was instructed to record on his prepared data sheet whether the second light was on for a longer or shorter period than the first. No equal judgments were allowed. The usual instructions prohibiting counting and so on were given, and two practice trials gave the Ss the sequence of events to be expected. Obviously, this experiment could be done without the light; E could use a stopwatch, simply saying "start" and "stop" to mark off the intervals. The use of the two lights and the two clocks was a matter of convenience.

Certain features of Table 5-4 may be noted before we go about determining the DLs from the data. First, the range of the variable stimuli used increases as the magnitude of the standard stimulus increases. This increase was used merely to accommodate the general fact (Weber's Law) that discrimination gets poorer and poorer as the magnitude of the standard stimulus along a given dimension increases. The actual range used around each standard was based on guesses by E, with the intent that the guesses would run from percentage values near zero at the "bottom end" to near 100 percent at the top. The results show that all the smallest variable stimuli were never judged longer than their respective standards, so for most purposes, they provide data of no value. The fact that this does not occur with the largest variable stimuli indicates again that as stimuli increase along a dimension, discriminability decreases. In terms of number of seconds between adjacent variable stimuli above and below any given standard, there is complete symmetry around the standard. Yet, discrimination is poorer above the standard than it is below.

Determining DLs. We may look first at the overall results graphically shown in Fig. 5-9. Smooth curves of the general ogive shape have been drawn through the empirical points, with a common baseline for the variable stimuli for all five standards. The fact that the curves slant more and more toward the horizontal as the length of the standard stimulus increases is another means of saying that discrimination becomes poorer and poorer as the length of the standard interval increases. Consequently, we may at once deduce that the size of the DL increases as the magnitude of

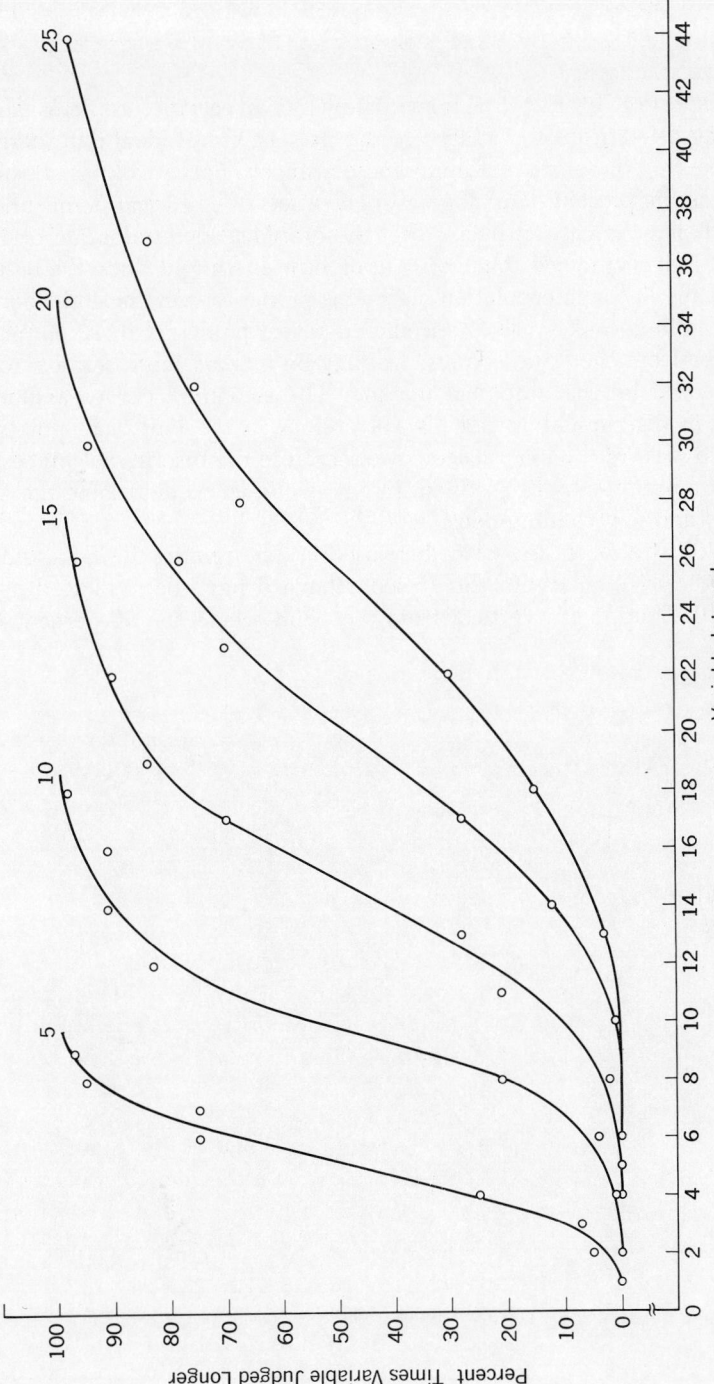

Fig. 5-9. Discriminability functions as related to the duration of the standard interval in time judgments. The standards were 5, 10, 15, 20, and 25 sec.

the standard increases. The particular question we ask is whether or not Weber's Law holds for the DLs. Is there a constant ratio between the DLs and the five standards?

An inspection of Fig. 5-9 immediately raises certain problems about determining DLs, problems which are not present in the ideal data derived from the method of constant stimuli where a smooth curve will pass through all points. In the present data, none of the five sets of empirical points allows this. This being the case, it means that the graphical determination of DLs may result in inaccuracies, depending upon how one might draw the curves. The use of the linear interpolation method is probably even more dangerous since this method makes use of specific empirical points. If these empirical points differ from the "true" points, we may be making more serious errors than we would by the graphical method. The smoothed curves assume a continuity in discrimination not always present in the empirical points as such, but in view of the long history of research in the discriminal processes, such an assumption may be justified. In any event, let us determine the DLs graphically and see what happens.

As an illustration of the procedure used in determining the DLs, the results for the judgments with the 15-sec. standard have been plotted again in Fig. 5-10. Dropping a vertical from the point where the 50 percent line

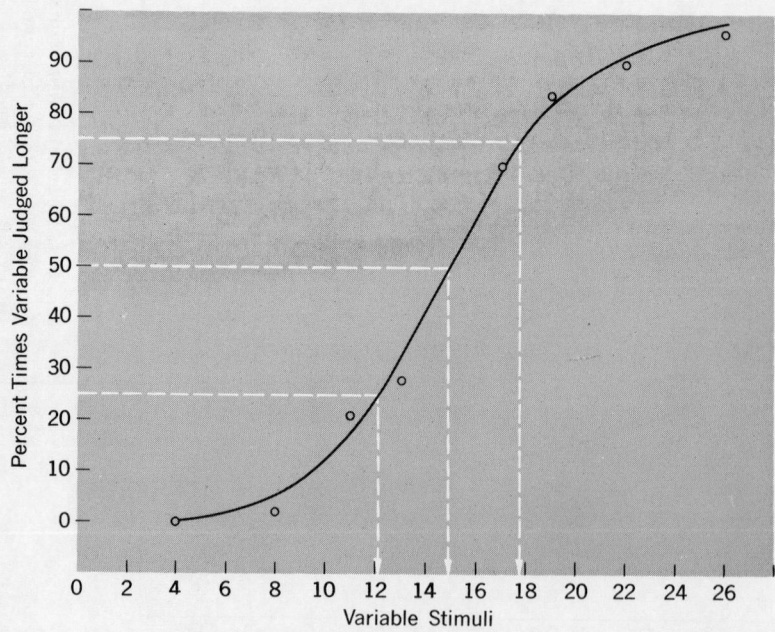

Fig. 5-10. Determination of the DL by the graphical method.

crosses the curve places the PSE exactly at 15 sec., that is, the PSE is equal to the standard. This in turn means there is no constant error involved. Verticals are dropped also from the 75 percent level and from the 25 percent level to obtain the upper and lower points of change, respectively. The upper DL is the difference between the PSE and the upper point of change. Since the upper point of change is 17.8 sec., the upper DL is 2.8 sec. Corresponding operations also show the lower DL to be 2.8 sec. (15—12.2).

If these procedures are carried out for all five sets of data, and if the lower and upper DLs are averaged, the DLs (in sec.) are 1.05, 1.75, 2.80, 3.90, and 5.30 for the five standard intervals in order of magnitude. Clearly, the size of the DLs increases as the magnitude of the standard stimulus increases. If Weber's Law describes this increase, the ratio between each DL and its standard should be constant. These ratios, in order, are .21, .18, .19, .20, and .21. We would conclude that these do indeed appear quite equivalent proportions and that Weber's Law appears to hold fairly well within the range of intervals studied. Roughly speaking, the ratio is 1/5; for every increase of 5 sec. in the magnitude of the standard, the magnitude of the DL will increase by 1 sec.

Numerosity DL

We will now describe an experiment in which the results, viewed as a test of Weber's Law, produced a minor puzzle. The task involved judgments of numerosity.

Materials and procedure. Slides were prepared on which the number of dots differed. Four standard stimuli were used on which the numbers of the dots were 16, 32, 64, and 128. Around each of these standards eight variable slides were constructed so that four had a greater number of dots than the standard and four had fewer. The four standards are shown in Fig. 5-11. The positions of the dots within the square were not left entirely to randomness. Instead, the dots were assigned to a position at random within a limited area. For example, in constructing the slide with 64 dots, a large square was divided into 64 small squares of equal size. One dot was to be placed within each square. Each of the 64 squares was in turn divided into nine smaller squares. The position of the dot within each of the 64 squares was determined randomly among the nine smaller squares. The purpose of this was to avoid unusual patterns which might result if the assignment of dots was strictly on a random basis.

The design of the experiment was similar to that used for determining DLs for time judgments. That is, it was basically a within-S design except that each possible comparison was given only once to each S. Therefore, the balancing of progressive error had to be accomplished by using different subgroups which were differentiated only in terms of the order of presenting the stimuli. A total of 100 Ss was run as four subgroups of 25 each. Block randomization of the order of presenting the stimuli, a different randomization tion for each subgroup, was used. In the block randomization each standard occurred once before any was shown the second time, then each was shown twice before any was shown the third time, and so on. The particular order of the four standards within a block of four presentations was determined

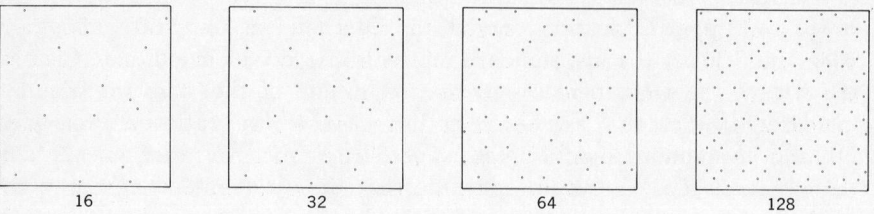

Fig. 5-11. Standard slides used to determine difference thresholds for dot density.

randomly, and the particular variable stimulus which occurred with the standard was determined randomly subject to the restriction that across the 32 trials (4 standards with 8 variable stimuli each) each occurred with the appropriate standard once. Let us look at the first eight trials for one of the four orders in order to make the block randomization clear.

TRIAL	PAIRS PRESENTED
1	106-*128*
2	*32*-34
3	61-*64*
4	*16*-18
5	*128*-134
6	82-*64*
7	25-*32*
8	20-*16*

The standard stimulus in each pair is italicized. It should be observed that in the first four trials (the first block) each standard was used once and that each was used once in the second block. Within each block, the order of the pairs is random, however.

It will be noted that the standard stimulus is sometimes presented as the first slide of a pair of slides, and sometimes, as the second. Across all four orders this was so arranged that on half the trials the standard occurred as the first slide and on half the trials as the second slide. Thus, considering the pair 61-64, 50 Ss made a judgment when the slides were presented in that order, and 50 made a judgment when the order was 64-61. Any effect of the short time interval between the two slides should not bias the judgments when all data are combined for the 100 Ss.

The Ss were given two pairs of practice slides and were instructed how to record their judgments. If they judged the second slide to have a greater density of dots than the first, a G was recorded; if they judged the second to have less density, an L was recorded. They were further told that even if they could not tell a difference between the density of dots on a pair of slides, they still must choose between G or L.

In presenting the pairs of slides, each slide was projected for 3 sec., with approximately .5 sec. between the disappearance of the first slide and the appearance of the second. The Ss were allowed from 5 to 8 sec. for recording their judgments. Always before presenting the first slide of a pair, a "ready" signal was given.

Results. For each pair of stimuli, the number of Ss judging the variable stimuli to have greater density than the standard was determined. Since there were 100 Ss, the number of Ss also represents the percent of Ss. The values for each variable stimuli are shown in Table 5-5.

A graphical picture of the results will not be presented here, although the careful student may find it quite useful to make plots of the data. Certain features of the results are worth pointing out. Although not producing "ideal" psychophysical curves, the relationships for the 16 and 32 standards appear to be fairly conventional. For the standard with 64 dots, however, the plot gives essentially a linear relationship, rather than the expected ogive curve. Why should this be? We cannot tell with confidence; however, if the range of variable stimuli had been such that at the extremes the judgments had been perfectly accurate (0 percent and 100 percent), it is possible that the ogive or sigmoid shape to the curve would be apparent.

A plot around the 128-dot standard produces some disturbing features. The maximum frequency that the variable was judged greater than the standard was 76 percent; it is clear, therefore, that the range of stimuli at the "upper end" was not great enough. Furthermore, it may be noted that the slide with 134 dots was judged greater than the standard (128 dots) only 41 percent of the time. This might suggest that there is a serious constant error involved in the judgments, since the PSE will be appreciably different from the standard. However, since there is no reason to believe that any such bias could be consistently present in these judgments because of the balancing of the order of presentations, it seems more reasonable to conclude that these judgments around this standard stimulus are simply quite variable and that to stabilize the curve would require many more Ss, or many judgments from a few Ss.

TABLE 5–5
Percentages of Times that the Variable Stimuli Were Judged to Have Greater Density of Dots than the Standard Stimuli in an Experiment to Determine DLs for Numerosity

Standard Stimuli

	16		32		64		128
VARIABLE STIMULI	PERCENT GREATER	VARIABLE STIMULI	PERCENT GREATER	VARIABLE STIMULI	PERCENT GREATER	VARIABLE STIMULI	PERCENT GREATER
9	0	20	0	46	4	92	5
12	0	25	10	53	16	106	16
14	7	28	22	58	29	116	21
15	21	30	45	61	36	122	35
17	54	34	70	67	53	134	41
18	73	36	68	70	61	140	65
20	87	39	71	75	78	150	74
23	94	44	91	82	92	164	76

Yet, accepting the results as obtained, let us proceed to obtain a DL for each standard. Smooth curves were drawn again, and the values for the upper point of change (75 percent) and lower point of change (25 percent) determined. An average DL would be one-half the distance between the baseline points dictated by the two points of change. Thus, from the curve around the standard of 16, the upper point of change is determined as 18.5 dots and the lower point as 15.3. One half of this difference is 1.6 dots; the DL is a change of 1.6 dots. For the other three standards, in order, we obtain the values of 4.7, 9.0, and 19.0. Clearly, as the number of dots on the standard slide increases, the number of dots required to produce a discriminable difference increases.

Does Weber's Law hold for these data? The ratios (DL/standard) are in order of the standards, .10, .15, .14, and .15. Except for the standard with fewest number of dots, the ratios do appear quite constant. Thus, Weber's Law does not seem to hold at the low end of numerosity; the DL is too small when the DLs for the other standards are used as a predictor. In order to confirm Weber's Law with the 16-dot standard, the DL should have been 2.4 dots rather than 1.6. This is an appreciable difference between theory and fact. What could produce this? There is reason to believe that when the number of dots was less than 16, particularly with 9 and 12 dots on the slide, the Ss had sufficient time within the 3 sec. that the slides were presented actually to count the number of dots or to estimate the number with high accuracy. Since this could not be done when the other standards were used, it seems likely that we were getting different judgmental processes involved for the judgments around the 16-dot standard as compared with the other standard. It is interesting to note that if only the upper DL is used for the 16-dot standard, the value is almost exactly 2.4, a value noted earlier as being needed to confirm Weber's Law across all standards. If we assume that counting could not occur when the variable stimuli above the 16-dot standard were shown, then we may discount the lower DL and conclude that our data are quite in line with expectations from Weber's Law.

Judgmental numerosity thresholds. In conjunction with performing the above experiment, another, a parallel one, was carried out. The procedure can be understood completely by examining what was asked of the S. A subject was handed a sheet of paper on which was printed the following instructions:

"Assume that you are an instructor for a class. Assume further that there are 16 students seated in a large classroom, these students being scattered throughout the room. You walk in and glance quickly over the classroom and then immediately walk out. While you are out, more students may have come into the classroom and taken seats. You walk back in and take another quick glance over the classroom. How many students do you think would now have to be seated in the classroom for you to just detect (from your brief glance) that more students had come in during your absence? Encircle the number below that you think would represent the number of students that would now have to be present for you to just barely detect that there had been an increase over the original 16."

Other Ss were given sheets on which the instructions were identical except that the number of students said to be seated originally in the classroom was 32. Still other groups had the number specified as 64 and 128. Thus, the "standard" stimuli were the same as those used in the dot-numerosity experiment. It should be clear that any given S made only one judgment; to ask him to make all four judgments might find him making his own law in some way so that he intentionally puts in proportionate increases as the size of the standard increases.

When the above data were collected, the four different sheets were interleafed and passed out among groups of Ss so that, essentially, the particular standard given a particular S was a chance affair. The numbers of Ss were 49, 51, 48, and 48 for the four standards in order.

The data yield what may be considered upper DLs, which may be calculated as the difference between the mean judgments of the number of students which must be in the classroom for a difference to be detected and the number said to have been seated originally. For the standards in order, the means were 4.57, 5.76, 8.46, and 14.29. It is quite apparent, therefore, that these judgments represent the "internalization" of the idea that the more "things" present to start with, the greater the number that must be added for a difference to be detected. However, the faint hopes that these judgments might confirm Weber's Law and might also parallel the DLs for the dot-numerosity experiment were thoroughly squelched. The Weber ratios are .29, .18, .13, and .11. The ratios clearly decrease rather than remain constant. But, let's examine the situation a little more carefully.

In the description, "large classroom," there may be some ambiguity in the instructions. What did S think of when visualizing a large classroom? Suppose those Ss given the instructions with the 64-student standard visualized the classroom as seating 100 students; or suppose those given the 128-student standard visualized the room as seating 150 students. Detection of change in number of students might be based on number of empty seats, and, if so, it changes the standard, making it smaller than intended. Even if only a small proportion of the Ss had done this, the mean judgments would be seriously affected. Therefore, we repeated the experiment and removed the ambiguity concerning a large classroom.

The procedure was exactly the same as before, but the instructions specified that the classroom seated 1000 students. A new group of Ss was used with 50, 53, 52, and 54 in the groups given the 16, 32, 64, and 128 standards, respectively. The mean increase in the number of students judged necessary to produce a JND was 8.00, 12.50, 14.96, and 24.88 for the four standards in order. The minor change in instructions clearly had an effect—

unexpected as it was. As compared with the first study, there was an appreciable increase in the absolute number of students believed necessary to add to the base in order to produce a JND. In the first study the values were 4.57, 5.76, 8.46, and 14.29, about half as large as those given in the second study. Apparently, the vision of a 1000-seat classroom "rubbed off" on the Ss in such a way as to affect their notions about the absolute number of students they believed must be added in order to produce a JND.

The Weber ratios for the second study were .50, .39, .23, and .19. Again, there is no constancy in these ratios. Both studies produced very lawful results, but they do not conform to the Weber Law. Clearly, these judgmental-type DLs do not follow the same laws as the sensory-type DLs.

A VARIETY OF THRESHOLDS

In order to further our appreciation of the concept of a threshold, and in order to show the great versatility of the methods used to determine thresholds, we will sample a variety of studies.

Word Frequency

Suppose you were asked to judge which of the two words, *fie* or *cat*, occurs most frequently in printed discourse (in books, magazines, newspapers). Although you have probably never been asked to make this judgment before, you would, without hesitation, say that the word *cat* occurs more frequently. This ability is rather amazing. It is as if every exposure to a given word has left its imprint on you; it is as if for each word you have a counter "inside" and every time you have seen the word the dial on the counter has advanced. Consequently, when you are asked such a question, you "read" your counters and produce an answer. It is a fact that we are quite sensitive to differential frequencies of environmental events even though we are not at all intending to be so; it just occurs.

But now, suppose you are asked about two more words, *bad* and *hot*. Which of these words occurs more frequently in printed discourse? Very likely your counters cannot produce a clear and quick decision, for, in fact, the two words occur with almost equal frequency (Thorndike & Lorge, 1944). Such observations indicate that given the appropriate technique we should be able to determine a difference threshold for word frequency.

For this study, the method of constant stimuli was adapted. The available counts of word frequency are expressed in terms of the frequency with which a word occurs per million words of text. For example, the word *lea* occurs once per 4.5 million words, while the word *the*, the most frequent three-letter word, occurs 236,472 times per 4.5 million words, or nearly once in every twenty words. For the present study, a standard stimulus of approximately 300 was used. Four variable stimuli with lower frequency and four with higher frequency made up a series that may be likened to any series of stimuli used in determining DLs by the method of constant stimuli. In order that the results not be dependent upon idiosyncratic factors associated with a single word, eight different series were used, but in all eight series, the standard was approximately 300. For example, here is one of the series with the frequency values also given:

WORD	FREQUENCY
nob	1
par	24
din	72
pet	162
cat	306 (standard)
tie	489
lay	984
see	6146
and	138,672

As noted, there were eight such series. In presenting the items for judgment, each standard was presented with each variable stimulus within its series. A total of 64 paired presentations would be required to pair each standard with each of its variable stimuli for the eight series. We chose to present these as a series of pairs of words mimeographed on a single sheet of paper. The S was instructed to encircle the word in each pair which he thought occurred most frequently in printed discourse. The order of the 64 pairs on the sheet was random, although this may be of little consequence since S was not required to make his judgments in the order in which the words were presented. A total of 50 Ss made the judgments.

The results for all eight series were combined; the basic data are the percentage of times that each variable stimulus was judged to have greater frequency than the standard. The relationship between the frequency of the variable stimuli and the percentage of times judged more frequent than the standard is shown in Fig. 5-12. It will be noted that the baseline is expressed in logarithmic units. The reason some such scale is absolutely necessary for the present data can be realized if you try to put the raw frequencies in the sample series shown above along a baseline and try to plot the percentages at the appropriate points. The frequencies of 1, 24, 72, and 162 would be "squeezed" into a minute section of the baseline, and it is doubtful that the points could even be separated. Obviously, we need a scale which stretches out the smaller numbers and compresses the larger numbers; common logarithmic transformation accomplishes just this.

The relationship in Fig. 5-12 appears very stable; a smooth curve essentially passes through all empirical points. From these data, we have determined the DL to be approximately 400; that is, the frequency between two three-letter words must differ by at least 400 occurrences per 4.5 million words before we can show greater than chance accuracy in our frequency judgments. As might be expected, the lower DL is appreciably smaller (290) than the upper DL (514).

Although the method of constant stimuli was used in this study, it seems quite feasible to use the method of limits to make the determination

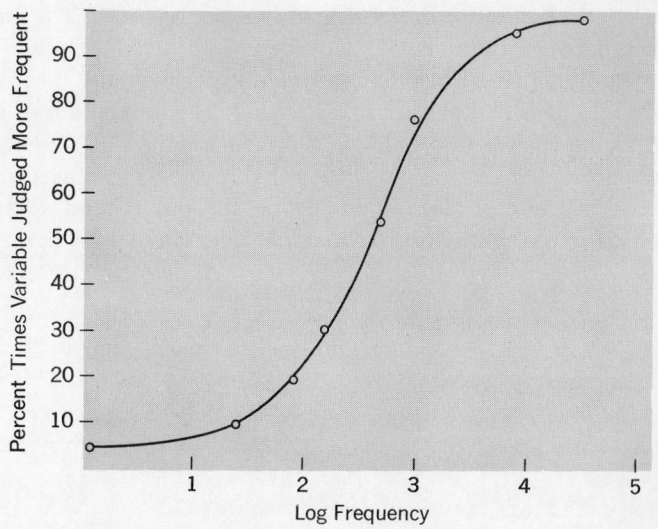

Fig. 5-12. Results of the use of the method of constant stimuli to determine discriminability in judging the frequency of three-letter words.

of the DL. Can you work out a procedure using the method of limits which seems appropriate?

Closure Threshold

One of the fundamental properties ascribed to objects in our environment is form. We describe objects as being round, square, triangular, hexagonal, jagged, and so on. But these names are clearly applied to modal objects, and it is apparent that forms exist for which we do not have names. Furthermore, forms having shapes "midway" between two standard shapes might be considered ambiguous figures. For example, suppose we have a circle and start "squeezing" it with equal pressure at four points, 0, 90, 180, and 270 degrees. At what point will it no longer be seen as a circle but rather as a square? At some point there must be a transition zone and a threshold which divides circleness from squareness. Or, consider a case in which the number of equal-length sides of a plane figure is increased.

At what point will a brief glance at the figure produce the response of "circle"? When there are 10 sides, or 15, or 20?

A behavioral tendency of importance in form perception is known as *closure*. This terms refers to the fact that we tend to perceive forms as being complete when in fact they are incomplete physically. If the outline of a circle is made up of discrete dots lying fairly close together, we do not see a myriad of discrete dots; instead, we see a circle. We tend to fill in the space between the dots.

Bobbitt (1942) has demonstrated experimentally that there is a definite threshold at which closure takes place in the perception of triangularity. To determine such a threshold, incomplete triangles as illustrated in Fig. 5-13 were presented. Figure *a* would probably not be seen as a triangle but rather as two discrete angles. Figure *b*, on the other hand, would probably be seen as a triangle—closure would occur. These two figures represent the

a   b

Fig. 5-13. Illustration of two extreme figures used by Bobbitt (1942) in determining the closure threshold for triangularity. Figure *b* is likely to be seen as a triangle, whereas this is not usually true of Fig. *a*.

extremes of the steps along the dimension defined in terms of the amount of the perimeter of the triangle present.

A series of these finely graded forms was presented in ascending and descending order (method of limits), each figure being exposed .1 sec. by a tachistoscope. The Ss were fully informed as to the nature of the experiment. In responding, S reported whether he saw "twoness" (two angles) or "oneness" (triangle). From this procedure, thresholds of closure of considerable stability were determined. Depending upon the size and shape of the "triangle," 68 to 72 percent of the perimeter had to be present before the figure was seen as a triangle.

Tactual and Kinesthetic Thresholds

Many environmental changes are appraised through the cutaneous (skin) sensibilities. Sensations such as heat, warmth, cold, surface pain, and light pressure (touch) are all mediated through organs lying near the surface of the body; and each of these sensations has a threshold value for the particular stimulus producing the sensation. For example, there are wide differences in the sensitivity of the skin on various areas of the body. The *two-point threshold* of touch is the distance between stimulating points applied simultaneously to the skin at which S can just discriminate that there *are* two points.

The device used to stimulate the two points is called an *aesthesiometer,* and it may take many forms. A micrometer may be used; a compass fitted with two blunt ends may serve satisfactorily; even two points of cardboard have been used. However, it is critical not only that the device must stimulate two points on the skin simultaneously, lightly, and briefly, but also that there exist some means of measuring the distance between the two points stimulated. Careful exploration of various surfaces of the body shows that there are wide and rather startling differences in sensitivity. For example, the lips are extremely sensitive; so also are the finger tips. But the surface of the back yields a very large threshold value.

We have identified two kinds of thresholds, namely, the absolute threshold and the difference threshold. The two-point threshold as well as many others (such as the closure threshold discussed above) may not seem to fit nicely into either of the two categories. Although a rigid classfication of a threshold into one or the other type is not at all necessary, many feel more comfortable when this can be done. The most satisfactory way to handle this classification is to use the measuring operations as the basis for classification. It will be noted that whether the two-point threshold is determined by the method of limits or by the method of constant stimuli, the operations are those used to determine absolute thresholds. In determining difference thresholds a standard stimulus is always present with variable stimuli judged against the standard. We *could* determine a difference threshold with an aesthesiometer. For example, suppose we used as a standard stimulus the stimulation of two points far "above" the two-point threshold. That is, we set the aesthesiometer so that S clearly perceives that two widely separated points are being stimulated. The variable stimuli then could be two-point stimulation of distances between the points which are both less and more than the distance between the standard stimulus. In each pairing, S would be asked to judge whether the second of the two stimuli had a greater or less distance between the two points than did the first stimulus. So far as is known to the present writer, such a DL has never been determined, but it is clear that one could do so, and clearly, we are asking about a threshold that is different from the usual two-point threshold.

As an example of what will be called here a kinesthetic threshold, consider the following situation. A 3-in. stick about pencil size, for instance, is used as the standard stimulus. Other sticks graduated in length above and below the standard are used as variable stimuli. A blindfolded S grasps the ends of the standard stick between the thumb and forefinger, puts it down, grasps a variable stimulus in the same manner, and then makes a judgment as to which was longer. Therefore, by using the method of constant stimuli, for example, it is clear that a DL for what is called finger span could be determined. Such a study shows that we can detect very small differences in length and that Weber's Law holds except for standards which are 1.5 inches or shorter (Gaydos, 1958).

Thresholds with Animal Subjects

It is quite possible to develop a communication system between a lower animal and E so that thresholds can be determined for the animal. We are all probably certain that we can detect at least gross differences in our own state of hunger. It is reasonable to expect that lower animals may also detect differences in their level of hunger or drive. In fact, the assumption of the ability of animals to behave differently under different drive levels (as calculated by hours of deprivation since last eating) is made by certain theories of learning. We may examine a study by Bolles (1962) as a test of the validity of the assumption.

The Ss were white rats housed in a small cage. From opposite sides of the cage, two alleys led to their respective goal boxes. Initially, the animal was taught to discriminate between low and high hunger. Many days were required to do this since only one trial per day was given. A trial consisted first of inducing high hunger or low hunger and started 23 hr. after the animal had last eaten. To induce high hunger, the rat was given only one-eighth of its daily ration in the home cage. Then after a 5-min. delay, two doors in the cage were opened making both of the alleys available to the animal. If the particular trial involved low hunger, seven-eighths of the daily ration was given before the doors leading to the two alleys were opened. The discrimination to be learned by the animal was, in a manner of speaking, "If I got only a small amount of food—if I am still very hungry—I will find additional food in the goal box of Alley A and none in Alley B. If I got a large amount of food—if I am not very hungry—I will find additional food in Alley B but none in Alley A." On one day, the animal was fed the one-eighth daily ration, on the next, seven-eighths, the next, one-eighth, and so on, although not in complete alternation throughout the training. This continued day after day until the discrimination was learned, learning being defined as the choice of the correct alley on nine of ten consecutive days.

Having established this discrimination between wide differences in hunger, E then started bringing the amount received in the home cage from day to day closer and closer in amount. For example, retaining the one-eighth daily ration as a standard, he reduced the feeding for low hunger to six-eighths, then to five-eighths, and so on, until the animal now was responding with 75 percent accuracy. This value would represent the upper point of change, and the difference between the amount of food given at this point and the amount represented by the one-eighth daily ration would be the DL. Different subgroups of animals had different standards, but in the middle range of hunger the DL amounted to about 30 percent of the total daily food consumption. Clearly, these animals made a discrimination which appears to be based on the level of hunger.

A long training procedure for rhesus monkeys produced a communication system whereby Schwartzbaum and Wilson (1961) could determine DLs for taste of salt with distilled water as the standard or comparison stimulus. As a result of several training steps, the monkeys were brought to the point where, on a single trial, they would quickly taste the solution in the two drinking tubes. One of the solutions was distilled water, and the other was a salt solution which was clearly discernible from the distilled water. The training was carried to the point where S consistently chose to open a food cup below the tube holding the salt solution and to ignore the food cup (which contained no food) below the tube with the water solution. Of course, the position of the tubes was changed from day to day, and other steps were taken to make sure that S was making the discrimination on the basis of salt solution versus distilled water and not on other cues.

Once the discrimination was established, the concentration of salt in the salt solution was gradually reduced but the distilled water was maintained in the other tube. Obviously, at some point the discrimination could no longer be made. The findings show that the DLs for salt for these monkeys is quite comparable to those for man.

In still another study (Payton & Blake, 1964), monkeys were first taught to discriminate a vertical line (food present) from a horizontal line (no food present). After this discrimination was well established, the test trials were given on which the horizontal line was tipped varying degrees toward the vertical orientation. These Es report that their eight monkeys had an average DL of 2 degrees. This means that a line only 2 degrees away from the vertical orientation will be seen as different from one in the vertical position.

The above samples of various kinds of thresholds that are engaging the attention of psychologists must, it should be repeated, be considered only samples. The number of potential thresholds that may be studied is enormous. In the discussion of thresholds, we have not attempted in all cases to point out why anyone would want to study a particular threshold. But like any phenomenon, a particular threshold will become of interest when theoretical or practical reasons, or both, make it important. For example, there is a rather large body of literature on DLs in visual perception of velocity (e.g., Brown, 1961). Not only does this body of knowledge of the variables influencing DLs of velocity aid in understanding visual functions per se, but it also has importance in designing machines where judgments of velocity differences are of importance, as, for example, in the movement of objects seen on a radar screen. So let us not leave the impression that investigators determine thresholds just for the "heck of it" (although this is a perfectly valid reason). Instead, let us emphasize that determinations are made to aid in solving problems about behavior and hence to contribute to the over-all understanding of behavior.

RESPONSE BIASES AND THRESHOLD MEASUREMENTS

Consider yourself an S in the following experiment. You are told that you will be presented a series of pairs of slides with a varying number of dots on the slides. For each pair of slides you are to make the judgment as to whether the second of the two slides had more or less dots than the first. You are told further that no equal judgments are allowed; if the number of dots on a pair of slides appears equal to you, you must nevertheless make a decision between more or less. As S you have a data sheet for recording your judgments, an M if you thought the second slide of the pair had more dots than the first or an L if you thought it had less. By the instructions, then, you are led to believe that sometimes you will find the second slide to have more dots than the first, sometimes you will find it to have less, and sometimes you will not be able to discriminate a difference.

The E in this case initially presents to you eight pairs of slides in which it is obviously apparent that the second slide has more dots than the first. Then, on the ninth trial, he presents two slides with an equal number of dots. If you, and the other Ss collectively, behave in a chance manner, we might expect that the division between L and M on the ninth trial would be 50-50. But let's review what you have done on the first eight trials. As you look at your data sheet you see that you have recorded an M on all eight trials. On the ninth trial you are given an ambiguous situation—one in which the number of dots on the two slides appears to be equal (assuming no time-order error). You are forced to choose between an L and an M. What will your choice be?

Such an experiment was performed by the author. For Group 1, consisting of 15 Ss, the numbers of dots on the first eight pairs of slides were 32-61, 15-30, 64-116, 75-128, 12-23, 16-32, 16-34, and 14-28. All 15 Ss correctly recorded an M for all eight trials. On the ninth trial a 32-32 pairing was given. For Group 2, consisting of 26 Ss, the order of the two slides within a trial for the first eight trials was reversed, and again, all Ss correctly recorded eight successive Ls. What predictions can we make about the performance of the Ss on the ninth trial? Actually, we could arrive at two opposing predictions. Loosely speaking, we might identify these with the error of expectation and the error of habituation as discussed earlier. In the latter case, on the ninth trial, S might say to himself, "I don't know what this character (E) is up to, but all the previous pairs of slides have clearly had the second slide having more dots than the first (or less dots than the first), and I suppose that is also the case for this pair." Now, of course, we do not presume that the S necessarily goes through this "reasoning," but a response tendency which reflects such thinking would lead to S's giving the same response (habituation) as he had given on the first eight trials.

On the other hand, a little consideration will also make it plausible that he might shift his response on the ninth trial. If you are taking a true-false test and you come to a statement that you clearly have no idea about its truth or falsity, what determines your response? Among other things, you may look back over the number of Ts and Fs you have given to the previous questions, and, apparently based on an assumption that the instructor would make about an equal number of Ts and Fs, you may choose the response which had occurred least frequently in your responses to earlier questions. Or, if for the immediately preceding four times you have given Ts with considerable confidence, then you may conclude that this one—the one for which you do not know the answer—must be an F. You are, in effect, showing the gambler's fallacy; if a coin comes up heads four times in a row, we sometimes feel that this increases the likelihood of tails on the fifth throw, although in fact it doesn't. In any event, such "forces" may be responsible for your choice of T or F. In a similar fashion, under the expectation that the pairs of slides will sometimes have more dots on the second than on the first, and sometimes the reverse, and seeing that you have recorded eight Ls (or eight Ms) in a row, you may switch to the other response when the pair with equal number of dots is presented on the ninth trial.

Although not highly significant statistically, the data show that expectation or switching is the predominant response tendency among these Ss. Of the 15 Ss in Group 1 who recorded (correctly) M on the first eight trials, 10 switched to L on the ninth, and 5 continued with M. Of the 26 Ss in Group 2, "primed" with Ls on the first eight trials, 17 switched to M, and 9 continued with L. Thus, the majority in both groups moved away from the response they had been using on the first eight trials.

To evaluate the implications of such findings, we must first repeat comments made earlier. As we studied the methods of determining thresholds, it was clear that the numerical value said to represent an absolute threshold (or a difference threshold) was a derived response measure. That is to say, from the direct response measure—number of times S reported a stimulus present in an absolute threshold experiment—a threshold is said to be that value at which the response is correct 50 percent of the time. There is nothing sacred about this; indeed, some investigators have occasionally used other criteria. The threshold is a statistical abstraction; it is a derived dependent variable. One may manipulate various independent variables and determine the influence on the threshold as defined in this manner. No one can seriously object to this.

However, some may wish to go further than this and think of the threshold as representing a particular cut-off point on a stimulus dimension which represents in the literal sense of the word a threshold—a point at which the energy of the independent variable first stimulated the sensory equipment. Or, in a manner of speaking, it takes "this much energy" to activate the sensory equipment. While accepting the fact that some minimal amount of stimulus energy above zero energy is required to activate the sensorium, such thinking as the above goes beyond the data and implies that there is a "true" threshold. Usually we do not find it advisable to carry our thinking quite this far, for we now fully realize that we cannot know phenomena except by the methods we use to measure them, and we know that different methods of attack may produce somewhat different values, not only in the case of thresholds, but for almost any phenomenon we study.

Why should different methods produce different conclusions about thresholds? The answer lies in the fact that decisions made by S in a threshold experiment are determined in part by nonsensory factors, and different methods may allow these nonsensory factors to operate in different amounts.

Nonsensory factors. By nonsensory factors or variables we mean factors which are not a part of the immediate sensory stimulus but which nevertheless influence Ss' responses. The switching behavior shown by the Ss in the simple procedure outlined earlier is an illustration of the influence of such a nonsensory factor. Whenever S makes a judgment in an experiment, we must recognize the possibility that this judgment may be in varying degree determined by nonsensory factors. It seems fair to say that the less the information for making a judgment supplied by the sensory input of a given situation, the greater the importance of nonsensory variables. This may be illustrated. Suppose we are measuring an absolute threshold for pure-tone intensity. If we present a tone of 100 db., it is almost certain that 100 percent of Ss with normal hearing would report the presence of the tone (just as all Ss made the correct decision on the first eight trials in the above study). There, then, the decision is largely determined by the sensory input. If, however, the intensity of the tone is so weak that S is in doubt as to whether or not he heard a tone, nonsensory variables may be important in his decision. Let us see what some of these nonsensory factors might be.

If S is in doubt as to whether he heard the tone, we might expect him to say 50 percent of the time that he had heard it and 50 percent of the time that he had not heard it. Thus, we might think that S's behavior would reflect a coin-tossing situation. This may or may not be true. Indeed, if S does treat it as a coin-tossing situation, it probably is not even true that his responses will be split 50-50 between the two categories. For if a group of Ss are told that a coin is to be flipped and they are asked to choose heads or tails, approximately 75 percent will choose heads. The fact is that we have response biases of a wide variety, and whenever we must make a decision in an ambiguous situation, these biases are likely to be involved in the decision. Even if the S is responding with "yes" or "no" and has to make a decision on an ambiguous threshold-measurement trial, we may find him saying "yes" more often than "no"; like the girl in the musical *Oklahoma*, S can't say "no."

We have already noted in an earlier section, in discussing word-recognition thresholds, that certain motivational variables may be involved in what at first appears to be a cold, neutral measurement situation. But even in an absolute threshold determination, some Ss may view making an error a more serious matter than do other Ss. Thus, some Ss may never say "yes" ("I heard the tone") unless they are quite sure they heard it. Other Ss live more dangerously and report the presence of the tone when they are quite unsure of themselves. Clearly, the thresholds for two such groups would differ, but we may be in error if we attribute the difference to differences in the sensory equipment per se.

Finally, we may note again that the response S makes on a particular trial may be in part dependent upon what response he has made on earlier trials. This was the outcome of the experiment reported at the start of this section. But such built-up biases could operate in the absolute-threshold measurement situation. If S has reported hearing a tone on all of the last few trials, it may make him more prone to say "no" on the current trial if he is uncertain.

We wish to make two major points as a consequence of the discussion of the nonsensory factors which may enter into threshold measurements. The first is that the influence of response biases is a widespread problem throughout all of psychology, and we will continue to run into it throughout this book. Tune (1964) has recently reviewed the literature on response biases or preference and uses experiments from many different areas in his review. Even work with animals does not avoid the problem; rats, for example, usually have a bias toward turning left as opposed to turning right (or vice versa) in a simple spatial choice situation. Over and over again we will find that we must design experiments so that the results for different conditions will not be differentially influenced by response biases (unless the intent is to study the biases). And we will find that some psychologists study the ways in which response biases develop. What conditions produce them? How might they be extinguished? It is of particular importance to note that response biases are of the first order of importance in the study of thinking where, we might presume, the logical might prevail over the illogical, the rational over the irrational. We will find that this is far from the truth as revealed by experimental work in the area.

The second point to be made by the discussion of nonsensory factors involved in threshold measurements pertains to recent developments in thinking and method which are found under the categorical heading of *signal-detection theory*.

Signal-Detection Theory

The realization that nonsensory factors are involved in threshold measurements by the classical method of attack (limits and constant stimuli) is not new (Corso, 1963). What is new in the movement known as signal-detection theory is the beginning of the development of techniques by which the influence of nonsensory factors can be removed or subtracted from the data, thus leaving a response residue that is believed to be dependent largely upon variation in the sensory stimulation. Apparently the immediate impetus for the development of signal detection theory came from practical problems associated with signal detection by radar operators. If a radar operator is reluctant to report an enemy "blip" until he is very sure that he has seen it on the scope, it may be too late. On the other hand, if an operator reports an enemy when in fact there was no signal on the scope, this also has undesirable consequences. Consider, too, the radar operators in a control tower of a busy commercial airport. One operator might have a very low "threshold" for reporting two planes on a collision course whereas another might have a high threshold. Such problems, produced by the response biases of the operators, led mathematicians and engineers to develop a theory to cope with the problems.

No attempt will be made here to present signal-detection theory in its detailed form, a form which is highly mathematical. We may, however, see the basic sort of data which may be handled by this theory. Visualize a situation in which S is undergoing measurements to determine his absolute auditory threshold. The S is told ahead of time that on some trials an auditory stimulus *will* be presented after a ready signal and that on some trials the auditory stimulus will *not* be presented after the ready signal. Since the intent is to measure the absolute threshold, S may be in doubt as to whether a stimulus was or was not presented even if the auditory stimulus was presented on every trial. It is already an ambiguous situation, a situation where response biases may influence the decision, and S's knowing that the auditory stimulus will not be presented on some trials only adds to the ambiguity.

From such a procedure, four different outcomes are possible: (1) the auditory stimulus is presented, and S reports its presence; (2) the auditory stimulus is not presented, and S correctly fails to report its presence; (3) the auditory signal is present, but S fails to report it; (4) the auditory signal is not present, but S reports that it was. This last outcome is the critical one, for the frequency of such occurrences may be taken as indicative of S's tendency to respond on the basis of nonsensory factors. If the entry in this outcome is zero, it would suggest that S is not at all influenced by nonsensory factors. If the frequency of this outcome is high, it must indicate a strong tendency to respond on the basis of nonsensory factors.

It is at once apparent that certain variables ought to influence the frequency of responses fitting this fourth outcome. If E punishes S for these false responses, they might be expected to decrease in frequency. If *E* varies the relative frequency of times that the ready signal is and is not followed by an auditory signal, the frequency of the false reports should vary. If *E* rewards *S* for decreasing the frequency of reports fitting the third outcome (signal present but *S* failed to report this), it would surely result in an increase in the frequency of the fourth outcome.

What we see is that *E* attempts to break the gross behavior, usually measured in threshold experiments, into sensory-determined and nonsensory-determined components. The gross nonsensory component will be in turn broken down into further subcomponents defined in terms of the independent variables which influence the frequency. Over and over again we will see that if there are what may be called breakthroughs in psychological research, they are identified with just such analytical advances.

It should be noted that the basic tools used in signal-detection theory have much in common with the tools used in certain theories of simple learning and in theories dealing with complex decision-making processes. The student with mathematical skills may wish to study some of these theories in detail, including signal-detection theory. Some representative reports are Swets, Tanner, and Birdsall, 1961; Luce, 1963; Edwards, 1962; Egan, Greenberg, and Schulman, 1961; Mueller and McGill, 1963.

SUMMARY

This chapter dealt with the techniques of measuring absolute and difference thresholds. The absolute threshold refers to the minimum amount of stimulus energy to which the organism is sensitive and is defined as the magnitude of the stimulus necessary to evoke a response 50 percent of the time. The difference threshold is the amount of change in a stimulus necessary to produce a phenomenal change. It is defined as the amount of change in stimulus energy necessary to elicit a report of change 50 percent of the time.

The method of limits and the method of constant stimuli are the two basic methods of attack used in measuring thresholds, and several illustrations of their application were given. A variant on the method of limits, the staircase method, was also discussed. Illustrations of the application of the methods included studies on critical flicker fusion, absolute word-recognition thresholds, absolute auditory thresholds, difference thresholds for temporal duration, numerosity, and word frequency, closure thresholds, tactual and kinesthetic thresholds, and various thresholds measured with lower animals.

Studies in which two independent variables were manipulated were examined with special attention paid to the interaction effects of the two variables. An interaction occurs when the magnitude of the effects of one variable are found to differ depending upon the setting of the other variable.

A series of studies on word-recognition thresholds as a function of word frequency were examined to show how the cumulative research over a period of several years may lead to a fairly complete understanding of how a particular independent variable produces its effects.

Weber's Law states that the size of the difference threshold is a constant proportion of the magnitude of the standard from which the difference threshold was determined. This ratio is said to be constant over a wide range of a particular stimulus continuum. Sensory thresholds appear to fit the law quite satisfactorily; the ratio for temporal discrimination was about 1/5, and that for numerosity, about 1/7.5.

Finally, the role of nonsensory factors (response biases) in threshold judgments was discussed with reference to signal-detection theory as a technique for coping with these nonsensory factors.

CHAPTER SIX

Scaling Methods

When we refer to scaling methods we mean techniques for sorting stimuli according to the amount of some specified characteristic these stimuli are said to possess. The result of the application of these techniques is a scale. The S, through whom the stimuli are filtered, is the go-between—the sorting agent. If the sorting is reliable we say that the set of procedures leading to the scale constitutes the definition of a dimension. In the minimal case, if two stimuli can be shown to possess reliably different amounts of a specified characteristic, a dimension is said to exist. Thus, if a group of Ss agree that Barry has a good sense of humor and Nelson a poor sense of humor, we say that a measurable dimension of humor exists.

We will see that scaling methods are applied to two general classes of stimuli. In one class, the stimuli presented can be described by a physical scale (feet, minutes, decibels, grams, and so on). The usual intent of the scaling method is to determine the relationship between subjective measurement of the stimuli (by judgment of S) and the measurement by a physical scale. This is, as we now know, the fundamental problem that has intrigued workers in psychophysics since the beginning of experimental psychology, and we shall see that it is still an extremely provoking issue.

The second class of stimuli to which scaling methods are applied is that class for which no known physical scale is appropriate. We do not have an available "yardstick" to measure sense of humor; we do not have a physical scale to evaluate beauty. For this second class of stimuli, therefore, the intent of the scaling method is to *provide* a measurement of the stimuli via the judgmental processes of the S. In our discussion of scaling techniques we will intermingle illustrations of these two classes of stimuli.

By way of further introduction, we must clearly state the limitations to be placed on the scope of the present chapter. In keeping with the major objective of this book, the emphasis will be on an examination of methods and procedures. Even so, we will fall short in at least two ways. First, there are many variants on scaling methods, and we cannot hope to cover them all. We will consider what might be called the modal methods. Second, the refinement of scales resulting from various scaling methods has been carried in some instances to a highly sophisticated mathematical level, and it is unlikely that many undergraduate students would be mathematically equipped to work with them.

It is a fact that the scaling methods have widespread use as practical devices. Industries make use of them for product evaluation; attitude measurement by various techniques derive in one way or another from the scaling methods to be discussed here. Yet, the usefulness of the scaling methods as mere devices for the measurement of behavior should not obscure the fact that their fundamental role is to aid in understanding behavior. The scales, in this role, become response-measuring devices, because they are used to assess the influence that various independent variables have on behavior. As the influence of various factors is determined, theories are developed to order these facts. There is no shortage of such theories. And although we will touch on certain phenomena of behavior which are studied by the use of the scales as the response-measuring device and upon some of the theories which have evolved, we will make no pretense of systematically covering fact and theory. Our major objective concerns the presentation of the methods.

THE METHOD OF RANK ORDER

This is one of the simplest of the scaling methods, but, at the same time, one which is highly effective in answering certain questions. In this method the S is presented a group of stimuli which are presumed to have some characteristic in common, and he is requested to rank the stimuli in order from high to low according to the characteristic being considered. If we were interested in a group evaluation, we would give the stimuli to a group of Ss and then, of course, obtain some measure of average rank to allow us to determine the group ranking of the stimuli. Although the matter of determining mean rank order is not difficult, let us follow through an illustration.

Suppose that an automobile manufacturer is interested in consumer beliefs about the durability of different makes of compact cars. He is interested in what the consumer *believes* about the durability or ruggedness of the autos. Note that he is not asking which make *is* most durable, for in order to answer this question he would make tests of the cars under identical conditions. This manufacturer knows full well that fact and belief are not always in a one-to-one relationship. He knows, too, that what people believe about the autos is an important factor in sales. In any event, he wants to learn what people believe about the durability of certain makes of compact cars. Let us assume there are five cars, which we shall call A, B, C, D, and E. The number of people that would actually be contacted would depend on a number of factors, but for our purposes we will consider the results from only 10 Ss.

The E types the name of each make of car on a card. The cards are presented to S with appropriate instructions to rank order the makes in terms of his (S's) belief about durability, and also, to assign the car believed to have greatest durability a rank of 1, that believed to be second most durable a rank of 2, and so on. Even if S feels two cars are equal in durability, we

TABLE 6–1
ILLUSTRATIVE DATA SHEET RESULTING FROM THE RANKING OF
FIVE COMPACT CARS (A, B, C, D, E) FOR DURABILITY BY
TEN SUBJECTS

SUBJECT	CAR				
	A	B	C	D	E
1	4	3	1	2	5
2	3	4	1	2	5
3	3	4	2	1	5
4	2	3	1	4	5
5	3	5	2	1	4
6	4	2	1	3	5
7	5	3	1	2	4
8	3	4	1	2	5
9	2	1	3	4	5
10	4	3	1	2	5
Sums	33	32	14	23	48
Overall Ranks	4	3	1	2	5

would probably request that he try to make a decision which would put one ahead of the other. We could, however, "split" the ranks if we wish. Thus, if S could not determine which should be ranked 3 and 4, because they appeared equal, we might record a score of 3.5 for each auto.

Table 6-1 gives the hypothetical results from such an experiment. This table might, in fact, be the "raw" data sheet which E uses as he records the ranks decided upon by each S. To determine the overall rank order we simply sum the columns of ranks, for it is apparent that the column with the lowest sum must represent the most preferred auto. In this case we see that Car C is most preferred and Car E, the least preferred. The scale resulting from the method of rank order is known as an *ordinal scale*, in which all we have is a rank ordering of stimuli on some characteristic; we do not have any quantitative information on the amount of the characteristic which separates the ranks. That is, a simple rank-order scale does not tell us, for example, that the difference in the amount of the characteristic separating Ranks 1 and 2 is equivalent to the amount separating Ranks 2 and 3. However, we are not without some information on such matters. For example, we would not hesitate to conclude that the difference in judged durability of Cars A and B (Ranks 3 and 4) is less than the difference between Cars A and E (Ranks 4 and 5). Indeed, we would probably conclude that there is not a group difference in judged durability of Cars A and B; if we took another sample of 10 Ss, the ranks for these two cars might well be reversed.

We must draw a working distinction between absolute and relative judgments in the various scaling procedures. Clearly, the method of rank order requires S to make relative judgments, and we cannot conclude that Car C is believed to be the most durable car on the market. All we know is that among these five cars it is believed to be most durable. There could well be another compact car, Car X, that is believed to be more durable than Car C. We do not even know from Table 6-1 whether Car C is, in any absolute sense, durable at all. The Ss may actually believe that Car C will "fall apart" in six months; all we know is that they do not believe that Car C will fall apart as quickly as the other four makes. In a certain sense, this lack of information provided by the method of rank order might not recommend its use. However, if E realizes the limited nature of what he will learn by use of the method, and if in spite of this he is satisfied that it will provide the information he wants, how can we say that the method should not be used?

Using data collected by the writer, we may now consider another illustration of the use of the method of rank order. We quote the instructions given to the Ss:

"Imagine that you move into an International House on a college campus. One of the rules of the House is that you must have as a roommate a foreign student of one of the seven nationalities listed. Look at the list carefully; then assign the number *one* to the nationality of the student you would most prefer to have as a roommate, the number *two* to the nationality preferred second, and so on, until the least preferred nationality is assigned the number *seven*. Take as long as you like to make the rankings. If two nationalities appear to be a tie as far as you are concerned, choose one or the other—don't rank them the same. All seven nationalities must be assigned a rank and no two ranks are to be the same."

Rankings were obtained from students enrolled in introductory psychology at Northwestern University. In 1947, 85 students made the rankings; in 1953, 187 students; in 1963, 196 students. To present the results, we have calculated not only the mean ranks for each nationality for each of the three years, but also the standard deviation of the ranking for each nationality. These data are shown in Table 6-2.

Now let us see what sort of information is transmitted by the data of Table 6-2. If we wish to draw conclusions about changes in preferences over the 16-year period, we must first make an assumption, namely, that had all three groups been elementary psychology students at the same time, the rank orders resulting would have been the same. That is to say, we must make an assumption about the equivalence of the three groups. Assume that in 1947 we had asked a group of senior political science students to rank order the nationalities; we might well expect their mean rankings to differ

TABLE 6–2
NATIONALITY PREFERENCES DETERMINED BY THE METHOD OF RANK ORDER FOR THREE DIFFERENT YEARS

	MEAN RANKS			STANDARD DEVIATIONS		
NATIONALITY	1947	1953	1963	1947	1953	1963
English	2.23	2.50	3.47	1.36	2.07	2.19
German	2.75	3.14	3.59	1.66	1.43	1.86
French	3.22	2.51	2.68	1.63	1.43	1.61
Russian	4.19	4.58	3.81	1.85	1.85	1.81
Chinese	4.42	5.23	5.56	1.66	1.58	1.69
Italian	5.14	4.41	4.33	1.33	1.49	1.77
Japanese	6.04	5.63	4.54	1.36	1.46	1.67

from those of the elementary psychology students in the same year. Such differences would probably be attributed to differences in the backgrounds of the two groups. Now then, if the elementary psychology students measured in 1953 and 1963 contained a larger proportion of political science students than did the comparable class in 1947, changes in the ranks "over the years" might be attributed to this rather than to any geopolitical events which might be hypothesized to lie behind—to cause—the changes in preferences in Table 6-2. But if one makes an assumption that the three groups measured differed only in exposure to the geopolitical events occurring, then certain of the changes in the rankings may be interpreted. However, even the acceptance of this assumption does not give us a clear-cut means of reaching firm conclusions. We need to pursue this matter further.

We will repeat, the rank-order method is a relative method. Suppose a single individual made the rankings in 1953 and again in 1963. Suppose further that because of a delightful trip to France in 1960, he felt more favorably disposed toward the French than he had 10 years earlier. So, when he ranks them the second time, in 1963, he maintains the same ranks except for an interchange of the English and the French. In 1953 he had ranked the English first and the French second; in 1963 he reversed these, making the French first and the English second. But suppose we did not know about the trip to France; suppose, rather, that we had only the two sets of data. We would be quite unable to draw a conclusion concerning the cause of the change. One possibility is that the attitude toward the French had, in an absolute sense, become more favorable; enough change had occurred to make it more favorable than the attitude toward the English, which had not changed. Another possibility is that there was no change in attitude toward the French but that there had been a decrease in favorableness of attitude toward the English. Either situation, or a combination, would produce a change in the rank order. We have, in effect, reciprocal measures; if one goes up, the other must necessarily go down.

In view of the above argument, we must be cautious about interpreting changes over years of the ranks in Table 6-2. For example, we note that the rank of Chinese becomes lower and lower between 1947 and 1963. This might be ascribed to political changes in China; indeed, this seems to be a very plausible hypothesis. However, we cannot tell whether or not the favorableness toward the Chinese has, in an absolute sense, decreased. Instead, there may have been subtle increases in favorableness toward one or more of the other nationalities. Even if the attitude toward the Chinese has remained constant, the rank order given the Chinese could be lowered because of the "moving up" of one or more other nationalities.

Let us consider another illustration of the dangers involved in reciprocal measures such as ranks. An investigator has a hypothesis that food advertisements would be much more effective if potential consumers saw them just before a meal rather than just after a meal. The notion was that the food advertisement would be enhanced in its appeal if seen by a hungry person. Let us say that E uses five advertisements of food and five so-called control advertisements of nonfood articles, such as refrigerators or autos. One group of Ss ranks all 10 advertisements just before an evening meal, and a comparable group of Ss ranks them just after the evening meal. The hypothesis predicts that the average rank order of the food advertisements will be higher (actually lower, numerically) before dinner than after. Now suppose that this is in fact found, the average rank of the 5 food pictures being 3 before dinner and 7 after dinner, and the nonfood ads showing a mean rank of 7 before dinner and 3 after dinner. Of course, the results are quite consonant with E's hypothesis, but an alternative hypothesis is not ruled out, namely, the hypothesis that the appeal of the food ads remained constant but the appeal of the nonfood ads increased. It is clear that if the appeal of the nonfood ads did increase from the pre-dinner to the post-dinner test, the *apparent* attractiveness of the foods ads *had* to decrease. We must be careful about drawing cause-effect conclusions from reciprocal response measures. We may now return to the data of Table 6-2.

Social attitudes which are held by a large majority of the people and which remain fairly fixed over time are often spoken of as stereotypes. There are in fact no violent changes in mean ranks in Table 6-2 over 16 years, so that we are probably dealing with attitudes that might be classed as stereotypes. If we attend only to mean ranks, however, we are not letting the data tell us all that they are trying to tell us. One can make a fairly strong case for an increase in flexibility of attitude if we examine the standard deviations in Table 6-2. The average standard deviations for 1947, 1953, and 1963 are 1.55, 1.62, and 1.80, respectively. How might this increase be interpreted? An increase in the size of the standard deviation for a given nationality would indicate that there is less agreement among the students—less stereotyped attitudes. It may well be that increased interchange among the peoples of the world is indeed having an influence. Such interchange may be breaking down some of the stereotypes which are handed down from generation to generation. If the variability among the students in ranking the nationalities is increasing, another change automatically follows, namely, an average decrease in the difference between successive ranks. This can be simply indexed by noting the mean value determining the highest and lowest ranks. For 1947 these two values were 2.23 and 6.04, or a difference of 3.81; in 1953 the extremes were 2.50 and 5.63, or a difference of 3.13; and the 1963 values were 2.68 and 5.56, or a difference of 2.88. If this trend is reliable, at some point far in the future the seven nationalities will all receive a mean rank of 3.5.

THE METHOD OF PAIRED COMPARISONS

The method of paired comparisons is exactly what the name implies; S is presented a pair of stimuli and is asked to judge which has the greater amount of a specified characteristic. Each stimulus in the group is paired, hence compared, with every other stimulus. We will examine how this method might have been applied to the initial problem used for the method of rank order, that of determining the beliefs about durability of five compact cars.

In the method of rank order, all five cards (on which the names of the autos were printed) were spread out before the S. In the method of paired comparisons, only two cards would be shown at a time, with S required to choose the one he believed to be more durable. How many pairs will have to be shown in order to meet the requirement that each auto is paired with every other auto? The formula is $\frac{n(n-1)}{2}$, n indicating the number of stimuli, which in this case is five. Thus with 5 stimuli, 10 pairs would be shown S. If there were 10 stimuli, all possible pairings would total 45; if 50 stimuli, 1225 pairings. It becomes apparent that we would not choose this method if we had very many stimuli to evaluate since the work involved becomes prohibitive. As one of the variants on the method, investigators have explored the use of incomplete pairings and have shown fairly high reliability. However, we will consider the method as applied in its pure form.

In evaluating the five autos, E would have listed on a data sheet the actual pairings required (A vs. B, A vs. C, A vs. D, and so on). To avoid any biasing by progressive error, he may vary the order in which the pairs are presented to different Ss. As S makes a choice for a given pair, E records which member of the pair is chosen. Thus, if A and B were presented, and S said A was more durable, E would record A on his data sheet.

The basic data which E obtains from the method of paired comparisons is a rank ordering of the stimuli. How is this determined? In the auto illustration, E would simply count the total number of times that each auto's letter was entered on his data sheet. The recording of a given letter, when a pair was presented, indicates that that stimulus was chosen over the one with which it was paired. Hence, the letter occurring with greatest frequency is given the rank of 1; the letter occurring with second most frequency is given the rank of 2, and so on. Again, we are dealing with relative judgments, and all the cautions which we have discussed with regard to the method of rank order hold for this method also. The ranks represent only an ordinal scale, although it is here that some advanced mathematical techniques have been used to derive a scale in which intervals along the scale are presumed to be equal; hence, the "distance" between successive ranks can be rather precisely stated.

An illustration. Judgments are always made within a context or background. This background or context may be only that representing the S's accumulated experience with objects and events which, so to speak, he "carries around with him in his mind." In addition, however, E may systematically vary the context or background on which the objective stimulus is placed for S to observe and judge. The objective of such variation is, of course, to study the influence of the context on the judgments. We saw in the previous chapter that two potential consequences may be discerned. If the stimulus to be judged appears to assume phenomenally the properties or characteristics of the context, *assimilation* is said to have occurred. On the other hand, if the stimulus to be judged appears to assume properties or characteristics opposite to or away from those of the context, *contrast* effects are said to have occurred. In the present illustration of the application of the method of paired comparisons, the contrast effect appears stronger than assimilation.

The seven stimuli (reproduced in Fig. 6-1) used in the experiment were 2 in. by 2 in. lantern slides. It will be noted that each slide has a central square within which are small circles or dots. The judgments of the Ss always referred to the density of dots within the central squares. In actual fact the number of dots within the central square is equal for all seven slides. This density will be referred to as a density of 4. It is apparent that the density of dots surrounding the central square differs from slide to slide, with the number below each slide (1 through 7) indicating increasing density. The middle slide, with a density of 4, has equal density within and without the central square. Some observers, in viewing Fig. 6-1, experience a contrast effect, namely, an apparent decrease in the density of dots within the central square as one moves quickly from 1 through 7. This indicates that the greater the density of dots of the context, the less the apparent density of the central square.

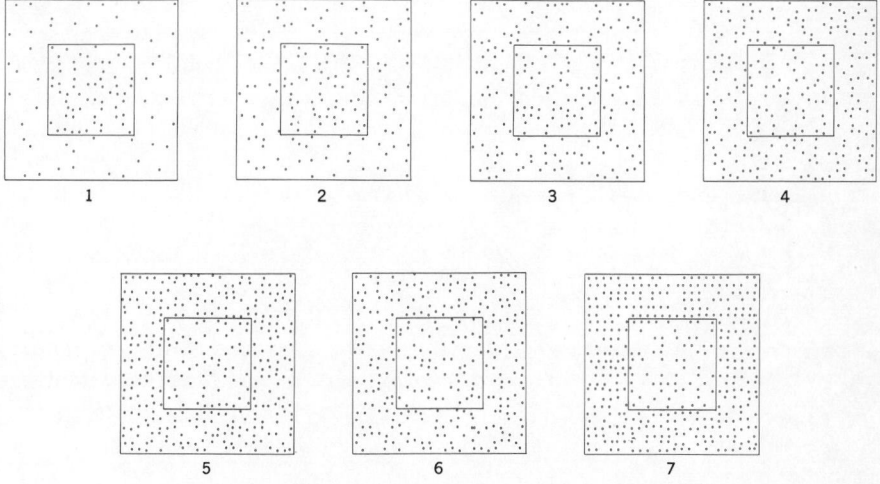

Fig. 6-1. Slides used to study contrast effects in the judgment of dot density. The density in the inner square is the same for all slides (4), and the surrounding density varies from 1 to 7 as indicated.

With seven stimuli, 21 different pairings are required for each stimulus to be paired with every other stimulus. In the experiment each pairing was repeated four times so that each S actually made judgments for 84 pairings. A minor deviation from the pure paired-comparison procedure occurred. The two stimuli of a pair on a given trial were not presented simultaneously; rather, they were presented in succession. Therefore, for any given pair, one of the slides was presented first on two of the trials, and the other was presented first for the other two trials. The first member of a pair was flashed on a screen for 1 sec. Two sec. later the second member of the pair was flashed for 1 sec. Immediately, S recorded his judgments as to whether the first or second slide had the greater density of dots within the central square. The instructions given to S led him to believe that the actual number of dots within the central square did in fact vary from slide to slide. In order to minimize the effects of dot pattern on recognition of a slide as having been seen earlier, the placement of the square slide in the projector was systematically rotated from trial to trial.

A total of 21 Ss completed the 84 judgments. For each S, each stimulus could have been chosen a total of 24 times, for that is the number of times each stimulus was presented as a member of a pair. If the context had no

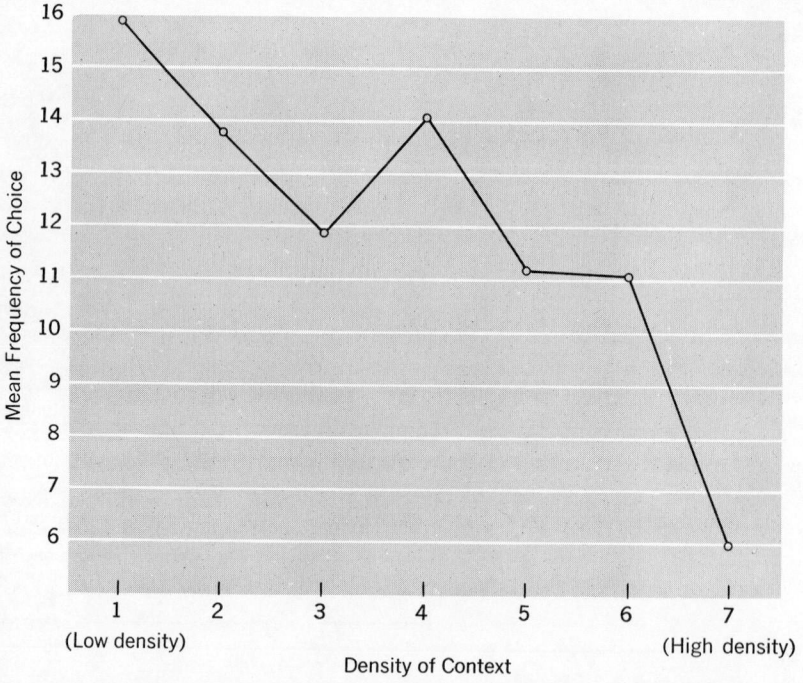

Fig. 6-2. A contrast effect. See text for complete explanation.

effect on the judgments—if S responded in a chance manner—each slide would have been chosen 12 times. If a contrast effect was present, the frequency with which the slides were chosen should differ, with Slide 1 being chosen most frequently and Slide 7, least frequently. As may be seen in Fig. 6-2, this is essentially what happened. The function is by no means regular, but across all seven slides there is clearly a decrease in frequency. Of course, what Fig. 6-2 shows is a correlation between two dimensions, namely, a negative correlation between the density of dots of the context and judgments of the density of dots in the central square.

In reading the procedure used in the above experiment, some may experience feelings of familiarity, as if such procedures had been discussed before. This probably results from the similarity of the procedures of the methods of constant stimuli used to measure difference thresholds and those outlined above for the method of paired comparisons. However, there is a difference. In the method of constant stimuli, a standard stimulus is paired with all variable stimuli in the series. In paired comparisons, each stimulus is paired with every other stimulus—there is no standard. Nevertheless, the results from the paired-comparisons procedure may be conceived of as measurements of a series of discriminability functions (with each stimulus a standard) in the same sense that the results from the method of constant stimuli is a discriminability function around a single standard.

CATEGORY SCALING

There are a number of different terms associated with category scaling. In certain forms of this scaling we speak of S's making an *absolute judgment* (as opposed to a relative judgment, which occurs in the methods of rank order and paired comparisons). The S makes judgments one at a time in succession, and, as a result, the term *single stimuli* has been associated with category scaling. Finally, *rating scales* represent a form of this type of scaling.

In category scaling, S sorts stimuli along a dimension defined by E. However, in its usual form, S places a given stimulus in one of a limited number of categories; that is, the dimension, although conceived of as continuous and with an infinite number of steps, is, in fact, broken into a restricted number of categories. Obviously, the limiting lower case is composed of two categories. There is no limiting upper case, although in practice it is rare to find more than 11 categories being used unless the number of categories is the independent variable. However, we see that E could merely identify two extremes of a dimension and then allow S to use as many categories as he wished, the number being determined by the fineness of the discrimination S believed he could make (Stevens & Galanter, 1957, Fig. 8D).

Some Illustrations

Food preferences. We will use a study by Peryam and Haynes (1957) as an initial illustration of category scaling. The Quartermaster Corps of the Army maintains a food and container institute laboratory in Chicago. Probably in no other single laboratory are the various psychophysical and scaling methods used so extensively with the intent of applying the results to the solution of practical problems. The particular topic of this study was food preferences. Basically, the question raised by these investigators concerned the applicability of laboratory findings to real-life situations. Rather than speculate about the matter, a direct test was made.

The twelve foods that were chosen for testing were of distinctly different types. Based on previous information, they were selected to represent a wide range of preference ratings (see Table 6-3). Two groups of Ss were used, each group being tested in different settings. The laboratory group consisted of 80 civilians employed at the institute, and the tests were carried out in secluded air-conditioned booths, quite apart from rooms in which the food was prepared. The other group was made up of 200 soldiers at Fort Lee, Virginia, and their tests were carried out with 50 Ss at a time seated in the regular dining room of the Fort. For both groups the tests were carried out at the same time in relation to regular mealtimes.

The tests were not abstract in nature, since S was actually presented samples of the food to eat prior to making his judgment. The same source supplied the food materials for the two tests, and the methods of preparing the food were equivalent. It would be expected that preferences for the foods might well differ as a function of number of other foods tested within a single period. Therefore, at a given sitting, S evaluated only three foods, returning on three following days to complete the evaluation of all 12. And of course, across all Ss, the order in which the different foods were rated was random. Between the eating and rating of one food and the rating of

TABLE 6–3

RATING SCALE AND MEAN RATINGS FOR 12 FOODS BY SOLDIERS
AND CIVILIANS. DATA FROM PERYAM AND HAYNES (1957).

Rating Scale	FOOD	CIVILIANS	SOLDIERS
__|__Like extremely	Meat Bar	3.62	2.46
__|__Like very much	Cabbage	5.15	4.26
__|__Like moderately	Milk	5.46	4.68
__|__Like slightly	Cheese Bar	5.69	3.48
__|__Neither like nor dislike	Sauerkraut	6.31	6.18
__|__Dislike slightly	Carrots	6.66	4.54
__|__Dislike moderately	Bread	6.75	6.50
__|__Dislike very much	Ham and Eggs	6.88	6.40
__|__Dislike extremely	Corned Beef	7.02	6.02
	Corn	7.14	7.38
	Salmon	8.08	7.12
	Peaches	8.43	8.23

another within a session, S took a drink of water to remove the residues of the previously eaten food.

The rating scale used in this study is shown in Table 6-3. Note that it is aligned vertically; frequently rating scales are presented horizontally. This is a nine-point scale, with each point given a descriptive rating. In making a rating, S simply checked one of the nine points to indicate his rating. In tabulating the data E assigned the values 1 through 9 to the nine points, with 1 being "dislike extremely." Finally, the mean ratings for each food were determined.

Table 6-3 shows that there is a high correspondence in the rank ordering of the stimuli, for the results of category scaling allow first a determination of the rank order of the stimuli. The product-moment correlation between the two sets of mean ratings is reported as .92, indicating that the civilian judges' tastes result in about the same relative preferences as do those of the soldiers. However, there is one difference. The mean scale value for all 12 items for the civilians is 6.43, whereas that for the soldiers is 5.61, indicating that the soldiers, on an absolute basis, disliked the foods as a whole more (or liked them less) than did the civilians.

Affectivity. As we will learn in more detail in later chapters, many studies of learning require the scaling of materials to be used in the experiment. For example, over many decades there have been experiments on the relationship between learning of words and their affective characteristics. Obviously, before such an experiment can be conducted, there must be a scaling of the affective responses elicited by words. That words will elicit different affective reactions is clear. The word *mother* will almost always elicit a pleasant rating; the word *vomit*, on the other hand, will inevitably elicit an "ugh" reaction. Since there is nothing intrinsically pleasant or unpleasant about the configuration of the letters in these two words as such, we must be responding to the meaning of the word. The writer asked 46 Ss to rate 100 adjectives along a pleasant-unpleasant dimension. A five-category scale was used, with the numbers 1 through 5 equally spaced along the scale. The label "unpleasant" was printed above the scale at the 1 end, "pleasant" at the 5 end, and "neutral" at 3. The Ss were asked to choose one of the five numbers as representing their reaction to the word. The mean category value for each word was calculated. Most people will probably find some agreement with the following words and mean values, ranging from unpleasant to pleasant: filthy, 1.1; stupid, 1.5; gaudy, 2.0; rigid, 2.5; pious, 3.0; astute, 3.5; slender, 4.0; cheery, 4.5; lovely, 4.8.

Loudness. The two illustrations above involved stimuli for which no physical scale was related to the judgments requested. We do not have a yardstick with which to measure the words and see how the judgments along the pleasant-unpleasant dimension correlate with this measurement.

But, of course, category scaling can be used when a physical scale is available. Without inquiring into the purpose of the experiment, we may look briefly at results presented by Galanter and Messick (1961) in order to illustrate the relationship between a physical dimension and category scaling of phenomenal experience related to the dimension.

By a noise generator, auditory stimuli having the same frequency components were presented at 20 different intensity levels varying from a low of 51.4 db. to a high of 88.0 db. Initially, E produced the softest stimulus and told Ss that this was to be called "1," and then produced the loudest stimulus and told Ss that this was to be called "11." All stimuli to be presented were to be assigned a number from the range 1 through 11. Each of the 20 stimuli was presented three times to 71 Ss, the order being different on each of the three series.

We should note that with certain types of stimuli, the same stimulus can be presented on several trials without S's being aware of the repetition. Such would seem to be the case in this experiment since to recognize a repetition would require absolute memory of loudness. When S is likely to recognize a stimulus as having been presented before, it is not considered wise to repeat it in scaling procedures. Why should this be? Essentially, the matter is one we might call *artificial reliability*. By presenting the same stimulus more than once to an S, we increase the reliability or stability of his judgments. Assume, however, that we repeated as stimuli the food items shown in Table 6-3. If S on the second presentation of one of the food items, remembers in which category he placed it on the first presentation, he may place it in the same category upon the second presentation merely to be consistent. Thus, even if upon second presentation he really reacted differently from the way he did upon the first presentation, he might still place it in the same category as he did the first time, if for no other reason than because he believed that E would not expect two different reactions. The consequence of this would be spurious reliability; S used the same category on successive trials but not necessarily because his reaction to the stimulus was equivalent on the two trials.

The results of the Galanter-Messick scaling are shown in Fig. 6-3. There is not a single reversal in the upward trend; each successive increase in intensity is accompanied by an increase in the mean category value. The relationship, however, is not quite linear since the weakest noises presented disturb the linear trend shown when the more intense stimuli are presented.

Anchoring and Frames of Reference

As a means of identifying the nature of the variable to be discussed in this section, let us return briefly to the experiment in which noises of different intensity were scaled. The Es in this experiment told the Ss that the loudest noise *within the series* was to be placed in category 11 and the softest, in category 1. These two stimuli were actually presented to the S for identification before judgments were made. Now let us change the instructions somewhat. We tell the Ss that their judgments are to be made along an 11-point scale in which category 11 is the *loudest* noise S has ever experienced, and category 1, the *weakest* noise that it is possible to hear. The range of intensities actually used was much less than the total range S has ever experienced. What will happen under these new instructions is, perhaps, obvious. All of the ratings will be bunched toward the center of

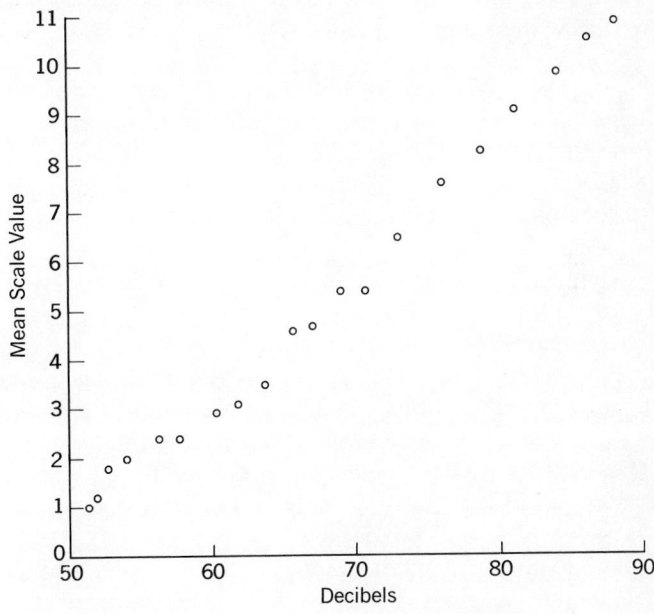

Fig. 6-3. Mean loudness scale values as a function of the intensity of noise. Data from Galanter and Messick (1961).

the scale; perhaps categories 1 through 4 and 8 through 11 would never be used. If so, this would leave only three categories (5, 6, and 7) for S to use. If S is not allowed to use fractional values, the resulting scale would be extremely insensitive. It would be insensitive in the sense that it would not be capable of fully reflecting S's discriminal abilities. Consider another case. We present the loudest noise in the series and tell S that this noise will be called 11 but that noises weaker than this are to be judged with reference to all possible weaker noises. The effect of this would be the use of only the upper part of the scale, perhaps only the upper half, for again we have *anchored* the bottom end to the softest noise S has ever experienced. By use of anchoring stimuli, we are changing S's *frame of reference;* we are changing the context limits within which the judgments are to be made.

Described in terms of experimental procedures, the study of anchoring in category scaling has taken two forms. First, for different groups of Ss different ranges of stimuli are used, with all Ss being required to use the same category scale to reflect their judgments. Second, Ss are given experience in sorting the stimuli of a given range of values along a scale following which the range is extended. In both procedures, of course, the effects of the different ranges are noted by examining the scale values of the stimuli. We will illustrate both methods.

Width of rectangles. In a study by Fillenbaum (1963) the stimuli were seven rectangles, all of which had the same height but varied in breadth. The height was 25 cm., and the seven different breadths were 5.00, 5.56, 6.17, 6.87, 7.62, 8.45, and 9.36 cm. We might think of the rectangles as columns of equal height but varying in width. The Ss were instructed to judge the slimness of the rectangles along a five-point scale, with 1 being *very slim*, 2 *slim*, 3 *medium*, 4 *broad*, and 5 *very broad*. The treatments given four groups will be examined.

No anchor: The Ss in this group were given only the seven basic stimuli.

Slim anchor: In addition to judging the seven basic stimuli, the Ss were also presented an eighth rectangle, whose width was 4.05 cm. It was presented twice as frequently as the seven basic stimuli.

Broad anchor: The procedure was exactly the same as for the slim-anchor group except that the extra rectangle was broader than any in the series, being 11.11 cm. in width.

Double anchor: For this group, both the broad and slim anchors were added to the basic seven stimuli, but each was presented with the same frequency as the seven stimuli.

In presenting the stimuli, block randomization was used, and a total of 140 ratings was given by each S. However, in order to work with data only after the ratings had become stabilized, Fillenbaum used only the last 100 judgments (approximately). There were 40 Ss in the no-anchor group and 21 in each of the other three. Just how the Ss were assigned to the various groups is not clear from the report.

The mean scale values as related to the width of the seven basic rectangles are shown in Fig. 6-4. The results for the group with no anchor are to be considered the control against which the effects of the anchoring in the other conditions may be assessed. The slim anchor increased the scale values for all stimuli, but the effect was greatest at the low end. The broad anchor had very little effect at the low end but decreased the scale values at the high end. The double anchor essentially combined the effects of the slim and broad anchor taken individually. With the double anchor the range of mean scale values is greatly restricted. For the control, the mean scale values for the slimmest and broadest rectangles are 1.3 and 4.2, respectively, for a range of 2.9. As a consequence of the double anchor, however, the corresponding end points are 1.9 and 3.4, for a range of 1.5. Clearly, the an-

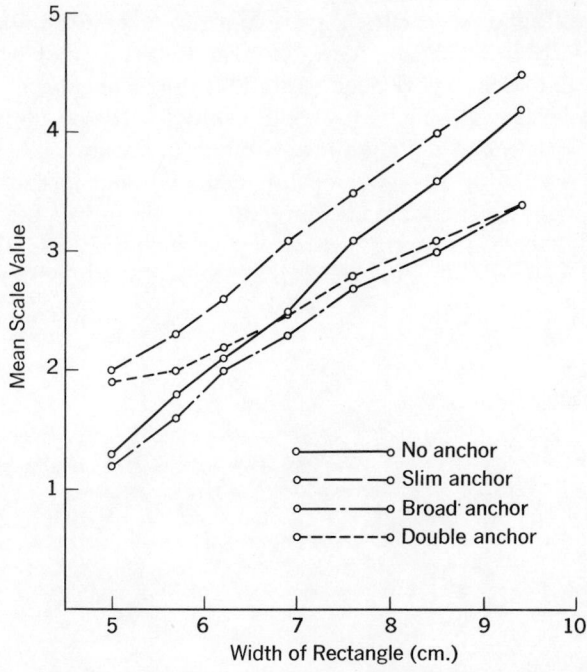

Fig. 6-4. The effect of various anchoring conditions on the judgments of width of rectangles having constant heights. See text for description of conditions. Data from Fillenbaum (1963).

chors provide quite different frames of reference for the various groups.

Affective tone of colors. Next we may consider a procedure wherein E builds up a particular frame of reference in S via a series of judgments and then introduces a new stimulus (an anchor) as a means of changing the frame of reference. In a study by Hunt and Volkmann (1937), 5 Ss judged the pleasantness and unpleasantness of colors along a seven-point scale. High numbers were used for the pleasant end of the scale, and low, for the unpleasant. The Ss were not told that the most pleasant color in the series was to be assigned the number *seven* nor the most unpleasant color, *one,* but neither were they told not to do this. However, the Ss did use the full range for the colors actually shown them, as seen by the fact that the most pleasant color had a mean scale rating of almost *seven* after 10 judgments on each of 10 colors and the most unpleasant color had a mean scale rating of nearly *one*.

After the initial series of judgments, Ss were given instructions to think of the most pleasant color they had ever seen and to hold this in mind as having a rating of *seven*. In the second series if they actually judged a color as having a value of *seven*, it would mean that this color was as pleasant as any they had ever experienced. Note that this is anchoring only at one end of the scale, like the anchoring in the study discussed above where a slim rectangle or a broad rectangle was used as an anchor.

The results for the series of judgments without instructional anchoring and following instructional anchoring are shown in Fig. 6-5. At the pleasant end of the scale, the introduction of the anchor clearly shifted the scale values downward, affecting the values for five of the colors at the pleasant end of the scale.

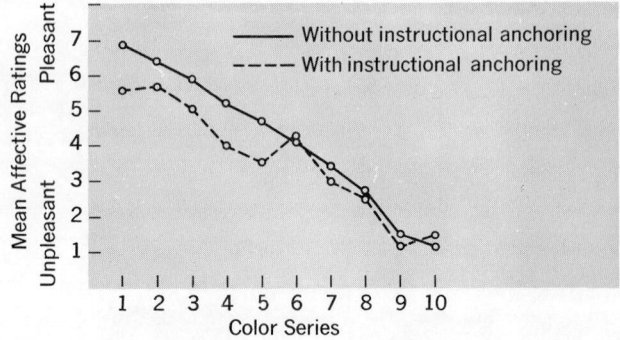

Fig. 6-5. An anchoring effect in the judgment of the affective tone of colors produced by specific instructions. Data from Hunt and Volkmann (1937).

Certain aspects of the Hunt-Volkmann procedure need further examination. The data may contain components of artificial reliability, as discussed earlier. In the initial series each stimulus was presented for 10 times. After a given color was presented a time or two, it is quite likely that S remembered the category to which he had earlier assigned the color and, therefore, subsequently always assigned it to that category. However, for this particular study the multiple judgments in the initial series works to an advantage. We note that a control group was not used; that is, a group of Ss that continued rating the stimuli in a second series *without* being given anchoring instructions was not used. Thus, we might suggest that the change in the ratings in the second series would have occurred without instructional anchoring since there is no control group to deny this possibility. It would appear highly unlikely, however, that such changes would occur if the Ss were, in fact, sorting a given color into a given category because they remembered that they had placed it in that category on earlier trials. Indeed, it is quite possible that the failure of the anchor introduced at the pleasant end of the scale to affect the ratings of colors at the other end may be attributed to memory for categories. It was as if at a certain point the anchor no longer had an influence, and, rather than a gradual convergence of the curves in Fig. 6-5, there is a sudden "coming together." At this point S sorts the colors into the same categories (by memory), as was true on the first series.

In the Hunt-Volkmann study, anchoring was introduced at only one end. It is, of course, quite possible to use their procedures (preliminary series followed by anchoring) and to use double anchors. For example, McGarvey (1943) had Ss rate a series of "behaviors" along a six-point scale from most desirable to least desirable. These behaviors were such events as: *fishing without a license, poisoning a neighbor's dog whose barking bothered you, killing an idiot baby, manufacturing counterfeit money,* and so on. Following an initial series of ratings for 12 such events, Ss were provided anchoring events at both ends of the scale, the anchor at the least desirable end being still less desirable than any of the 12 events, and the anchor at the desirable end being more desirable than any of the 12 events. The results were as expected and much the same as those found by Fillenbaum in the rating of rectangles, namely, a restriction in the range of the scale values in the second rating as compared with the first.

Anchoring effects are sometimes called contrast effects; it is as if the introduction of a new stimulus beyond the series being rated produces a contrast with these old stimuli and "shoves" the old toward the center of the scale. Some investigators (Sherif, Taub, & Hovland, 1958) have reported an opposite effect (assimilation) under special circumstances, although others have argued (Parducci & Marshall, 1962) that such results are merely a special case of contrast. We will not get involved in these rather subtle matters. For our purposes, it is enough to know the general experimental procedures used in manipulating anchors and to know that they may have a rather profound effect on results obtained in category scaling.

SOME COMPARISONS

The presentation of the various scaling methods will be interrupted briefly in order to make some comparisons of the results produced by two of the methods already discussed. Comparisons of results produced by different scaling methods may be made at several levels. At the "highest" level, E will be interested in comparing the precise mathematical statements expressing the relationships among the stimuli as measured by a physical scale and the psychological or phenomenal scale values. At a less sophisticated level, a comparison may be made of the rank orders of stimuli resulting from different scaling procedures. It is at this latter level that the present discussion is conducted.

For a number of years the writer has asked the members of his course in experimental psychology to make a comparison of the rank ordering of stimuli resulting from various scaling techniques. The procedures and results of one recent class will be discussed. Each member of the class was required to select his own stimuli and to carry out his own experiment. In this particular class each student was to provide at least 10 stimuli but no more than 12, and each was to have his stimuli "evaluated" by the method of rank order and by category scaling (using a seven-point scale). An independent group of Ss was to be used for each method. For the category scaling, the frame of reference was to be "all such stimuli with which the S had had experience." In addition, each S was to use one or more additional groups in testing the influence of some variable on category scaling. We will not be concerned with this latter requirement.

It may seem, offhand, that setting up an experiment like this would be relatively easy in the sense that it would be difficult to make an error in design. Yet, there are several troublesome points.

1. It is quite possible to choose stimuli in which the judgments may be confounded by extraneous or peripheral variables. For example, silverware patterns is one of the favorite choices of women students (whose single status apparently has only a short term to run). The usual procedure is to cut pictures of various patterns from magazines and then mount them on cardboard. Unfortunately, the silverware patterns are often placed on different backgrounds in magazines; one pattern might have a blue background, another a pink. It seems quite possible that S, although requested to judge only the patterns, might be influenced by the background.

One student once brought the front pages of several newspapers. He was interested in having his Ss judge the attractiveness of various headline types appearing on the front page. But this student left the mastheads intact, and some of his newspapers were published in Chicago where feelings are fairly strong for and against certain dailies. The judgment of the type might be influenced by the S's attitude toward the newspaper.

A student interested in having Ss judge the liking for various perfumes brought the various stimuli in the regular commercial bottles complete with trade names. Of course, the Ss may have preformed likes and dislikes for perfumes put out by certain establishments so that using these bottles would not allow an independent judgment at the moment.

2. Since a random-groups design is used, the student must set up a

procedure whereby the groups will not be expected to differ on any relevant characteristic. The student "picks up" his own Ss, usually at the student union; his scheme for placing the Ss in the two (or more) groups must be carefully worked out. Usually, a form of block randomization has been used.

3. In presenting the stimuli for category judgment there may be differences produced by the order in which the stimuli are presented to S. Indeed, there is some evidence (e.g., Willingham, 1958; Kamenetzki, 1959; Parducci, 1959) of within-series effects that are very much like contrast effects. If one extreme stimulus is presented for judgment just before a stimulus at the other extreme is presented, the judgment of the second may differ from what would be obtained if it followed one of about equal value. Therefore, Ss within the group using category scaling should have the stimuli presented in different order. The student usually handles this problem by constructing several random orders ahead of time and rotating his Ss on the orders.

Sample stimuli and results. To determine the degree of agreement of the rank orders resulting from the two methods, the rank-order correlation has been used. The stimuli used and the rank-order correlations obtained by the students in this class are shown in Table 6-4. Most of the correlations would be judged statistically significant, although several are far from what we would consider satisfactory if the two scaling methods are presumed to be measuring the same thing. However, one reason for doing such an experiment is to attempt to make the point that we must not automatically conclude that the two scaling methods "get at" different things if the correlation between the rank orders of the stimuli is low. What are the relevant factors which must be considered before reaching a conclusion that the two methods do not produce equivalent results?

First, of course, we must consider the possibility that either method, taken by itself and repeated on two different groups of Ss, might give correlations which are no higher than those obtained by comparing the results for two different methods. This is to say, then, that if we attribute a low correlation between the rank order produced by the two methods, we implicitly assume that the rank ordering by each scale is in itself perfectly reliable. In the above experiment we did not determine directly the reliability of each method. But there are internal checks which can be made and to which we will return in a moment. It should be noted that our interest here is in the consistency or reliability of the rank ordering of the stimuli along the scale. What might prevent a consistent rank ordering of a set of stimuli if the same method were used on two different groups of Ss for these stimuli?

The two groups of Ss could differ on characteristics that would lead to different rank orders. However, we presume that the groups were not statistically different since the Ss were assigned to the conditions by a random method. Still, some minor differences in rank order could be accounted for by this factor.

The most important factor to consider is the amount by which the stimuli differ, with particular attention paid to those which appear to be judged very much alike on the particular characteristic being scaled. Equivalent (or nearly equivalent) scale values or ranks may result from two distinctly different mechanisms. First, there may be wide differences among the stimuli

TABLE 6–4

STIMULI USED AND RANK-ORDER CORRELATIONS OF THE RANK ORDER OF THE STIMULI AS DETERMINED BY THE METHOD OF RANK ORDER AND BY CATEGORY SCALING

STIMULI	CORRELATION
Characteristics important for selecting a close friend, e.g., good-natured, trustworthy, wealthy	.95
Women's shoes; all the shoes had very similar styling but differed widely in color and decoration. Real shoes, not pictures	.88
Judged intelligence of people in different occupations, e.g., doctor, politician, nurse, janitor	.96
Preferences among 10 American authors	.78
Preference for various brands of cigarettes; brand names were on cards	.56
Prestige of various occupations; two different studies	.83 and 1.0
The "coolness" of certain habits at the present time, e.g., wearing sun glasses, going to foreign films, riding in sports cars, reading Sartre, playing a guitar	.65
Humor of limericks	.62
Preferences for 10 different breeds of dogs	.94
Academic excellence of Big Ten colleges	.85
Aesthetic attractiveness of various geometrical forms	.73
Cleverness of birthday cards	.82
Liking for 12 different contemporary musical artists	.90
Degree of applicability of common sayings to everyday life	.90
Liking for prints of well-known art works	.83
Preferences for silverware patterns	.79

for each S, but the differences are not the same (not stereotyped) among Ss. For example, we note in Table 6-4 that preference scaling among cigarettes produced quite a low correlation between the ranks for the two methods. It is possible that this results from the fact that by either method there are not clear *mean* differences among the brands. This may come about because one S has a strong preference for Brand A over Brand B, whereas the next S has an equally strong preference for Brand B over Brand A. The result for both Ss combined would be equivalent values for both brands, this in spite of the fact that each S judges the brands to be distinctly different.

The second way in which nearly equivalent scale values may be obtained is the obvious one; two or more stimuli are judged to be essentially equivalent by all Ss. If all perfumes smelled the same to the Ss, their forced rank orders would be relatively meaningless, and they would assign all perfumes nearly equivalent values in category scaling. It is quite possible to determine statistically whether two or more stimuli do or do not differ in scale value. If several such stimuli are not significantly different, their rank orders are essentially chance rank orders and would be expected to differ appreciably for another group of Ss even if ranked by the same method. Correlations between two methods cannot be expected to be high if a number of the stimuli do not differ appreciably.

We have noted that there are two routes by which stimuli may produce about the same value on the scale: (1) each S clearly rates them differently, but there is no stereotyping among Ss so that the group means indicate equal judgments of the stimuli; (2) the Ss may agree on the location of each stimulus on the scale, but several are judged to have the same value. How could we distinguish which of these two factors is responsible for two (or more) stimuli receiving about the same scale values (hence, unreliable rank orders)? Measures of variability of scale values have great worth at this point. It can be seen that if the first alternative applies, the variability of the scale values for a stimulus must be large. If one S likes Stimulus A very much and dislikes Stimulus B very much, and if another S has just the opposite opinion, the range of scale values for each will be essentially the range of the scale. On the other hand, if the second alternative is most appropriate, the variability in placement among Ss will be relatively small.

Again, we must repeat ourselves; we must allow any set of data to tell us all it can by slicing it in several different ways and thereby testing out alternative hypotheses. To obtain a relatively low correlation among the ranks derived by two different methods does not immediately tell us that the two methods are measuring things differently. First we must make certain that ranking of the stimuli by each method taken individually is reliable. The ideal way of doing this is to test two equivalent groups on the same stimuli by the same method. But apparent failure of reliability even by this technique must be viewed with caution, for it may simply mean that some of the stimuli are not reliably different. Therefore, even by using two different methods, as the students did in producing the results shown in Table 6-4, much can be learned about the reliability of the judgment of differences among particular stimuli. If these differences are found to be small, it is a reasonable conclusion that this is behind the apparent low agreement (which occurred in some instances in Table 6-4) in sorting the stimuli by the two methods. Only if a set of stimuli was shown to have reliable differences between adjacent stimuli as we proceed up the scale, and this was shown for both methods, then, and only then, would we conclude that the two methods were getting at something different if the correlation between the rank orders produced by the two scales was low. It is quite unlikely that such a low correlation would be found under such circumstances.

One final word, relating to matters somewhat more psychological in nature, must be spoken. Occasionally, such exercises as those producing the data in Table 6-4 eventuate in some rather remarkable findings. In another class, where the results of two different scaling methods were compared (one of which we have not discussed as yet), a student brought 12 pictures of women who were unknown to the Ss. The Ss were asked to rate each woman on her fitness as the first woman President of the United States. The correlation between the ranks resulting from the two scaling methods was .75. This must mean that there are some fairly standard or stereotyped notions concerning the attributes needed by a woman to be President and that the different degrees of the attributes are inferred from the pictures in a very similar manner by all Ss. Perhaps we should not be surprised by such results. We know from other work that whether or not a person wears glasses influences the judgments of others concerning his intelligence. The same person wearing glasses when appearing before one group of judges and not wearing them before another group was judged to be more intelligent by the first group (Thornton, 1944). We know further that judges differ in their assessment of some personality traits of girls depending upon whether the girls are or are not wearing lipstick (McKeachie, 1952). Such results must indicate that we all respond in some uniform manner to certain subtle cues even when the judgment required need not be *logically* based on these cues.

EQUAL-INTERVAL METHODS

Thus far in presenting the scaling methods we have been concerned primarily with sorting stimuli so that a rank order of these stimuli could be determined. In category scaling, of course, we also calculated scale values, and there are probably grounds for making decisions concerning differences in magnitude of differences between various stimuli depending upon the scale distance involved. Thus, if Stimulus A, ranked first, is given a scale value of 6.9 on a 7-point scale, and Stimuli B and C, ranked second and third, respectively, have scale values of 4.5 and 4.0, we might well conclude that A and B differ more than do B and C. Yet, essentially, we have only an ordinal, rank-order scale, with no precise information about the meaning of the magnitude of the differences separating the ranks. As already noted, there are procedures by which results from, for instance, a paired-comparison experiment can be translated into scale units which are presumably equal phenomenally (Guilford, 1954; Torgerson, 1958). But there are more direct methods of establishing equal-interval scales, and it is to these that attention is turned in the present section. To a large extent, we will minimize the discussion of the nature of the scales that result from the various techniques and emphasize, rather, the problems presented the Ss in order to bring out the remarkable flexibility and capacity of the human being in producing the judgments.

In category scaling, as discussed in the preceding section, E may request S to view the various points on the scale as representing equal psychological or phenomenal differences and to rate the stimuli accordingly. As a matter of fact, even when such instructions are not given, it is quite possible that S makes assumptions about the equality of units. Suppose one does instruct S that the scale units are to be considered equal psychological units. Are we then to assume that the difference between two stimuli with scale values of 5 and 6 differ by the same amount as do two stimuli with scale values of 6 and 7? We might assert that these are equal because we have instructed Ss to consider the units on the scale equal, but we have no way of telling from a single set of data whether or not they are "really" equal.

Equal-appearing intervals. We illustrate this method by citing the work of Stevens and Volkmann (1940). Two pure tones, 200 and 6500 cps, were presented; and in addition, three variable tones were available to S. The task assigned S was that of setting the three variable tones so that the "sense distance"—the pitch distance—between 200 and 6500 cps was divided into four equal phenomenal units. One might think of this as first bisecting the total distance with one of the variable tones, and then bisecting each of the two halves with the remaining two variable tones. The 10 Ss were given a number of trials, with the mean setting of the three variable tones being taken as the best estimate of the division points. A schematic drawing of the results is shown in Fig. 6-6. In this drawing the "distance"

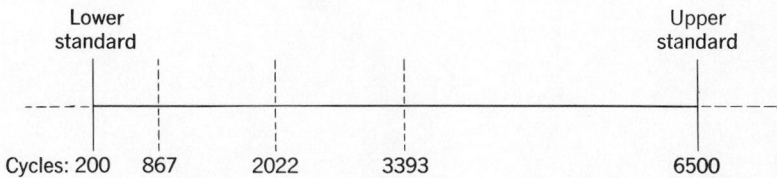

Fig. 6-6. The quadrisection of a sense distance. Ss were presented with two standard tones, 200 and 6500 cycles, and were asked to break the total pitch distance into four equal parts by setting three variable tones. Ss judged 2022 cycles to bisect the total distance, and judged 867 and 3393 cycles to bisect the lower and upper halves respectively. Data from Stevens and Volkmann (1940).

between 200 and 6500 cps is depicted, with the vertical dashed lines indicating the points at which the total distance was divided so that the four resulting smaller differences represent equal phenomenal pitch distances.

How would we construct a pitch scale which has greater generality than that for the four intervals actually judged to be equal? To do this we would plot the physical scale along the baseline, making the four frequency spans correspond to the equal phenomenal units which are plotted along the ordinate. Common logarithms were used for the abscissa, and the resulting plot is shown in Fig. 6-7. Now, presumably, if we take any two equal subsegments from the ordinate, determine the range in cps represented by each (by crossing horizontally to the curve and dropping vertically to the baseline), and then actually present these two spans to S, he would judge them equal.

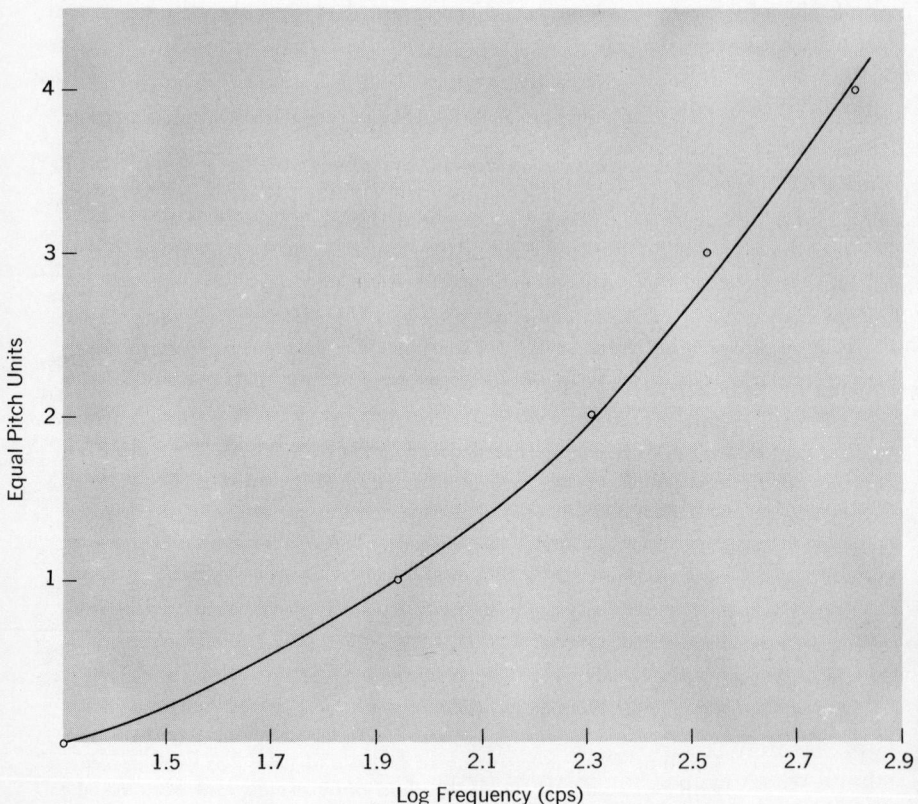

Fig. 6-7. Relationship between frequency and pitch, with the pitch units equal. The zero of the ordinate is not to be taken as zero pitch; it is a zero reference point (200 cps) for the total sense distance used here. Data from Stevens and Volkmann (1940).

Suppose we ask S, in the above experiment, to bisect further each of the four spans, then bisect each of the resulting eight spans, and so on. Eventually, we would reach a point where we had divided the total sense distance into the smallest unit detectable by S, and we could see that this would be a difference threshold—a DL. Thus, the ultimate in the reduction of a given sense dimension—the reduction to the smallest usable unit—would be a scale in which the units were DLs.

Technically speaking, the scale resulting from coordinating the axes in Fig. 6-7 is an *interval scale*. An interval scale is one in which there is an arbitrary origin, and the scale units above this origin are said to be equal. In the above graph, the arbitrary origin is 200 cps. It becomes apparent, therefore, that we might construct such a scale for stimuli which cannot be measured along a physical scale. Suppose, for example, we brought together 30 or 40 trait or aptitude names, such as intelligence, sense of humor, clerical ability, ability to concentrate, and mathematical aptitude. By the method of rank order we have determined that among college students intelligence is the trait held in highest esteem and clerical ability is the one held in lowest esteem. We present the following situation to S. We provide a pictured linear scale with 11 equal divisions on it. At the right end we place the trait of intelligence, and at the left end, clerical aptitude. From among the remaining traits S is to pick out one which he believes is just halfway between clerical aptitude and intelligence in terms of esteem. Then he picks traits which bisect the remaining two distances, and so on. In effect, what we are doing is establishing an interval scale. Very likely, these formalized successive bisections are probably what S does less formally when we require him to consider the units of the scale equal in category scaling. Note that if we carried out the above procedure the origin of the scale becomes quite arbitrary in that we decided that clerical aptitude would be the anchor point at the bottom end of the scale.

There is still a third type of scale, which is at a "higher" level than either the ordinal scale or the interval scale. This is called a *ratio scale* and differs from the interval scale only in that the origin is at a true zero point. What do we mean by true zero? In the case of physical scales, this is quite apparent; zero length has meaning, as does zero weight. What would a true zero point on a psychological scale be? If there is a corresponding physical scale to which the psychological scale can be coordinated, true zero might be placed at the level of the absolute threshold. In the case of pitch, this is approximately 20 cps. But what would be a true zero for a characteristic of stimuli which cannot be measured by an available physical scale? In recent years there have been some attempts to arrive at a zero value for such characteristics (Thurstone & Jones, 1959). Let us examine the logic of such attempts.

An interval scale is presumed to possess the property of *additivity*. On physical scales this is obvious. If we put two sticks, each 1 ft. in length, end to end and then measure the resulting total distance, it will be 2 ft. To say that intervals on a scale are equal means that a direct comparison of so-called equal units at different points on the scale will show them to be equal in fact. In the Thurstone-Jones procedure, this property of additivity is used to try to determine a zero point. Let us assume we have two objects, A and B (among several others), which represent gifts that S might like to receive. By a scaling procedure we derive a scale of equal intervals representing how much S would like to receive each object as a gift. Let us say that Gift A has a scale value of 2 and Gift B, a scale value of 3 on a 9-point scale. We now present S both A and B and ask him to consider them as a single gift and to rate it on the scale. If S gives the combined stimulus a value of 5, we would consider the scale to be additive (if, of course, such addition held up over various combinations of stimuli). But, if the scale is additive when gauged in this fashion, it must also mean that a zero point is set, for, phenomenally, S appeared to be adding 2 and 3 together when he gave the combined stimulus a rating of 5. The zero point would be one unit below the 1 point on the scale. Actually, some success has been achieved with such procedures (e.g., Hicks, 1962).

Division and multiplication. In the method of equal-appearing intervals, S clearly divides a given sense distance in half. This bisection procedure can be used by presenting S a single stimulus and requesting that he produce one which is half the magnitude—a stimulus which has half as much of the characteristic as the stimulus presented. If a number of different stimuli are given, with division requested in each case, a scale can be constructed on the basis of the equal units which are presumed to result when these half judgments are given. Another attack would be to have S multiply a stimulus so as to produce another stimulus which is twice as great. There is no reason why S could not be asked to multiply a stimulus so that the obtained one will be three times as great or four times as great.

Such procedures have usually been limited to stimuli which can be measured along a physical scale. However, one study used a unique characteristic and related it to a scale of dollars. In this study (Galanter, 1962), one group of Ss was told to assume that they were to be given an outright gift of $10. Obviously, such a gift would produce a certain degree of happiness. The Ss were then asked to estimate how much money they would have to receive to be twice as happy as they were when they received $10. For another group, the base gift was $100, and they were asked to say how much would make them twice as happy as the degree of happiness produced by a gift of $100. For a third group, the base was $1000. The Ss had difficulty making these decisions, but with some "pushing" by E, all Ss did produce a figure. There were 20 Ss in each group. For the base of $10, a median of $45 was given as the amount needed to make S twice as happy; for $100, a median of $350 was required to double the happiness; and for $1000, $5000 was required. From these data Galanter constructed a scale which he called a utility function for money and for which the unit was called "utiles." Apparently he preferred this to a happiness function in which the units would have been "haps."

Ratio judgments. As another somewhat different procedure, E may present S two stimuli which differ on some specified characteristic and ask S to specify how much greater magnitude of the characteristic is possessed by the greater of the two stimuli or what fraction is the smaller of the larger. A variation on the method is known as the *constant-sum method.* Here S is presented two stimuli and is asked to divide 100 points into two parts, the parts reflecting the ratio of the two stimuli. If two stimuli appeared equal, each would be assigned 50 points; if one appeared three times as great as the other, the points would be assigned 25:75. Usually, with the application of this method, the procedure is exactly the same as with paired comparisons. Each stimulus is paired with every other stimulus, and S makes the decision as to the division of the points for each pairing. We will examine one study in which the pairing was incomplete but which will provide us a "feel" for the manner in which the data are handled.

Baker and Dudek (1957) used 11 lines of different lengths and presented them to S via lantern slides. The actual line lengths are unimportant since the ratios of the 10 longer lines to the shortest line are given. The longest line had a ratio of 36 to 1 to the shortest line. If the shortest line was 1 in., the longest was 36 in. In each case the shortest line appeared on every slide with one of the longer lines. Each slide was presented for 30 sec., during which time S was to divide 100 points so as to reflect the ratios of the lines being shown. Each S was given 20 trials; on 10 of the trials the shortest line appeared above the longer one, and on 10 trials it appeared below.

In analyzing the data, the E, summing across all 49 Ss, first determined the total points assigned each of the 10 lines. Obviously, the line assigned the greatest number of points is the one judged longest and that with the smallest number, the shortest. Then the Es determined the ratio between the total points assigned the shortest line and the total points assigned to each of the other lines. These ratios, therefore, represent the group reflection of the ratio judgments as requested for each slide during the presentation. The relationship between the resulting scale and the actual physical length is shown in Fig. 6-8. The shortest line on both scales is arbitrarily set at 1. The diagonal in this graph shows what the relationship would be if there were a one-to-one correspondence between the two scales. Obviously, the psychological length does not increase in a one-to-one relationship to the physical length; as physical length increases, the underestimations become greater and greater.

MAGNITUDE ESTIMATION

We turn next to one final method of scaling, a method that is used for equal-interval scaling and is presumed to result in certain instances in a ratio scale. However, since it is almost a unique method and since it has been used to produce a new psychophysical law, it deserves somewhat detailed consideration. To say it is unique as a method is really not true, for, as will be seen, it has grown out of the other methods. As a scaling method, it appears to give the S the greatest freedom of all the

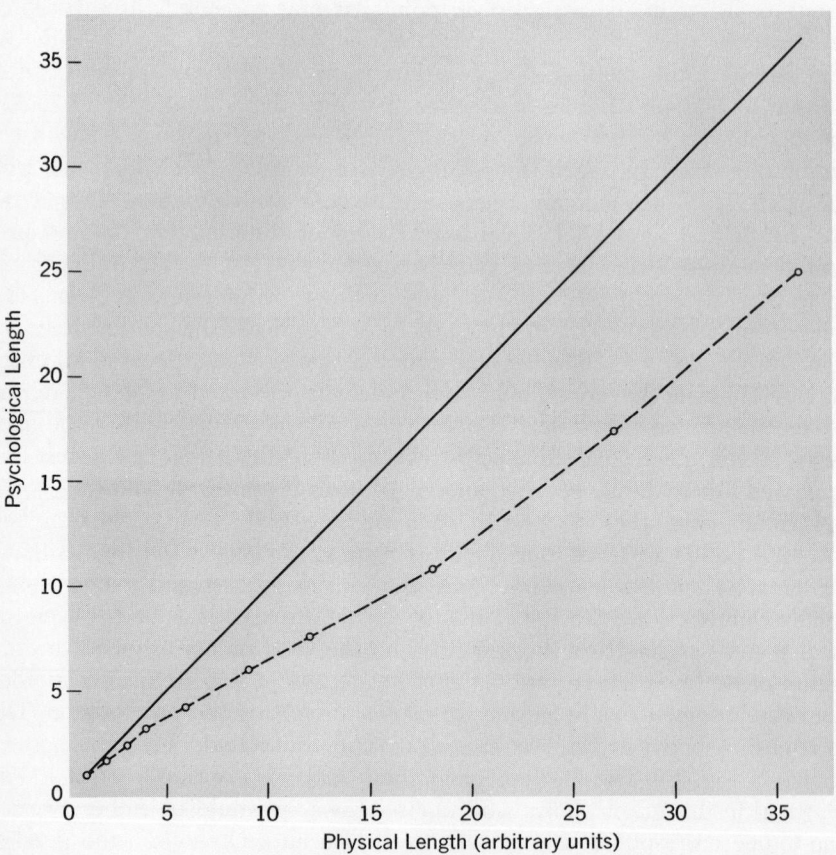

Fig. 6-8. Relationship between physical length of line and psychological length. The solid line indicates a one-to-one relationship, the dotted line, the relationship actually obtained. Data from Baker and Dudek (1957).

methods and may be more resistant than others to anchoring and related effects.

The modern development of the method is attributed to Stevens (1956). In the "freest" form of magnitude estimation, S responds to stimuli by assigning them numbers. The only restriction given by the instructions is that the numbers given to various stimuli should reflect the differences among the stimuli. In the initial experiments reported by Stevens, loudness judgments were used. The Ss were told that after tones of different loudnesses were presented they were to assign numbers representing these various loudnesses. And then, "Try to make the ratios between the numbers you assign to the different tones correspond to the ratios between the loudnesses of the tones. In other words, try to make the numbers proportional to the loudness, as *you* hear it." (p. 20)

The Ss had to assign a number to the first tone presented. Among the 26 Ss these numbers varied from 1 to 100, with 10 being the most popular. There were eight tones, differing in intensity, and each was presented twice to each S. The intensities of the 8 tones varied from 40 db. through 110 db., in 10-db. steps.

In handling the data, Stevens first reduced the number series used by the different Ss to a common reference point. To do this he averaged the two numbers assigned a given tone by S. (It will be remembered that each tone of a given intensity was presented twice.) Then he used a multiplier to reduce the value for the 80-db. tone to a value of 10. If for one S the average value assigned the 80-db. tone was 5, it was multiplied by 2; if for another S the average value assigned this intensity was 30, it was multiplied by .33. The average value for all other intensities for a given S was also reduced (or increased) by multiplying by the number necessary to produce a value of 10 for the 80-db. tone. Thus, for each intensity there was a series of 26 values, one for each S, and the median was used as the measure of central tendency.

The results of this experiment are plotted in two ways in Fig. 6-10. In the upper curve the median values are plotted against db., a logarithmic scale. The relationship is a smooth one and tells us that as intensity increases in equal logarithmic steps, there is a disproportionate increase in the differences between successive medians. We speak of such a curve as being concave upward. In the lower part of Fig. 6-10, we have plotted the same results in a slightly different manner. We have retained the log scale for the abscissa and have translated the median judgments into a log scale. (The medians were all first multiplied by 10 to avoid negative logarithms.) When the log of the median judgments is used, it appears that we have a linear relationship; equal log steps in db. are accompanied by equal loudness steps when expressed in logs. Such a log-log plot reflects a *power function,* and we will return to the implications of this function at a later point in the chapter.

As noted earlier, the above data were collected by the method of magnitude estimation as applied in its freest form. Indeed, in our laboratory we usually speak of it as "free scaling." Somewhat less freedom is allowed S when a restriction is used which consists of assigning a number (by E) to a given stimulus in the series. Thus, in scaling loudness, E might present an

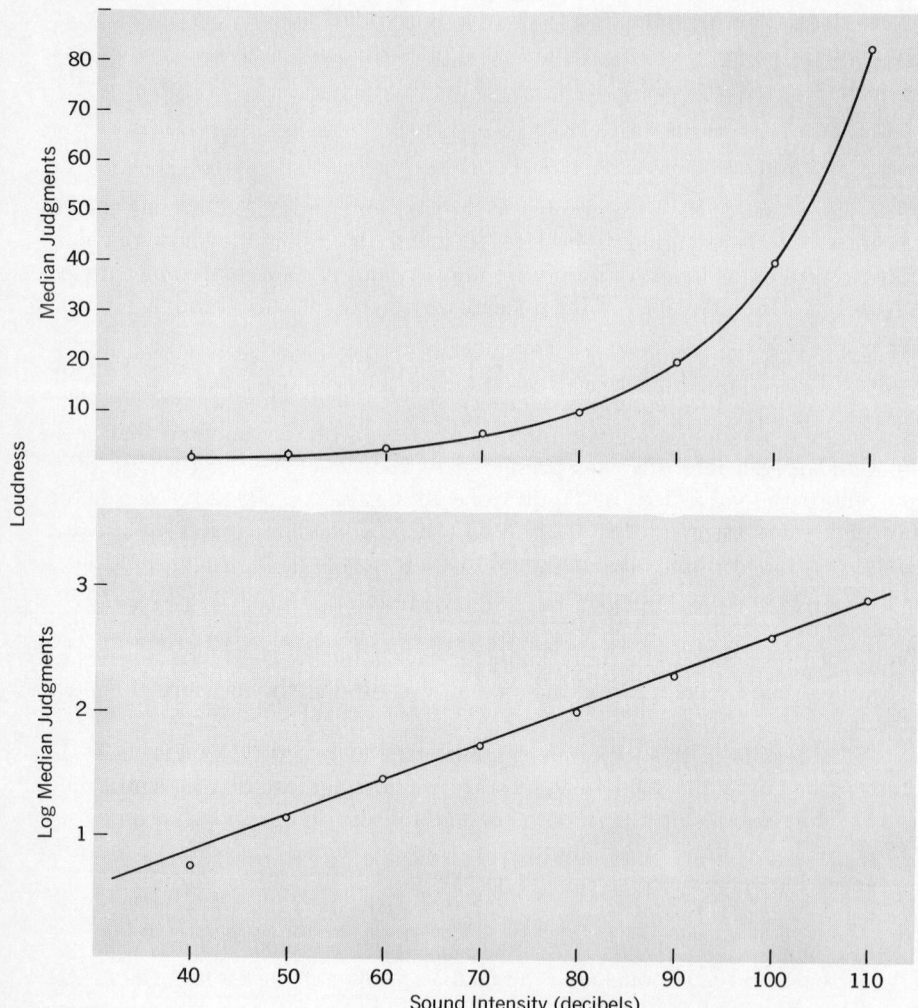

Fig. 6-9. The relationship between sound intensity and loudness as determined by the method of magnitude estimation. The data are the same in both plots, the only difference being that the ordinate in the upper curve is plotted on an arithmetic scale, while in the lower one it is plotted on a log scale. Data from Stevens (1956).

80-db. tone and inform S that this tone is to be given a loudness value of 100. In this case, this standard is always available to S throughout the judgmental series so that he can repeatedly "check" to determine the loudness of this tone which he must always think of as having a value of 100. By either the completely free method or the partially restricted method, the loudness scale remains much the same (Stevens & Tulving, 1957).

The restricted form of magnitude estimation may be illustrated by moving to quite a different judgmental task. This study was conducted by the writer with 78 Ss quite naive to scaling of any kind. They were given a sheet on which 72 three-letter words were listed. At the top of the sheet the following instructions were printed:

'A number of three-letter words are listed below. For these words we want you to think about how *frequently* each appears in *print*. That is, how frequently

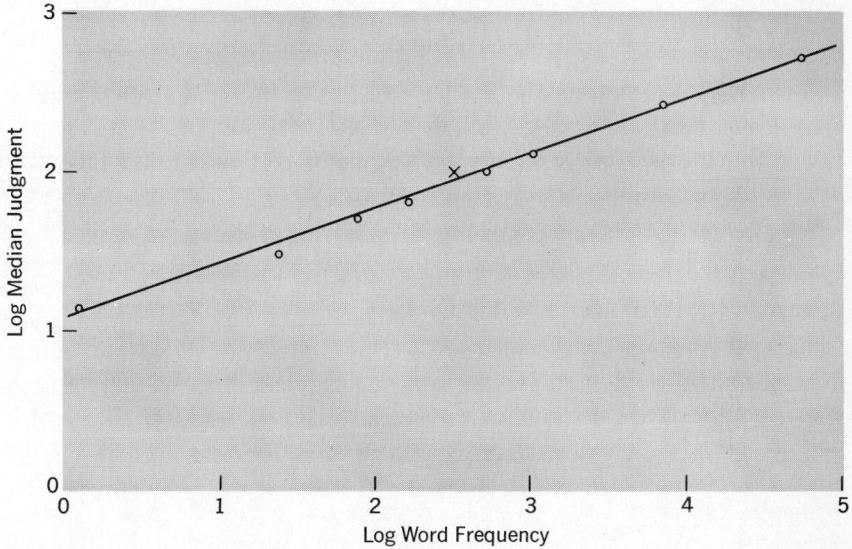

Fig. 6-10. The relationship between word frequency and judged frequency as determined by the method of magnitude estimation. The x represents the "anchor" words assigned a value of 100.

does each appear in books, magazines, newspapers, and so on. We are *not* interested in the frequency with which the words are spoken by you or by others; we are interested in the frequency with which the words occur in print.

'Your task is to assign a number to each word such that the number you assign represents your judgments of the frequency of that word relative to the other words. To give you an "anchor" for your numbering system, eight of the words (WIN, CAT, etc.) have already been assigned a value of 100. It is a fact that these eight words occur in print with about equal frequency. For each of the other words you are to assign a number which represents its frequency. Obviously, if you think a word occurs with a greater frequency than the eight 100 words, you will give it a value greater than 100; just how much greater than 100 is up to you. If you think the frequency is less than the eight words, you will give it a number less than 100. But, of course, the different values you assign the words should be in some way proportional to their frequencies as you judge them.'

The eight anchor words were scattered throughout the other 64 words to which S had to assign a number. Represented were nine different frequency levels with eight different words at each level. (These were the same words as used in the study employing the method of constant stimuli and reported in the preceding chapter.) The nine levels, expressed in number of occurrences per 4.5 million (Thorndike & Lorge, 1944), were 1, 25, 75, 165, 300, 500, 1000, 7000, and Very High. This latter class consisted of words which varied in frequency from 31,000 to 236,000. Actually, none of the levels was perfectly homogeneous with respect to the words in the class, the frequency varying somewhat, although each level was completely distinct from every other level. The eight anchor words constituted the class having a frequency of 300.

Although the words were ordered on the page randomly, randomization was probably not a necessary step since the Ss usually looked over the columns of words before starting to assign numbers. The ranges of numbers used varied markedly; the higher numbers assigned frequently ran into the thousands, and some Ss used negative numbers.

For each word at each level the log frequency was determined, and the mean of these eight log values was calculated for plotting along the abscissa. For each word we determined the median judgment directly, and for each of these judgments we determined the log and then the mean of the eight logs within the level. Therefore, there are eight points, but each point is based on eight different words. These eight points are plotted on the log-log coordinates in Fig. 6-10. A straight line appears to describe the relationship accurately; to say the least, we were somewhat surprised to discover that a log-log plot did result in a linear relationship.

In the two illustrations given of the application of magnitude estimation, the stimuli used were also measurable along another scale, that is, intensity by db. and words by frequency. It is, of course, quite possible to "sort" stimuli by magnitude estimation when these stimuli cannot be described by other scales. Suppose, for example, we wished to assess food preferences for a dozen specified foods. We could put the names of these 12 foods on cards and present the cards as stimuli. It is probably wise to show all the stimuli to S first in order to give him a notion of the range involved, particularly since we will probably allow him to make only one judgment for each food. To allow multiple judgments would, in this case, produce the artificial reliability discussed earlier. We may wish to assign a number to a particular food as a common anchor for all Ss, although there is no reason to believe that this should be a requirement. That is, we may just as well let S freely choose his own numbering system. In the instructions we would insist that S assign the numbers in a "ratio-like" manner so that if one food is preferred twice as much as another, it will be given a number that is twice as large. At the minimum, such a scaling procedure would produce a rank order of preference for the stimuli. And if we want to assume that S could and did follow the equal-unit instructions, we could insist that we have an interval scale. Using only the rank orders resulting from the method of magnitude estimation, students in the writer's classes have normally found quite high agreement with the rank order resulting from the method of rank order for dimensions ranging from degree of humor on greeting cards to preferences for brands of beer to benefits derived from attending college.

Two final points should be made. There are a large number of available studies reporting the application of the method to stimuli for which a physical scale is also available; they include roughness of sandpaper, vibration frequency, coffee odors, viscosity. The method, it appears, is a very viable one.

The second point is that magnitude estimation, like some of the other ratio-scaling methods, has its counterpart in what is called *magnitude production*. We will remember that, in the ratio methods discussed earlier, S may be required to double, to halve, or to quarter a stimulus. Furthermore, S may be given a tone stimulus and told, "Let's call this loudness 10; now you produce for me a tone which has a loudness of 20." In a series of trials S is given some different numbers (in random order) and is asked to produce the equivalent stimulus. Studies using this method have produced relationships quite parallel with those resulting from magnitude estimation.

Cross-Modality Scaling

An outgrowth of the method of magnitude estimation is the method of cross-modality scaling. This consists of matching sensations in one sense modality with sensations arising from another. Let us first see what faces the S in cross-modality scaling. The Ss in a study by Stevens and Guirao (1963) were asked to adjust a line so that the various lengths represented the various loudnesses of tones presented. The line was projected on a screen and could be varied in length by S's merely turning a knob. Initially, a line was shown on a screen and a tone of a given intensity sounded. The S was told he was to assume that the line length was equivalent to the loudness of the tone. He was further instructed that when successive tones were sounded, he was to adjust the line to maintain the equivalence, using the initial pairing as a base or anchor. A loud tone, of course, meant a long line, and a soft tone, a short line.

At first glance this task may seem like nonsense. How is length to be compared with loudness? Are we not comparing apples and oranges? Of course, the proof is whether or not S can produce reliable relationships, and it is clear that he can. However, a little reflection will show that we do in fact almost inevitably think in terms of correlated dimensions. For example, if we pose the completely nonsensical question "Which is heavier, a second or a minute?" most people are impelled to say a minute is heavier. In any case, a number of studies have shown that such cross-modality matching can be accomplished with considerable precision. One of the more widely used response modalities is the strength of grip as measured by squeezing a hand dynamometer. The S may evaluate different loudnesses by gripping the dynamometer at various levels, a very strong grip meaning a loud tone, a very weak grip, a soft tone; or stimuli varying in warmth are applied to a given locus on the body, and S indicates the differences in warmth by gripping the dynamometer with different forces. From such matches, a plot is made relating two physical scales. For example, grip force is measured in pounds, and intensity of the tone, in db. A plot of the relationship between these two scales gives a loudness scale expressed in pound units. It therefore seems quite possible that we could demonstrate a relationship between weight and time. We could say to S, "Here is a weight; lift it; we will call this weight 10 sec. I am going to present to you other intervals of different durations. After each interval is complete, find a weight which you think reflects the length of the interval." It is very likely we could show that a minute is heavier than a second, which is to say only that S can quantitatively relate sensations arising from one modality with sensations arising from another. And this is a point of considerable importance which arises from the results of cross-modality scaling. We have great flexibility in translating from one dimension to another, as from big and little to loud and soft or from heavy and light to long and short.

We may look at two illustrations of cross-modality scaling. These studies were conducted by the writer using Ss who were naive to the scaling procedure. The stimuli in the first experiment were nine slides which varied in the number of dots (16, 25, 32, 44, 53, 67, 82, 106, 128). The response measure used to reflect the judgments of the density of dots was that of drawing lines. The Ss were told that after the presentation of each slide they were to draw a line to reflect the density, with long lines meaning high density and short lines, low density. The lengths of lines drawn, they were further told, were to reflect the relative density of dots from slide to slide.

Obviously, in this situation one could not expect S to start drawing lines "cold." The length of line was limited by the width of the standard size sheet of paper on which the lines were to be drawn. Therefore, E showed all the slides to S once, in order to provide the range of densities involved. Only after this was done, did the experimental trials begin. The nine slides were then presented four times each with the order determined by block randomization. Each slide was presented for 2 sec., and then S immediately drew the line freehand. The origin of each line, namely, the period mark after the trial number of the left-hand side of the page, was the same for all Ss. The 40 Ss covered all preceding lines drawn so that they had to rely on their memories for the lengths drawn for preceding slides.

The lines drawn were then measured to the nearest 1/10 in. The mean lengths of the four lines drawn for each slide by each S was determined, after which the median length for each slide for the 40 Ss was calculated. The results are shown in Fig. 6-11. Both axes are an arithmetic scale. In drawing the

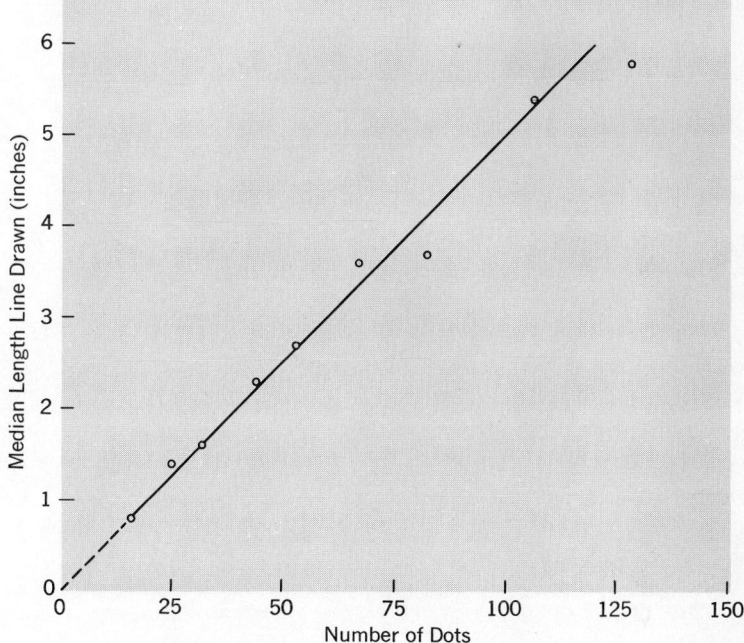

Fig. 6-11. The results of cross-modality scaling wherein S drew lines of different lengths to reflect judgments of different dot densities.

straight line we have "fudged" a little, as can be seen, so that if we extrapolate the curve to the baseline it intersects at zero. This implies that had a slide with zero dots been projected, S would have drawn a line of zero length, which seems quite plausible. Actually, if the curve is drawn properly, an extrapolation will give an intersection slightly above zero. Perhaps the best fit would result in a slight curve in the upper section. As the curve is drawn now, each inch, on the average, represents an addition of 20 dots on the slide; and no matter how the curve is drawn, this will not change appreciably, except for the uppermost section of the curve. It would appear that the results approximate a ratio scale, with an absolute zero and equal intervals. As we shall see, the second experiment also produces the same type of scale.

In the second experiment, drawing of lines was again used to reflect the judgments. The stimuli, however, were temporal intervals, and S was asked to reflect differences in the duration of the intervals by drawing lines. There were nine intervals: 8, 11, 14, 17, 20, 23, 26, 29, and 32 sec. Each interval was presented twice. Since we know (see Chapter Two) that absolute judgments of time intervals decrease with practice, we made the two blocks of trials sym-

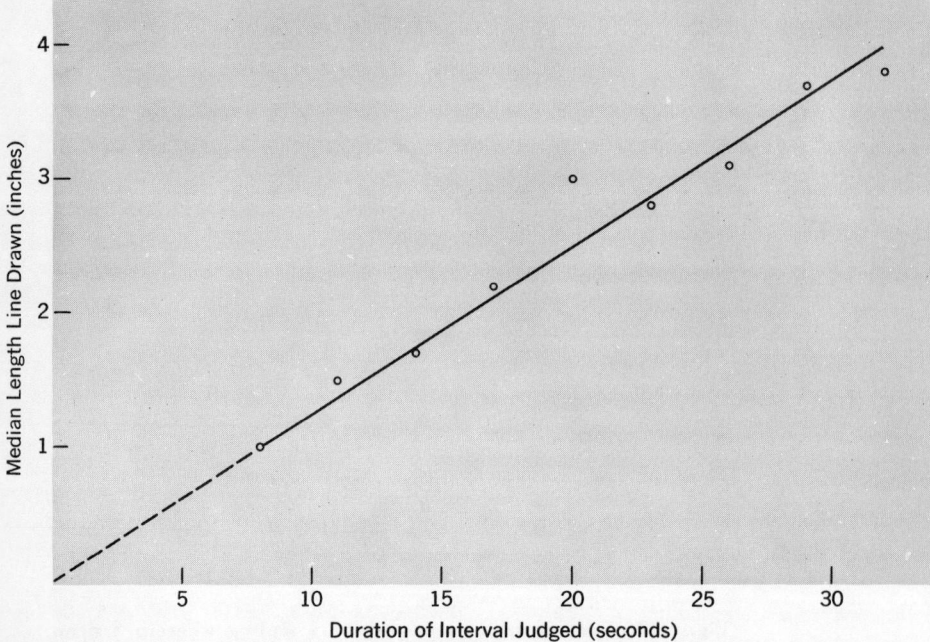

Fig. 6-12. The results of cross-modality scaling wherein S drew lines of different lengths to reflect judgments of the lengths of varying temporal intervals.

metrical. That is, a random order of the nine intervals was determined, and then the order was exactly reversed for the second presentation. In presenting the intervals, S timed the procedure with a stop watch, saying "start" to indicate the beginning of an interval and "stop" to indicate its end. Again it was necessary to give S the range of intervals to be used. To do this, S was twice given a 7-sec. interval and a 34-sec. interval and was told that the short one was slightly shorter than the shortest that was going to be used and that the long one was slightly longer than the longest that would be used. The other details of the procedure were the same as in the dot-density experiment, and the data were handled in the same manner.

The results are plotted in Fig. 6-12. In spite of the fact that there were 49 Ss involved, the data points show appreciable variation. Nevertheless, a straight line through a zero origin describes the relationship quite well. This is to say that 1 in. represents 8 sec.; 2 in., 16 sec.; 4 in., 32 sec. It will be noted that the longest line length is somewhat less for this experiment than for the preceding one, and the reason for this is not clear. Once again, however, a scale seems to have been produced which has all the characteristics of a ratio scale.

It is quite possible that some of the variability in the data could be reduced by modifying the procedure slightly so as not to require S to *produce* the line. To do this, we could have lines, running across the entire page, already printed on the sheet. Then when S makes his judgment, he merely puts a crosshatch on the line to indicate the length from the left that he is using to reflect his judgment of the stimulus. Such a procedure is essentially returning to category scaling with an infinite number of categories along the scale.

ISSUES AND THEORIES

We have spent considerable time in detailing and illustrating some of the frequently used scaling methods. A certain amount of tedium may have been generated by the almost endless passing on to another method, but even so, we did not by any means cover all the variants on the basic methods. Some of us receive at least a momentary aesthetic pleasure from a well-ordered relationship, several of which have been presented in the preceding pages. Yet, a restlessness must develop sooner or later, for we cannot be forever satisfied with particulars. Experiments must lead to principles or generalities which both supersede and encompass the particulars. As psychologists, we are interested in generalities about behavior, either generalized empirical laws or theories.

Theories, we know, may be controversy-producing agents. Whether the development of an area of research is advanced or hindered by such controversy has always been a matter of debate and will undoubtedly remain so since we do not have an appropriate control condition (one in which theoretical controversy is disallowed). The fact is that theories *are* constructed, and the fact is that controversy may occur because of the theory. So, good or bad, such controversies will probably always be with us. In this oldest area of experimental psychology (psychophysics), controversy over different issues has waxed and waned for 100 years. All the signs of the moment lead us to believe that we are well on an upward trend of disagreements at the general level. We should, therefore, sample (albeit tenderly) some of the issues which are involved. Since we cannot hope to settle these issues, we may sit back somewhat as spectators and see how the teams are shaping up. A scholarly controversy adds some spice, and for those involved it may produce the motivation to do research that might not have been done otherwise (providing enough spleen remains to afford the energy to do the research). Disagreements may lead to a clarification of differences which were unclear initially, and they may lead to more pointed research questions than were thought of before. History does not show that scholarly disagreements have led to mayhem, but unless a certain level of dignity attends them, they may fall to the "my-Dad-can-whip-your-Dad" level. In the issues we will discuss, mere mischief-making is minimal and dignity is maximal.

To imply that in examining these issues we will have no need to remember problems of method is not quite proper, for we shall see that the base of some of the differences in positions lies in the methods of investigation. And to repeat, we are sampling issues, without any attempt to cover any one issue in all of its implications, details, or historical perspective. Our purpose is to try to transmit a feeling for the nature of scholarly controversy.

The Power Law

Much of the history of psychophysics is related to attempts to state a general law which relates changes in stimulus energy to changes in sensation. For 100 years Fechner's Law has probably provided as good a summary statement as any that have been suggested as alternatives. Without considering how Fechner arrived at this law, and without considering the law in its mathematical form, we can say that the law asserts that sensation increases in equal arithmetic steps as the magnitude of the stimulus increases in ratio steps. This statement may have a familiar ring. We will remember that this, essentially, is the meaning of Weber's Law—the difference threshold is a constant proportion of the standard stimulus. Indeed, Fechner assumed the validity of Weber's Law to derive his more general law. Fechner's Law is stated to include any magnitude of stimulus change, not merely minimal change that can be detected. We know that equal ratios are represented by a logarithmic scale; if we plot the stimulus dimension in log units, these units should be paralleled by equal sensation units if Fechner's Law is valid, that is, the plot should be a straight line.

As noted above, there have been other statements of laws (e.g., Guilford, 1954) offered as substitutes for Fechner's Law, which did not always seem to reflect the way nature was organized. These laws did not "catch on." But now, S. S. Stevens has proposed a new law, and his intent for it is most clearly seen in the engaging but firm title of a report he wrote for *Science:*

"To honor Fechner and repeal his law" (1961). Stevens is quite aware of the fact that history shows, in the normal course of events in an empirical discipline, that a theory is not "repealed" unless another is offered as a substitute; therefore, he offers his power law as a substitute.

The power law states that equal stimulus ratios are paralleled by equal sensation ratios. The law is so named because the formulation asserts that sensation (response) is equal to the stimulus magnitude raised to the nth power. This function has the useful characteristic of producing a straight line when plotted on log-log coordinates (as seen in the lower curve of Fig. 6-9). The slope of the line is determined by the exponent. If the exponent is 1, both arithmetic coordinates and log coordinates produce a straight line. It so happens that the exponent for apparent length *is* 1, a fact which is undoubtedly involved in the linear plots of Figs. 6-11 and 6-12.

Stevens has amassed an extraordinary amount of data, all of which fit the power law (1960; 1962). In the course of arriving at this general law, Stevens also reached other conclusions, and it is to these conclusions that others have taken exception and to which we shall turn our attention.

In a series of studies, Stevens and Galanter (1957) showed that for certain continua, category scaling and magnitude scaling did not produce the same relationships. There was reason to believe that Ss could not maintion equal intervals in category scaling along these continua, whereas it was assumed they could when using ratio-scaling techniques, particularly magnitude estimation. In a manner of speaking, because ratio-scaling procedures resulted in a power function and category scaling did not, the latter method was rejected as an efficient method for discovering the laws relating stimulus change to sensation. It is as if Stevens assumed that because Ss were told to make the units equal in magnitude scaling they did, and if another method did not agree with the results produced by magnitude scaling, then the other methods were rejected as not allowing S to make the units equal in the way he was instructed to do. These statements are somewhat unfair to Stevens, for he advances plausible reasons (e.g., Stevens & Galanter, 1957) to explain why category scaling may not produce the same function as ratio scaling. Nevertheless, there is a certain arbitrariness involved in these decisions, for they rest on the presumption that S can more readily maintain equal intervals in ratio-scaling procedures than he can in category scaling.

Closely tied with the problem of maintenance of equal intervals by S is the notion that in ratio-scaling procedures S is minimally influenced by context factors, factors that produce anchoring, contrast effects, and so on. In ratio scaling—again, particularly magnitude estimation—there are, according to Stevens, fewer constraints on the S than in category scaling. And this brings us to one of the major points of disagreements, namely, the role of context in ratio-scaling techniques.

Context effects. Consider the following experiment by Garner (1954). The judgment given S was to determine whether the second of two tones was more than or less than *half* as loud as the first. The critical instructions given the Ss were as follows:

'You will listen to a series of pairs of tones, one pair every seven seconds. The first tone will always have the same loudness. The second tone will vary in loudness from one time to another. Your task is to decide whether the second tone is more or less than half as loud as the first. If it sounds more than half as loud as the first, you put a plus . . . on your record sheet. If it sounds less than half as loud, you put a zero . . . on your record sheet.' (p. 219)

The procedure, it can be seen, is that of constant stimuli, with a standard tone always presented first and the variable, second. The judgment required, however, was that of bisection or halving the standard, and the S had to decide whether the variable undershot or overshot half the sense distance between the standard and zero loudness.

Three groups of 10 Ss each were used. The critical aspect of the experiment lies in the different ranges of variable tones presented these three groups. The standard was always a 90-db., 1000-cps tone. For one group of Ss the variable tones ranged from 55 to 65 db., for another, from 65 to 75 db., and for the third, from 75 to 85. Within each range there were six variable tones, 2-db. steps apart. We can see the notion on which Garner was working. For the average S, half loudness must lie within one of the three ranges (or outside of any of the ranges) if S has any clear notion of what constitutes half loudness. Let us assume that "true" half loudness lies between 55 and 65 db. This means that the 20 Ss given the two ranges of greater intensity would not in fact be presented any tone that is half as loud; all should be more than half as loud. This should be true if S knows what the phenomenal experience of half as loud is. If the Ss in some absolute sense knew this, the 20 Ss assigned the two upper ranges should have given all pluses on their data sheets, indicating that all variable tones were more than half as loud. As we shall see, this did not happen.

Each S made 600 judgments, 100 for each variable tone paired with the standard. For the Ss within each of the three ranges, it was quite possible to determine the average loudness judged half as loud. If a plot is made of the percentage of judgments which were pluses (more than half as loud), and if an increasing function is found going from below to above 50 percent, the place at which the curve crosses the 50 percent point would indicate the average db. level judged half as loud. When such determinations were made, it was found that half-loudness judgments were essentially the midpoints of the three ranges. This is to say that the 10 Ss who were presented variable stimuli between 55 and 65 said the half-loudness point was 60; those presented the range from 65-75 said its was 70; and those given the range 75-85 said it was 80. It is clear that S's judgments of what was half as loud was wholly at the mercy of the context, and to say that Ss in such a situation can make valid half-loudness judgments is nonsense. The Ss did not respond randomly; they were very consistent. The correlation between judgments for the first 300 trials and the second 300 trials was $+.84$, showing that these half-loudness judgments are quite reliable. Or to paraphrase Garner, the Ss did not know what they were doing but they did it consistently.

There is a basic lesson in the Garner study: we must not assume the validity of a scale simply because S has been requested to make numerical-like judgments. Stevens was quite aware of the possible role that context could play in the judgments producing a loudness scale (or any sensory scale other than loudness, which has simply been an attribute frequently studied). He realized that a number assigned a previous tone (as in magnitude estimation) could influence what he calls the tone presented at the moment. Such effects, however, are said to be balanced out by the random presentation of the tones. He argues, too, that context effects should be minimized if judgments are requested for the very first stimulus presented S—before an experimental context is developed. Furthermore, Stevens was involved in a study (Stevens & Poulton, 1956) in which the very first judgment given in magnitude estimation was studied. The results produced the usual power law. Therefore, Stevens does not argue that context effects are to be ignored; rather, he argues that such effects can be minimized if the experiment is done properly. Subsequently, Garner (1958) did a further experiment, using the half-loudness procedure again but only for the very first judgments, and, like Stevens and Poulton, found lawfulness in his results. He points out, however, that among the various experiments on loudness, the absolute values (in db.) for half-loudness judgments have varied a great deal for a given standard from experiment to experiment, which again raises the question of what any given sensory scale can mean in an absolute sense.

Finally, one conclusion from still another experiment by Garner (1959) should be mentioned. In part, the study was comparable to that reported above in which different intensity ranges were used for half-loudness judgments. We noted the high consistency of the Ss; that is, if over a series of trials S reported, on let us say 80 percent of the presentations, that a given variable tone was more than half as loud as the standard, this percentage remained quite constant on subsequent trials. Garner found that a number of different changes in the conditions of the experiment did not change this fact. He therefore suggests that what may be determining the responses is a response bias like those discussed at the end of the previous chapter. In an ambiguous situation, where the sensory input does not provide a clear basis for a judgment, response biases may determine the judgment. When S is given a standard and a variable tone and is asked to decide whether the variable is more or less than half as loud, and when S does not have any clear notion about what half as loud is, his decision is based on nonsensory variables. One S may have, or may quickly develop, a reporting frequency of 80 percent greater than half as loud; others, will "hit upon" different percentages. Therefore, the data show highly reliable individual differences, and the average among a group of Ss within a given intensity range of the comparison stimulus is about at the midpoint. But what meaning does a sensory scale have if such biases are involved? This is the question that others have posed to Stevens. Stevens' reply has been a shrug and 10 more experiments on various sensory characteristics to show that the power law continues to hold.

Strictly speaking, the Garner experiments have not used the method of magnitude estimation, and it is this method that has been largely used in the development of the power law. But it can be seen that in the method of magnitude estimation, S must essentially make half-loudness judgments. If a given intensity is assigned a value of 100, S must assign a value of 50 when another tone appears half as loud. But it might be argued that S can assign numbers meaningfully by the method of magnitude estimation when he is properly instructed and that this does in fact differ fundamentally from the half-loudness judgments Garner required of his Ss. When Stevens was questioned about S's capacity to use the number system in the manner the instructions require for magnitude estimation, he pointed out that the power law is not tied to this question, for in the cross-modality matching studies S is not required to use numbers at all, and still the power law holds (Stevens, 1962). But let us return to the problem of context as it pertains strictly to the method of magnitude estimation.

One of the last available studies on the matter is the work of two English investigators, Poulton and Simmonds (1963), the same Poulton who worked earlier with Stevens. (The arguments revolving around the power law are not an intramural matter. In addition to the interest shown by the English, investigators at the University of Stockholm have published extensively in the field of scaling and have inevitably become involved in the methods and the results leading to the power law [e.g., Eisler, 1963].) In the Poulton-Simmonds study, Ss judged the lightness or darkness of gray patches. The S was shown a medium-gray patch and was told that this was to be thought of as having a value of 10. Then the Ss in some groups were shown a darker gray and were asked to assign it a number greater than 10 in order to reflect the difference between the standard (the gray assigned 10) and the darker one. Other Ss were given patches lighter than the standard and were asked to assign them values less than 10. For various groups, standards of different grayness were used. Each S also made a second judgment in which the gray was less than the standard if the first had been greater, and greater if the first had been less. There were also other conditions in this extensive experiment (1200 Ss) which need not concern us. There were three critical variables: first judgments versus second judgments, first variable lighter than standard versus first variable darker than standard, and the grayness of the standard. The term *first judgment* means exactly that, namely, the very first judgment S made. Thus, on this judgment there was no possibility that it would be influenced by prior presentations and judgments within the experimental situation.

For the various conditions the Es calculated the exponent needed to describe the law (assuming a power law) for the various conditions. The notion is that if the variables of the experiment are of no consequenece, the exponents should be equivalent (within statistical limits) for the various conditions. That is, if magnitude scaling is free of constraints and free of context effects, these exponents should be equivalent. The results show that a conservative summary would state that these exponents varied "all over the place." The investigators say, "It appears to be impossible to obtain a direct measure of sensory magnitude which is unaffected by the experimental conditions under which it is made. This raises serious doubts as to whether it is possible to obtain direct measures of sensory magnitude having any general meaning. . . ." (p. 303)

This is where the thinking about the role of context seems to stand at the moment. On the one hand, Stevens, while not denying that context effects can be demonstrated by nearly any scaling method, believes their influence is at a minimum in magnitude estimation methods. There are data other than his own which he can cite to support his position (e.g., Fillenbaum, 1963). Stevens believes that the methods allow derivation of general laws which can be taken to reflect fundamental properties of the sensory systems. On the other hand, there are those who feel that context effects and response biases are so important that it is quite improper to deduce anything fundamental about the sensory systems from ratio-scaling experiments, which is to say, they deny that sensory scales represent a truth about nature that is detachable from the methods used to derive them. Some would further say that it seems questionable whether Ss can handle sensory magnitudes in the quantitative manner requested of them by many of these experiments. And so it goes.

In the quotation above from the Poulton-Simmonds article, they say it is doubtful that direct measures of sensory magnitude have any general meaning. We also used the phrase "fundamental properties of the sensory systems." We must now turn to a consideration of what is meant by "general meaning" and "fundamental properties."

Sensory Transducers

Let us review briefly the conceptualizations involved in constructing sensory scales. We assume that when environmental energy to which the human organism is sensitive varies on some characteristic, such as intensity, this produces sensations which in some way covary in magnitude with the energy changes. Scaling methods represent ways of bringing the variations in magnitude of sensations "outside" so that E can study the relationship between them and the energy changes. The central question concerns the fidelity with which the sensations can be transmitted to E. The ideal transmission system represents one in which there is an exact correspondence between variations in the magnitude of sensations (a purely subjective matter) and the variations along the measuring device used by E. But alas, how do we discover the degree of correspondence? We don't. Stevens wants to believe (and proceeds as if he does) that there is very high correspondence when the direct magnitude-estimation techniques are employed. Those who have shown the powerful effects of context and response biases question Stevens' act of faith, implying that there may be serious distortion between the raw sensation experienced by S and the measurement used by E to reflect that sensation. This is where the fundamental question lies, for the position one takes at this juncture determines the direction of further thinking. We shall pursue the thinking which has resulted from Stevens' position.

We recognize that there are various levels at which one may investigate a phenomenon. Earlier, we saw that an illusion might be investigated at the strictly behavioral level or at the physiological level. It seems fair to say that there is a general belief that sooner or later a given behavioral phenomenon will be understood so well at the behavioral level that further work must shift to a physiological level, where the behavioral facts will direct the research. Essentially, Stevens, with regard to his power law, takes the position that we are far enough along at the behavioral level that further understanding will come primarily from the physiological level. This position is quite easy to understand given Stevens' premises, which may be described as follows: The scaling methods are refined to the point where we are able to obtain measures of subjective sensation with little or no distortion to be attributed to our measuring techniques; for many different modalities we find a power law applies; the exponents in the formula of the power law differ for the various sense modalities. He concludes that the sensory mechanisms (the end organs, and the other mechanisms which convert stimulus energy into sensation) must differ for the different modalities in ways that correspond to the differences in the exponents. In Stevens' terms, the differences in the exponents must indicate differences in the *sensory transducers,* and he offers some interesting speculations (which he clearly labels as such) about how the transducers may differ (1960). It is clear that those who believe that serious distortion may occur (due to context, biases, etc.) in measuring the sensations, deny that Stevens' work at the behavioral level gives him this license to point toward differences in sensory transducers. They accept his behavioral results for what they are; they accept willingly his right to speculate about the nervous system; but they deny that his empirical findings (different exponents) must necessarily reflect differences in the transducing systems. They would be much more comfortable if Stevens kept his general meaning at the strictly empirical level, for the fact remains that the demonstration of the applicability of the power law to a great variety of stimulus energies is an impressive achievement. Yet, given the premises which Stevens reaches, it is inevitable that thinking must be directed toward the physiology or neurology which underlies the law. And who can say that this is "bad"? Indeed, there have already appeared reports evaluating various ways by which the different exponents could be mediated physiologically (e.g., MacKay, 1963). Physiological discoveries of great importance may be made; they may show that Stevens was quite wrong; but they may be discoveries that would not have been made otherwise.

There are ways, other than those of physiology, to attack the sensory-transducer interpretation. For example, one might attempt to show that the laws could be mediated by (could be the consequence of) other judgmental processes which could not logically be tied to sensory transducers. It will be remembered that we found a powerlike law to hold for the judgment of word frequencies (Fig. 6-10). One might argue that a power law was found for these judgments and that it does not make physiological sense to tie them to sensory transducers because we are not dealing with raw sensory stimulation in this case. Instead, we seem to be "reading" something which has been accumulating over the years. But to argue that such results are "against Stevens" is fallacious reasoning; Stevens is not saying that power laws occur only for sensory transducer systems. It is quite possible for similar laws to be produced for quite different reasons.

There is one alternative interpretation of the power function, which, while not necessarily throwing Stevens off stride, has produced some valuable experiments. Let us look at the theory and one experiment.

The physical-correlate theory. The contemporary exponent of this theory is Warren (1958), although he is careful to point out that others have previously suggested much the same idea. The theory holds that judgments of sensory intensity are based upon experience with some variable characteristic which is correlated with the sensory intensity, and this characteristic need not be an attribute of the particular stimulus that E varies. A clear illustration of the application of the theory occurs with loudness judgments. The S has learned through experience that a tone of constant intensity sounds softer at a distance than when at close range. Therefore, in making loudness judgments, S (so the theory says) actually "thinks of" a distance or length dimension and makes his judgments accordingly. Warren offered this theory as a means of accounting for the power law. Stevens, however, rejects this notion and prefers to believe that the power law is a direct result of sensory transducers, with no secondary or intervening psychological processes involved. Stevens does not deny that past learning could conceivably be involved in some sensory judgments, but he points out that it seems quite impossible to show that the physical-correlate theory can be applied to all the various sensations for which the power law has been shown to apply. The power law holds for scaling of electric shock, for example, and Stevens is inclined to believe that it would take some powerful imagination to come up with a dimension correlated with electric shock since people have had so little experience with electric shock. Further, he wonders how the theory could account for the results of cross-modality matchings. His evaluation of the physical-correlate theory is, to say the least, negative: "A 'theory' of this sort, since it is probably not susceptible to proof or disproof, must be judged, if at all, on the basis of the demands it makes on our credulity." (Stevens, Mack, & Stevens, 1960, p. 66)

Warren and his co-workers do not, of course, believe that their theory is quite this bad and are incredulous at the notion that credulity is the only grounds for evaluating the theory. They believe, instead, that some of their experiments are relevant to the theory and can be interpreted as supporting it. We will examine one such experiment (Warren, Sersen, & Pores, 1958).

The method was quite similar to that used by Garner which was discussed earlier. A given standard tone was sounded, and S was to determine the loudness of a variable tone that was half as loud. However, these Es believed that they avoided the context effect which Garner showed worked so strongly. As in the procedure used for the method of limits, the variable tones were systematically either increased or decreased in intensities in 2-db. steps. Since the starting point differed from trial to trial, S would not know the range of the variable intensities involved. For one group of Ss the half-loudness judgments were determined in this manner.

Another group of Ss were given exactly the same stimuli but were asked to make judgments on the distance of the source of the tone. According to the physical-correlate theory, in judging loudness S "uses" the distance dimension for his judgments since intensity and distance are correlated in the experience of the Ss. To obtain measures that would be comparable to half loudness measures, S must make judgments of twice the distance. The S was told to consider the standard tone as coming from a fixed source, but to think of the variable tone as coming from distances further than the standard. The judgment to be made was whether the variable tone was more or less than twice the distance of the standard.

The results show that, on the average, the intensity of the tone judged by one group to be half as loud did not differ from the twice-distance judgments of another group. The Es conclude that the results are quite compatible with the physical-correlate theory. In judging loudness, S could make use of the distance-loudness correlation and make the judgments on the basis of distance. Of course, the data do not show that this is in fact how the loudness judgments were made, but as a hypothesis it remains tenable.

This, then, is the theory and the nature of the experiments offered as an alternative to going directly from the power law to sensory transducers. Has anything been settled? The answer depends upon who answers the question. Theories may have a tendency to make their makers a little stubborn. On the other hand, an investigator with a theoretical generalization that has some explanatory power ought not to be vapid about the matter and withdraw the theory because some data do not agree with it. The physical-correlate theory has not been extended to encompass nearly all of the many dimensions which are involved in the empirical generalization of the power function and the subsequent speculation about sensory transducers.

One final word should be said before we leave the disagreements which are growing around the meaning of the power law. To the uninitiated, it might seem that Stevens is being unduly "picked on." Do not be concerned. The stature of an investigator might be measured by the number of attacks directed at his ideas, a relationship which appears to result from a form of cross-modality matching. Furthermore, it appears that Stevens rather enjoys a productive confrontation in spite of the fact that he says ". . . there is no need to debate matters that have been or should be settled in the laboratory. Our important debates are not with one another; they are with nature." (Stevens, 1964, p. 385)

Adaptation-Level Theory

Judgments are relative. Such a statement has been made so frequently by so many people that it is almost a commonplace. Indeed, it is almost trite. Even so-called absolute judgments have some degree of relativeness in them. If we judge how fast a car is going, using miles per hour as the scale, the scale is anchored at one end in zero miles per hour (very, very slow) and at the upper end, let us say, at 100 miles per hour (very, very fast). If judgments are so relative in nature, it would seem that a theory about these judgments should most assuredly make the notion of relativity explicit, and it should be a pivot in the theory. At the moment S is given a stimulus to place along a nine-point category scale, we say that he is making a relative judgment, and when we say relative, we mean relative to the other stimuli he has been judging. But how are we going to summarize meaningfully all these other stimuli so that the referent for relative is something more than a trite saying?

The most prominent and currently active attempt to accomplish this summarization is known as adaptation-level theory. More particularly, adaptation level is the summarization of the effect of experience with all past stimuli of a given class so that adaptation level (AL) is the reference point against which the judgment of the moment is made. The AL, roughly speaking, is an indifference point dividing a dimension in half (psychologically speaking); it is a neutral point, or a fulcrum, around which all judgments revolve. It is the point at which weights are neither heavy nor light, experience neither pleasant nor unpleasant, lights neither bright nor dim. All judgments, according to the theory, are made relative to AL. The quantitative aspects of the theory consist of ways of calculating AL for a given class of stimuli, hence allowing predictions to be made of the judgment just being made.

The AL theory is the work of Helson. Introduced in 1947, the theory had been extended, refined, and experimented upon until it culminated into a book (Helson, 1964). Helson is generous when it comes to generalizing on the basis of the theory. Initially developed to account for certain phenomena observed in color judgments, it is now asserted to be relevant to the understanding of social behavior, behavior of groups, mental illness, and acquisition of skills. The serious student will surely want to pursue these matters, although here we will consider only the basic notions involved in the theory as applied to judgments in simple scaling procedures. And, of course, it goes without saying that not all workers in the field are as enamored with the theory as are Helson and his students. We will return to this later; first we must examine the theory and then see how it accounts for some judgmental phenomena.

Consider a simple judgmental situation in which S is judging weights along a 7-point category scale, with verbal labels at each of the seven points (very heavy, heavy, moderately heavy, and so on). According to AL theory there are three sources of stimuli involved in determining adaptation level, hence in determining the judgment of the moment. First, there are the residuals of past experience with weights which S brings to the laboratory. Second, there is the effect of stimuli which S had previously lifted in the experimental situation. Third, there are the contextual stimuli, stimuli which form a background. For example, we know that the size of the container in a weight-lifting experiment may be important. However, for our purposes, we may concentrate primarily on the role of the other stimuli which are present in the experimental situation and are in the same class as those being judged. Admittedly, in most situations it is difficult to deal with the residuals of the experience with weights which S brings to the situation, and we may, therefore, drop this from our consideration. The point is, once AL is calculated, E can determine what will happen in judging the "next" weight. Clearly, if the stimulus weight is heavier than that weight represented by AL, S will place it above AL; if lighter, below. Just how much above or below it is placed is also predicted by the theory, but we will not get into the detailed mathematics required for this prediction.

The AL is calculated as the weighted log mean of the stimuli as measured along a physical scale, for example, for weight lifting, grams or ounces. What is meant by a weighted log mean? Suppose we have just two stimuli, one of 200 grams and one of 800 grams. If in a series of judgments these two stimuli have been presented an equal number of times, their scale value (grams) would be equally weighted. Hence, AL would simply be the number of grams represented by the mean of the logarithms of the two stimuli. But if the 800-gram weight had been presented twice as frequently as the 200-gram weight, it must be given twice as much "weight" as the 200-gram weight in calculating AL.

We already know that a log scale implies equal rates. Helson has assumed the validity of Fechner's Law in formulating his techniques for calculating AL. He has been chided by some (e.g., Stevens, 1958) for making this assumption; in their minds, the theory has gone astray at the outset because (in their opinion) Fechner's Law is not valid. Still, even if Fechner's Law is not a perfect description, it may be close enough to allow some reasonably good predictions. According to the theory, AL is the mean of the logarithms of the stimuli. Thus, with two stimuli (200 and 800 grams) presented an equal number of times, AL is not 500 (an arithmetic mean), but 400 grams (a geometric mean). A log scale represents a geometric series, and the geometric mean for two values is the square root of the product of the two. For n values, the geometric mean is the nth root of the product of the terms (Lewis, 1960). With only two values, the geometric mean is simple to calculate; 200×800 is 160,000, the square root of which is 400. However, with several values, the easiest procedure is to determine the logs for each value, find the mean of the logs, and then translate back to the physical scale. If for these two stimuli AL is 400, it means that this is the neutral point on the scale for them. The use of such a scale is not new to us, for we know that discrimination becomes poorer and poorer (DLs get bigger) as we go "up" a sensory dimension, and the log scale is used to reflect equal ratios (Weber's Law). If we have been allowing S only two categories of judgment (heavy or light), and if after we have presented the 200- and 800-gram stimuli many times we present a 500-gram weight, it would be on the heavy side of AL, and he would certainly have to put it in the "heavy" category.

So much for a general notion of Helson's thinking. We may now look at a phenomenon (anchoring) which occurs in scaling as a means of demonstrating how the theory operates to explain the phenomenon. This particular illustration will also allow us to see the basis for two controversial matters surrounding AL theory.

We have already discussed anchoring, and we may review the phenomenon briefly by considering a hypothetical situation. Suppose we are scaling weights ranging from 200 to 800 grams along a fully labeled 7-point scale. Each of the several weights has been judged many times, but all equally often. We would know how to calculate AL, and after the large number of trials, it should be stable. Now, without warning S, we introduce a 1200-gram weight into the series. We know that by introducing this anchor we will, descriptively speaking, get a contrast effect as judging proceeds. Weights formerly put in the highest (heaviest) category will be dropped down the scale in order, so to speak, to make room for the 1200-gram weight. The AL theory explains these shifts quite simply. Introduction of the 1200-gram weight changes the AL, the direction of the change or shift being upward or toward the heavier stimuli. As this shift occurs, stimuli which prior to the introduction of the 1200-gram stimuli were above AL may be reduced to a point below AL (on the light end of the scale); hence, they are placed in "lighter" categories than was true prior to the introduction of the anchor stimulus. Thus, contrast or anchoring effects in this situation fall readily within the scope of AL theory.

This hypothetical experiment, however, introduces two problems, one of which concerns the role that semantics plays in the shifts. Helson tends to think of the perception of a given stimulus actually changing when there is a shift in AL. Other writers have suggested, however, that what we are dealing with is semantic confusion on the part of S. What is S to think when the 1200-gram weight starts appearing in the series and he recognizes it is clearly heavier than any he had been experiencing? Since the scale given him to use is "closed in" at both ends, he has to make the shift in assigning the old weights to the specific categories in order to accommodate the new weight on the scale. The old weights may be perceived in exactly the same manner as they were before the anchor was put in the series, but what can he do but shift downward?

The second problem indicated by the illustration concerns details in the formulation of the theory. When an anchor is introduced as in the above illustration, AL theory predicts a gradual change in AL; the effect of any stimulus in a series on AL is a function of the frequency with which it has been experienced. Essentially, no other characteristic of the presentation procedure is said to influence AL. As we shall see, there is evidence that several such characteristics do influence AL and, so it is argued, AL theory in its present formulation is incomplete. This situation (incompleteness) is not unusual for any theory. But let us return to the two problems in order.

Semantic effects. The AL is not tied to any particular form of scaling. Shifts in AL, according to the theory, are fundamental changes in the balance of the organism and will occur if there is a change in stimulation, such as a change by anchoring. If this is true, judgments which are made on an absolute basis (with no end limits to the scale being used by S) should be influenced by anchors as readily as should judgments in category scaling. On the other hand, if anchors do not influence the judgments on a scale with no end limits, it may suggest that anchor effects, assumed to be in support of AL theory (because they are assumed to indicate a true change in the perception of the stimulus due to shifts in AL), are, in fact, due to semantic confusion.

The evidence is by no means conclusive on this issue. We may examine some studies by way of showing the nature of the tests and the results they have produced. Earlier, the results of a study by Fillenbaum (1963) were presented to show the effects of anchoring in category scaling of rectangles (Fig. 6-4). In this same study, Fillenbaum had other groups make direct estimates of the height-width ratio of the rectangles with anchors introduced and not introduced. Essentially, the results show no effect of the anchors for direct ratio scaling and therefore support the notion that semantic effects or limited-response language involved in category scaling is responsible (at least in part) for the anchoring effects.

Quite a different finding resulted from an experiment by Krantz and

Campbell (1961). The task given the Ss was the judging of line lengths projected on a screen, the judgments to be reported in inches. There were two groups of 80 Ss each. One group was given seven different line lengths over a series of trials, the *longest* line of the seven being 20.2 in. when projected on the screen. Another group was also given seven different line lengths of which the *shortest* line was 20.2 in. Thus, for both groups a single line of exactly the same length occurred, but for one group this was presented among a series of shorter lines, and for the other group, among a series of longer lines. The S, of course, was completely free to judge the length; there was no restriction on his response language in terms of number of categories available, and the scale was "open" at both ends. If context effects operate in this situation, it could be taken to mean that S, depending on the context, actually perceives the line to be of a different length. And this was the outcome. Each of the seven lines was judged by each group 15 times with block randomization determining the order for presenting the lines. The average judgment for the common line when it was the longest line of the seven was 17.21 in.; when it was the shortest line, it was judged on the average to be 12.74 in. It would be difficult to attribute these results to semantic effects; it was, indeed, as if the Ss in the two groups perceived the common line to be of different lengths.

In this same experiment, however, Krantz and Campbell included another scaling method, a method which could be called a modified method of magnitude estimation. The two series of lines were used (for two different groups of Ss) with the line length common to both series being the longest in one case and the shortest in the other. The Ss in each group were told that the average-length line was to be given an arbitrary value of 100. Lines longer than the average were to be given numbers above 100, and those below, less than 100. They were told, furthermore, that whenever a line of a given length was repeated (when S perceived a line as being the same as one presented earlier), the number given the earlier line was to be assigned again. Under these circumstances, the context effects were greater than those found when S reported in inches. That is, the differences in judgments assigned the line common to both series were greater than the differences when the Ss reported in inches. Since there was no reason to believe that the perception of the common line should differ for the two types of scaling, Krantz and Campbell argue that the novel judgmental language used in the method of modified magnitude estimation must be partly responsible. Therefore, they conclude, both true perceptual effects and semantic effects are present. Perceptual effects occur in both methods, with semantic effects occurring only with the modified method of magnitude estimation.

At the present time, therefore, it appears that the issues are more complex than anticipated, and, clearly, no resolution is possible. More than simple differences in perception seem to be involved, but just what conditions are necessary for the appearance of the effects of these other factors is not clear. These extra-perceptual effects must be associated in some way with the scaling method used, but there is no way to specify at the present time precisely what characteristics of scales will produce the effects. Furthermore, a given type of scale may produce the effects for judgments along one dimension but may not do so for judgments along others. At this point we can say only that for Helson to assume that *all* anchoring or context effects reflect fundamental differences in perception is not wholly in accord with experimental findings. But that fundamental perceptual differences are involved to some extent for some judgments seems quite in accord with the available facts.

Incompleteness of AL theory. As was noted earlier, AL theory weights all past experience with stimuli of a class. The weighting is strictly on the basis of frequency of experience with a given stimulus within the class. Temporal factors do not enter into the equations for determining AL; experiencing a given stimulus 10 minutes previously is given the same weight in determining AL as experiencing that stimulus "right now." We may look at two sets of results which suggest that temporal factors are important in determining AL for at least some types of judgments.

In the Krantz-Campbell study, reviewed above, Ss were given further trials beyond those mentioned. It will be remembered that a line of a given length appeared in two series, one in which it was the shortest in the series and one in which it was the longest. Following the 15 trials (where a trial consisted of one presentation of each of the seven lines within a series), there were three trials in a transition phase of the experiment. In this transition phase, the composition of the series was changed in three gradual steps so that at the end of the transition the series were completely reversed. Consider an S initially given the series in which the common line was the shortest in the series. Following the transition phase, this line became the longest in the series. Likewise, for an S in which the common line was initially the longest, following the transition phase it became the shortest. Thus, for the first S shorter lines than he had previously experienced were added, and for the second S, longer lines were added. Following the transition phase, several more trials were given on the new series. Of course, the common line still remained for all Ss.

The critical question concerns the changes in the judgment for the common line on the trials after the transition phase. According to AL theory, there should be a gradual change in the judgments for this common line, because the new lines added had, at the start of the trials following transition, been experienced many fewer times than had the lines given during the initial 15 trials. Therefore, AL must change gradually as the new lines were repeated. However, for the Ss making the judgments in inches, this did not happen. Even by the end of the transition phase, the judgments for the common line in the two series had been reversed: the line which was initially the shortest in the series (but which had become the longest by the end of the transition) was being judged longer than the line which for the other Ss had initially been the longest in the series. In short, the reversal in the judgments took place very rapidly so that shortly after the transition phase the judgments of the common line were being made in much the same fashion as they had been originally. It would appear that AL was shifting very rapidly as a function of the recency of the experience with the new series, which is to say that temporal weighting seems necessary to account for these results. On the other hand, the groups who were making judgments by the modified method of magnitude estimation *did* show a gradual change in judgments of the common line in a manner that Krantz and Campbell judge to be almost exactly what would be predicted by AL theory in which temporal factors are not considered. Thus, these data suggest again that the method of scaling is important in determining AL.

The second illustration comes from the work of the students in the writer's class. The task required of S was judging the relative size of triangles, the method of presentation being essentially the method of constant stimuli. Equilateral triangles, constructed from white cardboard, had a small index tab glued on one side to be used as a "handle" for presenting the triangles for judgments. On each trial S was actually presented three triangles in succession before the judgments were made. The critical judgments consisted of deciding whether the third triangle was larger or smaller than the first. Now in fact the first and third triangles were of *equal* size, although by instructions S was led to believe that they could be different in size:

"You are to make a series of judgments concerning the size of triangles. On each trial I will present you three triangles, one after the other. As I present each one, observe and try to remember its size. After I have presented the third triangle, you are to tell me first whether the third was larger or smaller than the first. Then, you are to tell me whether the second was larger or smaller than the first. You must always make your judgments in that order—third against the first followed by second against the first. After you have given me both judgments, I will present you three more triangles for the next trial and again you will give me the two judgments in the order mentioned—three versus one followed by two versus one.

"Some of the judgments you are asked to make involve triangles which have only very small differences in their sizes. So, you must observe carefully. If you are in doubt concerning a judgment, let your first reaction guide your response. You can never say that the two triangles are equal; you must always report larger or smaller."

The variable in this experiment was the size of the second (interpolated) triangle. The first and the third triangles were always 4 in. on a side. The interpolated triangles were 3.0, 3.5, 4.0, 4.5, and 5.0 in. The question we asked, of course, was whether or not the variation in size of the interpolated triangle produced a difference in the judgment of the third versus the first, which were of equal size. Requiring S to judge the second against the first was merely a device to force S to attend to the interpolated triangle over the many trials given him. Each S was given a total of 100 trials, 20 for each size of interpolated triangle. Block randomization determined the order of the interpolated triangles. On a given trial, the first triangle was raised above the top of a small screen and held there in S's view for 3 sec. Then there was a 2-sec. blank period followed by the interpolated triangle for 3 sec., then a 2-sec. blank period, and finally, by the third triangle for 3 sec. The S then immediately made his judgment of the third versus the first.

The 11 Ss each made 20 judgments for each size of the interpolated triangle; therefore, for each size there was a total of 220 judgments. As the response measure, we used the percentage of times that the third triangle was judged larger than the first. If interpolating a triangle has no influence,

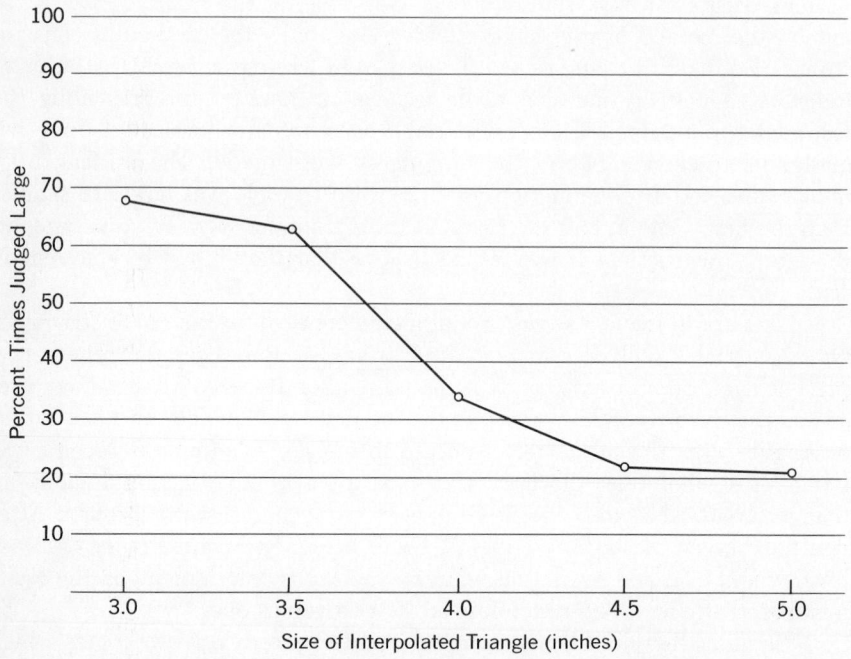

Fig. 6-13. Percentage of times the second of two equal-sized triangles was judged larger than the first as a function of the size of triangles interpolated between the two.

we would expect the percentages to be equivalent across the five conditions and, unless there is a constant error or some response bias involved, we would expect these percentages to hover around 50 percent. Figure 6-13 shows that the size of the interpolated triangle bore a very systematic relationship to the judgments. If the interpolated triangle was smaller than the first and third, the third was judged to be larger than the first; if the interpolated triangle was larger than the first or third, the third tended to be judged smaller than the first.

These results conform to the *general* notion of AL theory. When we present a large interpolated triangle, AL increases; therefore, the third triangle appears smaller than the first. Contrariwise, if the interpolated triangle is small, AL decreases making the third appear larger. It is as if the remembered size of the first triangle is a compromise between its actual size and the size of the interpolated triangle. We already know that this effect is descriptively termed assimilation—one stimulus appears to assume a property of another stimulus.

Although these results are in general agreement with the notion of AL theory, they are not in harmony with the detail which says that changes in AL are independent of the temporal order of stimuli which change AL. In the above experiment, because it seems as if the interpolated triangle *immediately* changes AL, a recency factor seems necessary.

Two other points are worth making about these data. First, it should be noted that when all three triangles are exactly the same size, the percentage judged larger is not 50 percent, as might be expected, but 34 percent. Why should this be? One possibility is that there is a time-order error involved. The apparent size or remembered size of the first triangle may change as a function of the interval between its presentation and the presentation of the third triangle. This would mean that the apparent size of the first grows larger over time so that we would have what is called a positive time error. Another possibility is that, again, we are dealing entirely with nonsensory factors or response biases. Faced with this ambiguous situation in which the three triangles are all the same size, and under instructions to say "larger" or "smaller," the Ss as a group may have a bias toward using the word smaller in preference to the word larger.

A second point concerns the near equality of the effects for the two larger interpolated triangles and the equality for the two smaller triangles. That is, there is very little difference between the effect of an interpolated triangle of 4.5 and 5.0 in.; likewise, there is very little difference in the effect of interpolated triangles which are 3.0 and 3.5 in. The data suggest, therefore, that if still larger and smaller triangles were interpolated, the direction of the curve might reverse itself at both ends, moving back toward 50 percent and perhaps even crossing this value, in which case we would interpret it as a contrast effect rather than as assimilation. At least, such an experiment looks worthy of a try.

The above two studies suggest that in the long run AL theory will have to provide some weighting in the formula for AL for temporal order of experience. We have chosen this particular factor merely as an illustration of potential modifications which may have to be made in AL theory if it is to survive. Other research is suggesting further changes. For example, extensive work by Parducci (1963) has led him to conclude that while his findings are in general agreement with AL theory, several factors, not now accommodated within the theory, must be "written into" the formulas. He finds that the end stimuli in a series are more important than are the others in determining AL. Furthermore, he finds that Ss have a bias toward using different portions of the scale with about equal frequency, and if there is not an equal number of stimuli with each value along a physical scale, AL will be distorted.

SUMMARY

Three scaling methods were presented as techniques for deriving a rank ordering of a set of stimuli:

(1) The method of rank order, in which S directly assigns ranks to the stimuli.

(2) Paired comparisons, in which S judges each stimulus against every other stimulus, with the frequency with which each stimulus is chosen determining the rank order.

(3) Category scaling, in which S is provided a rating scale, often with descriptive phrases for the category, and in which each stimulus is placed in a category. The assignment of numbers to the categories allows derivation of a scale value for each stimulus which in turn is used to determine the rank order of the stimuli.

The rank-order scale resulting from these methods constitutes an ordinal scale in which little is known quantitatively about the magnitude of the differences between successive ranks. The difficulties of drawing cause-effect conclusions from shifts in the rank ordering of stimuli as a function of independent variables were pointed out. The problems revolve around the reciprocal nature of rank orders—a change in the rank order of one stimulus must necessarily result in the change of the rank of at least one other stimulus. Which change was produced by the independent variable? This problem is not faced when scale values derived from category scaling are used as the dependent variable. Category scaling is the major scaling technique used to study anchoring effects—the effects of different frames of reference on scale values.

Equal-interval scaling techniques are presumed to result either in an interval scale, in which the units throughout the scale are psychologically equal although the origin of the scale is arbitrary, or in a ratio scale, which has equal intervals and an origin at zero. The following methods are used to produce such scales:

(1) Equal-appearing intervals, in which S fractionates or divides a sense distance into equal phenomenal units. In a variant on the method, S multiplies the sense distances, for example, doubles them.

(2) Ratio judgments, in which S gives direct ratios for the relative magnitudes of two stimuli.

(3) Magnitude estimation, in which S arbitrarily assigns numbers to stimuli, these numbers representing proportional magnitudes of the stimuli. A variant on the method is magnitude production, in which S is given a series of numbers and is asked to find stimuli which are in the same relationship to each other as are the series of numbers.

(4) Cross-modality scaling, in which the magnitude of sensations arising in one modality is used to indicate the magnitude of sensations arising in another modality.

Stevens' power law and Helson's adaptation-level theory were used to illustrate the nature of theoretical interchanges in the scaling area.

CHAPTER SEVEN

Elementary Displays and Reaction Speed

In the topics covered thus far, the S has been more or less a passive organism. He has been passive in the sense that he made simple judgments or discriminations without any emphasis upon the speed with which these were made and without his responses' changing the situation in any fundamental way. In a true sense, the topics covered were concerned with mapping the discriminal capacities of the organism. The topics of the present chapter are clearly an extension of this study but with a shift in emphasis to factors determining the *speed* with which the environment can be perceived and responded to. It is apparent, therefore, that we will be dealing with a response measure that we have thus far given little attention. We refer to *latency* of response—the time between the presentation of a given stimulus event and the response (as required by *E*) to this event. Latency, as a response measure, has widespread use in psychological research, and it will be the major response measure used in the studies to be discussed in this chapter.

We have heard a great deal about machines replacing men. Automation is the general term used, since it reflects the rapid technological changes which have led to computers, to assembly lines with machines doing the work that men previously did, and to complex weapons of war which in some cases cannot be handled directly by men. But men at least must monitor these machines; they must respond to them at given signals, changing this lever or pressing that button or turning this switch at the appropriate time. And the monitors, while relatively free from physical labor, may, in a manner of speaking, be cursed with another evil. For now they must wait for signals to appear and then respond, but the signals may occur only infrequently. Whereas previously a seaman would actively search the horizon for an enemy ship, now he must observe the signals on a radar screen, and to maintain his alertness or vigilance (as it is called) may not be easy. The technological changes have produced, if not a new field of research in psychology, at least a remarkable acceleration in an old one. It has become imperative to know the capacities of man in detecting and responding to stimuli; it has become imperative, for it is of little value to build a machine if it is beyond the capacity of the operator to "work it."

The word *display* has come into use to identify the stimulus situation to which S must respond. The display, as we shall see, may be simple (such as the onset of a single stimulus), or it may be complex in that many events may be occurring on the display but only certain of these are relevant for a given response. The phrase, "display-control relationships," is often used to refer to the fact that given certain displays, certain controls must be manipulated. When the displays are complex and frequently changing, it is quite clear that the requirements of the display-control relationships may be too great for one man to handle. As a consequence, some work is being done using teams of operators in which the different tasks demanded by the situation are given to different members of the team. Anyone who has visited the control tower of a large metropolitan airport will realize immediately that the problems of the man who is appropriately monitoring machines and taking appropriate action at the appropriate time are not a mere laboratory exercise. And, of course, it is obvious that in space flight, the principles of human behavior which might hold under "earthy" conditions may be modified when the man must operate in a world of little or no gravity, spacesickness, and stresses of an entirely new origin.

It is of immense practical value, indeed it is a necessity, that research aimed at making it possible for the operators to keep up with technological advances be maintained. Thus, when a new interceptor plane is developed, the display-control systems must be capable of being handled by the pilot. To a large extent at the present time, however, each new technological advance is treated as a new problem in behavior; the research and recommendations concerning the control-display requirements for that particular machine may not result in principles which can be generalized to machines not yet built. It has been quite apparent that those psychologists interested in the long-term development of principles of display-control relationships have turned to the laborious but necessary analytical approach wherein the complex behavior required in the operating situation is broken down into constituent behaviors in an effort to achieve a more fundamental understanding of behavioral capacities. From such work it is presumed that general principles will evolve which can be used in the development of any new machine. Probably no topic is more indicative of this trend than the first we will consider. This topic, reaction time, has a long history of study in experimental psychology, but when it became a central problem in display-control relationships, it became apparent that much more needed to be known about it. In a published review of the topic in 1954, Teichner says, ". . . there are still large gaps in our knowledge of the empirical relationships in which reaction time is involved." (p. 128) Scores of additional studies have been published since that time. What appears at first to be among the most simple of human behaviors turns out, in fact, to be quite a complicated matter.

SIMPLE REACTION TIME

The basic procedure in studying reaction time (commonly abbreviated RT) is to present a signal, for instance a light, with S instructed to make some response, such as pressing a key, as quickly as possible after seeing the signal. The time elapsing between the onset of the signal and the making of the response is the RT. In driving an automobile we often find ourselves in situations where we must respond as quickly as possible to a given stimulus. The response we make is usually a brake-depressing response with the stimulus being any of several: a red light, a car backing out of a driveway, or a child running from behind a parked car. If these situations contained the proper "wiring" so that RT could be measured, we would have data on RT under the various conditions of operating a motor vehicle. The simple RT setup is also the simplest display we may present to S. However, the display may be made more complex, and the behavior we measure may include more than simple RT. Displays often involve many events happening simultaneously with a decision by the operator as to just when to do what. If, during a rush hour, we are trying to drive across a heavily traveled boulevard from a side street, we experience a complex display of various vehicles coming from both directions. To decide when to cross requires judgments of the distances and speeds of the other automobiles as well as a knowledge of our performance capacity and that of our vehicle. These situations do indeed approach the complexity of the perceptual situation present in many of our complex machines. What we must do, as operators, is to assess quickly a horde of incoming information and to decide on a course of action. The term *information processing* is sometimes applied to these kinds of situations.

When RT is studied systematically in the laboratory, the obvious apparatus requirement is one which allows us to measure RT, for RT is the dependent variable. In the simple situation, the onset of a stimulus starts an electric clock, and the response (e.g., pressing a key) stops the clock. Therefore, RT is read directly from the clock and is commonly expressed in milliseconds (.001 sec., abbreviated msec.). By way of setting forth the experimental techniques in studying RT, we will sample some recent studies for various classes of variables.

SOME INDEPENDENT VARIABLES

Stimulus duration and intensity. In a study by Raab (1962), the stimulus was noise consisting of frequencies between 100 and 7000 cps. Bursts of this noise were presented to S via an earphone applied to a single ear. The intensity of this auditory stimulus was either 40 db. or 60 db., and the duration of the stimulus was 2, 5, 10, 20, 50, or 100 msec. Thus, there were 12 different stimulus conditions. In the usual RT study, a preparatory signal is given. That is, S is not left entirely in doubt as to when the stimulus (to which he is to respond as rapidly as possible) will occur. One could envisage a situation in which a stimulus occurred periodically to which S was to respond, and later we will examine such situations. In the usual RT study, we prepare S for the stimulus. In the present study, a 1000 cps warning tone was delivered to S through the "other" earphone. On successive trials, this preparatory signal occurred 1.75, 2.00, or 2.25 sec. before the noise stimulus occurred. Why vary the length of this interval (called the fore-period)? If you imagine yourself as an S in an RT experiment in which the preparatory signal always occurs 2 sec. prior to the RT stimulus, what may you do? If you are like some Ss, and if a series of trials is given on which the preparatory signal always precedes the RT stimulus by a constant interval, you will start responding to the 2-sec. interval rather than to the RT stimulus. In a sense, you will start "jumping the gun"; being told to respond as quickly as possible to the RT stimulus, you may start responding to your estimate of 2 sec., thus indeed producing a very short RT. To avoid this problem, a variable foreperiod is often used. In the present experiment, the length of the foreperiod had three different durations. The sequence of events, then, for a single trial was (1) a preparatory signal (100 cps tone in one earphone lasting for .75 sec.); (2) a variable blank interval, the foreperiod (of either 1.75, 2.00, or 2.25 sec.); (3) the noise stimulus in the second earphone; (4) S's response (pressing a telegraph key).

Only four Ss were used, all being highly practiced and given additional practice in the course of the experiment. Each S was tested for 12 days. On each day, 108 trials were given. Since there were 12 different conditions, each occurred nine times on a day. Each preparatory interval occurred three times with each condition on a given day, and the entire series of 108 trials was randomized. The report does not say whether or not a different random order of the 108 trials was used on each day. With each condition occurring nine times per day, for 12 days, there would be a total of 108 trials for each condition for each S. However, this E discarded the longest and shortest RTs for each condition for each day, leaving only seven trials for each condition per day, or a total of 84 for the 12 days. The reason for discarding the longest and shortest RTs is not given, but can you reason why E might have done this?

The means for the combined data for the 4 Ss are plotted in Fig. 7-1, with a log scale for the baseline. Both variables are related to RT. The stronger the intensity of the noise stimulus, the shorter the RT; the longer the stimulus duration, the shorter the RT; although it is apparent that a leveling off occurred so that beyond 100 msec. very little further reduction in RT would be anticipated.

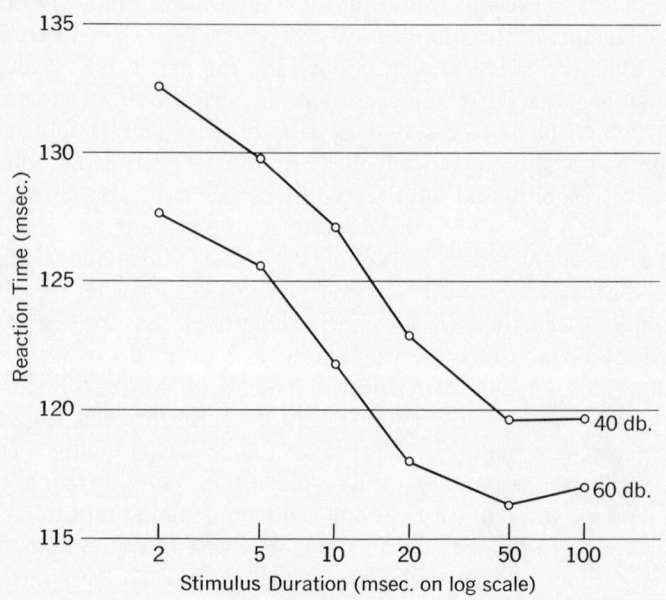

Fig. 7-1. Reaction time as a function of duration and intensity of the noise stimulus. Data from Raab (1962).

Practice effects. Offhand, we might suspect that RT (being an apparently simple and almost reflexive reaction) would be little influenced by practice. This is not so. Changes in RT do occur with practice, with RT becoming shorter and shorter. Of course, there must at some time be a limit to this improvement, but the amount of gain with practice is appreciable. Consider a study by Henderson (1952). He used a visual stimulus for key-pressing. A vocal "ready" was the preparatory signal; the time between this signal and the onset of the visual stimulus (the foreperiod) varied from 2 to 4 sec. Each of 20 Ss had 100 trials per day for six days. Henderson determined the mean of every tenth response on each day across the 20 Ss, and these values indicate the change in RT from day to day. For the six days in order, the mean RTs in msec. were 213, 186, 176, 179, 171, and 168.

We mention these practice effects here not only to indicate that this supposedly simple response does change with practice, but also to remind ourselves again that whenever we use the same S in various conditions within an experiment, we must be sure that we counterbalance or randomize the conditions so that no bias will occur as a function of progressive error (practice effects).

Foreperiod factors. As noted earlier, if a ready signal of some kind is used, the time between this ready signal and the appearance of the stimulus to which S is to respond is varied to prevent S from responding to the foreperiod interval per se (which he may do if it is constant). To check further on such "false reactions," E may also occasionally insert a false trial by giving the ready signal but not giving the RT stimulus. Or, as another technique, E may discard all responses which are apparently too fast on the grounds that these could not have been initiated by the RT stimulus. For example, Drazin (1961) discarded all responses to a visual stimulus if the response—the RT—was 100 msec. or less, or if they occurred before the RT stimulus. The fact that these constituted only 1.5 percent of all responses indicates that these false or premature responses are not a serious problem if the S is carefully instructed and practiced and if variable foreperiod lengths are used. But we may consider the length of the foreperiod as a variable per se. If the foreperiod is very short, S may not have time to "set" himself— to prepare himself. If it is too long, he may get himself set and then as the interval wears on lose his "edge" to respond; he, in a sense, becomes less ready than he had been. The data available on this matter are by no means consistent. In a study by Karlin (1959) with a tone used as both the warning or ready signal and the RT stimulus, RT increased (became longer) in a negatively accelerated manner across four foreperiod intervals (.5, 1.0, 2.0, and 3.5 sec.). Klemner (1956) also found this effect. But Raab, Fehrer, and Hershenson (1961) found the opposite, as did Drazin (1961); and no resolution of these contradictions is available at the present time.

There *is* agreement on one general principle concerning the foreperiod, namely, that RT is influenced heavily by the foreperiod of the preceding trials. It is as if an adaptation level develops for the mean foreperiod interval of a series of trials. Within this level, the foreperiod length of the immediately preceding trial is most heavily weighed (to judge by the RTs of the present trial). If a long foreperiod occurred on the previous trial, in contrast to a short one of the present trial, it is as if S is caught napping on the present trial, and as a result, his RT is longer than if a short foreperiod had occurred on the previous trial. Or if the previous trial had a short foreperiod and the present trial a long one, S will respond less quickly on the present trial than if the previous foreperiod had been long. These effects are more marked in schizophrenic patients than in normals (Zahn, Rosenthal, & Shakow, 1963). Simple reaction time is far from simple.

Inhibitory effects. The RT task given S by Helson and Steger (1962) was to press a button as quickly as possible when a stimulus light appeared. The independent variable introduced was a second light which appeared 10 to 180 msec. *after* the stimulus light. This second light might be thought of as a distraction, although this is merely descriptive of its influence, for it increased or inhibited RT to the first light, and the amount of inhibition was a very regular function of its point of onset following the onset of the RT stimulus. More particularly, if the distracting light appeared 90 msec. after the stimulus light, inhibition was maximal. At this point RT was increased from about 215 msec. to 240 msec., the value of 215 being determined for trials on which the distracting light was omitted. However, the distracting light increased RT regardless of when it occurred, but the amount of its influence was minimal when it appeared 10 msec. after the RT stimulus as well as 180 msec. after. Thus, inhibition of RT was related in a complex manner to time of onset of the distracting stimulus. This inhibitory effect persisted over 360 trials, so it is not a transient phenomenon tied only to early practice on an RT task.

What could be responsible for such effects? Helson and Steger offer some speculations. One of these speculations suggests that the distracting light sets off action in inhibitory motor-nerve fibers, the responses of which are *faster* than responses in the fibers which produce the voluntary RT response. Therefore, even though the inhibitory impulse is initiated later than the impulse producing the RT, a lengthening of RT may result. The Es indicate that if it is not known that such inhibitory fibers exist, it might be worthwhile to search for them by electrophysiological means.

In the sense that the inhibitory effect needs to be better understood at the procedural level, it is possible that Helson and Steger are theorizing prematurely at the physiological level. Lappin and Eriksen (1964) were unable to replicate the Helson-Steger effect. The Lappin-Eriksen procedures were not identical to those used by Helson and Steger, and it is inevitable that some one or more of these differences in procedure are responsible for the discrepancy in the findings. The inability to confirm a given set of results is sometimes distressing, but it also may have beneficial effects in that it leads to identification of variables which are relevant but which, previously, may have been judged otherwise. Lappin and Eriksen identify four differences between their procedures and those used by Helson and Steger, and it becomes apparent that future research will be directed toward determining which one (or more) of these differences is to be held liable for the failure to replicate.

Another inhibitory effect has been demonstrated in simple RT when S is given a long series of trials at a fairly rapid rate. Two Canadian investigators, Foley and Humphries (1962), used a visual stimulus and a keypressing response. The RT stimulus appeared, on the average, every 4 sec., and no warning signal was used. With these experienced Ss, there was no systematic change in RT over the 250 trials. However, it was noted that, periodically, S had a very long RT. That is, S would be "going along" producing RTs of from 150 to 160 msec. when suddenly his RT would become 350 msec., far outside the distribution of RTs he had produced earlier. Over the 250 trials, the number of such long RTs, or *blocks*, as they are commonly called, varied among Ss, with one S producing only one such deviant response and one S producing 10. In this study they did not occur more frequently as the trials increased.

Such blocking, while poorly understood, has long been known to occur in serial-reaction tasks (tasks where S must respond rapidly to each of a series of stimuli). Some of the earliest systematic work was done by Bills in 1931 on a variety of tasks. The blocking is so apparent that it can be "felt" by S. For example, we may use a color board constructed from a piece of cardboard on which several rows of patches of easily identifiable colors are mounted. As S, your task is to name the colors of the patches as rapidly as possible, following the rows as in reading. You will find that, basically, you can name them very rapidly, but as you continue the task you will occasionally find yourself blocking, actually unable to produce the name of the particular color patch you are observing. This blocking may last for a second or two, and then you may proceed as if it had not occurred. It can be seen that this is a different situation from that used by Foley and Humphries because one has to discriminate differences in the colors and name them appropriately. In the Foley-Humphries situation, S had only to discriminate between the light being on and not being on. Nevertheless, the blocking in both situations may be the result of the same basic mechanisms, although, as mentioned earlier, the phenomenon is not well understood.

Eye dominance. When we speak of handedness, we mean the preference for the use of one hand over the other for writing, eating, and so on. It is also true that most of us have a similar bias in our visual mechanism in that one eye is dominant over the other. Unlike handedness, however, where right-handedness is far more common than left-handedness, there is no majority rule in eye dominance; one is as likely to have left-eye dominance as right-eye dominance. In a study by Minucci and Connors (1964), RT was studied as a function of eye dominance. If a single eye is stimulated by a visual stimulus, will RT differ as a function of eye dominance? A condition was also included in which both eyes were stimulated. The RTs were taken at four different intensity levels of the RT stimulus, which, for our purposes, may be identified as 1, 2, 3, and 4, from lowest to highest intensity. On each trial E gave a verbal ready signal, S depressed a switch and then, upon the occurrence of the RT stimulus, released the switch as rapidly as possible. The data are based on 10 Ss each given 10 trials under each of the 12 conditions (four intensities and three visual conditions) by randomization of conditions.

The results are plotted in Fig. 7-2. We may note first that RT decreases as a function of stimulus intensity thus supporting the results shown in Fig. 7-1 where an auditory stimulus was varied in intensity. The data also show that the RTs were shorter for the dominant than for the nondominant eye, but that they were shorter still when both eyes were stimulated. As a result of some mechanism, there is a summation effect; it is as if the RT stimulus

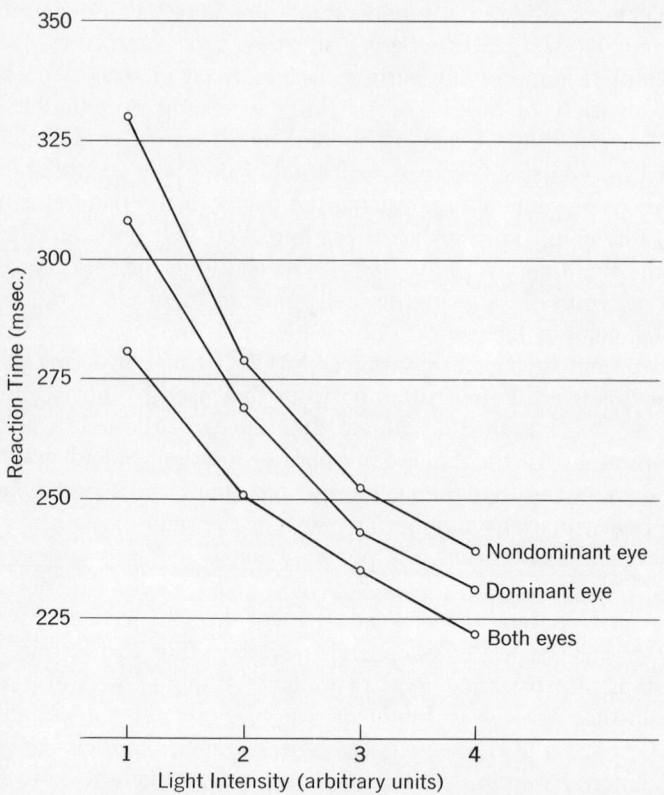

Fig. 7-2. Reaction time as a function of intensity of light stimulus and nature of viewing conditions. Data from Minucci and Connors (1964).

has greater intensity when presented to both eyes than when presented to each singly.

Other variables. Competition between Ss (seeing who can produce the shortest RT to a given stimulus) will result in shorter RTs than if S works individually (Church, 1962). If S is told whether his RTs are shorter or longer than they were on a previous series, the RTs become appreciably shorter than they do if such information is not afforded him (Church & Camp, 1965). Reaction time has been related to weather changes. Two German investigators, Muecher and Ungenheuer (1961), obtained RTs from 20,000 people attending an auto show in Munich during a 57-day period. The RTs were found to be longer on days when abrupt changes in weather were occurring. Should we draw cause-effect conclusions from such data? Should we conclude that the weather changes were the cause of the increased RTs? If not, how would you go about determining whether or not weather changes cause differences in RTs?

Component Analysis

We have repeatedly pointed out that the growth of an experimental discipline occurs as a result of breaking gross phenomena into parts for independent study. The study of RT as a component of more complex tasks is indicative of this kind of analysis. It might seem that RT is almost as "small" a component as it is possible to work with; that is, it might seem that it is not reducible to smaller components. However, this is not correct, and recent work is showing how RT has components which can be studied separately. The nature of the breakdown of simple RT may be illustrated by the work of Bartlett (1963).

The RT stimulus in Bartlett's study was a flash of light, produced following a ready signal. The S, as if ready to initiate a table-pounding response, sat with his elbow placed on the table. The response was the movement of the forearm. Bartlett measured three different components of the response. First, he measured muscle action potentials. Electrodes, attached to the muscles responsible for forearm thrust in this situation, "picked up" the initiation of muscle contractions. This first component represents the time between the onset of the visual stimulus and the moment at which the "message" produces the initiation of muscle contraction. Second, by a sensitive gauge, he measured the point in time following the RT stimulus at which the arm started to move, and third, the point at which the movement of the arm was sufficient to close a switch. This latter measure, of course, is what is commonly taken as RT—the time between the onset of an RT stimulus and the pressing of a switch.

For three Ss for a number of trials (extending over several days), the RT measure averaged 168 msec. This total time is broken down as follows: muscle action potentials appeared 114 msec. following the onset of the stimulus; the arm started to move at 142 msec.; and the movement was sufficient to depress the switch at 168 msec. The above data are for a dim visual stimulus. We have seen that RT decreases as the RT stimulus intensity increases. In this same study, Bartlett also used a bright visual stimulus, and the overall RT to it averaged 158 msec., or 10 msec. less than for the dim visual stimulus. This difference could be accounted for almost entirely by the difference in the point in time at which the muscle-action potentials first appeared for the two stimuli. For the bright stimulus they occurred, on the average, 105 msec. after stimulus onset, or 9 msec. sooner than they did for the dim stimulus.

This is a new area of analysis, and how consistent future results will be remains to be seen. However, if reliable components of overall RT can be assessed by the above methods, or by similar methods, research can proceed to determine where in the RT sequence the effects of various independent variables are located.

NOT-SO-SIMPLE REACTION TIME

What might we as *Es* do to complicate slightly the simple RT situation? Changing the RT stimulus from trial to trial would be one procedure we could follow. For example, the S could be instructed to respond as quickly as possible when *either* a visual stimulus or an auditory stimulus occurs. There is no obvious reason why RT should differ in this situation as compared with one in which the stimuli are always visual or always auditory. The evidence indicates that normal Ss do show comparable RTs in the two situations, but schizophrenic patients do not. With such patients, the RTs are shorter if successive stimuli are presented in the same modality than if the stimuli change from one modality to the other on successive trials (Sutton, Hakerem, Zubin, & Portnoy, 1961).

As a second change, we might keep the same RT stimulus from trial to trial but allow any one of several responses to be made to the stimulus. For example, S might have two keys, one for each index finger, so that he can respond with either key, always, of course, responding as quickly as possible. An experiment similar to this has been done (Morin & Forrin, 1963). Offhand, the results of such a procedure might seem quite uninteresting and unimportant. These two words, uninteresting and unimportant, sometimes appear in psychological literature as well as the literature of other disciplines, and it is appropriate for us to inquire into their meanings in such contexts.

To say that a given fact or relationship or phenomenon is uninteresting may mean at least two different things. First, it may mean that this fact must necessarily be so because of other facts. Assume that we know the distance to C and that this distance is constituted of distance A plus distance B. Assume further that we know distance A. It might be said to be uninteresting to determine distance B empirically because we know what it has to be.

A further illustration of this first meaning of uninteresting may be presented. Assume that you are the S. The E tells you two things: (1) the average height of adult men and women combined, and (2) the fact that the average height of men is greater than the average height of women. Then you are blindfolded, and *E* parades before you (one at a time) a series of 100 randomly drawn adult men and women. As each person pauses in front of you, *E* tells you his (or her) height, and your task is to guess the sex. After your 100 judgments are complete, the data are analyzed, and it is found that you performed well above chance expectancies. Such a finding might be said to be uninteresting because it had to occur if you applied the facts given you.

The discovery of the obvious, therefore, is the first meaning of the word uninteresting, and we may have a tendency to scorn the uninteresting. Yet we should not be smug about the matter, for the obvious is not always discovered to be as it should be. Sometimes when we measure B, we find that it is not the B we get by subtracting A from C. We may illustrate this. In word-association tests the *S* is given a stimulus word and is requested to respond as quickly as possible with another word which the stimulus word suggests to him. If the stimulus word is *man*, about 75 percent of adults will respond with *woman*, with perhaps one *S* out of 1000 Ss responding with *cow*. If the stimulus word is *lamp*, about 63 percent will respond with *light*, with one *S* out of 1000 Ss responding with *rug*. The most frequent response in each case (*woman* and *light*) may be thought of as strong associates, the infrequent responses (*cow* and *rug*), as weak associates. Now we construct a list of many pairs of stimulus words and their weak associates, and a list of many pairs of words and their strong associates. The lists are given to Ss to learn so that when each stimulus word is presented *S* must be able to produce the appropriate response word. In a high-associate list, for example, when *man* is presented *S* must respond with *woman*. In a low-associate list when *man* is presented, *S* must respond with *cow*. It would seem obvious, to the point of being uninteresting, that the list of high associates would be learned far more rapidly than the list of low associates. With adult learners, however, this may not occur; both lists will be learned with equal speed. The obvious is sometimes not so obvious.

A second use of the term uninteresting may occur when a given fact (or relationship or phenomenon) exists in isolation in that it does not seem to be related to anything else we know—it does not seem to have any relationship to existing theories or to existing interests of other Es. A single experiment which examines the influence of some independent variable on pogo-stick performance might be judged uninteresting in this sense of the term. Pogo-stick performance may be far afield from the behavior studied by other investigators, and just where pogo-stick behavior fits is unknown. Such isolated studies are not uncommon. Of course, experimentation must start somewhere, and a series of studies on pogo-stick behavior might lead to an integration of this behavior with other, better understood behaviors.

Turning next to the word *unimportant*, we can say without fear of contradiction that the most hideous insult we as investigators can receive is to be told that our research is unimportant. It is worse than being called stupid, for we might disclaim responsibility for being stupid, but when we invest time and effort in research we cannot disown it. What does unimportant mean? Sometimes it means much the same as uninteresting in that the research is said to demonstrate the obvious. In this sense the word trivial might be a synonym. However, perhaps the most uninformed use of the word *unimportant* comes from those who look at research results with a single criterion in mind, that implied by the question, "What good is it?" If no application of the findings to real-life problems can be found, the findings are automatically said to be unimportant. By this criterion, unless knowledge can be seen to be useful, the effort expended in obtaining that knowledge is not respected. There are two considerations which seem relevant to this use of the term.

First, at the general level, the accretion of new knowledge is the life-blood of modern civilizations where intellectual endeavors necessarily supersede all others. New knowledge may reduce fears caused by the unknown, and even though new knowledge may produce new fears, it at least tells us why there should be fear of it. New knowledge, whether useless or useful by practical criteria, provides aesthetic pleasures to many people in the same sense that a painting, a symphony, or a beautiful sunset offers pleasure to others. And, except for aesthetic purposes, "What good is a sunset?"

Second, and at the level concerned with knowledge developed by experimental procedures, the facts of history plainly and insistently tell us that we cannot at the moment judge the ultimate usefulness of an experimental discovery and expect that judgment to have validity. What may appear to be useless today may become very useful tomorrow. No one is so wise that he can view the future on this matter with any degree of certainty. The history of research is replete with illustrations.

Faraday, the man who contributed so much to our basic understanding of electricity, was not concerned with the usefulness of his discoveries. Gregor Mendel, the Austrian monk who worked out the basic laws of genetics, might have been judged at the time to be doing useless work, but the hybrid industries of agriculture today stem from what he did. Rutherford, who first understood nuclear transmutations and who first produced them experimentally in the early 1930's, believed no practical use would be found for nuclear energy. Psychologists have spent many hours in the laboratory studying the variables involved in animal learning. Even those who should have known better have decried this waste of energy; yet, when it became necessary to orbit an animal as a test before man's ascent into space, this accumulated wisdom was available and became immensely useful. Even a study of the factors involved in jumping on a pogo stick may be helpful as a starting point for estimating the problems a man will face in getting about on the moon where the gravity is slight.

Finally, let us consider a hypothetical illustration. Let us assume that during your junior year in college you find yourself majoring in biology. Furthermore, through some quirk, your interest begins to center on bugs. You decide to carry your studies on into graduate work. Your parents tolerate this, partly because it gives them an uneasy but definite feeling of status to have someone in the family engaged in research and partly because they think it is a momentary whim and that you will soon be back home to enter your father's business. But you don't come home, and it becomes apparent to them that you are thoroughly happy with your work. Your parents have inquired into the nature of your research, but you manage to sidestep this question for you are quite sure what their reactions will be. Finally, however, they corner you, and you have no recourse but to tell them that you are studying fireflies. Oh, how you wish you could say that the research is classified, or that you are working on a cancer cure. But you tell them that your central interest is fireflies. To say the least, this is somewhat puzzling to your parents, and they pursue the questioning with primary emphasis on why you are doing this research. You explain that you are studying the life cycles of fireflies, their methods of reproduction, territory covered by them, sources of the "fire," and so on. You have filled several notebooks with de-detailed observations on the firefly in its natural habitat and have done several experiments in which you have varied temperature, humidity, diet, and so on.

Your parents are insistent: "What are you doing this for?" You explain to them that not much is known about this insect and that you are attempting to fill this gap in our knowledge. "But," they persist, "what good is all this knowledge; what are you going to do with it?" You indicate to them that when your work seems fairly complete and when you are able to make the necessary comparisons with other species of the insect family, you may prepare a short book on your findings. At this your father lights up, and he suggests that you have been rather cagey about this whole matter. For, he continues, while he doesn't see right offhand who would buy such a book, he suspects that the sales will make you a nice little bundle of cash. Then you tell him that more than likely it will cost several hundred dollars to have the book published and that it is doubtful the sales will ever pay this back. Your bewildered father feels that life has dealt him a severe blow.

This hypothetical illustration, as well as those real ones given earlier, represent men doing research in its pure sense; that is, the work was not done because it was seen to have a practical application. They did not have to have an answer to the question "What good is it?" in order to justify the research. That it did in fact turn out to have great usefulness cannot be denied. In like manner, your knowledge of the firefly may ultimately be of great value in a practical sense. Let us not be hasty in judging a piece of research or a topic of research as being unimportant. Undoubtedly, much research in all disciplines slips away into oblivion, providing only momentary pleasure to a few, but much research is saved from oblivion because it sooner or later is perceived to be of aid in understanding nature as a whole or because the principles are found useful in a practical sense. Sidman (1960) has said this very nicely: "The cumulative development of a science provides the only final answer as to the importance of any particular data . . ." (p. 41)

Back to reaction time and to the particular experimental situation described. You will recall that we have a single stimulus and two response keys, one for each index finger. The S may respond with either key. We will use three groups of Ss, randomly assigned. One group is allowed to respond only with the key under the left index finger, a second only with the key under the right index finger, and the third, with either. We have said that superficially this situation might be judged by some as uninteresting and perhaps unimportant. As an antidote toward the use of such terms in connection with research results, you should "make up" a set of results from these three conditions which you might describe as being both interesting and important. In addition, let your imagination have free rein in speculating how certain findings might be used in the future in a very predictable manner, but do not allow yourself to insist that if you cannot see any ultimate use for the findings, they are unimportant; some other student may have a more vivid imagination than you have.

Choice RT

The next step in increasing the complexity of RT situations is that of having multiple stimuli in the display to which different responses must be made. The most frequently used situation is one in which there are two different stimuli, with S required to make a different response to each. The stimuli are always presented sequentially, never simultaneously, for the paradigms under discussion. Within this restriction, two paradigms have been used. Let the two stimuli be labeled S1 and S2, and the two responses, R1 and R2. In the first paradigm, two keys are available (and we use "key" as a general expression for any response device, for example, a button or switch). When S1 occurs, S is to respond with R1 (pressing the R1 key), and when S2 occurs, S is to respond with R2. On successive trials, S1 and R1 appear in a random order.

In the second paradigm, only one key is available. The S is instructed that when S1 occurs, the key is to be depressed but that when S2 occurs, the key is *not* to be depressed. Thus, the R2 response is that of *not* responding. Both paradigms represent a form of *choice* RT, as distinct from simple RT. We may call the first paradigm the *yes-yes* paradigm, meaning that a positive response must be made to each stimulus, and we may call the second paradigm the *yes-no* paradigm, indicating that a positive response is made to only one of the two stimuli. The effects of the two paradigms have been studied by Broadbent and Gregory (1962), two English investigators.

Their experiment employed three independent variables, one of which was the nature of the response system involved. For the auditory system the stimuli were two words, BID and DID, and the response was saying the word as quickly as possible when it was presented by a tape recorder. The order of appearance of the two stimulus words was random. Under the *yes-yes* paradigm, S responded by saying the same word that he heard. In the *yes-no* paradigm, S responded only when the word BID occurred; no response was to be made when DID was the stimulus.

In another set of conditions, representing a different response system from that above, the stimuli were tactile vibrations on the index finger of each hand. The S responded to this stimulus by pressing a key with the index finger. In the *yes-yes* paradigm he responded by pressing the key under the finger stimulated. In the *yes-no* paradigm he responded only when the right index finger was stimulated and did not respond when the left index finger was stimulated.

The two variables above yield four conditions—tactile stimulation with each paradigm and auditory stimulation with each paradigm. A third variable introduced in the Broadbent-Gregory study is known as *S-R compatibility*. The S refers to a particular stimulus and the R to the response control (e.g., a button) associated with the stimulus. If the stimuli of a given display and the response controls associated with those stimuli are aligned in such a manner as to be congruent with S's already established habits, we would speak of high S-R compatibility. If they are not so aligned, we would speak of some lesser degree of compatibility. For example, if there is a horizontal row of five lights below which there are five switches also in a horizontal row, and if the first light is associated with the first switch, the second light with the second switch, and so on, S-R compatibility is high. If the first switch is associated with the third light, the second with the first, and so on, S-R compatibility is low.

We have noted that when the spatial relationships between stimuli and the controls associated with those stimuli are in harmony with S's established habits, S-R compatibility is high. How did these habits become established in the first place? Probably they were established because the various display-control systems with which S is familiar have a certain commonality in their display-control relationships. To make a left turn, we turn the wheel to the left; to open a window of the car, we turn the crank below that window; to switch on a light in a bedroom, we normally expect to find the switch in or near the bedroom, not in the basement. At least the numbers, if not the letters, are aligned sequentially on a typewriter. From experience with many such systems as those illustrated, we probably build up habits of expecting spatial correspondence between the stimuli and the response controls. Spatial alignment as such may facilitate the development of these strong habits, but there are habits which do not have such intrinsically compelling spatial alignments. For example, there is nothing intrinsically compatible about hot water emerging from the left faucet and cold water from the right, but when a plumber inadvertently gets his pipes crossed, no end of grief occurs in such an incompatible system.

This third variable in the Broadbent-Gregory study, S-R compatibility, consisted of the two extreme values, compatible and not compatible. For the verbal response, the system was said to be compatible if S responded with the word shown; for example, to BID he responded BID. In the incompatible condition, S responded to BID by saying DECK and to DID by saying DIM. In the incompatible condition, therefore, S could not merely echo the stimulus presented but had to emit a different word. It should be noted that this form of incompatibility is not defined in terms of spatial correspondence. Spatial correspondence was used, however, in the other response system where the stimuli were tactual. In this system, compatibility was defined as responding with the finger stimulated. In the *yes-yes* paradigm S responded with the left finger when it was stimulated and with the right finger when it was stimulated. In the *yes-no* paradigm, of course, he responded with the right finger only when it was stimulated and did not respond at all when the left finger was stimulated. In the incompatible condition, stimulation of the left finger required responding with the right, and stimulation of the right required responding with the left (in the *yes-yes* paradigm). In the *yes-no* paradigm, S responded with the right finger when the left one was stimulated and did not respond when the right finger was stimulated.

In review, we see that three variables were manipulated and that each variable was combined factorially with every other variable. To combine factorially means that each level of a given variable occurs with each level of all other variables. In the present experiment, response system or modality (tactile and auditory) was first combined with paradigms (*yes-yes* and *yes-no*) to produce four different conditions, and then S-R compatibility (compatible or not compatible) was combined to make a total of eight different conditions. We would speak of this as a 2 x 2 x 2 design. As may be gathered, there is no end to the way in which variables may be combined. If E could expect to "make any sense" out of the results he might combine 10 levels of 10 different variables, thus having 10^{10} different or unique conditions. On second thought, E would not live long enough to finish gathering the data for such an enormous experiment, so we need not be concerned about his ability to interpret the results.

Four different groups of Ss were used to gather the data for the eight conditions. Two of the groups worked under the auditory-response system, one having the compatible condition and the other the incompatible. Two other groups worked under the tactile-response system, and, again, one had the compatible condition and the other, the incompatible. For these two variables, therefore, we have a random-groups design. However, the third variable (paradigm) was handled within each group by giving each S both the *yes-yes* and the *yes-no* paradigms. Each S was given two sessions, and it is reported that half the Ss received the *yes-yes* paradigm during the first session and the *yes-no* paradigm during the second session. For the other half of the Ss, the order was reversed. The purpose, of course, was to attempt to equalize the effects of progressive error for the two paradigms.

The Ss were Royal Navy enlisted men, divided among the four conditions as seen in Table 7-1. Just how the Ss were assigned to the four groups

TABLE 7–1
MEAN REACTION TIMES (MSEC.) AS A FUNCTION OF RESPONSE SYSTEM, COMPATIBILITY, AND RT PARADIGM. DATA FROM BROADBENT AND GREGORY (1962).

RESPONSE SYSTEM	S-R COMPATIBILITY	N	YES-YES	YES-NO
Auditory	Compatible	11	284	292
Auditory	Incompatible	6	444	354
Tactile	Compatible	12	193	194
Tactile	Incompatible	6	300	255

is not clear from the report; we can be sure only that they were not assigned randomly if the restriction was included that the number of Ss in each condition be equal. Also, since there is an odd number of Ss in one of the groups, the counterbalancing of the order of paradigms could not have been perfect, although we may presume that little bias would be present.

The nature of the comparisons between the *yes-yes* and the *yes-no* conditions requires discussion. For the verbal system, E scored only the RT to BID, since this was the only stimulus to which S responded in the *yes-no* condition. Thus, RTs to DID, a stimulus to which S was to respond positively only in the *yes-yes*, were ignored. Likewise, in the tactile system, E scored only the responses of the right finger, for again, in the *yes-no* condition, S did not (or at least, was supposed not to) respond with the left key. We would clearly anticipate that, at least early in the series, particularly under the incompatible conditions, S would make some errors. Nothing is said about such responses in this report. However, each S had 120 trials each session, and E used only the responses on trials 61-70 and 111-120 in presenting the data. Thus, the first 60 trials probably eliminated erroneous responses. Each stimulus was preceded by a "ready" signal approximately 2 sec. before the stimulus was presented, and the interval between successive stimuli was 5 sec.

Although we do not have direct comparisons with simple RTs, the choice RTs given in Table 7-1 can be noted to be appreciably longer than any we dealt with in the earlier section. This is merely to say that we may expect that choice RTs will be longer than simple RTs. In looking at Table 7-1, we may view the data for the auditory response system as one experiment and those for the tactile systems as another, for we have no reasonable grounds on which to compare one with the other because of lack of knowledge of equivalence of intensities of the RT stimuli in the two systems. Therefore, we have, in effect, two 2 x 2 experiments. However, for both systems it is quite apparent that RTs with compatible relations are much shorter than those with incompatible relations. Looking next at the influence of paradigm, we find that whether or not it influences RT depends upon whether the situation is compatible or incompatible. With compatible situations, there is essentially no difference between the two paradigms for either response system. But with incompatibility, the RTs are appreciably longer under the *yes-yes* paradigm than under the *yes-no* paradigm. This is to say, then, that the effects of paradigm and S-R compatibility interact, and this interaction is evident in the results for both response systems.

A puzzle. Consider yourself an S who is seated in front of a table. Mounted on the tabletop within a relatively small area are five small neon bulbs and two levers, as schematized in Fig. 7-3. You are told that for a

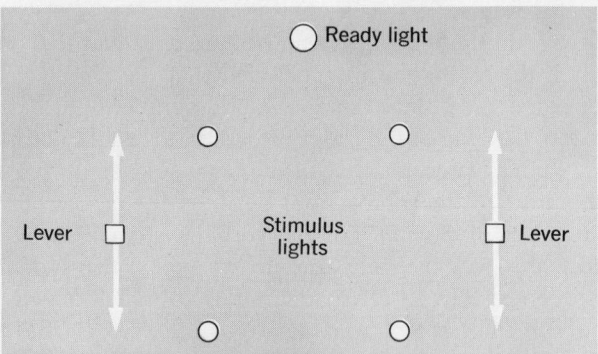

Fig. 7-3. Essentials of the choice reaction situation as used by Gottsdanker, Broadbent, and Van Sant (1963). The S responded to the two left lights by pushing the left lever toward the light which came on following the ready signal. The right lever was used for the two right lights in the same manner.

series of trials, one of the left two lights will come on 1 sec. after the ready light. With your thumb and index finger resting on the lever at all times, your task is to move the lever as quickly as possible *toward* the light when it comes on. A timer is started when the stimulus light comes on, and a slight movement of the lever stops the timer, thus allowing measurement of the RT. Fifteen sec. following a given response, the ready light glows again, and 1 sec. later, one of the two lights once more comes on. Which of the two lights will come on is the unknown from trial to trial. The two lights on the right could also be used for a comparable series of trials.

There were two basic conditions in this experiment, performed by Gottsdanker, Broadbent, and Van Sant (1963). In one, Ss performed just as described above, and this is referred to as the Single-Choice condition. In the other, the Double-Choice condition, both pairs of lights were used. The S sat with his left hand on the left lever, his right hand on the right lever. He was told that first one of the left two lights would come on and he was to respond as quickly as possible just as in the Single-Choice condition. However, in addition, he was told that .5 sec. after one of the two left lights came on, one of the two right lights would come on and he was to respond to that light in the same manner as in the Single-Choice condition. Of interest to these investigators was the critical comparison of the RT under the Single-Choice condition with the RT to the *first* light in the Double-Choice condition. Assume the Single-Choice condition used the left two lights, and the Double-Choice used these same two lights for the first response. How will the RTs compare? Obviously, the only difference between these two conditions is that S knew, in the Double-Choice condition, that he was also going to have to respond to the right lights after responding to the left lights.

It should be clear that there was no funny business in this procedure. In the Single-Choice condition S always worked with the same two lights over a series of trials, and he always knew that one of the two would come on. In the Double-Choice condition, S always knew which of the pair of lights would be used for the first reaction. Thus, S did not have to guess which of the pair of lights would be used first in the Double-Choice condition.

Six Ss were used, each S serving in both conditions. Actually, there were two subconditions under each of the two main conditions. For the Single-Choice condition, one session was given using the left two lights and another, using the right two lights. Under the Double-Choice conditions, one session was given in which the left lights were first and the right lights second, and another session in which the order was reversed. Therefore, each S served in four sessions, and 40 trials were given at each session. So that progressive errors could be balanced, the order of the conditions within the four sessions differed for each S. In addition, S was given two practice sessions during which time he had considerable experience with all conditions. Finally, at the beginning of each session some "warm up" trials were presented before the 40 experimental trials were started.

Even with practice, Ss made mistakes or errors, which consisted of moving the lever the wrong direction (away from the lighted bulb). For all Ss combined, 5.2 percent of the trials produced errors in the Single-

Choice condition, and 5.6 percent, in the Double-Choice. Whenever an error was made, S was not told, but the trial was rerun after the regular series of 40 trials.

In the report the RTs are given for each session, and within each session RTs are given for moving the lever up and for moving it down separately. However, we have determined the mean of these various subconditions in order to get a single value to represent the RT for the Single-Choice and another for the Double-Choice. These means are 250 msec. and 292 msec., respectively. It should be clear that the RT for the Double-Choice condition represents the RT for the first light, thus corresponding to the RT in the Single-Choice condition. The difference between the two means is highly significant statistically and occurred without exception in all subcondition comparisons. This experiment, therefore, shows that when S knows he is going to have to make another response shortly after making a first one, his RT for the first one is lengthened. This study when introduced was called a puzzle because, it seems, no ready explanation is available for it. The Es suggest that one might talk about differences in the concentration or attention between the two situations, but they point out that since we do not have independent measures of such assumed processes, we are not being helped very much.

How do we go about trying to get a better understanding of a new phenomenon? Usually, the procedure is to determine initially some of the variables which regulate or produce the phenomenon. Let us speculate briefly about some variables and what an exploration of their effects might tell us. First, as Gottsdanker and his co-workers point out, the time between successive stimuli in the Double-Choice condition should be a relevant variable. In the above study it was .5 sec. However, assume we were to allow 30 sec. to intervene; wouldn't it seem likely that the Double-Choice effect would disappear? Under such circumstances the second response would be like a new response, since it would not be tied intimately to the first. Therefore, an increase in the interchoice interval in the Double-Choice condition ought to produce a systematic reduction in the RT so that at some relatively short interval the first RT should be as short as it is in the Single-Choice condition.

Is the effect a modality effect? Suppose the second response in the Double-Choice condition is to be made by moving a lever to an auditory signal from one of two earphones. If the phenomenon does not occur under such circumstances, we might suspect that it is due to some lag or refractoriness in the visual system. Does the phenomenon occur only with bilateral responding? Suppose both the first stimulus and the second stimulus are on the left; would the effect be increased or decreased? Quite clearly we could lay out a program of research in an effort to "run down" this phenomenon. As a matter of fact, it would appear to be a most enjoyable enterprise.

"Same" or "different" judgments. The task facing S in a study by Nickerson (1965) was that of deciding whether the second of two sequentially presented English letters was the same as or different from the first. All of the 16 letters used were consonants, chosen to have minimal visual form similarity; for example, both C and G were not used. The first consonant appeared on a screen for 3 sec. Then a blank interval of 1 sec. occurred, and this was followed by the second letter which remained on until S responded. If the second letter was the same as the first, S pressed one key, or if different, a second key. The empirical question concerned the difference in RT for the two judgments.

The four Ss in this experiment served for 22 sessions. In each session 64 RT trials were given, in 32 of which the second letter was the same as the first and in 32 of which the second consonant was different from the first. The same and different conditions were randomized within each block of 16 trials and were subject to the restriction that each occur eight times. The particular letter used on a given trial was determined randomly by drawing from the pool of 16. If the trial required a different second letter, it was chosen by drawing randomly from the remaining pool of 15.

The mean RT for the four Ss under the two conditions was determined for each session. On all 22 sessions the RT was longer for the different judgment than for the same judgment. The data also show that the Ss improved (their RTs became shorter) from session to session, with the greatest improvement being made in the first three sessions. On the first session the mean RTs were 628 msec. and 656 msec. for the same and different judgments respectively; on the twenty-second session, the corresponding values were 329 and 382.

Similarity and choice RT. Similarity in one form or another is probably the most widely manipulated variable in experimental psychology. The study of difference thresholds is a study of similarity; the scaling of stimuli or attributes of stimuli along a dimension is in a sense a scaling of similarity. We will see in subsequent chapters many other illustrations of the effects of this variable. In any choice RT situations, similarity will likewise be a powerful variable. As an illustration, suppose we told the S that we would present either a circle or an ellipse as an RT stimulus. Further, we told him that if the figure is a circle, he must make response A, or if an ellipse, response B. It is apparent that if the ellipse was only slightly deviant from a true circle, S would take longer to respond appropriately than if the figure was clearly flattened. Length of RT (or decision time) is directly related to the similarity of the stimuli.

The illustration we will use here concerns similarity of meaning among words, as varied in two experiments by Slamecka (1963). On a given trial S sat poised with a finger of each hand on a different switch. In this case, S indicated his own readiness by depressing both keys and saying "ready." One second later a cover dropped revealing a card, and as it dropped, a clock was started. When S released one of the keys, the clock was stopped, providing the RT measure. In the center of the card was a key word, below and to the left, another word, and below and to the right, a third word. The S had to decide which of the two lower words was more similar in meaning to the key word. If he judged the lower left word to be more similar to the key word than the lower right word, he released the left key. If the right word was judged more similar, he released the right key.

The variable was the meaningful similarity between the two lower words. For all cards (in one experiment) one of the two words was a "good" synonym to the key word; therefore, variation in the similarity between the two lower words produced differences in the similarity between each lower word and the key word. The similarity was determined independently in a previous experiment. Three levels of similarity were used, with 12 instances (12 cards) for each. In the two experiments, there were two kinds of similarity. The first varied meaningful similarity, as described above. An illustration of each level of similarity follows.

High Similarity: key word, *unselfish;* lower or choice words, *generous* and
  giving.
Medium Similarity: key word, *brutal;* lower or choice words, *savage* and
  rude.
Low Similarity: key word, *clear;* lower or choice words, *distinct* and *obscure.*

In high similarity, both of the two choice words are about equally good synonyms of *unselfish.* In medium similarity, *savage* is a better synonym of *brutal* than is *rude.* In low similarity, *distinct* is the good synonym; indeed, the other word, *obscure,* is an antonym.

In the second experiment a form of similarity that we will call contextual similarity was varied. In this case, the same key words were used for all levels of similarity. Again, illustrations will indicate the nature of the similarity. For these three illustrations, *black* was the key word.

High Similarity: choice between *soot* and *coal.*
Medium Similarity: choice between *basement* and *cave.*
Low Similarity: choice between *cream* and *tar.*

As noted earlier, for each level of similarity there were 12 different choices, or a total of 36. For each experiment there were 12 Ss, and by the simple expedient of shuffling the cards, the order of presenting the cards was different for each S. The median RT for each S was determined for each level of similarity, and the means of these medians used as estimates of RT. The results for both experiments are plotted in Fig. 7-4. We have spaced the three levels of similarity equally along the baseline, although we do not in fact know that they are equally spaced psychologically. However, the results are quite evident; the more similar the two alternatives, the longer the RT. It should be noted that the RT is measured in seconds, not milli-

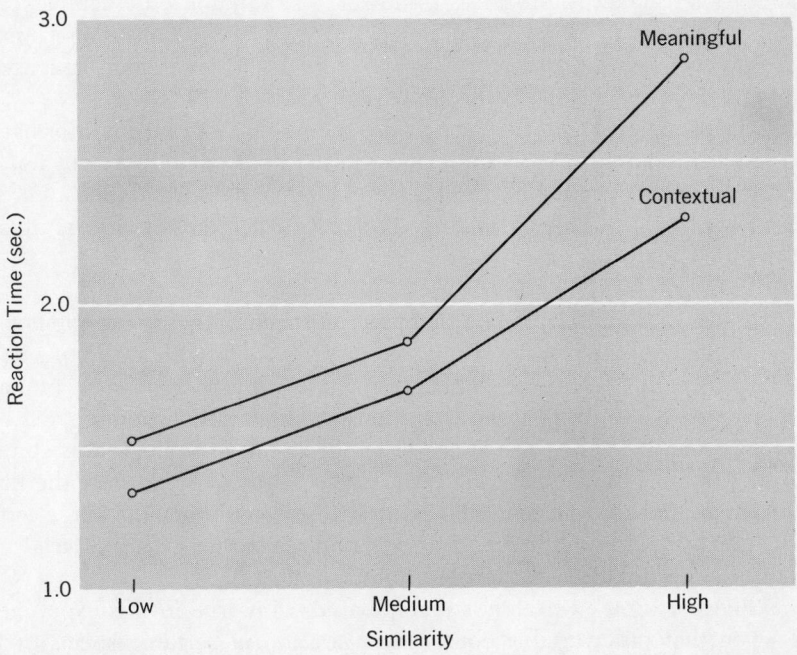

Fig. 7-4. Reaction time as a function of meaningful and contextual similarity between choice words. Data from Slamecka (1963).

seconds, indicating that the RTs are much longer in this situation than any examined previously.

STILL MORE COMPLEX

Once we go beyond the simple two-choice situation, the number of permutations among stimuli and among response alternatives is endless. Nevertheless, these expanded situations parallel many of the tasks which, in fact, do occur in reality, and, therefore, they must be simulated in some manner in the laboratory if an understanding of them is to be achieved. Not only do the situations become analytically complex, but the equipment necessary to simulate them also becomes complex. There is still another level of complexity which is accompanying research in the area, and that is explanatory complexity. It might seem on the surface that RT cannot possibly require a complex explanatory system, but the nature of recent attempts belies this. For example, the following statement occurs as a conclusion to a recent article: "The . . . processes assumed . . . are admittedly complex, but there is no reason to believe that the cognitive processes subsuming human behavior, even in the case of relatively rapid choice reactions, are necessarily any simpler." (Fitts, Peterson, & Wolpe, 1963, p. 432)

Some of the explanatory concepts use the mathematics from information theory, and apparently with some success. The present writer will not attempt to transmit even the flavor of these mathematical formulations. For the student with mathematical facility, two excellent sources are available: Miller (1953) and Garner (1962).

Familiarity and number of stimuli. In an experiment by Fitts and Switzer (1962), the stimuli used were single letters. When a shutter lifted revealing a letter, S was to respond as rapidly as possible by naming the letter. There were three conditions, each condition being given to a different group of 15 Ss. In one condition all 26 letters appeared as stimuli, the order of appearance being random. In a second condition only the three letters E, P, and B were stimuli, and in a third condition, the three letters A, B, and C were stimuli. Each S was given three sessions, with 80 trials per session. Certain features of this design must be emphasized.

Whenever a task variable is manipulated, as is true in this experiment, and when that task variable consists of variation in certain aspects of the language (words, letters, sentences, parts of speech, and so on), we face a real possibility of confounding by some other task variable. Let us examine how such confounding might occur in the present study. A college student would be expected to be very familiar with the letters of the alphabet since he would have seen each thousands of times. Nevertheless, it is apparent that there are very large differences in the absolute number of times each letter has been seen. For example, A, E, and T occur more frequently in words than do Z, K, and Q. Would RT vary as a function of this differential frequency in the past experience of S? The data show that it will. In the condition in which all 26 letters were used as stimuli, the correlation between the frequency with which the letters occur in printed English and RT was .60. It is as if the letters which have been most frequently experienced in the past are "nearer the surface," so that when they appear on the screen as a stimulus, they can be spoken more quickly than those which have been less frequently experienced. Of course, the differences in RT are not large; the most rapid RT was to the letter A (approximately 420 msec.), and the slowest, to Z (500 msec.). However, it is clear that the frequency of the letters is related to RT when all 26 letters are used.

Next, consider the other two conditions, the one in which the three letters E, B, and P were used and the one in which A, B, and C were employed. The variable which the Es wanted to manipulate was the familiarity of the subset. This is to say that they believed that as a subset of three letters, A, B, and C would be more familiar *as a set* than would E, B, and P. Or, to say this another way, A, B, and C have occurred more frequently together in the past history of S than have E, B, and P. Following the same line of thinking, we would suspect that X, Y, and Z have occurred more frequently together than have C, F, and Q. In any event, the Es predicted that RTs would be shorter to the letters A, B, and C when these occurred over and over again in random order than they would be to E, B, and P when these occurred over and over again. They predicted this outcome because A, B, and C is a more familiar subset than is E, B, and P.

The results confirm the prediction; over all three sessions the average RT to the letters A, B, and C was consistently shorter than the average RT to E, B, and P. Can we attribute this to the intended variable (familiarity of subset), or is there another variable that is responsible? What about frequency of individual letters? We have seen that this is a determinant of RT; perhaps, on the average, the letters A, B, and C occur more frequently in printed English than do the letters E, B, and P. This is not true. In fact, the Es selected E, B, and P because these letters do occur individually with almost the same frequency as A, B, and C. However, the design of this experiment is such that the issue of the frequency of individual letters as a possible confounding agent can be quickly set aside. This can be done because the letter B occurred as a stimulus in all three conditions. Therefore, the RT to B can be determined in all three conditions. If it differs across conditions, this must be due to the presence of the other letters on other trials; differences in RT could not possibly be attributed to differences in frequency, for the frequency of B cannot differ from itself. The results show that RT to B was fairly similar when all 26 letters were used and when B occurred along with P and E. However, the RT to B under both of these conditions was appreciably longer across all three sessions than the RT to B when B occurred with A and C.

When a task variable is being manipulated, the beauty and power of using a common item or items across all conditions cannot be overemphasized. Such a procedure immediately eliminates the possibility of confounding by certain other task variables. In this particular case, if differences in RT across the conditions appear when the RT for only B is considered, we immediately eliminate the possibilities of frequency as a confounding variable. However, this procedure will not take care of all possible confounding variables. In this experiment, the Es wanted to attribute the difference in RT for the two conditions having three letters to differences in the familiarity of the subset. So, we must ask about still other possible differences among the two subsets. We have seen that the more similar the stimuli, the longer the RT. Looking at the three letters E, B, and P, we might say that the forms or configurations of the three letters are more similar than the forms of A, B, and C. If this is true, RT to B might be lengthened because S had more trouble distinguishing B from E and P than he did in distinguishing B from A and C. However, the Es were quite aware of this possibility and cite previous evidence to support the conclusion that the discriminability or tendency to confuse the three letters within each set is comparable. In short, even in such a simple stimulus situation, the possibility of confounding the results for a given task variable by its covariation with other task variables is very real. Over and over again we will find that manipulating a task variable, and holding other potential task variables constant, is one of the trickiest aspects of the experimentalist's work. We would hope that we would always be able to carry it off with a finesse equal to that shown by Fitts and Switzer in the above experiment.

Differential frequency within sessions. We have seen that the more frequently experienced letters produce shorter RTs than do the less frequently experienced letters. In the present study, the relative frequency of stimuli was manipulated within experimental sessions (Fitts, Peterson, & Wolpe, 1963).

The stimuli were all single-digit numbers (1-9). There were four conditions, each condition being given to an independent group of 12 Ss each. The critical stimulus was 1; it was varied in frequency in the experimental sessions, and since number of trials was kept constant, a necessary variation in the frequency of all other numbers occurred. On each session there was a total of 126 trials. In Cond. 14, each of the nine numbers occurred equally often, namely, 14 times, the order being random, of course. In Cond. 30, 1 occurred as a stimulus 30 times, with each of the other numbers occurring 12 times each. In Cond. 94, 1 occurred on 94 of the 126 trials, with each of the others occurring 4 times each. Finally, under Cond. 118, 1 was the stimulus on 118 of the 126 trials, with each of the other numbers occurring once. The response required was that of speaking the number as quickly as possible when the number was exposed from behind a rapidly acting shutter.

There were four sessions. On the first session all 48 Ss were given Cond. 14. Only on sessions 2, 3, and 4 were the differential conditions introduced for the four groups. One of the groups, of course, remained under Cond. 14 throughout all four sessions. The average RT decreased only slightly over the four sessions for this group. For the other three groups, however, distinct differences appeared on sessions 2, 3, and 4. The greater the frequency with which 1 appeared in the 126 trials, the shorter its RT and the longer the RT to the other numbers. There were only slight changes across sessions; that is, on session 2 the above effect was essentially as great as it was on session 4. The following values are only approximations, but they provide a notion of the magnitude of the effect. For Cond. 30, RT to the stimulus 1 averaged

370 msec., while RT to the other numbers averaged 400 msec. For Cond. 94, RT averaged 330 msec. to 1, and 420 msec. to the other numbers. Finally, for Cond. 118, RT to 1 was about 290 msec., and to the other numbers, 440 msec. Thus, there was a reciprocity—the faster the RT to 1, the slower it was to the other numbers.

The data show that the more frequently 1 occurs in a series of trials, the faster the RT to it. (Another experiment used 5 as the critical number and obtained the same results as those found with 1, so it is not an effect peculiar to 1.) The Ss were told before each of the last three sessions just what proportion of times each number would appear, and they were shown a bar graph to illustrate the proportions. How, then, are the results to be interpreted? We have seen that the more frequently letters have been experienced outside the laboratory, the faster the RT. Perhaps in the same sense we are producing differential frequency for the letters within the laboratory, and since 1 occurs most frequently it will be responded to most quickly. We can see, however, that it cannot be *only* this factor which is involved. In the first place, if it is mere frequency, RT to 1 should continue to decrease over sessions more than it does. Second, and most important, a simple frequency hypothesis could not explain the increase in RT for the other numbers. So it seems we need a somewhat more complicated explanatory system to account for the findings. On all of the conditions where 1 occurred more frequently than the other numbers, S on any given trial would predict that 1 had the greatest probability of being the number revealed. This ability to predict would be present on the first trial since S was instructed concerning the frequency with which the numbers would occur. Furthermore, S's confidence in his prediction would increase as a function of the increase in the frequency with which 1 occurred in the various conditions. Let us assume, therefore, that this confidence is reflected in the manner in which S "set" himself to expect 1 to be shown. The greater the frequency with which 1 occurs in a series (relative to the other numbers), the more ready he is to expect 1. In fact, in Cond. 118 (where 1 occurred on 118 of the 126 trials), the situation may closely approximate a simple RT situation since a choice reaction is so rarely required if S expects 1 to occur. The greater the frequency with which 1 occurs, the more likely S is to expect 1 on any given trial and, conversely, the less likely he is to expect a different number. Given these assumptions, we see that when 1 does occur and when S is expecting 1 to occur, the judgment is a "same" judgment. When S is expecting 1 to occur and it does not, it is a "different" judgment. We have seen in an earlier study that a different judgment takes longer than a same judgment. If the above analysis is correct, therefore, the present study reflects mechanisms corresponding to those involved in making same-different judgments. Perhaps, therefore, if we could explain the difference in RT for same-different judgments we could explain the present results.

SEARCH TASKS

In RT studies, either simple or complex, S is presented only one stimulus at a time and is asked to respond to it as quickly as possible. He may have to select an appropriate response—he may have to choose between pressing this key or that key, or saying this letter or that letter. But objectively, which stimulus he must respond to in most RT studies is never in doubt to S. In complex RT studies, S must discriminate among the response alternatives and make appropriate responses as quickly as possible. Even in most serial-responding tasks, where S is presented a long series of stimuli to which he must respond differentially, only a single stimulus occurs at the moment, and S must select the appropriate response. In search tasks the emphasis is reversed, namely, the major emphasis is placed upon discriminating among the members of a group of stimuli with the response indicator a minor factor. As a general description of search tasks we may say that multiple stimuli are used with S's task being that of locating or discovering a particular stimulus or a particular series of stimuli as specified by E. The common response measure is the time required.

Finding a needle in a haystack is the most celebrated of all search tasks. Somewhat less impossible, although more dramatic, are searches which occur frequently in an effort to find a downed plane in mountain terrain, a capsule of instruments in the ocean, or a lost child in a forest. Sometimes the stimulus is not completely specified, as in the case of a detective looking for clues to a crime where the appropriate stimulus might be a footprint, a hank of hair, or a drop of blood. Sometimes there is a serial search task such as the search investigators must make after a plane has exploded in the air. After scouring a wide area for scattered parts, they try to reassemble the plane piece by piece in an effort to determine the cause of the explosion. Without the use of haystacks, oceans, or exploding planes, we may devise laboratory situations which will allow us to discover the important variables in search behavior.

Some of the variables involved in search behavior are obvious. For example, other things being equal, if we were to search for a specified object among 30 other objects, we would very likely find it more rapidly than if we searched for it among 100 other objects. Or, if the object of search is highly similar to the other objects in the display, it will take longer to find than if it is dissimilar. Easy and difficult jigsaw puzzles are primarily determined by this variable of similarity. As we shall see, however, one of the problems of study concerns the effective ways of reducing this similarity. We will look not only at some of the tasks used to study search behavior, but also at some of the findings, and in doing so, will distinguish between discrete search tasks and serial search tasks. In the former task, a trial consists of finding one given stimulus; in the latter, a trial consists of finding a series of stimuli, each successive one being determined by the previous one.

Discrete Search

Directional search. Neisser (1963) has worked with a search task that is simple and yet allows the study of the influence of several variables. It is directional search since S is required to search in a specified order. The basic task may be described as follows. Pairs of letters are arranged in a column on a sheet of paper, the number of pairs perhaps totaling 50. A specified letter, perhaps the letter Q, occurs in only one pair. The S is instructed to start at the top of the column and proceed downward as rapidly as possible until he finds the letter Q. He starts at a ready signal which also starts a timer, and with his hand on a switch, he stops the timer when he finds Q.

In this particular situation, one variable which must necessarily influence search time is obvious, namely, the position in the series of the letter being searched for. Neisser shows this variable (position) to be linearly related to search time. But consider another variable. Suppose all pairs of letters except one contained Q, and we compare search time with the case in which all pairs of letters except one did *not* contain Q. Keeping position constant, in which case would search time be more rapid? Is it easier to detect the *presence* of a letter which occurs only once in a series of pairs, or is it easier to detect the *absence* of the letter in a pair when it occurs in all other pairs? The answer is that the former situation produces more rapid search time, and by an appreciable amount. Looking for Q is easier or faster than looking for no Q. Even after several problems a day for 18 days the difference remains. Just why it takes more time to discover that an item is missing than to discover its presence is not clear. Can you formulate a hypothesis that is testable?

We mentioned that similarity is likely to be a relevant variable in search behavior, and for this directional search task, Neisser shows it is indeed a potent factor. The letter Q can be thought of as having circular form, the letter Z, angular form. In one set of conditions circular-like letters, C, D, G, O, R, and U, were used as the other or context letters. For angular context letters he used E, I, M, V, W, and X. In two conditions Z occurred as the search letter, occurring once in the circular context and once in the angular. In two other corresponding conditions, Q was the search letter. The results were as anticipated. Search time for Q when it occurred in the angular context was less than when it occurred in the circular context; search time for Z when it occurred in the circular context was shorter than when it occurred in the angular.

What are some of the other variables that might be manipulated with this basic task? The number of letters in each item in the column could be varied. We have discussed the situation in which each item consists of only two letters. Suppose each item consisted of five letters and there were 20 such items in the column. Would the search time for a single letter be equivalent to that shown when the column consisted of 50 pairs? Or, suppose we did not require S to search directionally. What predictions would you make about mean search time as compared with directional scanning, and what prediction would you make about variability within S on a series of nondirectional trials compared with directional trials? Of course, the search letter would appear in a random position in the column on successive trials. Is it more "natural" to search down than up? What if the materials were digits, in which the population is only 10 rather than 26, as in the alphabet? Clearly, this task is amenable to a wide variety of variable manipulation.

Number of items and color coding. We will use a report by Smith (1962) to illustrate another approach to the study of search behavior. The display consisted of varying numbers of three-digit numbers presented to S by means of lantern slides. The slide may be visualized as consisting of 13 columns and 27 rows, for a total of 351 tiny squares. The numbers placed on a given slide were assigned randomly to these 351 squares, with the first two numbers of all the three-digit numbers on the slide unique and with the third number equally represented among the 10 possible. On each trial S was told the first two digits of the number for which he was to search; when S found the number, he pressed one of 10 numbered buttons to indicate the third digit. Exposure of the slide started a timer; pushing the appropriate button stopped it to provide the search time for the trial.

One variable of the experiment was the total number of three-digit numbers that appeared on the display, this total varying from 20 to 100 in increments of 20. A second variable was color coding, in which each subset of numbers upon a slide appeared in different colors. There were also conditions in which all numbers appeared in the same color. We will consider only the conditions in which the total number of numbers varied and in which five different colors were used to define subsets of equal size. Thus, with a display consisting of 20 numbers, four of these were printed in orange, four in blue, four in green, and so on. With 100 numbers, 20 were orange, 20 blue, and so on. It should be clear that the subsets had no property in common other than color, since the colors were assigned at random to the digits subject to the restriction that each color was used for an equal number of stimuli.

Before a slide was presented, S was told the first two digits of the number for which he was to search, and this also appeared on a small panel. In addition, S was told that the color of the search number was unknown, or he was told what its color was. If S did not know the color of the search number, there would be no reason to believe that because different numbers had different colors, search time would be influenced, and it wasn't (when compared with search time when all numbers were of a single color). Of course, search time increased as a function of the number of stimuli on the slide, and again this relationship was approximately linear. With 20 stimuli, search time was approximately 4 sec., and with 100 stimuli, 17 sec.

As expected, when S was told the color of the search number, search time was drastically reduced. With 20 stimuli, mean search time was about 2 sec., and with 100 stimuli, 5 sec. Color coding, of course, reduces the number of stimuli among which S must search. In fact, we come fairly close to predicting the effects of color coding by this principle alone. For example, with 100 stimuli, 20 of each color, performance when S is told the color should be almost the same as that shown when 20 stimuli are used and S is not told the color. The data come close to this expectation; 4 sec. search time was required for 20 stimuli when S was not told the color, and 5 sec. was required when there were 100 stimuli and he was told the color of the search stimulus.

In common discrete search tasks, S searches for a single object or stimulus. However, it is a perfectly reasonable expansion of this procedure to require S to find more than one specified stimulus. These might be two or more stimuli differing in some manner, or they might be several identical stimuli scattered around the display. In this latter case a second response measure becomes available because if S is not told the number of identical stimuli present in the display, an omission measure or a failure-to-detect measure is obtained in addition to a search-time measure (e.g., Promisel, 1961).

Techniques of search. As a final illustration of a discrete search task, we will look briefly at a study by Turner, Santos, and Solley (1962). A board, 4 ft. by 4 ft., contained 100 holes in a 10 by 10 matrix. Pegs placed in these holes could be used to hold plastic figures of a wide variety. The board was painted white as were the figures. On a given trial S was given a figure and required to point to one like it among those on the board. Number of stimuli was varied, and again it was found that there was a linear relationship between search time and number of stimuli. These investigators interrogated their Ss carefully concerning search methods. Three search methods were distinguished. The first, and most systematic, was that of proceeding up and down rows (or columns). The use of this method increased as the number of stimuli on the board increased. The second method was called global by the investigators and was said to have been used if S scanned the board in single or double sweeps or if he scanned by quadrants. This method was used more frequently than the systematic method when there was a small number of stimuli but decreased in frequency of use as the number of stimuli increased. The third method, which was very infrequently used, was that of randomly skipping from one stimulus to another.

Two points should be made about these techniques of search. First, we must be careful in accepting what an S says he did as representing in fact what he did do. We are all more or less capable of making up a "good story" on the spur of the moment; we might tell E what we thought he wanted to hear, or we might tell him something that would make our search behavior seem rational. Nevertheless, there are many instances in which Ss have been shown to report very reliably and validly when the validation is determined by independent measures. For example, in the present study, one E, observing the eye movements of S and relating them to the reported techniques of search, found little discrepancy.

A second point concerns possible relationships between techniques of search and proficiency of search. Although these Es did not relate techniques used by various Ss to search time, this could have been done. Suppose it were done and we found that those who use the systematic method have shorter search times than those who use the global method. There is a strong "force" which tends to lead us to the conclusion that, therefore, systematic search is a better technique than global search. As strong as this force is we must resist it, for clearly no such conclusion is justified. It is not justified because two different variables are involved, namely, different Ss and different methods. Thus, it is quite possible that those Ss who used the systematic search technique would have faster search times than those who did not even if the former used the global technique. The only way to reach a sound conclusion on such an issue is to do an experiment in which two random groups are formed, one being forced to use the systematic technique and the other, the global technique. This forcing may not be easy if one method is more natural than the other, but with strong instructions and penalties for not following the instructions, a reasonably good split in the use of the two techniques could be achieved.

Two final comments may be made about discrete search tasks. In reporting the above studies we have paid but little attention to the design. The reason for this is that the designs did not offer us anything new. By and large, most of the studies of discrete search have used a single group of Ss, with all of these Ss serving in all conditions of the experiment. We would simply point out again that such a design is not necessary; independent groups can be used equally well.

It was noted earlier that in the study of RT, apparatus to measure latencies to at least .10 sec. was almost mandatory. However, in studies of search time, it is quite possible to proceed without having to assemble equipment of this nature. A stopwatch can be used quite adequately for most studies of search behavior.

Serial Search

A serial search task conforms to the saying, "One thing leads to another." It is like a treasure hunt in which the finding of one clue gives directions for finding the second, the second, for the third, and so on. It would be quite possible to construct any number of serial search tasks, but so far as the present writer knows, only two have appeared in modern literature. The first to be discussed is known as the Tsai-Partington Numbers Test. (See Ammons [1955] for background.)

In the Numbers Test a series of numbers, perhaps 2 through 25, are splattered or randomized on a sheet of paper. In the middle of the paper, the digit 1 appears, distinctly set off from the other numbers, by having, for example, a circle around it. Given a start signal, S places his pencil on number 1, then searches for number 2 and draws a line to it, then searches for 3, draws a line from 2 to 3, then finds 4 and continues the line from 3 to 4, and so on. There is no magic in running the series to only 25; it could run to a smaller number or to a larger. Either of two response measures may be used: the highest number reached by S after a constant period of time for a trial; or, in terms of true search time, the time required for S to find and connect all the numbers (in appropriate order, or course), the search time then becoming the time required to connect all numbers.

An experiment conducted by the writer with six members of his class may be examined to illustrate the task and the influence of two variables on it (Underwood, 1961). Suppose we use only one random positioning of the numbers of the sheet and require S to use this same sheet on a series of trials. We would expect that he would remember from trial to trial the location of some of the numbers. Therefore, performance should increase from trial to trial—learning should be evident. On the other hand, if different randomizations of the numbers are used on successive trials (sheets), any improvement in performance due to learning should be minimal as Ss are restricted to improvement in skill of searching or in quickly connecting successive numbers with the pencil. Let us call the first situation the constant form and the second, the variable form. A second variable was the time between successive trials. In one condition, S, after completing one trial, went immediately to the next. In another condition, 60-sec. rest periods were inserted between each trial. The former condition is commonly known as massed practice, and the latter, as spaced or distributed practice. (The choice of these two variables was determined by a hypothesis which predicted that there should be an interaction between the effects of the two variables; since this did not occur we need not trouble ourselves with the hypothesis.) The two variables were combined orthogonally to produce a 2 by 2 design. In addition, we designed the experiment to allow us to examine the effect of one other variable, namely, the effects of Es. All of the six different Es ran an equivalent number of Ss for each condition, namely, three for each condition or a total of 12. Thus, for each of the four conditions a total of 18 Ss was used, and no S served in more than one condition (random-groups design). Each E obtained his own Ss as best he could; hence, there were no grounds for assuming that the different Es would be sampling the same population (although all Ss were college students). Furthermore, it is quite possible that there could be systematic changes in the performance of 12 Ss that a given E runs. For example, he might ask his best friends to serve first as Ss and then gradually work down in his hierarchy of friends to complete the 12 Ss. Consequently, the first Ss, close friends, might be more cooperative or more alert than the last Ss, his casual friends. It is clear that this had to be considered in designing the experiment. Therefore, the 12 conditions (three of each of the four) that each E was to run were randomized on a schedule sheet, and E assigned Ss to this schedule in order in which he met them. The random order for each of the 6 Es was different.

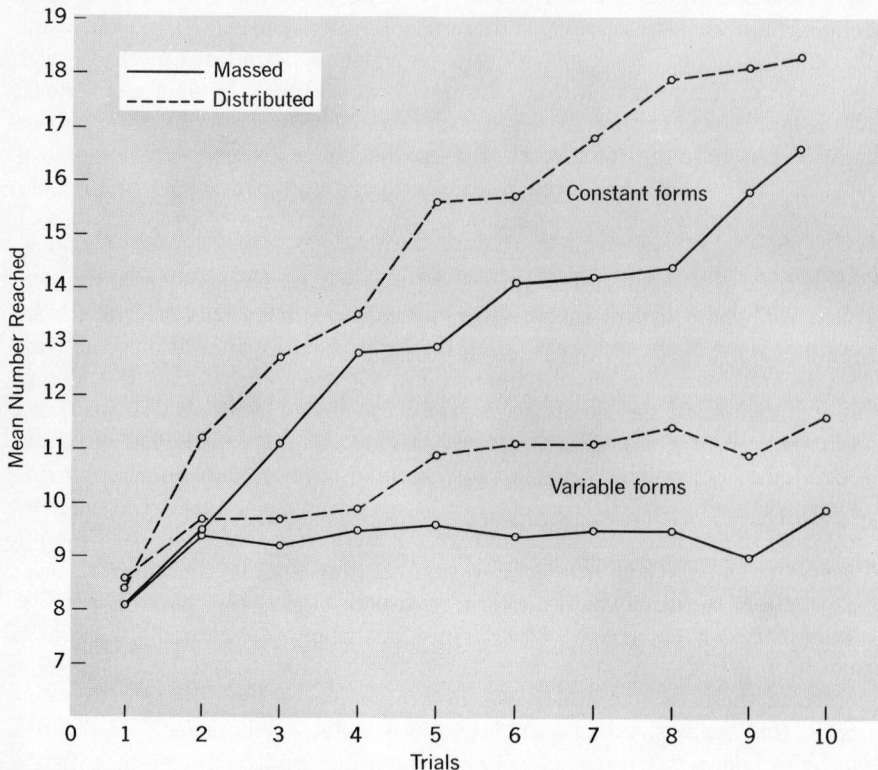

Fig. 7-5. Serial search performance as a function of variable versus constant forms and massed versus distributed practice. Data from Underwood (1961).

The numbers 1 through 75 appeared on the sheets used in this study. Five different random orders, hence five different sheets, were prepared. Each S was given 10 trials. If the S was under the constant-form condition, all 10 trials were given with the same form—same random order of numbers on the sheet. If the S was under the variable-form condition, each of the five forms was used twice in random order, subject to the restriction that the same form not be used on two successive trials.

The 10 sheets for a given S were stapled together. On each trial, S was allowed 30 sec. to go as far as he could, starting with the number 1, of course. Our response measure, then, was the number reached on each trial. In the 0-sec. condition (massed), E terminated a trial by saying "stop," whereupon S immediately turned to the next sheet and started the next trial. With the distributed or spaced condition, S, with the booklet removed, rested 60 sec. between trials.

An analysis of the results showed that differences among Es (which in-cludes differences in Es per se as well as possible differences among Ss they obtained) did not even approach statistical significance, so we may consider the results of the other two variables. These are shown in Fig. 7-5 where trials are plotted against mean number reached on each trial, with the means based on 18 Ss. Both variables influenced behavior. For both the variable and constant forms, distributed practice resulted in performance that was superior to massed practice. And the constant form resulted in a much higher level of performance than did the variable form. Performance improves from trial to trial with the constant form, whereas improvement is relatively slight from trial to trial with the variable form.

Almost any of the discrete search variables could be manipulated with this task. Various forms of coding could be used; for example, the numbers 2-9 could be printed in one color, 10-19 in another, and so on. Or numbers with-in a certain range might appear within one quadrant, another range within an-other quadrant, and so on, with S instructed or not instructed about this arrangement. Or suppose we use 25 letters rather than numbers: will search time for letters be different from search time for numbers?

The second serial search task to be presented was developed by Bakan (1955), but for our purposes the work of Kappauf and Payne (1959) will be used to illustrate the task. Below are listed several pairs of two-digit numbers:

39-64

16-41

42-26

10-39

81-19

22-51

64-73

To start the task, you as S would be told to find the number 10 as the first member of a pair. You would be told further that the *second* pair determines the next *first* pair you must find. Thus, after you find 10 in the above column, you know that you must find 39 next; after you find 39 you know that your next target is 64, and so on. Of course, to make the task more difficult many pairs of pairs occur on a page.

In the Kappauf-Payne study, all two-digit numbers from 10 through 99 were used. On a given page, each of the 90 two-digit numbers occurred once as the first two-digit number of a pair and once as the second two-digit number. The pairs of two-digit numbers, randomized separately on each page, appeared on a given page as six columns of 15 entries each. In this particular experiment 10 different pages were used.

The variable in the experiment was search speed as a function of time worked. After some initial practice, Ss worked 75 min. continuously. The Es controlled the time allowed per page but varied the time on successive pages so that for each set of two successive pages, 15 min. of search time were allowed. Thus, on the first page, S was allowed 10 min., on the second, 5 min., on the third, 8 min., on the fourth, 7 min., and so on. On each page S started with the number 10 and proceeded as rapidly as he could to find the successive numbers. Since the Es did not want to give S knowledge of his performance, they used varied time intervals for each page, a procedure which essentially made it impossible for S to know "how he was doing." Thus, with varied time, the number S had reached when told to turn the page could not provide S with information as to changes in his performance. A total of 60 Ss was given the task, the response measure being the number of numbers found during successive 15-min. periods. For the five successive 15-min. periods the means were 50.1, 48.1, 45.2, 45.5, and 44.2. A small decrement occurred in this serial search task over the course of 75 min.

No body of data is available from the use of this task. However, like the other search tasks we have examined, this one will allow the manipulation of a number of variables. Furthermore, since it is an easy task to construct, it is ideally suited for work in laboratories where equipment is scarce.

Further Comments on E Effects

In the experiment discussed earlier in which the Numbers Test was used, the results for six different Es were quite comparable. Furthermore, all of these Es knew about the hypothesis which led to a prediction that there would be an interaction between the effects of the two variables. The interaction did not appear. We were forced to conclude that Es were a neutral factor in this situation. Such neutrality is not always found. Indeed, some recent work shows some rather amazing effects that have to be attributed to E. A recent summary of this work is available (Kintz, Delprate, Mettee, Persons, & Schappe, 1965). An illustration may be taken from the work of Rosenthal (1963).

The task was the rating of photographs of people in terms of degree of success the pictured person had achieved in life. The rating was along a 20-point scale extending from −10 to +10. One group of Es was told that their Ss would probably produce a mean rating of about −5; another group of Es was told that their Ss would probably produce a mean rating of about +5. Of course the Ss actually making the ratings were assigned to the different *Es* on a random basis. All *Es* read exactly the same instructions to their *Ss*. With 30 *Es* running about 375 *Ss* (combining three different studies), the lowest mean rating obtained by any *E* expecting high ratings (when he was told that his *Ss* would give a mean rating of about +5) was higher than the highest rating of any *E* expecting low ratings. The source of such a "bias" is not known, but obviously it is a serious matter.

Rosenthal reports a number of other experiments he has conducted for studying the generality of the bias effects and demonstrates that they occur in quite a variety of situations. The possibility of bias, subtle and unrecognized by the person collecting the data, has always been a problem. It is a basic reason for using mechanical recording and stimulus programming whenever possible. We attempt by any means possible to eliminate procedures wherein the person must exercise choice or judgment in recording responses. Yet there are many problems demanding experimental work where it is not possible to mechanize, and it is for such situations that Rosenthal's findings remind us to exercise care if we wish to avoid subtle factors which may influence our results.

At the same time, however, it would probably be a mistake to over-emphasize the possible influence the person collecting the data may have. McGuigan (1963) has pointed out that when more than one *E* is used as a data collector in an experiment, the report usually does not contain an analysis of the effects of this variable. The point is that we must recognize that the data collector is a potential variable, and it is perfectly reasonable to expect that in certain situations he will be a relevant variable. However, if we use more than one data collector in an experiment, we treat them as we would any other variable—we neutralize them by having each complete an experiment unto itself. We do not allow one person to run all the *Ss* for one condition and a different person to run those for another condition. When we balance our conditions across data collectors, we can then determine whether or not the results differed for these data collectors. The fact that many experiments, done in different laboratories, show the same results indicates that the importance of the data collector as a variable must not be overemphasized. We cannot ignore this potential variable, but it need not frighten us.

VIGILANCE

Vigilance research concerns the attentiveness of the subject and his capability for detecting changes in stimulus events over relatively long periods of sustained observation. (Frankmann & Adams, 1962, p. 257)

The *S* in a vigilance situation is presented a display, and he waits (and sometimes waits and waits) for a change to occur in this display at which time he must respond as quickly as possible. The situation is, of course, analogous to that of a lookout, whether he searches for tuna, enemy ships, enemy planes, or for animals during a hunting expedition. There seems to be only one way to account for the great amount of research on this topic which has appeared in the last 10 years from the laboratories of British, Canadian, and American psychologists, namely, that it is a fundamental problem in military defense. The various radar lines used to warn of a possible attack are manned by military personnel who must observe radar scopes continuously in order to detect the approach of possible hostile objects. Indeed, many of the studies available have in fact used radar scopes as a means of presenting the display, and many of these studies have been done by psychologists at military research installations.

Only a few of the studies of vigilance have used tasks of an elementary nature; that is, most of these studies have used rather elaborate equipment. Nevertheless, we shall see that some of the tasks are of such nature that they could be adapted for use in most laboratories. Initially, we will survey some of these tasks in order to provide us with a "feel" for the problems facing an S serving in a vigilance experiment. We may note in advance that two response measures are used, both at some times, but separately at other times, depending upon the apparatus and the intent of the experimenter. If, on a display that S observes, a distinguishably different stimulus appears, the stimulus may remain until S responds to it. In such a case, the basic measure is the RT, and E observes changes in RT over the watch period. In other cases, however, the distinguishably different stimulus appears for only a short period of time. For such cases the response measure is the number of signals correctly detected, often expressed as a percentage of total signals presented. In a manner of speaking, the RT to the missed signals is longer than the maximum allowed by E to define a successful detection. However, the RTs may be obtained for the stimuli which S did detect within the time allowed. Thus, there would be two response measures possible, namely, percentage of correct detection and RT of signals detected. Under certain conditions, one of the response measures may be more sensitive in detecting changes in vigilance than will the other. For example, Adams, Stenson, and Humes (1961) found very little decrement in vigilance over a 3-hour period when measured by percentage of correct detection, but did find some increase in RTs.

Some Vigilance Tasks

Erratic clock. Various forms of an erratic clock have been used, the notion being developed originally by Mackworth, an English investigator. Consider a clockface with no markings on it and with but a single hand. The hand makes one revolution per second in a series of discrete but, of course, very rapid steps. Now, suppose that once in a while the step made by the hand is twice as great as the normal step. Would you, as S, detect this, and how frequently would you detect it over a 2-hr. period? For example, in a study by Wiener (1963), each step under normal circumstances was 11.25 degrees, there being 1/32 of a revolution in each step. The change to be detected in this display was a step of 20 degrees, or 1/18 of a revolution, or 1.78 times the size of the normal step.

The same idea has been used by Bergum and Lehr (1962), but instead of a clock, they had a series of 20 small light bulbs arranged in a circle. Under normal circumstances these came on in sequence, but the critical signal was the skipping of one of the lights in the sequence.

Digit sequence. As developed by Bakan (1959), this task involved S's listening to a long series of digits which were read at the rate of about 1 per sec. The S's task was to detect the reading of three odd digits in a row, which, of course, E allowed to happen only infrequently. Corcoran (1963) has used this task in visual form, presenting digits one at a time on a screen. It is clear that there is nothing magical about using three odd numbers; indeed, E could have made the infrequent signal a single digit.

Kappauf and Powe (1959) combined both the auditory and visual procedure. As digits, at the rate of one per second, were read to S, he followed along in a booklet in which the series of digits was printed to correspond to the spoken series. Occasionally, however, there was a discrepancy between the spoken digit and the written digit, and it was S's task to detect this. This task, therefore, is very much like a proofreading task.

Dials, gauges, and meters. These devices have been used in a variety of forms. For example, Broadbent (1954) assembled 20 steam gauges, all of which S was to observe, and asked S to respond when any one of them went over a specified danger mark. A little imagination will make it obvious that there are numerous variations that could be instituted with such devices.

Single light. A single light source has been used in either of two ways: namely, the light's being on continuously with the critical signal being a brief interruption, for example, .03 sec. in a study by Sipowicz, Ware, and Baker (1962); or the light's not being on most of the time but occasionally appearing for a short interval, for example, 100 msec. in a study by McCormack (1960). Assuming that S has to blink once in a while, it is quite apparent that he would occasionally miss a signal on these visual displays where the critical signal is of very short duration.

These, then, are illustrative of vigilance situations which S may face. We may now sample some of the variables that influence performance.

Some Vigilance Variables

Signal rate. The change in the stimulus event which S is required to detect is commonly called the signal. One of the most apparent variables in the vigilance situation is the frequency or rate at which the signal appears. A study by Jenkins (1958) illustrates the effect of a wide range of signal rates. The vigilance task was a modification of the erratic clock in which a voltmeter made a deflection of a given distance every second, and the signal to be detected was a movement of a greater distance. Four different rates were used, namely, 480, 60, 30, or 7.5 signals per hr. The Ss, enlisted men from the Air Force, were assigned to one of four groups in a random-groups design, and each group was given one of the four rates. The number of Ss in the groups varied from 35 to 26. All Ss were given practice before two experimental sessions, which were each 90 min. in length, one coming in the morning and one in the afternoon of the same day.

In programming the stimuli it is apparent that the critical signals, at whatever rate, should not be equally spaced in time. That is, this should not be done unless E wants to study time perception, for certainly after being exposed to a situation in which a signal occurred at regular intervals, S would soon learn about when to expect each signal. Vigilance studies, originally designed to simulate actual watch conditions where the moment for the appearance of a signal is indeterminate, have always used variable time intervals between successive signals. Nevertheless, behaviorally, the more rapid the signal rate, the more likely S will expect the appearance of a signal at any given moment. In the present study, at the 480 rate, a minimum of 2 sec. occurred between two successive stimuli, and for the three slower rates, a minimum of 5.4 sec. occurred. Some minimum time is necessary if S is to be allowed a chance to detect and respond to each stimulus.

In the present situation a stimulus in addition to the erratic voltmeter was used; it was a small light which came on at the rate of 10 times per hour for all conditions but without a consistent interval between successive appearances. There was no relation between the light and the other signal although the light was positioned close to the voltmeter. Whenever S detected the signal on the voltmeter, he pressed a switch held in his hand; whenever the light came on, he was supposed to press a button on the display panel, and the light remained on until the button *was* pushed. The purpose of this light was ". . . to permit an assessment of the frequency and duration of gross failures to attend to the area of the display. Such failures would be indicated by very long latencies of response to the pilot-light." (p. 648) However, it can be seen that RT to the light could also be used as a measure of deterioration of performance throughout the experimental period.

With different signal rates, behavior under the different conditions can be compared appropriately only by determining percentage of signals detected. The results show greatest superiority in percentage detected when the rate was 480 per hr. Performance started at about 90 percent detection, and by the end of the 90-min. morning period it was still above 80 percent. By the end of the afternoon it had fallen to 70 percent. For the slower rates, the detection percentages decreased more drastically. Initially, performance was approximately the same for all groups (near 90 percent), but by the end of 90 min., it fell to near 50 percent, with only small differences among the slower three rates. In the afternoon, performance again started at a fairly high level (with the exception of the performance for the 30-per-hr. group which started at about the same level shown at the close of the morning session). The lowest level of detection shown was about 25 percent by the Ss in the 7.5-rate group and occurred near the middle of the afternoon session.

Let us look briefly at some other findings of this study. The S in vigilance situations may report the presence of the signal when it was not present. In the current study these false reports were more frequent the higher the signal rate. For example, across both sessions, the median total false reports was 38.3 at the 480 rate and 15.4 for the 7.5 rate. The RT to the pilot light roughly paralleled the performance to the signal. That is, RT was faster the greater the signal rate and showed some increase throughout each session. One other finding is relevant for assessing the reliability of detection scores. Jenkins correlated individual performances (percentage of signals detected) for the morning and afternoon sessions and found these values to be .92, .82, .62, and .52 for the four signal rates from fastest to slowest, respectively.

Knowledge of results and reward. When S knows he is in an experimental situation and that the safety of his country does not depend on his alertness at the moment, it is quite understandable that he may lapse occasionally into inattentiveness. In the laboratory, therefore, it is sometimes necessary to make it pay for S to be as alert as possible over long periods in order to discover the maximally efficient vigilance behavior that might be expected in the "real" situation. The present study is relevant to such considerations. It was performed at Fort Knox, the armor-training center, with soldiers as Ss (Sipowicz, Ware, & Baker, 1962).

They used the single-light situation in which the light was on continuously except for occasional interruptions of .03 sec. The interruptions occurred at the rate of 12 per half hour, and since the Ss served for 3 hr. continuously, a total of 72 signals occurred. The S was to press a button whenever a signal occurred, and this was to be pressed within 5 sec. for the signal to be considered detected. Each S worked in an isolated booth and wore earphones to reduce ambient noise. There were four groups of 20 Ss each who were assigned the following conditions:

Group C: This control group worked throughout the 3-hr. period under the usual instructions to detect all the signals possible.

Group KR: This group was given knowledge of results. To do this a small light at eye level came on for 2 sec. if S *failed* to detect a signal; thus, if the light did not come on, he would know he had properly detected the signal.

Group R: The Ss in this group were told that they would be given $3 if they detected all signals but that this amount would be reduced proportionately to the number of signals missed. Actually, the reduction was by geometric steps so that if six or more signals were missed, S would receive no money. The amount to be lost for each miss was clearly explained to S.

Group R plus KR: These Ss were given the combined conditions of KR and R.

We noted above that a long vigilance session could lead to inattentiveness. In the present situation, the Es eliminated the records of all Ss who missed 12 or more consecutive signals on the grounds that such Ss were either asleep or were being downright uncooperative while remaining awake. (The S was isolated in a booth not accessible to direct observation by Es.) Five such Ss were eliminated, two from Group C, one from Group KR, and two from Group R.

The effectiveness of both knowledge of results and reward is shown in Fig. 7-6. All three experimental groups performed at a much more proficient level than did the control group. Reward appeared to be a little better than knowledge of results, and the combined effect of both reward and knowledge of results gave maximally efficient performance.

The above variables might appear to influence behavior only during the session in which they are operative. At least with knowledge of results, this is not true, for Wiener (1963) has shown that knowledge of results given during a session on one day results in better performance on the following day even when knowledge of results is not given on the second day. It is therefore not clear whether knowledge of results is effective because it sustains attentiveness and this carries over to subsequent sessions or whether knowledge of results actually results in some increase in the skill of detecting. Of course, it may influence both. The Es for the above study interpret the effect of both knowledge of results and reward as being motivational in nature. The findings of the following experiment might also be considered to result from sustained motivation.

Threat. In this study by Bergum and Lehr (1963), there were two groups of Ss. One group, essentially a control, worked through a vigilance session under normal instructions to detect as many signals as possible. The Ss in the other group were informed that they would be visited occasionally by a lieutenant colonel or a master sergeant, and indeed they were so visited about four times each through the 135-min. vigilance session. It was presumed that such visits might sustain vigilance behavior in view of the fact that all Ss were soldiers. The display was a circular pattern of lights which came on successively; the signal was the failure of a lamp in the series to light. The signal rate was 12 per hr., and the S pressed a button to indicate detection.

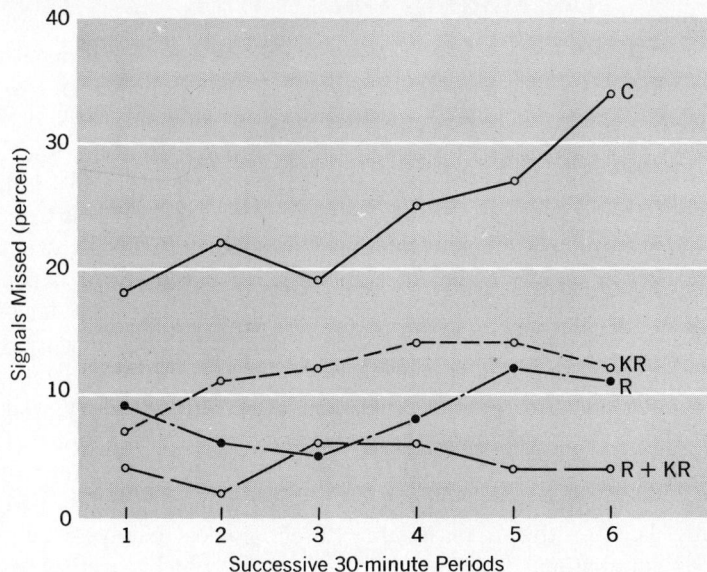

Fig. 7-6. Signals missed in a 3-hour vigilance session as a function of knowledge of results (KR), reward (R), and both (R + KR). The curve labeled C represents the control group. Data from Sipowicz, Ware, and Baker (1962).

The results leave no doubt about the effectiveness of the variable. The total period was divided into five successive 27-min. periods, and the response measure was percentage of signals detected. Under the control condition the five percentages were, in order, 77, 50, 30, 34, and 34. Under the threat condition the corresponding values were 97, 77, 72, 71, and 80. However, even with the threat condition, there was a significant deterioration in performance.

We will stop at this point. Many other variables have been manipulated. Indeed, if one systematically analyzes the vigilance situation in terms of task, environmental, and S variables, it is very likely that someone has done an experiment on most of the variables which such an analysis suggests would be relevant. There have also been theories of sorts concerning vigilance which we have not considered; discussions of these may be found in Broadbent (1958) and Frankmann and Adams (1962). One final fact must be registered. Almost without exception, Es in their studies of vigilance have used independent-groups designs rather than within-S designs. Can you see why this practice has been followed?

Concluding Observation

The vigilance situation is a work-type situation in reverse. In the work situation S performs the same task over and over, and, as Es, we ask what variables will sustain performance, or prevent work decrement. Such descriptive terms as boredom, fatigue, loss of attention, and lowered motivation would seem to be applicable to the work situation in much the same manner as they are applicable to the vigilance task. This is true in spite of the fact that in the vigilance situation S does not actively perform the task over and over as rapidly as he can (unless persistent attention is considered to be the task). Instead, S waits for the appearance of a particular stimulus. It is the waiting which seems to take on the characteristics of work.

Work tasks which have been used in the laboratory vary from those in which S must perform repetitive physical work (lifting heavy weights) to those in which the momentary physical energy required is minimal (writing the letters of the alphabet over and over). In recent years, very little systematic experimentation has been done on work decrement as studied in such situations. Perhaps this is reasonable. Technological changes (lumped together as automation) have resulted in jobs in which repetitive work, at least work of a heavy physical nature, is at a minimum. The worker observes displays and pushes buttons; he manipulates machines which do the heavy work. With tasks where there is much repetition but minimal physical output, it is less clear why the research seems to have died out. In any event, we will deal with such tasks in the next chapter.

SUMMARY

Three basic types of studies, all using reaction speed as the response measure, were analyzed in this chapter. These three types were identified as reaction-time studies, search-time studies, and vigilance studies.

Simple reaction time deals with the speed with which S can respond to an expected stimulus. In choice reaction time, S must respond differentially to either of two (or more) expected stimuli. The effect of a number of independent variables (stimulus duration, stimulus intensity, practice, length of foreperiod, and so on) were examined. A way in which simple reaction-time behavior could be analyzed into components was presented. Certain inhibitory effects in reaction-time studies were also examined.

Search time is concerned with the speed with which S can find a unique stimulus embedded in a group of stimuli. Again, experiments showing the effects of certain independent variables on search time were presented.

Vigilance deals with the ability of S to detect infrequently occurring stimuli, and the measurements of performance are normally taken over relatively long periods of time (hours).

The marked interest shown by contemporary investigators in the above three types of studies appears to stem directly from technological advances collectively called automation.

CHAPTER EIGHT

Perceptual-Motor Learning and Performance

We will describe a simple experiment which produces quite predictable results. The Ss are given the task of printing the letters of the alphabet over and over; however, they are required to print each letter upside down and, as they print successive letters, to move from the right to the left side of a sheet of ruled paper. This is called the inverted-alphabet task. When the sheet is turned 180 degrees, the letters appear as the alphabet normally does with the letters running from left to right.

The S is instructed to print as many letters as possible in the time allowed. In addition, he is told that if he makes and detects an error (a letter improperly printed if the paper were turned 180 degrees), he should correct it before proceeding to the next letter in the alphabet. In the present experiment we will assume that two groups of Ss were used, a particular S being assigned to a group on a random basis. First, all Ss in both groups were given 10 min. of uninterrupted practice (no rests). After the 10 min. of practice the E Group (experimental group) was stopped and given 5 min. of rest during which these Ss relaxed but were not allowed to inspect the printing they had done during the 10-min. practice period. After the rest interval they were given 5 min. of additional continuous practice on the inverted-alphabet task. The C Group (control group) was not stopped after the initial 10 min. of practice; instead, they continued without a break for 5 min. more. Both groups, therefore, had 15 min. of practice on the task; the only difference in the treatment of the two groups was that the E Group had a 5-min. rest between Trials 10 and 11 and the C Group did not.

How can we speak of trials on this task when the work or practice is continuous? In the usual experiment E contrives a means whereby the total work period can be broken into subunits of time, with a performance measure obtained for each subunit. We noted above that the E Group had a rest between Trials 10 and 11, implying that the subunit of analysis was a minute. In some manner, E must be able to mark the end of each minute on S's sheet so that following the experiment he can count the number of letters printed in each successive minute. One way to handle this is for E to signal the end of each minute so that S upon hearing the signal can make a differentiating mark on his paper, a hash line, perhaps. The hash line would be made quickly, and S would continue printing. Another technique is to require S to drop down to the next line on the paper when he hears the signal. However it is accomplished, E must be able to break the total time into equal subunits of time if he wishes to examine the changes in performance over time.

The idealized results of such an experiment are shown in Fig. 8-1. During the first minute of practice the average college student will print approximately 36 to 37 letters—he will get through the alphabet once plus 10 or 11 letters of his second run through the alphabet. There will, of course, be wide individual differences, not only on the first trial but on later trials. Between the first and the fourth or fifth trials, there may be a rather sharp improvement in performance after which further gains are relatively slight. After 10 min. of continuous practice, the average S will be printing about 45 letters per min.

Since both groups were treated identically through the first 10 trials, a single performance curve for both the E and C Groups for the first 10 trials is depicted in Fig. 8-1. Following the tenth trial, the two groups differed dramatically. The performance of the E Group "jumped" following the 5-min. rest period to a level of about 55 words per minute and remained near that level for the five postrest trials. The C Group continued to show only slight improvement on Trials 11-15.

As noted earlier, the basic facts shown by this experiment are easily repeated. These facts, and the procedures used to produce them, raise a number of issues which we must discuss in detail. Some of these issues have been glossed over in previous discussions. Others are raised by the fact that we are, with this chapter, beginning the study of learning; and certain distinctions between learning and other concepts must be made at the outset. There will be, therefore, some diversions before we return to a specific consideration of experiments in perceptual-motor learning. First we will indicate the issues to be discussed.

The phenomenon demonstrated in Fig. 8-1—the difference in performance between the rest and no-rest groups on Trials 11-15—is known technically as reminiscence. Over the past seven chapters we have become acquainted with a number of terms or concepts which may be considered technical terms. Constant error, counterbalancing, anchoring, reaction time, adaptation level, figural aftereffects, and so on, have all been used in some

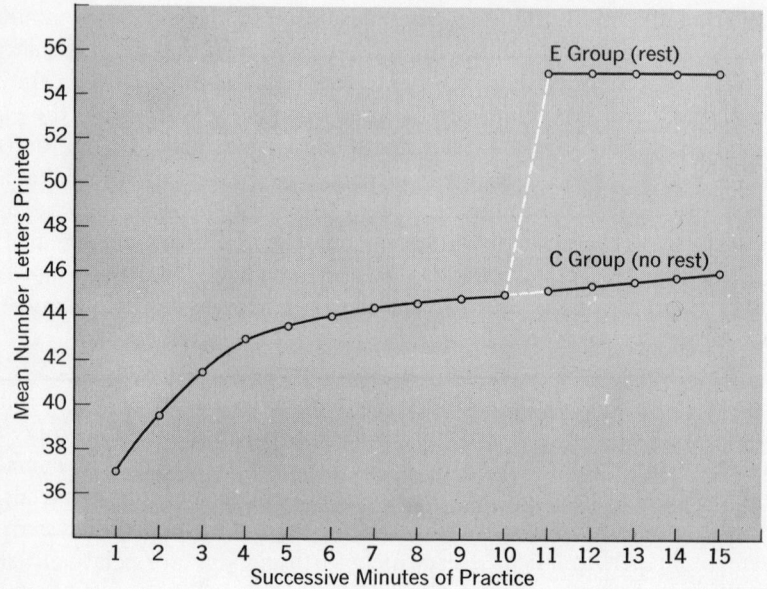

Fig. 8-1. The effect of a 5-min. rest interval following 10 continuous minutes of work on performance on the inverted-alphabet task (schematized).

technical sense. But in what technical sense? Are all of these terms to be considered equivalent in that they all have the same "status"? Why is a technical term different from a nontechnical term? These questions are indicative of the problems which we have skirted thus far. We have made no serious attempt to differentiate in a formal sense among the various technical terms we have employed; neither have we been meticulous in our definitional procedures. It is time that some tidiness be introduced.

In the discussion of definitional procedures it will be seen that, essentially, we are discussing experimental designs used to demonstrate or exhibit empirical phenomena. We need to contrast such empirical phenomena with theoretical explanatory notions, and the results of the experiment as depicted in Fig. 8-1 will be our "jumping off" point for this discussion. Finally, we must, insofar as present experimental techniques allow, be able to distinguish experimentally between learning, which may influence performance scores, and other factors of a nonlearning nature (sometimes called nonassociative factors) which also influence the performance measures we record in an experiment.

OPERATIONAL DEFINITIONS

A part of the process of doing experimental work is that of reporting the results of experiments. A person who does a sound piece of research is under some obligation to make his results public. A research community would not survive if each worker kept his results to himself; it would not survive because, if for no other reason, it would lose the support of society. Generally speaking, this does not seem to be a serious problem. Research workers, while not necessarily loquacious, need little urging to transmit orally the results of their researches. Quite naturally, most of us get excited with our findings and we *want* to tell others. One need only note the hundreds of research reports given at national and regional meetings of a research discipline to recognize this lack of recalcitrance. On the other hand, the reporting of results of experiments in final written form does not happen quite so easily. Perhaps the oral reporting removes the initial excitement attending the data so that the time and patience needed to write up the experiment in final form becomes a chore. Many fine sets of data must be languishing in laboratory files all over the world. But let us push ahead without trying to analyze the psychology of the penless researcher and look at one particular problem we face when we *do* write finished research reports in which we wish to be as precise as the available language allows. The problem revolves around the use of concepts which must inevitably appear in our writings.

Most experimentalists in all disciplines tacitly or actively accept operational definitions as a means of specifying the empirical basis of a discipline. That is, they use operational definitions in order to define the phenomena of nature with which a discipline concerns itself. Psychologists concern themselves with behavior, and the empirical behavioral phenomena which they deal with map the domain of psychology. There is some overlap, of course, with other disciplines. Biologists, physiologists, and neurologists may deal with behavior which is also the bailiwick of the physiological psychologist; the experimentally minded sociologist may be working with the same behavioral phenomena as a social psychologist. The so-called cross-disciplinary research indicates that there exists a set of behavioral phenomena common to the interests of two or more disciplines. Thus, we often find psychologists, sociologists, and anthropologists working as teams. It is quite possible that in the long run certain disciplines which are now distinct may develop so many common interests—so many behavioral phenomena studied in common—that one name will eventually be used for all. Fission may also occur. In its early days, psychology was closely associated with philosophy, but as psychology became more and more empirical, the commonality of interests was lost, and two strikingly different independent disciplines now exist.

What is an operational definition of a behavioral phenomenon? An operational definition identifies a phenomenon by specifying the procedures or operations used to measure it. An operational definition is contrasted with a literary or dictionary definition in which the measuring procedures are normally not specified. A literary definition of anxiety as "painful uneasiness of mind" does not specify measuring procedures. The dictionary meaning of ego as "the entire man considered as union of soul and body" does not specify measuring operations. Regression defined as "return of the libido to earlier stages of development or to infantile objects of attachment" is experimentally meaningless until we can measure both the libido and its return. We must look at some operational definitions in order to see what we mean by measuring operations. We will identify three classes of operational definitions, but because the differences between them are not easily identified by a simple verbal label, we will call them Class I, Class II, and Class III. The various characteristics of the classes will be pointed out as each is taken up in order.

Class I

In identifying phenomena by Class-I operations, E is interested fundamentally in determining if there are reliable individual differences in response to a specified stimulus situation. The stimulus situation is identical for all Ss, and E measures some response to this situation. If he can show that Ss differ consistently (reliably) in their responses to the situation, he has identified a behavioral phenomenon, and his operational definition consists of a specification of the stimulus situation and the distribution and reliability of the responses to it.

Assume that we construct a questionnaire to measure anxiety. There are 20 questions, questions such as "Do you frequently have nightmares in which you fall from a tall building?" "Do your palms always seem to be damp?" "Do you sometimes take sleeping pills?" The 20 questions are printed in random order in a booklet and presented to a group of Ss, perhaps to the 200 students taking elementary psychology at a given time, at a given school, and taught by a given instructor. We score the questionnaire by counting the number of "yes" answers to the 20 questions. Then we demonstrate reliability (consistent individual differences) by showing that there is a high correlation between the number of "yes" answers to the 10 odd items and to the 10 even items. After asserting that what we mean by anxiety is the score (number of "yes" answers) on this test, we may define the level of anxiety of a particular S by relating his score to the scores of others (as by percentile rank) who took the test.

The logic of operational definitions is such that the definition might become extremely detailed and thereby long and burdensome. For our definition of anxiety it might seem that we would be forced to give the details of the construction of the test, the scoring, the method of determining reliability, the nature of the distribution of scores, and so on. Normally, such detailed specification of operations is not required; rather, we are allowed to abstract the essentials of our procedures. Operational definitions are intended to facilitate understanding of concepts, and we need only enough detail to assure that this understanding is transmitted. For the definition of anxiety we may say, "Here is a questionnaire; here are the instructions to the Ss; it was scored in this manner and this is the reliability. What we mean by anxiety is the score obtained on this questionnaire."

It must be quite apparent that a phenomenon defined by Class-I operations does not, when considered in isolation, give us much understanding of behavior. These operations show that behavior is usually consistent, but this fact does not require new demonstrations. The operations allow us to state a mean value for a group (average number of "yes" answers in the case of anxiety), but the meaning or implication of such a value is difficult to assess. To know that Egypt exported 75,000 bales of cotton in 1951 does not have much meaning until it is related to other events, for example, the number the country shipped in other years or its proportion of world exports represented. To know that the mean reaction time to an auditory stimulus is 200 msec. might have some meaning for the understanding of neural transmission speeds, but it is minimal meaning. The point is that phenomena defined by Class-I operations are given psychological meaning only when they are related to other phenomena, and few investigators would stop with the simple defining procedure (as we apparently stopped with our definition of anxiety). We seek reliable individual differences in our phenomena defined by Class-I operations so that we *can* relate the behavior to other behaviors.

To define intelligence as the score on a particular test is quite acceptable if we are concerned only with definitions, but, of course, we are concerned with more than this. We are interested in other behaviors with which the score on the intelligence test might be related, for it must be related to something else if it is to be useful. We may construct a reliable test to measure anxiety, but it must be related to other phenomena to be useful. To be useful implies either of two outcomes. It may be useful in a practical sense—the scores on an intelligence test may predict academic performance in college. In a second meaning, the relationship between behaviors measured by Class-I operations help us to understand the organization of aptitudes and skills. One of the major objectives of the correlational approach to research (as discussed in Chapter One) is that of understanding the organization of abilities.

Two further points must be made with regard to Class-I definitions. First, we note that the operations involved do not meet our specifications of an experiment, for an experiment, we said, requires at least two different stimulus situations—two different treatments. In Class-I operations we present all Ss with a single static stimulus situation; we are not examining the influence of an independent variable. To determine the mean reaction time to a static situation is not equivalent to determining mean reaction time as a function of the length of the foreperiod. The latter type of operation is included in Class III. The difference is apparent in another manner. Only in terms of frequency distributions are the results of Class-I procedures amenable to graphing. For example, if we had given 200 Ss a reaction-time test, we could plot the response measure in millisecond ranges, or categories (e.g., 151-160, 161-170, 171-180, and so on), along the abscissa, and the number of Ss falling into each category, along the ordinate. With a true experiment the response measure is on the ordinate, the independent variable, on the abscissa.

The second point concerns a matter to which we alluded in an earlier chapter. It is probably quite natural to ask, for example, in referring to the definition of anxiety as discussed earlier, "But does this questionnaire really measure anxiety?" At this point we must keep a clear separation between the meaning of a concept as given by an operational definition and the meaning of a concept in other senses. An operational definition is useful only in specifying what E means when he uses the term at a strictly empirical level. That is the only purpose of an operational definition. The meaning of such a concept in other senses may take several forms. When a given E constructs a questionnaire or test which he will assert measures anxiety, he must have had a literary conception of anxiety, or a casual observational conception of anxiety, or some notion derived from some source which led him to put the particular questions on the questionnaire. It is quite possible that another E, starting from a different conception, would arrive at a different set of items. Furthermore, it is quite possible that the scores on the two questionnaires would not correlate and hence must be considered to be measuring different things. This is a little confusing since we would have two independent definitions of anxiety. At this point, however, each is an equally "good" definition. Only if subsequent research showed that they differed in usefulness (as discussed above) would we have empirical grounds for preferring one over the other.

In another vein, some person might object to any measure of anxiety on the grounds that one cannot capture the true essence of anxiety by any measurement procedures. To such a person the meaning of anxiety is like the meaning of soul to us—we do not quite know what operations we could use to measure souls. In still another sense, some may have a belief that there is something that is *really* anxiety or "true" anxiety, and the question posed initially asks whether or not we have succeeded in measuring it. Let it be clear that the use of operational definitions is not concerned with the meaning of concepts in these senses. Any empirical meaning for the experimentalist over and above that given by the operational definition comes from further research, and this meaning can only consist of relationships with other behaviors or relationships between independently manipulated events and behavior.

Class II

The operations typifying Class II are those involved in scaling objects or events for which no known physical scale is appropriate. Such procedures were discussed in Chapter Six. Let us use an illustration, the scaling of words for affective connotation, to focus on. By some method of attack (category scaling, rank order, or paired comparisons), we present a number of words to a group of Ss who are under appropriate instructions to scale these words for affectivity. Just as in Class I, the operations require the presentation of the same stimuli to all the Ss in a single group. But the hoped-for outcome as far as definitions are concerned is quite different from that of Class I. In Class-II definitions we hope that not only will individual differences in response to a particular stimulus (a word) be minimal but that the mean group response to different stimuli will be reliably different. Thus, we expect that the words will be reliably sorted along a scale which we will then call a scale of affectivity.

For all classes of operational definitions we often use an if-if-then type of wording. For the above illustration we might say, "*If* I ask Ss to rate these words on this scale according to these instructions, and *if* I obtain reliable differences among the scale values for various words, *then* I will call this an affective scale along which words may differ." The if-if-then definitions are obviously of a provisional nature, for if in fact the differences do not occur as a consequence of the operations, nothing has been defined in an empirical sense. If, for example, we found that the scale values for all the words were essentially the same, the *then* aspect of the definition cannot be completed, because the second *if* provision is not satisfied. If this happened we would not necessarily conclude that words do not differ in affective connotation, but we would certainly conclude that our operations did not demonstrate it. (Without elaboration, we can see that in most scaling studies, such as the above, we would expect some stimuli to be given comparable scale values; for example, two words may be judged to have about the same affective connotation. The minimum requirement of reliability is to give at least two stimuli different scale values, the difference between them being of such magnitude that it is unlikely that chance factors were responsible for the difference.)

Like Class-I operations, those of Class II do not allow graphical expression in the usual sense; that is, we are not obtaining a relationship between a dependent and an independent variable for which scale values are available *prior* to the research. We are, in effect, determining whether we *can* assign scale values in a reliable manner. However, unlike Class-I operations,

Class-II operations meet the requirements of an experiment. Each word *can* be considered a different stimulus situation. Suppose we have 10 different words we want to scale for affectivity. We can, if we wish, randomly draw 10 different groups of Ss and give each group a single word to scale. If we get significant differences among the mean scale values for the different groups, it is the same as saying we have different affective values for the words. The use of a single group of Ss in the usual scaling study is a matter of convenience. In Class-II operations we have an experiment in which there are distinctly different treatments (e.g., different words), but the differences cannot be specified ahead of time along a dimension. As we said, the purpose of the operations is to try to establish a dimension.

The perceptive student might now say that perhaps we should apply the above reasoning to the Class-I operations. We have said that the Class-I procedures do not meet our conception of an experiment, but in the illustration using the anxiety questionnaire, there were 20 different questions asked of the S. Why do we not consider each of these a different stimulus situation—different treatments? By analogy with the above reasoning, we could give a single question to each of 20 groups of Ss. However, if we did do this we would be getting quite a different end product from that intended by the usual Class-I operations. The purpose in using 20 different questions is to get 20 different measurements of the same thing. Indeed, often in the process of refining tests and questionnaires, E will eliminate items when the responses to them do not correlate with the responses to the test as a whole. The use of 20 different items is analogous to E's giving each S 20 different trials in a simple reaction-time situation because 20 measurements give a more reliable measure than does a single measurement. It is, for example, very difficult to conceive of any reason why E might want to use different groups of Ss in giving a Class-I operational definition of reaction time, and of course, the major intent of Class-I operations involving multiple items or questions is that of establishing reliable individual differences. This cannot be done if 20 different groups of Ss are measured on only one item.

If E's intent *is* to establish differences in responses to 20 different items (such as questions on an anxiety scale), then, clearly, the operations fit Class II. In fact, such a procedure might be used in the initial stages of constructing a scale. For example, E might bring together a large number of questions and give them to experienced clinicians for scaling in terms of the degree to which the questions are believed to be relevant for measuring anxiety. Then he would construct his initial scale from questions which are reliably sorted and, at the same time, are said to be highly relevant for measuring anxiety. Such a procedure would represent an attempt to purify the items so that all would be measuring the same state (anxiety). It is remotely possible that the purification, carried to its extreme, might lead to a single-question questionnaire. Generally speaking, therefore, the Class-I operations indicate that E does not intend to give different treatments, whereas in Class-II procedures, he clearly does.

The operations which fit under Class II are more general than indicated by our illustrations, which have been limited to the scaling of stimuli. This class includes any experiment in which the differences between (or among) experimental treatments cannot be quantitatively specified. Such experiments may produce results of practical value but, perhaps, of little analytical value. An experiment which studies learning as a function of visual versus auditory presentation is of this nature. If differences do occur, to what do we attribute them? We cannot attribute them to anything other than the gross differences between what is meant by the visual system and what is meant by the auditory system. We might obtain reliable differences in preferences between two grossly different works of art or between two boxes for packaging breakfast food and, at the same time, be quite unable to relate these differences to a quantitative factor. We might measure differences in performance on two typewriters of different makes without being able to specify in a quantitative fashion the multitude of differences involved. We might measure differences in the performance of two randomly drawn classes of pupils in the same course taught by different teachers without being able to specify in a quantitative manner what the differences between the teachers are which led to the difference in performance. This is not to say for any of these illustrations that appropriate analysis and refinements and many experiments will never allow E to relate the differences found to quantitative variables.

Class III

We place in Class III operations in which an independent variable is manipulated in a quantitative manner causing differences in behavior to occur. Most of the phenomena which we will consider in subsequent chapters fall into this class; therefore, we will be frugal with illustrations at this time. Again we may use the if-if-then paradigm in formulating the definitions: if we vary the intensity of a visual stimulus, and if simple reaction time changes as a function of this stimulus variation, then we will say that we have operationally defined $xgq7!\$$. In other words, $xgq7!\$$ is defined by these operations. Of course, before the operations were carried out, the definition of $xgq7!\$$ was provisional; if no difference occurred as a result of manipulation of stimulus intensity, there is no phenomenon to be defined and $xgq7!\$$ as a concept would be psychologically meaningless.

These peculiar symbols have been used to illustrate a point, namely, that we have many phenomena which are operationally defined which have no name; each is simply a relationship between a dependent and independent variable. On the other hand, Es sometimes assign descriptive names to phenomena. Certainly *anchoring*, as discussed in Chapter Six, is descriptive of the results of the set of operations. So, too, is *threshold* descriptive of the phenomenon. However, there are many phenomena for which names have not been applied, although they hold the same status as those for which names have been used. Indeed, there is some basis for suggesting that one should not use descriptive names because their literary meanings and operational meanings are not entirely comparable. If a name must be assigned, so this argument runs, we should assign one which is neutral and will not be confused with the literary term as used by the man on the street. For example, reminiscence as a technical term has quite a different meaning from the meaning it has in a literary context. The name assigned to the above phenomenon ($xgq7!\$$) is not likely to be confused with any other words known to the present writer. Of course we do not have to assign any name; but a name can be used as a symbol to indicate that there is a relationship between an independent and dependent variable, although the name alone can never describe the precise relationship.

We noted earlier that Class-II operations may precede Class III. In the previous chapter we saw how Slamecka scaled the similarity of words (Class II) and then determined the relationship between reaction time and similarity by Class-III operations. The Class-II operations produced an ordinal quantitative scale which became the independent variable for the Class-III procedure.

Many basic Class-III definitions are given by use of an E Group and a C Group. Such a definition specifies only that E has discovered a relevant variable but does not tell what the relationship is between the variable and the behavior. For example, consider the study in the previous chapter in which two stimulus lights were flashed in succession and reaction time to the first light was shown to vary as a function of the time between the two lights. If we translate this phenomenon into the minimal possible operations, we might say that, if an E Group is given two light stimuli separated by 100 msec., and if a C Group is given only the first stimulus, then a difference in reaction time between the groups to the first stimulus defines phenomenon X (to use a neutral name). Basically speaking, the C Group's "second" light was separated by zero time from the first, so we still maintain the quantitative aspect required by Class III. Many Class-III definitions of phenomena imply a quantitative dimension in that the C Group is given a zero amount of a specified stimulus and the E Group, a finite amount. The two-group definition, of course, does not require two different groups. We could use a single group and give the control treatment at one time and the experimental treatment at another (within-S design).

It is sometimes helpful to use a diagram of the operations as an adjunct to the verbal statement. If we are studying the influence of two stimuli, 100 msec. apart, on the reaction time to the first stimulus, our diagram might be as follows:

	FIRST STIMULUS	SECOND STIMULUS
E GROUP	yes	yes
C GROUP	yes	no

We have noted earlier that to produce an exhaustive operational definition one must give the complete details of an experimental procedure and relate these to the results (measures of behavior). That is, we must relate the entire procedure section of an experimental report to the results section in order to define the phenomenon. We have also noted that we do not have to do this. We sharply abbreviate the report of our operations, but if understanding breaks down (if you do not know what I mean by my operational definition), it implies that I have abbreviated too much. To correct this we would expand in detail as much as necessary to produce understanding. In areas where research has been carried on for many years, understanding is easier than it is in newer fields. In fact, many shorthand descriptions are used. Thus, if I say I have used the method of limits to determine thresholds in an experiment in which I manipulated a specified variable, we normally do not ask for more information concerning the method of limits. Knowledge of the method is accepted as universal among people in the field, so the simple phrase, method of limits, carries in its meaning a number of subsidiary operations. Of course, if you do not know about the method, the meaning of the phenomenon being investigated will be somewhat obscure. Nevertheless, you as a reader can look to other sources for your definition of the method of limits in order to arrive at an understanding of the definition of the phenomenon involved.

Operational Definitions and Experimental Design

Our premise has been that the minimum requirement for an experiment is two conditions or two different treatments. The diagrammatic operational definition describes, in essence, an experimental design, with the E and C Groups given the different treatments. We may ask if we can ever do an experiment in which a C Group is not required. We can, although a value for a control group (had there been one) must always be inferred with some degree of confidence. Let us refer back to Fig. 8-1, where reminiscence was demonstrated by the use of E and C Groups. We note that all Ss in both groups were treated in the same manner for the first 10 trials. The performance curve over these 10 trials, if a large number of Ss is used, is quite stable. If the C Group had not been used, we would be in little error to project the performance curve of the E Group to the eleventh trial in order to indicate what the performance would be without the 5-min. rest. That is, we could extrapolate the performance curve of the E Group to the eleventh trial to estimate the performance which would have been observed had the 5-min. rest not been given. Thus, this value could be compared with the eleventh trial performance actually obtained after the 5-min. rest. It is apparent, however, that the further ahead we attempt to predict or project the performance, the greater the likelihood of error. We would probably be on quite shaky grounds to predict what a group would have achieved on the fifteenth trial without rest.

Generally speaking, then, if we have a stable performance curve over a period of time for a group, and if an introduction of an independent variable produces a clear discrepancy between the projected and measured performance, we are on fairly safe grounds in assuming the independent variable to be an effective one. Consider an extreme case of this as given in another source:

Suppose we have a group of adults who by standard testing procedures have been classified as imbeciles for 20 years. Each year for 20 years they have been tested and each year the test record shows no appreciable change. Then a new drug ("anti-imbecile") is placed on the market. On one day all members of the group are given an injection of the drug, and on the next day the test scores all fall within the normal range. Although it is remotely possible that something other than the drug caused the change, it is highly unlikely that anyone would care to defend this position strongly. (Underwood, 1957, p. 133)

We conclude that while we must continue to insist that an experiment consists of a minimum of two conditions, there are times when the effects of one of the conditions (usually a control condition) may be accurately inferred from the measurements actually obtained under the other condition.

Operational Definitions and the Discovery of New Phenomena

To say the least, this heading is presumptuous. It implies that there are rules or prescriptions by which one may make discoveries. This is manifestly untrue. At one extreme, discoveries happen by accident; at the other, they may be pointed to by the inexorable logic of a formal theory. Nevertheless, in psychology, where formal theory of a generalized nature is at a minimum, there are certain modes of thought with which we should be familiar since these modes in the past have been very useful in broadening the empirical base of psychology, and it is in the interests of broadening the base of experimental psychology that we venture to be so bold as to discuss ways of discovery.

What is meant by the phrase, "broadening the base of experimental psychology"? There are many forms of behavior which have not been brought under experimental scrutiny. What is the difference between two supervisors, one of whom can obtain willing and maximal performance from those under his supervision and another who cannot? Why are only a few people paranoid, but most are not? What are the variables producing love? What is the basis of humor? Why is one person courageous and the other not? It is now perhaps evident what is meant by broadening the base of experimental psychology. We will broaden the base when we provide provisional operational definitions for new phenomena, many of which we know exist and would be new only in the sense that they are brought under experimental study. Once appropriate operations for study can be specified, we can proceed to examine each phenomenon in terms of the variables which influence it, its relationship to other phenomena, and so on. How does one get started on such an enterprise? Where does one look for these so-called new phenomena?

Our own observations should be a prime source of hypotheses about behavior which has not been studied experimentally. But there are others who can offer many of these observations to us. Good novelists are acute observers of human behavior, and many of them offer interpretations of this behavior, interpretations which are couched as cause-effect statements. At the very least a good novelist may offer vivid descriptions of behavior from which we might be able to supply hypotheses about the causes of that behavior and then translate the hypotheses into experimental operations. For some unknown reason the present author remembers a phrase from an "action" book he read as a boy. The hero had to make a decision about the proper moment for attacking an outpost that was not expecting an attack. He decided that the right time would be just before dawn because, he believed, men sleep most deeply just before dawn. This is a testable proposition.

We are all more or less acquainted with the writings of those who set about to explain behavior, particularly deviant behavior, without the benefit of systematic data but with a background of clinical observations. Freud's work is illustrative. He "thought up" many mechanisms and "laws" about those mechanisms to account for certain forms of deviant behavior. Many research workers have since tried to give these mechanisms an empirical base, which is to say they have tried to supply provisional operational definitions and then, of course, carry out the operations to see if a phenomenon can be demonstrated under controlled conditions. We need only mention such terms as regression, repression, and rationalization to capture the spirit of such inquiries.

Over the years many supposed laws of behavior have become commonplace sayings and are used by many as if they were in fact reliable laws of behavior. It is said that "all work and no play makes Jack a dull boy," but, so far as is known, no one has put this hypothesis to an experimental test. Is a little knowledge a dangerous thing? Do too many cooks spoil the broth? Is out of sight out of mind?

Although you might not judge such sayings to be important propositions about behavior, it is quite a worthwhile exercise to try to devise provisional operational definitions to test their truth or falsity. For example, one old saying declares that "a bird in the hand is worth two in the bush." Quite unwittingly, apparently, this provisional law has been tested. Thus, an S can choose between accepting $1 now for having done a simple task or $2 if we will wait two weeks. The evidence indicates that this saying must have originated with a psychopath for they behave more in conformance with the proposition than do normals.

Any experimental discipline, to remain viable, must persistently attempt to bring new phenomena under experimental inspection. One way to do this is to attempt to formulate provisional operational definitions for supposed cause-effect relationships and then, of course, carry out the operations. The cumulative history of ideas has undoubtedly carried along with it many falsities about human behavior; but it has also undoubtedly carried many truths. The beauty of these truths need not be tarnished in the least by demonstrating them experimentally, and clearly the falsities need exposure.

LEARNING, PERFORMANCE, AND WORK

Learning so pervades human activity that any curiosity about the nature of man and his behavior leads sooner or later to inquiry about how his habits are formed, how his skills are acquired, how his preferences and tastes develop, how his knowledge is obtained and put to use. Equally important is how he becomes enslaved by prejudice and bigotry and other learnings which lead to trouble instead of to a satisfactory solution of problems. (Hilgard, 1948, p. 1)

Learning is something we infer to have occurred by observing changes in performance. We do not observe learning directly, although we often speak as if we do. We measure an S's performance, and if this performance shows certain characteristics, we say that learning has occurred. Learning is thus a construct, or, as we often say, it is an intervening variable which links performance changes and practice. This makes it no less real but forces us to be analytical in our thinking about how much of the performance change which we observe can in fact be attributed to a relatively permanent change in behavior which we call learning. Several considerations must be kept in mind if our analytical thinking is to be appropriate.

We know that the performance change from which we infer learning must result from practice or repetition of a specifiable behavior sequence. We cannot measure performance change without at least two successive measurements—two conditions—and so our operational definition must depend upon two "trials" of practice for a single group (the two trials constituting the two conditions) with performance on the second being superior to the first. As an alternative, we may think of a definition in terms of a control group not given practice and an experimental group given practice and then both tested. If there is a difference in the performance in favor of the experimental group, we say that learning has been demonstrated, hence defined.

Sometimes the amount of learning may be considered quantitatively identical to the change in the performance measures. Such an inference is at other times quite inappropriate. This is clearly demonstrated in the results of the experiment reported at the start of this chapter and exhibited in Fig. 8-1. Are the performance measures at the end of 10 trials to be used to infer the amount of learning which had occurred? No, the level of learning attained is not indicated by the performance, since following a rest interval, performance "jumped" to a higher level. We infer from this fact that S had in fact learned more than could be inferred from the performance on the tenth trial. Some factor must have been depressing performance on this trial so that the full amount of learning which had occurred was not measurable. Note that we cannot even say that the performance on the eleventh trial for the E Group (the group having the 5-min. rest) is indicative of the true amount of learning, for we have no basis for saying that the depressive factor was completely eliminated by the 5-min. rest. In the most extreme case we may find performance curves actually decreasing—performance getting worse—with practice but with learning still occurring.

The above discussion implies that we must be extremely cautious about identifying amount of performance shown after practice with the amount of learning which has occurred. We must be cautious because we know that factors other than associative or learning factors may influence performance. The above illustration indicated that a factor which depressed learning performance was present. In the same sense, other factors may enhance performance (but not learning) and give us an overestimate of the amount of learning if we insist upon equating amount of learning with amount of performance. That learning occurs in most situations which E devises as learning situations cannot be denied, but extracting the amount learned from the performance measure is another matter. As we discuss various learning situations in subsequent chapters, we will point out those situations in which the problems of separating changes attributable to learning from changes due to other factors are particularly acute. It should be noted that we would not have to use the term *learning* at all, and some investigators do not. Instead of speaking about learning, they prefer to inquire into the independent variables which influence performance, especially those which improve performance. Nevertheless, we will use the term, although we must be aware of the distinction between learning and other factors which may influence the overall performance curve. If the inverted-alphabet task is indicative of perceptual-motor tasks in general, we must be keenly aware of the distinction in this chapter.

Performance measures from which we infer learning will differ as a function of the task used. Sometimes a task is such that S either makes a response or he doesn't, and we could infer learning from the changes in the probability of making the response. Other tasks may require a speed measure of learning, the inverted-alphabet task being an illustration. Still others may have a precision measure, such as changes in the accuracy of shooting at the usual round target on the rifle range. Often two or more different measures may be used.

The study of learning shades over into the study of work behavior. Ideally, to study work behavior we study performance on a task after performance has ceased to improve as a result of practice—learning is at an asymptote. In actual practice this condition is seldom met. Given a sensitive response measure there is every reason to believe that performance would improve almost indefinitely with practice. Nevertheless, work behavior is normally studied after major improvements due to learning have occurred. Work tasks and perceptual-motor tasks have much in common, and, in addition, work behavior and perceptual-motor learning share common explanatory concepts.

TASKS

The tasks discussed in the previous chapter place very little emphasis on skill involved in responding. Emphasis was on detection of stimulus changes or on discovery of stimuli with the response measure being detection or reaction speed. As we move to a study of perceptual-motor learning there is a shift in emphasis. Here, many of the tasks may emphasize precision of movement as well as speed of movement. Many sports would be considered good illustrations of perceptual-motor skills, for they may require the hitting of a moving target with a bat or racket, thus emphasizing close coordination between perception of stimulus events and timing and movement of musculature. Sometimes the perceptual aspects are minimized, as in certain track and field events. Sometimes the tasks allow very little learning, and the interest is in the change in behavior associated with rapid repetition. It is thus apparent that the tasks involved vary along many dimensions and cannot be simply characterized.

Out of necessity the usual elementary laboratory class must work with tasks which do not require complex stimulus events, because the production of these events requires complicated apparatus which is not only expensive but in many cases difficult to maintain in good working order. Most of the 10 types of devices listed by Bilodeau and Bilodeau (1961) as being in common use in the study of motor skills between 1950 and 1960 are of this nature. Without doubt many of these tasks afford a study of skill learning that is at a higher level than that observed with simpler tasks which the usual laboratory possesses in multiple units. Compare, for example, the skill learned in inverted-alphabet printing with that learned on the following piece of apparatus. The S is seated before a gunsight and some 20 ft. in front of the sight is a large semicircular screen. A camera is coordinated with the gunsight so that periodically a small image of an airplane appears at one edge of the screen and "flies" rapidly across the screen, disappearing at the other edge. Each "flight" may originate at a different position and may take a different course. The S's task is to get the plane in the sights of the gun and shoot it down. A score can be determined as the percentage of successful hits.

It should be apparent that such apparatus is necessary to study certain forms of complex skill learning. Yet it is not at all certain that the use of such tasks facilitates the acquisition of skill in designing sound experiments, and since that is our major goal, we may, perhaps, without serious harm, largely ignore the work that has been done with such tasks. In any event, tasks which we will use in this chapter to illustrate various experimental procedures and phenomena will be, relatively speaking, quite simple tasks, ranging from those which require only pencil and paper (such as inverted-alphabet printing) to those in which a minimum of "hardware" is involved.

A HYPOTHETICAL CONSTRUCT

A considerable amount of the work in motor learning has, in one way or another, been concerned with a particular explanatory notion. Because the thinking lying behind this notion is somewhat different in character from other explanatory techniques we have discussed, we will examine both the thinking and the technique at some length. Initially, we need to refer again to the results of the hypothetical experiment reported at the start of this chapter in Fig. 8-1. We note first that at the empirical level we define operationally the phenomenon of *reminiscence*. Reminiscence is defined as the difference in the performance of the C and E Groups following the 5-min. rest given the E Group. Thus, we say, "If two groups are given 10 min. of continuous alphabet printing, and if one group is then given a 5-min. rest and the other is not, and if following the rest the performance of the group given the rest is superior to the group not given the rest, we say that reminiscence has taken place." But suppose we had given 8 min. of continuous work, or a 10-min. rest, or had used a different task. Would we still define the difference as reminiscence? Of course. A phenomenon is defined by a general set of operations, and we allow the details to vary greatly. The critical operations for the definition are only that a rest interval of some length be introduced after some amount of work on some task and that the performance of the group given the rest be superior following the rest to that of the group not given it. If the performance of the group given the rest is inferior after the rest, we have defined another phenomenon (perhaps forgetting). Our operational definitions must often specify a directional difference between E and C Groups, but given that specification, the operations involved may vary widely in detail, and we still admit the phenomenon under the general name (in this case, reminiscence).

We have seen that one form of explanation is *empirical extension.* Another name for this could be *operational identification,* meaning that E, in studying a given set of operations defining an empirical phenomenon, realizes that the operations can be fitted under those used to define what had hitherto been thought to be quite a different phenomenon (as judged by the operations). It was this form of explanation which we traced in Chapter Three in Künnapas' attempts to account for the horizontal-vertical illusion. Künnapas suggested that the operations commonly used to measure the horizontal-vertical illusion fit, when stripped of their nonessentials, the operations used to define the phenomenon of *contrast.* If he could make this identification "stick," the end product would be a reduction in the number of independent phenomena. He has explained the horizontal-vertical illusion by saying that it is really a contrast phenomenon, which is to say, when contrast is explained the horizontal-vertical illusion will be explained.

The approach to explanation of reminiscence has taken a different turn. We noted that Fig. 8-1 suggested that during the 10 min. of continuous practice, "something" appeared to be depressing performance; this was inferred from the fact that a 5-min. rest for one group resulted in the performance's rising to a level appreciably higher than that of the no-rest group. The theoretical notion, or hypothetical construct as such notions are often called, used to explain the reminiscence in such situations is called *reactive inhibition.* The investigator postulates a hypothetical process (reactive inhibition) to account for the empirical phenomenon. This process is assigned characteristics *needed* to account for the obtained results. What do we mean when we say it is assigned characteristics? Even from the simple experiment producing Fig. 8-1, the essential characteristics to be assigned can be identified. First, the reactive inhibition must inhibit performance. Second, it must disappear or dissipate or go away with comparative rest. Third, it must result in some way from the act of responding—from printing—for we would be quite sure that giving a rest interval before any printing was done would not have resulted in a difference between the performance of the two groups. It is apparent that these characteristics are gross; they do not state such things as the rate at which reactive inhibition builds up, what tasks causes it to build and what tasks do not, or the rate at which it dissipates. But if one uses such a theoretical notion, his research may be directed toward specifying these characteristics in more precise or quantitative terms.

Although sometimes given other names (e.g., work inhibition), reactive inhibition has had fairly widespread usage in psychology in accounting for some superficially diverse phenomena. Some of these we will point out later. For the moment, we need to discuss how one "thinks" about such a construct. Some theorists will insist that it is to be used only as a coordinating idea and that nothing need be implied about the reality or palpability or physical existence of the process implied by the idea. It is a coordinating idea because it may be used to explain a number of different phenomena. There are others who would say that the process is as real as any process (such as learning) and that in fact a part of the research work involved should be that of attempting to identify the physiological counterpart of the process. Whatever position one takes on this matter does not seem to influence research done at the strictly behavioral level, but it appears to be true that those who think in terms of reactive inhibition come to treat it in conversation, at least, as if it were indeed very real.

What about Es who do not like to think in terms of hypothetical constructs in any form? There are some who feel that nothing is gained by the use of such notions and in extreme cases indicate that the use of such constructs is akin to invoking spirits, spooks, gremlins, or ploglies to account for behavior. They prefer to work strictly at the empirical level, plotting laws to show the relationships, for example, between amount of work and reminiscence, amount of rest and reminiscence, and so on. If they find different amounts of reminiscence across various tasks, they analyze the tasks to determine the distinguishing characteristics and relate these characteristics to reminiscence or the other phenomena associated with perceptual-motor learning. Who can say that in the long run the end product of the work of such investigators is going to be different in any fundamental way from that of those who assiduously use hypothetical constructs in directing their research?

But the fact remains that reactive inhibition has had and still has a rather firm hold on many investigators. Therefore, as we sample some representative studies, we will not avoid showing how reactive inhibition may be coordinated with the empirical results.

WORK AND REST AS VARIABLES

Persistence of Reminiscence

A short rest interval following relatively continuous practice will, as we have seen, produce a sharp increment in performance. Obviously, such an increment operates in opposition to another well-established phenomenon, forgetting. It might be expected, therefore, that if the interval between work and the test for reminiscence is extended long enough, net forgetting would eventually be observed. However, if the practice before rest is continuous or massed, reminiscence persists for an amazingly long period of time. The evidence comes from a study by Koonce, Chambliss, and Irion (1964).

The task on which Ss worked is known as the *rotary pursuit* or *pursuit rotor*. This device consists of a circular disc about the size of a phonograph turntable and is usually made of a nonconducting material, such as bakelite. A small metal target about the size of a dime is imbedded in the turntable, flush with the surface and an inch or two from the periphery. The disc will, of course, move in a circular path when the turntable moves. The S is asked to keep a metal stylus on the target, a task which is more difficult than it may appear since the stylus is jointed or hinged between the handle and the tip so that the tip cannot be pressed down on the target. It is necessary that S make a circular motion with his entire arm, coordinating the movement with the circular motion of the target in order to rest the stylus tip lightly on the turntable (hopefully on the small metal disc). When the stylus touches the disc, an electrical circuit is completed, thus activating a timer; when the stylus leaves the disc, the timer stops. The score, therefore, is the number of seconds or percentage of time on target for a given trial period (perhaps 1 min.). The two critical task variables would be the rate of rotation of the target and the size of the target. In usual work, when speed of rotation is not a variable, the rate is 60 revolutions per min.

In the present study, all groups were given 5 min. of continuous practice prior to the introduction of the rest interval; and the scores, taken every 30 sec., were expressed as time on target in units of .001 min. After the rest intervals the groups were given 5 min. of continuous practice again. The rest intervals were 0 (control), 10 min., and 1, 7, 35, 70, 175, 365, and 730 days. With such long intervals the problem of maintaining the original equality of groups is a serious one. Even if, originally, the Ss are assigned to the groups on a random basis, there might be a selection factor involved in the loss of Ss over the long intervals. Since the Ss were college students, some could be expected to leave school (voluntarily or involuntarily), and there might be a difference in the ability level between those who remained in school and those who left. These Es fully recognized the serious implications of such selection. However, the Ss who *did* return after the various intervals were shown not to differ significantly in performance on the 10 trials of prerest practice. That is, the performance of the nine groups, constituted of those who actually returned for the postrest trials, did not differ on the prerest trials. There were 15 Ss in each group, except for the longest interval which had only 10.

The control group, given continuous practice, scored 130 on the eleventh trial, the trial which corresponds to the first postrest trial of the other groups. In Fig. 8-2, this level is shown by the dotted horizontal line. For plotting purposes, number of days has been transformed to logs, with the 10-min. group not shown. The ordinate gives the mean time on target on the first postrest trial. Reminiscence has occurred for all intervals, although there is an apparent decline in the amount of reminiscence with the longer intervals. Nevertheless, somewhat startling to contemplate is the fact that performance after two years is better than if no rest intervened. The superiority of the rest groups persisted over all 10 relearning or postrest trials, the control group scoring 162 on the last postrest trial while the mean of all experimental groups was 228.

Warmup. It was noted that if forgetting of a motor habit occurs, it will counteract the effect of reminiscence. If it occurred in the above study, it was not sufficient to overcome the positive effects of reminiscence (or, dissipation of reactive inhibition). Another phenomenon which has been identified as occurring in some motor tasks, particularly the pursuit rotor, is known as a decrement due to lack of warmup. In the same sense that warmup is assumed to facilitate athletic performance, it is presumed that if Ss come back to a pursuit rotor after a rest in an appropriately

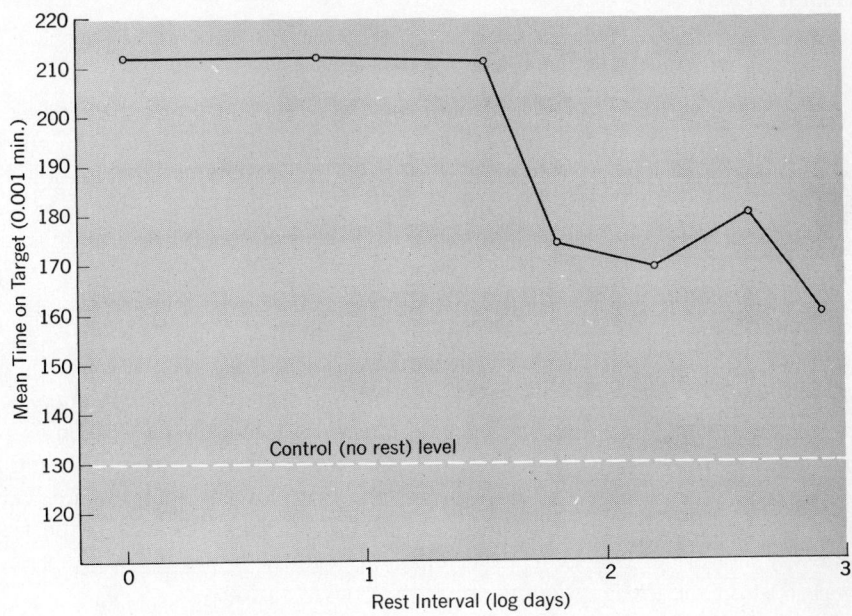

Fig. 8-2. Reminiscence in pursuit-rotor performance as a function of the length of the rest interval. The shortest rest interval was 1 day, the longest, 730 days; the performance scores are compared with a control group given no rest. Data from Koonce, Chambliss, and Irion (1964).

warmed-up state, their initial performance will be better than with no warmup. As it is, it is assumed that the initial practice after rest serves as a warmup period for S, and this is inferred from the fact that after a rest the performance curve rises very sharply for tasks such as the pursuit rotor. If this rise is sharper than expected at a comparable level of performance without there having been a rest, it is taken as evidence that the initial performance after rest was depressed by lack of warmup. For example, in the above study, the mean performance of all experimental groups on the first five 30-sec. trials after rest was 194, 228, 237, 234, 237. The jump between the first and second trial is much greater than would be expected had S been performing at a level of 194 during continuous practice. Therefore, it is assumed that the jump is primarily due to warmup on the initial trial, and had lack of warmup not been involved reminiscence would actually have been greater than when measured by the scores plotted in Fig. 8-2. A review and more thorough discussion of warmup phenomena may be found in Adams (1961).

Distributed Practice

Reminiscence is defined by a single rest interval introduced following relatively continuous practice. A closely related effect is the effect of distributed practice. Distributed practice involves the introduction of two or more rest intervals during a practice period. The performance under such a schedule is usually compared with that of a continuous or massed-practice group. It seems evident that if reactive inhibition builds up with work (practice) and dissipates with rest, the introduction of a number of rest periods during practice should result in a performance curve that is appreciably higher than that shown by groups with no rest. But how long should the rest intervals be? For optimum performance (performance not depressed by reactive inhibition) the interval should be long enough to allow all of the reactive inhibition to dissipate so that S, after rest, starts with no or little reactive inhibition present. How long is such an interval? One would suspect that the longer the period of work, the longer the rest interval should be. However, let us examine a study where the work period was constant and the length of the rest interval was varied.

In a study by Kientzle (1946), ten 1-min. trials on inverted-alphabet printing were given. Nine different groups (35 to 63 Ss per group) were differentiated by the length of the rest period introduced after *each* 1-min. trial, the rest periods being 0, 3, 5, 10, 15, 30, 45, 60, and 90 sec. Obviously, the group with 0-sec. interval between trials is a continuous or massed group. The effects of the varying lengths of rest intervals as assessed by performance on the tenth trial is shown in Fig. 8-3. A smooth curve has been drawn through the empirical points. If we infer that performance reflects the rate at which reactive inhibition dissipates, then we will conclude that the amount built up during a 1-min. work period is largely dissipated with a 30 sec. rest, since intervals beyond that produce only a slight increase in performance.

One might infer from Fig. 8-3 that if one is to learn a perceptual-motor skill (distributed practice has been shown to facilitate performance on many different motor-skills tasks), the skill will be acquired much more rapidly by distributed practice. Two considerations deny any such conclusion. First, consider the condition in which 90 sec. occurred between each trial. The total experimental time was 23.5 min. Suppose that S had practiced the full 23.5 min. While performance would probably be lower at the end of practice than at the end of 10 trials with 90 sec. between trials, the amount learned would be appreciably more, for we know, and this is the second

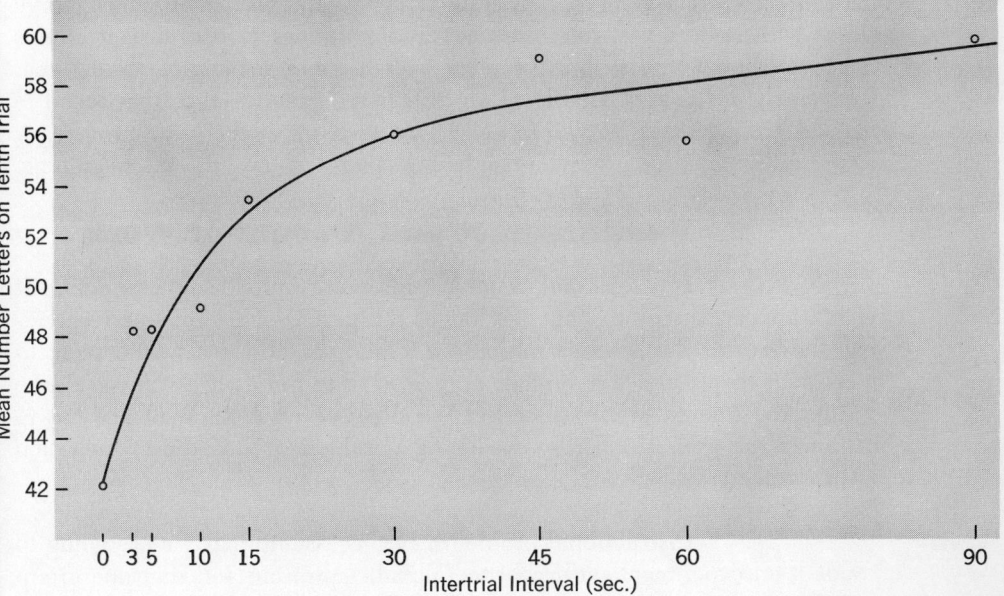

Fig. 8-3. Reversed alphabet printing as a function of time between each 1-min. trial. Data from Kientzle (1946).

consideration, that we cannot equate learning with performance under massed practice on a motor-type task. For pursuit-rotor learning there is some evidence that the amount learned under massed practice is somewhat less than under distributed practice (Archer, 1958; Jahnke & Duncan, 1956). For other tasks the amount learned appears to be the same. In any event, if one adds resting time to work time to determine total time for distributed practice and allows S in the massed group to work this total time, the amount learned will be greater for the massed S.

Switching intervals. Suppose as S is going along in his practice on a motor task under distributed practice, we suddenly switch him to completely massed practice. Or suppose the reverse is true—following practice under massed procedure, S is switched to distributed practice. Studies examining the effects of such shifts at various stages of practice have been done using the pursuit rotor (Reynolds & Adams, 1953) and inverted-alphabet printing (Kaufman, Smith, & Zeaman, 1962) with much the same results. In these experiments a distributed group and a massed group are consistently given their respective conditions throughout the practice period, and their results serve as boundary performance curves. When a group initially given massing is switched to the distributed condition, his performance curve rises (with some initial reminiscence) and continues to rise until it attains the level shown by the group having had distributed practice throughout. Conversely, if the S is initially given distributed practice and is switched to massed, his performance will fall and then level off at the same proficiency level exhibited by the group having had massed practice from the beginning.

Reminiscence and Amount of Work

It is said that reactive inhibition results from responding. It would appear, therefore, that the longer the period of continuous responding, the greater the reactive inhibition. Experimentally this would seem to mean that the greater the number of massed trials before a rest interval, the greater the amount of reminiscence. We shall see what the evidence has to say about this proposition after examining a problem of procedure which such an experiment raises.

Instructional problems. Let us assume that we are going to conduct an experiment with inverted-alphabet printing and that one group is to be given 5 min. of continuous work, another 10 min., and another 20. Following the work periods we give all three groups a 10-min. rest interval before returning to the task to obtain reminiscence measures. Normally, as a part of our instructions, we request the Ss to work as rapidly as possible—to print as many letters as possible—until told to stop. After the formal instructions, it is customary to ask if there are any questions. Suppose at this point an S asks how long the continuous work period will be. If we give him this information, we would be telling one group that they will print for 5 min., another for 10 min., and another for 20 min. Should we give this information? We have evidence which says we should not.

The logic of the situation can be seen if we take an extreme case. Suppose that one group of Ss were instructed to run 100 miles as fast as they could and another group, 100 yards as fast as they could. It seems safe to predict that the group instructed to run 100 miles would run the first 100 yards (if they ran at all) at a much slower pace than the group instructed to run 100 yards. The same effect occurs when comparable operations are introduced into the laboratory. First, we will examine a study in which inverted-alphabet printing was used (Saufley & Bilodeau, 1963).

These *E*s reasoned that, for a given task, S might pace himself (as a conservation measure) only if he had a fair notion of the nature of the task and what he was going to conserve himself against. Therefore, telling S how long he was going to work on a task about which he knew little would produce very little change in the rate at which he attacked the task. But if S had experience with the task, knowledge of how long he was going to have to work might well change his initial rate of attack. We may consider three conditions from the study.

Group C (naive control): These Ss, when first introduced to the task, were told that they would have to work for 20 min., printing as rapidly as they could.

Group E-1: These Ss were given 12 min. of practice without being told how long the period would be. This was followed by a 10-min. rest, after which they were told, before starting to print again, that they were to print as rapidly as they could for 20 *sec.*

Group E-2: These Ss were treated like those in Group E-1, except that, following the rest, they were told to print again as rapidly as possible for a period of 20 min.

If performance of naive Ss is influenced by knowledge of how long the practice or work period will be, the performance of the C Group should be less than that of either Groups E-1 or E-2. This was not true. The performance curves for 12 min. of practice were essentially the same. However, differences between the performance of Groups E-1 and E-2 occurred soon after rest and must, therefore, be attributable to the differential instructions concerning amount of time they had to work. Actually, Group E-1 was given 30 sec. of work, and the performance over the 30 sec. can be compared with that of Group E-2, instructed to work 20 min. The performance of the Ss in Group E-1 was significantly higher than that of Group E-2 during this 30 sec.

This study would seem to indicate that if naive Ss are used in inverted-alphabet printing, knowledge of amount of time to be spent in practice will not influence performance. Within the limits of expected work periods given here, this conclusion cannot be denied for this task. But there may be a limit to the generalization. If a naive S knew he was to work for 60 min., it is quite possible his performance on early trials would be influenced. As for other tasks, it would seem that if S has some realization of the nature of the task and how working on it may make him "feel," knowledge of how long the work period will be will influence early performance. Thus, although Krueger (1937) used experienced Ss and showed that knowledge of the length of the work period in doing simple addition problems influenced initial rate of performance, it is quite likely that a naive S would respond in much the same way since he has had a great deal of experience with addition problems outside of the laboratory.

Illusory work. We may consider a study which deals with

lifted weights, as pure a work task as is normally used in the laboratory. Here, skill is minimal, sheer muscular work, maximal. The device used to study work is an *ergograph*, which, in its simple form, consists of a cord attached to an arm, a finger, or a leg. A weight is suspended at the end of the cord which runs over a pulley. The S's exciting task is lifting the weight a given distance, then letting it down, lifting it again, and so on at a prescribed rate. The crudest response measure is simply the length of time that S can continue to raise the weight. If the lifts are not paced, another measure could be the number of pulls in successive units of time. Or, if the criterion for distance of pull is not maintained, work output in terms of size of weight and distance pulled can be determined for successive units of time.

Very gross as well as very subtle variables may change work output. An S working under no particular incentives for a period necessary to produce apparent exhaustion will suddenly be unexhausted if offered a valuable incentive for additional work. The sample study we will consider is at a more subtle level but clearly shows that the amount S works depends upon his conception of the amount of work to be done or the conception he has of the difficulty of the work. In this study by Jarrard (1960) a finger ergograph was used. The S placed his hand, palm up, on a flat surface with the cord attached to the middle finger. Then he raised and lowered a 1000-gm. weight a given distance by alternately contracting and relaxing the finger.

If two objects have the same shape and weight, but are of different sizes, S will judge the larger object to be lighter than the smaller. This, we will remember, is known as the size-weight illusion. If one beer can is crushed from end to end in a large vice, and if this crushed can is compared in weight with a noncrushed can, the illusion is quite apparent; the crushed can will appear heavier than the noncrushed can. In the present experiment, Jarrard had two wooden blocks, one 15 cm. high with a base that was 10 cm. square, and another that was 7.5 cm. high with a base 5 cm. square. By filling the latter with lead shot, it was made to weigh the same as the former (1000 gm.).

Initially, by direct lifting, all Ss were given experience in comparing the weights of the two blocks. This produced the size-weight illusion so that S undoubtedly entered the experiment proper believing the small block to be heavier than the large one. In the main part of the experiment, some Ss worked initially with the small block and then changed to the large; others worked first with the large and then switched to the small. The Ss could see E change the weights. The hypothesis was that S would work longer when being switched from small to large than when being changed from large to small. Control groups had either the larger or the smaller weight throughout.

The results confirm expectations; the number of trials (lifts) to exhaustion was less than that for the control group when the shift was from large to small, and the opposite held when the shift was from small to large. Indeed, the illusion was so compelling for the Ss switched from the large to the small block that their muscle action potentials (electrical discharges produced by contraction of the muscles) showed that they worked harder, which may account for the more rapid loss of "ability" to lift the weight.

Our general conclusion must be that caution is in order in giving instructions which might directly or indirectly inform S of the length of the work period or the amount of work to be done, unless, of course, the purpose of the study is to examine the effects of such information. Therefore, in studying the rate of buildup of reactive inhibition by varying the length of the work period before the rest interval, we should avoid giving knowledge about the length of the work period if we expect the Ss in all groups to attack the task with equal vigor. Inverted-alphabet printing may not be influenced by this problem when naive Ss are used and the work period is no longer than 20 min. Nevertheless, we should probably avoid answering the question about the length of work period if we as Es are asked about it by the Ss.

Amount of work. As illustrative of the work on varying the number of massed trials before a rest, we will use a study by Wasserman (1951). He used the inverted-alphabet task with 30-sec. trials and gave the nine groups different numbers of trials, namely, 2, 5, 10, 15, 25, 30, 35, 40, prior to the introduction of a 10-min. rest interval. Wasserman also introduced a second variable, a motivational variable. The implication of this variable for reactive inhibition will be discussed later. The operations for introducing high and low motivation in this experiment consisted of differential instructions. The instructions designed to produce low motivation told the Ss that the task was being tried out for future use and that they were merely helping out in determining whether or not it could be used in future research. The instructions designed to produce high motivation informed the Ss that the task was a new type of intelligence test. Differential instructions of this nature are considered to produce differences in degree of ego-involvement. High ego-involvement is said to be produced if S believes he is being measured on some trait on which society places a high premium. Generally speaking, high intelligence is desirable and society does prize it. Therefore, it is assumed that if S takes E at his word when E says the task measures intelligence, he will, so to speak, work hard to show that he has high intelligence. It is quite possible to establish a dimension of traits varying in the premium which Ss place on the possession of those traits. Any of several scaling methods discussed in Chapter Six could be used.

Telling S that a given task measures intelligence when it is not known to do so might cause a lifted eyebrow or two. It is a fact that such white lies are not unusual in experimental work, for it is necessary to produce a reasonably realistic situation. Although the research community will accept such procedures, there is, at the same time, a responsibility imposed on E—

a responsibility to "remove" the white lie before releasing S from the experimental situation. If S believes that a task is an intelligence test, and if he believes he did very poorly (whether he did or not), some depression, perhaps painful, may result if the misconception is not corrected. It is quite unfair to allow S to leave the experimental situation without removing any such deleterious effects. The E can inform S just what he did and why he did it and, in addition, point out that the task is not in any way known to measure intelligence. However, because S may then say to a friend who is still expecting to serve in the experiment, "He tells you it is an intelligence test but in fact it isn't," E must request cooperation from the S in keeping the situation inviolate until the experiment is completed. Most Ss will respond appropriately to such requests.

But let us return to Wasserman's study. There are nine degrees of prerest practice, given to nine groups with high-motivation instructions and to nine other groups with low-motivation instructions. The basic concern is with the amount of reminiscence over a 10-min. rest. The data are presented in Fig. 8-4 in terms of the increase in performance from the last prerest trial to the first postrest trial.

It was noted earlier that if reactive inhibition builds up in some direct fashion with amount of continuous work, reminiscence should become greater and greater as practice before rest increases. Quite obviously this expectation is not borne out. Maximal reminiscence occurs after only a few trials. Wasserman points out that the amount of reminiscence estimated after two trials is probably an overestimate. This results from a very peculiar fact that has been noted by a number of investigators using this task: performance on the first 30-sec. trial is superior to that on the second 30-sec. trial. Possible reasons for this dip have been advanced by Saufley and Bilodeau (1964). The implication of the dip for the data of the moment is that since the reminiscence in Fig. 8-4 is calculated from the last prerest trial to the first postrest trial, the difference is magnified for the two-trial groups because of the depression on Trial 2. However this may be, the fact is clear that we do not get more and more reminiscence as the amount of prerest practice increases. For Ss under low motivation there is an appreciable decrease after reaching the initial peak, although the amount for Ss under high motivation remains fairly constant.

No final accounting of such data via the reactive inhibition construct can be given. However, here is the way Wasserman's thinking ran. An S will tolerate only so much reactive inhibition. When it reaches this maximum level, he may provide himself with very short rest intervals, sometimes called bootleg rests. In a manner of speaking, therefore, S is making it possible for reactive inhibition to dissipate during the period when he is supposed to be working as rapidly as he can. Such an explanation would account for the relative constancy of the reminiscence for the high-motivation Ss, but what about the continued decrease for the low-motivation Ss? Some investigators (including Wasserman) have introduced an additional concept to aid in handling such facts. We will not discuss it, because it has generally been discounted in more contemporary work. It is possible that Ss under low motivation keep shifting downward the level of the amount of reactive inhibition they will tolerate before taking a bootleg rest.

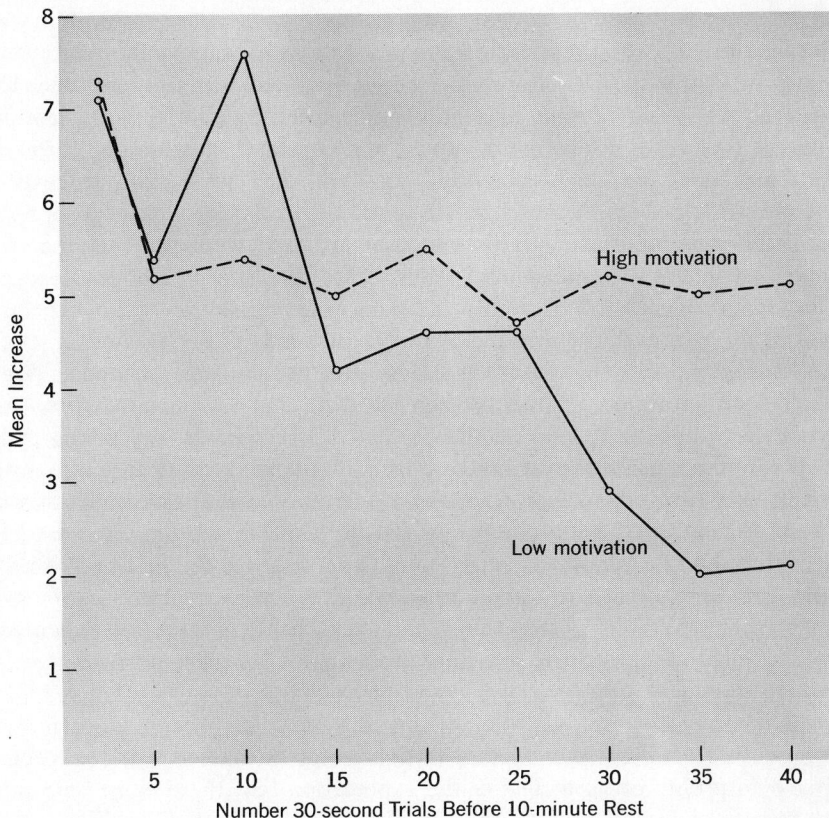

Fig. 8-4. Reminiscence as a function of number of prerest trials and level of motivation. Data from Wasserman (1951).

Is the bootleg-rest notion a reasonable one? Any E who has run Ss in this task will point out instances of such rests. Even though Ss are instructed to work as rapidly as they can, it is not a rare thing to see an S lift his hand, shake it a couple of times, and continue work. After several minutes of continuous printing, there are clear subjective feelings of fatigue in the writing hand. However, by the development of a very clever device for measuring not only the time to print letters but also the time to travel from one letter to the next, Archer and Bourne (1956) were unable to obtain any evidence that there was an increase in average travel time (indicating increasing numbers of bootleg rests) as work continued under massed practice. Indeed, there was a reduction in travel time. So, in fact, we do not have evidence that S administers his own rests to fit the demands of the situation.

Wasserman's notion in comparing Ss of high and low motivation was that the former Ss would tolerate a greater amount of reactive inhibition than would the latter Ss. He interprets his results to support this position. The relatively constant amount of reminiscence after the initial large amount suggests that a given level is "hit upon" and constantly maintained throughout the practice period. Just how it is maintained, if not by bootleg rests, is not known. One possibility is that S rests by involving muscle groups not normally used in printing. This might be inferred from the fact that the quality of letters printed seems to deteriorate as massed practice proceeds. This is most clearly seen when S is asked to write, say, *a* and *b* over and over again as rapidly as possible. As work proceeds under massed practice, the letters tend to get bigger and bigger and less smoothly formed, letters which look like those we made when we were first learning to write. One hypothesis (Robinson, 1934) could be that this represents the "taking over" of more gross muscle groups than are usually involved, resulting in a poorer quality of writing. However, this taking over may at the same time provide a resting time for the muscle groups usually used in writing. It should be clear that this is a hypothesis attempting to account for the fact that there is a limit on amount of reactive inhibition built up with continuous practice. Investigators have suggested that S may take bootleg rests, but when one tries to measure these rests (as did Archer and Bourne), no evidence for them is found. An alternative suggestion is that S takes bootleg rests for particular muscle groups while shifting the work in part to other muscle groups. In any case, other factors (which enter as massed work proceeds) appear to prohibit a clear test of the expectation that there is a direct relationship between amount of reactive inhibition and length of continuous work on a task.

One last point should be made. Wasserman also showed that performance was better during prerest practice for his high-motivation Ss than for his low-motivation Ss.

FURTHER CHARACTERISTICS OF REACTIVE INHIBITION

We have seen that certain phenomena of motor learning, defined by relating certain stimulus manipulations to differences in performance scores, have led to the assignment of certain characteristics to a hypothetical process called reactive inhibition. Reactive inhibition is said to build up with work, to depress performance (hence mask some of the learning that has occurred), and to dissipate with rest. In this section we will rather briefly treat other approaches which are being used to investigate the properties of reactive inhibition. We should remember at all times that the experiments resulting from these approaches produce results which stand for what they are (relationships between independent variables and performance), and one need not refer at all to reactive inhibition if one does not choose to. In most of these studies, however, notions about reactive inhibition have prompted the investigations.

Specific Repetition and Reactive Inhibition

The following experiment was performed by the writer's class, and part of the thinking which led to it includes a guess about conditions in which amount of reactive inhibition will vary.

We have seen how inverted-alphabet printing has been used to study perceptual-motor learning. But we also noted that there is no clear distinction (as far as reactive-inhibition phenomena are concerned) between tasks said to be learning tasks and those said to be work tasks (where learning is at a minimum). In the present study the task would normally be said to be a work task. It involves the writing, over and over, of the same small group of letters in alphabetical sequence. There is improvement on this task in early trials, which might be due to warming up or to overcoming certain interference effects. Concerning the latter, it can be seen that if S is asked to write *abcde* (in that order) over and over again, there might be some interference in going from *e* back to *a*, since this breaks the alphabetical sequence. Whatever the cause, it only serves to remind us again that we cannot, a priori, draw a sharp line between tasks presumed to involve learning and those that do not.

The basic fact which prompted the present experiment was produced in a study by Robinson and Bills (1926). In one condition S wrote *ab* in longhand over and over again as rapidly as possible under massed conditions. (Note that S wrote; the results would probably be the same if printing were used although this has not, to the best of the writer's knowledge, been demonstrated.) In another condition, S wrote *ab cd ef* over and over again as rapidly as possible under massed practice. The performance (total letters) of the group writing the six letters over and over again was superior to that of the group writing the two letters. Why should this be? Thinking in terms of reactive inhibition, one could say that the more exact the repetition of successive responses, the greater the reactive inhibition. We assume (1) that the printing of several different letters involves more different muscles or more different patterns of muscular involvement than does the printing of one or two letters and (2) that the greater the work imposed on a particular musculature, the greater the reactive inhibition. Printing *ab* over and over more likely forces S to use the same responding mechanisms than does printing *ab cd ef*. In terms of the earlier discussion of bootleg rests, and speaking more in an all-or-none fashion than is warranted, we might say that while writing *cd*, S is resting the responding mechanisms used to produce *ab*. Bootleg rests in this case are not really bootleg rests; they are granted S by the nature of the task.

If the results of the Robinson-Bills study are due to differences in amount of reactive inhibition generated in the two instances, then an obvious prediction follows, namely, that the effects of distributed practice (as compared with massed) should be greater when only two letters are printed over and over than when three or more are printed. By any conception of reactive inhibition, the less the amount of reactive inhibition accumulated, the less should distributed practice facilitate performance. We are assuming that the amount of reactive inhibition accruing to a given letter is inversely related to the number of different letters printed. The reactive inhibition generated in writing a particular letter dissipates somewhat while other letters are being written. The critical prediction is an interaction in performance between number of letters and length of intertrial rest.

Four groups of 19 Ss each were used in the 2 x 2 design. Two of the groups repetitively wrote eight different letters (*abcdefgh*), and two other groups wrote two letters over and over. For the two-letter groups, the letters written were *ab*, *cd*, *ef*, or *gh*, with 5, 5, 5, and 4 Ss assigned to each. Therefore, differences in performance between the two- and eight-letter groups should not be attributed to differences in speed with which different letters may be written. The other variable was length of intertrial rest, 0 or 30 sec. One of the groups given eight letters had continuous work, the other had 30-sec. rest after each minute of work. The two two-letter groups were assigned in the same manner to either a massed-practice procedure or a distributed-practice procedure. The total work period was 15 min., and the response measure was the total number of two-letter units printed in 15 min.

The results are shown in Fig. 8-5 where it can be seen that the predictions are supported. When S wrote eight letters over and over, distributed practice was only slightly superior to massed practice, whereas a large difference is apparent when only two letters were written over and over. In a similar study (Nohara, 1965), the interaction seen in Fig. 8-5 was not significant. However, there are several differences in the procedures for the two studies so that it is not possible to identify the possible source of the discrepancy.

The above experiment rested on certain assumptions about the similarity of response patterns. It can be seen that assumptions about the effects of similarity (or dissimilarity) of motor patterns could be tested by another approach. First, we might take a certain selected number of letters and scale these for similarity of movements required to produce them. Certainly, we would suspect that the movements required to produce a c and an o are more similar than those required to produce a c and, say, a k. Next, suppose we give two groups of Ss 10 min. of continuous work in writing c over and over again. Following this, one group fills the next 5 min. writing o over and over,

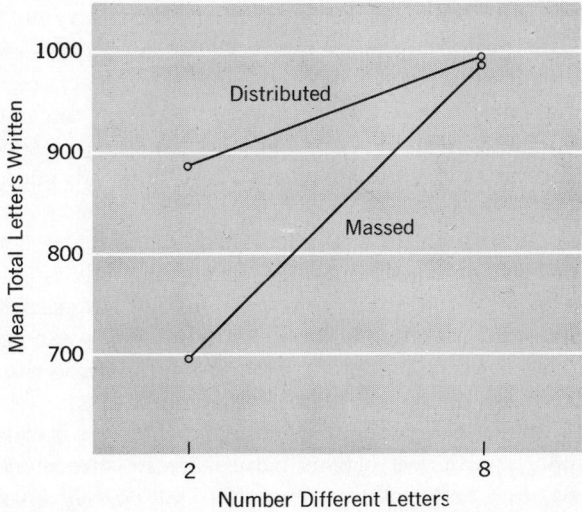

Fig. 8-5. Number of letters printed in 15 min. as a function of massed and distributed practice and as a function of number of different letters.

after which they return immediately to writing c. The other group fills the 5-min. interval with the writing of k. When both groups return to the printing of c, we would have to predict that performance would be better for those who had filled the 5-min. period with k.

The Locus of Reactive Inhibition

The tendency of investigators to think of reactive inhibition as a substantive process is shown most clearly in studies designed to provide evidence on its locus. Some of the impetus for this work seems to have been provided by Hull (1943), who used the concept extensively in his general theory of learning and performance, and who localized it in the effector systems. But even without this impetus, it is clear that sooner or later investigators would ask questions about locus if they thought of reactive inhibition as a real process. Two major experimental approaches have resulted from these questions. One concerns various ways of filling a reminiscence rest interval. The other concerns bilateral reminiscence.

Filling the reminiscence interval. In a study by Duncan (1957), three groups of Ss were given 3 min. of continuous work on the pursuit rotor. Then a 5-min. reminiscence interval was introduced. During this interval the control Ss did in fact rest, but a second group, properly instructed, visually followed the target of the pursuit rotor during the 5-min. interval. The third group made rotary movements, exactly the same as those made if they were on target 100 percent of the time. This was accomplished by a special circular track which guided the stylus in the correct orbit and which forced S to make the circuit at a rate commensurate with the rate that the actual rotor made. Following the "rest" interval, additional trials were given on the pursuit rotor.

Although all three groups performed at about the same level immediately after rest, as trials continued, the group having made the circular motions with the arm during the rest fell behind the other two groups. Duncan concludes that reactive inhibition as generated by the pursuit rotor does not reside in the visual system (for the group following the target with their eyes suffered no decrement), but the hypothesis that it is generated by kinesthetic stimulation of the responding mechanisms is quite tenable.

Not all experiments of this nature are in agreement. Adams' results (1955) led him to conclude that the visual system *was* involved; Humphries and McIntyre (1963) concluded that neither the peripheral motor nor visual systems was involved. We have no resolution of these differences since the rest-interval tasks were not all comparable from experiment to experiment.

An alternative to localizing reactive inhibition in the peripheral motor systems is to say that it is a central process, and this apparently means the central nervous system. Thus, reactive inhibition, although generated by the act of responding, has its representation in the central nervous system. To some the issue of a peripheral locus versus a central locus has a certain component of nonsense in it, not only because it is difficult to draw a distinction between what is peripheral and what is central, but also because the experimental results themselves are not always capable of mediating a clear decision. Still, relationships as a function of independent variables are produced, and whether or not the theoretical notions are valid inferences is a separate issue.

Bilateral transfer. In the study of learning, transfer designs are widely used as a means of making inferences about the nature of the habits or other processes involved in learning. Two different tasks are commonly used, and some specified relationship exists between them. The basic question is whether or not practice on the first task will influence performance on the second task. At the gross design level we have an experimental group given both tasks and a control group given only the second. If the performance on the second task differs, transfer is said to have occurred. If the performance of the experimental group is superior to that of the control, positive transfer is defined; and if it is inferior, negative transfer is defined. It was noted that the above is a gross design; this is to say that it is the general operational definition of transfer. But as we shall see, primarily in later chapters, the level of analyses has advanced to the point that we rarely use the gross design, for we rarely ask about gross transfer. Rather, we are usually interested in the amount contributed to transfer by a particular factor, and when we ask this question we must, by addition of appropriate groups, eliminate the differential influence of all other factors on transfer.

If age is an index of honor, bilateral transfer has an honored status in experimental psychology. The classical laboratory exercise for exhibiting or demonstrating bilateral transfer is mirror star-tracing. A star outline, printed on a standard sheet of paper, is placed on a table before an upright mirror. A shield is attached to a support of some kind in such a way that it completely obstructs S's direct vision of the star but allows him to see the entire star by looking in the mirror. The task is to trace around the outline of the star by directing the pencil movements from the mirror images of the star, the hand, and the pencil. Usually, the outline of the star consists of a narrow pathway, and S must traverse the outline by keeping within the path. The E usually scores by trials, a trial consisting of the time required for one circuit of the pathway. On each successive trial a new star outline is given. Initially, at least, there is considerable interference in making the appropriate movements caused by the necessary reversal of movements as compared with those required by direct vision.

Bilateral transfer is demonstrated if practice at mirror tracing with one hand transfers to the other hand. The E Group first practices with the right hand, then with the left, and the C Group has only the second or left-hand trials. If the performance of the former group is better than that of the latter, bilateral transfer is defined. Moreover, it is usually found; it will occur not only bilaterally (from arm to arm or arm to foot on opposite sides of the body), but also unilaterally (from arm to foot on the same side of the body).

The results of an experiment performed in the writer's laboratory course may be used to illustrate the method and results of a simple bilateral-transfer investigation. The students, after reading about bilateral transfer, were in considerable disagreement as to what caused it. Some felt that it was due entirely to the learning of a general principle, the principle of mirror reversal, and that if one learned this, transfer would be complete from one hand to the other. Other students believed a certain amount of skill was required which would be specific to a given hand and that this would not transfer to the other. Accepting the fact that bilateral transfer occurs, no student suggested the hypothesis that acquisition of a habit by one hand would not transfer at all to the other. However, this third possibility could be set up as a hypothesis along with the other two, so three hypotheses were stated:

1. In learning mirror star-tracing, S learns only the general principle of mirror reversal. Transfer from one hand to the other should be 100 percent.

2. In learning mirror star-tracing, S learns not only a general principle but also skills specific to the practicing hand. Bilateral transfer will thus take place, but it will not be 100 percent.

3. In learning mirror star-tracing, S learns a skill specific to the practicing hand. No bilateral transfer will take place.

Three groups were used to test these hypotheses, one control group and two experimental groups. All Ss were given a preliminary practice trial and then performance on a second trial was used to match the three groups of 14 Ss so that mean performance and variability of performance of the three groups were equivalent. The conditions for the three groups were as follows:

Trial 2

	MATCHING TRIAL	TRIALS 3 TO 12	TRIALS 13 TO 15
GROUP I (CONTROL)	preferred hand	no practice	preferred hand
GROUP II	preferred hand	nonpreferred hand	preferred hand
GROUP III	preferred hand	preferred hand	preferred hand

The critical data come from trials 13 to 15. If Hypothesis 1 is to be substantiated, the difference in performance on these trials should not be significantly different for Groups II and III, and both should produce higher scores than Group I. If Hypothesis 2 is to be substantiated, performance of Group III should be better than Group II, and that of Group II better than that of Group I. If Hypothesis 3 is to be substantiated, Groups I and II should be equal, although both would be inferior to Group III.

Figure 8-6 shows Hypothesis 2 to be in best accord with the data. It is clear that there is bilateral transfer (Group II is better than Group I) on Trials 13 to 15, but Group II is inferior to Group III, indicating that practice with the preferred hand facilitated later performance with that hand more than did practice with the nonpreferred hand. Something was learned by Group III that was not learned by Group II.

Now, what does bilateral transfer have to do with reactive inhibition? Mirror star-tracing has not been frequently used as a task in studies of perceptual-motor learning where reactive inhibition is a matter of issue, but there is no reason why it would not be so used. The point of introducing bilateral transfer comes about because studies concerned with the locus of reactive inhibition have used the occurrence of *bilateral reminiscence* as evidence that reactive inhibition must be at least partially central in nature. This is to say that if bilateral reminiscence is to occur, practice under massed conditions with one hand will, if followed by rest, be followed in turn by an improvement in performance with the other hand. The minimum operations necessary for demonstrating bilateral transfer of work decrement have been given by Kimble (1952):

E Group: Practice with nonpreferred hand—rest—test with preferred.

C Group: Practice with nonpreferred hand—no rest—test with preferred.

(Initial practice could also be with preferred hand, with testing on nonpreferred.) If the performance of the E Group is superior to that of the C Group

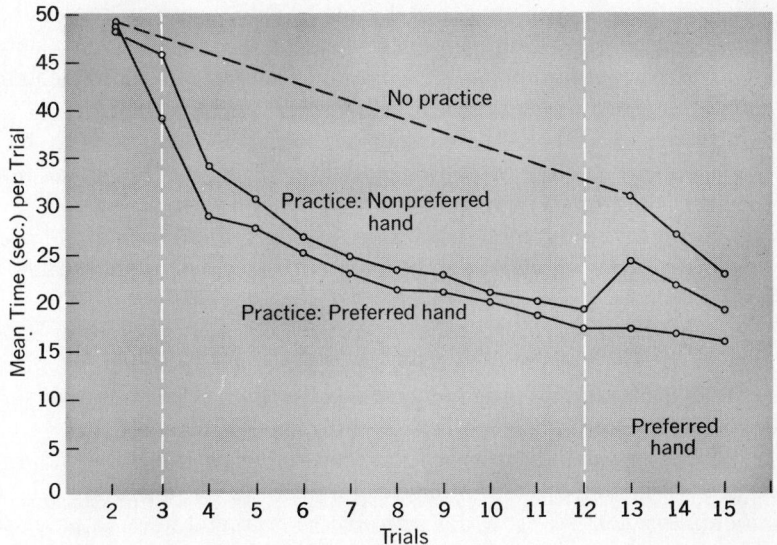

Fig. 8-6. Transfer in mirror star-tracing. Trial 1 was a practice trial; Trial 2 was used as a source of data for matching the three groups of 14 Ss each. Tracing was with the preferred hand on Trial 2.

after the rest, bilateral transfer of reactive inhibition is demonstrated, as it was in Kimble's study using the pursuit rotor. Other investigators have extended these observations and have shown that the variables influencing bilateral reminiscence have much the same effect as those influencing conventional reminiscence in the responding arm (e.g., Grice & Reynolds, 1952; Rockway, 1953). However, as these investigators point out, such results need not lead to the conclusion that reactive inhibition is central. It is probably next to impossible to restrict activity to one hand and arm *only*, so it is possible that some reactive inhibition could develop in the bilateral member. That it would be less in amount is in accord with the findings that bilateral reminiscence is less than conventional reminiscence. However, even with a task where motor activity is relatively restricted, such as in inverted-alphabet printing, evidence for bilateral transfer has been found (Albright, Borresen, & Marx, 1956). The issue of locus of reactive inhibition is still with us, although no conclusion about it can be firm at this time.

Generality of the Reactive-Inhibition Notion

It was noted earlier that the basic notion of reactive inhibition, although perhaps called by other names, has widespread use in psychology. We shall simply note some of the evidences for this statement.

1. Reactive inhibition has been used to account for certain phenomena of conditioning, such as extinction (Hull, 1943).

2. Duncan (1956) has noted the close correspondence between the properties assigned reactive inhibition and those assigned to *neural satiation,* a construct used to account for certain perceptual phenomena.

3. Certain visual aftereffects (spiral aftereffect) are being interpreted in terms of reactive inhibition, and reminiscence has been demonstrated (Holland, 1963).

4. The behavior of pigeons in certain situations has been shown to demonstrate reactive-inhibition-like phenomena, including reminiscence, very much as found with the human S following practice on the pursuit rotor (Boneau & Axelrod, 1962).

5. Even personality theorists have made use of the concept. Introverts and extroverts are asserted to have different rates of generating reactive inhibition (Eysenck, 1956), with extroverts generating it more rapidly. Tests of the hypothesis are sometimes interpreted as being favorable (e.g., Star, 1963), and sometimes unfavorable (e.g., Yates & Laszlo, 1965), to the hypothesis.

KNOWLEDGE OF RESULTS

One of the most widely investigated variables in the area of perceptual-motor learning is knowledge of results, commonly abbreviated KR. Another term, *feedback,* is sometimes applied to the procedures. In terms of these procedures, KR always involves giving S some information about his performance on successive trials. Bilodeau and Bilodeau (1961) say, "Studies of feedback or knowledge of results (KR) show it to be the strongest, most important variable controlling performance and learning." (p. 250)

There have been many ideas advanced about the role of KR in terms of how it may (through what mechanisms) influence work, learning, and performance (e.g., Ammons, 1956), but two factors rather persistently stand out in most discussions. One is that KR may produce an increase in motivation, and insofar as increases in motivation will enhance performance, KR may be expected to enhance performance. When tasks are used in which the acquisition of skill is minimal and emphasis is on sheer speed or work output, KR may be expected to produce enhanced performance because of increased motivation. If a person working on such a task knows from time to time how well he is performing, he may be motivated in a very simple fashion to "beat my previous score." When, however, we are in the process of learning a task that emphasizes precision and coordination of movements, it is questionable whether high motivation will facilitate the learning. When such a task is well learned, increased motivation might facilitate the speed of its execution, but the actual speed of learning initially may not be influenced at all by increased motivation and may even be retarded (as reflected in the idea of "trying too hard").

The second route by which KR may enhance performance results from the information value of KR. On some tasks performance is automatically followed by KR. When one shoots an arrow at a bull's-eye 30 ft. away, he receives immediate KR from observing the position of his arrow in the target. On the other hand, when he shoots a rifle at a bull's-eye 200 yards away, he is not usually provided KR in the immediate visual display. Some situations may provide only crude KR. For example, S probably can tell when his performance on the pursuit rotor deviates markedly from one trial to the next, but he would probably be quite unable to detect an improvement of 1 sec. time on target if each trial is 60 sec. The information value of KR as provided by E, therefore, becomes of relevance to learning a skill when S cannot obtain such information directly. The giving of KR often provides S with information about the discrepancy between his performance and some criterion of performance set by E. As a consequence, it is presumed that on successive trials S will in some way be able to modify his behavior so as to perform at a level closer to that set by E. Just how S may translate the KR into behavior that does represent increased skill is an issue that is quite unsettled, for it represents the crux of skill learning, and this is true whether the task is one in which S can provide his own KR or a task which requires that E give KR. We will return at a later point to a further consideration of this difficult problem. For the time being, we wish to identify some of the variables associated with KR.

Tasks, Response Measures, and Variables

A great variety of tasks has been used to study the role of KR in perceptual-motor learning. The most dramatic effects can be shown for tasks in which the precision of the response is initially very poor and for which S can give himself at best only minimal KR. One such task is line drawing. The S, blindfolded, is asked to draw a line of a specified length. After each attempt—each line drawing—S is given information about the accuracy of his performance. How will performance changes be measured? Several methods have been used. Changes in average deviation from the specified line length is one. Changes in the mean constant error, which, as we will remember, takes into account the direction of the deviation, is another. Or, E might set some arbitrary standard of a "correct" response and measure the increase in frequency of correct responses over trials. Thus, if the line length specified were 3 in., E might arbitrarily say that any line drawn which was between 2.9 in. and 3.1 in. would be called correct. If such a criterion is set for a correct response, E might set a criterion of performance, such as five successive correct responses, and then measure differences among groups in terms of trials to reach the criterion.

The response measures for other tasks will usually be comparable to those mentioned for line drawing. Here are some other simple tasks that have been used: drawing a yardstick out of a sheath a specified distance; pushing a lever or turning a knob a specified number of degrees; exerting a certain degree of pressure on a spring or bulb. It may be noted that E would not necessarily have to specify the length of line to be drawn or the distance or degrees for a lever to be moved. He could, for example, simply ask S to draw a line and then tell him how much he was off. Indeed, one group of investigators, being somewhat concerned by the fact that S brought a fairly precise knowledge of inches to the line-drawing situation, asked S to draw a line that was 60 glubs long and gave all KR in glub units (Denny, Allard, Hall, & Rokeach, 1960).

As tasks become more complex, the giving of KR may become more complex. A bulb may be lighted when S is tracking a target correctly or when he has a plane accurately in a gun sight. There are, then, innumerable ways in which knowledge of results may be given. Even teams of men involved in air defense exercises have been given KR concerning the adequacy of the various functions they were supposed to carry out. Their subsequent performance was better than that for teams not given such KR (Alexander, Kepner, & Tregoe, 1962). Still with major emphasis on simple tasks, let us look at some of the different ways in which KR may be given.

Frequency of KR. McGuigan (1959) gave Ss 70 trials at drawing a 6-in. line. For one group, KR was given after each trial, for another, after 55 percent of the trials, and for another, after only 10 percent of the trials. As might be expected, at the end of 70 trials performance by the 10 percent group was poorer than that shown by the other two groups.

Precision of KR. At the extremes of precision of KR, E could simply tell S he was "wrong," or, as in line drawing, he could tell him that the line drawn was "one-eighth too short." If the same criterion of proficiency is set, the ultimate accuracy for two groups treated in these manners would be expected to be equivalent, although the rate at which peak proficiency is reached will be more rapid for the group given precise KR.

Augmented KR. There are a number of studies in which E has manipulated cues during the acquisition of a skill in such a way that these cues augment the KR with which S can provide himself during practice. Thus, these studies deal with tasks on which S can give himself KR, at least KR about his performance at the moment. Augmented feedback, if it is to influence performance, must do something over and above telling S when he is performing properly or improperly. Several of the recent studies have used what is called a compensatory tracking task. Such a task requires considerable equipment, both for presenting the display and, above all, in measuring the performance. However, we may describe the basic task that faces S without worrying about how all of the electronic equipment handles the problems of measurement. In one form or another, a compensatory tracking task will conform to the following description. Suppose you as S are seated before a small-screen television set. A very narrow vertical line, almost hairlike, divides the screen into two halves. A small blip or dot appears on the screen next to the line but starts moving to the left and away from the line. By manipulating a small knob in the appropriate direction, you can move the blip back toward the line. And that is your task—to keep the blip directly on the hairline. Changes in the system that operates the position of the blip cause it to move either way and at different speeds. But, by manipulating the knob you can counter these movements.

Given this situation, a situation in which it is quite clear that S can tell with considerable precision when he does and does not have the dot touching the hairline, Es have asked about the effect of augmenting cues. As an illustration we will consider a study by Karlin and Mortimer (1963). There were four conditions. First, there was the inevitable control group, whose members were given no augmented cues. Members of an auditory group received a tone through headsets whenever they held the blip within a certain zone, defined as ¼ in. on either side of the hairline. For a third group of Ss given visually augmented cues, E defined the zone by two additional hairlines, red in color, positioned ¼ in. on either side of the target line. The fourth group received no augmenting cues during actual practice, but at the end of each trial Ss were told by E what their scores had been on that trial. The acceptable score was within the same zone as that defined for the other two experimental groups, although the Ss in this fourth group did not know this. They were simply told that they would receive a score for length of time they maintained the blip within some zone.

Each group practiced for three days, with 15 trials of 36 sec. each per day. At the end of three days all augmented groups were superior to the control group, but performance of the verbal group—the group informed of their scores after each trial—was superior to either the visual or auditory group.

All studies have not shown that augmenting cues will facilitate performance. Whether or not these cues will facilitate appears to be tied to the nature of the task. Pursuit-rotor performance does not seem to be benefited by augmenting the KR (e.g., Bilodeau & Rosenquist, 1964), whereas performance on compensatory tracking tasks is usually benefited. Thus, augmented KR appears to be highly intricate in its effect on performance.

Delay of KR. Consider the simple task of learning to draw a line of a given length with KR after each attempt. The S draws a line, and E tells him, "You were one inch short." How does S make use of this information? How does he translate the KR into an adjusted response on the next trial? Somehow he must have a memory of the stimuli occurring (the "feel," a visualization of the line drawn) during the act of drawing the line which allows him to adjust his line on the following trial so as to relate the memory to the KR. If this is in any sense an accurate description of what goes on, the critical component is the memory for the feedback stimuli occurring during the act of drawing, for the next line must in some way be drawn with these previous feedback stimuli in mind. It would seem, therefore, that insofar as memory accuracy diminishes with time, a delay of KR would impede performance. With a delay in KR, S will institute a "correction" factor against a different memory base from one existing when KR is given immediately. The facts show, however, that this expectation is not normally borne out; delaying KR in a simple task, such as line drawing, does not seriously damage the rate at which S learns to become accurate. Five experiments, using delays as long as a week, were used by Bilodeau and Bilodeau (1958) in support of this conclusion. But that something does change with time is also apparent, and to understand this we must look a little more closely at the problem of design in the experiments in which KR is delayed.

Suppose we are going to give S 10 trials in a line-drawing experiment. For one group KR is given immediately, for another it is given after 10 sec., and for a third, after 30 sec. Now, it can be seen that if S draws each new line immediately after being given KR, the effect of delay of KR is confounded by differences in intertrial interval. The solution would seem to be that we must keep the intertrial interval constant, perhaps at 1 min. But the moment we do this, we introduce another possible confounding. The group that receives immediate KR would have a 60-sec. interval before the next trial, and the group that receives a 30-sec. delay of KR would have only a 30-sec. interval before drawing the next line. Suppose KR is forgotten. If so, differences in accuracy over trials may be due not to delay of KR per se, but to the delay between KR and the next trial. Or, if no differences in accuracy appear, it may be due to the fact that the effects of one factor counteract the effects of another. Is forgetting of KR a reasonable expectation? Yes. If over a series of trials S is given a series of KR reports (1 in. too long; ½ in. too short; ½ in. too long), it is quite possible that with a delay he might well become confused as to just what was the last report. Indeed, we shall see in a later chapter that the situation is a fairly typical one for studying forgetting of verbal materials. Bilodeau and Bilodeau suggest that such forgetting did occur in their studies. They reasoned as follows. A group given immediate KR, but with 24 hr. between successive trials, failed to show learning. However, if S was given immediate KR and then 24 hr. later a reminder of what the KR report was, learning did occur. Or, if KR was given only after 24 hr., learning also occurred.

The evidence does show that the length of the intertrial interval does influence acquisition of accuracy in a simple task in a deleterious fashion, in spite of the fact that the location of KR within the interval does not (except insofar as the KR report is forgotten, as noted above). So something is being forgotten. What appears at first to be a relatively simple situation is, in fact, a very complex one. It is for this reason, perhaps, that some investigators have turned their attention to experiments designed to bring an understanding of just what *is* forgotten when memory for a simple movement response is tested (e.g., Bilodeau, Jones, & Levy, 1964).

Another type of KR delay. Again visualize a series of trials on a simple task, such as line drawing. The S is given delayed KR, but during the delay other trials are occurring. In the simplest case, KR for performance on Trial 1 is given after S makes the response for Trial 2, for his performance on Trial 2, after making the Trial 3 response, and so on. We must note that E is not hoodwinking S, since S is fully informed about the procedure ahead of time. That is, he is told that the KR he receives is to be related to the trial preceding the one just completed.

This type of delay has a profound effect on the rate at which accuracy in making simple responses is achieved (e.g., Bilodeau, 1956). The longer the delay (the greater the number of previous trials to which KR is referred), the slower the rate of learning. The interpolated trials, and the KR given after those trials, present a confusing situation for the S. It is clear that the effects are due to the interpolated trials, for we saw above that merely waiting for KR has little if any effect on achievement of accuracy.

Maintenance of Accuracy

If KR is given as a means of training S to make accurate movements when he cannot make such movements initially, it is a natural next step to ask questions about the maintenance of accuracy when KR is removed. We have already touched upon this topic in speaking of retention or forgetting of skills, but the operations normally coming under this topic of maintenance of accuracy involve more than a simple test of retention. Primarily they are concerned with the performance over a series of trials after the removal of KR. Furthermore, it is obvious that the problem is of interest primarily for tasks or skills for which S cannot provide his own KR. In general, the results are clear. If KR is introduced during training, accuracy will increase rapidly; but if after achieving some specified level of accuracy

KR is no longer provided, the performance will deteriorate. This deterioration is sometimes very rapid; performance will quickly fall back to a level that was present before KR was given in training. Sometimes this inevitable deterioration occurs more gradually. One of the most dramatic instances of this deterioration is provided by Annett (1959). The task was that of pushing a plunger against a spring to a specified level of pressure. In one condition S was provided continuous information during the act of exerting pressure so that by watching a display provided him, he could push the plunger and tell exactly when he had achieved the requisite pressure. Thus, during the training trials accuracy was perfect on each trial. Although S was fully informed that he would, on later trials, have to perform without this information and that his task was to "get the feel for" the proper pressure, when the KR was removed, some of the pressures exerted by some of the Ss were so great as to be outside the capabilities of the recording apparatus, and the equipment was damaged several times. The Ss reported that the feel of the pressure was totally different with KR than without it. Despite the fact that during training S was essentially 100 percent correct on each trial, little if any learning occurred. Apparently in skill learning, careful guidance of the response by extrinsic means is not an efficient way to produce learning.

It is quite natural that Es have sought conditions of training in which KR can be given and which will result in the maintenance of high performance after the removal of KR. It is natural because the search for such conditions will allow inferences about the critical stimuli or cues involved in acquiring the skill. The success in these ventures has been minimal. It is generally believed that when KR is given, S in some way attends to feedback that is associated with KR, and this feedback differs in part from that essential to maintenance of the performance after KR is removed. Telling S that KR will be removed on later trials and that, therefore, he should not become dependent upon cues associated with it may make some difference (e.g., Lavery, 1964), but the fact seems to be that either S does not know what to attend to or else he cannot dissociate himself from KR feedback. Some differences in performance after removal of KR have been produced by varying the conditions of giving KR (e.g., Annett, 1959; Lavery & Suddon, 1962), but these conditions only influence the rate of deterioration, not its inevitability. Perhaps in the search for conditions which will prevent deterioration entirely, we are quite unrealistic; perhaps the human organism is really not capable of such behavior regardless of the conditions of learning.

THE ANALYSIS AND SYNTHESIS OF A MOTOR SKILL

A highly practiced complex motor skill is beauty. The beauty appears to be inherent in the flow of behavior—in the continuity of the interaction between the perception of changes in the environment and the adjustment to fit these changes. The expert skier making a run down a mountain shows this interaction in a most prolonged and observable manner, but it is also present in the more momentary acts of hitting a golf ball or shooting a clay pigeon. However, if the continuity of the movements, seen as the end result of great amounts of practice, is emphasized too strongly in our descriptions of the behavior we wish to understand, it may retard the growth of this understanding. This may result from the belief that such behavior, being based on a flow of complex interactions, will not yield to experimental analysis. The continuity, it is said, is the essence of the behavior, and to attempt to break it down into parts is to lose the behavior we are trying to understand. The analysis might lead to an understanding of something but not that which we set out to understand. Who can deny that such an argument has no validity? But if one's goals are analysis and also synthesis, in which the continuity is to be accounted for, the validity of the argument will be given an ultimate test. To set about on such a research program requires the development of a scheme or model which prevents one from *not* forgetting the continuity to be explained. And so it seems that many investigators in the field of motor skills are proceeding with the whole picture of the skill in mind, but at the same time they are not letting it frighten them away from analyzing the parts and speculating how these various constituents can go together to produce the continuity.

One may conceive of a smooth movement as consisting of a series of discrete responses, responses which through long practice have lost the discreteness which characterized them in the beginning. That beginning is usually very early in the life of an organism, as he develops simple skills which will later be combined into more complex skills. In other words, a smooth and continuous complex skill can be conceived of as representing a series of subskills, each readily available to "run itself off" when the appropriate stimulus is present. By appropriate models or conceptual schemes about how behavior achieves its continuity, the investigators proceed to their experimental analyses as first steps. For a thoughtful appraisal of this approach, which includes a discussion of the many aids available to the investigator in terms of computers, information analysis, and so on, one may refer to Fitts (1964).

We have not attempted to survey all the variables which Es have manipulated. Analysis must necessarily proceed in certain directions. The perceptual capabilities of Ss must be determined. For example, many skills have moving targets, and these targets may vary in speed, direction, and trajectory. The appropriate execution of a skill with moving targets often involves anticipation as to where the target will be when another event occurs. In baseball, for instance, the batter must predict where the ball will be at a certain time and coordinate the other event (swinging the bat) with his prediction. As we noted in the previous chapter, the contemporary work on reaction time is in part directed toward discovering the reaction capabilities of Ss in various situations and how these can be fitted into more complex skills where speed of reaction is of importance.

If, as suggested earlier, complex motor skills are thought of as representing many sets of subskills, then in attempting to synthesize the complex skill from its parts, one must study not only the parts, but also how they interact with other parts when put together. One line of attack on this problem is to determine under what conditions overall learning is facilitated when practice occurs on the separate parts prior to putting them together and, also, under what conditions or for what type of tasks it is better to practice the entire task from the beginning. This variable, known classically as the whole-part variable, is receiving attention in motor skills laboratories. And so it goes; the experimental analysis of behavior is inevitable, that of synthesis, probable.

SUMMARY

If a group of Ss is given a short rest after practicing continuously for several minutes on a perceptual-motor task, performance will rise dramatically when practice resumes after the rest interval. This phenomenon, called reminiscence, was used as a basis for discussing three general matters which arise in doing experimental work: operational definitions, distinction between learning and performance, and the use of hypothetical constructs as explanatory devices.

An operational definition specifies the meaning of an empirical phenomenon by stating in abstracted form the procedures and measurements used to identify it. Three classes of such definitions were described and contrasted.

Since reminiscence indicates that S has learned more than was shown by the performance scores on the trial before the rest interval, the need for drawing a distinction between learning and performance was apparent.

To explain reminiscence, some investigators have used a hypothetical construct named reactive inhibition. Unlike explanatory attempts examined in earlier chapters, this approach postulates the existence of a process which has certain characteristics, and the characteristics assigned are those needed to mediate the experimental findings. That reactive inhibition must build up with responding and must dissipate with rest are the two basic characteristics.

An examination was made of a number of experiments, the results of which have been used to characterize more fully the nature of reactive inhibition. The two critical variables are the length of the work period and the length of the rest period. Other phenomena which entered into these experiments included warmup decrement, rate of initial work as a function of amount of work anticipated, the role of similarity of responses in the generation and dissipation of reactive inhibition, the role of motivation on reminiscence, and bilateral transfer of reminiscence.

The final section of the chapter dealt with the effect of knowledge of results on the learning and the maintenance of a perceptual-motor skill. The effects of a number of different variables associated with knowledge of results were examined: frequency of knowledge of results, precision of the knowledge, augmenting stimuli or cues, and delay of knowledge of results.

CHAPTER NINE

Animal Learning

Man is an animal—except in the learning laboratory. There, man as an object of study becomes a human, and all other organisms become animals. Birds, fish, reptiles, and insects have all contributed members to the cages of the learning laboratory. To attempt to list every animal would serve no purpose, but we may sample a few: dog, cat, rabbit, guinea pig, skunk, squirrel, gerbil, raccoon, monkey, baboon, orangutan; pigeon, chicken, goose, duck, parrakeet, dove, myna; goldfish, eel, octopus, guppy, salmon; earthworm, cockroach, bee, paramecium, stentor. So diversified is the list that it would come as no surprise if a fading parchment among the Dead Sea Scrolls were to report observations on the learning of a unicorn.

One name obviously missing from the above list is the white rat. This animal has eaten more food pellets, traversed more mazes, and pressed more levers in the study of learning than all other organisms combined. A learning laboratory without a bank of cages for rats is atypical and, some might say, cannot rightly claim its appellation. The learning of rats has produced more hypothetical constructs than has the learning of humans. It is no wonder that as long as 30 years ago investigators began dedicating books to the white rat. But, as is clear from the above listing, animal learning is not to be considered entirely white-rat learning, and there are numerous signs that the empirical base of learning will be markedly broadened in the future as other organisms, if not replacing the white rat, at least supplement him. As one sign of this we cite the 1957 publication of a book of well over 700 pages dealing with learning studies in which the major organism used was the pigeon (Ferster & Skinner, 1957). As another illustration of this trend, we note the systematic study of the effects of certain variables on many different organisms being conducted by M. E. Bitterman and his students at Bryn Mawr. So, even though the white rat has little chance of fading into oblivion, his reign as king may sooner or later be challenged.

Why all this enormous output of energy over the years on the study of learning in animals? There is no single explanation, but we may indicate some of the more prominent positions taken in answer to such a question.

Animals as Ss allow for precise control of a host of variables which may be associated with learning. We discussed in an earlier chapter what is usually meant in practice by the holding of all conditions constant except the variable being manipulated. We say that few if any of these variables are in fact held constant; instead, they fluctuate in magnitude for different Ss, at different times, and for different conditions. What we do is arrange our conditions so that there will be no bias in behavior associated with these variables for different conditions. Yet, these variables, fluctuating in magnitude or extent, will produce both inter-S and intra-S variability in the performance measures. An investigator wants stability in his response measures, whether for statistical purposes or in order to aid predictability from situation to situation. It would appear that the use of animals could result in this precision because of the potential for control of these extraneous variables. It is possible that we might truly approximate what we mean when we say we hold all other variables constant. By using the white rat as the exemplary animal, let us see how this might come about.

The genetics of the rat can be governed so that the genetic background of the animals in the various conditions will be essentially identical, and by this we refer not only to "mean" genetic background but to the fact that all Ss in all groups have very homogeneous genetic characteristics. Insofar as learning is influenced by genetic characteristics, the variability of learning scores among Ss should be reduced by this procedure. Furthermore, there can be precise control of such variables as age, rearing, and food intake, so that at the time an experiment is performed, all animals in all groups can be equivalent on many variables. The logic of the reasoning is inescapable.

We have persistently pointed out in previous chapters that experimental analysis necessarily means simplifying experimental situations so that the subprocesses or subphenomena observed in complex behavior can be "taken out" and studied independently. An extension of this thinking may be used to reach the position that animals will be better Ss for studying certain phenomena (such as learning) than will humans. The white rat is not so "encumbered" with past learning, with symbolic processes, and with language as is the human S. To study learning at a simple level—to study learning in the "raw"—the human adult S may be too complex a "situation." All of the overlay of symbolic capacities and language of the adult human may even prevent the study of basic principles of learning. We might study newborn infants and achieve the same purpose as that achieved by studying animals, but the supply of newborn babies available for unfettered research is distinctly limited.

A third reason for the extensive use of animals in research on learning is that many experimental operations can be carried out on animals which cannot be carried out with human Ss. The more extreme illustrations would be, for example, the effect of brain lesions on learning. Sometimes human Ss are available for such studies (as when shrapnel may have destroyed certain segments of the brain), but, generally speaking, our society does not tolerate experimental production of such lesions. Somewhat less extreme would be the determination of the effect of certain deprivations on learning, for example, food deprivation. Some such studies can and have been conducted with human Ss, but again, at the extremes, these studies are not feasible. For quite another reason, there are certain problems basic to understanding learning which can *only* be accomplished with certain forms of lower animals. Most of these revolve around genetic problems. To understand genetic characteristics as related to learning requires the study of many generations of a given organism and thereby requires organisms whose life spans are relatively short. Or, if we ask questions about the genetic transmission of acquired habits, only certain organisms provide the appropriate vehicle. For example, we might teach a simple habit to an elementary organism that reproduces by fission—by splitting. Will the habit be retained by both new organisms resulting from the fission?

Finally, it is perfectly justifiable to study animal learning for no other reason than to gain an understanding of how animals learn.

Many investigators firmly believe that learning is learning, whether it be in the cockroach or the eighth-grade student. A basic cluster of laws must, it is said, underlie all learning, and the vehicle (the S) through which these laws are derived is irrelevant. Particular features of different organisms may modify but not change the law. Some have felt that the way to approach human learning is to obtain the basic principles of learning from simpler organisms and then use these basic principles as a foundation for deriving the more complex aspects of learning presumably reflected in human Ss. It is a fact that common laws of learning for humans and animals, as expressed in terms of functional variables between independent and dependent variables, have been found. It is also a fact that laws of learning derived from studies of animals have been applied to human learning situations. The recent emphasis on teaching machines, or programmed learning, resulted from the application of certain techniques and principles derived from extensive studies of animal learning.

We immediately realize, of course, that the question of whether or not the laws of animal learning are applicable to human Ss is no more than an extreme case of how far experimentally derived laws can be generalized. It is the same question we ask ourselves, for example, when we inquire if reminiscence, observed in pursuit-rotor learning, will also occur in learning a list of words. Any ultimate and completely definitive answer to such questions can be given only by experimental tests. Any generalization is tentative; it is a hypothesis that a given result found in one situation will also be produced in others, but the validity of the hypothesis can be determined only empirically. The investigator will have varying faith in his generalizations, the faith being determined by similarities between the situation in which a law has been derived and the situation to which the generalization is extended. An empirical relationship determined on college-student Ss would probably be more readily generalized to a senior in high school than to an earthworm. A principle derived from inverted-alphabet printing might be more readily generalized to inverted-number printing than to a child's learning to speak. And so it goes. No E is content with his particular findings; at least in his own thinking he generalizes. No one, so far as the present writer knows, has ever suggested that we will have as many different laws as we have experiments. Nevertheless, in the long run we must determine the boundaries beyond which our generalizations are no longer valid, and such determinations are a part and parcel of experimental work. To ask whether principles of learning derived from animals are applicable to human Ss is to ask a question of the type which investigators continually put to themselves and which leads them to seek empirical answers.

We may wish to test the generality of a principle emanating from experimental work on one organism by testing it on another organism and still find it quite impossible to make a satisfactory test. A task or situation quite satisfactory for working with one species may be nearly impossible to simulate adequately when dealing with another. Offhand it would seem difficult to study pursuit-rotor learning in the goldfish. But the ingenuity of investigators in the area of animal learning is remarkable, and translations of tasks have been made which to this writer, at least, seemed both impossible and preposterous before they were accomplished. So, do not prejudge these matters with finality. The writer once pointed out how valuable it would be for analytical research on forgetting if we could study the retention of a single word. The implication of the statement, as well as the affective tone in which it was wrapped, made it clear that it was believed something quite impossible to do. But less than a year later an investigator proceeded to show how it *could* be done, and an entirely new area of research was opened up. Therefore, it would be foolish to say that we will never have a study reporting reminiscence in the pursuit-rotor learning of goldfish; this seemingly impossible technological height may yet be scaled.

COMMON TASKS AND RESPONSE MEASURES

Classifications of tasks used to study animal learning, or classifications of the learning occurring in various tasks, or both, are, like all forms of classifications, subject to many arbitrary decisions. There are many dimensions or characteristics of tasks and the behavior they elicit so that we might well expect little unanimity among various classificatory schemes. Inevitably, it seems, something will not quite fit a scheme, and we wish we could solve the problem by ignoring it. Classifications of animal learning may be made on the basis of certain theoretical assumptions about the learning, and insofar as these assumptions may vary from person to person, the classifications will vary. We will not get involved in these matters, although it is well worth any serious student's time to examine recent classificatory attempts to realize fully the problems one faces; some examples may be found in Kimble (1961), Bitterman (1962), and Grant (1964).

Our purpose is to place before us some of the common tasks or problems presented animals as vehicles for the study of learning. To break up what will be a rather long discussion, three sections will be identified. In the first section we will look at tasks which are alleys and mazes. In the second section we will discuss problems as they are presented to animals in boxes. Finally we will look at situations that are commonly said to study classical conditioning, but we will consider these only briefly because few, if any, elementary laboratories are likely to carry out experiments in classical conditioning. If there is a dimension running through these three classes of tasks, it is in terms of the locomotion required of the animal in exhibiting learning which in turn is related to the nature of the response measures used.

Alleys and Mazes

The straight alley. Relatively speaking the straight alley or runway is a newcomer (appearing in the early 1940's), but it had to come sooner or later for it represents the ultimate in simplicity (Fig. 9-1). The essentials consist of a starting box and a goal box connected by an alley. The sides of the boxes and the alley may be 8 in. to 10 in. high, and normally the whole is covered with glass or hardware cloth, which prevents the animal from climbing out but still affords observation by E. Obviously, the tops of both boxes must be removable or constructed for opening so that the animals may be put into the start box and taken out of the goal box. The door "guarding" the start box is usually a vertical sliding door controlled by pulleys and cords and is sometimes called a guillotine door. In the usual procedure the animal is dropped into the start box, and when he orients toward the door, it is quickly opened; the door in front of the goal box is commonly closed after the animal enters. The length of the alley may vary, of course, but typical lengths are from 4 ft. to 8 ft. Investigators are inclined to keep the width fairly narrow, perhaps 4 in. None of these dimensions is sacred, and E may introduce considerable variation depending upon his purposes.

What does an animal learn in a straight alley? In a manner of speaking he learns to run—to run from the start box to the goal box. Some might say he learns that there is food in the goal box, and some might prefer merely to speak of runway performance without reference to what is learned. However this may be, the fact is that the animal's performance will change over successive trials. This performance change is measured in time scores. There

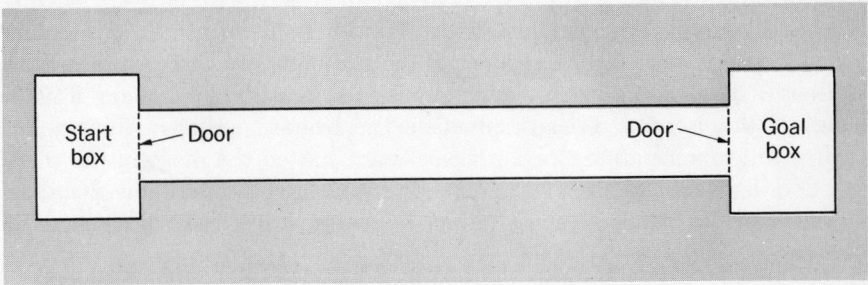

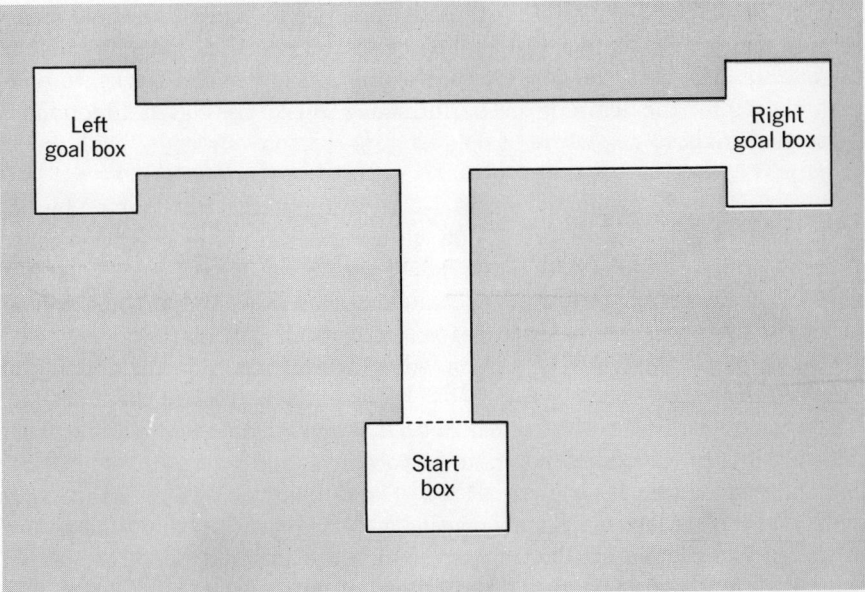

Fig. 9-1. A straight alley (upper) and a T-maze, both used in studying animal learning.

is no other alternative, since there is not, as we usually speak of it, a correct or an incorrect response. The animal can go only from one box to the other, if he goes at all. The gross measure is the time required for the animal to traverse the runway from the moment the door is opened allowing exit from the starting box until he enters the goal box. But this measure can be broken up into as many components as desired by E. He may, for example, determine the time required to *leave* the starting box, and he may, in addition, measure speed of running various segments of the alley. An E can, with separate stopwatches or with a rapid pencil and one watch, measure starting time and running time independently. However, if he wishes to measure running speeds in successive sections of the alley (time to traverse successive sections), more complex instrumentation is required. A common way of handling this is by a series of photoelectric beams, perhaps a foot apart, each wired to a separate clock. All clocks are started the moment the start-box door is open, and as the rat proceeds out of the box and down the alley, he successively "breaks" the photoelectric beams, stopping each clock as he does so.

If performance improves over successive trials, time measures will decrease—time to traverse the alley will become shorter and shorter—and if many trials are given, under constant conditions, a speed that is essentially asymptotic will be reached. It is common practice to express the time measures as reciprocals (1/measured time). Thus, as speed of going from start to goal box increases, the converted measures get larger and larger. In plotting, therefore, the learning or performance curve rises as a function of successive trials.

Single-choice mazes. In the straight alley there are no formal right and wrong responses, unless one wishes to call running a right response and not running a wrong response. The decision the animal makes, be it a decision, is to run or not to run. The single-choice mazes require the animal to choose between two alternatives on each trial. The most widely used device to study the behavior associated with such decision making is the simple T-maze, pictured in Fig. 9-1. The essential parts are the start box with a door to restrain the animal until E is ready, the stem leading from the start box to the choice point, and two alleys, one leading to a left goal box and one leading to a right goal box. The dimensions of the T-maze vary widely, and many accouterments may be added, depending upon the nature of the problem being studied. Doors, which are lowered once the animal commits himself, may be placed near the choice point in each alley leading to the respective goal boxes. Curtains are occasionally hung near the choice point in each goal-box alley so that the animal cannot see the goal box, hence the food, and for certain problems the goal boxes may be removed and interchanged from trial to trial.

Single-choice mazes sometimes take other forms. In the Y-maze the goal box alleys may meet the stem at a 45-degree angle instead of a 90-degree angle as in the T-maze. In the U-maze the alleys, rather than terminating at the goal boxes as in the T-maze, continue after making 90-

degree turns at the locus of the goal box in the T-maze.

What are the problems presented the animals in such devices? The most obvious one would be the learning of a spatial habit—learning to go right versus going left. The animal might be taught to go right when hungry and left when thirsty. He might be given a brightness-discrimination problem in which, for example, the correct response is to take the white alley at the choice point and not to take the black alley. Such a problem, it can be seen, would require interchangeability of the alleys so that the animal does not acquire a spatial habit correlated with the brightness. These latter types of problems are more frequently given in discrimination boxes (treated later). For certain problems E may use *forced trials*. On a forced trial the animal has no choice because one of the alleys is blocked at the choice point making the maze a straight alley with a 90-degree turn. There are a number of reasons in particular cases why E might want to use forced trials, but basically he uses them to control the frequency of experience with each goal box or its contents.

The common response measure used to show change in performance over trials is change in frequency with which the animal makes the correct (as defined by E) choice. These frequencies are often expressed as percentage correct in blocks of trials. We would expect the animal to be initially correct on 50 percent of the trials if he responded randomly. Unfortunately, this is often not the case, for animals may have right- or left-going biases so that the initial performance might be well below or well above 50 percent in acquiring a spatial habit. For certain problems E may give each animal a number of free runs (no reward in either goal box) in order to determine the turning bias. Then, in the experiment proper, E will put the reward in the goal box that will cause the animal to learn a spatial habit that is opposite his preference. In any event, it is clear that E must not allow biases to bias performance more for one experimental condition than another.

In studying the acquisition of a particular habit, E may run the animal for a constant number of trials, measuring the change in percentage correct in successive blocks of trials, perhaps 10 trials to a block. Or, he may let the number of trials vary from rat to rat by setting a criterion of performance, such as nine correct turns on 10 successive trials. Here, then, the response measure is the number of trials required to reach the criterion of performance set. Correct-response measures may be supplemented by time scores; for example, E might record the time from the moment the animal leaves the start box to the time he commits himself (enters one or the other arms leading to the goal box).

Two phenomena, normally occurring in simple-choice situations, may be mentioned. We spoke as if the animal had to make a decision at the choice point, which indeed he does. It is sometimes noted that before the correct response is well learned, the animal will stop at the choice point, look toward one goal box and then toward the other, and make tentative movements toward one and then the other, as if he were trying to "feel" what to expect if he took each alley. Such behavior is called *vicarious trial and error*. It is a miniature conflict situation in which neither alternative response has gained ascendancy over the other; and, as with humans, in making a choice between two nearly equal stimuli, the latency of the response is increased. The vacillatory behavior may be both indicative of the conflict and the means by which it is resolved.

The second phenomenon is called *spontaneous alternation*. Suppose a rat has no strong bias for the left or right turn. On each trial we place the same amount and kind of food in each goal box. We might presume that on successive trials the animal would get fixated on either a right turn or a left turn. This may not happen. Instead, the animal may take the left turn on one trial, the right turn on the next, the left on the next, and so on, in a fairly regular pattern of alternation. This phenomenon has intrigued investigators, particularly those with a theoretical bent. We will not get into these theories except to note that reactive inhibition has sometimes entered into the explanations.

Multiple-choice mazes. If the problem is one of learning serial habits, or the chaining of habits, multiple-choice mazes will be used.

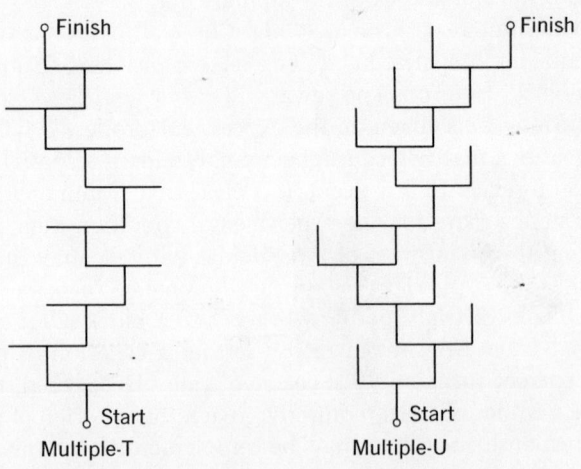

Fig. 9-2. Two types of multiple-unit mazes.

These usually consist of "stacking" T's or U's as pictured in Fig. 9-2. The usual alley structure may be employed, although sometimes the maze may be elevated some distance above the floor with the path consisting of a single narrow board. The elevation is effective in preventing the animal from leaving the experimental situation by any route other than that intended by E.

The response measures are elaborations of those used in the T-maze. The E will record whether or not an error was made at each choice point so that a learning record over trials would indicate error reduction or increase in proportion of correct responses. Time measurements may also be taken to supplement the correct-response measures. One of the classical phenomenon associated with multiple-unit mazes is the *goal gradient*. If E records the errors at each choice point on successive trials, he finds that the animal eliminates errors (avoids taking the blind alley or cul-de-sac) in a backward direction from the goal box. Thus, over trials, there is an inverse relationship between the elimination of errors at the choice points and the distance of the choice point from the goal. Obviously, this means that the most difficult error to eliminate (or to say it positively, the most difficult correct turn to learn) is the first one after leaving the start box.

Boxes

Skinner box. Best known of all the tasks in the box family is the Skinner box, named after its originator. In many classification schemes it is said to evoke *instrumental learning*; it is called this, in contradistinction to classical conditioning, because in instrumental learning the organism must produce the particular response called correct before it is rewarded—the response is instrumental in producing the reward. In classical conditioning, as we shall see, the response and the reward are literally forced on the organism. Skinner himself prefers to call the procedures *operant-conditioning* procedures.

A diagram of a Skinner box as it might be used for a rat is shown in Fig. 9-3. The particular response to be learned is that of pressing the lever. When the lever *is* pressed, a pellet of food drops out of the small tube near the bottom of the cage into the food cup, although the apparatus can be arranged so the reward is a drop of water. The response measure is the number of responses per unit of time. Initially, the animal will respond infrequently (why he responds at all in the beginning is a matter for later discussion); as learning occurs, the frequency increases. The frequency may be recorded on counters, with E reading the counters at set points, perhaps every 3 min., during a session. With proper instrumentation a cumulative record can be obtained on a roll of paper that is fed through a roller at a constant rate. Initially, a pen, marking continuously, is positioned at the bottom of the paper. When the animal responds, the pen is moved a slight distance upward. The faster the animal responds, the steeper the slope of the record. In effect, the learning curve for the animal is obtained directly by this procedure. Since the paper is fed at a constant rate, time is represented on the baseline, with frequency of responding on the ordinate. Differences in slopes will represent differences in rate at which different animals learn, or changes in slope during a session for a single animal will indicate differences in rates of responding at various points during an experimental session. It will be realized that frequency of responding per unit of time could be viewed as latency between successive responses.

The above situations are capable of many variations. Specific stimuli can be introduced. For example, the animal may be taught to respond only

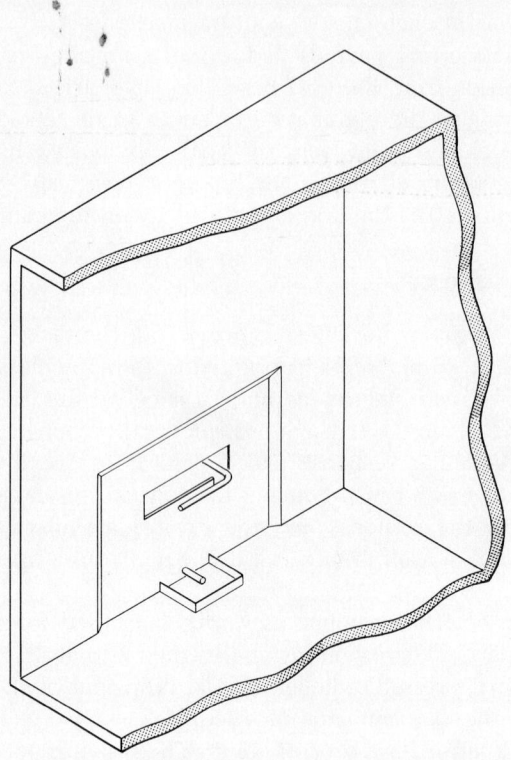

Fig. 9-3. Cut-away diagram of a Skinner-box.

when a light is on or he may be taught to respond when a square figure is present but not when a circle is present. Shock may be introduced either through the floor of the boxes or through the lever itself.

Shock boxes. This device has also taken many forms, but the most common one consists of an oblong box divided into two halves, perhaps by a hurdle. The grid floor in one half produces a shock, but the other compartment is "safe," and in a typical trial the animal is placed on the "hot" side. This usually produces considerable activity, and the animal will, in the course of the activity, get over the hurdle to the safe end. On successive trials the measure of learning would be the latency of reaching the safe box. The task can be made somewhat more difficult by introducing an instrumental act more complicated than simply jumping over a hurdle. The division between the two compartments might consist of a door which can be opened only by pressing a lever. But again, in the act of moving around as a consequence of the shock, the animal will eventually hit the lever, the door will open, and he can enter the safe compartment. We may note that in the situation just described there is no way for the animal to avoid being shocked; it is placed on a hot grid and can learn only to minimize the duration of the shock. Such procedures are sometimes called *escape-training* procedures. A slight modification produces *avoidance learning* or *avoidance conditioning*. Suppose a rat is dropped on a cold grid, but 10 sec. later the shock comes on. In this case S can learn to get to the other compartment in order to avoid the shock. A specific stimulus might be used, for instance, a buzzer which sounds for 2 sec. and then is followed 5 sec. later by the shock. The buzzer becomes a signal, a *conditioned stimulus*, to "move out of here." As we shall see, this procedure is quite comparable to classical conditioning.

Classical Conditioning

Classical conditioning procedures orginated with Pavlov. Most students are well aware of this and are acquainted with the essentials of the procedure. A neutral stimulus, which before training will not elicit the response to be learned or conditioned, is called the *conditioned stimulus* (CS). On a given trial the CS is presented, and shortly after or in conjunction with it, the *unconditioned stimulus* (UCS) is initiated. The UCS will naturally elicit the response to be conditioned, and this response is called the *unconditioned response* (UCR). Conditioning occurs if, after pairing of CS and UCS over a series of trials, the CS alone will elicit the response, the *conditioned response* (CR). In Pavlov's studies the UCR was usually salivation, with dogs used as Ss. Meat powder or acid, either of which will produce salivation, was commonly employed as the UCS, with a buzzer as the CS. The sequence of events was the sounding of a buzzer, followed by meat powder placed in the dog's mouth, followed by the UCR produced by the powder. If after several trials salivation began to occur before the meat powder was given, it was taken as an indication of conditioning. Or if salivation occurred on a test trial on which only the CS was given with the UCS omitted, it was taken as evidence of conditioning. The previously neutral stimulus had gained the "power" to produce the salivary response.

Classical conditioning procedures often require extreme physical restriction of the animal, accomplished by stocks or slings when larger organ-

isms are used. American investigators, in their studies of classical conditioning with animals, have most frequently used avoidance conditioning. In
such a procedure with a dog, the UCS will be a shock to the foot (which
produces leg flexion—the UCR), with a neutral stimulus preceding the onset
of the shock. Learning is indicated when the dog lifts the foot (avoiding
the shock) when the CS occurs alone. However, some studies have been
done in which the animal was shocked regardless of whether or not the
dog lifted his foot.

As indicated above, frequency of CRs as a function of trials is a common response measure. For certain responses, the amplitude of the response
may be used, for example, in salivary conditioning the number of drops of
saliva. It is presumed that the greater the magnitude of the CR, the better
the conditioning. This cannot be accepted for all situations. A dog, well
trained in foot flexion by avoidance-conditioning procedures, has a minimum
amplitude of response—the paw is lifted just far enough to avoid being
shocked. Latency measures may also be misleading for certain responses.
The well-trained dog may not lift the foot immediately upon the occurrence
of the CS but may wait until just before the shock occurs.

One of the problems in using classical-conditioning procedures with
animals in which the UCS is food (or water) is to find a response measure.
Pavlov, as we noted, used salivation in dogs, but with smaller animals this
may be quite impossible. Recently, however, classical-conditioning procedures were used with pigeons (Longo, Klempay, & Bitterman, 1964). A
neutral stimulus (buzzer) preceded the appearance of grain by 10 sec. over
a series of trials. We note that the pigeon did not have to do anything to get
the grain—the grain always appeared in the food cup 10 sec. after the onset
of the buzzer. On test trials, given periodically, the interval between the
buzzer and the appearance of food was lengthened to 40 sec. The response
measure was the activity level shown by the pigeon during the 40-sec. interval. This activity level was measured via a stabilometer. The floor of the
cage was mounted on a sensitive spring which transmitted movements of
the pigeon to a recording apparatus. The data show an increase in this
activity over the series of trials and, in addition, an increase during the 40-
sec. period; this evidence is taken to indicate that conditioning of anticipatory activity occurred. It is to be noted, however, that this response is not
the response produced by the UCS in the same sense that salivation is produced by a UCS. This is to say, therefore, that the UR to food does not become the CR. To say that the procedures do not fit the classical-conditioning
procedures exactly is not to deny their usefulness in studying learning.
Nevertheless, the bulk of classical-conditioning work at the moment is being
done with human Ss, where the eyelid reflex and the psychogalvanic response
are the two major URs used.

These, then, are some of the tasks used to study animal learning. We
could not hope to describe all possible variations that have been employed

or all modifications that have been made to fit particular organisms. One may study avoidance conditioning in the goldfish by devices suitable to its habitat, but these devices may appear superficially quite different from those used for studying learning in the cat. A monkey may be given operant training in a device that resembles a chair more than a box. Subsequent discussions will bring out some of these variations on the more frequently used devices.

One of the virtues of classical-conditioning situations, as well as those using shock or other aversive stimuli, is that the response to be learned is literally forced on the S. Either the shock causes foot withdrawal or, in the shock box, the appearance of the correct response is not long delayed. However, when a rat must find his way through a multiple-T maze on the first trial, it would seem that very patient Es are necessary. Is there any reason to believe that a pigeon would start pecking a little circle the moment it is placed in a Skinner box? Of course, we would expect that a hungry organism placed in such situations will be active, and that such activity, like activity produced by shock, will sooner or later produce the desired response. But as we shall see in the next section, there are many techniques now commonly employed to reduce the tediousness of these early stages of learning.

As was noted above, aversive stimuli will usually produce the behavior necessary to "hit upon" the correct response. To certain animals, stimuli which to us are quite innocuous have aversive properties. A cockroach may learn a maze if the maze is brightly lighted and the goal box kept dark; the cockroach has a natural aversion to light. Recent accidental discoveries have shown that ionizing radiation will serve as an aversive UCS, although through what mechanisms it operates is unknown (Garcia, Kimeldorf, & Hunt, 1961). Water mazes are sometimes used in which cold water serves as an aversive stimulus so that a rat will swim through the maze to reach a platform (the goal box) which is out of the water.

For rewards or positive stimuli, we naturally think of food and water when rats or other larger animals are used as Ss. But how shall we reward an earthworm at the end of a maze? Ratner (1964) found that a box of damp moss at the end of a straight alley (12-in. plastic tube) resulted in faster "running" than did a moist paper towel spread out at the end of the alley. Monkeys seem to be willing to perform various tasks merely to be able to get a look at something "interesting." The presence of other rats near a nominal goal may serve as a reward for the rat. It has been shown that thirsty rats will "drink" from an air jet, and this appears to serve as a reward (Hendry & Rasche, 1961). An increment in the brightness of the light in a Skinner box as the bar is pressed also seems to act as a reward (Berlyne, Salapatek, Gelman, & Zener, 1964). In short, when thinking of aversive stimuli that may be used to elicit behavior, we need not restrict our thinking to shock, although shock is very frequently used; nor should we limit our thinking of rewards to food and water, although again, food and water are by far the most frequent rewards used to produce behavior in learning situations.

PLANNING AN EXPERIMENT IN ANIMAL LEARNING

We have already discussed in detail in earlier chapters some of the decisions which must be made in planning an experiment. Many decisions, we saw, are quite arbitrary. Others, however, are made on the basis of accumulated knowledge. This accumulated knowledge is of two types. First, there is the recorded knowledge and experience, the knowledge we are trying to pass along in this book. But there is a second type that rarely if ever appears in the written reports of experiments. This knowledge, which might better be called laboratory lore, is highly specific to areas of investigation and can be obtained only by talking with or observing the specialist in the area. In animal learning the lore consists of techniques of research. How *do* you get a sleepy rat to leave the start box of a straight alley? How do you pick up a rat—by the tail? Will a rat bite? Does *E* wear gloves in handling the animal? How long should a rat be left in the goal box? When, in timing running speed, do you say that a rat has entered the goal box? How does *E* keep track of which rats belong in which group? Many such questions can be answered only by the person experienced in the animal laboratory.

The author has had very little experience in the animal laboratory and is, therefore, quite incapable of recording the lore. This lack of experience was demonstrated quite nicely by a recent incident. Two of the author's undergraduate students wanted to do a study on the role of novel stimuli on performance in the straight alley. The notion was to train two groups of rats to a high level of performance after which food was to be removed and novel stimuli substituted for the food in the goal box in order to see if performance would be maintained by such stimuli. One group was to receive the novel stimuli, the other group (the control) was to get nothing. The novel stimuli consisted of brightly colored small plastic toys and figures, and the plan was to place a different stimulus in the goal box on each successive trial.

The results were quite positive initially—the group given the novel stimuli continued to run at the same high rate as they had for food, whereas the control animals showed a reduced speed. However, the experiment had to be terminated before it was completed because we rapidly ran out of stimuli. Upon reaching the goal box the animals proceeded to chew and ingest the toys, and soon none was left for further trials. The purpose of reporting this aborted study is to emphasize that the unfortunate ending would never have occurred had an experienced animal researcher been in charge. Such a person would have known that the rats would probably eat the stimuli, and steps would have been taken to prevent this (perhaps by enclosing the novel stimuli in a small wire mesh cage).

General Design

Animal experiments are most frequently conducted by the random-groups design. A given number of animals is available, and these are assigned randomly to the two or more conditions of the experiment. When the animal involved is very expensive, for example, a chimpanzee, the same animal may be used in several conditions by a within-S design if the conditions permit it. It is not always clear just when the conditions will permit the use of this design because, as we have earlier discussed, it is sometimes difficult to know when differential transfer effects will occur in moving from one condition to another.

A modification of the random-groups design called the *split-litter* technique is sometimes used when the Ss are rats. If animals are bred in the laboratory, E may split a given litter of eight rats so that two from the litter are assigned to each of four conditions. Which two rats are assigned to a given condition is determined randomly. The number of Ss in each condition is increased to the desired level by using several litters. Obviously we would not assign all of the rats from one litter to one condition or those from another litter to a different condition.

An extensive experiment with animals may require successive shipments from a supplier. If E is going to run a four-condition experiment and wants to asign 24 rats to each condition, he may order four successive shipments of 24 each, to arrive on the first of four consecutive months. Each order carries the same specifications, such as, "Sprague-Dawley, 90-day-old females." Nevertheless, E would not assume that each successive shipment contained equivalent animals. He would not, for example, use the first shipment for one condition, the second for another, and so on. Rather, he would arrange his assignments in such a fashion that each successive shipment of animals is equally represented across all conditions.

Different strains of rats do differ, some in known ways. If for some reason different strains of rats are used in the same experiment, they should be assigned equally to all conditions. However, most investigators would probably frown on such procedures since certain unwanted interactions between strain and experimental conditions might result. Indeed, some of the differences among strains are a little disconcerting in view of the earlier discussion about generalizing the results of an experiment. For example, Nakamura and Anderson (1964) have shown that performance of two strains of rats in two kinds of avoidance-conditioning apparatuses are quite different. Such findings not only make us cautious about our generalizations, but also may make us suspicious that contradictory results for a given vari-

able in different experiments in different laboratories might not have occurred had the animals used in the two experiments been equated on strain.
On the positive side, however, we see again that this lack of equality from
experiment to experiment and from laboratory to laboratory is one way in
which the identification of relevant variables occurs. For example, if over a
period of years a number of different investigators have worked on the
influence of a given variable, and if in viewing the findings we discover
that discrepant results are always associated with a given strain of animals,
the very tenable hypothesis presents itself that the discrepancies are a result
of strain differences. In effect we have arrived at a causal hypothesis much
as we do when we analyze a series of naturalistic observations as discussed
in Chapter One.

An omission. In discussing problems of experimental design
in this book, we have assumed the use of several Ss in the various conditions,
both for the within-S designs and for the independent-groups designs. Mean
performance scores are normally obtained for the various conditions, and
statistical tests are used to help reach a decision concerning the effect of the
independent variables on mean performance. There is a group of investigators who eschew this approach—they do not use multiple Ss in the above
sense, nor do they use statistical tools in the evaluation of their data. Simplified, the approach they take is as follows. The effect of an independent
variable or several independent variables is determined for a single S. If
more than one S is used, the data would be kept separately for each. The
effects of an independent variable are determined by a careful inspection
of performance curves, usually cumulative performance curves. Reliability
of performance is not ignored, but it is not assessed by statistical procedures.

Much of the work carried on by this group of investigators employs
animal Ss, and that is the reason for bringing up a certain matter at this
point. The present writer cannot adequately represent their point of view,
although it is a point of view with considerable force in experimental studies
of learning today. Sidman (1960) has provided a spirited outline of the
position of this group and at the same time has provided an equally spirited
criticism of the theme that research is best done by using groups of Ss, a
theme which is implicit in the present book. We all have the same long-
term objective, namely, that of understanding behavior, but the strategies
to be used in reaching the objective differ.

Adaptation Procedures

Let us say that we have chosen our problem, the rats have
been assigned to groups, and we are ready, presumably, to start collecting
the data. At this point we find that considerably more preparation is needed
—we are not yet ready to drop the rat in the maze or in the Skinner box

and watch the anticipated learning unfold. For most experiments a certain amount of preexperimental training is necessary to make the animals appropriate Ss for our experiment. We will speak of this training as resulting from adaptation procedures.

Deprivation schedule. It is common practice to place rats on a deprivation schedule at least several days before introducing them to the experimental conditions. Typically, a 23-hr. schedule is used in which the animal is allowed free access to food 1 hr. out of each 24 hr. The animal serves as S just prior to the 1-hr. feeding period so that it is under maximum deprivation for this schedule. Immediately after serving as S on a given day the animal is given all the food it can eat within the 1-hr. period, *ad libitum* or *ad lib* feeding as it is often termed. At the end of the 1-hr. period the food is withdrawn for 23 hr.

We noted that the learning trials are usually given just prior to feeding, a point at which the animal is under maximum deprivation for this schedule. The reason for this is probably apparent: a deprived animal is active, and for the instrumental learning tasks it is necessary that the animal be active if the instrumental response is to be produced. Within limits, there is a direct relationship between time of deprivation and activity level. The activity level may be measured by any one of several types of stabilometers (as discussed earlier) or by rotary cages. In the rotary cage, which is mounted on a horizontal axis, the active animal will run, as if he were on a treadmill. Each rotation of the cage activates a counter so that activity level may be measured in terms of rotations of the cage per unit of time. Food deprivation, therefore, is a way of inducing the animal to be active, and a 23-hr. deprivation schedule is commonly used to produce the activity. Curiously, this relationship between activity level and deprivation time does not seem to hold for water deprivation (Campbell & Cicala, 1962). However, both water deprivation and food deprivation are systematically related to weight losses in animals, and specifying the deprivation in terms of percentage of normal weight at which the animal is maintained is another common way of specifying deprivation.

Some investigators, after reporting the deprivation schedule, may introduce such words as motivation or drive, relating deprivation time directly to amount of motivation or drive. For some this may be a matter of taste, but for others the different terms are assigned subtle distinctions for theoretical reasons. It does not seem necessary for us to get entwined in these distinctions for the time being. Insofar as we can, we shall adhere closely to the experimental operations, and, at the moment, we are discussing deprivation as an experimental procedure.

For many years it had been generally assumed that an animal placed on a given deprivation schedule would rather quickly become a stable animal with regard to the effects of this schedule. It was assumed that his weight, eating activity, and so on, would quickly reach a stable level so that if he were on a 23-hr. deprivation schedule, he would be a "constant" animal. However, investigators in the middle 1950's began to question the validity of this assumption (e.g., Reid & Finger, 1955), and the resultant data have clearly shown that the period required for an animal to become a constant animal is much longer than was originally presumed. We may illustrate this using data presented by Dufort (1964).

One group of rats was placed on a 23-hr. schedule as discussed above, the *ad lib* feeding period occurring between 9:00-10:00 A.M. Another group, essentially a control, was under *ad lib* conditions at all times. Each rat was housed individually in a cage, and each day E weighed the rats at 9:00 A.M. and measured the amount of food intake between 9:00 A.M. and 10:00 A.M. Both groups were initially on *ad lib* feeding for 5 days prior to the introduction of the 23-hr. schedule for one group. At the end of this 5-day period, the two groups were matched on body weight, following which measurements were taken over an 18-day period. The results over these 18 days are shown in Fig. 9-4, the means being based on 9 Ss in each group.

The body weight of the Ss on 23-hr. deprivation schedules drops throughout the 18-day period, but at the end of 18 days is at or near a constant level. The body weight for the control animals increases slightly. For the deprived Ss, food intake drops initially and then rises to a point of stability after about 12 days. The food intake for the controls, of course, merely represents the amount they happened to eat between 9:00 and 10:00 each day since they could eat at all times.

What are the implications of such data? Insofar as differences in body weight and food intake may be reflected in performance scores, we may expect differences to occur across days for reasons attributable to other than the manipulated variable, whatever it might be. Such differences in performance have been found (e.g., McMahon & Games, 1964) when performance was measured on a learning task for groups differing only in length of time on a deprivation schedule prior to being introduced to the task to be learned. However, if all groups have the same deprivation schedule and are run in the experiment for the same number of days, there should be no bias *unless* the effects of the particular variable being studied interact with the effects of the level of adjustment to the deprivation schedule. On the other hand, suppose we are going to study the effect of massed versus distributed trials on runway performance, giving 10 trials a day for three days under massed practice and one trial a day for 30 days under distributed practice. If the trials for both groups are initiated one day after the 23-hr. schedule is started, it becomes quite obvious that some of the differences in performance, differences which we wish to attribute to massed versus distributed practice, could be due to level of adjustment to the schedule.

There is no general solution to the problem. One must study the conditions to be used in an experiment and evaluate the possible influence of

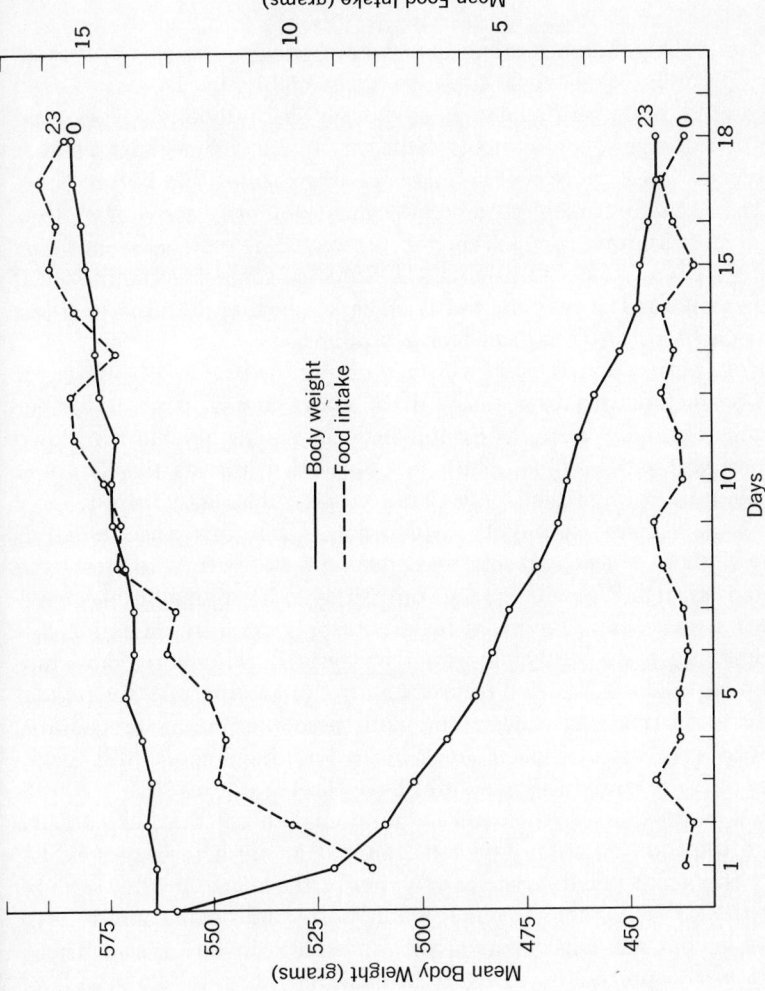

Fig. 9-4. The effects of a 23-hr. deprivation schedule on body weight (left ordinate) and food intake (right ordinate). The zero group had food available at all times, and the 23-hr. group, only between 9:00 and 10:00 A.M. each day. Data from Dufort (1964).

deprivation schedule. For some independent variables, no bias will occur, but for others, a bias may be present. We realize, however, that there are two decisions which must be made in planning an animal experiment where food (or water) is used as a reward: first, what deprivation schedule is to be used and, second, how long before the experiment proper begins should the schedule be initiated.

Pretraining. Assume that we are going to do an experiment using a straight alley. We have 90-day-old rats available that have been well fed and watered since birth, have been housed in individual cages, and have little or no experience in being handled by *E*. If such an animal is placed in the start box, there will be evidence of behavior that investigators call fear. The rat will crouch; then it may make tentative movements forward and then withdraw; defecation may occur. If it eventually finds its way to the goal box, it may not notice the food for some time, and even if it approaches the food, it may not eat it. A hand reaching into the goal box may serve as a stimulus for further fear symptoms.

An investigator must decide whether or not he wants this stage of learning to be included in his records. If the above animal is given further trials, he will eventually come to exhibit little fear, will quickly run down the alley, and will eat the food. The fear observed in the starting box will sooner or later be extinguished or superseded by other activity-producing stimuli, such as stimuli leading to exploration. Each time the animal is handled by *E* there is less and less resistance. So, if *E* wants to study the learning from "scratch," he will use the completely naive animal in his experiment. But it is generally found that little is to be gained by including this aspect of learning in the learning which interests *E*. Therefore, most animal experiments include a period of pretraining designed to take the animal through this early phase of adjustment, and these pretraining procedures, while a matter of report, are not included in the learning records. Still speaking in general, the pretraining procedures have three purposes.

The first purpose may be to teach the animal to eat the food pellets. The form of the food normally given the animal in the home cages is different from the small pellets used as rewards in the maze or alley or box. One might think that a hungry animal would seize and devour any type of food available, but this has frequently been shown to be untrue. Therefore, a part of the pretraining consists in exposing the rats to the pellets, perhaps in the goal box or a box similar to it. Given time, the rat will come to eat the pellets with relish.

A second purpose of pretraining is to adjust the animal to the experimental apparatus. The required extent of this adjustment will vary considerably depending upon the purpose of the experiment and how much the pretraining experience with the apparatus may "water down" the subsequent results. For example, if *E* were interested in finding out whether nonrewarded experience in a maze facilitated subsequent acquisition, pretraining in the apparatus might eliminate the effect of his variable. In classical conditioning, when the anmal is restricted by stocks or straps, a considerable number of adaptation trials is almost mandatory.

For animals such as the rat, the third purpose of pretraining is to adjust the animal to being handled. Rats, being what they are, initially show an aversion to being picked up and transported in the human hand. However, with sufficient exposure to this means of transportation, they apparently become resigned to it and, in comparison with their initial behavior, appear gentled. There is a rather large body of literature concerning the effect of handling; clearly there are effects, but we will not discuss them here. (The following reports show the direction the research is taking: Sperling and Valle [1964]; Denenberg and Kline [1964]; Du Preez [1964].) It is sufficient to know that handling will influence later behavior and that most *E*s will make handling a part of their pretraining procedures.

Each pretraining procedure which can be distinguished operationally from others is to be considered an independent variable, either as a potential independent variable or as one whose influence has been demonstrated. We sometimes call them method variables, and to some, such an identification is equivalent to saying that they either are not interesting variables or are not important theoretical variables. But, of course, whether or not a variable is interesting is a matter of personal taste, and sooner or later all variables may be shown to have theoretical relevance. We must recognize that pretraining as a whole, and the operationally distinguishable subparts, are independent variables. Like any potential variable they must be held constant for all conditions of an experiment. Therefore, unless pretraining procedure is the variable of study in an experiment, all groups will be given exactly the same pretraining, and its nature becomes a matter of record in reporting the experiment. It is inevitable that sometimes the same variable will produce different results in different experiments. A relationship found in the Iowa laboratory may not correspond with that found in the Stanford laboratory. Such contradictions must be resolved. One of the potential causes for such contradictions lies in differences in pretraining procedures, which is to say that the effect of a given variable may differ as a function of the kind or amount of pretraining. Therefore, we must treat pretraining as we do any other variable. Strictly speaking, there are no right and wrong pretraining procedures; there are, however, conventions and preferences. Pretraining is held constant when it is not being studied, but the level at which it is held constant is based on an arbitrary decision made by *E* before he undertakes the experiment.

We noted three purposes for pretraining animals, and we also noted that the extent of pretraining procedures to be used cannot be given a general statement because they will vary as a function of the particular experiment. We will have occasion to see illustrations of just how they are worked out in particular experiments. Sometimes the pretraining procedures are very extensive if E is not interested in the initial learning but is primarily concerned with the performance of the response after it is learned. Such was the case for Ferster and Skinner (1957) in their extensive studies with the pigeon. In a sense, to teach the pigeon to peck a key was a necessary nuisance pursuant to the study of the influence of various reinforcement schedules on the rate and maintenance of the pecking response. Therefore, their pretraining procedures took the pigeon through the complete acquisition phase to a point where it would readily peck the key to obtain food when placed in the box.

We do not wish to leave the impression that the various pieces of equipment used to study animal learning have any particularly aversive properties (save when shock is used). Even if a rat is never rewarded in the goal box of a straight alley, he will come to reach a low level of performance in going down to the goal box when placed in the start box (e.g., Logan, 1960, Fig. 6). A rat will also reach a low frequency level of pressing a bar in the Skinner box in spite of the fact that he has never received any obvious reward for doing so. As a matter of record, Jensen (1963) has argued that pressing a bar has considerable intrinsic appeal to the animal since it frequently chooses to press the bar to get food rather than to eat it out of a readily available dish.

That a rat will press the bar in a Skinner box at a low level of frequency even if food has never been given in the box or that he will make an occasional trip down a straight alley even though food has never been present in the goal box suggests that there may be deprivation conditions leading to activity other than the obvious ones of food, water, and sex. There indeed may be. Hill (1956) confined rats for varying intervals of time in very small cages which, from the rat's point of view, would be said to be cramped quarters. Subsequent testing in activity wheels showed that the amount of activity was directly related to the period of previous confinement in the small cages. There is also evidence that activity in rats may occur from an opportunity to explore novel objects or situations (e.g., Berlyne, 1960). Still, unless the intent of E is to study such behavior, food or water deprivation is ordinarily used in the study of animal learning.

In our discussion of planning an experiment with animal Ss, we have covered the general design of the experiment and problems of adaptation, including deprivation schedules and pretraining procedures. The discussion has centered largely on rats, but there is no reason to believe that the essential problems differ for other animals. We turn next to specific experiments on learning as a means of discovering how the procedures are handled in detailed form. At the same time we will get acquainted with some phenomena of animal learning on which contemporary investigators are working. The topics to be covered in the remainder of this chapter revolve around deprivation and incentive variables. In the following chapter other variables will be discussed.

The number of studies which have been performed to determine the influence of amounts and kinds of deprivation on learning and performance and the number of studies in which incentives have been varied can only be described as enormous. There are probably three major reasons for this outpouring. First, the number of different independently defined deprivation and incentive variables which can be manipulated is great. Second, it has appeared easy beyond expectations to get conflicting results, and conflicting results almost always generate a new series of experiments in an attempt to resolve the dissonance. The fact still remains, however, that there are a number of flat contradictions in the literature which have not been resolved. A third reason is that theories of learning are often closely tied to deprivation and incentive variables, and these theories have been responsible for many of the experiments.

No attempt will be made to summarize empirical findings. Fortunately, with regard to some of the variables we will consider, fairly recent reviews and summaries are available; these may be consulted to fill in the empirical gaps which will be evident in the present writing. We retain as our major purpose that of understanding research procedures.

MAGNITUDE OF INCENTIVE

By incentive we mean, of course, the food or water which appears in the goal box or which is delivered by pressing a bar. We may become precise and speak of positive incentives and negative incentives. A positive incentive is one that the organism will approach (and often seize and consume). A negative incentive is one which the animal will actively avoid. If a given stimulus is one which the animal will neither approach nor avoid, we would say that it has neutral incentive value.

Given an incentive, its magnitude may be varied. In the case of food we could vary the size of a single unit or we could vary the number of units of the same size. In the case of a negative or aversive incentive, such as shock, the magnitude may be varied by varying the number of volts. The question we ask concerns the influence of magnitude of incentive on performance, and a study by Ehrenfreund and Badia (1962) will help provide an answer.

The straight alley, or runway, was the testing device, with rats as Ss. Two variables were manipulated at each of two levels, thus requiring four groups of Ss. The two variables were deprivation level and magnitude of incentive. Deprivation level was defined by the amount of food given to maintain the rat at a specified weight *below* the weight which the rat maintained under *ad lib* feeding conditions. Two groups of animals were maintained at 95 percent of *ad lib* weight, and two others, at 85 percent. Obviously the latter groups were receiving less food and thus were under greater deprivation than the former groups. The manner by which these Es managed to maintain the appropriate weights is of some interest. First, the *ad lib* weight of each animal was determined after which each was housed in a special weight-control box. The mechanics of this box were such that when the weight of the rat fell below the specified level, pellets were automatically delivered every 12 sec. until the weight was regained. At this point the dispenser stopped delivering pellets until the weight of the rat again fell below the specified level. The device is said to be accurate within 1 percent of specified weight.

During the runway trials, one group under each deprivation level received a 45-milligram (mg.) pellet in the goal box on each trial, and members of the other group received a pellet of 260 mg.

A problem of procedure presents itself in any experiment in which reward magnitude is varied. If two groups of animals are being run under the same deprivation condition but receive incentives of different magnitudes, after a single trial the deprivation levels will differ. The animals receiving the incentive of larger magnitude will, after eating it, be under a less intense deprivation level than the animals receiving the incentive of smaller magnitude. It would seem, therefore, that in running a series of trials, one immediately after the other, the deprivation levels could differ to such a degree that a confounding would be produced and our response measure would not be a function wholly of the direct effect of incentive magnitude but would in part be a function of different deprivation levels. One might solve the problem by running one trial a day, with the daily rations of the two groups being adjusted to take into account the different amounts of reward on the single trial. There is another possible solution. After each trial the rat receiving the smallest incentive is removed to a special cage where it is fed food of an amount represented by the difference between the large and small incentive. For example, if the large incentive were 100 mg. and the small, 25 mg., the animals given 25 mg. would be given 75 mg. immediately after the trial but in another location. At this point, therefore, as members of both groups would have had the same amount of food, the deprivation level would be said to be the same, and another trial could be given immediately. Actually, Es shy away from such a procedure. It may be that the rats getting the 75-mg. "make-up" pellet would learn to run rapidly down the alley so that they could be taken out to receive the big pellet. However, if some delay occurred between removing the rat and giving him the extra food, it is unlikely that the above effect would occur, so that several trials could be run each day. Of course, if many trials are run on a single day, the deprivation level may be reduced in both groups to such an extent that performance would be seriously influenced.

The above problems are not as serious in practice as they might appear to be. In recent experiments *E*s have given several trials a day without even attempting to compensate for differences in magnitude during the actual series of trials. It is believed that the amount of food received will have so little effect on deprivation differences that it is hardly worth being concerned about.

In the Ehrenfreund-Badia study, a total of 90 runway trials was given, under the four conditions outlined above, followed by 25 additional trials in which the incentive magnitudes were reversed for the various groups. Those that received 260 mg. on the first 90 trials received 45 mg. on the 25 additional trials, and those originally getting 45 mg. received 260 mg. All 115 trials, run in four days, were distributed over the four days as follows: 20, 30, 30, and 40. Five trials were given in fairly rapid succession on a given day, and then the animal was placed back into the weight-control apparatus where it remained for ½ hr. to 1 hr. The *E*s argue that the use of these boxes will keep the deprivation level quite constant for the groups at their required level. Those animals getting small rewards in the runway will receive more pellets of food in the weight-control apparatus than will those getting large amounts of incentive in the runway.

The response measure was the speed through the middle 2-ft. section of the 5-ft. runway—neither starting times nor total times to traverse the runway were used. The median speed for each successive block of five trials was determined, and this value was converted to its reciprocal. The means for each group on the last five trials before magnitude switch, which would be trials 86-90, are shown in Fig. 9-5. These values, taken on the last trials, are considered asymptotic values by the investigators. We note that both variables influence performance. The higher the deprivation, the faster the running, and the greater the reward, the faster the running. It may be noted that with high deprivation and a 45-mg. incentive, performance is equivalent to that with low deprivation and a 260-mg. reward. Too, there is an interaction in the effects of these variables on performance: differences in incentive magnitude produce bigger differences in performance at a low-deprivation level than at a high-deprivation level.

The results relating asymptotic performance and incentive magnitude are fairly representative of results found by other investigators—the greater the magnitude of incentive, the faster the ultimate speed of running. Pubols (1960) gives this as a firm conclusion, a consequence of his survey of a number of studies.

As a next step we must consider the results found by Ehrenfreund and Badia when, after 90 trials of training, reward magnitudes were switched. For those animals under high deprivation, the switch from the small to large incentive caused a rather quick upward change in running speed, *beyond* the level (speed) shown by the group that had had the large reward throughout the 90 trials. This has sometimes been called an "elation" effect. Contrariwise, the groups switched from large to small incentive showed a "depression" effect in that their performance fell to a level *below* that shown by the group at the end of 90 trials with the small incentive. Such changes were also evident in the performances of the low-deprivation groups, but these changes were somewhat less dramatic than those seen in the high-deprivation groups. Not all studies have demonstrated that the performance curves stabilize above the level (or below the level) shown by the group

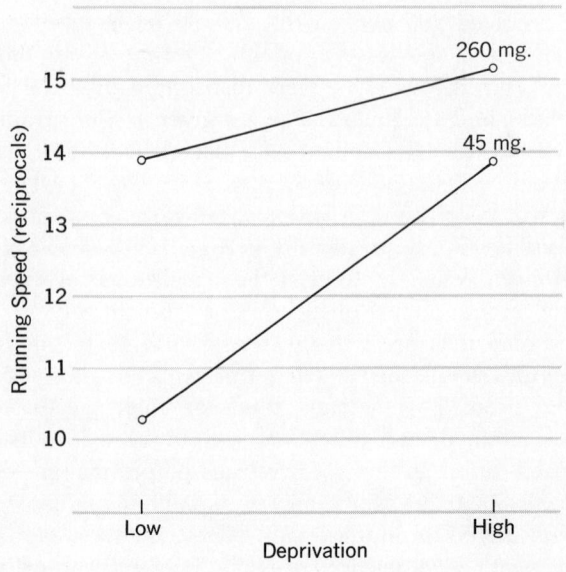

Fig. 9-5. Running speed in a straight alley as a function of deprivation and magnitude of reward. Data from Ehrenfreund and Badia (1962).

having had the given magnitude before the switch, which is to say that elation and depression effects are not always found. However, the data from many studies are quite consistent in showing that the changes in performance reach at least to the level produced by a given magnitude of incentive before the switch. The rate of change in performance following a switch in the magnitude of an incentive has varied markedly in different experiments. Sometimes the change to a new level will be complete after only a few trials whereas in other studies the change may take place very gradually. Reasons for these differences are unknown.

Investigators have reported certain changes in the observable behavior of the rat on the first few trials after a change in the magnitude of an incentive following many trials with a constant incentive. Descriptively, the rat appears quite upset if not downright mad, for he seems excited, is more difficult to handle, and is resistant to being placed in the start box.

Learning or Performance?

The discussion in the previous chapter made us aware of the distinction between learning and performance. We ask at this point whether or not the obtained differences in performance resulting from differences in incentive magnitude can be taken to represent differences in learning. Most have said no, and certain theoretical formulations have been based on the assumption that differences in incentive magnitude produce only differences in performance. It is commonly assumed that differences in deprivation time do not influence learning directly and that variations in incentive magnitude act in the same way. A large incentive simply energizes the animal more than does a small incentive, and this is reflected in the different running speeds. Of course, it is troublesome to specify just what habit is learned in the straight alley in the sense, for example, that one can specify the learning of a particular habit in a T-maze. The bulk of the evidence shows that incentive magnitude does not influence associative processes in the straight alley, whatever they are.

The reasoning about learning and performance often takes the following course. If there is a switch in the magnitude of incentive from small to large following the attainment of asymptotic running speed, and if the performance change to a higher level following the switch occurs quickly, it would appear that little if any new learning is involved, for such learning, it is argued, would not be expected to occur so rapidly. On the other hand, if there is a gradual change in performance to a higher level, new learning might be indicated. As noted earlier, some Es have reported such gradual changes (e.g., Homzie & Ross, 1962). Also, recent evidence has suggested that learning differences may, in fact, be involved in differences in performance associated with deprivation level (e.g., Brush, Goodrich, Teghtsoonian, & Eisman, 1963). The issues, therefore, are far from settled even with the straight alley.

Further complications have arisen in recent work using other tasks. Pubols, in his 1960 review, reached the conclusion that the data warranted a decision that incentive magnitude did not influence learning, and that this conclusion could be generalized across tasks. However, a number of recent studies have quite clearly demonstrated differences in performance as a function of incentive magnitude when the performance is measured in terms of acquisition of correct turns. Wike and Farrow (1962) found that thirsty rats learned a T-maze (right or left turn) more rapidly with 3.25 cc. water as incentive than with 0.25 cc. A similar finding is reported by Hill, Cotton, and Clayton (1962), who examined the effects of one versus four ᴊod pellets. Cross and Boyer (1964) found learning of a four-choice multiple-Y maze faster with four pellets of food than with one. Therefore, if we assume that differences in speed of acquiring *correct* responses (as opposed to running-speed scores) represent differences in associative processes, we must conclude that there is some evidence that incentive magnitude is related to learning and not just to performance. At the same time, however, granted certain theoretical assumptions, one may reach the conclusion that even differences in speed of acquisition of correct turns as a function of incentive magnitude need not be taken to represent differences in learning or differences in associative strength.

Why, one may ask, is there so much ado about deciding whether or not performance changes associated with variation in incentive magnitude represent an effect on learning? There are two reasons why investigators have been concerned with this problem. The first is strictly an empirical one, namely, that the analysis of behavior requires us to separate variables which produce a lasting effect on behavior (learning) from those which have a temporary effect. The second reason concerns theoretical attempts to account for behavior by combining the influences of the independent variables in the usual learning situation. The method of summing the influences of these different variables will differ depending upon whether a variable is said to influence learning or whether it is said to influence only performance. For example, if incentive magnitude is assumed to influence only performance, we might say that the overall measured performance speed is some simple additive function of amount learned (which in turn might be related only to number of trials) and performance speed associated with a given incentive. On the other hand, if incentive magnitude influences learning as well as performance speed, we have to include some formulation of how trials and incentive magnitude interact to produce learning; then this effect must be summed with any additional influence incentive magnitude has on performance. The assumption one makes about how a given variable produces its influence on behavior will normally come from available data. If the data can be viewed in such a way as to conclude that incentive magnitude influences only performance, the theoretical formulation is simpler than if it is necessary to "have" incentive magnitude also influencing learning. Spence (1956) provides a good discussion of these issues.

Other Manipulations

We cannot dwell unduly long on this single variable (incentive magnitude). There are scores of studies in which it has been manipulated, often in conjunction with other variables, and many of these studies have asked about the effects on aspects of behavior other than simple acquisition. If one "thinks of" a study of incentive variation which is believed to be an interesting one to do, the chances are that it has probably been done.

Let us sample quickly some of the other manipulations which are, in one form or another, related to incentive magnitude.

1. We may analyze the source of magnitude effects. A big piece of food takes longer to eat than a small piece; a big piece may have more nutritive value than a small piece; a big piece may gain its effect either for one of these reasons or, perhaps, because it looks bigger. Experiments have been done to attempt to determine if each or all are involved in the incentive-magnitude effect. Actually, a liquid incentive is best for such analyses. Kraeling (1961) used sucrose as the incentive and varied three aspects. First, the sucrose concentration level in a given water amount allowed determination of the effect of the intensity of incentive stimulation. Second, by varying the time allowed to consume the liquid, two things could be determined: the effects of this variable for each level of concentration and the effects of amount of caloric intake. Running speed in a straight alley was found to be directly related to concentration of sucrose, and there was very little relationship with either exposure time or caloric intake.

2. In single-choice situations we may reward each choice but use rewards of different magnitudes. If the rat makes the right turn, for example, we could give him four pellets; if he makes the left turn, we could give only three pellets. If the rewards are discriminably different, learning rate is directly related to the magnitude of the difference (e.g., Hill & Spear, 1963). If the discrimination is fairly difficult, perhaps a choice of four versus three pellets, the animal acquires the discrimination more rapidly with low deprivation than with high deprivation (Bower, 1964).

3. Goldstein and Spence (1963) gave an animal experience in two runways, one painted black, the other, white. The magnitude of the incentive was different for each. The animal was given experience on each runway from trial to trial, essentially in a random order, and the running speed varied depending upon the particular incentive. If the animal was placed in the white alley containing 10 units of food, he ran faster than if he was placed in the black alley containing only 5 units. Of course, it took a number of trials before the animal was discriminating properly. Or, to say this another way, it took a number of trials before the animal associated white with large incentive, black with small. But the results showed that it was not simply a relative matter of large and small which determined the animal's asymptotic running speed. Rather it was the absolute value of the incentive. For example, the running speed to a 5-unit incentive was essentially the same when the comparison was 10 versus 5 as it was when the comparison was 5 versus 1. Therefore, the running speed to the larger of the two incentives was not the same just because it was larger; there appeared to be an absolute running speed associated with a given incentive magnitude, and this did not vary as a function of the magnitude of the other incentive.

4. There have been many experiments on *delay of reward*, or delay in

giving the incentive after the animal reaches the goal box. A recent summary of the empirical findings on this variable is available (Renner, 1964). It is a very potent variable (the longer the delay, the slower the learning), and the effects interact with the effects of magnitude of incentive when the animal is learning to discriminate between two incentive magnitudes (Davenport, 1962; Logan, 1965).

5. We have seen that a hungry rat will run down an alley to obtain food and that the greater the magnitude of the food, the faster he will run. It appears that he runs to obtain the food. But there are situations in which the habit of running, once established, becomes unadaptive to the point that the animal will overlook a lot of food merely to reach the goal box. Stolz and Lott (1964) trained rats to run down a straight alley to obtain a small pellet of food, and then they piled a heap of pellets across the runway about halfway down. Many of the rats proceeded to climb over the pile of pellets and continue on to the goal box. Even after they had eaten some food from the pile, they often "preferred'" on following trials to run on down to the goal box for the tiny pellet present there. Furthermore, there is some evidence that a rat will run faster to get an incentive for which in the past he has had to work hard than to get one which he obtained earlier with ease (Lewis, 1964).

Magnitude Of Negative Incentives

If an animal will run faster to get to a large piece of food than he will to get to a small piece, then it would seem that he would run faster to avoid a strong shock than to avoid a weak one. However, the effect of punishment on learning is an extraordinarily complicated topic because of the great variety of results emanating from experimental attempts to determine the effects of shock (for shock has been the primary aversive stimulus used) on learning and performance. These results show, at one extreme, that if the animal is shocked for making the wrong responses in choice situations, learning will be facilitated; at the opposite extreme, shock for correct responses facilitates learning (e.g., Fowler & Wischner, 1965). Obviously, when such results obtain it can only mean that there are many other variables which interact with punishment. Solomon (1964), in a recent survey of this situation, lists 12 such variables and indicates that these are "some" of the interacting factors. Attempts are being made to "make sense" out of the available evidence; Solomon's is one, and a review by Church (1963) is another.

Escape learning. Shock as a means of producing behavior to be learned has certain advantages over food and water as a means of producing such behavior. There does not seem to be a problem of deprivation control, and although there may be some changes in the animal's sensitivity to shock over a series of trials, we can give many trials a day without being concerned about changes in deprivation level (as we must be when varying the magnitude of food incentive). Consider a study by Trapold and Fowler (1960). They studied the effect of strength of shock on escape learning. The straight alley was so constructed that the animal received continuous shock from the start box and from the main alley, but not from the goal box. The animal was dropped into the start box with the door closed, and when the animal oriented toward the door, it was opened. The Es measured latency in leaving the start box and speed of running down the alley. All animals were given 20 trials on a single day. Five different groups were treated identically except for the intensity of the shock. Over the 20 trials the results show that running speed was a direct function of intensity of shock; the more intense the shock, the faster the running. This finding seems perfectly sensible; were we placed in such a situation, we would behave in a comparable manner. However, when measured in terms of starting speed—latency in leaving the start box—no simple relationship was found. Rather, the relationship was complex; first there was a decrease in latency (starting time was faster), and, then, an increase as shock intensity increased. So, even with this relatively simple escape task, a complication arises in determining the effect of shock intensity on escape learning.

In another experiment these same Es (Fowler & Trapold, 1962) used the same apparatus but had it wired so that shock could also be given in the goal box. Shock intensity was held constant, the independent variable being the duration of the shock in the goal box. Six different groups were used, differing in the aforementioned duration, from 0 sec. to 16 sec. Thus, at one extreme, one group had no shock while remaining 30 sec. in the goal box, while at the other extreme, the animals had to endure 16 sec. of shock, after which they remained in the goal box for an additional 30 sec. The procedures, therefore, are comparable to delay of positive incentive—here, delay of escape. Again, the results on running speed were very clear-cut; the longer the delay in the goal box before shock terminated, the slower the running speeds. The differences in starting speed were not as great as those for running speed, but no reversal of the function was evident as was true in the former study.

We must look at the above procedures a little more closely. In this experiment, all animals were left in the goal box for 30 sec. after the termination of the shock. At the extremes, therefore, with 0-sec. shock, the animal remained a total of 30 sec. in the goal box; with the 16-sec. shock, the animal remained a total of 46 sec. This has two implications. First, time spent in the goal box is confounded with length of shock. Second, since animals were placed immediately in the start box after being removed from the goal box, intertrial interval and intensity of shock are confounded. The question is, therefore, are the results due to delay before termination of shock as such, or are they due to the correlated events (length of time in goal box and length

of intertrial interval)? These investigators were quite aware of these con-
foundings. Therefore, they ran two additional groups in which the shock was
terminated after 8 sec. and after 16 sec., with *total* time in the goal box being
30 sec., the first group remaining for 22 sec. after the shock terminated and
the second, for 14 sec. This procedure obviously makes the intertrial interval
constant also. The performance of these two groups did not differ from the
performance shown by the 8-sec. and 16-sec. groups in the main experiment.
Therefore, these investigators concluded that it was quite unlikely that the
correlated variables of goal-box time and intertrial interval were responsible
for their findings.

Avoidance learning. The above studies dealt with escape
training—the animals were always shocked, regardless of what they did. We
will now consider a study (Moyer & Korn, 1964) using *avoidance training* in
which the instrumental response allows the animal to avoid being shocked.
Again the variable was intensity of shock. The shock box consisted of two
sections, separated by a hurdle 5 in. high. Jumping the hurdle was the
avoidance response. Both sides of the box consisted of grids through which
shock could be administered; on successive trials the animals went from Side
A to Side B, then from Side B to Side A, and so on, so that no handling within a session was required once the animal was placed in the box.

The CS consisted of two components. Assume that the animal was placed
initially on Side A and that when put there a light above that grid was on
but the light above the grid on Side B was off. At the start of the trial, three
events happened simultaneously: the light on Side A went out, the light on
Side B went on, and a 600-cps, 73-db. tone started sounding. Exactly 5 sec.
after these changes, the grid under the rat was charged and remained so
until the animal jumped the hurdle into the other half (Side B) which was
lighted. As the animal jumped, of course, the shock was terminated, and
simultaneously the tone ended. It is apparent that if the animal got to the
other side within the 5-sec. interval, shock was avoided. It is not clear why
the compound CS, both light and tone, was used (but see below). To simplify this we will speak only of the tone as the CS. The onset of the tone
would serve to signify that the shock would be coming, and avoidance learning would be demonstrated by an increasing frequency of jumping the
hurdle during the 5-sec. period between onset of tone and onset of shock.

We noted above that the procedure allowed a series of trials to be
run without removing the animal from the box. Once the series of events
defining one trial is completed, the series can again be initiated for the next
trial, the only difference being that the animal must jump back to the box in
which he had just been shocked. Two questions are raised. First, this procedure may produce results which would differ from those obtained if the
animal always jumped from A to B or from B to A, but not both directions.
With unidirectional jumping, one compartment is always the shock compart-

ment, and the other, always the safe compartment. The procedure used by Moyer and Korn is asking the animal to return to a compartment in which he has just been shocked. However, the use of the lights is probably related to this matter; the animal could learn that "light on" is a signal for a safe compartment.

The second question concerns the programming of the trials. Once the animal gets to Side B from Side A, how long do we allow him to remain there before initiating a trial which will end when the animal returns to Side A? Moyer and Korn say that they varied the length of the interval, from 10 sec. to 30 sec., with an average of 20 sec. This means that once the animal jumped the partition there would be, on the average, a lapse of 20 sec. before the light went out above him and the tone sounded. Why use a varied interval? Why not always make it 20 sec.? The reason for this lies in another form of conditioning known as *temporal conditioning,* a phenomenon mentioned briefly in Chapter Two. Assume that we have a hungry rat in a box and that every 20 sec. we deliver him a small food pellet. Over a period of time the rat's behavior makes it unmistakably clear that he is beginning to "tell time." Near the end of the 20-sec. period he will approach the food box as if he is expecting the food at that time. As another, perhaps more objective, procedure, we may wire a Skinner box so that it will produce pellets between the fifty-fifth and sixtieth sec. of every minute only. The animal may press the bar all he wants to between 0 and 55 sec., but no food will appear. Only if he presses it after 55 sec. have elapsed will he receive food. A rat placed on such a schedule will eventually show bursts of lever pressing starting just before the 5-sec. food period out of each minute. In such instances the CS has become the period of time; the animal is responding to passage of time, or, more precisely, the events occurring in time allow him to learn to tell time.

Because of the fact of temporal conditioning, classical-conditioning experiments routinely vary the length of the intertrial interval so that temporal conditioning will be minimized. The E wants to bring the behavior under the control of the CS he is presenting and to prevent the behavior from being controlled by the passage of time. If the shock came on every 30 sec. in the Moyer-Korn experiment, the animal might learn to jump the hurdle with time as the CS, not with tone as the CS. If the time interval between trials is erratic, temporal conditioning is presumed not to occur.

The variable in the Moyer-Korn experiment was the intensity of the shock, which was varied from 0.5 milliamperes (ma.) to 4.5 ma. across seven groups of animals. The animals were given 30 trials a day for four days. The results (Fig. 9-6) are plotted in terms of percentage of trials on which avoidance occurred (trials on which the animal jumped the hurdle within the 5-sec. period between the onset of the CS and the onset of shock). A smooth curve has been drawn through the empirical points. The stronger the shock, the *less* the percentage of avoidance responses. The reason for this, according to Moyer and Korn, is that as shock intensity increases, behavior of a disorganized nature occurs; the animals bite the bars, bump into walls, run around, and also jump, but unless the jump occurs quickly and gets them over the hurdle, there is a lot of other behavior, perhaps naturally produced by the strong shock, which is inimical to jumping. Shock does not

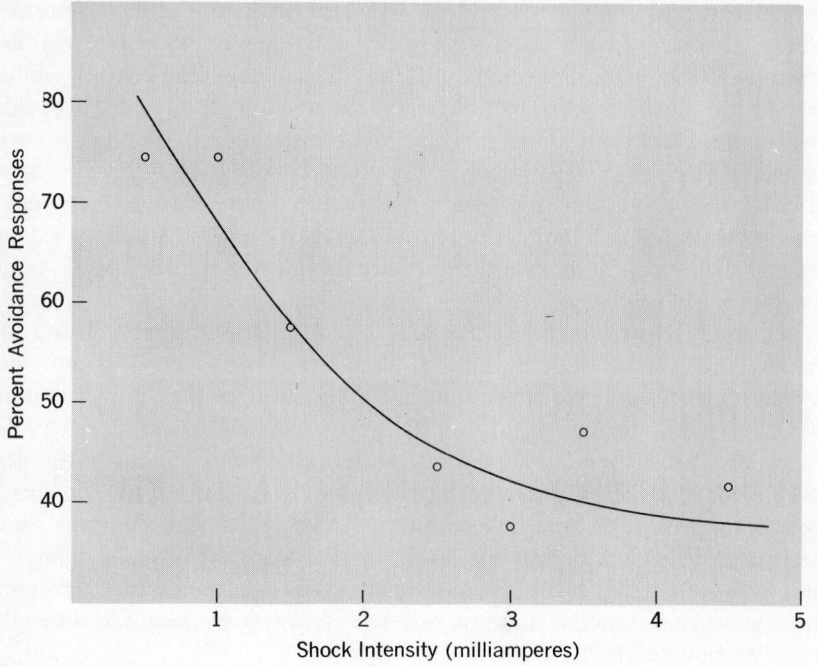

Fig. 9-6. Avoidance learning as a function of shock intensity. Data from Moyer and Korn (1964).

always produce the behavior E wants it to produce, and this is probably one of the major reasons why the role of punishment in behavior has been so difficult to pin down.

INTERMITTENT REINFORCEMENT

In the situations discussed thus far, the animal, if given a food reward, is given this food on each trial that he makes the correct response. What is correct is arbitrarily specified by E. In the usual straight-alley experiment, the mere act of reaching the goal box is the correct response, and upon so doing the animal receives a piece of food or a lick of water. It is quite possible, however, to set arbitrarily the correct response as that of running within a specified range of speeds. Under these restrictions the animal is rewarded if he runs within this range of speeds and is not rewarded if he runs more rapidly or slowly. In a T-maze we call one response correct, the other, incorrect, and give reward accordingly. In other words, by giving a reward or incentive (or reinforcement, as many call it) for a specified behavior, we see that learning consists in an increased likelihood that the reinforced behavior will occur and in a decreased likelihood that the non-reinforced behavior will occur. It is obvious that by using incentives we gain control over the behavior of the animal. There are, however, certain limitations to this control, and it is to the variables influencing this limitation that we turn our attention in this section.

In all of the experiments discussed thus far, reinforcement has been 100 percent—the animal always received the food if he made the correct response, or he was always shocked if he did not make the response. It is quite apparent that we need not give the reward on all correct trials; we could give it only occasionally, or intermittently. This variable, intermittent reinforcement, often called partial reinforcement, is a very powerful one when we gear our thinking to the long-term control of behavior initially acquired by reinforcing correct responses. More particularly, the most profound effect of intermittent reinforcement is found when reinforcement is discontinued. The discontinuance of incentives after they have been provided during acquisition is the defining operation for *experimental extinction*. More specifically, if we remove the incentive (US in classical conditioning) following a certain number of acquisition trials, and if on the following trials performance falls below the level of that shown with continued incentive, experimental extinction is defined. If we cast this into diagrammatic form, we have the following:

	TRAINING	REMOVAL OF INCENTIVE
E GROUP	Yes	Yes
C GROUP	Yes	No

If the performance of the E Group following removal of the incentive is poorer than that of the C Group, experimental extinction has been demonstrated. As might be expected, most studies do not include the C Group. Enough experience has been built up for Es to realize that the C Group would not fall because they have not had the incentive removed. Therefore, experimental extinction is often measured as the fall in performance shown by the E Group, using the performance on the last training trial as the base. Only occasionally has evidence been presented for extinction *not* occurring, so that the most frequent experimental question is not whether or not it occurs, but what the factors are that produce differences in the rate at which it occurs—the rate at which performance falls following removal of the incentive. It can also be seen that the study of extinction is not the study of forgetting. Extinction is an active process in that trials are given in which the incentive is removed and performance is measured on these trials. In forgetting, we merely let time elapse between the learning of a task and the test of performance.

When fixed numbers of trials are used with such tasks as the straight alley and the T-maze, intermittent reinforcement is expressed as the percentage of trials on which the incentive is present. Continuous reinforcement is, therefore, 100 percent, and partial reinforcement is any percentage that is less than 100 percent. If the partial reinforcement schedule is 50 percent, every other trial involves, on the average, an incentive, but rarely would E use alternating trials of incentive and not incentive. Instead, he would determine a random order so that over a given number of trials 50 percent will have been reinforced.

When discrete trials are not used, as in the Skinner box, two major types of intermittent reinforcement have been employed. With a *fixed-ratio schedule,* every nth response is followed by a reinforcement. For instance, E might reward every tenth response. In the *fixed-interval schedule* a response occurring a given period of time after the preceding reinforcement is also reinforced. A fixed interval of 1 min. would mean that following a previously reinforced response, 1 min. is allowed to elapse and then the first response occurring after that point in time is reinforced. The fixed-interval procedure is comparable to the method for producing temporal conditioning discussed earlier.

Scores of studies have shown (with only rare exceptions) that resistance to extinction is higher following intermittent reinforcement than when following 100 percent or continuous reinforcement. To say this another way, rate of extinction is more rapid following continuous reinforcement than when following partial reinforcement. This seems to make a certain amount of sense. If during acquisition an animal has not received food on every trip down the runway, he will be somewhat less concerned about this when he does not receive food on an extinction trial. He will, so to speak, have another go at it because that is what he has been accustomed to. An animal that has been reinforced continuously, however, might take a somewhat different view of the situation. He has received food on every previous trip, and the failure to find the food on the first extinction trial represents a clear change.

It becomes clear that if we wish to maintain or control behavior (as represented in a given response) over long periods of time, intermittent reinforcement is necessary. By gradually changing from continuous to intermittent reinforcement over many trials and then making the intermittency more and more extended, it is possible to develop behavior that will go on and on before extinction starts to occur. Ferster and Skinner (1957) have some striking illustrations of this. One pigeon had been given 800 reinforcements on various schedules. Then it was given 400 reinforcements on a fixed ratio of 170—every one-hundred-seventieth response (the pecking response) was reinforced. Initially, in extinction 1000 responses occurred at the rate which was comparable to that under the last fixed-ratio schedule. Then, after a short pause (the pigeon may have been tired) another run of 900 responses occurred. Extinction became evident only in the long pauses between the successive bursts of responding. It seems apparent that if near the end of the first 1000 extinction responses a reinforcement had been given, the response would have been maintained even longer. This is to say that by gradually working the organism to a point where reinforcements are very rare, behavior can be maintained over long periods of time.

Once a given schedule of reinforcement has been employed over many hours of training, the behavior which accompanies it is quite resistant to outside influences. Some of these behaviors were shown most dramatically in the chimpanzees used as Ss in the Mercury Project leading to the first manned orbital flight. During the orbital flight of Enos, this chimpanzee carried out many tasks (Rohles, Grunske, & Reynolds, 1963), one of which was pressing a lever to obtain food on a fixed-ratio schedule. A yellow light coming on was a signal to press the lever, but in order to obtain the food, he had to press 50 times. The response measure was the time to make the 50 responses. That he was traveling through space 100 miles or so above the earth seemed to be of little consequence to the orbiting Enos; the time to make the 50 responses showed little change when measured at various points in the flight.

Lewis (1960) has reviewed studies on partial reinforcement in discrete trial situations, and has also reviewed a number of theories purporting to account for the fact that extinction is prolonged following intermittent reinforcement. None of the theories satisfied Lewis when he placed them against available data, and this situation has probably not changed. His review may also be consulted with regard to studies with human Ss, for the intermittent reinforcement effect is quite apparent with such Ss. Indeed, studies using the slot machine can lead one to believe that gambling behavior in humans may be the counterpart of the partial-reinforcement effect on extinction as noted with animals. A payoff, coming only periodically, keeps the gambler gambling. However, no one has suggested that a gambler who wins on every card hand, on every pull of the slot-machine handle, on every throw of the dice, or on every horse race will stop gambling.

Sample Studies

We will examine three studies. Two of these, each making a test of a theory, were concerned with the rat in a straight alley. The third used earthworms as Ss, and it will not only show us the generality of the partial-reinforcement effect, but it will also introduce us to some additional experimental controls that are required in certain studies.

Discrimination hypothesis. In the above discussion we implanted the idea that the partial reinforcement-extinction effect might occur because the animal can more easily tell when extinction starts following 100 percent reinforcement than when following partial reinforcement. This common sense point of view can be given firmer status by specifying that the effect results from differences in the change in moving from the training to the extinction trials and that the greater the amount of change, the more easily is the change discriminated. If there is little change, the rat will continue behaving as he has on training trials; if there is much change, his behavior will change. (This hypothesis can be stated in terms of another behavioral phenomenon, *generalization*, which we will discuss in the next chapter.) A test of this hypothesis has been made by Theios (1962), and the hypothesis takes a fairly severe thrashing.

Theios used a straight alley, with five groups of rats. All animals were tamed by handling and were given five trials to learn to eat the food pellets in the goal box. Then 30 preliminary training trials were given to all animals, with 100 percent reinforcement. After this preliminary training, Theios matched five groups of rats on the basis of their performances on the 30 preliminary trials, and the experimental variables were introduced before further training. These conditions are outlined in Table 9-1. All groups were given 70 training trials (original training) at the rate of five trials per day. Groups 1, 2, and 3 had a partial-reinforcement schedule of 40 percent; Groups 4 and 5 had continuous or 100 percent reinforcement. Following these 70 trials, three of the groups were given additional training, all with 100 percent reinforcement. Group 2 had 25 additional trials, Groups 3 and 5, 70 additional trials. Then all groups were given extinction trials.

TABLE 9–1

THE EFFECT OF 40 PERCENT AND 100 PERCENT REINFORCEMENT
IN ORIGINAL TRAINING ON EXTINCTION AND THE EFFECT OF
ADDED TRIALS OF 100 PERCENT REINFORCEMENT. DATA FROM
THEIOS (1962).

GROUP	REINFORCEMENT ON ORIGINAL TRAINING	REINFORCEMENT ON ADDED TRAINING	EXTINCTION SCORES
1	40%	No Training	61
2	40%	25 Trials—100%	66
3	40%	70 Trials—100%	50
4	100%	No Training	33
5	100%	70 Trials—100%	31

Here is the reasoning behind these procedures. Although Groups 1, 2, and 3 originally had a partial-reinforcement training procedure, the addition of 100 percent reinforced trials for Groups 2 and 3 should, when the extinction starts, make the change more noticeable for these groups than for the group not given these additional trials. Furthermore, the change may be as great for these groups as for a group given 100 percent reinforcement on both original and added training (Group 5). If this is true, then Groups 2 and 3 should, in extinction, behave as if they had never been partially reinforced.

The extinction scores in Table 9-1 represent mean number of trials required to reach the criterion arbitrarily set up by E. This criterion of extinction was the fifth trial on which S failed to enter the goal box within 60 sec. after the start door was opened. Thus, a large score means slow extinction, a small score, fast extinction. We may first compare extinction for Groups 1 and 4 since these two groups represent the extinction effects following partial and continuous reinforcement. The difference is apparent; nearly twice as many trials were required to reach the extinction criterion following 70 trials of which 40 percent were reinforced than following 70 trials all of which were reinforced. With 25 added trials of 100 percent reinforcement (Group 2), no change occurs; extinction is as slow as for Group 1. The 70 additional trials do, however, increase the rate of extinction somewhat, but extinction takes longer than if partial reinforcement had never been given. Thus, if the change between training and extinction is involved in the partial-reinforcement effect, it is not by any means the entire source of the effect according to the data of this study. The Theios findings have been confirmed by others (e.g., Sutherland, Mackintosh, & Wolfe, 1965). However, it should be noted that the discriminability hypothesis retains considerable validity in the classical conditioning of human Ss (Bridger & Mandel, 1965).

An analytical problem. We have previously discussed the problem of transfer-type designs, designs where we attempt to learn about some process which has occurred in one stage of learning by switching to a second stage in which conditions differ in such a way as to (we hope) lay bare the mechanisms operating in the first stage. The studies in which intermittent reinforcement is varied in the first stage and in which extinction rates are studied in the second stage fit the transfer design. Are any problems raised by such procedures? The answer is yes, but the problem of predicting when they will arise is difficult. Let's see why this ambiguous answer must be given.

We have not considered the effect of intermittent reinforcement on acquisition. Let us suppose that 40 percent reinforcement resulted in a higher level of performance than did 100 percent reinforcement. Then we introduce extinction trials and find that the group having 40 percent reinforcement takes longer to extinguish than does the group having 100 percent reinforcement. Perhaps the difference in extinction, we might argue, is not due to some aftereffects of partial reinforcement which persist into extinction but rather to the fact that partial reinforcement led to a higher level of performance in the acquisition phase than did 100 percent reinforcement. This assumes that if we gave two groups of animals training under 100 percent reinforcement, giving one a greater number of trials than the other, until they reached the level of performances shown by the 100 percent and 40 percent groups as indicated above, the same differences would be found in extinction. If this were true, we could not attribute partial reinforcement any effect other than that leading to a higher level of learning. If the above state of affairs in fact obtained, we would be faced with a serious analytical problem. What are the facts? We can conclude only that they are confused on both issues.

First, the data on the effect of partial versus 100 percent reinforcement on acquisition in a straight alley are contradictory. Some *E*s have found that partial reinforcement leads to a higher performance level; some find that 100 percent reinforcement leads to the higher performance level. No blanket statement can be made about the asymptotic level of performance to be expected under partial and 100 percent reinforcement.

The second issue concerns the relationship between level of performance before extinction and rate of extinction. Up until a few years ago it is probably fair to say that most *E*s accepted the fact that the higher the level of performance before introduction of extinction trials, the slower the extinction. With certain tasks (e.g., the Skinner box) the evidence clearly appeared to support this position. But there have been a number of recent studies with the straight alley which have shown either that a higher level of performance was followed by more rapid extinction than was a lower level of performance or that no consistent differences occurred in extinction following different levels of acquisition performance.

This perplexing state of affairs can only bring a note of reasoned caution. Differences in rate of extinction may occur as a function of differences in original level of acquisition. Differences in reinforcement schedules may produce differences in level of performance at the end of acquisition. Therefore, caution must be entertained in interpreting differences in rate of extinction as a function of a residual effect of reinforcement schedule if level of acquisition performance differs. In any two-stage experiment where performance differences are present at the end of the first stage, extreme caution must be exercised in interpreting the source of the differences which may occur on the second stage.

Frustration. If a rat runs down an alley on the first trial and gets a piece of food but on the next run finds no food, we might, in a manner of speaking, say he is frustrated because he expected to find food. Starting with this notion, a number of theorists have worked out schemes to account not only for the slower extinction following partial reinforcement, but also for other phenomena. Perhaps Amsel's schemes are best known (1958; 1962). We are not going to concern ourselves with the details of these theories since it is sufficient at the moment to indicate that after a number of trials under intermittent reinforcement, the theories indicate the development of anticipatory frustration. Frustration, and then anticipatory frustration, has motivation-like properties in that anticipatory frustration will result in more vigorous responding. If this is true, we will expect that after a long series of acquisition trials, the animal will run more rapidly under an intermittent-incentive schedule than under a 100 percent schedule. As noted earlier, the data are not consistent on this matter, but the lack of consistency may be due to differences in number of training trials at the time of termination of training.

It was reasoned (Wagner, 1963a) that if anticipatory frustration has motivation-like properties, the frustration should respond to a drug that depresses activity of the central nervous system. Alcohol would be one such drug, but in the present experiment sodium amytal was used. This drug, it was believed, should depress the activity associated with the motivation-like characteristics of anticipatory frustration. If this is true, animals given the drug and having partial reinforcement should run more slowly than animals given the drug and having 100 percent reinforcement since the latter group would not have (theoretically) anticipatory frustration. To test this, four groups of animals were used, two under a 100 percent schedule and two under a 50 percent schedule, and all given 64 trials on a straight alley. One of the groups under each schedule received an injection of sodium amytal 10 min. prior to the first run of the four given on each day. The other two groups were injected with a saline solution to control for any side effects of injection itself.

The results are a classic picture of complete interaction between the two variables. For the saline-injected groups, 50 percent reinforcement resulted in faster running (clearly evident at the close of training), while the 100 percent schedule produced faster running for the animals injected with sodium amytal. Such results are considered by Wagner to be quite in support of the notion that partial reinforcement will lead to a motivation-like state which results in a stronger overall level of motivation than that associated with 100 percent reinforcement.

Rearing of a worm. The use of certain animals other than rats for the study of learning is sometimes associated with advantages not available with the rat. Following an experiment in which perhaps chickens or ducks have been used, the underfed graduate student may no longer remain so. Another advantage associated with certain animals is availability. In many sections of the country the earthworm is available for the turn of a spade. And apparently the earthworm is teachable, as witness the study by Wyers, Peeke, and Herz (1964). (See Jacobson [1963] for an exhaustive review of learning studies on worms in general.)

The technique used was classical conditioning. The UCS was a photoflood bulb which produced a rearing response (UCR) in the anterior section of the earthworm. The worm was placed in a small plastic tube mounted on a plywood block a foot square. A vibrator, used as the CS, was attached to the base so that the vibrations were transmitted to the worm in the tube. On a given trial the CS was turned on for 6 sec., and during the last 2 sec. of this period, the UCS was flashed on. If after a number of trials the worm was observed to rear during the 4-sec. period prior to the appearance of the light, a CR was said to have occurred. The UCR is often followed by a withdrawal movement, but in the present study the data are evaluated in terms of rearing.

The two basic groups of worms consisted of one given 100 percent reinforcement (the UCS always following the vibrator) and another given 50 percent reinforcement. These two groups received 50 trials a day for three days followed by 50 trials of extinction on the fourth day (with the UCS never given, of course). The results show learning for both groups over the three days, with performance leveling off at about the 75 percent level— on 75 percent of the trials the CR occurred and only one worm is reported to have failed to learn. At the end of the three days the 100 percent group was a little superior to the 50 percent group, but not significantly so. However, during the extinction trials the 50 percent group performed at a considerably higher level than did the 100 percent group; that is, intermittent reinforcement prolonged extinction.

Had the above two groups been the only ones employed in this experiment, an experienced investigator in the area of conditioning would surely raise the question as to whether or not any learning had been demonstrated. He would accept the fact that there was an increase in the frequency of rearing responses to the vibrator over trials, but the question on which he would perseverate would be whether or not there had been associative formation that could be called learning. We are once again back to the issue of performance versus true associative formation. Could the performance of the worm, a performance that increased with trials, be due to some process other than an associative process?

A number of years ago a phenomenon was discovered which is known as *pseudoconditioning*, obviously meaning false conditioning. Pseudoconditioning is a conditioning-like phenomenon. but it cannot easily be attributed to the formation of an association, and it is most likely to occur when an aversive stimulus is the UCS in classical conditioning. One of the most dramatic demonstrations of pseudoconditioning comes from an older study by Wickens and Wickens (1940). Infants were given trials of withdrawal conditioning in which a buzzer was the CS followed by a mild shock to the foot as the UCS. The shock, of course, produced foot withdrawal. Twelve trials a day were given for three days followed by a test for responses to the buzzer alone. Many of the infants withdrew their feet when the buzzer sounded, suggesting that conditioning had occurred. However, in this study, a pseudoconditioning control group was given the same number of "training" trials, but on these trials only the shock was given—the buzzer was never sounded. On the test trials to the buzzer alone these infants produced as many foot withdrawals as had those in the other group. Since the buzzer and shock had never been paired, the foot withdrawals for this group cannot be said to be due to associative learning. Without this pseudoconditioning control the Es probably would have concluded that they had conditioned foot withdrawal, but with the control results, they could not conclude that conditioning had been demonstrated. It appears that when an aversive stimulus is used as a UCS, the organism may give the response produced by the UCS to almost any change in the environment. This is somewhat analogous to the sprint man who, waiting tensely against the starting blocks, may "jump the gun" to some stimulus other than the gun.

The existence of pseudoconditioning has forced investigators to elaborate their operational definition of learning in situations where pseudoconditioning may occur; they must add control groups where conditions are such that the formation of an association between the CS and the response could not occur. The number of responses that are made in these control conditions to the CS alone must, in effect, be subtracted from the number of CRs which occurred in the true conditioning conditions.

It may have been noted that the plural form, control groups, was used above. The reason for this follows. In certain situations the mere presentation of the CS over and over may produce what might appear to be a CR. This is sometimes called sensitization but is a form of pseudoconditioning. We have said that in classical conditioning the CS must be one which before training will *not* elicit the CR, but in certain situations it is possible that after it is presented a number of times alone, it will elicit the response despite the fact that it did not do so initially. In any event, in the rearing of the worms, the Es felt it to be a distinct possibility that the vibrator, after being presented many times, might itself cause the rearing movement. Therefore, two pseudoconditioning control groups were added.

For one group over the three training days, only the vibrator was presented—the UCS (light) was never turned on—and for another group, a series of trials was given in which only the UCS was presented. On occasional trials, of course, only the vibrator was presented, a necessity if Es were to discover if pseudoconditioning had occurred. Analysis of the responses for both of these groups showed that "conditioned" responses had occurred; in some blocks of trials they were as frequent as 20 percent but averaged about 10 percent across all three days of training. Of course, since these frequencies are much less than shown by the true conditioning groups, the Es concluded that conditioning had occurred, but it is clear that the frequency of true CRs can be determined only by subtracting the frequency of responses occurring in the pseudoconditioning control groups.

Although the two pseudoconditioning controls in the above experiment may have been adequate, a little reflection will lead to the conclusion that they are not ideal controls. In the true conditioning procedure both a CS and a UCS are presented to S. It would seem most appropriate, therefore, to present *both* the CS and UCS to a pseudoconditioning control group since it is possible that when both act on the organism, more pseudoconditioned responses will occur. In using such a control it is required that the UCS *precede* the CS. It is known that little if any conditioning (backward conditioning) occurs under such an arrangement. At the same time, however, if the action of the CS and UCS summate in some way to boost the number of pseudoconditioned responses above the combined number occurring after the presentation of each alone, we will have the best estimate of the number of responses which may be attributed to pseudoconditioning.

SECONDARY INCENTIVES

A hungry rat will learn to run through a multiple-T maze if a piece of food is at least sometimes found at the end of the maze. We know that the food is related in some way to the rat's running through the maze, for if the food is never found, the rat will stop running. This does not necessarily mean, of course, that the food, or its consumption by the rat, is responsible for the learning of the sequence of the turns in the maze, but we know that under normal circumstances, at least, the presence of the food is necessary to make the animal perform. The food is termed a primary incentive because it is directly related to the needs of the animal. We have, however, many terms that are used more or less interchangeably. Need for food, need for water, and so on, are often called primary drives; and for a hungry rat a piece of food is a primary reinforcer or primary incentive. A secondary incentive is one that is not related directly to a primary drive; it is only indirectly related as a consequence of learning. A secondary incentive is also known as a secondary reinforcer or conditioned reinforcer. It is a stimulus that serves as a symbolic incentive; it is not itself edible or drinkable but has been associated with stimuli which are. A penny is a secondary incentive to a child because it may be associated with a piece of candy. It is apparent that secondary incentives must be involved in most human behavior, and therefore, the understanding of how a stimulus becomes a secondary incentive becomes important in understanding human behavior. The animal laboratory provides a ready place to study such learning "in the raw."

The defining procedures for a secondary incentive require the pairing of a neutral stimulus with a primary incentive for a number of trials. One paradigm which may be employed is as follows:

	TRAINING	TEST
E Group:	Primary incentive plus neutral stimulus:	Neutral stimulus only
C Group:	Primary incentive plus neutral stimulus:	Neither incentive nor neutral stimulus

If on the test the E Group performs better than the C Group, the neutral stimulus is said to have become a secondary incentive. To translate the paradigm into specific procedures, we might use a Skinner box wired in such a way that when the animal presses the bar, food appears at the same time a tone sounds. Both the E and C Groups are given a number of training trials under this arrangement. On the test no food appears when the lever is pressed, and the tone sounds for only the E Group. If the E Group makes more presses than the C Group within a given interval of time, the tone is said to have become a secondary incentive. A more stringent test would be to determine if a new habit could be learned with only the tone as an incentive. For example, we might place the lever at the end of a straight alley to make such a test. When members of the E Group arrive at the goal box and press the lever, the tone sounds, whereas a similar response by the C Group produces no tone. Will the speed of running increase more rapidly for the E Group than for the C Group?

There are a number of possible variations on the basic paradigm, and other controls may be required, depending upon the nature of the neutral stimulus. In the above paradigm we might find it desirable to add a control group which did not have the tone during training but did have it on the test trials. It is possible that a tone might have some intrinsic incentive value (it is not a true neutral stimulus). Some investigators believe that the above operations are inadequate for the establishment of a secondary incentive in that there will be no difference in the behavior of the E and C Groups on the test. There is evidence to indicate that for the most effective establishment of a secondary incentive, the E Group must be given training that will establish the neutral stimulus as a discriminative stimulus. Thus, included in the training should be trials on which the bar is pressed and *neither* food nor light is present. However, recent evidence indicates that secondary reinforcers can be established without such discriminative training (e.g., Reynolds, Pavlik, Schwartz, & Besch, 1963), although they may not be as effective or as strong when established in this manner. As usual, there are many more variables involved than we will cover here. Kimble (1961) and Meyers (1958) have reviews of the field. We will examine a few studies to provide an acquaintance with the research in the area.

Secondary Reinforcer as an Informer

Egger and Miller (1963) advanced a point of view that any neutral stimulus will become a secondary incentive only when it signals the arrival of a primary reward. The critical occurrence is not merely having a neutral stimulus and primary reward paired; the neutral stimulus must always give information that a primary reward will follow. This led them to an experiment the conditions for which are outlined in Fig. 9-7. Initially, their animals were well trained in a Skinner box until they were performing under a fixed ratio of 4 to 1 (4 presses for each pellet). Then the bar was removed, and the secondary-reinforcement training sessions occurred without the animal's ever pressing the bar. The neutral stimulus was either flashing lights or a tone, and on a given trial the stimulus was on for 2 sec.

For Group I, the redundant group, the neutral stimulus was always

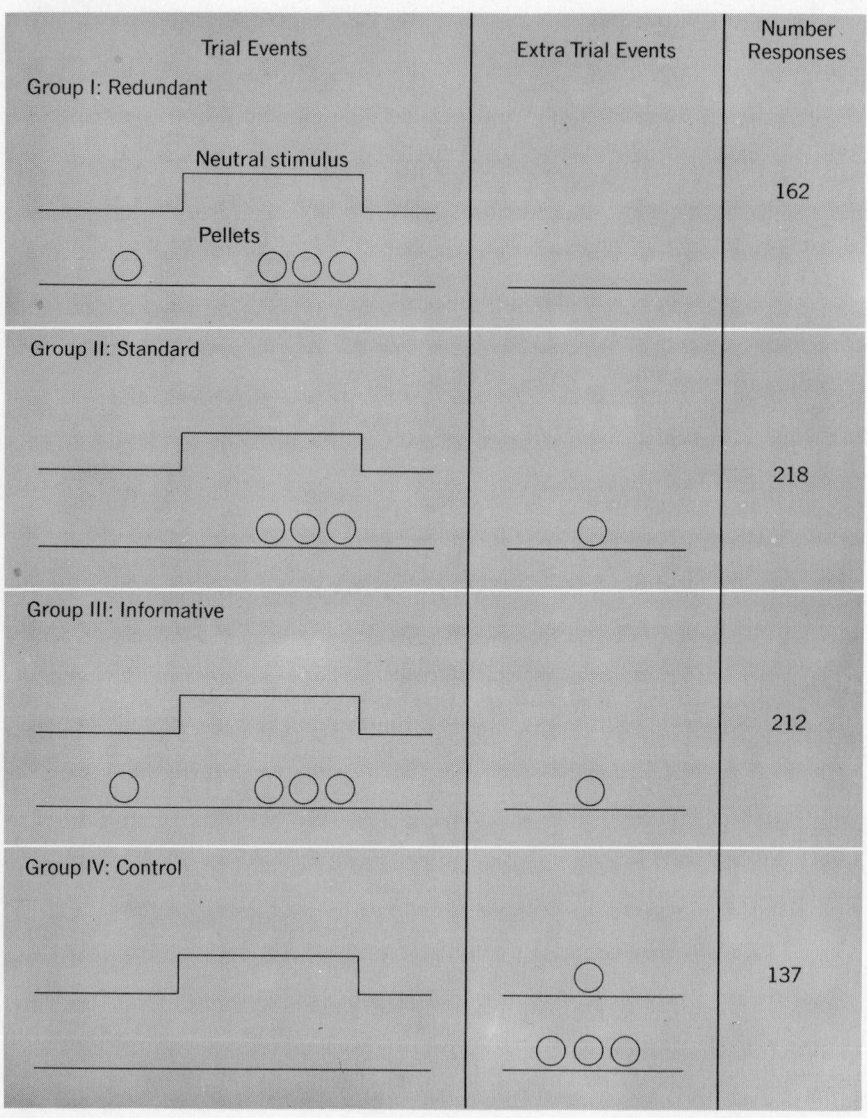

Fig. 9-7. Conditions and results of a study on secondary reinforcement. Adapted from Egger and Miller (1963).

preceded by the delivery of a single pellet of food, and then 0.5 sec. before the termination of the neutral stimulus, three more pellets were delivered. Egger and Miller call this the redundant group because the neutral stimulus adds no information—the appearance of the single pellet of food signals the subsequent occurrence of the other three pellets. Thus, according to their point of view, in spite of the fact that the neutral stimulus appears concurrently with primary reward, it will not become a secondary reinforcer because it does not give the animal any information he does not already have.

Group II was given the standard procedures for conditioning. Here the neutral stimulus *is* an informer; it tells the animal of the subsequent appearance of the three food pellets. These animals were also given an extra pellet between secondary-reinforcement training trials, and, of course, the neutral stimulus did not occur at that time.

The animals in Group III were treated exactly the same as those in Group I except that they received a pellet of food at various times between trials. Since this extra pellet was never followed by the three pellets, it destroyed the information or signaling value of the initial single pellet on the training trial. Under these conditions the only consistent informer was the neutral stimulus since its onset was always followed by the three pellets. Finally, the Control Group (IV) received the neutral stimulus, but never concurrently with food pellets, which were given between trials.

The above conditions were imposed after the animals were well trained in the Skinner box, and, to repeat, the bar was not present when the conditions were administered. There were nine training sessions during which each animal was given 15 secondary-reinforcer training trials. Following these training sessions, the bar was again introduced into the box, and the animal was allowed to press for 30 pellets with a fixed ratio of 3 to 1. Then 10 min. of extinction were given followed by tests for the effects of the training conditions. On these tests, when the animal pressed the bar, the flashing light came on or the tone sounded, whichever was appropriate for that animal, but the occurrence of the lights or tone was also on a fixed ratio schedule of 3 to 1. Since some extinction trials had been given just prior to the tests to determine the secondary-reinforcement strength of the originally neutral stimulus, the measurements were being made in retraining to press the bar. Following the first test session, two additional sessions were given 48 hr. and 86 hr. later. The response measure used was the mean total number of presses made during the first 10 min. of the test sessions.

The means are shown in the right column of Fig. 9-7. The results are quite consistent with the Egger-Miller point of view. It can be seen that Group I did press somewhat more frequently than did Group IV but not nearly as much more as did Groups II and III. For Group I the neutral stimulus was redundant; it did not tell the animal anything that he did not already know. For Groups II and III the neutral stimulus was the only consistant signal to indicate that three pellets would arrive shortly. The importance of the signaling characteristics of a would-be secondary reinforcer is also shown in the following experiment.

Familiarity of a Neutral Stimulus

The groups of animals in this study (Marx & Knarr, 1963) were treated to different secondary-reinforcement operations over many days. All animals were born and raised in complete darkness except for the experimental introduction of light, for light was the neutral stimulus to be used as the secondary reinforcer. About 25 days after birth the experimental program began. During a given 24-hr. period 96 feeding opportunities were afforded each animal. For a feeding opportunity a buzzer sounded, a door opened leading to a food box, and food was available there for 23 sec. The 96 food opportunities were irregularly spaced through the 24-hr. period.

The groups were differentiated by treatments given over 22 weeks. For one group, the onset of light from a 6-watt bulb preceded the opening of the door, hence signaling food. For another group, the onset of the light came 5 sec. after the opening of the door, therefore coming on while the animal was feeding. For a third group, the onset of the light came *between* feeding opportunities, and so temporally was always separated by at least 2.5 min. from any feeding. For all three groups the light remained on for 9 sec. A fourth group, a control group, never received light.

Tests of the secondary-reinforcing properties of the light were started two weeks after the animals were placed on the above schedules and then were given once a week for 20 weeks. For these tests, a bar was inserted in the home cages for 20 min. If the animal pressed the bar, a light came on and remained on as long as the bar was pressed. As the results turned out, only the number of bar presses, not the duration of the press, differentiated the groups.

The results show that the group in which the light was a signal for the appearance of food made far more presses than any other group over the 20 weeks, but there was a decline from week to week. The decline occurred in spite of the fact that the training procedures continued throughout the 20-week period. The group which received the light while they were feeding was not superior to the control group, hence, there was no evidence that the light had gained secondary-reinforcing properties. Again it appears that the most effective way for a secondary reinforcer to develop is to have it signal the imminent appearance of a primary reward. The unusual finding was that the group receiving the light between feeding sessions showed an increase in the frequency of bar presses throughout the 20 weeks, and the frequency at the termination of the experiment was comparable with that shown by the group for which the light was a signal for the appearance of food.

These investigators suggest that this finding offers some support for the proposition that familiarity of a stimulus is a sufficient condition for it to develop secondary-reinforcing properties. There is a puzzle associated with such an interpretation. Why did the group receiving the light during the feeding period not respond with comparable frequency to the light on the tests since familiarity would have been as great for this group as for the other group? Let us consider an alternative interpretation for the increase in bar presses for the group in which the light came between feedings.

In classical conditioning the interval between the onset of the CS and the onset of the UCS may be varied as one varies any other factor. In the usual conditioning procedures the CS remains on until the UCS is terminated. The two overlap, and regardless of the temporal separation of the onsets, when the two overlap the procedure is called *simultaneous conditioning*. As might be expected, there is a particular interval between the onset of the CS and the onset of the UCS which results in a maximal rate of conditioning. This varies somewhat for different responses (responses elicited by the UCS), but as an approximate figure, 0.5 sec. may be taken as the optimal interval. If the CS and UCS do not overlap—if there is a blank interval between the cessation of the CS and the onset of the UCS—the operations are termed *trace conditioning*. Not very much is known about trace conditioning when the interval extends beyond a few seconds, but it is generally assumed that when the interval is of such length, it is very difficult, if not impossible, to establish a CR. But perhaps if enough training is given, such conditioning will occur. We may examine this possibility for the group of animals in the above experiment which had the light coming between feeding periods but which showed a steady increase in frequency of bar pressing throughout the 20-week period.

As noted above, at least 2.5 min. separated the light from any feeding period, so that the minimum "trace" time (time between the light and the food) would be 2.5 min., and on most trials appreciably longer. But note that the light always signaled the appearance of food to come later, sometimes quite a bit later, but at other times not as much later. It is not at all clear that these variable intervals, when they all exceed the minimum length of 2.5 sec., will prevent conditioning. The critical aspect would seem to be the number of training trials, and in the experiment under discussion, the number of training trials was very great. There were 96 trials a day, or 672 a week, and by the end of the 22-week period a total of 14,784 training trials had been amassed. Our speculation is, therefore, that trace conditioning was being established, and that this is why the curve for the group having the light between feedings shows a rise throughout the period.

An Imprinting Object and Secondary Reinforcement

If in the early hours after a chick has been hatched, an object (any old object, including a human) is moved past the chick, it will follow the object. Furthermore, if on successive days the object moves past, the chick will persist in this following behavior. This is called *imprinting*. Much of the earlier evidence on this phenomenon came from naturalistic observations. Most species of birds, although not all, will imprint, but mammals apparently will not. Favorite subjects have been chickens, ducks, geese, and turkeys. In recent years, considerable work of an experimental nature has been undertaken to attempt to determine relevant variables, and naturalistic observations continue to be reported. This work up to 1960 has been summarized by Moltz (1960). Imprinting has become of interest to learning theorists because it appears to represent learning that has occurred without apparent reinforcement. Furthermore, there is a critical period of a few hours after hatching that imprinting will be most strongly "set"; that is, the following behavior in later life will be much more persistent if the imprinting object is introduced during this critical period. However, attempts are being made to bring imprinting into the system of thinking surrounding other forms of learning (e.g., Moltz, 1963). Our interest here is in the use of an imprinting object as a secondary incentive in the acquisition of a habit. We will review a study by Campbell and Pickleman (1961).

The subjects were chicks, and the task was that of learning a right turn in a T-maze. The stem of the T was 24 in. long, as was each arm, but the goal boxes were a little unusual, being 10 ft. long and 24 in. wide. The imprinting object was a blue cube 7 in. on a side and was suspended above the alley (goal box) in such a manner that it could be moved back and forth the full length of the alley. The cube was moved at a speed of 8 in. per sec.

The experiment started 20 hr. after the chicks hatched. The E chicks were placed in the right goal box for 10 min. During this time the cube moved and stopped alternately at 15-sec. intervals. Such an imprinting session was also given on the following three days. The C chicks were placed in the left goal box, which was quite empty, for 10 min. on each of the four days in order to correspond to the time of the imprinting sessions for the E chicks. The T-maze learning trials were initiated on the fifth day. The imprinting object was always in the right goal box but in a position where it could not be seen by the chick until the goal box was entered. Five acquisition trials were given each day for 10 days. If the chicken entered the left goal box, nothing was available. When an E chick entered the right goal box he was allowed to follow the cube for 2 min., but when a C chick entered the right goal box the cube did not move.

The results are clear. By the end of 50 trials the E chicks were choosing the right turn about 90 percent of the time, and the C chicks, about 60 percent of the time. The running speeds of the E chicks increased markedly over the 50 trials, but those for the C chicks, only slightly. There can be little doubt that the imprinting object had positive incentive value for the imprinted chicks.

It is doubtful whether an imprinting object, as used in this experiment, should be placed in the class of operations used to establish the usual secondary incentives. We have seen that in establishing the secondary-reinforcing properties of a neutral stimulus it must occur in conjunction with a primary reward. In the case of the imprinting object we cannot specify the deprivation state for which it is a reward (if it is), and, of course, it cannot be both a primary and secondary reinforcer at the same time. But the fact is that the chicks learned a new response as a consequence of the presence of an object which by the usual criteria cannot be considered a primary reward. So, whether or not the use of an imprinted object as an incentive fits the operations for establishing a secondary reinforcer, we do have a secondary-reinforcer-like phenomenon. Nevertheless, there are a number of further experiments which seem necessary. Suppose we have a neutral stationary stimulus present during the period that a moving object is being imprinted. Would this neutral stimulus now have secondary-reinforcing properties? In the Campbell-Pickleman study with the chicks, would learning of the T-maze have occurred if the imprinted object was not moved when the chick entered the goal box? Would a new moving object have produced positive results? Compared with the usual secondary-reinforcing effects, those found in the Campbell-Pickleman study are of great magnitude so that there is considerable room to investigate the influence of such variables as suggested.

Other Secondary-Reinforcing Operations

We have been dealing with the influence of a positive secondary incentive, one which produces approach responses. It is apparent that we could also study the effect of a neutral stimulus after it has been paired with a negative incentive. Will a neutral stimulus, after pairing with a negative incentive, gain aversive-producing properties? The answer is yes, but the interpretation of this effect has rather universally been that of the transference of drive-evoking properties to the neutral stimulus, and as such we will consider it in the following section. There is ambiguity present, however, for we may also interpret the influence of secondary positive reinforcers as being due to the increased drive or motivation which they produce.

There are other operations which may be used to study the development of both positive and negative symbolic incentives. It would seem reasonable to believe that if a neutral stimulus is present when a shock *terminates*, the neutral stimulus might become a positive secondary reinforcer. The notion is a little like hitting your thumb with a hammer because it feels so good when it stops hurting. A neutral stimulus, associated with the cessation of hurting, might become a secondary reinforcer. A number of experiments have worked with such a paradigm, but a critical survey of these experiments by Beck (1961) concludes that "there is almost no evidence to show that secondary reinforcement can be established by the association of a neutral stimulus with noxious drive-reduction." (p. 43) Difficulties are encountered when one attempts to set up an experiment designed to demonstrate such a secondary reinforcement. If we assume that such a demonstration is most likely to succeed if the neutral stimulus serves as a signal for pain cessation, it means, operationally, that the stimulus must be present while the pain is still occurring and, therefore, may become an aversive stimulus. If it occurs after the termination of pain, we have essentially a backward-conditioning procedure where the primary reinforcement (pain reduction) precedes the CS (the neutral stimulus), and it has been quite impossible to demonstrate backward conditioning by any technique (e.g., Kamin, 1963). So while logically it would appear that a neutral stimulus associated with pain reduction would become a positive secondary reinforcer, it is difficult to devise satisfactory operations to demonstrate it.

SECONDARY DRIVES OR MOTIVES

The notion used for developing a secondary drive or motive is comparable to that for developing a secondary reinforcer because in both cases we present a neutral stimulus when the animal is under a given deprivation condition, a deprivation perhaps of water. Trials are difficult to define in such cases, but we could set up a program wherein the neutral stimulus is always present when the rat is thirsty and not present when not thirsty. The test would be to satiate the animal on water (allow it to drink all it wishes in a given period of time), present the neutral stimulus, and then see if drinking is resumed. Tests for the development of such a secondary appetitional drive by such methods have been negative (e.g., Novin & Miller, 1962). Evidence for secondary or learned drives comes almost exclusively from shock studies in which fear is presumed to be conditioned to an originally neutral stimulus.

The conditioning procedure is quite straightforward. A neutral stimulus is presented, and perhaps 3 or 4 sec. after its onset, the animal is shocked. After a number of such trials the animal is given a new test task to learn for which the only stimulus is the originally neutral stimulus. On this test the animal would be placed in a box very similar to the one in which he had previously been shocked. However, the box is devised so that an appropriate instrumental response (e.g., turning a wheel or jumping a hurdle) following presentation of the originally neutral stimulus will allow the animal to reach a "safe" compartment. The safe compartment will normally be distinctly different from the one in which shock had been administered. These procedures have been generally successful in that the animal *will* learn to make an instrumental response with only the originally neutral stimulus as a goad. Briefly, we may examine the effects of some independent variables.

It will be remembered that in avoidance conditioning, learning is inversely related to the intensity of the shock. It has been generally found that the opposite function holds for fear conditioning in that the stronger the shock, the better the subsequent learning performance to the neutral stimulus (e.g., McAllister & McAllister, 1962). This seems quite reasonable. In the acquired-fear procedure the animal cannot avoid the shock and escapes from it only when it is turned off. The stronger the shock, the greater the amount of pain, hence the greater the fear associated with the onset of the neutral stimulus. A sudden onset of the shock produces better conditioning than if the same intensity is reached gradually (Fromer, 1962). One of the odd findings is that there may be little or no evidence for conditioning if the tests come immediately after shock training. At least, learning is much more rapid if the tests are made 24 hr. after shock trials than if they are made immediately (e.g., McAllister & McAllister, 1962; McAllister & McAllister, 1963).

In discussing intermittent reinforcement, we mentioned that one of the explanatory notions used was based on frustration. When a previously rewarded response is not rewarded, frustration occurs and behavior is energized. If this is true, frustration should be capable of being conditioned to neutral cues. And it seems to be. We will examine a portion of an experiment by Wagner (1963b) to demonstrate this. Two groups of animals were trained in a straight alley on a 50 percent reinforcement schedule. For the E Group, on each nonrewarded trial the CS (neutral stimulus) was present while the rat made the trip to the goal box. For the C Group, it was not present on any trial. The notion was, of course, to make this neutral stimulus a signal that "the food isn't there" for the rats in the E Group. A total of 116 runway trials was given.

The first effect of the neutral stimulus (which was a compound of flashing lights and intermittent sound) to be expected is the slowing down of the animals in the E Group on the later runway trials when the CS is present. This they did, showing a decrease in speed on nonrewarded trials from about Trial 60 on but a continued increase in speed from trial to trial on the rewarded trials (when the CS was not present). It is clear, therefore, that the CS came to "mean something" to the rat.

The second and critical finding concerns the acquisition of a new instrumental response with only the neutral stimulus as the drive producer. For this test, a two-compartment box was used, the response being that of jumping a hurdle to get from one compartment to the other, presumably motivated by the neutral stimulus. Performance was measured in terms of time to reach the other compartment following the presentation of the stimulus. Sixteen trials were given. Wagner divided these trials into two successive blocks of eight each, and the mean speeds for each block for the E and C Groups are presented in Fig. 9-8. There is no doubt that the performance of the E Group is much superior to that of the C Group. Furthermore, there is an actual increase in speed from the first to the second block for the E Group, an increase which is expected by the theory involved. It is assumed when the animal jumps the hurdle to the other compartment,

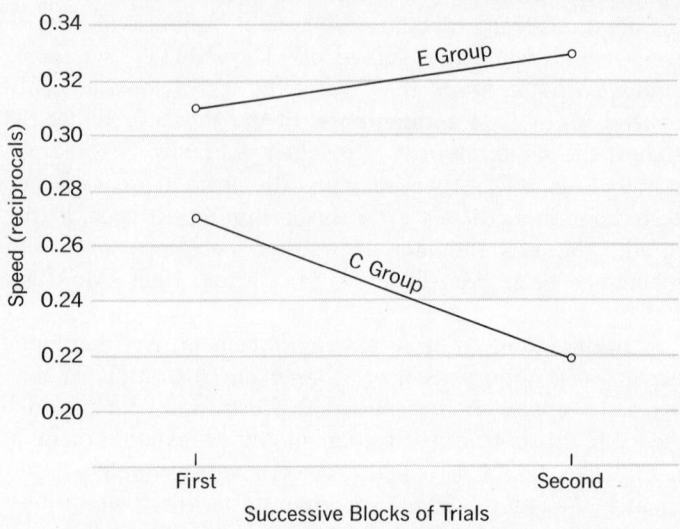

Fig. 9-8. Performance on an instrumental learning task as a result of a conditioned drive associated with frustration. See text for full explanation. Estimated from Wagner (1963b).

at which time the stimulus is terminated, that there is a reduction in the frustration drive. Onset of the stimulus produces the drive; its cessation reduces the drive. If one assumes, as some theorists do, that drive reduction is a favorable condition for learning, then the fact that the rats improved over the test trials (rather than extinguishing) is understandable.

SUMMARY

There are at least three reasons for the widespread use of animals in the study of learning. Animals are used because (1) they allow more precise control of extraneous variables, (2) they are presumed to be simpler organisms and thereby allow the study of learning at a very elementary level, and (3) they may be used to study the influence of certain variables (e.g., brain lesions) which cannot be studied with human Ss.

The most commonly used apparatuses for studying animal learning are alleys and mazes (straight alley, single-choice maze, multiple-choice maze), boxes (Skinner box, shock and avoidance boxes), and classical-conditioning apparatuses.

Most experiments in animal learning involve a form of independent-groups design. Considerable preliminary work is required in adjusting deprivation schedules (when food is a reward) and in pretraining the animals to eat pellets, to being handled, and to being reasonably docile in the apparatus used.

Experiments were reviewed on the role of magnitude of positive incentive on performance and led to an inconclusive discussion as to whether or not the better performance normally found with the larger incentive indicates better learning. It was shown that escape learning is directly related to the magnitude of the shock and to its duration, whereas avoidance learning shows increasingly poorer performance as shock intensity increases.

Intermittent, or partial, reinforcement refers to a schedule wherein reward is not given after every trial as is the case for continuous, or 100 percent, reinforcement. Intermittent reinforcement is almost always followed by extinction that is slower than the extinction following 100 percent reinforcement. Three studies were reviewed in detail in which partial-reinforcement procedures were used. In the process of reviewing one of these, pseudoconditioning was discussed in terms of the controls required to separate pseudoconditioned responses from true conditioned responses. We also noted the problem involved in measuring differences in rate of extinction when performance levels differed prior to extinction.

A secondary incentive, or secondary reinforcer, is an originally neutral stimulus which assumes reinforcing power by being associated with a primary incentive such as food. Some of the studies reviewed suggested that a secondary incentive will be developed maximally if it informs S of the momentary arrival of a primary incentive. One study was reviewed in which an imprinted object appeared to serve as a reinforcer for learning.

Finally, studies were considered in which an originally neutral stimulus might become a cue for evoking fear and frustration.

CHAPTER TEN

Further Conditioning Phenomena

In the previous chapter the emphasis was on the procedures used to study learning or conditioning in animals. In the present chapter we will allow the human S to join the animals as we discuss further conditioning phenomena.

STIMULUS GENERALIZATION

To define stimulus generalization we need an E Group and a C Group, with the E Group being trained to make a CR to a specific CS and the C Group not being given this training. After training, both groups are tested (without the presentation of the UCS) on a stimulus that is different from the original CS. If the performance of the E Group (by any acceptable response measure) is greater than the performance of the C Group, generalization is defined. Generalization, we see, indicates that as a consequence of training with a particular CS, other stimuli also gain some tendency to elicit the CR. The relationship between these other stimuli and the CS will be discussed shortly.

The C Group procedures may not be the most appropriate ones if we wish to measure the amount of generalization. Depending upon the nature of both the CS and the UCS, we may want the C Group to be a full pseudo-conditioning control group. If we are dealing with an aversive UCS or a strong CS, we may choose to present these stimuli in erratic order to the

C Group so that no associative connection will be established between the CS and the response and yet, at the same time, S will be fully sensitized to these stimuli.

Gradient of stimulus generalization. In the definition of generalization, the critical procedure, hence the critical defining operation, is that of making the test stimulus in some way different from the CS. The difference between the two stimuli could be very gross; for example, the CS might be a tone, the test stimulus, a light, and still meet the definitional requirements. However, it is doubtful if such a difference would result in the behavioral difference (a difference between the performance of the C Group and the E Group) which is necessary to complete the definition. In practice the difference between the CS and the test stimulus is specified by the units of a single dimension along which both lie, with the magnitude of the difference representing degree of similarity of the CS and the test stimulus. If we test at two or more points, differing in degree of similarity to the CS, and if we find there is a systematic relationship between performance to the test stimuli and the degree of similarity to the CS, we speak of a *gradient of generalization.* Suppose the training stimulus—the CS—is a 1000-cps tone. On test trials we use stimuli which vary (in cps) both above and below the CS: 900, 925, 950, 975, 1000, 1025, 1050, 1075, and 1100 cps. If performance is directly related to the similarity of the CS and the test stimuli, we will produce a double-winged gradient, since tests are made both above and below the CS on the frequency dimension. It can also be seen that we do not need a C Group in this situation to infer generalization as long as we find a difference in performance associated with the test stimuli.

The relationship between performance and similarity of training and test stimuli is normally expected to be a direct one. Within this gross relationship, however, one may find data which would describe all of the specific relationships shown in Fig. 10-1. The top horizontal curve represents 100 percent generalization across all test stimuli (assuming that control performance was lower). The slopes of the successive curves increase, indicating a decrease in the width of the band of stimuli to which S will respond. If generalization were zero, there would be no response to any test stimuli which would be of greater magnitude than that shown by a C Group.

The relationships between performance and similarity in Fig. 10-1 are linear. However, this need not be the case; the relationships may be negatively or positively accelerated. Given any relationship, we know that its exact form depends upon the choice of units along the baseline and whether or not the scale is transformed. The shape of the generalization gradient can be changed by changing the nature of the baseline (e.g., White, 1962) just as any other relationship can be changed by such procedures. What is the proper way to handle the baseline? Should the units be physical units? Should the units be psychologically equivalent (such as JNDs)? If the obtained relationship is not linear, should the scale be transformed if it will produce a linear relationship? Or should we turn the problem around and say that tests for generalization may be used to scale similarity?

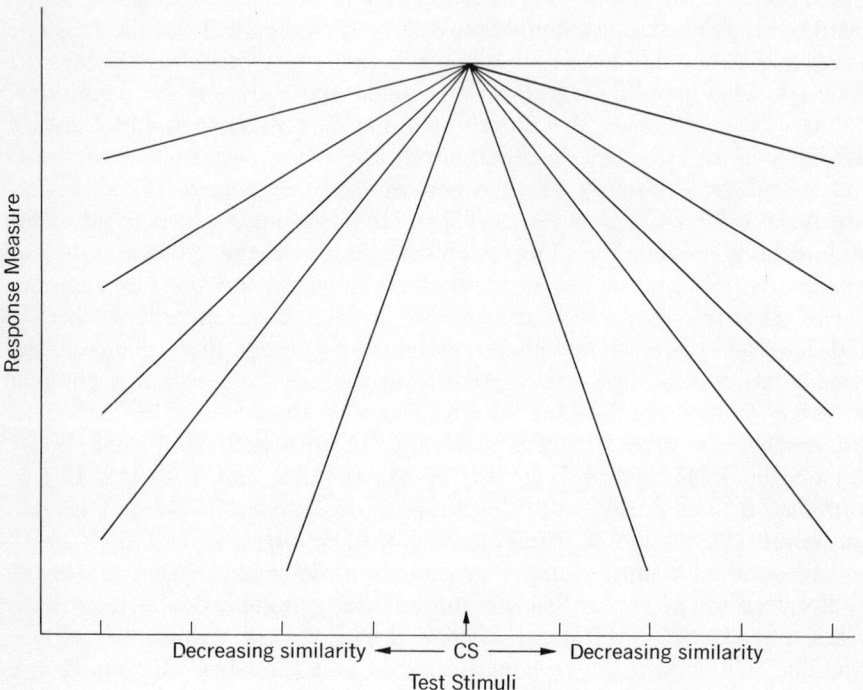

Fig. 10-1. Possible gradients of generalization following training on a conditioned stimulus (CS) and testing on other stimuli having decreasing similarity with the training stimulus.

The precise nature of any relationship depends in some degree upon the choice of units, and to change the details of a relationship by changing the units does not make it any truer, that is, it does not make it a more accurate description of a natural relationship. Changing the details of a relationship by changing the units may make it easier to work with, easier to use in theory, or easier to make it mathematically simpler, and all of these are quite worthwhile; but we must not represent such changes as bringing us closer to abstract truth.

Spread differences. As exhibited in Fig. 10-1, gradients of generalization have shown differences in the amount of spread. How can gradients vary from flat gradients indicating 100 percent response to all test stimuli down to a very narrow band of stimuli which will elicit the response? The answer, of course, is that the relationship between similarity and generalization is in turn influenced by many subsidiary variables, some of which are directly related to method of measurement, and these we will consider here. A review (Mednick & Freedman, 1960) may be consulted for a thorough coverage of the other variables involved.

One of the obvious reasons why we might get a flat "gradient" is that the band of test stimuli is narrow. If one investigator uses a narrow band and another a broad band, the latter may well get a decreasing gradient, and the former may not. This is obvious when the manipulations are along a common dimension (e.g., intensity of a tone). But it is not as obvious when two different dimensions are involved in the two studies. For example, if one investigator is working with the wavelength of light and another with intensity of tone, how do we place these two dimensions on a common baseline so that we know the units are equivalent? One might think that we could express the baseline in a common psychological unit, such as a difference threshold or JND, and, indeed, such a procedure will come almost as close to a solution of the problem as we can reach. But it is not a perfect solution by any means, because certain assumptions are involved which may result in a distortion of the obtained relationships.

The determination of JNDs requires an active comparison of stimuli by S. In the usual test for generalization where this comparison is not present, we need not expect that JNDs will reflect themselves in a one-to-one relationship in generalization differences. In a psychophysical procedure S may easily discriminate between a 1000-cycle tone and a 1005-cycle tone. But following training with a 1000-cycle tone as a CS will he, if asked, detect that a 1005-cycle tone is a different tone? Nevertheless, there is a certain amount of sense in using JND units as a baseline, but our steps will normally have to be much larger than a single JND. That is, we might use steps of 10 JNDs as determined in a psychophysical experiment. So much for one dimension. However, if we want to compare the generalization along two dimensions, such as wavelength of light and intensity of tone, and if we use JNDs as common units for plotting, can we assume that 10 JNDs along the wavelength of light is psychologically equivalent to 10 JNDs along the dimension of tonal intensity? If by such a procedure we obtained the same gradient of generalization, we might feel fairly confident about the matter. But if the gradients differ, are we to conclude that generalization along one dimension differs from that along the other, or are we to conclude that we do not really know because we do not know that our units are equal? These problems of metricizing different dimensions so that the units of the metric will be equivalent are difficult ones, but lack of equivalence of the metrics across different dimensions may be responsible for the reports of different shapes of gradients of generalizations.

In testing for generalization with multiple test stimuli, we have, at the extremes, two ways of carrying out the tests. Either we may test the same S at all of the points, with the order of testing randomized for each S, or we can use each S in a test at only one point. It can be seen that on the test of generalization, when the UCS is omitted, we are, essentially, giving an extinction trial. Therefore, when the same S is tested several times, his performance should be lower and lower for each successive trial because of extinction. If we combine all data across Ss we may, therefore, expect a fairly sharp gradient because we assume that responses to a generalized stimulus extinguish more rapidly than do responses to the training stimulus. In effect, we are measuring rate of extinction of responses as a function of their similarity to the training stimulus. The facts show that the gradient inferred from a single test trial is much broader than a gradient inferred from the pooled results of several test trials (e.g., Wickens, Schroder, & Snide, 1954) and may be essentially flat. Therefore, another variable involved in determining the shape of the generalization gradient is the method used (multiple versus single tests) in testing for generalization.

Another factor involved in multiple testing which may produce changes in the shape of the gradient from study to study again concerns the nature of the unit. Mednick and Freedman (1960) suggested that Ss may respond in a systematic fashion to the number of different stimuli on either side of the training stimuli rather than to the absolute differences between the stimuli. For example, assume the training stimulus is a 1000-cycle tone. One investigator may use 1100, 1200, and 1300 as testing stimuli, and another, 1200, 1400, and 1600. In both cases there are three test stimuli, but they differ in the span they cover. If S responds in terms of number of units "away" from the training stimulus, the generalization would be equivalent for each successive test value regardless of the span covered. But if the values are plotted above the absolute values of the stimuli used, the gradients would show different slopes. There is evidence that with human Ss for certain situations, at least, this notion of number of test stimuli (as distinct from the span covered) does influence the measured generalization, hence, the shape of the generalization gradients (Thomas & Hiss, 1963). Pigeons, on the other hand, give no support to the idea (Friedman, 1963).

Still another issue arises when considering multiple testing. Suppose that we are going to have four test points along a dimension. We may test all Ss on all points several times, or we may divide our Ss into four subgroups, giving each subgroup a number of tests on the same point but using a different group to represent each point. When this is done and the gradients resulting from the two methods are compared, they are quite different (Kalish & Haber, 1963).

The above illustrations indicate that many variables are involved in determining the shape of any gradient of stimulus generalization.

Some Representative Studies

Size generalization. In a study by Grice and Saltz (1950), rats learned to run a straight alley and push open a small door behind which was a pellet of food. The small door was set flush with, and in the center of, a circular disc whose size was the dimension along which tests for generalization were made. All circular discs were mounted so that their centers were the same distance from the floor, and the small door was also always the same distance from the floor regardless of the size of the disc. Eight groups of rats were involved. After preliminary training, four groups were given 60 training trials in which the circular disc was 20 sq. cm. in area. The other four groups were given an equal number of trials with the circular disc being 79 sq. cm. in area. The generalization tests were extinction trials. On an extinction trial the door in the circle could be opened only one-eighth in. If the rat pushed the door this distance, it was counted as a response. Of course, no food was obtained at any time during extinction.

For extinction, the four groups trained on the 20-sq.-cm. stimulus were assigned to extinction trials with stimuli of four different sizes, 20, 32, 50, and 79 sq. cm. The four groups trained on the 79 were extinguished to the same stimuli. Thus, two gradients were investigated, one extending above 20 on the size dimension and the other extending below 79 on the size dimension. It should be clear that during extinction a given rat always had the same size circle at the end of the runway. A total of 25 extinction trials was given, and the response measure was the mean number of trials on which the animal tried to push open the door in the disc. If 60 sec. elapsed without this attempt it was scored as a failure (no generalization).

The results are shown in Fig. 10-2. A conventional baseline has been used, and straight lines are drawn through the points. The two lines are fairly symmetrical, and for both training points it is clear that extinction rate and distance from training point are inversely related. Generalization gradients appear to be clearly demonstrated. Nevertheless, it is apparent that there was considerable response strength toward pushing the door even for the stimuli at the size most extreme from the training stimulus. In the 25 trials only 4 animals (out of a total of 30) represented in the groups tested at the extremes failed to push the door at least once.

Spatial generalization. Assume that as S you are facing a curved panel on which a horizontal row of seven lights is mounted. Since the panel is curved, each light is the same distance (5 ft.) from your eyes. If the center light is considered to be at zero degrees from your direct line of vision, each light proceeding away from the center is spaced 8 degrees apart so that, spatially, they are 8, 16, and 24 degrees from your central line of vision and extend to both the left and the right. Just above the center light is a small green light which you, as S, are instructed to watch, since it serves as a ready signal. Your fingers rest on a reaction key. You are told that shortly after the green light comes on, the center light will also come on and you are to respond

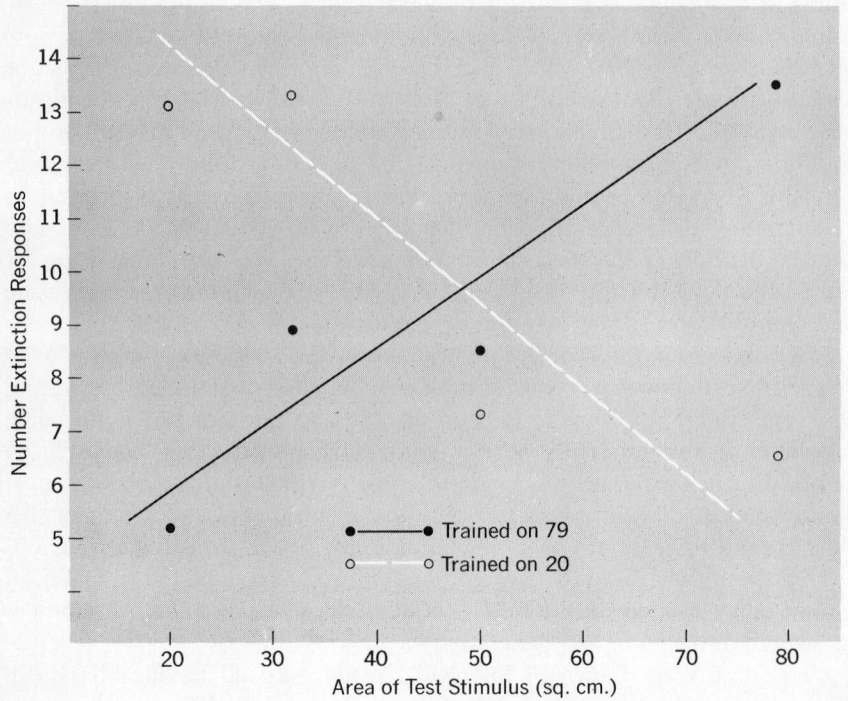

Fig. 10-2. Generalization along a size dimension. Data from Grice and Saltz (1950).

(as in a reaction-time procedure) as quickly as possible by releasing the key which you depressed when the green light went on. Finally, you are told that the other lights will come on but that you are *not* to respond to them; you are always to respond to the center light and respond as quickly as possible, but you are never to release the key for any of the other six lights. This is the situation devised by Brown, Bilodeau, and Baron (1951) for studying a generalization-like phenomenon along a spatial dimension.

The procedure used by these investigators gave S a number of initial

trials on the center light only; then, without warning S, the Es started a series
of trials on which one of the other six lights came on about once in four trials.
In one experiment, this procedure was continued until each of the six test
lights had come on four times each. A total of 24 Ss was used, and the response measure was the percentage of the tests on the forbidden six lights
to which S in fact responded by releasing the key. The values are plotted in
Fig. 10-3. Since the S always responded to the center light, its value is 100

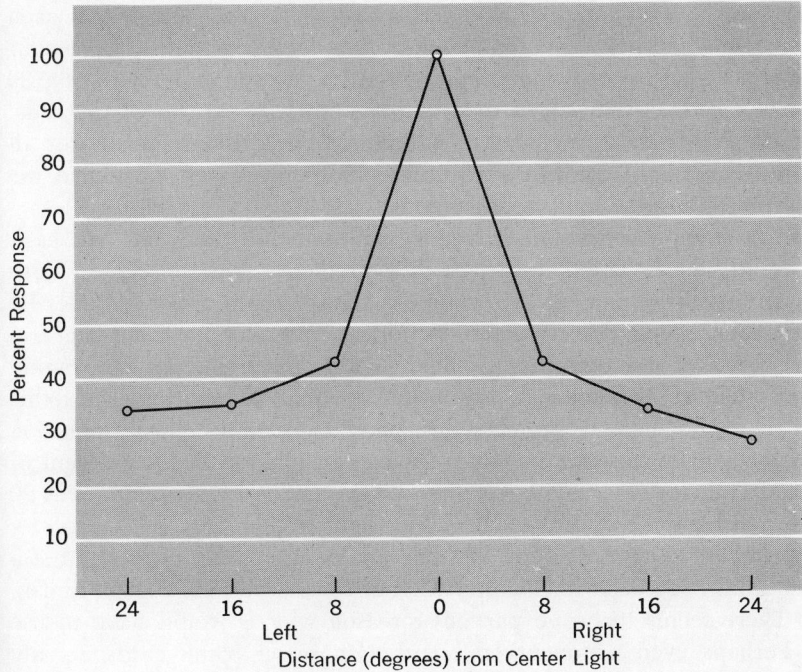

**Fig. 10-3. Gradient of spatial generalization. Data from Brown,
Bilodeau, and Baron (1951).**

percent. This figure shows that the Ss did respond to the other lights, and the
frequency of responding decreased as the distance between the training light
and the test light increased.

It was concluded that the above procedure was not ideal
for studying spatial generalization (Brown, Clark, & Stein, 1958). For the
procedure to "work," S had to be under a speed-of-reaction set. Furthermore,
although S was specifically instructed not to respond to the other lights, E in
fact did nothing about it when S did and would have been disappointed, no
doubt, had he not so responded. To avoid some of these problems, the pro-

cedure was modified. The S was told that each of the seven lights represented a horse and that on successive trials the appearance of a given light meant that the horse was running in an imaginary race against other imaginary horses, although not against the horses represented by the other lights. The S was to judge whether the horse would win or lose the race. In the beginning, of course, this was a sheer guess, and S was so told; however, he was further told that over a number of trials he would begin to get some notion about each horse's ability to win. He "built up" this notion since E told S after each trial (a trial consisting of a single light coming on with S guessing "win" or "lose") whether the horse *had* won or lost. The outcome of each successive race had been decided ahead of time by E and, in this particular experiment, called for the horse represented by the center light to win 80 percent of the time, with all of the others winning 20 percent of the time. During the 210 trials or races, each light came on 30 times; hence, for all except the center light, 24 of these races were lost and six won. Of course, the order of presenting the lights was random.

The question concerns the frequency with which S predicted that each horse would win. Over all the trials, they predicted that the center horse would win about 80 percent of the time, which is the number of times he did win. Thus, S was able to match his guesses very closely to the true frequency. However, for the other six lights, where the frequency of winning was equivalent at 20 percent, S did not guess equal frequencies. The lights nearest the center light were guessed to be winners on a higher proportion of their races than those further from the center light, so that a gradient of response frequency was found. For the two extreme lights the value was 20 percent, and for the two next to the center light, 45 percent.

This racing situation should be quite amenable for use in most laboratories and has been used for manipulation of several variables (e.g., Simon, 1964). There seems to be no particular reason why E would have to use lights. Perhaps even a noncurved board with seven blank cards equally spaced across the board would suffice. The E could simply point to a card as the horse racing at the moment. After S made a choice of win or lose, E could verbally inform E whether the horse *did* win or lose according to his prearranged schedule. It is possible that a group of Ss could serve at one time, recording their guesses on a prepared data sheet. The most obvious variable is the proportion of times that each horse wins. Suppose that the middle horse wins only 20 percent of the time, and all others, 80 percent. Would an "upside down" gradient result?

Other procedures for voluntary responses. The above illustrations of generalization along a spatial dimension dealt with a voluntary response. The S could choose whether to respond or not or whether to predict a win or a loss. This technique is adaptable for use with other stimulus dimensions. Kalish (1958) showed Ss a given color and instructed them to remember it and to respond only to it on subsequent trials. On successive trials he presented other colors varying on how closely their wavelengths approximated that of the one shown first. This procedure is somewhat like the method of constant stimuli discussed in earlier chapters. The technique produces generalization gradients, and if we wished we could determine difference thresholds from these gradients. The difference threshold would be the wavelength span between the training stimulus and the point at which S identifies the test stimulus 50 percent of the time as being the same as the training stimulus. For a bidirectional gradient this could be determined both above and below the standard.

Another technique sometimes used requires S to make a movement of the hand a specified length for a training stimulus; then test stimuli are interspersed among the training stimuli, with S, of course, instructed to respond only to the training stimulus (Rosenbaum, 1953). With this procedure two response measures are available, namely, whether or not S made any movement at all (a frequency measure) and the distance of movement.

LaBerge (1961) used the vertical spatial position of a small rectangular-shaped light source in a darkened room as the dimension for studying generalization. In addition, he used *two* positions for training. Initially, S was taught to move one lever, L1, when the light was in one position, P1, and to move a second lever, L2, when the light was in P2 (4 in. lower than P1). However, after training in learning to push L1 and L2 to the appropriate stimuli, test stimuli were interspersed, these test stimuli, of course, differing in position from P1 and P2. Test stimuli whose positions were between P1 and P2 were used, as well as test stimuli whose positions were above P1 and below P2. Given a large number of test trials at a number of different positions, LaBerge could plot two gradients of generalization. The ordinate for one represented the number of times S responded with L1, with the positions of the training and test stimuli appropriately spaced (in inches) along the abscissa, and the ordinate for the other represented the number of times S responded with L2.

It should be noted that the procedure used by LaBerge represents generalization measured following a form of discrimination training. If only a *single* training stimulus had been used, with S instructed to respond *only* to the stimulus when in that position, it would be essentially the same situation discussed earlier in which lights were spaced along a horizontal spatial dimension with S trained on the center light. For reasons we will note later, the generalization gradients resulting from the use of a single training stimulus will not be expected to have the same shape as those resulting from two training stimuli; the latter will be steeper.

Generalization of suppression. It would appear reasonable to expect that if S is taught not to respond in the presence of a given stimulus, this teaching being helped along by use of shock, tests for responding in the presence of stimuli similar to the CS ought to produce a gradient in which the frequency of response becomes greater as the test stimuli are further and further removed from the training stimulus. This expectation is borne out, and we will use a study by Desiderato (1964) as an illustration.

Hungry rats were taught first to press a bar to receive food. Then they were trained on a variable-interval schedule so that for a press, food pellets were delivered each minute, on the average, but the interval varied from less than 1 sec. to 419 sec. This schedule resulted in the rat's pressing regularly and with little extinction even over fairly long intervals. After performance reached a stable level, E introduced a 60-sec. tone, at the termination of which he gave a shock. The purpose of this was to reduce bar pressing during the 60-sec. interval that the tone was on. This training was continued until a substantial reduction in bar pressing occurred. Furthermore, the shock was on an intermittent schedule; sometimes it followed the tone, and sometimes it did not. The purpose of this was to prolong extinction of suppression during the tests for generalization, making use, therefore, of the law which states that intermittent reinforcement is followed by slower extinction than is continuous reinforcement.

On test trials S was presented not only the tone used in suppression training but also tones differing in frequency from the training stimulus. The five tones used in tests were 670, 1000, 1500, 2280, and 3500 cycles per sec. Actually, half the rats had 670 as the training stimulus, and, half, 3500, but for presentation here we will combine the results for both in terms of number of log units that the test stimuli were removed from the training stimulus, since the five stimuli are separated equally along a log scale.

The response measure was a derived one called a suppression ratio. If the animal made no responses during the presence of the training stimulus (or test stimuli) the ratio was 1; if the animal responded normally, the ratio would be zero. Tests were carried out over five days, with each of the five tones being used once each day. The results as plotted in Fig. 10-4 are the combined results for all tests. The gradient is sharp; the further the test stimuli were removed (in frequency) from the training stimulus, the lower the suppression ratio—the less the reduction in frequency of bar pressing. With the log scale the gradient is quite linear.

One of the persistent issues involved in the study of generalization is whether or not a gradient of generalization is found when discrimination training is not involved. Discrimination training means the reinforcement of responses to a training stimulus and nonreinforcement to a stimulus some distance removed on a common dimension from the training stimulus. We noted earlier that on the very first test trials when formal discrimination training was not used prior to the tests for generalization, the gradient is sometimes essentially flat, meaning that S responds to all of the test stimuli with equal frequency. But this is not always true. Yet, as others have pointed out, in situations where discrimination training is not used formally, there may in fact be discrimination training in a gross sense. If the CS is a tone, the lack of a tone between trials is, in this gross sense, discrimination training in that responses occur when the tone is present but not when it is absent. However this may be, all considerations insist that the gradient of generalization must be steeper following formal discrimination training than when not following such training. Tests for generalization around the training stimulus are a reflection of two gradients, namely,

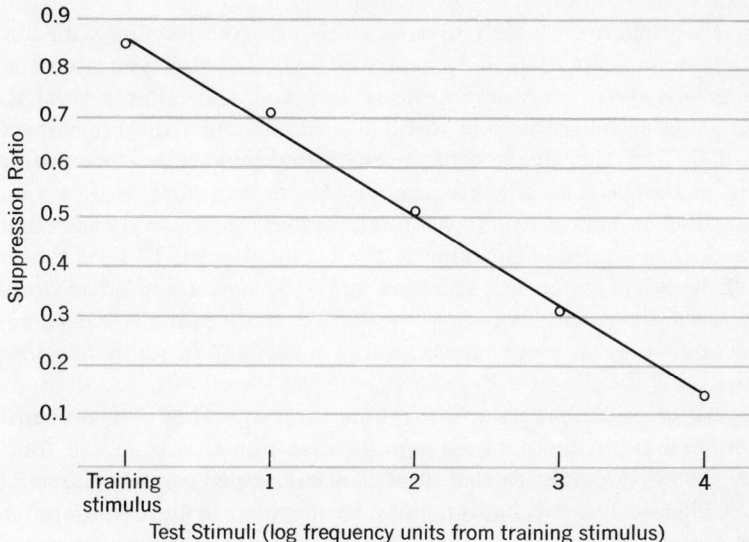

Fig. 10-4. Generalization of suppressed responding. Data from Desiderato (1964).

the tendency to respond to stimuli similar to the reinforced stimulus and the tendency not to respond to the nonreinforced stimulus and stimuli similar to it. That a number of experiments have found generalization gradients to be steeper following formal discrimination training than those found when formal discrimination training is not used is, therefore, to be expected.

       Semantic generalization. Again, visualize yourself as an S in the following situation. As E, I present to you a word on a screen, and after it has been there for a few seconds, I give you an uncomfortable but not painful electric shock. The shock causes you to emit certain responses. Some of these are obvious. If you are shocked on the hand, you will probably withdraw your hand; you may also squirm regardless of the point of application of the shock. In addition to these obvious responses, however, some that are not so obvious occur. Among these is a change in skin resistance, usually measured on the palms of the hands. This response, called the psycholgalvanic response or galvanic skin response, and often abbreviated either as PGR or GSR, has frequently been used in conditioning studies. Simply speaking, change in the skin resistance results from changes in palmar sweating and so changes the resistance to a subthreshold current being passed through the hand from one electrode to another. This change in resistance is measured by a galvanometer.

The PGR has been widely used in studies of conditioning with human Ss. In the present situation, the chances are good that if you are shocked when a given word is flashed on the screen, you will, after several trials, begin to show a change in skin resistance merely upon the appearance of the word—before the shock occurs. This would be called classical conditioning of the PGR to a word stimulus. If we are going to test you for generalization of conditioning, we might present test words which have high and low similarity of meaning to the training word. Thus, if the training word were *cold*, one test stimulus might be *icy* and another *blunt*. If there is semantic generalization, your PGR is more likely to occur to *icy* than to *blunt*. If so, we might speak of it as a gradient of semantic generalization.

Results of such procedures have not always shown generalization (Feather, 1965), but there are enough positive results (e.g., Lang, Geer, & Hnatiow, 1963) to indicate that it will occur under appropriate circumstances. Either of two mechanisms may be involved in the appropriate circumstances. If during training the CS is *icy*, and if when *icy* occurs S implicitly responds with *cold*, *cold* as an implicit response may become a part of the CS. On a test for generalization when *cold* is actually presented, the CR should occur. Another mechanism, of the same type, has its locus of action on the test for generalization. Assume that *icy* was the CS but that it did not elicit *cold* implicitly during training. Assume further, however, that when *cold* was presented on a test trial it *did* elicit *icy* implicitly. Since the CR had been established to *icy*, it would be expected to occur when *icy* occurred implicitly.

The notion that generalization may be mediated by implicit verbal responses has also been applied to the situation where colors are stimuli (as discussed earlier). Assume that the training stimulus is green and that on test trials colors with wavelengths moving away from green are used. Thomas and Bistey (1964) obtained gradients of generalization of such nature that they could conclude generalization occurred when the test stimulus also elicits the response "green." This is to say that the generalized response was mediated through an implicit response to the test stimulus, the implicit response being the same as that which occurred to the training stimulus.

Failure

Occasional reports appear in which no evidence for a generalization gradient is found. For example, Jensen and Cotton (1963) used a procedure quite similar to that used by Grice and Saltz, as described earlier. Rats were trained to run down an alley in which a square white stimulus surrounded the food well. Tests for generalization were made with squares of different sizes. No evidence for a gradient was found on either the early trials, over 20 extinction trials, or by any method of selecting animals in terms of performance during acquisition. The authors were baffled since no apparent reason could be discovered for their failure versus others' success. But as we know by now, it is out of such puzzles, frustrating as they may be at the time, that discoveries of new relevant independent variables are made.

The "Use" of Generalization

The above samples have given us some notion of the different types of situations in which generalization is studied. Generalization is an empirical phenomenon just as any other relationship between a dependent and independent variable is an empirical phenomenon. This particular relationship happens to have a name, but this changes nothing. We have seen that the critical defining variable is some specifiable change between the training and test stimuli. The situations we have examined have been elementary in the sense that the change can be specified as occurring along a unitary dimension. However, it is quite possible to study the effects of a complex training stimulus (one with two or more identifiable components) and then test with changes along one or more of the dimensions. Therefore, we must not limit our thinking about generalization to elementary relationships between training and test stimuli.

The phenomenon of generalization, and of a generalization gradient, has widespread use in explanatory attempts of other phenomena. Essentially, this is a form of empirical extension or operational identification that we have previously discussed. These theoretical attempts may be supplemented by certain assumptions about the shape of generalization gradients, about the interaction of avoidance or negative gradients and positive gradients, or about addition or summation of gradients which overlap. Without considering in detail any of these theoretical attempts, let us sample a few of the phenomena in which generalization has been used as an explanatory notion.

Two-stage experiments. In a general sense, any time we study the effects of a change in procedure, we may wish to think of this change in terms of generalization, hence "explain" the behavior resulting from the change by generalization. This is to say, the moment a change in

instituted, the defining conditions for generalization are met.
extinction trials are started following acquisition, we have
hange in stimulation as a consequence of removing the UCS,
ent in performance may be expected because of this. We have
differences in extinction rate, following intermittent and 100
‿‿‿‿rcement, might be interpreted in terms of differences in amount
of change occurring between acquisition and extinction trials. Since intermittent reinforcement is more like extinction trials than is 100 percent reinforcement, there should be less generalization decrement in the former than
in the latter. (But we remember from the previous chapter that this does not
seem to be entirely responsible for the differences in rate of extinction.)

So, whenever a phenomenon is defined by a change in procedure for a
given group of Ss, we should be sensitive to the possibility that this phenomenon may in part at least be a manifestation of stimulus generalization.

Discrimination learning. In its simple form, discrimination
learning is learning not to generalize. If we reinforce a response to one
stimulus and do not reinforce (or punish) this response to a highly similar
stimulus, we could visualize the learning process as one in which not only
the span of the positive gradient to the reinforced stimulus but also the span
of the negative or suppression gradient must be narrowed. Obviously, we
will predict that the more similar the two stimuli, the slower the learning.
In fact, the procedure for establishing neuroses experimentally as evolved
by Pavlov was to start with an easily established discrimination and then
make the two stimuli more and more alike. For example, a discrimination
was first established between a circle and an ellipse, the latter being initially
very obviously an ellipse (to the E). Then the horizontal and vertical axes
of the ellipse were made more and more similar in length (thus making it
appear more and more like a circle). When the ellipse became very much
like a circle, discrimination broke down and the behavior of the animals
(dogs) suggested a neurotic-like breakdown.

Another phenomenon which may be studied following discrimination
training is known as *transposition behavior*. Suppose an animal is initially
presented two stimuli, perhaps a 40-watt light and a 60-watt light. These are
presented together, and the S must learn to respond to the 60-watt light
and not to respond to the 40. After this discrimination is established, a test
trial is given on which E presents the 60-watt light and a 100-watt light.
Which will the animal choose? Many studies have shown that the animal
will choose the 100-watt, and this is called transposition; the animal seems
to transpose his response to the brighter of the pair regardless of the absolute
intensity. It appears as if S has learned a relation (the brighter one is correct), and this rule is applied on the transposition test. However, some investigators have attempted to explain this in terms of an interaction between
positive and negative generalization gradients without, thereby, assuming
relational learning. (See a review by Hebert and Krantz [1965].)

Another type of discrimination problem in which generalization is assumed to play a decisive role is known as the *oddity* problem. In this situation S is presented three stimuli, two of which are alike, and one, different. The correct response is that of choosing the odd one, regardless of what the stimuli are. If there are two apples and an orange, the orange is correct; if there are two oranges and one apple, the apple is the correct choice. Needless to say, perhaps, relative to a simple choice situation, this presents a fairly difficult task and is not one that is usually presented to a rat. However, monkeys can solve such problems, and as we shall see, so can children.

In the study by Lipsitt and Lolordo (1963), two oddity problems were used, each problem being represented by three lights; red, green, and blue were used for the easy problem, and red, pink, and orange for the difficult one. The difficulty of the oddity problems, therefore, was manipulated by

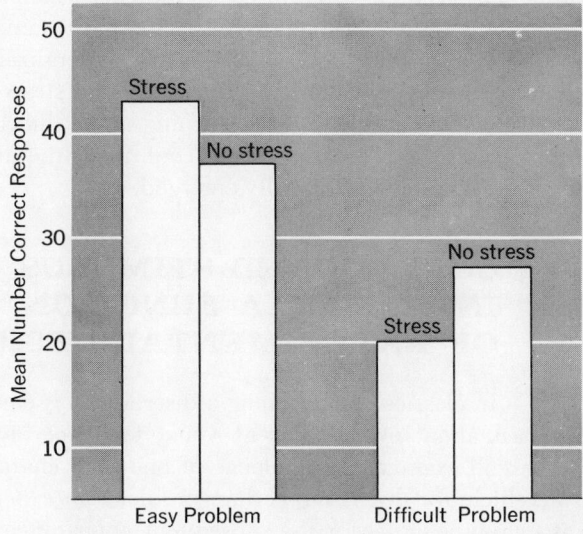

Fig. 10-5. Effect of stress on the learning of easy and difficult oddity problems. Data from Lipsitt and Lolordo (1963).

varying the similarity of the three lights. Generalization should be greater among the similar-colored lights than among the dissimilar ones. On any given trial S was presented three lights, such as two blues and a red; the odd one (red) was correct. On successive trials each color was correct equally often, and each position was occupied by the correct light equally often. On any given setting of three lights, S was allowed only one choice and was told whether he was right or wrong. A total of 54 trials was given, and the basic measure was the number of correct responses.

There were four groups of Ss, fourth-grade students. Two of the groups received 54 trials on the easy problem, and the other two, the same number on the difficult. In addition, members of one of the groups given each problem were put under severe time pressure to make their choices quickly on each trial. This technique was used to induce stress. We will recognize that this is the 2 x 2 design with which we are already familiar. The thinking behind the study was that stress would have a different influence on learning the two problems. More particularly, it was predicted that stress would facilitate learning of the easy problem but inhibit the learning of the difficult problem.

We will not consider the assumptions made by these investigators in arriving at these predictions. Actually, there are several ways of reaching the predictions, some of which involve assumptions about generalization and generalization gradients. The serious student may find it of value to try to construct a theory based on generalization gradients which will produce the predictions made by these investigators. That is, what assumptions could you make about the relationships between stress and generalization or generalization gradients which would allow you to deduce that stress would facilitate learning of the easy task and inhibit the learning of the difficult task? As may be seen in Fig. 10-5, the predictions were confirmed; the anticipated interaction between stress and task difficulty emerged.

CONDITIONED STIMULUS INTENSITY: A FUNCTION OF EXPERIMENTAL DESIGN

In classical conditioning a discrete CS is employed, and it is reasonable to ask about conditioning as a function of certain characteristics of the CS. We will examine the influence of one such characteristic, CS intensity, as a vehicle for discussing certain problems in experimental design. If the CS is merely a signal for the subsequent appearance of the UCS, its intensity should not be related to conditioning performance beyond the minimum intensity level necessary for it to be perceived by the organism. On the other hand, intensity might be related to learning in a more fundamental way—the CS may be more than a signal, with its intensity directly related to the rapidity of conditioning. Experimentation ought to be able to determine which of these two positions is most appropriate, but as we shall see, difficult problems arise in carrying out the research.

Response Strength Versus Associative Strength

Classical conditioning procedures most frequently used with human Ss involve the PGR or the eyelid reflex. We have already outlined the procedure for studying PGR conditioning, so we may note here the essential steps in eyelid conditioning. Eyelid conditioning represents a highly specialized area of research and requires considerable equipment for programming the stimuli and recording the responses. The UCS most commonly used is a puff of air directed at the cornea, a stimulus which invariably produces a closing of the eyelid. The CS is normally a weak tone or a weak light. The onset of the UCS follows the onset of the CS by approximately 0.5 sec. in the usual experiment since this interval is associated with optimal conditioning rate. Obviously, the CR is the closing of the eyelid, and if conditioning occurs, the lid will close before the onset of the UCS—the puff of air. Conditioning may be indexed over trials by an increase in the frequency of anticipatory closures, closures which occur after the onset of the CS but before the occurrence of the UCS.

One of the obvious problems is how to measure lid closure. It is sometimes done photographically; all events (onset of CS, lid closure, onset of UCS) for each trial are photographed in appropriate temporal order. More common, perhaps, is the use of mechanical devices for recording lid closure. To simplify somewhat, it can be seen that if a tiny thread is attached to the eyelid with paste, and if this thread is attached to a sensitive recording device, eyelid closure may be transmitted to a record sheet. This record would also show the onset of the CS and the UCS. Amplitude measures, too, may be obtained by measuring the amount of closure. However, the frequency measure is most common, and E will state precisely the amount of closure used as a criterion for calling a given response a closure response. It goes without saying that for all techniques S's head must be held in a fixed position.

The eyelid can be closed voluntarily, and it is to be anticipated that these voluntary closures are a source of irritation to E since he does not want to include them in his count of true CRs. Indeed, we might ask whether S *really* is conditioned or whether he just voluntarily closes his eye when the CS occurs since this would avoid the slight irritation caused by the puff of air on the cornea. However, a voluntary response can be distinguished from a true CR in the records. Several studies have shown that even if S is instructed to try to avoid blinking, he will still show an increase in the frequency of CRs over trials. Some Es use a ready signal with S instructed to blink voluntarily at the occurrence of this signal, a signal which may occur 2 to 3 sec. before the CS. This would eliminate some natural blinks which occur after the appearance of the CS and which might mask true CRs. As a further means of avoiding voluntary factors, E may give S another task to perform in order to hide the true purpose of the experiment. In one such approach (Spence, Homzie, & Rutledge, 1964) this task required S to try to predict on each trial of a series of trials which one of two lights would come on. By being told that the purpose was to study problem solving (which of the two lights would come on) under distracting circumstances, the S was led to believe that this task was the central one in the experiment. The distracting circumstances consisted of the usual events in eyelid conditioning—the CS followed by a puff of air. That such procedures may be successful is indicated by the report of one S given directly to the present writer. This S, when asked about what had happened in the session, described the problem-solving task and further reported that she thought she would have solved it had it not been for the fact that E kept trying to distract her by blowing a puff of air against her eye. We will conclude that the eyelid can be conditioned and that the major technical problems in measuring the conditioning have been handled.

We may now return to the problem of performing an experiment in which we vary the intensity of the CS. Suppose we use a tone of a constant frequency as the CS, with the intensity of the tone set at different levels for different groups. All groups are given the same number of trials, and we obtain the mean frequency of occurrence of CRs for each group. Finally, suppose we find that the greater the intensity of the CS, the greater the frequency of CRs. Are we to conclude that conditioning (associative strength) is a direct function of CS intensity? Probably not, for again we are faced with problems similar to those revolving around the learning-performance distinction discussed earlier. In this case the response strength due to nonassociative factors may differ as a function of CS intensity whereas associative strength or learning strength may not. To say this another way, CS intensity might cause a greater amplitude of response, but this may not indicate a greater strength of the association between the CS and the response. Since the amount of closure must reach a certain level before E will identify it as a CR, it follows that the greater the intensity of the CS (if related to magnitude of closure), the greater the number of responses which will be called CRs by E, even though the associative strength was the same for all levels of CS intensity. One of the better possible solutions to this problem was worked out by Grant and Schneider (1948). Because their reasoning is applicable to many similar problems in psychology, we will follow it in detail.

A possible solution. The problem is to separate the influence of temporary or nonassociative factors, factors which we will identify as influencing response strength, from factors influencing associative strength or true learning. In this particular case, performance measures obtained as a function of varying the intensity of the CS may include both changes in response strength and changes in associative strength. The solution proposed by Grant and Schneider involved the orthogonal design (with which we are already familiar) in which CS intensity was varied both during conditioning and during extinction. Grant and Schneider used four different levels of CS intensity; however, the route to the solution may be simplified if we speak of only two levels. Let us call these H and L, for high and low intensity. During training, half the Ss had H, half had L. For the extinction trials, each group was broken into two subgroups, one subgroup having H, the other, L. The matrix for the experiment for the four groups would appear as follows:

EXTINCTION

	H	L
H		
L		

TRAINING

Let us assume that all Ss (who were assigned randomly to the four cells) were given a constant number of training trials and 15 extinction trials, with the response measure the number of CRs on the 15 extinction trials. Grant and Schneider assumed that rate of extinction was a good index of associative strength developed during learning; the higher the associative strength, the slower the extinction. In terms of the response measure used, the greater the number of CRs given during extinction, the higher the associative strength (the slower the extinction). Associative strength can develop only during training trials; therefore, if there are differences in the row totals in favor of the H stimulus during training, it would mean that associative strength was developed to a higher level with the H stimulus than with the L stimulus. This would be true because, in summing across the two cells for each row, we are including both H and L stimuli during extinction, and thus the intensity during extinction does not enter differentially into the row totals. By the same reasoning, if there are differences in the column totals it would mean that intensity of CS influences response strength, for these sums "neutralize" differences due to CS intensity during the acquisition phase. Of course, it would be possible to get differences in both row and column totals, in which case, apparently, we would conclude that CS intensity influences both associative strength and response strength.

Unfortunately, this design may allow the differential effects of another phenomenon, generalization, to enter. If S had H during training and L during extinction, it would essentially be a generalization test. Or, to say this another way, we know that generalized CRs may extinguish more rapidly than original CRs, and differences in the cell means may reflect this. More particularly, the H-H group—those having high intensity both during training and during extinction—and the L-L group should show maximal generalization since they are tested on the stimulus on which they were trained; the H-L and L-H groups, on the other hand, should be somewhere on the generalization gradient, and their performances should be lower for that reason alone. However, if generalization occurs, a significant interaction in the extinction scores would emerge; H-H and L-L combined should be higher than H-L and L-H combined. This was the reasoning which Grant and Schneider brought to this difficult experimental problem.

Let us consider four idealized outcomes from this procedure, outcomes which are shown in the four panels of Table 10-1. The mean number of CRs

TABLE 10–1

FOUR IDEALIZED OUTCOMES FOR THE GRANT-SCHNEIDER DESIGN

See text for complete explanation

		Results			*Conclusions*

Results

		EXTINCTION			
		H	L	TOTALS	
TRAINING	H	12	12	24	
	L	6	6	12	
	TOTALS	18	18		

Conclusions:
1. CS intensity *does* affect associative strength
2. CS intensity does *not* affect response strength
3. No generalization

		EXTINCTION			
		H	L	TOTALS	
TRAINING	H	12	6	18	
	H	12	6	18	
	TOTALS	24	12		

Conclusions:
1. CS intensity does *not* affect associative strength
2. CS intensity *does* affect response strength
3. No generalization

		EXTINCTION			
		H	L	TOTALS	
TRAINING	H	12	6	18	
	L	6	12	18	
	TOTALS	18	18		

Conclusions:
1. CS intensity does *not* affect associative strength
2. CS intensity does *not* affect response strength
3. There is generalization

		EXTINCTION			
		H	L	TOTALS	
TRAINING	L	9	9	18	
	L	9	9	18	
	TOTALS	18	18		

Conclusions:
1. No affect of CS intensity on response strength, associative strength, or generalization

given during the 15 extinction trials is entered in each cell for each of the four groups. (These values are quite hypothetical.) In the first panel, it can be seen that the intensity of the CS during extinction (column totals) does not influence behavior, but intensity of CS during training does (row totals). The conclusion would be, therefore, that CS intensity influenced associative strength but not response strength. To the second panel we apply the same reasoning to reach a conclusion that only response strength was influenced; to the third panel, we reason that neither was influenced but that generalization occurred; and to the fourth panel, that CS intensity was not an effective independent variable and no generalization occurred. It is this fourth panel which represents the results of the Grant-Schneider experiment. Using four different CS intensities during training and during extinction (a total of 16 cells, hence 16 groups), they were unable to show any significant effect of CS intensity.

Some final comments should be made with regard to this design. As noted, it may be used to solve problems where transferlike designs are used and performance and learning distinctions are important. For example, it may be used to study the effect of magnitude of incentive as discussed in the preceding chapter; it will help answer the question of whether magnitude of incentive influences the strength of association or whether it merely influences performance. Yet, we should not leave the impression that such designs cannot yield ambiguities. Let us consider one such possibility for the outcome of the CS-intensity experiment. Suppose our values showed 15 in the H-H cell and 7 in each of the other three cells. Assume further that not only both main effects (column differences, row differences) but also the interaction were significant statistically. Such a result would hardly make sense in terms of the factors thought to be involved. The significant interaction would mean that generalization occurred, but the odd thing about it is that it occurred for H-H, not for L-L. As a matter of fact, if you try assigning various values to the cells so that both row and column differences are present, it is quite impossible to avoid a significant interaction that would *fail* to be a puzzle if the interaction is interpreted only as representing differences in generalization. Fine designs do not always solve our problems, but fine designs can often tell us where the problem lies.

A CS Intensity Effect

The Grant-Schneider conclusion that CS intensity was not involved in strength of conditioning was supported by other experiments and remained a firm conclusion until a discovery made by Beck (1963) suggested a hypothesis to Grice and Hunter (1964) which they set about to test. As a part of a larger design, Beck had two levels of CS intensity. However, both intensities were presented to the same S in an irregular order over a series of conditioning trials. The outcome of this procedure showed that CS intensity was directly related to the frequency of CRs. Thus, it appeared that a reasonable hypothesis to accomodate these findings, when compared with earlier findings that CS intensity had little if any effect, concerned the nature of the design. If a single S is exposed to different intensities during acquisition trials, the intensity function is sharp; if different intensities are given to different Ss by a random-groups design, little relationship between performance and CS intensity is observed. Grice and Hunter tested this proposition.

They used four groups of Ss for their eyelid-conditioning experiment. One group had a 50-db. tone as CS on all 100 training trials; a second group had a 100-db. tone on all trials. We may speak of these groups as having unmixed presentation of CS intensity. Two other groups had mixed presentations in which they received 50 trials with the 50-db. tone and 50 with the 100-db. tone, randomly ordered. In computing the results the Es determined the frequency of CRs to the 50-db. tone for one of these latter two groups and also determined the frequency to the 100-db. tone for the other. In each case the percentage of trials on which a CR occurred was calculated. The

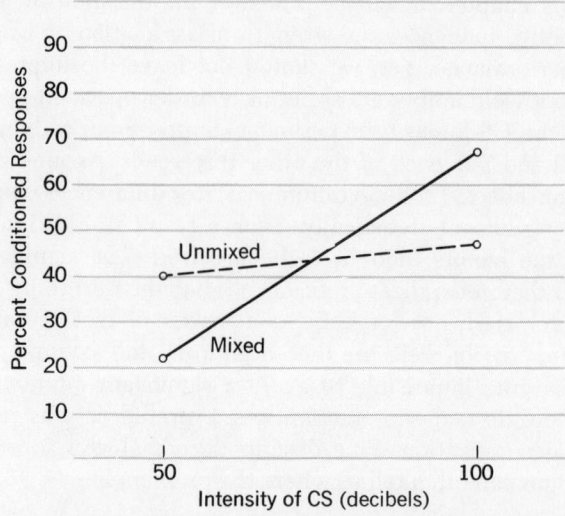

Fig. 10-6. The effect of CS intensity on conditioning performance as a function of mixed and unmixed presentation of stimuli during training. Estimated from Grice and Hunter (1964).

change to percentages makes all four groups equivalent, although mixed-presentation groups were involved in only half as many trials as were the unmixed-presentation groups. The results (percentage CRs over the last 60 training trials) are plotted in Fig. 10-6.

With unmixed presentation we see that there is only a slight effect of CS intensity, whereas for those Ss having mixed presentation, the effect of CS intensity is quite large, there being over 40 percent difference in the frequency of CRs. Although acquisition curves show that frequency of the CR increases over trials for the mixed groups for both the 50- and 100-db. stimuli, they increase at a greater rate for the latter. It is apparent, therefore, that we get two different laws relating CS intensity to conditioning performance, depending upon the nature of the design used. This is a striking illustration of the role of the design in determining laws. We should note that we are not dealing here with design errors; both designs are equally sound in that there is no confounding of variables. The two procedures simply yield different results. We will have occasion in later chapters to see how this may occur in other areas.

Two other matters should be mentioned with regard to the Grice-Hunter results. First, the performance differences in Fig. 10-6 cannot be attributed to differences in associative learning, for this design did not attempt to separate the associative factors from the nonassociative factors as was true in the Grant-Schneider procedure. The separation of these two possible contributors to the overall effects still needs to be handled. The second matter concerns factors which might produce the differences in the results emanating from the mixed and unmixed designs. We will only mention here that Grice and Hunter lean favorably toward an interpretation which stresses an adaptation-level approach, a concept which we discussed in an earlier chapter. With the mixed presentation of two stimuli, the adaptation level is somewhere between the two intensities, and with this as a reference point, each of the two stimuli provides considerable contrast. This interpretation obviously places the effect with mixed presentation on a relative basis and not upon the absolute intensities. One simple test of this would be a procedure wherein one group with mixed presentation is given 20- and 70-db. tones, and another, 50 and 100. Both should produce the same CS-intensity functions if absolute intensity is of little importance.

In concluding this section we should note that an effect of CS intensity has been demonstrated even with unmixed presentation for other tasks and organisms. For example, Kamin and Schaub (1963) studied the effect of CS intensity on suppression conditioning in rats. In suppression conditioning, it will be remembered, the rat is first taught to respond (in a Skinner box) to receive food and then is taught *not* to respond when a given stimulus is present. In the Kamin-Schaub study the intensity of this stimulus (white noise) was varied. The results clearly demonstrated that acquisition of the suppression response occurred more rapidly with the more intense stimulus. However, the Grant-Schneider type of design and analysis did not allow a definitive conclusion as to whether the effect was an associative effect or a response-strength effect, or both, although generalization differences were plainly evident during extinction. This is to say, the source of the performance differences could not be unambiguously identified.

THEORETICALLY SENSITIVE
ACQUISITION PHENOMENA

In the years immediately preceding and following World War II much of the energy devoted to animal experimentation was generated by desires to make crucial tests of opposing theoretical points of view. These theoretical points of view were general in the sense that they included statements about the critical factors involved in the formation of associations; they were not general in the sense that the white rat was the center of thinking. At the present time it is fair to say that these particular theoretical issues have to some extent lost their fervor-producing characteristics. Crucial experiments somehow never quite turned out to be crucial as the lack of precision in the theories allowed appreciable leeway in incorporating within them new phenomena which at first seemed quite incompatible with the theory; too, some of the strong personalities who produced the theories passed on. Whether or not a strong attachment to a theoretical position is a "good" thing or a "bad" thing is itself occasionally debated, but one fact remains, namely, that for a graduate student studying at a university where a particular theoretical position is espoused, the excitement may become heady. The interplay between the theory and the experiment has a certain elegance and, at the same time, an aesthetic quality that is not quite matched in other areas of human endeavor.

No experimental discipline proceeds without some theoretical orientation. Therefore, we may ask what characterizes the theoretical trends which are emerging as replacements for those which generated the experimental problems only a few years back. Three such trends may be noted. First, theories are being devised to account for a very limited number of phenomena. Although these theories may have their roots in the earlier, more general theories, they are applied only to certain aspects of learning. Thus, an investigator may spend many years attempting to understand how intermittent reinforcement retards extinction; another may concentrate on the role of motivation (whether it influences learning or only performance); another may work on factors involved in the development of secondary incentives. Each investigator has certain hypotheses of limited scope, and he has a laboratory; as he proceeds with his research, he modifies his hypotheses as demanded by the data, or he discards them as demanded. The propositions which remain relatively unscathed over the years he retains, and he may look around to see how they may be applied to other phenomena. This might describe the typical researcher in learning.

A second trend which may be noted is the development of statistical and mathematical learning theories. If there is an emerging replacement for the generalized theories of two decades ago, it probably lies here, although it seems too early to be confident of this prediction. At the present time these theories are being tested primarily on very simple phenomena, but they have within them the potential for wider application. Even so, they have already been applied to animal learning, to simple human learning tasks, and, in some cases, to concept formation. They have some very vigorous and able proponents so that the future of learning theory cannot help but be heavily influenced by them.

A third trend which has been increasing its scope for a number of years is the use of conditioning principles to explain a wide variety of what may be called personality mechanisms. In these mechanisms we would include reactions to conflict, the mechanisms of fear and the overcoming of fear, and certain psychoanalytic mechanisms such as displacement and masochism. Theorizing of this nature is, as we have seen, a form of empirical extension and has proven an extremely fruitful way of trying to understand behaviors that normally are thought of as being very complex. For a comprehensive view of this approach the student should refer to Miller (1959).

The fact remains that certain phenomena are more sensitive theoretically than are others in that they are more pertinent for the shaping of theoretical points of view or modifying those that exist. The effect of intermittent reinforcement during acquisition on the rate of extinction, as discussed in the previous chapter, is one theoretically sensitive phenomenon. In the present section we will consider others.

Most learning experiments with animals involve incentives or reinforcers. The rat runs down an alley and receives a piece of food or a sip of water; if he takes the correct turn in a T-maze he is also rewarded; if he makes an incorrect response he may be shocked. What role does the food or water or the shock play in learning? This has been, and remains, a critical theoretical issue. In order to teach an animal to perform with any degree of consistency, we must necessarily give him food or water or shock, and thus it might appear that these incentives are critically involved in the learning. But it is difficult to demonstrate this because of the natural confounding of the presence of reinforcers and learning in most experiments. How do we make an animal perform without giving him food? And if he does perform without apparent reward, cannot this be taken to mean that there must have been some reward that we as Es did not detect? It is difficult to produce a "pure" situation in which it can be said with considerable conviction that no reward was present. However, let us look at some of the situations which probably approach the ideal and then see if learning did occur.

Contiguous Conditioning

Brogden (1962) used kittens as his Ss and employed an E Group and a C Group. The basic equipment was a rotating cage, and the conditions were set up to see if the cage-turning response could be acquired without apparent reward. The CS was a 1000-cycle tone at 60 db. The cats were placed in the rotator and were tested initially to determine their reactions to the tone. On none of the tests did the animal start running in the rotator at the sound of the tone; therefore, it was concluded that there was nothing about the tone per se that would cause a cage-turning response. At this point the acquisition trials involved a waiting game. The E simply observed the kitten carefully, and in the natural course of events the animal would (for unknown reasons or because of unknown stimuli) start walking in the cage, thus turning it. The moment E observed this response he sounded the tone. This procedure continued until each kitten had accumulated at least 30 such trials. The kittens in the C Group were in the rotator for the same period of time and, of course, made a number of cage-turning responses, but at no time did E sound the tone. The critical stage, then, was the test stage during which E waited until the kitten had been inactive for at least 30 sec. and then sounded the tone. Would the kittens in the E Group make a cage-turning response at the sound of the tone? Did the pairing of the tone with the natural cage-turning responses result in conditioning such that the tone would now elicit the cage-turning response?

The answer according to Brogden's data is yes. Twenty test trials were given to the kittens in each group. Members of the E group averaged 3.46 cage-turning responses to the tone, members of the C Group, 0.58. It can be seen that the learning was not great, but, as Brogden points out, the temporal relationships between the tone and cage-turning were not conducive to much learning. We will remember that optimum conditioning occurs when the CS precedes the response to which it is to be conditioned. In the present study the tone actually followed the initiation of the response but clearly occurred while the response was in progress. Brogden concludes that the contiguous relationship between the tone and the response was sufficient to produce some learning. Is there some subtle incentive operating in this situation? Is there a secondary incentive of some kind involved? Brogden does not think so; he believes the learning occurred without reinforcing consequences.

Sensory Preconditioning

Sensory preconditioning has a fairly long history, but only in recent years have conditions evolved which allow the production of a stable phenomenon. The basic notion of sensory preconditioning is to present, over and over, two neutral stimuli together, for instance a tone and a light (in the presence of S of course). After many such presentations one of the stimuli, let us say the tone, is used as a CS in a conditioning procedure. After the CR is developed, test trials are given with the other stimulus, in this case, with the light. If the CR occurs, sensory preconditioning is said to have been demonstrated. Obviously, the appropriate control is the presentation of each stimulus alone—temporally separated—so that the two cannot be associated.

A discussion of just how or by what mechanisms sensory preconditioning may occur will be delayed until we have examined a particular experiment, since the results of this experiment will be of aid in conceptualizing what may be "going on." In this study by Wickens and Cross (1963), four groups of Ss were used. In the sensory-preconditioning phase these groups differed in the temporal relationships between the two stimuli, a light and a tone. These relationships are diagramed in Table 10-2. The light was always presented

TABLE 10–2

DIAGRAM OF THE TEMPORAL RELATIONS FOR A LIGHT (L) AND TONE (T) IN SENSORY PRECONDITIONING. ADAPTED FROM WICKENS AND CROSS (1963).

for 600 msec. for all groups, the groups differing in treatment only in the point of onset of the tone prior to the onset of the light. For Group 1, both came on simultaneously, hence both were on for 600 msec. For Group 2, the onset of the tone preceded the onset of the light by 100 msec., for Group 3, by 400 msec., and for Group 4, by 600 msec.

The Ss in each of the four groups were given 10 pairings of the light and tone, with irregular intervals separating the pairings. Following this phase, all Ss were given PGR conditioning with the light as the CS and a mild shock as the UCS. Ten such trials were given. Finally, tests for sensory preconditioning were made by presenting the tone for four trials without shock being given. The critical data concern differences among the four groups on the PGR on these four test trials. Over the test trials the PGR was greatest for Groups 2 and 3 and least for Groups 1 and 4. Thus, it appears that the temporal relationships obtaining between the two stimuli in the sensory-preconditioning phase is an important determinant of the amount of conditioning or association which occurs in this phase.

Why should these temporal relationships be so important? To understand this we need to have some notion of the events which may be occurring during the sensory-preconditioning phase, and to do this we have to broaden our conceptions of stimuli and responses. We think of an association as being established between a stimulus and a response. How, then, can we establish an association between two stimuli—between the light and tone? We don't. The association is not "out there" between a light and tone; it is, so to speak, within the organism. The light and the tone cause the organism to respond; in the simple sense this is what we mean by seeing and hearing. The light produces a seeing response, the tone, a hearing response. Furthermore, a response may serve as a stimulus for further responses, and this is often regarded as a response-produced stimulus eliciting another response. A skilled series of movements, as in typing or playing the piano, can be thought of as a series of responses producing stimuli producing responses producing stimuli and so on. This is to say, it seems reasonable that a response produces neural consequences which may be thought of as stimuli for further responding.

With the above notions in mind, we may guess about the internal events which led to sensory preconditioning and why the amount should vary as a function of the temporal relationships. When the tone precedes the light, we may have something like this:

$$\text{Light----}r\text{----}s\text{----}$$
$$\text{Tone----}r\text{----}s\text{----}$$

Note that the s (the stimulus properties of the response r) to the tone temporally just precedes the r to the light. Given this situation, an association may be established between the s to tone and the r to light, as follows:

$$\text{Light----}r\text{----}s\text{----}$$
$$\text{Tone----}r\text{----}s \;\nearrow$$

When the light is used as the CS for PGR conditioning, the events may be as follows:

$$\text{Light----}r\text{----}s\text{----PGR}$$

Then, on the test for sensory preconditioning, we have:

$$r\text{----}s\text{----PGR}$$
$$\text{Tone----}r\text{----}s \;\nearrow$$

This scheme may not be the appropriate one, but something like this must occur in sensory preconditioning. One point which may strain our credulity is having the stimulus properties of a response to tone elicit the response normally made to a light, for this is what the above scheme indicates is occurring in sensory preconditioning. However, even if taken literally there is evidence that such is possible. The extreme cases are called *synesthesia*, the most common form being colored hearing, in which visual and auditory responses become associated. A few people may have the entire piano keyboard associated with the color spectrum, but even those of us who do not, quite well understand what is meant by a blue note. However this may be, the above scheme requires only that the tone produce a response which in turn has stimulus properties which became connected to some response produced by the light.

We know that there are optimal relationships for establishing conditioning in the usual sense. Simultaneity of the CS and UCS is not a favorable condition, nor is too long an interval between the onset of the two a favorable condition. The optimal situation appears to be one in which the CS precedes the response to be conditioned by a very short interval. We presume that variation of the onset of the two stimuli in the above study varies the temporal relations of the s and r which are assumed to become associated in the sensory-preconditioning phase. It can be confidently predicted that had the tone been used as the CS in PGR conditioning, with the tests being made with the light, little or no evidence for sensory preconditioning would have been found, since backward conditioning rarely if ever occurs.

Whatever the mechanisms involved in sensory preconditioning, it is very difficult to identify primary or secondary reinforcers, and thus sensory preconditioning is a phenomenon which is difficult to handle within certain theoretical schemes where reinforcers are assumed to be fundamental in establishing associations. Wickens and Cross conclude that reinforcement is not involved in the sensory-preconditioning phase. Yet a good reinforcement theorist might find that the light or tone has slightly aversive properties so that cessation of it (or them) is reinforcing in the same sense that shock cessation is said to be reinforcing. So, conclusions from such experiments can never be completely definitive.

Stimulus Cessation as a Reinforcer

As indicated above, we might view reinforcement more broadly than merely obtaining food, cessation of shock, or relief from fear. What might appear to be neutral stimuli may have slightly aversive characteristics. The cessation of any stimulus, whether or not viewed as an aversive stimulus, might empirically be shown to be associated with the learning of the responses they follow. We may illustrate the problem by examining the results of a study by Cooper (1963).

The apparatus was a simple shuttle box, the two compartments separated by a 2-in. hurdle. The response to be learned was jumping the hurdle. No shock was used, no food was present, and the animals had free access to food and water in the home cages. The "reinforcing" stimuli were of three kinds. One was the vibration of the cage, another, a buzzer clamped to the outside of the box, and another, a light (7.5 watts) within each compartment. As in the Brogden experiment discussed earlier, E was to play a waiting game in presenting these stimuli; more particularly, when the animal jumped the hurdle naturally from one compartment to the other, the stimuli were to be presented. As a baseline, Cooper determined the natural level—the operant level—of hurdle jumping. To do this he used 20 trials of 1 min. each and determined the number of hurdle jumps and the latency of each. The latency was determined from an arbitrary point in time. Thus, E started a clock for the start of the trial. If the rat jumped the hurdle within 1 min., he recorded this as well as the latency—the time from the moment of starting the clock. After an irregular interval, varying from 50 to 70 sec., the clock was started again for the next trial. Thus, 20 trials were given in this manner to determine the number and latency of hurdle jumpings.

On the experimental days, the 1-min. trial procedures were used again. On these trials, however, as the clock started, the stimulus appropriate to the animal's group was also turned on. Thus, if the animal was in the light group, as a trial started, the lights in both compartments came on. If the animal jumped the hurdle within 60 sec., the jump was accompanied by termination of the stimulus, that is, the lights went off. If the animal did not jump within 60 sec., the stimulus and trial were terminated. A total of 20 such trials was given on each of five successive days, with the interval between trials averaging 60 sec. but varying from 50 to 70 sec.

There were seven different conditions, hence, seven groups of rats, making use of the three stimuli alone and in combinations (buzzer, vibration, light, buzzer and light, buzzer and vibration, vibration and light, and light and buzzer and vibration). The data are presented in terms of the mean latencies for the 20 trials. (We may presume that on trials in which S did not jump the latency was counted as 60 sec., although this is not stated in the report.) No data are given on the actual number of hurdle crossings within the 60-sec. trials, but it is reasonable to assume that the shorter the average latencies, the greater the number of jumps. The mean latencies for 100 trials for each of the seven stimulus conditions are presented in Table 10-3. Data on successive blocks of 20 trials show that most of the differences reflected in Table 10-3 occurred during the first 20 trials. From that point on the latencies were quite stable over the remaining 80 trials. Differences are large among conditions. The vibrator alone produced latencies that were almost the same as those obtained for operant level, which is to say that there is no evidence that the vibrator alone had any effect. This is not completely clear, however, since had operant level been measured over 100 trials corresponding to the 100 experimental trials, the latencies might have differed from those obtained in the single session of 20 trials prior to the experimental trials.

The data in Table 10-3 suggest that a compound stimulus is much more effective than is each element of the compound. The effects of the compounds represent approximately an addition of the effect of each element alone. The fact that this also holds for the vibration suggests that it too did have some effect.

TABLE 10–3
MEANS LATENCIES (SEC.) IN HURDLE JUMPING AS A FUNCTION OF SEVERAL STIMULUS CONDITIONS AND THEIR COMBINATIONS. DATA FROM COOPER (1963).

STIMULUS CONDITIONS	LATENCIES
Vibration	43.25
Light	31.09
Buzzer	28.02
Buzzer and vibration	15.77
Light and vibration	12.72
Light and buzzer	7.51
Light, buzzer, and vibration	5.27

It appears that the differences among the stimuli in this experiment provided some basis for learning differences. Each may have some aversive qualities so that jumping the hurdle terminated the stimulus and provided some reinforcement. However, there is no independent evidence that the stimuli have the aversive characteristics, and we are caught up in a circle. If we believe that learning requires reinforcement and if learning occurs, then we conclude that there must have been some reinforcement. On the other hand, the reinforcement theorist may request that an equally plausible alternative explanation be given for the learning observed, and this becomes difficult. We cannot simply say that an animal naturally avoids such stimuli; otherwise the avoidance would have been complete and immediate, and no learning would have occurred. A theory must have a way to get the animal to increase the frequency of the hurdle jump, and it must also account for the decrease in latency over trials. The assumption that the stimuli had aversive qualities would appear, at the moment, to be the simplest explanation of the fact that the animal made the jumps with greater than operant frequency, but the mechanisms for the increase in frequency with trials might be handled in several ways. For example, some would say that the result of the jumping is the removal of the slight fear or pain produced by the stimuli and that this removal is responsible for the development of the association. Some might say that given the fact that the animal jumps because of the aversive stimuli, the tendency to jump more frequently and with shorter latencies occurs because the stimuli present become associated with the jumping response by simple contiguity of the response and the stimuli. There are other possibilities; perhaps the stimuli increase the general activity level, which, in turn, results in more jumps because there is an accumulative effect of the repeated stimuli on activity level. It is very difficult to devise a situation which will eliminate all but one of the alternatives. We have reported this study in order to demonstrate that learning in considerable amounts will occur in situations where the reward or punishment is not obvious and where the level of learning also varies appreciably as a function of the nature of the stimuli involved.

Latent Learning

In its basic form, latent learning is learning which occurs without positive or negative reinforcers being present. As in the case of sensory preconditioning, experiments on latent learning represent attempts to see if learning will occur without reinforcers, secondary or primary. However, as will be demonstrated shortly, there are variants on the basic form of latent-learning experiments. We will attempt neither to describe the various situations used nor draw any conclusions about the influence of results on theoretical formulations. Kimble (1961) has an extended discussion of both. We will illustrate one set of procedures used to study latent learning when such learning is viewed as acquiring differential response tendencies without differential reward (Gleitman & Herman, 1962).

The apparatus was a T-maze, with one goal box painted white, and the other, black. The animals were given pairs of trials, differentiated by forcing or not forcing the animal to a particular side. On the first trial of each pair the animal was free to choose either side, and in whichever side he chose he found food. On the forced trial, the arm chosen on the previous trial was blocked so that the animal had to go to the goal box of the other arm, but here too, he found food. Thus, over a series of trials, the animal had equal experience and equal reward in both goal boxes.

Following training (10 trials to each goal box), the goal boxes were removed to quite a different spatial location where each animal was given two intermittent shocks in one goal box and food in the other. The question is, of course, which turn will the animal make when once again placed in the T-maze. On this test trial 71 percent of the 38 animals chose the arm to the goal box in which they had not been shocked. It appears, therefore, that the animals during the initial training had learned the positions of the black and white goal boxes even though such learning was not necessary to obtain the reward. When shocked in the white box, for example, pain became associated with white; on the test trial, therefore, the "knowledge" of the location of the black and white boxes was put to use, and the animal went to the black box.

By making certain assumptions (which we will not consider), theorists who hold that reward is fundamental in learning can handle certain latent-learning results. Perhaps it is true, as Kimble (1961) concludes, that the studies of latent learning, while not proving one theory and disproving another, have forced all theorists to make their theoretical thinking more and more refined. One consequence of this is that the positions have become less and less distinct. Still, a fundamental question remains: Is reward (in the sense of obtaining food or escape from pain) necessary for learning? The latent-learning experiments were at one time viewed as the vehicle by which this question could be answered once and for all; they are no longer so viewed.

Drive and Learning

In the general sense a reinforcement theorist holds that a positive incentive which the animal obtains following a response is in some way responsible for the learning that occurs. He may also hold that the cessation of an aversive stimulus (a shock) is also responsible for learning, but we will be concerned here only with the role of positive incentives. Undoubtedly, many psychologists are reinforcement theorists in the general sense. However, a learning theorist would not be satisfied with the general statement; rather, he would feel some responsibility for making assumptions concerning how the reward could result in learning.

Hull (1943) was a reinforcement theorist who assumed that drive or motivation was necessary before learning would occur and who also assumed that a reward produced learning because it produced a reduction in drive. One of the problems involved in testing whether or not drive is necessary for learning is getting the animal to perform in the absence of drive. Obviously, the animal must be exposed to all the stimuli of a situation if learning is to occur in the situation, but this exposure is difficult to produce if drive is lacking. N. E. Miller at Yale has been one of the most persistent workers in attempting to solve these problems in order to determine the roles of drive and drive reduction in learning. We report here one of the studies conducted in his laboratories, a study which appears to give a crisp answer to the question of whether or not drive is necessary for learning (DeBold, Miller, & Jensen, 1965).

Classical conditioning was used, in which the CR was a licking response. By operative procedures, a fistula (tube) was inserted through the rat's snout in such a way as to allow water to be injected directly into the mouth. The device was positioned so that the rat could lick the metal tip of the fistula and the frequency of these licks could be recorded. The CS was a buzzer, and 3 sec. after its onset a small amount of water (UCS) was injected into the animal's mouth. Naturally, the rat would lick (UCR) the point of the fistula from which the water had come. If conditioning occurs it will be shown by the licking of the fistula when the buzzer sounds and before the water is injected. The critical feature is that the stimulus events necessary for conditioning can be forced on the animal. Therefore, drive is not necessary to get the animal to expose himself to stimuli, and if learning occurs in the absence of drive it should occur here.

Training was conducted under four drive levels, but we will consider only two extreme conditions, namely, 22 hr. of water deprivation and satiation or zero drive. This latter group had free access to water during the 1-hr. period just prior to the conditioning session. Pseudoconditioning control groups were used in which the CS and UCS were given in a backward order.

A total of 120 conditioning trials was given, with 30 test trials (UCS omitted) interspersed. The high-drive group showed a marked increase in the frequency of licks over the 30 test trials; the satiated group showed no increase, and the relatively constant rate of licking was essentially the same rate as that shown by the control. However, perhaps the satiated animals did learn, but because of the lack of drive they did not perform the licking response with increasing frequency. Perhaps if the satiated animals had been made thirsty, they would have shown that they had learned the CR. These Es were prepared to handle this matter. On the day following the training trials, the drives for half the animals in each group were switched, and five test trials were given. If learning occurred for the satiated animals, it should be exhibited when these animals were placed under 22-hr. water deprivation. The results show that such learning was not exhibited—performance still remained at the level shown by the control animals. However, those animals trained under high drive and tested while satiated showed a large reduction in CR frequency, indicating that drive level is important for the performance of the CR.

These Es conclude that learning did not occur under conditions of zero drive in spite of the fact that the CS and UCS were paired for 120 training trials. Or, in terms of the concept used in the previous section, there was no latent learning in spite of the fact that the animals had been exposed to all critical stimulus events. To be fully convinced, a professional skeptic might insist upon one additional step, but it is a step that may be impossible to achieve. The animals under zero drive did perform the licking response during training, but at a very low frequency level. What would have been the outcome had an increasing rate of frequency with trials been forced on these animals, a rate increase corresponding to the one shown by the deprived group as they exhibited learning? Following such treatment would the zero-drive animals show no evidence of learning when switched to a deprived condition for test trials? During the conditioning trials as given, the two groups of animals differed on two factors, drive level and number of licking responses emitted. Which difference is responsible for the failure to show conditioning in the zero-drive group?

Perceptual Learning

Perceptual learning is learning which occurs without S's overtly making the response to be learned. One way of studying perceptual learning is by using curare, a drug which totally immobilizes the skeletal musculature so that the animal cannot respond. While immobilized the animal is given a series of conditioning trials, perhaps shock avoidance to a given CS. Now, of course, the animal does not avoid since he cannot do so while under the influence of the drug. However, following a number of training trials, the animal is allowed to recover from the effects of curare and is tested again. Has he learned in spite of the fact that he could not respond? The answer is yes; the animal does not have to make the instrumental response (which demonstrates that learning has occurred) in order for learning to occur. Under the influence of curare the animal will even learn to discriminate between two stimuli (Solomon & Turner, 1962).

Another technique for studying perceptual learning is characterized by just a bit of the comic. Consider a multiple-unit maze which the animal is to learn. We want to see if he can acquire information about the maze without allowing him to run through it. What do we do? We haul him through the maze and reward him in the goal box. If learning occurs this should be evident in the subsequent performance when he himself must locomote through the maze, the performance being compared with that of a control animal which had not received the free rides. There are reports of positive results in the literature. For example, Dodwell (1964) carried the rats on a trolley just above the water of an eight-choice water maze. Their subsequent swimming performance was better than that of a control. In another case (Schaeffer, 1964), a simple Y-maze was used. The rat was held snugly in a small restraining cage with just his head sticking out. However, the cage was stationary, and the maze was pulled so that the animal was rewarded in one arm and not the other. Tests showed that some learning had occurred.

That a rat will learn a maze by being hauled through it may or may not appear striking, depending upon one's theoretical dispositions. However this may be, we must sound a warning about striking results or results which may place a strain on one's credulity. It is, perhaps, understandable why investigators may not submit negative results (no differences in behavior as a function of treatment differences) for publication. Furthermore, it is understandable why editors may choose not to publish experiments with negative results which are submitted to them. Limited space and availability of scores of manuscripts with positive results may justify the policy of not accepting experiments with negative findings. Nevertheless, these filtering mechanisms may result in some undesirable consequences. We cannot tell, for example, how many experiments have been performed in which an animal was hauled through a maze and no effect on subsequent behavior was noted. We are thus partially deprived of information which in the long run will be necessary to have—information about conditions under which a phenomenon does and does not occur. Publication of positive findings tells us the conditions under which a phenomenon does occur, but the failure to publish negative results does not allow us to tell under what conditions the phenomenon will not occur.

Furthermore, we know that significant differences between two groups will occur with a certain frequency as a consequence of sampling error. One significant difference in twenty, we say, may be attributed to sampling error rather than to a true effect of an independent variable. Therefore, if there is a bias *for* publishing positive results and *against* publishing negative results, the published literature must carry positive chance findings with a frequency that is greater than the frequency of chance positive findings expected by sampling theory. In short, the published literature must lead to the conclusion that there are more relevant independent variables than in fact is true. Of course, in the long run, any experimental discipline will correct itself by insisting upon replication of its findings. The failure to make public negative results simply slows down the correction process.

It should be stated that the above comments about negative results do not imply that an animal does not learn a maze by being hauled through it. The rather striking results of such experiments were merely used as an occasion to bring up the implications of loss of negative findings.

EXTINCTION AND RELATED PHENOMENA

It is perhaps natural for us to think of extinction initially from a common sense point of view. An animal has been running down a straight alley for a series of trials and has always found food in the goal box. When the extinction trials are begun, he no longer finds food in the goal box. Why should the animal continue running when the act of running is no longer followed by food? To say that the fact of extinction squares with common sense does not in any way explain extinction. Explanation requires that we try to understand the mechanisms which produced the cessation of running. Over the years at least four different mechanisms have been proposed to account for extinction.

1. Extinction may be viewed as a passive process in which the response gradually weakens and eventually dies out.

2. Extinction may be viewed as an active process in which a new response is acquired. If nothing else, this new response could be said to be learning not to respond.

3. Extinction has been said to result from the buildup of an inhibitory process such as reactive inhibition.

4. Extinction is related to the frustration or the emotional effects which occur when the animal, expecting food, no longer finds it. Further elaboration is required to show how expectations are acquired and how extinction could result when these expectations are not fulfilled.

None of the four positions is completely satisfactory, primarily because none can account for all of the facts associated with extinction. The general belief at present seems to be that a satisfactory explanation will have to include at least two independent mechanisms or processes, but just what they will be, or how they will be coordinated, is quite undecided. Theorizing about extinction is troubled in part because, as we shall see, it is difficult to state a simple set of empirical laws relating extinction to various independent variables.

Level of Acquisition and Extinction

It would seem reasonable to expect that the greater the number of acquisition trials, the slower the extinction. Indeed, such a relationship had for many years been accepted as a straightforward, uncomplicated relationship. The reasoning behind the Grant-Schneider design, as discussed earlier in this chapter, assumed a direct relationship between number of acquisition trials and number of trials to extinguish. At the present time the empirical picture is thoroughly confused. (See Sperling [1965] for a review.) The particular relationship between acquisition level and extinction rate seems to vary as a function of the nature of the task. For a simple instrumental-conditioning situation, such as the Skinner box, there is replicated evidence that the greater the number of acquisition trials, the slower the extinction. Recently, however, just the opposite results have been reported for the straight alley (e.g., Siegel & Wagner, 1963; Madison, 1964). In certain discrimination tasks the relationship is complex; the time to extinguish first increases and then decreases as the number of acquisition trials increases (D'Amato, Schiff, & Jagoda, 1962). Since the relationship appears to depend upon the nature of the task used, and since task differences must reflect the learning of different habits, the analytical problems facing investigators would appear to be centered in the nature of the habits involved.

Suppose we train a rat initially to make a right turn in a T-maze and then subsequently switch the reward to the left goal box. In effect, the animal must extinguish the right-going habit and replace it with a left-going habit. It would seem that the rate of learning the second habit would be influenced by the number of reinforced trials given in learning the first habit. Again, however, the findings do not yield a consensus. All three possible outcomes have been reported; many trials given in learning the first habit have, when compared with few trials, resulted in (1) faster learning of the second habit, (2) no difference in learning the second habit, and (3) slower learning of the second habit (Paul, 1965; Sperling, 1965). Certainly this puzzling state of affairs is closely related to the conflicting results on extinction as a function of number of training trials, and when one puzzle is unraveled the other will be also. But until this is accomplished, it is a little difficult to say what a theory of extinction must account for when it must deal with the relationship between level of acquisition and rate of extinction.

Latent Extinction

The operations for latent extinction require that members of the E Group be placed directly in the goal box for a period of time prior to the initiation of regular extinction trials. The members of the C Group are not given these placements. If, on the regular extinction trials, extinction occurs more rapidly for the E Group than for the C Group, latent extinction is demonstrated.

The studies of latent extinction are nearly unanimous in showing a latent-extinction effect. The magnitude of the effect has also been shown to vary in an expected way as a function of certain variables. For example, we would expect that the greater the number of placements of the animal in the goal box prior to the regular extinction trials, the greater the amount of latent extinction; or the longer the animal remained in the goal box for each placement, the greater the effect anticipated. Both expectations have been supported (e.g., Thomas, 1958; Dyal, 1962). At the same time, however, the magnitude of the maximal effect obtained has not been great in an absolute sense, and in some cases peculiar effects have been noted. For example, in the Dyal study, maximal effects occurred on extinction trials 1 and 2; after that point the control and experimental groups were equivalent, and the equivalence was, in part, accounted for by the fact that the performance of the experimental animals actually got better (reverse extinction).

Spontaneous Recovery

Spontaneous recovery (if it occurs) follows extinction. The necessary operations require only that an interval elapse between the last extinction trial and a test, the length of the interval being longer than the intertrial interval used between extinction trials. If performance is better than it was on the last extinction trial, spontaneous recovery is demonstrated. A systematic study would, of course, vary the length of the interval between the end of extinction and tests for spontaneous recovery, with different groups being used for each interval. Spontaneous recovery is presumed to increase as the interval increases.

It can be seen that spontaneous recovery should tell us something about the factors involved in extinction. For example, if extinction results from the accumulation of reactive inhibition, and if the inhibition dissipates with rest, spontaneous recovery is explained. If whatever produces extinction is said to be forgotten over time, spontaneous recovery would follow. So it would seem that laws governing spontaneous recovery would be important sources of inference concerning the processes involved in extinction. However, there are not a great many studies available. A study of spontaneous recovery requires extended work. The E has to take the animals through

not only an acquisition period (after all of the various pretraining pr[
dures), but also an extinction period before he reaches the point where
obtains data relevant to spontaneous recovery.

Bar pressing. Ellson (1938) gave four groups of rats 30 reinforcements in a Skinner box and then an extinction period which continued
until the animal failed to press the bar during a 5-min. period. This first
extinction period averaged 50 presses. A second extinction period was given,
but the groups differed in how soon it was given following the first extinction period, the intervals being 5.5, 25, 65, and 185 min. The index of spontaneous recovery was the number of presses to extinguish to the same criterion
as that imposed for the first extinction. The results, shown in Fig. 10-7, indicate that the longer the interval, the greater the number of trials required
to extinguish. With the longest interval (185 min.), approximately 25 trials
were required to meet the extinction criterion, half as many as were required
for the first extinction.

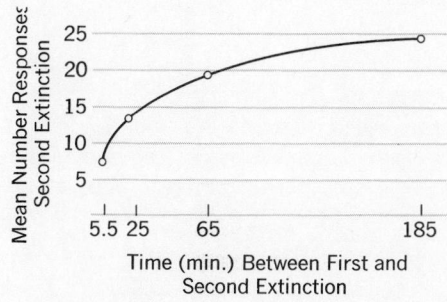

**Fig. 10-7. Spontaneous recovery as a function of time following
extinction. Data from Ellson (1938).**

T-maze. In a study by Cotton, Jensen, and Lewis (1962),
100 rats were taught initially to take the arm of the T-maze opposite to the
preferences shown on pretraining trials. After 30 acquisition trials, 30 extinction trials were administered. At the end of acquisition the animals were
running at a speed of approximately 40 in. per sec., and choice behavior
was nearly 100 percent correct. At the end of extinction the speed was
approximately 10 in. per sec. At this point the 100 animals were divided
into five groups of 20 Ss each, and tests for spontaneous recovery were made
at five different intervals, 0 min., 10 min., 3 hr., 1 day, and 1 week.

The first test trial after the interval was used to measure spontaneous
recovery. The speed scores for this trial are plotted in Fig. 10-8. Statistically speaking, only the change in speed from the zero interval to the

other four is significant as the four do not differ among themselves. Thus, all spontaneous recovery seemed to have occurred within 10 min. It will also be noted that at maximal recovery the speed was approximately 20 in. per sec., half the speed shown at the end of acquisition.

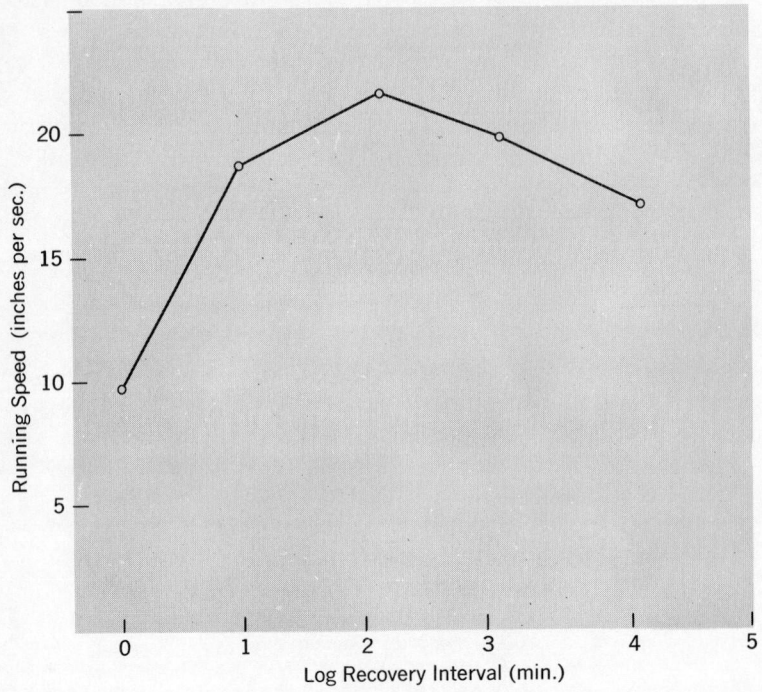

Fig. 10-8. Spontaneous recovery as a function of the length of interval between extinction and the recovery test. Data from Cotton, Jensen, and Lewis (1962).

The turn data give no evidence for spontaneous recovery. On the first test trial none of the groups differed from chance (50 percent). If spontaneous recovery occurred, the frequency of choice of the correct response should have been directly related to the length of the recovery interval. Indeed, there is some evidence for forgetting in the data. These Es gave 30 reacquisition trials following the initial test for spontaneous recovery, and the trends indicate that the longer the spontaneous-recovery interval before the 30 reacquisition trials, the fewer the number of correct turns made. It may be, therefore, that speed measures (running speed or rate of bar pressing) are sensitive indexes of spontaneous recovery whereas correctness of response is not.

Failure of Extinction

Finally, we may note that under certain training conditions habits can be established which give no sign of extinction over several hundred trials. The conditioning procedure must involve an extremely strong shock as the UCS in an avoidance-conditioning procedure. A CS is used, followed shortly by the very strong shock, which the animal may escape by jumping a hurdle. Perhaps only a few trials are needed before the animal jumps the hurdle and thus avoids the shock. Once he does do this, the situation represents the procedures for extinction since the UCS is not administered. It would seem, therefore, that after the animal jumped a few trials he would start showing a longer latency and after a few more trials simply would not jump when the CS was presented. This does not usually happen. Even while successfully avoiding the shock, the latency of the jump may continue to decrease over many trials. Extinction may never occur in some animals; several hundred trials have been given with the animals showing no signs of extinction. Traumatic avoidance learning, as it is often called (Solomon & Wynne, 1954), seems almost completely resistant to extinction.

TWO OTHER CONDITIONING-LIKE PHENOMENA

Probability Learning

Assume that you are the S in the following situation. Facing you is a panel on which there are two lights, one to the left (L) and one to the right (R). As a part of the instructions, E tells you that this is a guessing game. At a given signal on each trial, you are to guess which one of the two lights will come on and, over the series of trials, to guess as accurately as you can. On the initial trials, your responses will indeed be guesses, tempered by any bias you may have for one light over the other. In this experiment E has programmed the lights so that the L comes on for 75 percent of the trials and R, for 25 percent. Within this restriction, the ordering is random.

Let us presume that you, and a large number of other Ss, are given 100 trials; we determine the percentage of Ss choosing L and the percentage choosing R on each successive trial. If we plot the results, they would appear similar to those shown in Fig. 10-9. Initially, assuming no bias, each light has a 50-50 chance of being chosen. But as trials continue, there is a noticeable tendency to choose L more frequently than R, and after still more trials percentages level off at a point that represents almost exactly the true environmental frequencies—the relative frequencies programmed by *E*. This fact is sometimes called *probability matching*, and such a simple procedure has served as a starting point for a rather large number of studies appearing in the past 15 years, studies which in the aggregate are spoken of as dealing with probability learning.

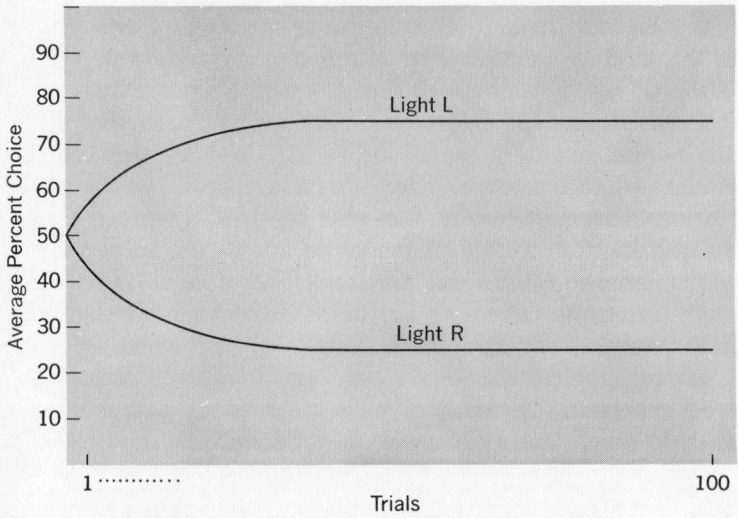

Fig. 10-9. Hypothetical results of a light-guessing experiment in which the left light (L) comes on 75 percent of the time and the right light (R), 25 percent.

The analogy between probability learning and conditioning is fairly straightforward. The signal to make the guess on a given trial can be likened to a CS; the choice is the response, and if you have made the correct response, you are presumably reinforced for choosing it when the light does in fact come on. But this may be no more than an analogy, and we will not pursue the matter more deeply. (See Estes [1964], who *has* pursued the matter.) The area of probability learning has come to stand on its own results and procedures, for it has overtones relating to conditioning, to psychophysical judgments, to gambling behavior, and to problem solving. To a large extent the recently developed mathematical learning theories have had their roots in the results of simple probability-learning experiments.

A first glance at the probability-learning situation might elicit, "Well, once the experiment has been done, what more is there to do?" In answer, we might inquire about variables related to the learning. A few possibilities may be mentioned, without citing particular studies but calling upon Estes' summary as a source of information. Two alternatives make the situation simple, but there is nothing magical in two. Three, or four lights, or 10 lights might be used. However, in all cases we should be aware of a certain problem of method. It will be remembered that in the discussion of generalization, we presented a study in which S guessed whether or not a given light in a series of lights, symbolizing horses, would win a race. Different lights were assigned different probabilities of winning in a situation that was quite comparable to probability learning. But we saw that horses which won infrequently but which were spatially contiguous to a horse that won frequently were judged to win more frequently than they did. If, then, in a probability-learning situation we are interested in the preciseness of probability matching over a series of trials, we have to balance out any differential effects of generalization by systematically changing the programmed frequencies on each light for various subgroups of Ss. With three or more lights, each light should be used equally often for each frequency when all Ss are considered. For example, if we have three lights and program .80, .10, .10 proportions, three subgroups of Ss should be used in which, viewing from left to right, one has the above order, another, .10, .80, .10, and a third, .10, .10, and .80. It would be of some interest to examine the results for each subgroup separately. If generalization is occurring in the first and third subgroups, we would clearly expect the "outside" light with the .10 proportion to have a lower-guessed proportion than the light with the same objective proportion that is contiguous to the .80 light.

If we use three lights with proportions of perhaps .70, .15, and .15, the guessing frequency for the most frequent light tends to run somewhat above the true frequency, perhaps as much as 5 percent, if trials are continued over a long period of time. Just why this happens is not clear; descriptively, it is as if there is a contrast effect between the frequencies which spread them apart; the most frequent one is guessed more frequently than it should be for perfect probability matching, and the two infrequent ones are guessed less frequently. One might try varying this three-light situation by instructing the S that he must consider the two infrequent lights as if they were one (as if he were to sum their frequencies), but that he must make independent guesses for each.

The plot in Fig. 10-9 is a smooth curve. If the random order of the two lights were different for each S, a smooth curve would be expected. However, if all Ss are given the same random order, there would probably be clear peaks and valleys, implying that on particular trials many Ss behaved the same way, choosing, for example, the same light, as if this particular trial had some general significance. Why should this be? Again, we must remember earlier discussions. If we flip an unbiased coin several times, and if it shows heads on five successive trials, we have a strong tendency to predict that it will show tails on the following trial. This occurs in spite of the fact that we know that each flip is independent of the previous ones and that on any given flip the probability of a head (or a tail) is .50. We saw how this might operate to bias responses in psychophysical judgments. The same bias has been shown to operate in probability learning. If S is on a .75-.25 schedule, and if the left light has come on 10 times in a row, it is almost a sure bet that he will guess that the right one will come on in the following trial. Since most Ss will "fall" for this, we would expect the .75 curve to show a sharp drop on that trial and the .25 curve to show a peak.

There are a number of other variables that can be and have been manipulated. We might give intermittent reinforcement (tell S the "correct" light on only 50 percent of the trials) and study both acquisition and extinction, just as we do in the usual conditioning study. Instructions have been shown to influence the choice behavior. If S can be instructed in a way that will get him to maximize the number of correct choices over a series of trials, his choice should be the most frequent light on every trial (after he discovers which one is the most frequent). If one were to be paid $1 for every correct choice, and if the proportions were split. .80-.20, we know we would maximize our "take" by guessing the left light on every trial. It apparently has been almost impossible, however, to get Ss to do this with 100 percent frequency; it is as if we like to gamble on the "long shot" once in a while.

Verbal Conditioning

Studies which fit under the general heading of verbal conditioning have certain similarities to probability learning. Again, let us presume that you are an S. As E, I tell you that I am going to present to you a series of cards, each card representing a trial. On each card are two numbers, clearly separated, one being a two-place number and the other, a three-place number. You are asked to choose either of the two numbers. If you choose the two-place number, I say, "Good"; if you choose the three-place number, I say nothing. Over a series of trials you might be expected to show a gradual increase in the frequency with which you choose the two-place number.

To say "Good" may seem a little obvious as a reinforcer, so I might turn a light on when you choose the two-place number and let it remain off when you choose the three-place; or I might say "Uh-*huh*" when you choose the two-place number. In addition, the stimulus cards might be more subtle. I might have two words on the card, one of which is a first-person pronoun (*I* or *me*) and the other, a third-person pronoun (*he* or *they*); I reinforce you for choosing the first-person pronoun. As another alternative, the card might contain an adjective and a noun, and the choice of the adjective would always be reinforced. As still another alternative, you might be instructed to emit words at a steady but specified pace, and each time you emitted a plural word it would be reinforced. In this case the question is whether or not you will increase the frequency of plural words as a result of the reinforcements. It is this type of procedure, more than the others noted, which has given the name *verbal* conditioning to the area of research.

It is perhaps not necessary to include the usual reminder that increases in frequency of the chosen class of words must be assessed against any changes in frequency shown by a control group, a group which is not given any form of reinforcement.

What are we dealing with in the above procedures? Basically, it is a problem-solving situation if E assumes that the so-called reinforcers (and a great many more have been used than those mentioned above) are interpreted by S as indicating correctness—as providing knowledge of results. It then becomes a matter of S's trying to discover what characteristic or characteristics of the stimuli E is calling correct. In the case of the illustration of two numbers given on a card, this may become apparent very quickly. In the case where plural nouns are reinforced, the discovery may not occur so quickly. However, these types of experiments have not been viewed as problem-solving situations by many investigators. Instead, they have been viewed as simple discriminative-conditioning procedures in which S is reinforced for making a response to one class of materials and not making the response to another class. There is still nothing unusual or unexpected about his conception until it is also reported that S may be quite unaware not only of what he has learned, but also of the fact that he has learned. It is reported that S does not state that he discovered that E said "Good" every time a plural was emitted; he did not decide that plurals must be the responses E wanted. It is as if learning, as measured by conventional standards, was observed but S could not report a principle for classifying the stimuli presented him and gave no indication that he had interpreted the buzzer, the "Good," or the "Uh-*huh*" as indicating a correct response.

The basic elements of the procedures have been extended to a wide variety of situations, both in the laboratory and in more naturalistic settings. Here is a procedure which *might* result in the conditioning of a friend during a period of conversation. Every time he uses a sentence in which "I" appears, you nod or smile; and you never nod or smile when he uses a sentence in which the word "I" does not occur. The expectation is that your friend will show an increase in the frequency of use of sentences in which "I" occurs.

You might also try to condition a response that is less directly tied in with the conversation. For example, assume you nod or smile every time S scratches his head. The rate of head-scratching may increase appreciably over time. There are unwritten reports of such types of conditioning which are rather dramatic, and there are a few that are written. For example, Verplanck (1955) reports that Ss in normal conversation can be caused to increase their frequency of statements of opinion if E gives some form of approval for each opinion and does not reinforce conversational units which do not include opinions.

There is apparently considerable experimenter skill involved in carrying out such procedures successfully. Verplanck (1956) has given in considerable detail the particular techniques which appear most successful, and his work may be consulted for these details. There are, furthermore, two fairly recent summaries of the literature on the topic (Krasner, 1958; Salzinger, 1959); and Postman (1962a) has viewed the phenomenon in the broader context of the role of reinforcement in general.

One of the central issues in current research is whether or not S *does* become conditioned without being aware of the class of responses to which he is responding with greater and greater frequency. Of course, the studies dealing with this problem are of the formal laboratory type and have used situations similar to those discussed early in the section (e.g., giving plural nouns) rather than those dealing with motor behavior (e.g., head-scratching). Recent reports (e.g., Spielberger & Levin, 1962; Dulany & O'Connell, 1963) produce results which throw considerable doubt on the proposition that the learning occurs without awareness of the principle involved. However, specifying degree of awareness is a tricky matter, and we know that people do solve problems without being able to tell how they solved them.

It is probably only proper to introduce a word of caution about verbal conditioning. The present writer has had a number of people tell him that they have been unable to produce conditioning in some of the situations reported above. The writer has never had much "luck" with it when applied by the students in his experimental course. To study a variable which may influence the amount or rate of verbal conditioning, one first has to devise a situation in which it will consistently occur; and to make it a situation which is not simply problem solving, we want to use one of the more ambiguous situations described above, where the response class is not obvious and where the reinforcement is not obviously indicative of correctness. Yet, to repeat, there seems to be considerable experimenter skill involved in producing the phenomenon, and perhaps the present writer has not been able to acquire the skill.

SUMMARY

This chapter continued the study of procedures used in conditioning and the study of phenomena emanating from the conditioning laboratory.

In studying generalization we noted the problem of obtaining equal units across modalities and how this problem may prevent meaningful comparisons of the shapes of generalization gradients. Several studies which have demonstrated generalization gradients were reviewed, studies which included physical scales for relating the stimuli (size, space, color) and studies which did not involve physical scales (semantic generalization). It was also seen that inhibitory responses will generalize in much the same manner as positive responses. Generalization involves a change in the stimulus conditions. Therefore, it was noted that many phenomena which are based on two-stage experiments may use generalization as an explanatory device.

The role of conditioned-stimulus intensity was examined as a means of discussing certain design problems. When the intensity of either the conditioned stimulus or the unconditioned stimulus is varied, a problem of interpretation arises. Changes in intensity may influence the response strength but not the associative strength of the response. One design was discussed in detail as a possible solution to the problem. In this design, the effect of response strength can be separated from the effect of associative strength, and both can be separated from generalization effects. Many studies have shown that the intensity of the conditioned stimulus does not influence performance when random-groups designs are used. However, it does influence performance when a within-S design is employed.

The conditioning laboratory has always been a prime source of data for evaluating learning theories. After noting certain changes which have been taking place in the nature of the theories advanced, several theoretically sensitive phenomena were presented by examining recent experiments. These phenomena included contiguous conditioning, sensory preconditioning, latent learning, perceptual learning, the role of cessation of a stimulus, and the role of drive.

It was noted that data are conflicting as to the role of level of acquisition in extinction and that the reasons for these conflicts are not clear. We dealt briefly with latent extinction and with spontaneous recovery. Finally, we gave a brief description of two other conditioning-like phenomena: probability learning and verbal conditioning.

CHAPTER ELEVEN

Verbal Learning

In 1885 a German psychologist, Hermann Ebbinghaus, published a book entitled *Memory: A Contribution to Experimental Psychology*. In this book he set forth both procedures for studying verbal learning and retention and the results of a number of experiments he had performed. His data were based on one S, himself, and the materials he learned consisted of another product of his inventive mind, the nonsense syllable. Ebbinghaus, as a result of his extended work, became not only the greatest nonsense-syllable learner of all time but also the pioneer investigator in an area which remains very active today.

Ebbinghaus believed his work represented an investigation of the higher mental processes. Perhaps, in comparison to the other experimentalists' work of the time, he was correct. However, over the years the work in verbal learning has become synonymous with rote learning, and, to many, rote learning is some distance removed from higher mental processes. Regardless of the position taken on this matter, the fact remains that verbal learning is a form of learning in which we all engage, which is an integral part of educational procedures, and in which many find tantalizing research problems.

Here are the plans for the present chapter. Initially, we will discuss four different types of verbal-learning tasks, emphasizing the methods used to present the tasks and the response measures employed to index learning. In a second section we will present an experimental design which will complete the survey of the major types of designs used in experimental work. Then, we will examine some of the variables which influence verbal learning, and, finally, we will touch upon certain theoretical issues which are contributing some spice to the experimental work.

TASKS AND PROCEDURES

Often in discussing verbal tasks, we will speak of verbal units, units that may vary in size and in characteristics. By size we mean the number of letters; by characteristics we mean certain attributes which may be related to the ease or difficulty of learning the unit. The unit PEN should be much easier to learn than the unit RZL. The latter unit is known as a consonant syllable—all three letters are consonants—and it represents the most difficult of all verbal units to learn. The nature of the characteristics involved in differences in difficulty will be discussed later.

Experiments have been performed in which single letters constituted the unit; others have employed two-letter units (bigrams). However, the most frequently used unit is a three-letter sequence called a trigram. The consonant syllable RZL is a trigram, and so is a three-letter word. Another widely used trigram is the nonsense syllable, a unit which has a consonant-vowel-consonant structure, but which, at the same time, does not constitute a word. The consonant syllable is sometimes referred to as a CCC, the nonsense syllable as a CVC. Occasionally other three-letter combinations are used (e.g., CCV) as well as multisyllable nonsense units (e.g., *zumap, supercalifragilisticexpialidocious*). Therefore, the size of the verbal unit used in verbal-learning experiments may vary from one to many letters, and it may or may not form a word.

It is common practice to form the verbal units into lists, the number of units in a list varying from three or four to over a hundred, although the typical experiment involves 8 to 15 units. The manner in which the units are formed into lists represents one of the characteristics used to identify different types of verbal-learning tasks.

Free Learning

The free-learning task, also called the free-recall task, is the simplest verbal-learning task we can present to S. Its nature is most easily seen by the instructions given to S, which may be something like the following:

"I am going to present to you a series of words, one at a time, for a few seconds each. After I have presented them all once, I will ask you to write down all you can remember. Then I will present them to you again, and following that you will once again write down all you can remember. The order in which you write the words is entirely up to you; each time I present them to you they will be in a different order, so don't try to learn the order in which they are presented; simply try to learn the words as individual words so that you can write them all down correctly after as few trials as possible."

How do we present the units one at a time? There are many ways, but a common means is by the use of a device called a *memory drum*. The units are printed on a tape which is wrapped around a drum driven by an electric motor. The drum rotates in a start-stop fashion so that each unit may be exposed for perhaps 2 sec.; then the drum moves to the next unit which is also exposed for 2 sec., and so on, with S viewing each word individually through a small aperture. The memory drum is a common device for presenting the lists, but it is by no means essential. For example, E could face the S across the table and expose each word successively on cards, perhaps timing the presentation of each card by a metronome. Or units might be spoken by E; or they might be recorded on tape and played to S; or each word could be printed on successive pages of a booklet with S instructed to turn each page when an appropriate signal is given by E; or lantern slides may be employed, with or without an automatic projector. There is almost no limit to the number of different particular techniques which might be used to present successive verbal units at a relatively constant rate for free learning.

Although it is common to present each verbal unit in succession for a constant period of time, the method of complete presentation is satisfactory for some purposes. By this method we would give S the full list of units on a sheet of paper, allowing him to study the list for perhaps a minute and then asking him to produce as many of the units as possible when the sheet is removed. A second sheet, with the words in an order different from the order on the first sheet, could be used for a second study trial. A drawback of the method of complete presentation is that it allows no control over the amount of time S spends on each unit, and since time spent in study is a highly critical variable in learning, the method does not allow us to draw conclusions about differences in difficulty of the items within the list. However, if we wish to compare the learning of different lists, the method of complete presentation may be quite acceptable, although it is not frequently used for this purpose.

How long do we allow S to write the units after each study trial? This is quite an arbitrary matter, varying from sharply limited time to all the time S wants—until he reports he does not remember any more units. In practice, the time allowed is usually between these extremes—long enough to be sure that S has been able to write all he knows without a long search of his memory, but not so long as to allow him to dawdle. It can be seen that if S wished, and if unlimited time were given, he might use the period to study the items he had already written down so that he would know them better on the next trial. Sometimes a paced recall is used which minimizes learning during the process of recall. In paced recall S may be allowed 2 or 3 sec. per item. A timing device gives a signal every 3 sec., and S must orally recall a unit during each period between signals (if he can). Only as many periods as units are given. All things considered, it is usually better to have S recall orally rather than in writing since the oral recall minimizes the amount of new learning which may take place during the recall period. Another distinct advantage of oral recall lies in the fact that E may record recall by using a check list made up of the words in the list. Furthermore, anyone who has observed the handwriting of the college sophomore when he is under speed pressure will recognize that it is not always a simple matter to score the responses produced in written recall.

In free learning, as well as all other forms of learning of lists to be discussed, E may use either of two criteria for terminating the alternating study and test or recall trials. He may decide beforehand that all Ss will be given a constant number of trials, for example, five study and recall trials, regardless of the performance shown. Or, as the alternative, S may be required to keep at the task until he reaches some criterion of learning, such as all units correct on a single recall trial. By either method E will have the number of correct units recalled on each trial, and, in addition, he may have a few overt errors. If the units are words, the giving of a wrong response—a word not in the list—is a very rare event. The S will give the words he can remember and that is it, although there will be an occasional repetition of a word on an oral recall trial. If, however, the units are trigram consonant syllables, a number of errors may appear, errors that consist of three letters that do not constitute a unit in the list. For example, if two of the units in the list were RZL and ZWP, S might give the response, RZW.

If a constant number of trials is given, E may plot an acquisition curve for the group of Ss by placing trials along the abscissa and mean number of items correct along the ordinate. If, however, the Ss are taken to a performance criterion, a comparable plot would not be very meaningful because Ss who learned quickly would contribute scores only for the first few trials, and on the later trials the scores for only slow-learning Ss would be involved. Indeed, using this procedure and given certain distributions of learning abilities of the Ss, we could imagine an acquisition curve that first rose, then fell before rising again. Clearly, if we wish to represent the progress of acquisition so that all Ss are represented at all stages of acquisition, we need some other technique when a performance criterion is used. The technique that may be used, not only for free learning but also for other forms, involves the determination of trials to attain successive criteria.

Trials-to-criteria curve. To illustrate the manner in which a trials-to-criteria curve is derived, we will assume that a 10-item list of fairly difficult verbal units was learned by 5 Ss. Each S was given alternative study and recall trials until all 10 items were correctly reproduced on a single recall trial. We would expect, as usual, that the number of trials to reach this performance criterion would vary among Ss. The 5 Ss, A, B, C, D, and E, required 5, 14, 9, 7, and 10 trials, respectively, to attain the criterion. In the upper part of Table 11-1 the number of correct units on each trial is indicated for each S. For example, the first S (A) got 3 correct on the first trial, 6, on the second, and so on. By looking at these scores you may perhaps understand why it would not seem meaningful to obtain the mean number correct on each trial and to use these values to plot an acquisition curve. On the first five trials, all Ss would be represented; on trials 11 through 14, only one S would be represented. A technique is needed to "stretch out" the

TABLE 11–1

CALCULATION OF VALUES FOR PLOTTING A TRIALS-TO-CRITERIA CURVE

See text for complete explanation

SUBJECT	TRIALS													
	1	2	3	4	5	6	7	8	9	10	11	12	13	14
A	3	6	8	9	10									
B	0	1	3	4	5	4	6	7	7	7	9	6	9	10
C	1	3	4	6	5	8	9	9	10					
D	2	5	6	8	7	9	10							
E	1	3	3	5	7	6	8	8	8	10				

	SUCCESSIVE CRITERIA									
	1	2	3	4	5	6	7	8	9	10
A	1	1	1	2	2	2	3	3	4	5
B	2	3	3	4	5	7	8	11	11	14
C	1	2	2	3	4	4	6	6	7	9
D	1	1	2	2	2	3	4	4	6	7
E	1	2	2	4	4	5	5	7	10	10
Mean	1.2	1.8	2.0	3.0	3.4	4.2	5.2	6.2	7.6	9.0

learning for the fast Ss and to contract the learning for the slow Ss. This is essentially what the trials-to-criteria curve does. All Ss are alike in that they were all taken to the same level of learning (all 10 items correct), and in the process of reaching that criterion, all Ss successively attained 1 correct response on a trial, 2 correct responses on a trial, 3 correct responses, . . . and 10 correct responses on a single trial. Therefore, we use these successive performance criteria as common criteria for all Ss and determine the number of trials to reach each.

The conversion for each S is made in the lower section of Table 11-1. The question we ask in making the conversion is how many trials were required by each S to reach 1 correct response, how many trials to reach 2, how many to reach 3, and so on. We may examine the conversion for the first S. On the first recall trial he gave three correct responses. Therefore, it took him 1 trial to reach the criterion of 1 correct, 1 trial to reach 2 correct, and 1 trial to reach 3 correct, and a value of 1 is entered for the first three successive criteria. On the second trial A got 6 correct, so we must enter 2 for the criteria 4, 5, and 6—meaning that it took only 2 trials to reach those criteria. On the third trial, 8 correct responses were given; hence, a 3 is entered for criteria 7 and 8. On the fourth trial 9 items were correct, and on the fifth trial, all 10 were correct.

Subject B presents a problem not observable in A. Note that in the upper part of the table, B, after reaching 5 correct on the fifth trial, fell back on trial 6 and did not reach the criterion of 7 until trial 8. This is reflected in the conversion, where 5 trials are entered for the criterion of 5 correct and 7, for the criterion of 6 correct. As we see, B was a slow learner, and this is reflected in the conversion table by the large numbers—indicating that the number of trials to reach the successive criteria are higher than for fast-learning Ss.

The mean number of trials to reach the successive criteria is shown in the last row of Table 11-1. Now we may plot these, placing the successive

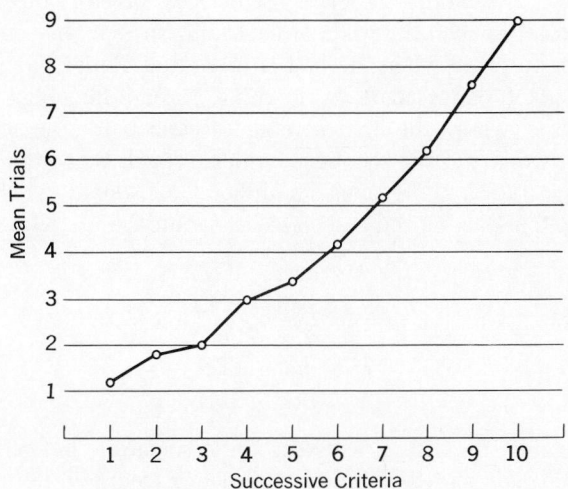

Fig. 11-1. A trials-to-criteria learning curve plotted from the data of Table 11-1.

criteria along the baseline and the mean number of trials to reach the successive criteria along the ordinate. Certain characteristics of the resulting curve (shown in Fig. 11-1) should be pointed out. If we plotted a curve for an easier list on the same graph, it would fall below the present curve; this would be proper because the easier list would require fewer trials to reach each successive criterion. However, we often associate better performance with a "higher" curve so that we must be careful in examining a trials-to-criteria curve; we must not make the mistake of inferring that good performance is represented by a curve that goes high. Some *Es* have reversed the axes to avoid this problem; that is, they plot successive criteria along the ordinate and mean trials to reach these criteria along the abscissa. This is one of those very rare cases where the dependent variable is plotted along the abscissa. There is another reason which might recommend switching the axes. The learning represented in Fig. 11-1 appears to have occurred at a positively accelerated rate since with each successive trial the gain is greater and greater. In fact, however, the learning is negatively accelerated— each successive unit of practice is accompanied (on the whole) with less and less gain in number of items correct. Reversing the axes gives the curve the negatively accelerated form.

Paired-Associate Learning

A paired-associate list consists of pairs of units; S acquires an association between the units of each pair so that the second member of the pair can be given when the first is presented alone. The paired-associate list is an exact counterpart of learning foreign-language equivalents of English words, where the first member of each pair (the stimulus term) is the English word and the second member of each pair (the response term) is the foreign word. If we consider difficult consonant syllables the foreign language, a five-pair paired-associate list would be as follows:

arm – RZL
pen – PNB
dog – QKX
hat – JTZ
bag – SMH

In learning the list S acquires an association between the stimulus term of each pair and the response term; for example, he must learn to be able to produce RZL when *arm* is shown alone. Normally, as with free learning, we will present the list for several trials and obtain a measure of performance on each trial. The order in which the pairs are presented from trial to trial is varied; if this were not done, it can be seen that S could learn the order of the response terms and essentially ignore the stimulus terms. In producing the responses orally, at least for response terms such as those above, *E* will require S to spell them since it would obviously be very difficult to pronounce them. The material may be presented in a variety of ways (by use of memory drum, cards, projectors) as discussed earlier for free learning, but there are two ways in which the learning trials may be carried out on whatever apparatus is used.

Alternate study and recall. This procedure is quite similar to that used in free learning. A study trial is given first, each pair being shown successively for a few seconds; S is fully instructed that he is to learn to associate the members of each pair so that the second can be produced when the first is shown alone. After a study trial, each stimulus is shown successively, and as each stimulus appears, S attempts to produce the response term with which it had been paired. The E will record the response S makes to each stimulus and note whether it is correct, a misplaced-response error (e.g., giving JTZ when *pen* is the stimulus term), or an integrative error (e.g., JKX, a trigram not in the list). Unless the instructions specifically require it, S need not respond at all to a stimulus if he feels he does not know the correct response. After the first recall trial, another study trial is given, which is followed by another recall, and so on, with the order of the pairs varying from study trial to study trial and the order of the stimulus terms varying from recall trial to recall trial.

Anticipation. In the anticipation method, a measure of performance is obtained on each presentation of the list except the first. The sequence of presentation of a trial would be as follows:

$$arm -$$
$$arm - RZL$$
$$pen -$$
$$pen - PNB$$
$$dog -$$
$$dog - QKX$$

Each successive event might occupy a 3-sec. period; for instance, *arm* may be presented for 3 sec., and *arm–RZL*, for 3 sec. The S is instructed that he is to attempt to produce the response term when the stimulus term is shown alone. Of course, on the first trial, S simply studies the list, but on the second and all subsequent trials, when *arm* is presented, S attempts to produce RZL *before arm–RZL* is shown together. If S does produce the response term, he immediately finds out that he was correct; if he cannot produce it or produces a wrong response, he immediately finds out what is correct.

The anticipation method has been used more frequently than the study-recall method. However, it can be argued that the study-recall method allows a clear separation of acquisition and recall performance, whereas the anticipation method does not. The anticipation method requires that on each trial S must try to recall associates he knows and must also learn new ones or strengthen weak ones. On the other hand, the study-recall method separates these two processes. On a study trial S can devote his attention to recalling the response terms. A number of comparisons have been made of the rate of overall learning produced by the two methods, and the results of these comparisons are horribly confused. If there is a consensus, it is that the study-recall method produces somewhat more rapid learning than the anticipation method, but what associated variables are required for this to happen is unknown.

Verbal Discrimination

This method of presenting verbal material has not been used frequently, but as a method it has certain properties that make it a valuable adjunct in studying verbal learning. In the verbal-discrimination list, pairs of units are presented S, one member of each pair having been arbitrarily designated by E as the correct member. Unlike paired-associate learning, there is not a stimulus term as distinct from a response term, and either the left- or the right-hand member of the pair may be the one arbitrarily designated by E as correct. Furthermore, on successive trials the position of the correct item is changed. If on one trial the pair is *arm-pen*, on the next trial the order might be *pen-arm*. We must say "might" because E would never shift all items in the list systematically on a given trial. Rather, he would shift them nonsystematically but in such a manner that over the several trials each item would occur in each position (left or right) about equally often. As in paired-associate and free learning, the order of the pairs varies from trial to trial.

On the first trial of a verbal-discrimination task S makes a guess for each pair, spelling or pronouncing the unit which he chooses as a guess. After each guess E informs S as to whether he was right or wrong. This may be done vocally by E or it may be done by showing S which member of the pair is correct. On all subsequent trials S also responds to each pair; he is not allowed to pass a pair if he does not feel he knows which member of the pair is correct. Half the pairs will be correct by chance; therefore, learning is normally measured above this 50 percent baseline.

A study-recall procedure could be used to present the verbal-discrimination list. This method would present each successive pair with, perhaps, the correct member of the pair underlined, with S trying to learn the correct member of the pair on the study trial. On the test trials the pairs would be presented without the correct unit underlined, with S instructed to identify the correct unit.

Let us return briefly to paired-associate learning and free learning by way of leading up to an examination of the learning involved in mastering a verbal-discrimination list. In paired-associate learning, we can identify two gross subprocesses. First, S must learn the response terms as responses—he must acquire them so that he can recall them. This phase, often called the response-learning phase, is, in some instances, the major component in the overall learning process. This would be the case with the five-item illustrative list given earlier. Those consonant syllables represent unusual combinations of letters, and to be able to learn the correct ordering of the three letters for each is a fairly difficult task. The second gross phase is that of "hooking" the response term to a particular stimulus term, a phase that is sometimes referred to as the associative phase. Free learning may be used as a method of studying the response-learning phase independent of the associative phase since in free learning S acquires response terms without having to associate them to a particular stimulus. In verbal-discrimination learning, on the other hand, response learning is entirely eliminated; all S has to learn is to choose the correct member of the pair. Even if the units were very difficult, for example, RZL, he would merely have to look at it and spell it—he would not have to recall it. Therefore, verbal-discrimination can be viewed as a way to eliminate response learning completely. However, exactly how or what S does learn in the verbal-discrimination task in order to be able to identify quickly and perfectly the correct member of each pair is not well understood at the present time.

Serial Learning

Serial learning was used by Ebbinghaus and was for many years the most frequently used technique for studying verbal learning. In serial learning the units are presented in the same order from trial to trial, and S must reproduce them in the order presented. The recitation of the alphabet represents the end product of a serial-learning task.

The anticipation method is commonly used in studying serial learning. The list is shown once to S, and on the second trial and every trial thereafter, he is under instruction to try to keep "one jump ahead"; when he is shown the first unit, he is to produce the second; when he sees the second, he must produce the third, and so on. Some may say that each unit is both a stimulus term (since it is a signal to produce the next unit) and a response term (since it is produced when the one before it is shown). This would be true for all items except the first and last one in the list since the first would serve only as a stimulus term, and the last, as only a response term if there is a break between successive presentations of the list. One could, of course, have the list as a continuous band, or circle, with no break between the first and last item. This conception of serial learning, in which each item is the stimulus for the next, has long been held, but recent work (to which we will address ourselves at a later point) raises certain doubts about it.

As can be seen, serial learning is very similar to free learning. The major difference lies in the order of the items, which is always constant in serial learning but is varied in free learning, and in serial learning S must produce the order as presented. Actually, similarities may hide large differences in the learning process, but recent work has suggested that these similarities between free learning and serial learning are also reflected in similarities in at least the end product of learning. For example, Tulving (1962a), as a result of his analysis of recall trials in free learning, has shown that S tends to repeat the order in which he recalls the units; he does not necessarily recall in a random order that differs from trial to trial, but, rather, imposes an organization on the recall that tends to produce a constant serial order. Let us consider a particular problem in reasoning about such matters, a problem with which we have already had contact but which we need to bring up periodically since it is an important one.

It is possible to study the organization of verbal units in the recall protocols over trials and derive an index of degree of organization. We will not consider how this may be done. As a result of studying such protocols, Tulving showed that individuals differed in the degree of organization they imposed on the recall. And, generally speaking, those who showed the greatest degree of organization also learned most rapidly. At this point, as we know, we are impelled toward the conclusion that those with high organization learned faster *because* of the high organization. However, we also know that we must not reach this conclusion; those who learned most rapidly might still learn most rapidly if a way were found to prevent the organization which they showed. High organization as a cause for the faster learning must, at this point, be considered only a hypothesis. Can we remove it from this level? Can we obtain data which will either support the hypothesis or deny it? There are ways. For example, Tulving (1962b) formed two random groups, one group instructed to recall the words in the free-learning list in alphabetical order according to first letters and the other group given no special instructions. By this instruction E attempted to provide the Ss an organizational scheme which was a meaningful one for this list and which might not have been discovered without the instructions. The results showed that Ss in the instructed group did show more rapid learning than did the other group, and the recall protocols showed that the frequency of use of the alphabetical scheme was greater in the instructed group than in the non-instructed group. Such evidence is quite in line with the hypothesis that Ss who "naturally" impose an organization on their recall learn more rapidly, because of the organization, than those who do not. This, then, is the approach we attempt to use to make decisions about cause-effect possibilities between correlated response measures. By forming random groups, we remove individual differences as a variable. Then we attempt to manipulate a variable which we think will produce a difference in one of the response measures (e.g., organization) and follow this with an examination of the difference in performance on the other response measure (learning). If there is a difference between the two groups on the latter response measure, we are inclined to conclude that the two processes are causally related—one produces the other.

The above discussion indicates that free-learning recall protocols may show some degree of serial organization. Now, suppose we presented a serial list for alternate study and recall trials, with, of course, the order of the units the same on each study trial. We use two groups; one group is instructed that they must recall the units in the order presented, and the other is instructed that they may recall the units in any order they wish. What expectations would we have for the outcome of such an experiment? Offhand, it would appear that the group which is required to recall the items in order has more to learn than the group not so required. The former group must not only learn the units as units, but must also reproduce them in a given order for them to be counted as correct. This expectation is by no means clearly supported by experiment. Waugh (1961) showed that although the group allowed to give the items in any order was initially superior to those who had to give the items in the order presented, as trials continued the latter group caught up with and then surpassed the former. The finding was confirmed by Dallet (1963). These results suggest, therefore, that when S is forced to use a given organizational scheme (as in serial learning), his learning will be facilitated in the long run despite the fact that there is nothing intrinsically meaningful about the scheme.

COUNTERBALANCED DESIGNS

The discussion of counterbalanced designs will complete our presentation of the major types of designs used in experimental work. We see in summary that these designs are four in number and may be identified as follows:

INDEPENDENT-GROUPS DESIGNS

1. Random groups
2. Matched groups

WITHIN-SUBJECT DESIGNS

1. Within-S balancing
2. Between-S balancing

The counterbalanced design is a within-S design, but it differs from the within-S design which we discussed in detail in the early chapters. The major problem posed by a within-S design concerns the appropriate balancing of conditions so that progressive errors do not bias the results for a condition. We are familiar with the within-S balancing; the data from each S comprises an unbiased estimate of the effect of the independent variable. It will be remembered that within-S balancing was accomplished by counterbalancing the order of conditions, completely randomizing the order of conditions, or block randomizing the order of conditions. In the present design, often spoken of in general as a counterbalanced design, each S serves in all conditions, but the data for any given S is biased by progressive errors. Only by combining data for a number of Ss do we achieve a balancing of the progressive errors, and so we speak of between-S balancing. The way in which this balancing is achieved is the central issue in the counterbalanced

design. Two general techniques are used: complete between-S counterbalancing and incomplete between-S counterbalancing.

Complete Between-Subject Counterbalancing

In the pure form of this design each S serves in all conditions
of an experiment but serves in each only once. Obviously, since practice
effects (or progressive errors from other sources) are likely to occur, the
results of the different conditions for a single S will be biased, and the
amount of the bias will be a direct function of the extent of the progressive
error. Between-S counterbalancing is presumed to eliminate this bias when
the data for all Ss are combined. The application of the design differs, depending upon whether a task variable or an environmental variable is being
manipulated, so we must illustrate the application for each type of variable.

Task variables. We will assume first that we are doing a
two-condition experiment in which the variable is the meaningfulness of the
verbal units. One list is made up of common three-letter words, and the
other, of CCC trigrams, but there is an equal number of units in both lists.
We will call the first, List H (high meaningfulness), and the second, List L
(low meaningfulness). Each S must learn both lists. With only two conditions, complete between-S counterbalancing is achieved with only two Ss.

	FIRST LIST LEARNED	SECOND LIST LEARNED
S No. 1	L	H
S No. 2	H	L

The first S learns the lists in the order L-H. Even if the two lists are known
to be equal in difficulty, the H list should be learned more rapidly than the
L list because it is favored by practice effects. Therefore, the results for S
No. 1 do not tell us about the influence of only H and L; rather, they tell us
about the influence of H and L plus practice effect—a simple case of the
confounding of the effect of two variables. However, S No. 2, given the lists
in H-L order, would have practice effect favoring the L list. If the practice
effect in moving from H to L is close to the magnitude of the effect in moving from L to H, and if we combine the scores for the L list for the two
Ss and the scores for the H list for the two Ss, we should have an unbiased
estimate of the influence of high and low meaningfulness on learning. As
we know by now, we would use far more than two Ss in such a design. In
assigning Ss to sequences (L to H, and H to L) we would use a random
procedure with the restriction that each sequence is to be used equally often.

In a statement above, we "slipped in" the qualification that the design
balances practice effect across the two conditions *if* the magnitude of these
effects is the same for the H to L sequence as it is for the L to H sequence.

If the effects are not equivalent, we may not get an unbiased estimate of the effect of the variable, although if the variable is a relevant variable—if it does influence learning—we will demonstrate it by the design.

How do we tell whether or not there are differential practice effects in the L to H sequence versus the H to L sequence? With only two conditions, as in the illustration we are discussing, the determination is relatively simple. We compare the difference in performance between L and H when these are first-learned lists with that between L and H when these are the second-learned lists. If these two differences are of the same magnitude, we would conclude that differential practice effects were not present. Suppose there are differential practice effects; what do we conclude? We should note that differences in performance on the first-learned lists conform to the random-groups design, and we could always limit our conclusion to such differences, essentially throwing away the data on the second-learned lists. Or, we could report the difference on the second-learned lists as a separate datum. This whole matter of possible effects of differential transfer is a difficult one and one on which we do not have much information. There are, however, additional comments which should be made about the matter, and we will return to it at a later point.

The formal characteristic of the between-S counterbalancing scheme is most clearly seen when we examine the nature of the experimental matrix when more than two conditions are employed. Let us assume that we have three levels of meaningfulness, H, M (medium), and L, each represented by a different list. Our matrix would appear as follows:

	FIRST LIST	SECOND LIST	THIRD LIST
S No. 1	L	M	H
S No. 2	L	H	M
S No. 3	M	L	H
S No. 4	M	H	L
S No. 5	H	L	M
S No. 6	H	M	L

As usual, the pairing of an S with a given sequence would be done randomly, and again we should note that when this is done, differences in performance on the first-learned lists would be equivalent to the outcome of a random-groups design. However, in using all of the data resulting from each S's learning all three lists, we bring the scores for the L lists into one distribution, those for the M lists into another, and those for the H into another.

The one basic characteristic of the experimental matrix for a between-S complete counterbalancing scheme is that all possible orders of the conditions are used. This results in each condition occurring equally often at each stage of practice and, therefore, being equally influenced by practice effects. As can be seen, with three conditions (in this case three variations on a task variable), each occurs twice at each stage of practice when 6 Ss are used. Of course, we would probably use more than 6 Ss, and in order to retain complete counterbalancing, we must use some number that is a multiple of 6 (12, 18, 24). There are only six possible ways in which three conditions can be ordered; there are only two possible ways in which two conditions can be ordered. If we use four conditions we will find that there are 24 possible ways in which these may be ordered, and if we should be so bold as to use complete counterbalancing with five conditions, we would discover that we would require 120 Ss since that is the number of different orderings of five conditions which are possible. (The student of mathematics will recognize that the rule involved between number of events and the number of different ordering of those events is factorial r, usually expressed as $r!$.)

Environmental variables. The counterbalancing matrix for an environmental variable is somewhat more complicated than it is for a task variable. When a task variable is manipulated, the different lists constitute the independent variable; therefore, the lists are counterbalanced. If we are manipulating an environmental variable, we must counterbalance that variable across Ss. But to examine the influence of an environmental variable we also must have lists—a different list for each condition—and this produces the complication. Assume that we are going to manipulate the rate at which items are exposed in free learning, one being a 2-sec. rate and the other a 4-sec. rate. With this two-condition experiment we need only two Ss to effect the counterbalancing as follows:

	List 1	List 2
S No. 1	2 sec.	4 sec.
S No. 2	4 sec.	2 sec.

If we include a 6-sec. condition to make three conditions, the matrix would be as follows:

	List 1	List 2	List 3
S No. 1	2 sec.	4 sec.	6 sec.
S No. 2	2 sec.	6 sec.	4 sec.
S No. 3	4 sec.	2 sec.	6 sec.
S No. 4	4 sec.	6 sec.	2 sec.
S No. 5	6 sec.	2 sec.	4 sec.
S No. 6	6 sec.	4 sec.	2 sec.

The problem concerns the lists. When we are manipulating an environmental variable, we are not interested in lists as such, but they are necessary for providing the learning tasks under which we are going to determine the influence of rate of presentation. With two conditions we choose two lists, and with three conditions, three lists. All Ss learn the lists in the same order. Suppose the lists differ in difficulty. Would this bias the rate conditions in some way? Differences in difficulty will *not* produce a bias since each condition (each rate) occurs equally often with each list.

To make sure that we understand how to collect the scores from the above three-condition matrix and also to lead us into further questions, we will assign arbitrary scores for each S for each condition. We will assume that E took Ss to a criterion of performance so that the response measure is number of trials to reach the criterion. Let the first number in the matrix represent the rate (in sec.), and the second, the trials to reach the criterion.

	LIST 1	LIST 2	LIST 3
S No. 1	2-10	4-8	6-4
S No. 2	2-15	6-8	4-8
S No. 3	4-6	2-6	6-2
S No. 4	4-9	6-5	2-7
S No. 5	6-4	2-8	4-6
S No. 6	6-6	4-7	2-10

We collect all the scores under a given rate:

	2 SEC.	4 SEC.	6 SEC.
S No. 1	10	8	4
S No. 2	15	8	8
S No. 3	6	6	2
S No. 4	7	9	5
S No. 5	8	6	4
S No. 6	10	7	6
Means	9.3	7.3	4.8

Such results would clearly allow us to conclude that rate of learning is inversely related to rate of presentation. Can we obtain other information from such a set of scores? Can we determine, for example, what the practice-effect curve is across the three stages? We cannot. Lists, which may differ in difficulty, are confounded with stages of practice since the same list is always used at a given stage of practice. Can we tell whether the three lists differ in difficulty? For the same reason we cannot since the fact still remains that lists and practice effects are confounded. However, if we wished to use 36 Ss, we could answer both questions and, in addition, determine the relationship between rate of presentation and learning. We would counterbalance the order of the three lists, and under each of the six possible list orders, we would counterbalance the three rate conditions as in the matrix presented above. If, across all 36 Ss, we sum the scores made on the first stage of practice (the first list learned), the second stage of practice, and finally the third stage, we would have values representing the true practice curve for these lists and rates. Since each rate and list occur equally often at each stage of practice, any differences as a function of stage of practice must represent the true practice effect.

By bringing together all scores obtained on List 1, on List 2, and on List 3, we can determine whether or not the three lists differ in difficulty. This again is a "clean" measure since each list has occurred equally often at each stage of practice and each list has been used equally often with each rate.

As we can see, a carefully conceived counterbalanced design can provide us with a great deal of information over and above that required to determine the effects of the variable of immediate interest.

Incomplete Between-Subject Counterbalancing

We noted above that with five conditions a total of 120 Ss would be required for complete counterbalancing. It would be uncommon for an E to feel that such a great number of Ss would be needed in order to assess the influence of an independent variable. Therefore, when five or more conditions are required, a form of incomplete counterbalancing is used. The incompleteness stems from the fact that all possible orders of the conditions are not used. However, to avoid confounding by differences in practice effects, each condition occurs equally often at each stage of practice. To accomplish this, the minimum number of Ss required is equivalent to the number of conditions. Assume we have five conditions for a task variable and these are identified as A, B, C, D, and E, each representing a different list. The matrix may be as follows:

S No. 1	A	B	C	D	E
S No. 2	B	C	D	E	A
S No. 3	C	D	E	A	B
S No. 4	D	E	A	B	C
S No. 5	E	A	B	C	D

All considerations we have given to the completely counterbalanced designs also hold for this design in bringing the data together, balancing practice effects, and so on. In fact, we could use incomplete counterbalancing with three or four conditions in the experiment, and it would be quite satisfactory. There is nothing magical in having all possible orders of the conditions represented, although there may be a compulsion to use such designs when possible because of the aesthetic elegance.

An extreme case of incomplete counterbalancing would be to assign each S a different random order of the conditions. If we use a reasonable number of Ss, perhaps 30 to 40, we can be fairly confident that each condition will occur about equally often at each stage of practice so that little bias will result. In practice, however, such randomization is rarely used if the magnitude of the practice effects is unknown or is known to be fairly large for the material and type of task involved.

Evaluation of Counterbalanced Designs

Until relatively recent years, counterbalanced designs were widely used in the study of verbal learning. Then, almost overnight, they were dropped by many investigators and replaced by the random-groups design. However, during very recent years, some Es have returned to the use of the counterbalanced design, particularly in studies involving free learning and in studies of short-term memory (Chapter Thirteen). There seem to be two major reasons why the design fell into disfavor. One concerns the effect of differential transfer which was mentioned earlier. Actually, the issue is more complicated than implied earlier, since it deals with matters of statistical analysis, matters which we will not attempt to discuss here. It can be said, however, that the implications of differential transfer effects within the counterbalanced design may have produced more fear than is warranted since we have not made a concerted empirical attempt to measure the extent of differential transfer in a variety of situations and to assess the influence it may have on conclusions about the effect of an independent variable. Such studies are badly needed.

The second reason why the counterbalanced design fell into disfavor is a reason we discussed in an earlier chapter in dealing with conditioning as a function of the intensity of CS. There we saw that intensity of the CS did not influence performance when S was given only one level of intensity but did influence performance when two levels were presented. We spoke of this as representing a design-specific phenomenon, and we concluded that the design characteristics must be viewed in the same way as we view any potential independent variable. If a phenomenon disappears or varies in magnitude as a function of the nature of the design, we have identified a relevant independent variable, and further work may tell us a great deal, not only about the conditions producing the phenomenon but also about the design itself.

There are phenomena in verbal learning which will vary in magnitude as a function of the nature of the design. For example, the author has done studies on the effect of distributed practice (as opposed to massed practice) on paired-associate learning. If S serves in more than one condition, as by a counterbalanced design, the variable may be effective, whereas if S serves in a single condition, as by a random-groups design, it will not be effective. Such a finding tells us that the phenomenon is based on an interlist effect of some kind. Certain retention phenomena also vary in magnitude as a function of the design. In short, counterbalanced designs may, in a manner of speaking, complicate our phenomena, and at certain stages of research E may prefer to avoid this complication.

Should we use between-S counterbalanced designs routinely in our research? Such a question will elicit different answers. These designs have certain advantages which cannot be gainsaid. If we have a small number of Ss available and a number of different conditions to investigate, the counter-balanced design is very efficient. We also gain a certain precision when we compare each S's performance under one condition with his performance under another. The writer's belief is that for many experiments in the under-graduate laboratory we should not shy away from the use of the counter-balanced design.

SOME CHARACTERISTICS
OF MEANINGFULNESS

In illustrating some of the design matrices in the previous section, the term *meaningfulness* was used to indicate a characteristic on which verbal units may differ. It seems self-evident that two units, such as KBZ and CAT, may differ in meaningfulness according to the literary mean-ing of the term. However, we must specify the measuring operations which are used to quantify differences in meaningfulness. We will see that we must speak of meaningfulness as a composite of characteristics, each characteristic given an independent operational definition. However, because the scales for the different characteristics are not independent (scale values on one scale are correlated with those on another), we have no recourse but to define meaningfulness as the aggregate of these characteristics, if we are to use the term at all. As we examine the scaling techniques, which may be done briefly since we have some acquaintance with them, it will be noted that most of them represent Class-II operational definitions.

Number of associates. The S is given a series of verbal units and for each is allowed a given period of time (e.g., 60 sec.) to write down all of the names of objects or events of which each unit reminds him (Noble, 1952). For each item the mean number of associates elicited is determined for a group of Ss, and the units are ordered along a scale in terms of this measure. This procedure is rather tedious for both the S and the E (who must count the associates). Therefore, an alternative procedure may be used in which S rates each unit as to the number of associates which he thinks each will elicit (Noble, Stockwell, & Pryer, 1957). A five point scale may be used in which the five categories are labeled *few, less than average, average, more than average,* and *many;* and to obtain a numerical index for each item, the values 1 through 5 may be assigned the categories.

Yes or no. This procedure was the one first used to define a dimension of meaningfulness (Glaze, 1928). Glaze used nonsense syllables and presented each syllable for a maximum of 3 sec. during which interval S was to indicate whether or not the syllable meant something to him. The so-called association value of a syllable was the percentage of Ss who gave an association to that syllable. Recently, Archer (1960) has evaluated all possible CVCs (including words) by using a technique very similar to the one Glaze used; the method has also been applied to consonant syllables (Witmer, 1935).

Pronounceability. The Ss rated the ease or difficulty of pronouncing verbal units on a nine-point scale; the score for each unit is the mean scale value (Underwood & Schulz, 1960).

Familiarity. We have seen in an earlier chapter how Ss are able to rate, with considerable accuracy, the frequency with which words occur in printed text. If familiarity is defined as the frequency with which S has come into contact with a word, we would expect S to rate the familiarity of verbal units with precision, and he does (Noble, 1953).

Other frequency relationships. It is possible to determine the relative frequencies with which two- and three-letter sequences occur in words. These frequencies show relationships with the other characteristics of verbal units as defined by the various techniques noted above. For example, if we count the number of times various nonsense syllables occur as portions of words, the frequencies show a direct relationship with values determined by all of the above procedures (Underwood & Schulz, 1960).

Stability

We have noted that the scale values obtained by the various techniques will normally show high correlations for any group of verbal units. Furthermore, the scale values are remarkably stable across the years. For example, Glaze accomplished his original scaling using 15 Ss, and in 1960, Archer used essentially the same technique with 216 Ss. For 1933 nonsense syllables scaled by both Archer and Glaze, the correlation (as reported by Archer) between the two sets of values was .79. One might expect some changes to be produced by brand names of soaps, since it appears that soap manufacturers use a list of nonsense syllables to obtain their brand names, for example, DUZ, FAB, VEL. Meaningfulness values are also stable for different age groups. Noble (1952), using basic airmen at an Air Force base in Texas as Ss, determined the number of associates elicited by 96 two-syllable units (including words and nonwords). Rocklyn, Hessert, and Braun (1957) used the same procedure for 24 of these units with Ss between the ages of 50 and 66 years who were unemployed residents of the Pittsburgh area. The correlation between the mean scale values for the 24 items for the two groups of Ss was .92.

Sources

We cannot reproduce in this book the vast tables which are available showing the scale values for many different types of verbal units scaled by several different procedures. However, some of these sources are listed in an appendix at the end of this chapter, with a note on the scaling procedure, and the sample units are provided to give a "feel" for the dimension involved. It might be useful to look at these sample units before proceeding with the next section in which we ask about the role of meaningfulness in learning.

MEANINGFULNESS AND LEARNING

There is an exceptionally strong relationship between the scaled attributes of verbal units, known collectively as meaningfulness, and the rate of learning the units. We will be quite unable to do justice to the scores of experiments which have examined this relationship. Our purpose will be to examine the relationship for free learning and for paired-associate learning and to discuss the explanatory problems which the relationships pose.

Free Learning

The author performed a study (Underwood, 1966) using free learning of 27 trigrams which cover the complete range of meaningfulness. Five different groups of Ss were involved, and we may symbolize these groups according to particular tasks given them.

Group CM. This group of 54 Ss scaled the 27 trigrams by a form of cross-modality scaling. They were presented with the items, listed on the left side of sheets of paper, and were instructed to judge the speed with which they thought they could learn each trigram if given the task of learning them as a free-learning list. To indicate the speed, they were to draw lines, a short line indicating that it would take only a short time to learn and a long line to indicate that it would take a long time to learn. The line drawn for each trigram was measured to the nearest 1/10 in., and the average length for the 54 Ss was determined. These means are shown in Table 11-2 under the column headed CM.

Group ME. This group of 69 Ss used a form of magnitude estimation in order to reflect the speed with which they thought they could learn the trigrams. The instructions required S to assign the value of 100 to units of average difficulty, values greater than 100 for items which were more difficult, and values less than 100 for the items which were less difficult. Of course, the instructions indicated that the numbers were to reflect as precisely as possible the differences in difficulty; for example, an item twice as difficult as another should be given a number twice as large. For the group, the mean value assigned each trigram was determined, and these are listed in Table 11-2 under the column headed ME.

Group PR. This group of 20 Ss gave pronounceability ratings to the 27 trigrams, the ratings being made along a 9-point scale on which 1 was easiest to pronounce, and 9, most difficult.

Group AV. This group of 20 Ss rated the items as to the relative number of associations each was believed to elicit. Again, a 9-point scale was used, with 1 representing few if any associations, and 9, many associations.

TABLE 11–2

THE RELATIONSHIP BETWEEN FREE LEARNING OF 27 TRIGRAMS AND VARIOUS PREDICTIVE INDEXES

See text for complete explanation

	CM	ME	PR	AV	LEARN
ING	5.57	60	2.75	7.60	5.19
MEL	6.15	68	1.60	6.80	4.83
BUG	4.02	23	1.65	6.45	4.76
KIT	5.56	33	1.70	6.75	4.72
LOT	4.37	32	1.65	7.65	4.57
HOB	8.74	91	1.95	5.60	4.54
OUS	9.11	90	4.35	6.35	4.44
JOK	9.00	88	3.80	5.80	4.30
DGM	19.20	165	7.50	4.05	4.26
VER	10.65	97	2.45	6.60	4.09
YIN	11.96	113	3.75	3.15	3.94
OWT	16.61	146	5.35	4.20	3.91
CES	13.05	120	3.00	5.90	3.89
RCH	17.85	144	5.65	4.50	3.52
TAF	10.61	116	2.15	5.60	3.44
TLY	18.04	150	6.15	4.75	3.35
USK	15.17	130	4.05	4.50	3.35
UNH	24.15	166	6.85	3.70	3.31
IDW	23.56	172	7.55	3.55	2.94
PKF	19.06	181	7.70	3.10	2.59
EQR	23.48	200	7.85	4.15	2.56
SJL	28.28	202	7.85	2.30	2.46
XFH	30.94	246	8.80	2.05	1.69
NDF	26.61	191	6.85	2.90	1.65
RZQ	30.35	244	8.55	2.80	1.61
KBV	23.78	199	7.75	2.25	1.52
VXK	32.33	234	8.15	1.95	1.35

Learning. A group of 54 Ss learned the 27 trigrams by a free-learning procedure. The trigrams were spelled to S via a tape recorder at a 5-sec. rate, and S wrote his responses on recall trials. Six study and recall trials were used, and the values in Table 11-2 show the mean number of times each item was correctly recalled, the maximum possible being six. The items are ordered in terms of difficulty. Thus, the trigram ING was the least difficult (given the most times correctly), MEL, the next least difficult, and so on, revealing KBV and VXK to be the most difficult items.

Even a casual inspection of Table 11-2 shows that the learning measures are correlated very highly with all scaling measures. Remember that the learning measures are ordered in terms of difficulty. We can see that as we go down the column, the CM measure, as well as the ME measure, increases. By the nature of the scale, the PR measures increase and the AV measures decrease in the downward direction.

The product-moment correlations (signs ignored) among the various distributions produces a matrix as shown in Table 11-3. The lowest correlation in the matrix is .88. Clearly, all scales predict the learning with very high fidelity, and as must necessarily be so, all scales are highly related. In spite

TABLE 11–3
INTERCORRELATIONS AMONG THE DISTRIBUTIONS GIVEN IN TABLE 11–2

	CM	ME	PR	AV
LEARN	.92	.91	.90	.88
CM	–	.97	.94	.92
ME	–	–	.94	.91
PR	–	–	–	.88

of the fact that the relationships are striking between learning and the scales, a somewhat different procedure would probably have resulted in the correlations being still higher. In learning, all Ss received the same ordering of the trigrams, and although the orders were different for each of the six study trials, some slight favoritism may have occurred for some items. The ideal procedure would have been to use a different six orders for each S.

From such results we can conclude only that all measures are, in effect, measuring learning. We ask S to rate how fast he expects to learn the item; his ratings must mean that he is indicating how much about the item he has already learned. The PR measure must also measure learning indirectly; pronounceability must be almost perfectly related to how much S already knows about the item, such as how well the letters go together. Similarly, ratings of number of associates can mean only that those items with the greatest number of associates are items which S already knows the most about, or is most

familiar with. We know the inherent danger in drawing cause-effect conclusions from correlational data. The correlations in Table 11-3 are simply
correlations among various response measures—various dependent variables.
The scales appear to measure the learning which took place prior to the
formal learning sessions, and the formal learning session simply measures
additional learning which is, so to speak, piled on top of the learning which
had already occurred. We need to know what factors were important for the
learning that had already occurred. We will discuss possible approaches to
this difficult problem somewhat later.

Paired-Associate Learning

In the paired-associate list, meaningfulness may be varied
among the stimulus terms or among the response terms. Of course, we could
vary meaningfulness simultaneously among stimulus and response terms,
but this does not provide us with very analytical data. Let us consider the
purer case in which we vary meaningfulness either among the response terms
or among the stimulus terms while keeping the opposite terms at a relatively
constant level of meaningfulness. Available data, of which there is a great
deal, are schematically summarized in Fig. 11-2. We will assume that the

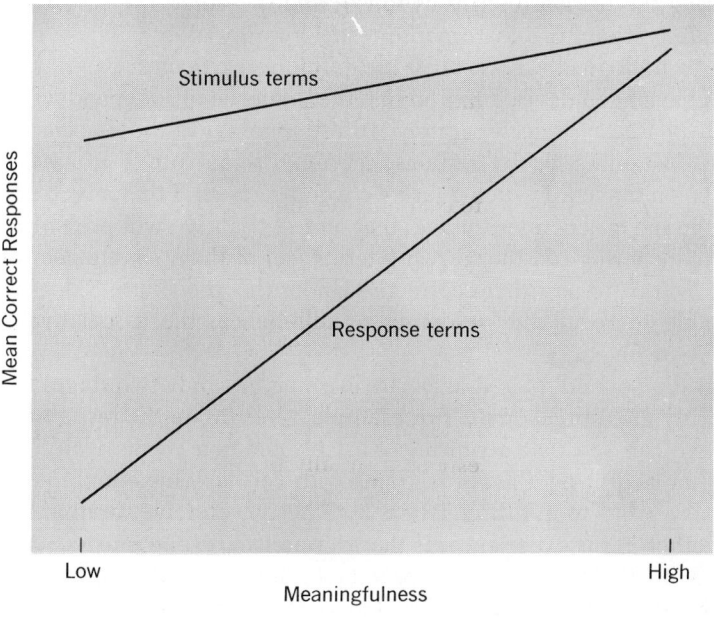

**Fig. 11-2. Schematic representation of the relationship between
meaningfulness of stimulus terms and of response terms, and
learning.**

lists were presented for a constant number of trials so that the response measure is the mean number of correct responses made over all of the trials. Two facts are apparent from Fig. 11-2. The first is that both stimulus meaningfulness and response meaningfulness are related to the amount learned in a positive manner. The second is that learning is more dramatically influenced by meaningfulness of the response terms than by corresponding changes in the meaningfulness of the stimulus terms. The slopes of the two curves will change but little as the opposite term is varied in meaningfulness; for example, if, when we vary stimulus meaningfulness, the response terms have very low but constant meaningfulness, the upper curve might shift downward dramatically, but the slope would remain essentially the same.

An Analytical Approach

We are well aware that one of the objectives of experimentation is to break gross phenomena down into their constituent parts. If the learning of a paired-associate list is considered a gross phenomenon, what are its constituents? What are the subprocesses or sublearnings which occur in the overall process of acquiring a list of paired associates?

Let us review briefly. It is common practice to break down paired-associate learning into two stages. One of these stages is response learning (acquiring the response terms as such), and the other, the associative stage (associating stimulus and response terms appropriately). These two stages appear to be logically necessary; furthermore, particular experimental procedures have been devised to examine the influence of independent variables on each phase or stage separately. In order to study the associative phase without contamination by response learning, some sort of a matching task would be employed. In such a task we would present S the pairs to study but include in the instructions the fact that on test trials we will present him both the stimulus terms and the response terms (all of them simultaneously), and his task will be to pair them correctly. Under this procedure S does not have to be able to recall the responses at all; hence, the associative stage is primarily involved.

Dividing overall paired-associate learning into only two stages is actually still a fairly gross breakdown. For example, referring to the response-learning phase, we can see that acquiring a list of common words would be much easier than acquiring a list of trigrams with very low meaningfulness. In the latter case, S has to put three letters together which have rarely if ever been put together in his experience. If the trigram is KBV, he must associate B to K and V to B; there would appear to be an associative stage within the response-learning stage for such verbal units. Thus, it is possible to make the breakdown much more elaborate than that implied by the gross division between response learning and associative learning, and, indeed, this has been done (e.g., Morikawa, 1959; McGuire, 1961; Cook & Brown, 1963). Nevertheless, we can go quite far in our understanding of paired-associate learning with just the two-component breakdown. For example, let us consider the results of the manipulation of stimulus meaningfulness and response meaningfulness as shown earlier in Fig. 11-2. An obvious explanatory problem is specifying why the two curves should differ in slope. One of the major factors which must be involved is that S has to be able to reproduce the responses—he must be able to recall them. Such is not required in the case of stimuli where S has only to be able in some way to discriminate among them—he does not have to be able to reproduce them. If differences in meaningfulness produce very little difference in the ability to discriminate among the stimuli, we would not expect meaningfulness among the stimuli to have very much effect. But if free learning is taken as the index of difficulty of response learning in a paired-associate list, we know that differences in meaningfulness among the response terms should produce enormous differences in difficulty to learn paired-associates.

Stimulus analysis. In thinking about stimulus terms in a paired-associate list, we may sometimes speak as if the "real" stimulus is out there—on the memory drum, on the card, on the screen. Of course we know that this is not proper. The functional stimulus is initially the response that is produced by the stimulus term as presented. If the stimulus term as presented is DOG, the functional stimulus is whatever response one makes to DOG, which is likely to be an implicit response "DOG." However, once one makes the implicit response "DOG," it may serve as a stimulus for another response, perhaps "CAT" or "ANIMAL." Such implicit responses are sometimes very compelling. If a stimulus word is HOT, one's perceptual response of "HOT" is almost inevitably followed by a further implicit response, "COLD." We must recognize that we carry around with us a vast repertoire of associations, and any verbal unit presented as a stimulus in a verbal-learning task may elicit some of these associations implicitly. We know that one of the dimensions of meaningfulness is the number of associates which a verbal unit evokes. It is quite possible, therefore, that stimulus meaningfulness influences learning somewhat because of these associates. In effect, these implicit associates may provide a bridge to the response term. If the stimulus term is DOG and the response term, the number 9, the association might be a two-step affair—from DOG to CAT to 9, on the assumption that there is already an association between CAT and 9. Such associations are often called mediated associations. The point we wish to make is that our thinking about the functional stimulus, the stimulus that actually enters into the association with the response term, cannot be limited to the stimulus term as presented. The functional stimulus may be an expanded stimulus in the sense that it elicits other verbal units which may be involved in the associative connection.

The functional stimulus may also be a contracted version of the stimulus term as presented. This is sometimes termed stimulus selection or stimulus fractionation. It is as if S selects out one unit of a multiple-unit stimulus which then becomes the functional stimulus. Consider a study by Jenkins (1963). The stimulus terms in the paired-associate list were seven three-letter consonant syllables made up of the 21 different consonants. The response terms were single-digit numbers. All Ss learned the list until they could recite it perfectly. Then, on test trials, each letter of each syllable was presented separately, and S was asked to give the number which was paired with the syllable in which the letter appeared. The results show that more correct responses were given to the first letters of the syllable than to the last and more to either than to the middle letter of the syllable. It appeared, therefore, that the functional stimulus for some Ss, at least, was a single letter, with the letter in the first position being preferred. In view of such findings, we can see another possibility why stimulus meaningfulness should have relatively little effect on learning. It appears that S, when we present him with low-meaningful stimuli, may not use the entire stimulus. He may fractionate a difficult stimulus such as KBV and use only the K, thereby negating the low meaningfulness of the trigram as a whole. Will S select the most meaningful element of a multiple-element stimulus? He certainly will. For example, if S is presented a compound stimulus such as COW-XOC (or XOC-COW) and after learning the list is presented with each component separately on a test trial, COW will produce many more correct responses than will XOC (Cohen & Musgrave, 1964).

The lesson from the above illustrations is that we must be thoughtful about our conclusions concerning the functional stimulus in verbal learning. We are presenting verbal units to organisms which possess an associative network among words, and thus a stimulus as presented may be expanded to include some portions of this network. These organisms also appear to have acquired habits of stimulus selection which may be elicited in verbal-learning experiments; and by being elicited, these habits may change the characteristics of the stimulus as presented.

The Origin of Meaningfulness Differences

We return now to the knotty problem posed earlier. We have seen that meaningfulness indexes resulting from the scaling operations can most simply be interpreted as representing differences in learning which have already occurred. Therefore, when we relate these indexes to learning measures, we are simply introducing more learning in a formal way. An item which has high meaningfulness must necessarily take a shorter period of time to reach a high level of learning than must an item of low meaningfulness. The critical experimental problem lies in trying to determine what produced the meaningfulness differences in the first place. What sort of approaches might be used to attack this problem?

The approach which seems to have the best possibilities of being fruitful is that of taking units which initially have equal meaningfulness and trying to induce meaningfulness differences in these units experimentally. More specifically, we might choose a group of very low-meaningfulness consonant syllables and treat half of them experimentally in an effort to change their meaningfulness and use the other half as controls. But what do we do to try to change the meaningfulness? We must recognize first that all scaled meaningfulness measures must reflect differences in experience with the verbal units. A common word has been experienced as a unit much more frequently than has a difficult consonant syllable. The question is whether or not there is a *particular kind* of experience that is fundamentally and causally related to the difference in meaningfulness. The experimental problem is to induce one kind of experience with the units while holding other kinds constant, and, in the vernacular, such procedures ain't easy to come by. Let's see why.

Suppose we have a hypothesis proposing that the critical and causal characteristic of meaningfulness is the number of associates an item elicits. Therefore, to our experimental consonant syllables we require S to learn a number of different associates, perhaps common words. He learns that when KBV appears, he must say COW, PEN, CUP, LAW, CAB; when RZL appears, he must say DAD, CAT, GAS, ROT, SUN. Then we use these syllables as response terms in a paired-associate list and compare the rate of learning of the list with another in which the control syllables are the response terms. Suppose we find that learning is faster for the list with the E syllables; have we shown beyond reasonable doubt that number of associates is at least one critical factor in meaningfulness? Probably not. Suppose another investigator holds the hypothesis that the critical factor which is directly related to experience with a unit is its pronounceability. He might well argue, therefore, that when S was learning the associates to KBV, he was also learning how to pronounce the item in a consistent fashion. He could further argue, therefore, that the associations may be irrelevant.

This illustrates the type of problem faced when trying to endow verbal units with a single attribute in an attempt to discover what effect this has on learning. That such operations have not as yet been carried out to everyone's satisfaction does not mean that they will not eventually be. The problem is of relatively recent origin, and investigators have by no means exhausted their ingenuity on it.

INTRALIST SIMILARITY

A second task variable which has considerable influence on learning is known categorically as intralist similarity, but this includes a number of quite independent defining operations used to differentiate among kinds of similarity.

Types of Similarity

Formal similarity. Formal similarity refers to the number of different letters used in making up a list; the fewer the number of different letters for a constant number of units, the higher the similarity. The following two lists would be extreme cases of the dimension:

LOW SIMILARITY	HIGH SIMILARITY
QJH	ZGJ
ZDW	GQJ
KBF	JFQ
XSG	QFZ
TLN	FQJ

The low-similarity list is made up of 15 different letters; the high-similarity list is made up of only five different letters.

Meaningful similarity. The dictionary could be used as the criterion for establishing differences among meaningful similarity, or rating procedures might allow specification of quantitative differences in meaningful similarity. A list made up of the following words would be said to have high similarity: *elated, gleeful, carefree, jolly, laughing, happy, genial, smiling, cheerful*. A low-similarity list would be one in which there was little or no synonymity among the items in the list.

Our language is such that there are not many instances in which many different words all have the same core of meaning, as in the list given above. Therefore, it has often been necessary to use subgroups of similar items to make up a word list, which, for example, might be *icy, frigid, cold; royal, regal, kingly; double, dual, twofold*.

Conceptual similarity. The greater the number of words within a list which belong to the same category or represent instances of the same concept, the higher the conceptual similarity. If all the words in a list are names of animals, we would have high conceptual similarity; if each word represents an instance of a different concept or category, we would have low conceptual similarity.

Analysis of the Effects of Intralist Similarity

In considering how intralist similarity may be expected to influence verbal learning, it will again be useful to think of two aspects of the overall learning, namely, that of acquiring verbal units as units and that of acquiring an association between two verbal units. The evidence indicates that intralist similarity will influence both aspects of the learning, but the nature of the influences depends upon the nature of the similarity. We may first consider meaningful and conceptual similarity, since they have much the same effect on both aspects of the learning.

Free learning. Conceptual and meaningful similarity are positively related to free learning; that is, the higher the similarity, the more rapid the free learning. If we accept the free-learning technique as the technique which allows us to study the acquisition of verbal units as units, with a minimum number of specific associative connections being involved, we may conclude that meaningful and conceptual similarity give us a positive factor which will have to be considered when assessing the role of intralist similarity in serial learning or in paired-associate learning (where specific associative connections *are* required). At the same time we must not overlook the necessity of explaining why free learning is positively influenced by conceptual and meaningful similarity. A number of investigators have directed their energies toward a search for a satisfactory explanation of the relationship, and we should sample these efforts briefly.

Consider a study by Cohen (1963). The Ss were given a 70-word list for a single study and recall trial. The list consisted of 20 different categories of words, some categories being represented by three words, some by four. Ten of the categories were said to be exhaustive categories and 10, nonexhaustive. An exhaustive category is one in which all or nearly all of the words which can fall within the category are used. The nonexhaustive category would be one with many more instances fitting it than were actually used in the list. An example of an exhaustive category is provided by the words *freshman, sophomore, junior,* and *senior.* A nonexhaustive category is represented by the words *sardine, minnow, perch,* and *salmon.*

Cohen actually performed several experiments with such materials, but all produced the same general finding, namely, better recall of words from exhaustive than from nonexhaustive categories. The average S was able to recall 18.7 items from the exhaustive categories and 14.2 from the nonexhaustive. The difference was produced primarily by the fact that S was more likely to give all items from the exhaustive category than from the nonexhaustive; the number of different categories represented at recall was approximately the same for both types. Cohen further proceeded to obtain word-association data for his lists. That is, Ss (who had not learned the lists) were asked to give the first word which each of the 70 words made them think of. These data show that S is more likely to respond with another word within the category for the exhaustive categories than for the nonexhaustive categories. Such differences are said to represent differences in interitem associative connection. In the present case it appears that these interitem associative connections allowed S to recall most or all of the instances within a category if at least one of the instances was specifically remembered.

Now we see, therefore, the possibility that conceptual similarity and meaningful similarity may produce a positive effect at recall because the higher the similarity, the greater the likelihood that one instance of a category will elicit another member of that category or that one word will elicit its synonyms. Thus, associative connections already exist among similar items, and these appear to be involved in the relationship between similarity and learning. If this is true, words which are associatively related but not similar in the two ways we have been discussing should produce the same effect as high similarity when placed in a list. They do (Deese, 1959).

Free learning and the frequency with which words appear in print are also directly related. However, the higher the frequency of the words in the list, the more likely it is that each word will elicit another in the list, this likelihood being determined by word-association norms. This relationship, therefore, allows the argument (Deese, 1960) that the frequency effect in learning is also produced by the differences in interitem associations which covary with frequency.

If the interitem associative connections are the important mediators of the similarity relationship in free learning, do they produce their influence at recall, or during the learning trial, or both? If lists are used in which there are subgroups of similar words (as in the Cohen experiment), there is clear evidence that the words at recall will be clustered, in the sense that S will recall words together which fit a given category or which are similar in meaning with greater than chance frequency. Much of the work on recall clustering has been done by W. A. Bousfield and his students at the University of Connecticut (e.g., Bousfield & Puff, 1964). Clustering in recall can be simply demonstrated. If you are given 10 min. to write all the names of cities in the United States that you can think of, you will probably discover when you examine your recall, that you have remembered them in certain groupings, perhaps geographical groupings. Midwestern cities would tend to be grouped together, eastern cities together, and so on. Or, you might group cities within states (Dallas, Austin, Fort Worth, San Antonio), or by their size. We cannot be sure, then, that because free learning usually shows clustering in recall, we should draw any causal relationship between the amount of clustering and the amount recalled. Clustering might be what we call an epiphenomenon; it is real and reliable, but it may be quite incidental to the recall found better for high-similarity lists than for low-similarity lists. We do know that if all items in a list are similar, thus minimizing any possible effect of clustering, free learning is still more rapid with high-similarity lists than with low, even when the recall is paced at a rapid rate (Ekstrand & Underwood, 1963). We cannot, then, answer the question posed earlier with any high degree of confidence—we cannot tell how much of the similarity effect in free learning is produced at the time of recall and how much is due to processes which took place during the learning trial.

When we turn to formal similarity, the available data say that with low-meaningful units, high similarity retards free learning (Underwood, Ekstrand, & Keppel, 1964). The reason for this is fairly clear. The acquisition of low-meaningfulness units such as RZL requires an associative phase—the learning requires the association of letters which rarely appear together. Learning that Z follows R is like having a paired-associate list in which Z is the stimulus term and R is the response term. We will see that establishing specific associative connections between units is inhibited by all kinds of similarity. In the case of RZL we have to think of each letter as a unit, whereas with a common word, such as RED, the word as a whole is the unit. A list of consonant syllables of low meaningfulness but with high similarity (such as listed earlier) becomes a very difficult associative-learning task, and high similarity inhibits the learning. We could make a comparable list with words somewhat as follows:

red—cat—pen
tub—ash—cat
pen—red—tub
ash—tub—red
pen—cat—ash

We would confidently predict that such a list given for free learning would be more difficult to learn than if there were five units made up of three three-letter words each, but with no word repeated.

Associative learning. We may now ask specifically about similarity as it influences the development of associations between units. We noted earlier that it has an inhibitory effect, and we may illustrate this for formal similarity as manipulated by Horowitz (1962). Two lists were made up, each consisting of 12 pairs. The critical members of the pairs were consonant syllables. In one case the 12 items included only four different letters; in the other case 12 different letters were used. Thus, the 12 high-similarity items were such syllables as FVX, XVS, XSF, and SFX. These syllables were each paired with a common word. In learning, S was shown each pair on a card for 4 sec. each. On the test trial following each study trial, E placed the 12 stimulus words on a board. The response terms, one each to a card, were given S, and he was asked to place them opposite their appropriate stimulus terms. Thus S did not have to recall the response terms; he merely had to learn the association between a particular stimulus term and a particular response term. This technique provides almost as pure a form of studying associative formation (the associative stage) as it is possible to devise. Half the Ss learning each list had the words as formal stimulus terms and the trigrams as formal response terms, and the other half had the reverse; however, this is of little consequence for such a task.

The results showed very large differences in acquisition rate over 10 acquisition and test trials, with acquisition being much faster for the low-similarity list. Roughly speaking, for the low-similarity trigrams, all Ss were matching the 12 pairs perfectly after five trials; for the high-similarity trigrams, the average number correct on the tenth trial was still only about 10.

Putting the parts together. We have stated the effect of various forms of similarity on response learning, and we have noted that associative learning is impeded by the various forms of similarity. If these two forms of learning represent the major factors involved in learning a paired-associate list, we should be able to make some predictions about paired-associate learning as a function of stimulus-term similarity and as a function of response-term similarity. We would expect to have continuous functions for each case as similarity is gradually varied, but for discussion purposes we may speak only of high and of low similarity.

When stimulus terms are neutral (and have low similarity), differences in formal similarity among response terms will produce maximum differences in learning. Formal similarity impedes acquisition of responses, and it also impedes associative learning. If the similarity holds among stimulus terms, with response terms neutral, a high-similarity list will be more difficult to learn than will a low-similarity list, but the differences between the two will be less than for the corresponding similarity among the response terms. Stimulus similarity will not influence response learning, only associative learning.

The above expectations will probably be confirmed only with units of low meaningfulness. As the units are given higher and higher meaningfulness, the negative effect on response learning of the formal similarity will become less and less. Furthermore, formal similarity will have little, if any, effect on the associative stage when the units are common words. For example, a series of words made up of only five letters, words such as *rat, tar, par, top, tap, pot, pat,* and *rot,* would produce little if any associative interference if these were stimulus terms in a paired-associate list. What we are saying, of course, is that with formal similarity there is an interaction between the effects of formal similarity and meaningfulness; the higher the meaningfulness, the less the associative interference for a given level of formal similarity.

In contrast to formal similarity, the difference in learning between high- and low-meaningful or conceptual similarity will be greater when the similarity is varied among stimulus terms than when it is varied among response terms. Either of these types of similarity influences response learning in a positive manner; that is, the higher the similarity, the more rapid the response learning. On the assumption that associative learning will be equally influenced in the negative direction by similarity among stimulus terms and among response terms, we would have to subtract the positive effect of response learning from the negative effect of associative learning when dealing with similarity among response terms. Therefore, stimulus-term similarity will produce a greater effect on paired-associate learning than will response-term similarity. In fact, with response-term similarity, resultant learning might be faster for high-similarity units than for low-similarity units; it would all depend on the magnitude of the positive effect on response learning versus the negative effect on associative learning.

The above discussion represents a way of thinking about how similarity may influence paired-associate learning. It should be evident that similarity will also influence serial learning, but because we cannot isolate stimulus terms from response terms, serial learning does not give us very much analytical power. Verbal-discrimination learning will also "respond" to variations in similarity, but little analytical work has been done with this task. Finally, it should be noted that intralist similarity, particularly formal similarity, has an enormous effect on learning if used in extreme form. For example, if we have similarity "splattered" in a list, so that it holds within and among stimulus and response terms, the list, even a short list, becomes almost impossible for most college students to learn. You may test this by trying to learn the following short paired-associate list, the items of which were taken from the Horowitz study reviewed above:

$$FVX - XSF$$
$$XVS - SFX$$
$$SXV - FXV$$
$$FSV - SVF$$
$$VSX - FXS$$

Somewhat less extreme would be having simultaneous similarity of stimulus terms and of response terms, but with low similarity between stimulus and response terms. Various procedures of this kind clearly influence learning (e.g., Umemoto, 1962) with meaningful and conceptual similarity as well as formal similarity. In a study by Newman and Saltz (1960), learning the appropriate locations of adjectives in a paragraph was severely retarded when different sentences in the paragraph used synonymous adjectives as compared with sentences where the adjectives were not synonyms. Considering the results of such procedures, as well as others not mentioned, we must conclude that the various forms of similarity collectively represent a most powerful variable in verbal learning.

Sources of associative interference. We have assumed that high similarity will produce associative interference in establishing specific associations between verbal units. We may, of course, inquire into the mechanisms behind the associative interference. There are several alternatives. In dealing with formal similarity, some investigators may use classical sensory generalization as a mechanism lying behind the effects. Semantic generalization is sometimes used; two words may elicit a common response (implicitly), and since this common response is nondifferentiating with regard to establishing new associations, "confusion" results. In conceptual similarity, *cat* and *dog* may not only implicitly elicit each other, but they may also elicit the common implicit response, *animal*. Again, such implicit responses will interfere with the development of associations. It is even possible that the implicit responses may not be verbal in nature. Thus, *icy* and *cold* may both produce the same "feeling tone." However one chooses to view these matters, it is clear that in order to produce the interference, two (or more) units must elicit a common response (usually an implicit response), and this common response cannot be a differential cue for establishing the two associations.

The interference produced by associations among words may sometimes be made explicit by a method of crossed associates (e.g., Spence & Lair, 1965; McCullers, 1965). Pairs of words which are strongly associated (*table-chair*, *horse-buggy*) are used, but the associated words are not paired in the list. To illustrate:

table—light
horse—thread
needle—glass
cup—chair
window—saucer
lamp—buggy

If the strong associate of a word is not in the list, it does not seem to produce much interference, but if it *is* in the list, it does. Thus, with *chair* as a response term in the list, interference by the strong association between *table* and *chair* is produced as S tries to learn *table-light*.

The Isolation Effect

Suppose we use a list of 20 words in a free-learning procedure. For the C Group, all items are printed in black ink; for the E Group the twelfth item is printed in red ink, and all others are in black. We give a single study trial followed by the usual recall. We can expect with a high degree of confidence that the twelfth item will be given correctly more times by the E Group than by the C Group. These operations and results define an isolation effect. The basic operations require that one item (sometimes two) is cast in some way to be distinctly different from (have low similarity with) the other items in the list. A nonsense syllable in a list of words will produce the effect and so will a three-digit number in a list of syllables.

Various hypotheses have been advanced to account for the isolation effect, but none seems to have handled all of the facts satisfactorily. The isolated item may be said to have greater attention value, but attention is a difficult variable to manipulate experimentally and to show, therefore, that it influences learning. If the isolated item is viewed as being less similar to the other units than the other units are to themselves, the isolated item should suffer less interference when, for example, it is a response term in a paired-associate list. However, studies have not given much support to the idea that reduced interference is the critical factor in the isolation effect (Saltz & Newman, 1959; Erickson, 1963). At the moment, the reasons why the isolation effect occurs are unclear.

A recent review (Wallace, 1965) of the empirical and theoretical issues involved in the study of isolation may be consulted for further information, and only one additional comment needs to be made here. Although the isolated item is learned more rapidly than the same item in the control list, the list as a whole shows no facilitation in learning. It is as if the acquisition of other items in the list suffers at the expense of the isolated item, or, as the saying goes, we rob Peter to pay Paul.

OTHER TASK VARIABLES

Although meaningfulness and intralist similarity have been the task variables most frequently worked with in recent years, there are other attributes of verbal units which have been investigated and which should have brief mention here.

Form class. Form class means the class of words to which a given word belongs (nouns, adjectives, verbs, and so on). It is reasonable to ask whether there is a relationship between learning and form class. The answer is yes. These may be further combined into two broader classes known as content words and function words. The content words are nouns, adjectives, and verbs; the function words are pronouns, prepositions, and conjunctions. Glanzer (1962), using paired-associate learning and with conditions in which words representing the form classes appeared either as stimuli or as responses (and the results were the same), showed that content words are associated with more rapid learning than are function words. Actually, the nouns and adjectives resulted in the most rapid learning, the verbs producing about the same rate of learning as the function words. Other evidence also indicates that prepositions and conjunctions are, for some reason, particularly difficult to "hang on to" or to "hang something on to" in paired-associate learning (Epstein, Rock, & Zuckerman, 1960).

There is another curious finding related to form class. If paired associates are presented in the adjective-noun order and the learning compared with the noun-adjective order of the same pairs, the latter pairings are learned more rapidly (Paivio, 1963). This seems curious in view of the fact that in sentences the noun generally follows the adjective leading us to believe that the adjective-noun order would be favored over the noun-adjective order. The phenomenon may in some way be related to a concrete-abstract dimension, with the nouns being more concrete than the adjectives, but just how this will influence the learning is a matter for speculation. Some have said that it is related to the greater imagery associated with concrete words (Paivio, 1965).

Affectivity. We have seen in an earlier chapter that words may be reliably scaled on the attribute of affective connotation varying from very pleasant to very unpleasant, for example, from *lovely* to *vomit*. However, when words are equated on other task variables known to be related to learning, there appears to be no consistent relationship between rate of learning and level of affectivity (e.g., Kott, 1955; Klugman, 1956).

TWO PROBLEMS IN LIST CONSTRUCTION

Having seen how certain task variables influence verbal learning, we must now consider two problems in list construction when task variables are manipulated.

Representativeness versus Analysis

Let us assume that we are going to study the effect of meaningfulness on serial learning. Let us assume further that our interest is in consonant syllables, and so we select Witmer's tables as a source of our syllables. As a sampling of the dimension of meaningfulness we decide to use association values of from 0 percent through 8 percent for low, 50 percent for medium, and 92 percent through 100 percent for high association value. How will we go about selecting the particular syllables from the many which fall within these specified levels? There are two approaches.

The first approach would recommend that we construct our three lists by drawing syllables randomly, perhaps by drawing 10 syllables from each of the three levels and letting one list represent each level. If we want to be a little more confident of representativeness within the levels, we might draw more than one list from each level and use the average learning scores for all lists within the level as indicative of the average learning rate associated with that level. There can be no doubt that if our interest is in getting representative syllables—syllables which represent the population of syllables at a given level—this procedure must be followed. Analytically speaking, however, it cannot be recommended if we want to study the effect of meaningfulness in pure form. Assume that the number of different letters involved in the syllables varies for different levels of meaningfulness. When we draw randomly, the intralist similarity will vary inversely to the number of different letters. Hence, our results will be a confounded relationship, the learning being a combined function of meaningfulness differences and differences in intralist similarity.

Consider another illustration. Assume that our interest is in free learning as a function of word frequency and that we form our lists by drawing randomly from specified levels of frequency. But we know that the more frequent the word, the less its length (the fewer the number of letters), so word length is confounded with frequency, and form class may also be confounded with frequency. Therefore, our learning results will be a function of frequency, word length, form class, and perhaps other attributes which are also correlated with frequency.

The analytical approach sacrifices representativeness in order to avoid the confounding of attributes. If we are going to study meaningfulness at three levels, we *choose* syllables from those levels which produce lists in which intralist similarity is constant as indexed by number of repeated letters. If we are going to study the effect of word frequency on free learning, we choose from the various levels of frequency the words which will allow us to construct lists which do not differ on other attributes insofar as those attributes are known. It is clear that analytical selection sacrifices representativeness.

Mixed versus Unmixed Lists

In manipulating a task variable, we have another decision to make in constructing lists; to illustrate let us again consider the manipulation of meaningfulness at three levels. We might construct a paired-associate list of 12 pairs, four pairs representing low meaningfulness, four representing medium meaningfulness, and four representing high meaningfulness. The average learning scores for the four pairs at each level could be used to index the rate of learning associated with the three levels of meaningfulness. Such a list is called a mixed list and is contrasted with an unmixed list where all items in the list come from the same level of meaningfulness and where, therefore, we need three different lists for the experiment.

The mixed list has a very distinct advantage. It is, in effect, a counterbalanced design—each S is given all three levels of meaningfulness or all three levels of frequency—and at the same time there is no problem of controlling for practice effects. We achieve statistical precision in comparing each S's score on one level of meaningfulness with his scores on the other levels. It would seem to be a fairly ideal procedure.

Recent thinking and findings, however, have made us less sure of this conclusion—the conclusion that a mixed list is the ideal procedure. The thinking is somewhat like that involved in the performance-learning distinction discussed in earlier chapters. Suppose you are an S in a free-learning experiment in which you are given 50 verbal units, 25 common words and 25 consonant syllables, with the words and syllables randomly ordered. Such a long list cannot be learned in one trial; it will take many trials. Most of us have study habits of sorts. Suppose your habits led you to decide to concentrate on the consonant syllables first and get those out of the way before you paid much attention to the words. The learning scores would show that you apparently learned the consonant syllables more rapidly than the words. Your particular habits led you to give the consonant syllables higher priority in learning, but had your habits led you to decide to learn the words first, quite the opposite finding would have occurred. These performance habits, therefore, may influence the results over and above any influence the task variable as such may have. Such priority habits cannot be dismissed as unimportant even if we instruct Ss to pay equal attention to all units.

The question of importance, of course, is how to tell whether or not such priority habits exist. If we find a substantial difference in the effect of a task variable when manipulated in a mixed list as compared with the effects in unmixed lists, the operation of priority habits is a likely hypothesis to account for the difference. In the unmixed lists, even if priority habits are operating, a bias is not produced because we average the scores for all items. Therefore, the critical operation for the identification of priority habits is to compare the laws obtained with mixed lists and those with unmixed lists for the same materials representing a given task variable. If these laws differ—if the magnitude of the effects of the variable differs for the two types of lists—it is a reasonable conclusion that priority habits are involved.

At the present time we do not know much about such priority habits. We do know that they have operated in certain situations (e.g., Postman & Riley, 1957), but we have no knowledge which allows us to predict their operation. This is to say, we do not know what cues must be present before the habits will be elicited. Furthermore, even when they are elicited, we do not know whether they will produce the same biasing effect for all Ss. Data were presented earlier from a mixed list of 27 trigrams varying in meaningfulness. Could these differences be due to priority habits and not to differences in the difficulty of acquiring the units? For this variable (meaningfulness) the findings using mixed lists and unmixed lists parallel each other very closely, so it is doubtful that priority habits are involved differentially in the relationship. But for most task variables, we do not have such evidence. Until we do, it seems most prudent to use unmixed lists, unless, of course, we wish to study priority habits.

SOME FURTHER VARIABLES

Time

The role of time factors in learning is often taken for granted; with possibly no exceptions, the longer we practice on a task the better we learn it. What is less well realized, however, is that if task variables as discussed earlier are held constant, we can state some rather definite relationships between time and learning, even when other factors are allowed to vary. If we present word lists for a single study and recall trial, and if these lists differ in length (number of words), S will recall a larger number of words from the longer list, although he will recall a smaller percentage. Murdock's work (1960), however, allowed him to show that if total time to study is used as the independent variable, there is no difference in the number of words recalled. Let us see how he did this.

Murdock performed a series of experiments, using in most of them complete or incomplete between-S counterbalancing. Among these experiments was one in which the length of list varied (20, 30, 40, or 60 items), and, simultaneously, the rate of presentation time per item was varied. The 20-word list was presented at a 3-sec. rate, the 30-item list at a 2-sec. rate, the 40-item list at a 1.5-sec. rate, and the 60-item list at a 1-sec. rate. If we multiply the number of items in each list by the rate per item, we find that all lists were presented for a total of 60 sec. If total time is the critical variable, the mean number of items recalled should be equivalent for the four lists. The results show this to be true, the average recall being 9.3, 9.3, 9.6, and 8.4 items for the lists with 20, 30, 40, and 60 items, respectively.

Murdock produced the same result in still another manner. The Ss were given a list of 25, 50, or 75 words and were allowed 30 sec. to study the list before being asked to recall as many as possible. The recall did not differ for the lists of different length.

The role of total time in learning, versus time per item, has also been demonstrated by Bugelski (1962) using paired-associate lists. Eight pairs of nonsense syllables made up the lists, and learning under all conditions was carried to a criterion of two successive perfect trials. There were five conditions representing differences in rate of presentation, and each condition was represented by a different group of Ss. Anticipation learning was used, and 2 sec. were always allowed for anticipation for all conditions. However, after the anticipation interval for a given stimulus term was over, the stimulus term and response term were shown together for study; and it was this study time, 2, 4, 6, 8, or 15 sec., that was varied for the groups. There was always a 2-sec. interval between pairs. Therefore, counting the anticipation interval and the time between pairs, we find the total time per pair was 6, 8, 10, 12, or 19 sec.

The results are plotted in Fig. 11-3, where the left ordinate identifies the mean number of trials required to reach the criterion set for learning. The relationship is clear with regard to this measure; as time per pair increases, number of trials to learn decreases. However, when total time per pair for all trials is calculated for each item by multiplying the number of trials by time per pair, the resulting curve shows no systematic relationship. This curve is shown as the dotted line in Fig. 11-3 and is plotted against the right ordinate. Although the curve is not horizontal, Bugelski reports that statistically speaking it may be considered a horizontal line, meaning, of course, that total time to learn did not differ. Thus, again, the critical factor appears to be the total time.

In a further experiment, Bugelski and Rickwood (1963) got at the problem in still another way. They let S control his own study time; although he was given only a 2-sec. anticipation period, when the stimulus term and

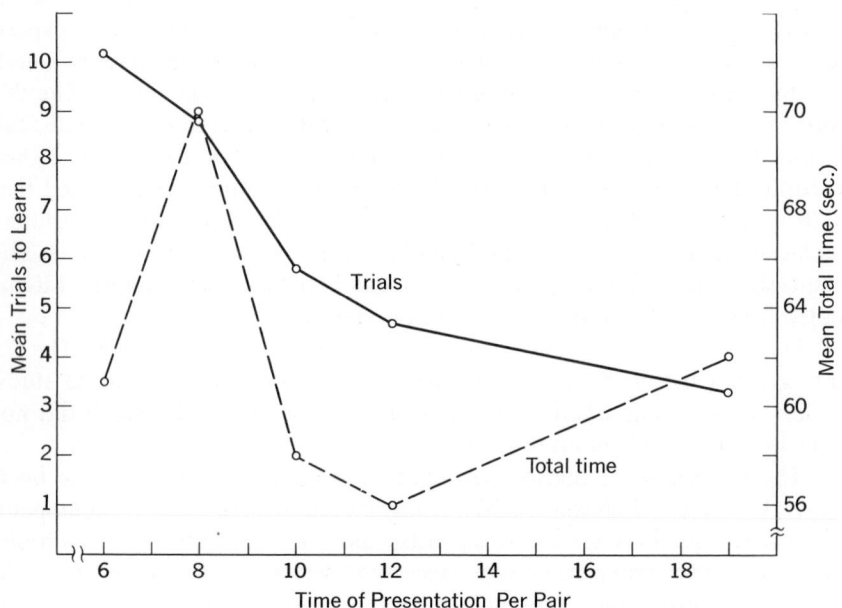

Fig. 11-3. Trials to learn and total time to learn as a function of time of presentation of each pair in a paired-associate list. Data from Bugelski (1962).

response term appeared, he could study them as long as he wished before moving on to the stimulus of the next pair. The group of Ss required 8.1 trials per item and the total time to learn per item was 65 sec., a time which is quite comparable to those shown in Fig. 11-3. Thus, even when S goes at his own pace the average time to learn turns out to be approximately the same as the time required when time is under E's control.

Intent to Learn

By appropriate operations we may present verbal materials to S without instructing him to learn the material but then testing him for how much he has learned. Such procedures are usually carried out with free learning and are often referred to as incidental learning, in order to distinguish them from studies or conditions in which S is instructed to learn (intentional learning).

In an incidental-learning procedure the list presented to S following instructions called covering instructions, which justify to S the need to observe the materials but carry no instructions to learn. The control group would be given essentially the same instructions but, in addition, would be told that they would be tested for recall of the items. As an example of covering instructions, Ss in the incidental-learning group might be told that E is interested in the pronounceability of the nonsense syllables to be presented. As each syllable appears, S is to rate it for pronounceability, which allows him to be exposed to each item, but he is not told that he will later have to recall the items. The intentional-learning group would also rate the items but in addition would be trying, presumably, to learn them, since they had been told that a recall would be taken.

Those who have worked most extensively in the field have concluded that, in general, the variables which influence intentional learning also influence incidental learning in the same manner (Postman, 1964a). But as a general finding, the total amount learned is less under incidental than under intentional learning. Nevertheless, the fact that under certain circumstances incidental learning is as great or nearly as great as intentional learning makes it doubtful if intent to learn is necessary for learning. Rather, it appears that if E can get S to make the responses to each unit which are appropriate for learning, S will learn, whether he intends to or not, and the amount learned may be as great without intention as with intention. Two studies may be used to illustrate this.

In a study by Postman and Adams (1960), a 214-word prose passage was used, but from it 35 words were deleted. The instructions for the Ss for both the intentional and incidental groups required them to fill in the blanks with words which they believed to be appropriate. In addition to such instructions, the intentional group was told that after they finished they would be asked to recall the words they inserted in the blanks. After S had finished filling in the blanks, he was given 5 min. to recall all of the words possible which he had inserted. Of course, this request came as a surprise to the incidental Ss. The intentional group recalled a mean of 16.80 words, and the incidental, a mean of 15.32. While the difference is just significant statistically, the critical fact is that there is very little absolute difference. We presume that the incidental Ss, in filling the blanks, said the words and saw them as they wrote them, that these are quite appropriate responses to make for learning, and that whether S intends to learn or not is not highly relevant.

Mechanic (1964) used a somewhat different procedure to produce responses to the items which he believed were appropriate for learning. A list of 24 trigrams was presented once, each trigram for 9 sec. The E told S that he was interested in the effects of fatigue and practice on pronunciation and that as each trigram appeared, S was to pronounce it over and over again throughout the 9-sec. period. A microphone was used to record (presumably) the pronouncings. In addition, the intentional group was told that they would be asked to recall the trigrams after all had been presented. The intentional and incidental groups did not differ in their recall after a single presentation of the 24 units, the means for both groups being 8.85 items.

Serial Position

One of the most striking variables in verbal learning is the position held by an item in a serial list. We remember that in serial learning the items are presented in the same order from trial to trial and that S must learn the order of the items. The rate of learning the items within such a list is very predictable from the serial position each holds. The first items

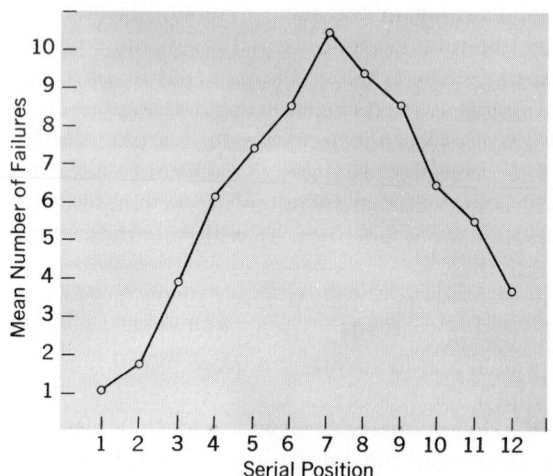

Fig. 11-4. The bowed serial-position curve. The values are from 64 Ss learning lists of 12 nonsense syllables. Data from Hovland (1938).

in the list will be learned most rapidly, those at the end of the list, next most rapidly, and the item just past the middle, most slowly.

A fairly typical curve representing the relationship between serial position and rate of learning is shown in Fig. 11-4. There were 12 nonsense syllables in the lists, and the response measure used was the number of failures at each position, a failure including an overt wrong response or S's saying nothing. We could also plot the mean number of times an item was correctly given in each position, in which case the curve as shown in Fig. 11-4 would be inverted. We often speak of the relationship between position and learning a serial list as the bowed serial-position curve. Even if the serial list is presented as a continuous task, S appears to "pick out" a starting point and develops the bowed curve. The basic relationship is normally apparent in the data sheet of single Ss. It also appears in the spelling errors of long words (Jensen, 1962). While not necessarily invariant, the bowed curve in the usual serial-learning experiment is a highly predictable phenomenon even in its details.

How would we account for the bowed serial-position curve? It appears to us the way the common cold does to the medical profession—an obvious phenomenon surrounded by many hypotheses, none of which seems to work out. In truth, it is extremely difficult to test hypotheses about the bowed curve of serial learning because it is relatively invariant; it cannot be "pushed around" very much by manipulating other variables. There is no shortage of theories about the relationship; they range from those which view the nervous system as an information-processing system (like a computer) to those which attempt to explain it in perceptual terms. As no purpose will be served by discussing these theories, suffice it to say that the person who originates a theory that works out to almost everyone's satisfaction will be in line for an award in psychology equivalent to the Nobel prize.

Very likely the ultimate understanding of the bowed curve will be related to an understanding of what is learned when a serial list is acquired. We have previously noted that the serial list is not a very analytical task since the stimulus functions and the response functions of the items are confounded. This assumption rested on the notion that S learns a chain of associations in which the first item is the stimulus for the second as a response, the second item, a stimulus for the third, and so on. Recent research has indicated that the situation is much more confused than this, for this research shows that it is very difficult to identify a stimulus for each unit in the serial list. We may sample this research to see both where the problem lies and what some of the variables are in serial learning.

The Stimulus in Serial Learning

Let us assume that S does learn a chain of associations as described above. If we label the successive items in the serial list as A, B, C, D, one association is said to be established between A and B, another between B and C, and another between C and D. Until recent years it seems to have been implicitly assumed that such associations *were* formed, but a study by Young in 1959 caused the first modern head-scratching about this assumption. Young reasoned that if such associations were formed in serial learning, a paired-associate list constructed of the relevant pairs should be learned very quickly. That is, following serial learning, a paired-associate list was to be constructed of the pairs, A-B, E-F, B-C, and D-E, so that each association required in the paired-associate list was presumed to have been acquired in learning the serial list. The results show that although there was some initial positive effect in learning the paired-associate list, in terms of trials to reach a criterion there was no benefit over that of learning the list when not preceded by the serial learning. It did not seem, therefore, that S *had* learned a chain of associations in the serial list.

One objection might be raised to the above study. In the paired-associate list each item occurred both as a stimulus term and as a response term (except the first and last item of the serial list, the first being used only as a stimulus term, the last only as a response). This is an unusual paired-associate list, and it can be said to have very high similarity. Such lists are known to be very difficult to learn (Umemoto & Hilgard, 1961), and perhaps this was "messing up" the associations that were presumed to have existed in the serial list. However, when the experiment was repeated, using each item only as a stimulus term or as a response term, essentially the same result was found (Young, 1962). If an association is established between A and B, and between B and C in serial learning, it would seem that the learning of the paired-associate list ought to be facilitated markedly; it is not. Such a result leads to a questioning of the assumption of serial associations in serial learning.

Another approach to the problem has shown that although S appears to be able to learn sequential associations between successive items in a serial list, it is difficult for him. In order to force S to learn sequential associations, we use a different item as the first one on successive trials. Of course, the order of the items remains the same on all trials; S merely starts at a different point in the series on successive trials. The evidence indicates that learning rate is severely retarded under such conditions as compared with the usual method of presentation where the same item is always used as the starting item (Ebenholtz, 1963; Winnick & Dornbush, 1963). Such findings also lead to the hypothesis that *position* along a spatial continuum may serve as a stimulus for each item in a serial list. When a different item is used as the starting item on successive trials, position for any given item varies from trial to trial and thus becomes an inconsistent cue. When the starting item is constant, as in conventional serial learning, a given position and a given item are always paired. In effect, S may learn a paired associate list in which the first position is the stimulus for A, and the second position, a stimulus for B, as follows:

STIMULUS "TERM"	RESPONSE TERM
1st position	A
2nd position	B
3rd position	C

How would such a hypothesis be tested? The basic notion would be to shift S to a second list following learning of a conventional first list. In this second list, some of the items would be items from the first list, occupying the same serial position as they had in the first list but so chosen that sequential associations would be inappropriate. For example, the second list might retain the items from the first list holding the odd positions (1, 3, 5, 7, and so on), and they would be in the same positions in the second list. New items would be used for the even positions (2, 4, 6, 8). The rate of learning the second list is then compared with the learning of a second list by a control group in which all arrangements are the same except for the serial position constancy. You may be able to determine just how this control list should be constructed to obtain this objective. However, since the procedure is a transfer procedure, some of the fairly delicate problems of control for transfer effects must be delayed until the next chapter. We will say only that investigations of this type (Ebenholtz, 1963; Keppel & Saufley, 1964; Battig, Brown, & Schild, 1964) have led to the conclusion that position *does* serve as a cue in serial learning. At the same time, the evidence does not allow the conclusion that it is the *only* cue; sequential associations still appear to play some role, and there may be other as yet unidentified sources of stimulus constancy which S "uses." We must, therefore, arrive at the accurate but unsavory conclusion that serial learning is a very complex affair. The bowed serial-position curve and all of the attendant processes which underlie it are likely to fascinate and frustrate investigators for a number of years to come.

THE FORMATION OF AN ASSOCIATION

We present to S a paired associate list for a series of trials, and sooner or later when each stimulus term occurs S will promptly and regularly produce the response. How does this come about? What is responsible for this learning? We have not really touched upon this problem; instead we have asked about factors which influence the rate at which associations are formed without inquiring about the critical process or processes necessary for their formation. This avoidance response is perhaps understandable since it is very difficult to devise a hypothesis about the critical processes and make an adequate test of it. In studying verbal learning we cannot easily prevent S from using the associations which he has already acquired. When the college sophomore comes to the laboratory, he possesses a great network of associations; unfortunately, he brings this network with him, and in most instances, it will enter into the "new" learning we ask of him. The relationship between meaningfulness and learning, we have seen, is largely a reflection of associations already learned. We do not think it is possible to present S with a verbal unit which will not in some way involve previously learned associations—we cannot start the learning at zero.

If a stimulus term is *dog* and the response term is *cat*, we cannot expect that the already established association will not play a role in "acquiring" this paired associate. Such direct associations may be more subtle, however. For example, Baddeley (1964) paired nonsense syllables so that in one case the last letter of the stimulus term and the first letter of the response term "went together," whereas in another case he paired them so that this was less true. The criterion of togetherness is the likelihood with which the two letters follow each other in words. For example, consider the pair QEM-POG. In words, P is the sixth most likely letter to follow M. If the pair is POG-QEM, we have a situation in which Q is the twenty-second most likely letter to follow G. If experience with words has established contingency habits between letters, habits whose strengths are based directly upon frequency of experience, QEM-POG should be learned more rapidly than POG-QEM. Baddeley shows that this is exactly what happens.

If there is not a direct association between the two terms, or parts of the two terms, mediating associations may be used; that is, an additional term may be interposed between the stimulus term and the response term. For example, in a very simple case, the pair *poi-girl* becomes *poi-boy-girl*. That such associational aids, as they are commonly called, occur there is no doubt since careful interrogation of Ss shows this (e.g., Bugelski, 1962). At the same time we should not conclude that all associations learned in the usual verbal-learning experiment involve associational aids (prior learning). Some Ss report no such associations, saying instead that they simply learned the associates "cold" which, when translated, appears to mean that A simply came to elicit B without addition of, or help from, any previously learned associations.

It will be remembered that the evidence produced by incidental learning of trigrams suggested that if E could get S to make responses to the trigrams believed critical for learning, the learning occurred without intent and to as high a level as with intent. In those experiments a pronouncing response was used as the vehicle for learning. Perhaps some such procedure could be used to get S to repeat the two units of a pair without his intending to learn an association between them, after which he would be tested for the development of an association between them. Such attempts have been made.

In one study (Spear, Ekstrand, & Underwood, 1964), Ss were first required to learn a verbal-discrimination list composed of pairs of words. It will be remembered that in a verbal-discrimination task, S merely has to learn which member of each pair E is calling correct for this task. It was presumed that in the act of learning such discriminations, S perceives and probably implicitly pronounces both units of the pairs to himself and that the responses to each word in a pair will occur in close temporal contiguity.

Will an association develop as a consequence? To test for this, the pairs of words from the verbal-discrimination task were used as pairs in a paired-associate list following learning of the verbal-discrimination task. Of course, S did not know that he would be shifted to a paired-associate task so there is no reason to believe that he intentionally tried to learn associations between the members of the pairs while mastering the verbal-discrimination list. The results were positive; the learning of the paired-associate list was substantially facilitated by the prior learning of the verbal-discrimination list. Such evidence would seem to support the notion that an association may be established between two verbal units merely by responding to each member of the unit in close temporal contiguity. The difficulty with this conclusion as a general one is that investigators using nonsense-syllable pairs have failed to find the facilitation in paired-associate learning (Battig & Brackett, 1963). Nevertheless, the incidental-learning approach may be the way to minimize the influence of associational aids in learning and thus allow us to discover the critical conditions involved in learning an association from scratch. Work with very young children, where the associational network is minimal, should lead to the same end.

All-or-none formation of associations. Advances in an area are often made by challenging long-held conceptions. A conception which has had quite wide acceptance for many years concerns the manner in which an association is formed. According to this conception, associations are said to increase gradually in strength over a series of trials; the idea was applied to many kinds of learning, not simply verbal learning.

In recent years the notion that associations show a gradual increment in strength has been challenged, and as a consequence, scores of studies have been undertaken in an effort to reach the truth of the matter. Apparently the initial challenge came from Rock (1957), who used verbal-learning data to support his argument; but he was followed by Estes (1960), who used both verbal-learning and conditioning studies as his source of evidence. These investigators offered as a substitute for the incremental position the idea that either associations are formed to full strength or they are not formed at all, and this position is known as the all-or-none conception of the formation of associations. The question is, "Does the strength of an association build up gradually or is it an all-or-none process?" We cannot hope to cover all of the nuances involved, but we do want to try to make one point. To do this, we must look at the procedure used to provide the demonstration that led to the notion of all-or-none learning of pairs of words.

In Rock's procedure, he asked S to learn a paired-associate list and used alternate study and recall trials. After each study trial, S was tested by being shown the stimulus terms and being requested to produce the appropriate response to each. The unconventional technique Rock introduced for the E Group was that of *replacing* the missed pairs. If, on the first recall trial, S made three correct responses but missed five out of an eight-item list, the five pairs were replaced with five new pairs drawn from a pool of pairs made up before the experiment started. The S then had a second study trial on the eight pairs (three old and five new), followed by another test trial; the pairs missed on the second test trial were replaced. This process continued until S mastered the list. The C Group learned in the usual fashion.

Rock reasoned that if learning is occurring gradually, all pairs should have some associative strength after the first trial. The fact that an item is missed does not mean that there is zero associative strength; it may be simply a weak association, too weak to result in the response being elicited. Now, if learning is occurring gradually and the missed pairs are replaced, S will have to start from the beginning for the replacement pairs. Consequently, it will require longer for him to learn the list than it will for a control S to learn it. On the other hand, if learning is occurring in an all-or-none fashion, items missed have zero associative strength, and to replace them is of no consequence. Therefore, Rock reasoned, replacing missed items should not slow down the learning one bit, and the list should be mastered as quickly by the E Group as by the C Group. His results show no difference in the rate at which the list was learned by the two groups. The data, therefore, were interpreted as contradicting the conception that associations gradually increase in strength but were held to be quite consonant with the alternative hypothesis that an association, when acquired, is acquired at 100 percent strength.

Plotting of a group learning curve shows that performance gradually increases. Plotting of the learning curve for a single S will also show this upward trend, although it will not be smooth. How can the individual learning curve show gradual improvement if learning occurs in an all-or-none fashion? All-or-none learning refers to a single association, but the associations for different pairs may be formed on different trials. Think of eight associations being formed on six successive trials as follows: 3, 2, 0, 1, 1, 1. On the last trial, all eight responses were given correctly. If we plotted the number correct for each successive trial, we would have 3, 5, 5, 6, 7, 8, thus producing the usual upward learning curve. Therefore, the idea of all-or-none learning is quite compatible with gradual learning curve.

In an earlier chapter we discussed the benefits which gradually accrue as a method of attack on a problem becomes widely used, hence well understood. Its pitfalls, its weaknesses, and its strengths become matters of public record, and an investigator knows what he can and cannot do with it. The classical psychophysical methods represent such methods of attack, as do classical conditioning, runway learning, and paired-associate learning. At the same time, we reminded ourselves that it is sometimes only by breaking away from traditional procedures that we can get at processes that are resistant to study by those procedures. Such flexibility is an absolute prerequisite for a viable experimental discipline. If we do not have this flexibility, along with new ideas and new notions about behavior which often demand new methods of attack, an experimental approach soon reaches a point where it churns within itself and does not produce the new knowledge necessary to sustain the use of the approach.

New methods of attack must carry with them an appreciation of the dangers which are inherent in the use of the method. Since its pitfalls or weaknesses are not known, the investigator must be particularly concerned that the method does not violate the fundamental tenets of experimental research, namely, that it does not allow, often surreptitiously, a confounding of independent variables. Or, to use the caution we have used several times before, we must be extraordinarily thoughtful about the implications of a new method of attack.

It appears now that the method introduced by Rock in his attempt to reach a decision on all-or-none versus gradual formation of associations probably allowed for a confounding of variables. It will be remembered that a pool of pairs of items was used as a source for replacement items. It will also be remembered that pairs from this pool were used to replace the items missed by the Ss in the experimental group. Items missed, or given incorrectly, were of necessity more difficult for the S than were those which were given correctly. Over a series of trials, it would seem that the replacement pairs must, on the average, represent easier pairs than those they replaced. Therefore, the list of pairs constituting the final list should be easier than the initial list. The control-group Ss were bound to the initial list. Consequently, it seems quite possible that gradual learning could have been occurring, that the E Group was "set back" when items were replaced, but that the replacement items, being easier, compensated for the setbacks. The end product was essentially equivalent rates of learning for the two groups.

It should be noted that Rock fully recognized the possibilities of this item selection, but the manner in which he attempted to determine whether or not it was occurring in his experiments did not allow him to detect it. Subsequent research has made it quite clear that such may have occurred. In fact, the manner in which the selection occurs is somewhat more complicated than indicated above (see Postman, 1963). Our purpose, however, is not to consider these matters in detail; our purpose is to make it clear that we must continually introduce new experimental techniques but, at the same time, to realize that extreme thoughtfulness must accompany such introductions.

Does formation of an association take place gradually or does it take place in an all-or-none fashion? Data can be brought together to support either position, and while the phrase is a bit shopworn and gray, it is probably correct to conclude that there is truth in both positions. It is not likely that nature is so constituted as to be either black or white; continuous changes are much more typical. In this case, the reference to continuous changes means that associations may be formed at one extreme so rapidly that they have the appearance of all-or-noneness. At the other extreme, the time required is such that the gradualness is quite evident.

SUMMARY

A fourth and final major type of design was introduced, a design which is often called a counterbalanced design. In this design each S serves in all conditions, but his data are not balanced against progressive errors. Rather, a between-S balancing is used in which the effect of progressive errors is neutralized by combining the data for all Ss. If complete counterbalancing is used, all possible orders of the conditions are used; if incomplete counterbalancing is used, all orders are not used, but each condition occurs equally often at each stage of practice. The appropriateness of the design is in doubt when differential transfer is present, but fear of such transfer, without evidence for it, may too frequently deny the use of a highly efficient design.

Verbal learning is normally studied with verbal units (having varying numbers of letters) formed into lists. Four types of lists are used: (1)free-learning lists; (2)paired-associates lists; (3)verbal-discrimination lists; and (4)serial lists. In constructing lists from verbal units having specified characteristics, E may strive for representativeness of his materials for the characteristic or may choose the analytical approach in which representativeness is sacrificed.

Task variables, particularly meaningfulness and intralist similarity, have very powerful effects on learning. Meaningfulness is a complex set of highly correlated attributes, but all attributes appear to be the result of prior learning which has occurred outside of the laboratory. The effect of meaningfulness on learning a paired-associate list can be said to be the product of its effect on two subphases, response learning and associative learning.

Three types of intralist similarity (formal, meaningful, conceptual) were discussed, and it was shown how each type influences associative learning and response learning and how, therefore, overall paired-associate learning may be predicted.

Learning time was shown to be a very accurate predictor of the amount learned in paired-associate and free learning, and the prediction is independent of the rate of presentation and the length of the list. Studies of incidental learning show that S may learn as much when not instructed to learn as when instructed, providing E can get S to make the appropriate responses to the material. Serial learning was shown to be a source of two critical problems, namely, the reasons for the bowed serial-position curve and the nature of the stimulus involved for each item in a serial list.

Finally, problems involved in attempting to determine fundamental

variables in establishing an association were discussed, along with problems
in determining the nature of the association when being formed.

APPENDIX TO CHAPTER ELEVEN

SOME SOURCES OF SCALED VERBAL UNITS

Trigrams

1. NOBLE, C. E. Measurements of association value (a), rated associations
   (a'), and scaled meaningfulness (m') for the 2100 CVC combinations
   of the English alphabet. *Psychol. Rep.*, 1961, 8, 487-521.

      The Ss rated 2100 CVC combinations as to number of associates
   they thought each would elicit. A five-point descriptive scale was
   used, labeled *none, below average, average, above average,* and *very
   many.* Scale values were determined by assigning a number 1 through
   5 to the descriptive categories. Sample items, with scale values in
   parentheses:
   XOJ (1.06) ZAR (2.04) SOF (2.89) RES (3.55) PUT (4.09) MAN
   (4.78)

2. ARCHER, E. J. Re-evaluation of the meaningfulness of all possible CVC
   trigrams. *Psychol. Monogr.*, 1960, 74, No. 10.

      Archer used the yes-no technique for scaling with the measure
   being the percentage of Ss reporting an association for each item.
   Sample items:
   XYH (1%) WEQ (20%) PAF (40%) DOX (60%) ROV (80%) MAD
   (100%)

3. WITMER, L. R. The association value of three-place consonant syllables.
   J. genet. Psychol., 1935, 47, 337-360. These syllables are also reproduced in Underwood & Schulz (see next entry).

      Witmer evaluated 4524 consonant syllables (CCC) by the yes-
   no procedure. Sample items:
   QJF (0%) FXB (21%) KDP (42%) THC (58%) BSH (83%) WHP
   (100%)

4. UNDERWOOD, B. J., & SCHULZ, R. W. *Meaningfulness and verbal learning.*
   Philadelphia: Lippincott, 1960.

      Pronounceability ratings were obtained for 239 trigrams, using a nine-point scale in which low numbers indicate easy pronounce-ability, and high numbers, difficult pronounceability. Samples items: RZQ (8.59) MPO (7.23) QAZ (5.95) LIR (4.03) MOG (3.06) CAT (1.60)

Tables in this book also show the frequency with which various two- and three-letter combinations occur in words.

Words

1. NOBLE, C. E., & PARKER, G. V. C. The Montana scale of meaningfulness (*m*). *Psychol. Rep.*, 1960, 7, 325-331.

    A total of 96 two-syllable units was scaled, with S writing down all associates to a unit he could think of within a 60-sec. period. Only 80 percent of the units are found in dictionaries, the other 20 percent being units which sound like words but are not. The values represent the mean number of associates produced in 60 sec.
    Meardon (2.56) *Icon* (3.95) *Rostrum* (5.07) *Pigment* (7.15) *Kitchen* (11.72)

2. JOHNSON, R. C. Meaningfulness of eighty English words. *Psychol. Rep.*, 1961, 9, 431.

    Johnson used the same technique as Noble and Parker.
    Astound (3.23) *Ninety* (5.43) *Fumble* (6.00) *Shatter* (7.03) *Hammock* (9.20)

3. CIEUTAT, V. J. Association indices for 446 randomly selected English mono-syllables, bisyllables, and trisyllables. *J. verb. Learn. verb. Behav.*, 1963, 2, 176-185.

    Cieutat used a seven-point descriptive scale indicating the num-ber of associates which S thought each word would elicit. The mean scale value is given for each word. Samples of each class of word are given here:

MONOSYLLABLES	BISYLLABLES	TRISYLLABLES
Saj (1.58)	Unau (1.67)	Mujtahid (1.63)
Tace (2.42)	Sumpage (2.39)	Biternate (2.31)
Cant (3.60)	Mythist (3.46)	Eliquate (3.02)
Quail (4.40)	Deerskin (4.45)	Thuggery (3.72)
Card (5.02)	Order (5.02)	Persevere (4.56)
Sin (5.79)	Lady (5.74)	Standardize (5.17)

4. THORNDIKE, E. L., & LORGE, I. *The teacher's wordbook of 30,000 words.* New York: Columbia Univer. Press, 1944.

    The frequency with which words occur in printed discourse is given in terms of frequency per million words.

5. PALERMO, D. S., & JENKINS, J. J. *Word association norms.* Minneapolis: Univer. Minnesota Press, 1964.

The word associations elicited by 200 words are listed. The associations were collected for 1000 college students and also for students in grade school and high school.

Numbers

1. BATTIG, W. F., & SPERA, A. J. Rated association values of numbers from 0-100. *J. verb. Learn. verb. Behav.*, 1962, *1*, 200-202.

A five-point descriptive scale was used, with S rating the number of associates elicited by each number. The descriptive categories were assigned the numbers 0 through 4, and a mean scale value was determined for each number. Samples:
31 (0.72) 78 (1.19) 63 (1.34) 96 (1.91) 45 (2.21) 100 (3.56)

CHAPTER TWELVE

Transfer

Parking-lot attendants are able to start and drive any make of auto, made in any year, with little or no hesitation. Having learned to drive one auto they have many habits that are quite appropriate to the driving of any auto. In spite of the fact that our automobiles do not always emerge unscathed from these parking lots, there is heavy *positive* transfer from the act of driving one automobile to the act of driving another. Any new skill which we undertake to acquire at the moment may be influenced by the habits developed in acquiring other skills in the past. Although the net effect of this transfer is usually positive, there may be *negative* transfer in certain of the component habits if the habits acquired in the past conflict with those required at the moment. A good tennis player can utilize many of his skills when learning to play badminton. Nevertheless, because of the differences in the flight characteristics of a tennis ball and a shuttlecock, it is not unusual to see the tennis player swinging "too soon" as he starts to learn to play badminton.

In a general sense, some of the phenomena we have studied in earlier chapters are transfer phenomena. Differences in learning as a function of the meaningfulness of verbal units are indicative of differences in the transfer of habits. We have been concerned at all times in designing experiments (in which S serves in more than one condition) about progressive error or changes in performance with practice, which is to say, we have been concerned with transfer effects. We have seen that notions about what is being learned in acquiring a given task may be tested by transfer tests. Therefore, when we arrive at the formal study of transfer, we are not, in the general sense, concerned with anything basically new. But, of course, when we formally set about to examine transfer, we go about it in an analytical manner as we attempt to determine the variables which influence the amount and direction of the transfer.

All areas of learning have, to some extent, included the study of transfer, but the level of analysis achieved in the area of verbal learning so far surpasses the level achieved in other areas that we will give most of our attention to transfer in verbal learning. In the immediately preceding chapter we dealt with methods and materials in verbal learning. So, now, we make an assumption that there will be heavy positive transfer to the present chapter from the information acquired in the previous chapter. If this assumption is not valid, our whole educational system is built on rather shaky tenets. We expect that a mastery of algebra will proceed at a more rapid pace because of a knowledge of arithmetic; some knowledge of spelling and punctuation is presumed to be of benefit in writing a story. In the present instance, it is hoped that the knowledge of paired-associate learning as presented in the preceding chapter will show heavy positive transfer, for it will be of great benefit in the present chapter. The study of transfer is built around paired-associate learning because of the analytical flexibility provided by the paired-associate task.

KEY PARADIGMS

The gross operational definition of transfer is provided as follows:

	Task X	Task Y
E Group	Yes	Yes
C Group	No	Yes

The E Group is given both Task X and Task Y, and the C Group, only Task Y. If there is a difference in performance between the two groups on Task Y, the procedures, viewed in conjunction with the result, provide the definition of transfer. We would look immediately at the direction of the difference; if the performance of the E Group is better than the performance of the C Group, we have defined *positive transfer,* but if the C Group is better than the E Group, we have defined *negative transfer.* If there is no difference between the groups, we would conclude that we have not demonstrated a transfer effect, although at the same time we might well recognize that both positive and negative effects of the same magnitude could have been present to produce a net effect of zero magnitude.

We called the above definition a gross definition. By this we meant that the operations involved can answer only a gross question—the question of whether or not the procedures will produce transfer effects. In the early stages of experimental work in an area, such a gross question is quite appropriate; we often attempt to determine if there *is* a phenomenon before we proceed with more analytical procedures, hence definitions of subcomponents of the overall transfer effects. At least, we will give independent operational definitions to the subcomponents if we can isolate them and measure them experimentally. We would then attempt to account for the overall transfer effects by the compounding of the subcomponents. The status of the study of transfer at the present time is that of attempting to isolate experimentally the subcomponents, and our major attention will be directed toward these efforts.

If even momentarily we study the gross operations for transfer, we can see that one variable must necessarily be of great importance in the study of transfer. This variable is the similarity between the two tasks—between Task X and Task Y. If Task X is that of learning a Latin vocabulary list and Task Y, learning to kick a football, it is quite unlikely that the two groups will differ on Task Y. If Task X is learning to kick a football and Task Y is also learning to kick a football, we could be quite confident that we would measure a difference in the performance of the two groups on Task Y. Thus, we expect transfer to vary as we move from rather complete dissimilarity of the habits involved in the two tasks to the other extreme, identity of habits, where we expect transfer to be maximal. It is clear, therefore, that similarity in the habits between tasks is a critical variable influencing amount and direction of the transfer. In recent years, however, with the work being directed toward an understanding of the subcomponents or subprocesses or subhabits involved in transfer, certain key paradigms have been used to represent certain points on the similarity dimensions. We will, therefore, build our initial discussion around these paradigms.

A-B, C-D

We will be dealing with paired-associate lists consisting of pairs of verbal units in which we have a stimulus term and a response term. It is common practice to identify the stimulus term in the first list in a transfer paradigm as A and the response term as B. Thus, the symbol used for the first list in a transfer experiment is A-B. If the second list is now identified as C-D, with C indicating the stimulus term in the second list and D the response term, we say that there is no similarity between the stimulus terms in the two lists and no similarity between the response terms. The statement "no similarity" is not entirely accurate when viewed in an absolute sense. Certainly the material will be verbal material in both lists, and in that sense the first and second list will be highly similar. However, this paradigm means that other than the fact that the terms are verbal units, there is no apparent similarity beween the two lists. To give an illustration, two pairs in each list may be as follows:

FIRST LIST		SECOND LIST	
Stimulus Term (A)	Response Term (B)	Stimulus Term (C)	Response Term (D)
pen	dog	ice	two
wry	law	rug	map

The A-B, C-D paradigm is now commonly used as a control paradigm for "extracting" certain transfer components when we wish to study the effect of similarity in the other paradigms to be discussed. Since all paradigms use A-B as the designation for the first list, we may identify the A-B, C-D paradigm distinctively by using only the second-list designation (C-D).

A-B, A-D

Using the C-D or zero-similarity paradigm as the starting point, we may move along similarity dimensions relating stimuli in the two lists until we reach identity of stimuli, A-B, A-D:

FIRST LIST		SECOND LIST	
A	B	A	D
pen	dog	pen	two
wry	law	wry	map

We note that the responses paired with the identical stimuli are different in the two lists; as S moves from the first list to the second list he must associate a new response term to a stimulus to which he had already associated a response term in the first list. It would appear that this might produce some difficulty in the second list, as, indeed, it does. We often speak of the A-B, A-D paradigm as the basic negative-transfer paradigm, and again we eliminate A-B in shorthand notation and speak of it merely as the A-D paradigm.

Still considering only variations in the similarity of the stimulus terms in the two lists, we have identified the extreme paradigms as C-D and A-D. We might manipulate similarity systematically between these extremes, either formal, meaningful, or conceptual similarity. For example, if A-B were *icy-dog*, the corresponding item in the second list might be *cold-two*. Or, if A-B is *RZL-dog*, the corresponding pair in the second list might be *ZRP-two*. Finally, if A-B is *sparrow-dog*, the corresponding pair in the second list might be *robin-two*.

A-B, C-B

Returning to the C-D paradigm as an anchor point, we may now think of increasing the degree of similarity of the response terms in the two lists. Again, the extreme point is identity, and we have the A-B, C-B paradigm, which we will speak of as C-B. Thus:

FIRST LIST		SECOND LIST	
A	B	C	B
pen	dog	ice	dog
wry	law	rug	law

Now we may summarize the position of the three key paradigms as we increase stimulus and response similarity. This is done by diagram in Fig. 12-1, in both symbol form and in illustrative form. Remembering that A-B

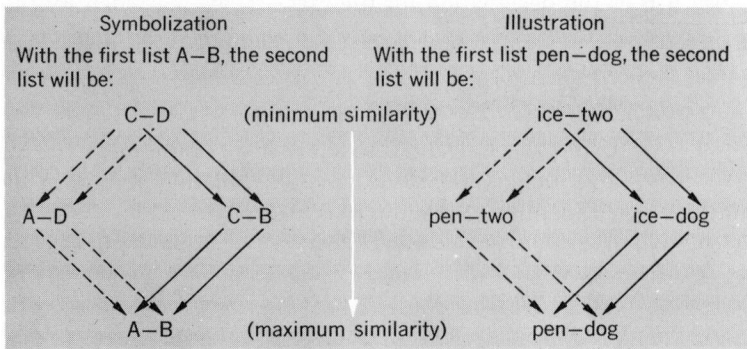

Fig. 12-1. The symbolization and illustration of key transfer paradigms in the study of transfer as a function of similarity in paired-associate learning.

represents the first list, we can see that in moving from the C-D to the A-D paradigm, we are increasing the similarity of the stimulus terms of the two lists. In moving from C-D to C-B, we are increasing the similarity of the response terms. From these two paradigms we may move toward still higher similarity. From the A-D paradigm we may move toward an increasing similarity of the response terms, and from the C-B paradigm, toward an increasing similarity of the stimulus terms. When these changes are carried to the extreme, we terminate with A-B, which is exactly the same as the first list, or complete identity. It would be simple if the amount of positive transfer increased as we move from C-D down the two tracks to A-D and C-B and on to A-B. This is not the case, for as we take either route we move from zero transfer (due to similarity) for C-D, to negative transfer for both A-D and C-B, and then to a rapid change into maximum positive transfer for A-B. Later we will see why these changes occur.

A-B, A-Br

We have noted that if the paradigm is symbolized A-B, A-B we have complete identity; with such a paradigm we are not studying transfer except insofar as all changes from trial to trial in learning a given task are said to be due to transfer. So, the A-B, A-B paradigm does not play a role in transfer studies. At the same time, however, for analytical reasons we need a paradigm in which the same verbal units used in the first list are also used in the second. For this purpose the A-B, A-Br paradigm has come into frequent use. In this paradigm, we use (in the second list) the same stimulus and response terms as those used in the first list, but these are re-paired so that S must learn new associations in the second list. To illustrate with two pairs:

FIRST LIST		SECOND LIST	
A	B	A	Br
pen	dog	pen	law
wry	law	wry	dog

There are not too many situations in "real life" of a general nature which correspond to this paradigm. If, however, a law were suddenly passed which required that green be used as a stop light and red as a go light, we would have the A-B, A-Br paradigm and probably also have considerable chaos.

Before moving ahead with the analyses of the subcomponents of transfer which may operate in differential magnitudes for the various paradigms, let us look at one study which shows the overall transfer differences to be expected from the four key paradigms. This study was done in the writer's laboratory (Twedt & Underwood, 1959).

Both the first and the second (transfer) lists consisted of 12 pairs of two-syllable adjectives. The first list was presented for anticipation learning until S correctly anticipated all response terms on a single trial with the second list presented for 10 trials and S instructed to make as many correct responses on each trial as possible. A random-groups design was used with 18 Ss assigned to the lists representing each of the four key paradigms we have discussed, the assignment being made by block randomization.

A point of method for transfer studies must be emphasized. It is common practice, and we have followed that practice, to symbolize the first list as A-B and the second list to fit the appropriate paradigm (e.g., C-D, A-D, C-B, and A-Br). Translated into two-syllable adjectives of the present experiment, with two pairs taken as representative of each list, we would have the following arrangement:

PARADIGM	FIRST LIST	SECOND LIST
C-D	honest-frantic	senior-rotten
	certain-aloof	ready-severe
A-D	honest-frantic	honest-rotten
	certain-aloof	certain-severe
C-B	honest-frantic	senior-frantic
	certain-aloof	ready-aloof
A-Br	honest-frantic	honest-aloof
	certain-aloof	certain-frantic

With A-B standing for the first list, the words in the second list complete each of the four paradigms. Our interest is in differences in performance on the second list. Assume we have done the experiment; could we attribute differences in performance on the second list entirely to differences in the paradigmatic relationships between the first and second list? A little consideration will show that we probably could not because the second lists differ for the various paradigms, hence there may be differences in difficulty among the second lists. Therefore, a portion of the performance differences which occur on the second list might not be due to transfer differences. Thus, if we had control groups who learn only the second lists, differences in difficulty among the four second lists might be shown.

There is a very simple solution to the problem, and as we look back now, we wonder how we could have been so slow in arriving at the solution. We must make the second list identical for all the paradigms, and let the first list vary. This is to say that in the above illustration the first list is used as the second list and the second as the first; therefore, all Ss under all paradigms learn exactly the same second list, and any differences which occur in learning this list cannot be attributed to any factor other than differences in the paradigms. In most experiments there would be little concern even if there were differences in difficulty of the first list since learning is normally taken to a criterion. Now, because the critical performance occurs on the second list, we always attempt to design our experiments to have a common second list for all conditions.

The results for this experiment are shown in Fig. 12-2, where the mean performance over the 10 transfer trials for each paradigm is plotted. If we consider C-D as the control paradigm (since it has no repeated words), we see that all of the paradigms produced negative transfer, with maximum negative transfer occurring with the A-Br paradigm. Just why each paradigm results in negative transfer will be discussed later. For relatively meaningful material and low *intralist* similarity, the results in Fig. 12-2 are fairly typical of the effects of the paradigms. However, we shall see that the transfer performance can be handily "shoved around" by manipulating certain variables.

The results shown in Fig. 12-2 were duplicated almost exactly by the use of mixed lists. For the mixed-list conditions the pairs on the transfer list were so arranged that in relationship to the pairs in the first list, three pairs were C-D, three A-D, three C-B, and three A-Br. Although it was comforting to discover that the mixed- and unmixed-list designs produced comparable results, we are not at all confident that this finding will obtain for all types of materials for all other paradigms. In the previous chapter we concluded that because we do not have general principles to govern us in the use of mixed and unmixed lists, our best approach at the present is to be thoughtful about the use of mixed lists. The same conclusion must be reached in designing mixed-list transfer experiments. We cannot simply assume that mixed and unmixed lists will always produce equivalent results.

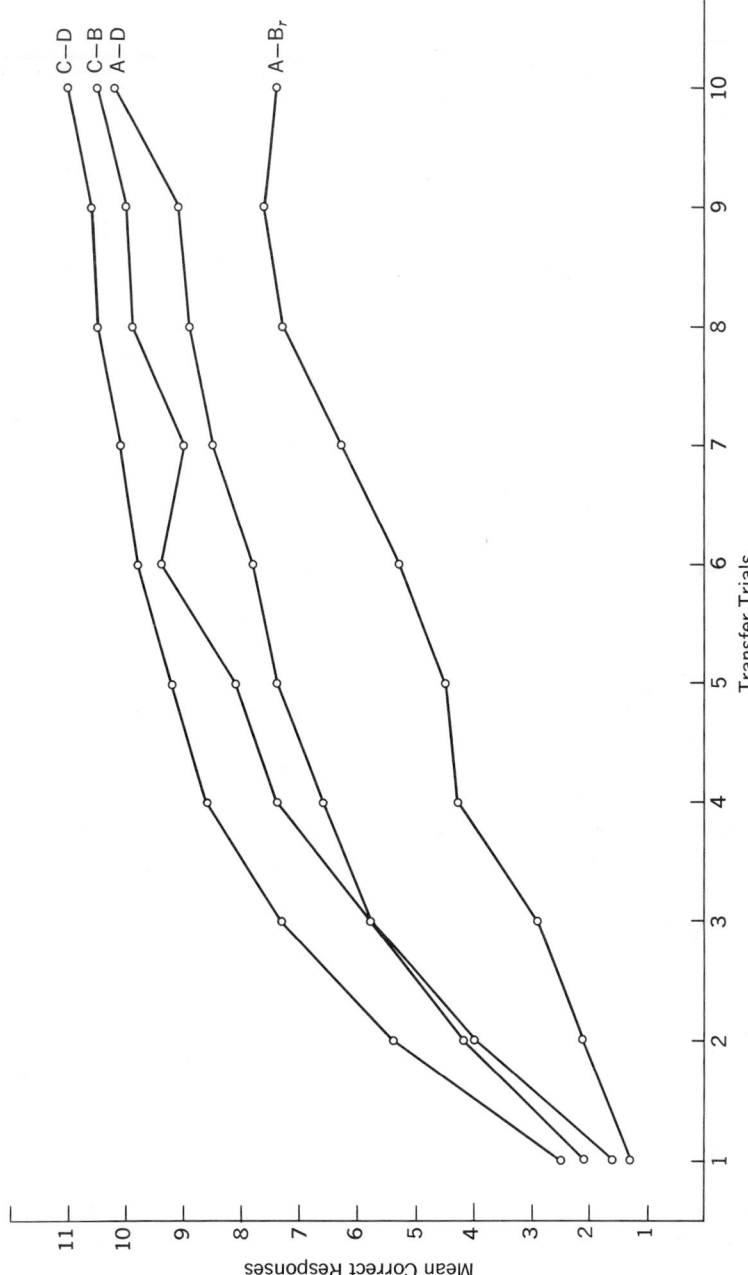

Fig. 12.2. Transfer performance under four key paradigms. Data from Twedt and Underwood (1959).

NONASSOCIATIVE COMPONENTS
IN TRANSFER

By nonassociative components in transfer we mean sources of transfer which are independent of the particular associations or discriminations required in the learning and which are, also, presumably equivalent for all paradigms. Two such factors, *learning-to-learn* and *warmup*, have been identified.

Learning-to-learn

Learning-to-learn (LTL) is simply another name for our oft-discussed practice effects. In verbal learning we say that LTL is the improvement in performance on successive lists when (1) the successive lists represent samples of items of the same class of materials and (2) no systematic similarity exists between the successive lists other than the commonality which allows them to be said to be of the same class of materials. Neither criterion is unambiguous. Are nonsense syllables and consonant syllables members of the same class? Are nouns and adjectives? Obviously, some arbitrariness is involved in specifying the class. At the same time, interlist similarity must necessarily vary as a function of the number of representatives in a class. If one class consists of single-digit numbers and another consists of the letters of the alphabet, the former is bound to produce greater interlist similarity as we construct successive lists (let us say, eight-item serial lists) by drawing numbers randomly from those available and by drawing letters randomly from those available. To recognize that the size of the class may influence amount of LTL is merely to suggest a variable influencing the amount of LTL, and to recognize that classes may be arbitrarily designated is likewise to suggest experiments in which LTL is studied within and across various arbitrarily designated classes.

A simple experiment on LTL is a rather unique one in terms of the design of the experiment. It is one of the rare cases where we *must* use the same S in all conditions because the problem is that of studying his change in performance across successive lists. The conditions of the experiment become the successive lists, or, as we often say, stages of practice. This being the case, unless we know that the lists are equivalent in difficulty, we would counterbalance or randomize the order of the lists so that across all Ss each list will have occurred an equal number of times at each stage of practice.

Illustrations of learning-to-learn. Meyer and Miles (1953) studied performance in free learning of 12-unit nonsense-syllable lists for 20 lists. The 20 lists were constructed to minimize interlist similarity, and

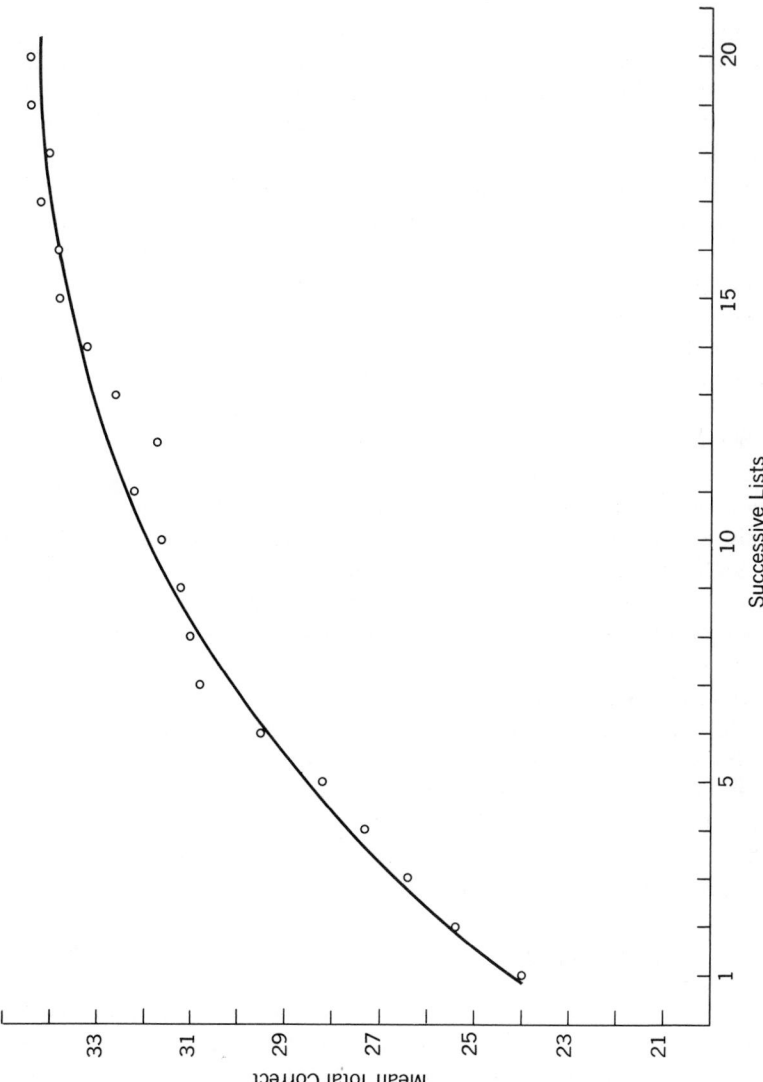

Fig. 12-3. Learning-to-learn (free learning) across 20 lists of nonsense syllables. Meyer and Miles (1953); data courtesy of Drs. Meyer and Miles.

the syllables had an average association value of 27 percent. Twenty different orders of the lists (not items within a list) were prepared, with each order used about equally often for the 64 Ss. A 30-sec. study trial and also a 30-sec. recall trial were used, with five trials given on each of the successive lists. One list was given each day.

To measure the LTL in this situation the mean total number of syllables correctly reproduced on the five trials of each list was used. The LTL curve is shown in Fig. 12-3. Clearly, performance on successive lists gradually improved with a suggestion that by the end of 20 lists little further change would be expected with additional lists.

Is Fig. 12-3 to be taken as representative of the LTL to be expected in free learning of all types of material? Probably not. In the free learning of word lists LTL is very small and may not occur at all unless several trials on each list are given (Dallett, 1963). The difference in the LTL for syllables and words strongly suggests that the higher the meaningfulness of the material, the less the LTL.

Enormous amounts of LTL have been shown in serial learning. Ward (1937) had Ss learn 16 successive serial lists of 12 nonsense syllables, one list a day. Learning was carried on until one perfect recitation was achieved. On the first list learned, approximately 38 trials were required on the average; there was a negatively accelerated decrease in trials to learn successive lists until, on the sixteenth list, an average of only 16 trials was required. Paired-associate learning also shows clear LTL, although no study is available in which it has been studied across many lists. We may only presume that other types of lists too (e.g., verbal-discrimination lists) will show LTL. Great gains attributed to LTL have also been shown in nonverbal paired-associate tasks (e.g., Duncan, 1960).

We will not be concerned here with the question of what produces the improvement we call LTL. Actually, we know very little about this matter as yet, although recent work has outlined an approach to the problem (Postman & Schwartz, 1964). What we must recognize is that whenever we are studying transfer and S learns two or more lists, a part of the overall transfer effects will probably include a component of LTL.

Warmup

We have seen in an earlier chapter how warmup may influence motor learning. Now we point out that evidence is available which suggests that a comparable phenomenon may occur in verbal learning. Suppose S comes into the laboratory for the usual transfer experiment and learns two successive lists. In the act of learning the first list he becomes "warmed up" so that a positive component will be contributed to the second list that was not present on the first, or at least was not present early in learning the first list. As an illustration, we may look at a study by Thune (1950).

Each S was given 10 trials on each of two paired-associate lists, List A consisting of paired adjectives and List B made up of one-syllable nouns. Six different groups of Ss were employed to implement the six conditions shown in Table 12-1. The difference among the conditions rests in the number of trials given on List A on Day 1 and in the number given on Day 2 prior to receiving 10 trials on List B. For example, the Ss in Condition 0 had 10 trials on Day 1 on List A, but zero trials on List A on Day 2. The Ss in Condition 2 had 8 trials on List A on Day 1 and 2 trials on List A on Day 2 immediately preceding the learning of List B. Here is the reasoning Thune

TABLE 12–1

CONDITIONS USED BY THUNE (1950) IN STUDYING WARMUP
AS A FUNCTION OF NUMBER OF WARMUP TRIALS

	DAY 1	DAY 2	
CONDITION	LIST A	LIST A	LIST B
0	10 trials	0 trials	10 trials
2	8 trials	2 trials	10 trials
4	6 trials	4 trials	10 trials
6	4 trials	6 trials	10 trials
8	2 trials	8 trials	10 trials
10	0 trials	10 trials	10 trials

brought to this situation. First, he assumed that whatever is involved in LTL —whatever skills or habits constitute it—would not be forgotten. This assumption implies that the amount of LTL is equivalent for all groups; those that had 10 trials on List A on Day 1 "put" just as much LTL in List B as did the group that had 10 trials on List A on Day 2, just prior to learning List B. On the other hand, he assumed that warmup is lost over time. In fact, he assumed that the warmup generated by learning on Day 1 would be entirely lost by Day 2. Not only does such an assumption seem perfectly sound if we view warmup in verbal learning as we do in motor learning, but there is also evidence to justify the assumption. Hamilton (1950) had shown that after about 60 min., there is no evidence of a carry-over of warmup effect.

Now we can see the full logic of Thune's conditions. If LTL is not forgotten, it is equivalent for all groups since all groups had 10 trials on List A before learning List B. But if warmup is lost within 60 min., there will be no carry-over of the warmup from learning List A on Day 1 to the learning on Day 2. Therefore, by varying the number of acquisition trials on List A on Day 2, Thune was essentially varying the amount of warmup just prior to learning List B. The question he was asking concerned the effect of number of warmup trials on learning. As may be seen in Fig. 12-4, there is a direct relationship; the greater the number of learning trials (warmup trials) on List A, the greater the learning of List B within the 10 trials.

The warmup effects as shown in Fig. 12-4 come about as a by-product of associative learning. Is it possible to warm a person up by use of a non-associative task? The answer is yes. In the same experiment, Thune had other conditions to study this problem. The warmup task consisted of guessing which of five colors would appear on the memory drum when the stimulus term was X. Now X was always the stimulus, and one of five colors might

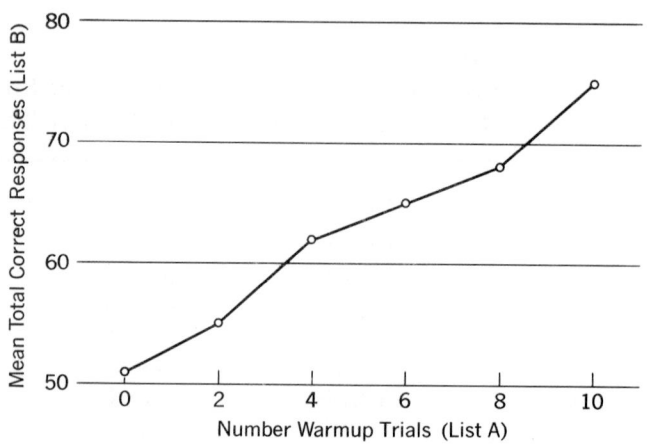

Fig. 12-4. Warmup as a function of number of learning trials on List A immediately prior to learning List B. Estimated from Thune (1950).

appear. Since X was nondifferentiating with regard to what *would* appear, S could only guess and could not possibly learn anything associatively; in fact, he was instructed to use extrasensory perception to guide his guesses. The notion of this task is to provide S the means by which he can establish a set for anticipating, as he will have to do in learning. We note that in the warmup task, S has to select a response (just as in the learning task), but he could not learn anything.

Two groups were used and their conditions are as follows:

		Day 1	Day 2	
	LIST A	COLOR GUESSING	COLOR GUESSING	LIST B
GROUP I	10 trials	10 trials	none	10 trials
GROUP II	10 trials	none	10 trials	10 trials

As can be seen, both groups had exactly the same tasks; they differed only in the temporal relationships between the tasks. If color guessing provides warmup, Group II should be better on List B than Group I, since color guessing for Group II was given immediately before the learning of List B. Group I scored 49.9 correct responses on List B, and Group II scored 71.4 correct responses. Clearly, the guessing task had an effect, and the performance shown by Group II is just about the same as that shown by the group having 10 learning trials as warmup in Fig. 12-4. From these data we conclude that warmup can be given quite effectively without having S learn specific associations, although we must not conclude that a nonassociative warmup task will always be as effective as an associative one.

Let us return to the original gross operational definition of transfer:

	TASK X	TASK Y
E GROUP	yes	yes
C GROUP	no	yes

Now we can observe that the performance on Task Y for the E Group is influenced not only by specific similarity relationships which exist between Task X and Task Y, but also by LTL and warmup, and performance on Task Y for the C Group does not have a positive effect from these two sources. If, therefore, we wish to study transfer effects which can be ascribed only to the specific similarity relationships between Task X and Task Y, we will want to "extract" the transfer effects due to LTL and warmup. It is for this reason that the A-B, C-D paradigm has come into widespread use. For example, if we intend to study the effects of the A-B, A-D paradigm, our defining operations become:

	FIRST LIST	SECOND LIST
E GROUP	A-D	A-B
C GROUP	C-D	A-B

Assuming that LTL and warmup will be produced in equivalent amounts for the two groups by the learning of the first list, the difference in performance on the second list cannot be attributed to differences in LTL and warmup. We have removed LTL and warmup as differential factors in learning the second list by the two groups and have, therefore, purified the measure of amount of transfer which can be attributed to the specific similarity relationship inherent in the A-B, A-D paradigm.

SPECIFIC SOURCES OF NEGATIVE TRANSFER

Still using the key paradigms as reference points, we will continue our discussion of the subcomponents of transfer. In this section we will consider the specific sources of negative transfer or interference present in the various paradigms. The two major sources of interference arise from *forward* associations and from *backward* associations.

Forward Associations

Whenever we are required to learn a new response to a stimulus to which we had previously associated a response, interference from the forward association is likely to occur. The classical paradigm is A-B, A-D, but, of course, we can see that the same source of interference is present in A-Br. When S is forced to learn A-D after having established an association between A and B, it seems quite apparent that some difficulty would be experienced; the old association, A to B, must be broken or extinguished or circumvented in some fashion before he can readily produce D when A occurs. Suppose we suddenly have to learn a new system of arithmetic which dictates that 2×2 is now 11, $8-4$ is now 1, and $3+3$ is now 27. Interference, indeed, frustration, might well occur.

We have all experienced the A-B, A-D type of interference in simple motor habits. If an object that is frequently used, such as a comb, after long being present in one drawer of a bureau, is moved to another drawer as a consequence of a general rearrangement, we may find ourselves returning to the original drawer to the stimulus "comb." As a matter of fact, it is rather remarkable that this paradigm produces so little interference—that the old habit persists such a relatively short period of time. Nevertheless, the interference which may occur can, under certain circumstances, be serious or lethal. It is a recorded fact that a large airplane was seriously damaged while taxiing when the pilot pulled a lever for "wheels up" when he intended to pull the lever for "flaps up." Investigation showed that the "flaps-up" lever on an earlier model on which the pilot had been trained was in the spatial location of the "wheels-up" lever on the present model. It would be convenient if in clutchless automobiles the brake pedal were moved to the left to be operated with the left foot, leaving the right fool entirely free for the accelerator. Yet, it would be difficult to predict how many accidents might occur as a result of pushing with our right foot to stop the car—because in the past we have always pushed with our right foot. There is some evidence that the tendency for earlier-learned habits to reassert themselves is enhanced by sudden stress or fear. Under usual driving conditions we might manage quite well with a left brake pedal, but the sudden presence of conditions ripe for an accident might lead us to revert to the old habit of pressing with the right foot. However, we must not overdo the macabre aspects of the A-B, A-D paradigm. The fact is that in our lifetimes we learn many new habits to old stimuli, and we do so without serious problems.

We should point out another characteristic of behavior which accompanies the learning of A-D following A-B. The fact that B does occur to A in the process of learning D to A is a rare event. We do not *frequently* reach into the now wrong bureau drawer following the change in the location of the comb; airlines do not go out of business because pilots keep destroying planes by pulling the wrong lever. And in the learning of verbal lists, only occasionally will S give the B response when learning A-D. If he does, we speak of it as *intrusion* of first-list responses during the act of acquiring the second list. In the usual experiment, perhaps one out of six Ss might produce a single intrusion. At one time we believed this might be due to a simple instructional set which S provided himself. Thus, having learned A-B and now given A-D, S noted that all the response terms were different and therefore he said to himself, "Don't give any of those responses I just learned." But when a test of this hypothesis was made, there was no change in the number of intrusions (Twedt & Underwood, 1959). The method of testing was to use a mixed-list design in which the second list included both A-D and C-B pairs. In the case of the C-B pairs, the first-list responses *were* appropriate, so S could not use a generalized principle about giving or not giving the first-list responses. The number of intrusions did not differ under these conditions and under the unmixed-list (all pairs fitting the A-D paradigm) procedure.

The component in overall transfer we have been discussing refers to the associative interference which results when in learning successive tasks S must acquire new responses to stimuli to which he had previously acquired a different response. We must think of this as interference from forward associations—from A to B—in order to distinguish it from another source of associative interference.

Backward Associations

In the act of acquiring an association between A and B, such that B can be produced when A alone occurs, S also acquires some capability of producing A when B is shown. It appears, then, that an association becomes established not only in the forward direction (A→B), but also in the backward direction (B→A). The forward association is sometimes called the S-R association (stimulus term to response term), and the backward, an R-S association. In recent years the study of the variables influencing backward associations has become almost an area of research unto itself. Our interest here is in the role which backward associations play in the key transfer paradigms, but, of course, we should independently establish the fact that backward associations are "real."

The reality or existence of a phenomenon may be established at various levels of inference. The least amount of inference is required when we attempt to measure a phenomenon directly. Somewhat more inferential thinking is required when we take two steps, namely, assuming the existence of a phenomenon and, then, deducing what must happen in a given situation if the assumption is correct. For example, we might assume that backward associations develop in the process of learning forward associations and then deduce what must happen in certain transfer paradigms if this is true. If the expected results are found, we might then assume that our assumption about the development of backward associations was tenable. This approach is widely used in experimental investigations of all kinds. It is usually less convincing than the direct approach of trying to measure the phenomenon directly because we may not always be able to exclude alternative interpretations. But sometimes, because we do not see ways of measuring the phenomenon directly, we go to a more inferential level.

The modern study of backward associations began at the inferential level of assuming the existence of backward associations and then testing their presumed effect on certain transfer paradigms (Harcum, 1953). For example, suppose the paradigm is A-B, B-C. If an association is established from B to A in learning A-B, when S must learn B-C, interference should result because a new response must be attached to a stimulus which already had a response attached to it. Such reasoning led to results which were positive, that is, they tended to support the assumption that backward associations were formed, although they did not rule out entirely alternative explanations for the transfer effects. Yet, as additional work using this approach (e.g., Murdock, 1956) gave further confirmation to the assumption, it became clear that the more direct approach would clearly show that backward associations were formed in the act of forming forward associations. The direct approach (e.g., Richardson, 1960) requires that following learning of a single list, S is given each response term in turn and is asked to produce the stimulus term with which it was paired. Such procedures amply affirmed the implications of the transfer studies; backward associations were indeed developed in the act of learning forward associations. One precaution must be exercised in the direct tests for backward associations. Suppose when S is given the test for backward associations he attempts to remember the stimulus terms and then runs through them until he comes to one that leads (by a forward association) to the response term being shown him at the moment. Clearly, this would not be evidence for backward associations. We believe that these "illegal" backward associations can be minimized by forcing S to produce the stimuli to each response term at a fairly rapid pace, perhaps at a 2-sec. pace.

Backward associations appear to develop inevitably in the process of the formation of forward associations. No one yet has discovered a way to prevent their development. At the same time, however, studies show that the strength of the backward association appears to be less than that of the forward association. That is, operationally speaking, S will normally not be able to produce as many stimulus terms when the response terms are presented as he can produce response terms when the stimulus terms are presented. The reason for this is apparent in some cases. For example, if the stimulus terms consist of low-meaningful trigrams, we know that S may select a portion of the nominal stimulus (e.g., a single letter) as the functional stimulus. He may be quite able to produce the single letter which served as the functional stimulus, but he cannot produce the other two letters. In a more general sense, therefore, we have to consider the problem of stimulus-term availability before we conclude that the backward association is weaker than the forward one.

The last statement implies that two associations are involved. This may not be the case. Instead, a single association with bidirectional properties could be used to describe the situation. At the present time we do not have definitive evidence on either of the two issues about forward and backward associations; we cannot tell whether two associations or one association is involved, or whether or not under favorable conditions of testing, the forward association and the backward association will be equivalent in strength.

Accepting the fact that backward associations are formed, we ask what implication this has for transfer in the key transfer paradigms. It is now believed that the negative effects in the A-B, C-B paradigm are produced by associative interference from backward associations. When A-B is learned, B-A is also acquired. Then, when the association C-B is required in the transfer list, the B-A backward association will interfere with the acquisition of the B-C backward association. In terms of backward associations we have B-A, B-C; S must learn a new response to a "stimulus" to which he has just learned a different response. In other words, the backward associations form an A-B, A-D paradigm, and we know this produces associative interference.

In the A-Br paradigm, associative interference stems from both forward and backward associations. It seems quite reasonable, therefore, that the amount of negative transfer in this paradigm should be greater than in either the A-D or C-B paradigm. As we have seen earlier (Fig. 12-2), this expectation is borne out by the data. Generally (although not always) the amount of negative transfer observed in C-B is less than in A-D. This might be a result of the fact that backward associations are weaker than corresponding forward associations, but another factor might also be involved, as we will see at a later point.

Are there other sources of interference in the key paradigms? There may be, but at the present stage of understanding we are inclined to believe that any such sources contribute a relatively small amount of interference. There is some quite inferential evidence that in acquiring a list of items, the response terms may to some degree become associated with the general experimental situation. This might be most clearly visualized in a free-learning procedure. What is the stimulus which evokes these responses on a recall trial? It is possible that the stimulus is the general experimental context and S learns these items to this context. Now suppose he is given a second list to learn. With the experimental context considered as the stimulus for both lists, it means that the second list must be attached to the same simulus to which the first list had originally been attached. In our symbols for the paired-associate list, it is an A-B, A-D paradigm, and some interference might be expected. If this is translated to the response terms of a paired-associate list, the different paradigms give different expectations. That is, if we assume that the response terms of a paired-associate list become associated to the general experimental context (as well as to the specific stimuli in the list) in the act of learning the list, and if the transfer list has a different set of response terms, an A-B, A-D paradigm is formed, and interference may result. There would be no interference from this source in the C-B paradigm (since the same set of responses is used in the second list), but there would be interference in the A-D paradigm since a new set of response terms is involved. Furthermore, it can be seen that the C-D paradigm would be subject to interference from this source. That is why we have said earlier that although we believe the A-B, C-D paradigm is the best control we have at the present, this does not imply that it is a perfect control, for a small amount of interference may be present from the interference produced by contextual associations. However, as indicated, we believe that this source of interference (if present at all) is very small, and we will not refer to it again. If there are other sources of interference in the key paradigms, they have not as yet been identified.

SPECIFIC POSITIVE FACTORS

We have identified learning-to-learn and warmup as general positive nonassociative factors influencing the learning of successive lists. We have identified forward and backward associations as sources of interference in learning successive lists. Now we will identify two variables which will "throw" varying amounts of specific positive effects into certain of the paradigms. One of the variables is intralist similarity, and the other, meaningfulness. The former variable, when viewed in the transfer situation, is involved in the transfer of discrimination; the second variable (meaningfulness) is concerned with the transfer of response learning.

Transfer of Discrimination

We have seen that in learning a single list, interstimulus similarity produces a large effect on rate of learning; the higher the similarity among the stimuli in a list, the slower the learning. Carried to the extreme, if all stimuli were identical, learning could not occur for there would be no way of establishing discrimination among the stimuli. Before learning of a list can be complete, each stimulus term must elicit a stable response which differentiates that stimulus from other stimuli in the list. The response term is, in turn, associated to the stable response elicited by each stimulus. Now, consider the A-B, A-D paradigm. Suppose there were high similarity among the A terms—among the stimulus terms. In the act of learning A-B, differentiation or discrimination among these terms must be established. This discrimination among the stimuli should transfer to the second list, since the stimuli are identical. Thus, in any paradigm where the stimulus terms are identical in the two lists (A-D or A-Br), a positive effect should be present which is not present when the stimulus terms are different (C-D and C-B). The amount of the positive effect should be directly related to the degree of interstimulus similarity.

The idea that stimulus discrimination should produce a positive effect on transfer was first advanced in a systematic fashion by Gibson (1940). Yet, in fact, over the years since then very little consistent evidence has been obtained in support of the phenomenon. However, the approaches may not have been adequate. One common procedure was to take a list of similar units (geometrical forms were frequently used) and present them to S in varying order from trial to trial, following which some technique was used to determine whether they had been discriminated (such as a recognition test). The forms then became stimuli in a paired-associate list, and the learning of the list was compared with the learning of the list by a control group which had not received the discrimination or predifferentiation training. The results were by no means always positive, and when positive, the effects were not large (Arnoult, 1957).

Another approach to the study of transfer of stimulus discrimination may be more fruitful. We would use the A-B, A-D paradigm, in one case with high intralist stimulus similarity and in another case with low intralist stimulus similarity. As a base, two other groups would be given the A-B, C-D paradigm, one with low similarity among stimuli and one with high. It should be clear that for this paradigm the similarity would hold among the stimului within each list, although the similarity between the stimuli in the two lists would be low.

A comparison of the transfer performance for the two paradigms when stimulus similarity is low should give us the expected negative transfer because performance under the A-D paradigm will be inferior to that shown under the C-D paradigm. However, with high similarity among the A stimulus terms, a positive transfer component (transfer of stimulus discrimination or differentiation) should be present in the A-D paradigm that is not present in the C-D paradigm. Therefore, negative transfer should be less with the high similarity than with the low, and if the transfer of stimulus discrimination is great, positive transfer might even result in the A-D paradigm with high similarity.

Tests made in the writer's laboratory, tests which are as yet unpublished, suggest that the mechanisms are operating as expected, but the magnitude of the positive transfer effect produced with high stimulus similarity is much less than expected. As yet we do not know whether this is a result of inadequate procedures or whether the theory has been overrated and the amount of the positive effect *is* very small. In any event, let us presume that there is a positive effect, magnitude unknown, from the transfer of stimulus differentiation. This positive effect will hold for any paradigm in which the stimuli are identical in both lists and the similarity among the stimuli is high, although, theoretically, a small positive effect should be expected even if similarity is low. In terms of the key paradigms, therefore, we will say that positive transfer performance in the A-D and A-Br paradigms will have a positive component attributable to the transfer of stimulus differentiation.

If there is transfer of stimulus discrimination, there should be a corresponding transfer of response discrimination. The reasoning would use the A-B, C-B paradigm as a focus in the same manner in which it used the A-B, A-D paradigm as a focus for evaluating transfer of stimulus discrimination. Furthermore, it can be seen that if there is a transfer of response discrimination, it would occur in both the C-B and A-Br paradigms. Without evidence for the transfer of response-term discrimination, let us assume that appropriate tests will show that the reasoning is sound and that, therefore, a positive factor is added to the transfer performance whenever response-term similarity is high and the paradigm maintains the same responses in both lists.

Transfer of Response Learning

In the previous chapter we discussed the problem of response learning as representing an independent and isolable process in acquiring a paired-associate list. It would seem, therefore, that any variable which influences response learning is going to influence the transfer when the same response terms are used in both lists (as in C-B and A-Br). We know that meaningfulness is one variable which does have a powerful influence on response acquisition. It follows, therefore, that if response learning transfers, the amount of apparent negative transfer should decrease as response meaningfulness decreases. Or to say this another way, as meaningfulness of the response terms decreases, the positive transfer component in the C-B and C-Br paradigms should increase (as compared with C-D). If the positive effect is great enough, the performance under these paradigms might actually be better than under the C-D paradigms. We shall see how these expectations work out.

Jung (1963) studied the effects of high and low meaningfulness of the response terms. He used the C-B paradigm, with the C-D paradigm as a control. In that portion of the experiment with which we will be concerned, four groups were used, two serving under C-D, two under C-B. The response terms in all lists were trigrams, the stimulus terms being two-syllable adjectives. The terms of low meaningfulness were SBL, MQK, OCJ, HFW, RDG, and TXP. Those of high meaningfulness were JAK, ENT, XYW, IMP, UVR, HOS. The learning of the first list was carried until one perfect recitation was achieved, and then 10 trials were given on the transfer list. Obviously, two of the groups learned under the C-D paradigm, and two, under the C-B. The response terms in the C-D paradigm were either of low mean-ingfulness in both lists or of high meaningfulness in both lists. The items given above were the ones actually used on the transfer list, and with the C-B paradigm, of course, they were used as response terms in both lists.

The mean numbers of correct responses on the first two transfer trials for the four groups are shown in Fig. 12-5. We may note first that the C-D

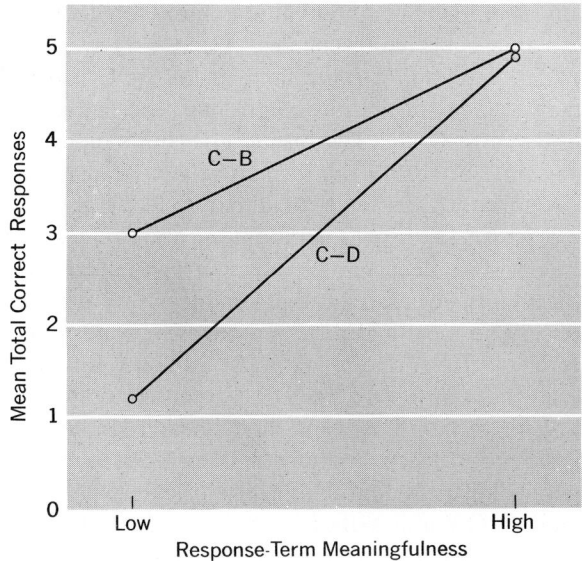

Fig. 12-5. Transfer as a function of response-term meaningfulness in the C-D and C-B paradigms. The data are for the first two trials on the transfer list. Data from Jung (1963).

relationship represents simply the role of response-term meaningfulness in learning. We note that performance under C-B is appreciably higher than under C-D when the responses have low meaningfulness, and this is taken as evidence of the transfer of response learning which produced a positive effect of such magnitude as to more than overcome any negative effect of backward associations. With high meaningfulness there is still some evidence of a positive effect since the transfer is not negative, but essentially zero. However, when correct responses over the 10 transfer trials were considered, there was a negative effect for high meaningfulness, but the positive effect for low meaningfulness was maintained throughout all transfer trials. Although we must conclude that there is a transfer of response learning, we must note in Fig. 12-5 that this transfer was not 100 percent when viewed against the learning of the high-meaningful list. It might possibly become 100 percent if the degree of first-list learning was taken to a higher level so that all response terms were strongly integrated.

Merikle and Battig (1963) examined the role of transfer of response learning in the A-Br paradigm. Meaningfulness was varied from high to medium to low. High meaningfulness was presented by common words, medium, by medium-association value nonsense syllables, and low, by low-association value consonant syllables. Again C-D was used as the control condition. The prediction was the same as for the C-B paradigm in the Jung study, namely, the lower the meaningfulness, the better the performance on transfer (relative to C-D). The results give full support to the expectation. With low meaningfulness of the response terms, transfer performance under A-Br was significantly *better* than under C-D, with high meaningfulness, significantly worse, and with medium meaningfulness, about equivalent. Clearly, the transfer effects can be moved around a great deal by manipulating meaningfulness. A paradigm that produces severe negative transfer with high response-term meaningfulness produces high positive transfer with low response-term meaningfulness. We must attribute this to the differences in the effect of the transfer of response-term learning present in the A-Br paradigm. With response terms of high meaningfulness the transfer of response learning is of little consequence since S can learn new response terms of the same level of meaningfulness very quickly. With low meaningfulness, however, in both C-B and A-Br, S, in learning the transfer list, does not have the problem of learning the difficult items which the S in the C-D paradigm has.

A Summary of Positive and Negative Factors

Let us now summarize (Table 12-2) the effects of the sub-components of overall transfer on the four key paradigms we have been using as focal points of the discussion. We may compare each of the paradigms with the control paradigm (C-D). Although a plus indicates a positive effect, we cannot insist that the effect is equivalent for all pluses (transfer of stimulus discrimination may not be equal quantitatively to the transfer of response learning). Indeed, we know that the magnitude of any given positive effect will vary. Nor can we say that the negative effect of backward associations is equivalent to the negative effect of forward associations. Clearly, this is a quasi-quantitative summary. It is, however, given as a demonstration of how experimental analysis over a period of several years produces data which allow us to fractionate a gross phenomenon into subprocesses or subcomponents which make up the gross effect. Each of the subcomponents can be studied independently and, indeed, one investigator may spend several years on such a component.

As we indicated earlier, there may be other sources of transfer which will eventually be added to the table if they can be identified and manipulated independently. But even at the moment, working only with the sources of transfer given in the table, one can make quite a number of predictions which are testable. For example, we note that while the A-Br paradigm has

TABLE 12–2

SUMMARY OF THE EFFECT OF COMPONENT PROCESSES ON OVERALL TRANSFER EFFECTS

An = sign means that this component does not differ for the paradigm; a — sign indicates a negative effect when compared with C-D [control] paradigm; a + sign indicates a positive effect when compared with C-D.

	PARADIGM		
TRANSFER FROM:	C-B	A-D	A-Br
Learing-to-learn	=	=	=
Warmup	=	=	=
Stimulus discrimination	=	+	+
Response discrimination	+	=	+
Response learning	+	=	+
Forward associations	=	—	—
Backward associations	—	=	—

two sources of negative transfer, we also see that it has three sources of positive transfer. In the data we examined earlier in the chapter, we found that negative transfer was greater for the A-Br paradigm than for the other two. However, it may well be that we could devise a situation where the positive transfer would be greater for this paradigm than for the other two. If we have high stimulus similarity, high response similarity, and low response meaningfulness, we would be throwing three rather powerful sources of positive transfer into the A-Br paradigm, whereas we can throw only one such in the A-D paradigm and two in the C-B.

Or, suppose we use a new paradigm, A-B, B-C. Suppose we vary response-term similarity; what would we predict about the transfer effects? Or, A-B, C-A? By examining the sources of transfer in Table 12-2, and perhaps by making some additional assumptions, it is clear that we can arrive at certain predictions about the transfer effects when we vary such factors as intralist similarity and meaningfulness.

FURTHER VARIATION
IN INTERLIST SIMILARITY

In the previous section we talked about intralist similarity, that is, similarity among the stimulus terms within a list (interstimulus similarity) or similarity among the response terms within a list. We have seen that such similarity manipulations have a secondary influence on transfer. Now we return to the problem of *interlist similarity*—similarity between corresponding terms in two paired-associate lists. In the manipulation of similarity, we pointed out that C-B and A-D represent intermediate degrees of interlist similarity when changes in similarity, each independently, occur between response terms in the two lists and between stimulus terms in the two lists. Thus, if the first list is symbolized A-B, we have two independent routes for manipulating similarity:

ZERO SIMILARITY	PARTIAL IDENTITY
C-D . . . . C-B	
C-D . . . . A-D	

In the first case, the response term D becomes more and more similar to the response term in the first list until it becomes identical and we have C-B. In the second case, the stimulus terms in the two lists become more and more similar until identity is reached and we have A-D. Now we have seen that we can produce negative transfer in both the C-B and A-D paradigms when C-D is used as a base for zero transfer. If, therefore, we manipulate similarity between these extremes on the two routes, we would expect a gradient of transfer effects running from zero effects at C-D to negative effects at C-B and A-D.

Still keeping two routes, we can proceed beyond partial identity to complete identity:

ZERO SIMILARITY	PARTIAL INDENTITY	COMPLETE IDENTITY
C-D . . . . C-B . . . . A-B		
C-D . . . . A-D . . . . A-B		

Since we know that complete identity must produce maximum positive transfer, we assume a gradient of transfer between partial identity and complete identity. Let us be sure we understand the meaning of the transfer paradigms which we might insert between the anchor points. Remembering that the first list is always A-B, we could have the following between C-D and C-B:

A-B	C-B′
X - *cold*	Y - *icy*

We assume that *icy* and *cold* are similar, but they are not identical. The similarity is often identified by a prime (as in B'). Or in the lower route, between C-D and A-D, we could have:

A-B	A'-D
cold - X	*icy* - Y

Moving back to the upper route again, between C-B and A-B, we might have:

A-B	A'-B
cold - X	*icy* - X

And in the lower route, between A-D and A-B:

A-B	A-B'
X - *cold*	X - *icy*

The full or complete relationships along these dimensions have not been worked out with strictly verbal materials in which formal, meaningful, and conceptual similarity have been manipulated. But there is enough "spot" evidence to indicate that expectations will be supported. That is, as we move along both routes from C-D, we will get poorer and poorer transfer performance until at C-B and A-D, the performance will be maximally poor. Then, as we continue the variation along both routes, transfer performance will start to improve, and we will get maximum positive effects with complete identity. We could, of course, vary similarity along both routes simultaneously. For example, an in-between paradigm falling between partial and complete identity might be:

A-B	A'-B'
cold-tired	*icy-weary*

MECHANISMS OF TRANSFER

In the case of the key paradigms, it is not difficult to see the source of associative interference. However, when we are dealing with similar rather than identical terms, we have to have, or at least would like to have, some mechanism or process to relate to the variations in similarity which will produce the observed transfer effects. Moreover, in moving from zero similarity to partial identity, we see that the mechanism must be able to mediate increasing associative interference. And if we wish to keep a single process throughout the entire range of similarity, the mechanism must be such as to start producing positive transfer as we move from partial identity to complete identity. To say the least, this theoretical problem is not simple, and it is fair to report that there is not a high degree of agreement among investigators on this matter. Nevertheless, let us look at some possibilities and see how they might mediate the transfer findings as similarity is changed.

Generalization

In an earlier chapter we discussed stimulus generalization. Among the illustrative studies was one dealing with semantic generalization. Given the development of an association between a word and a conditioned response, we saw that a synonym of the stimulus word would also tend to elicit the response. The mechanisms which produced this generalization allow different interpretative possibilities, a matter to which we will return later. Nevertheless, it can be seen that given the fact of generalization, one could use it as a theoretical device in order to account for transfer differences when similarity of verbal units between two lists is varied. For the moment, however, we shall turn our attention to the use of generalization as a theoretical device when formal similarity between verbal units is varied.

Illustrations. In a study by Abbott and Price (1964), the nonsense syllable XUH was used as the CS for establishing a conditioned eyelid response. The Ss were given 90 training trials to establish nearly 100 percent conditioning for all Ss, and then the 80 Ss were broken into subgroups for generalization test trials. One group was tested on the training stimulus, and a second group was tested on XUV, XEH, or QUH. Each of these syllables has a one-letter change when the reference is the training stimulus. The three different syllables were used to control for the particular letter changed (first, second, or third). A given S was tested on only one of the three. The Ss in a third group were tested on syllables in which two letters had been changed (XIY, ZUJ, JYH), and a fourth group was tested on a syllable in which all letters were different from the training stimulus (QOJ). Thus, it can be seen that there is decreasing similarity between the training and test stimuli as we go from Group 1 to Group 4. Ten test trials were given, with the percentage of conditioned responses on the 10 trials being the response measure. The results are shown in Fig. 12-6. As the formal similarity decreases, number of conditioned responses decreases, although there is little difference between one letter in common with the training stimulus and no letters in common.

Quite a different technique was used by Postman (1951) to measure generalization as a function of changes in formal similarity. Six-letter nonsense units were constructed, for example, RIJKAF. The 36 Ss were presented a list of 24 such units six times, each time in a different order, and were under instructions to remember the units since memory for them was to be tested. The test was carried out by a recognition procedure. On a sheet of paper 48 six-letter units were listed, of which only six were identical to those in the list given S to learn. Six units had one letter changed, six had two consecutive letters changed, six had three consecutive letters changed, and 24 were relatively new units in that the average of these had 1.3 letters in common with the original 24 units, or an average change of 4.7 letters. Thus, the changes in similarity in terms of letters were 0, 1, 2, 3, and 4.7.

On the test for generalization, S was given both the sheet with the 48 units printed on it and a sheet with 24 blank spaces on it. He was instructed to pick out the 24 units which had been in the original list. Obviously, since only six of the units *did* occur on the list given for learning, it was impos-

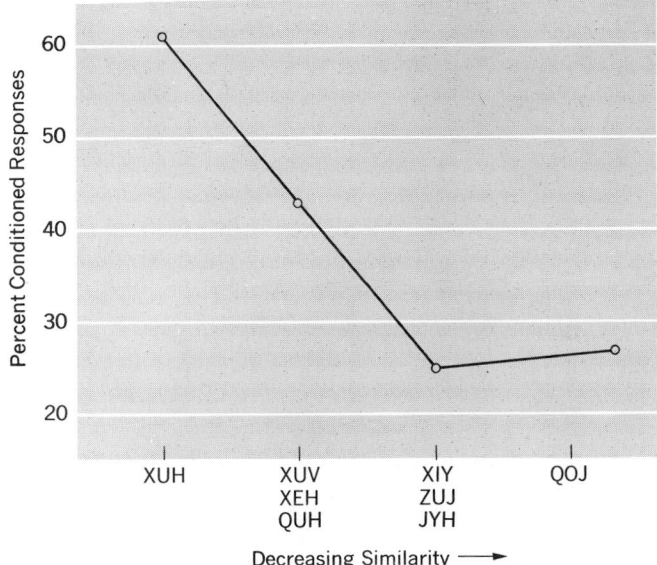

Fig. 12-6. Generalization of a conditioned eyelid response as a function of the formal similarity between training and test stimuli. XUH was the training syllable. Estimated from Abbott and Price (1964).

sible to pick out the 24. However, S was not told that all 24 units were not present and was given rather strong instructions that he *must* choose 24 units. Rather careful questioning showed that six of the 36 Ss were aware that all 24 words were not present, so we will consider the results for the remaining 30 Ss. The response measure used was calculated by asking the question, "What percent of the 24 items chosen as correct fell in each of the similarity groupings (0, 1, 2, 3, or 4.7 letters changed)?" The results are plotted in Fig. 12-7. We see that the probability of calling a given item correct decreases as a function of its similarity to the original training items.

Theoretical application. Having shown that variations in formal similarity of verbal units will produce gradients of response potential much as in classical sensory generalization, we may next use this fact to see how adequately certain facts of transfer may be handled.

We must first conceptualize the situation as it exists following the learning of the first list in a transfer study. As usual, we will symbolize the first list as A-B. In the left panel of Fig. 12-8 is shown the potential gradient of

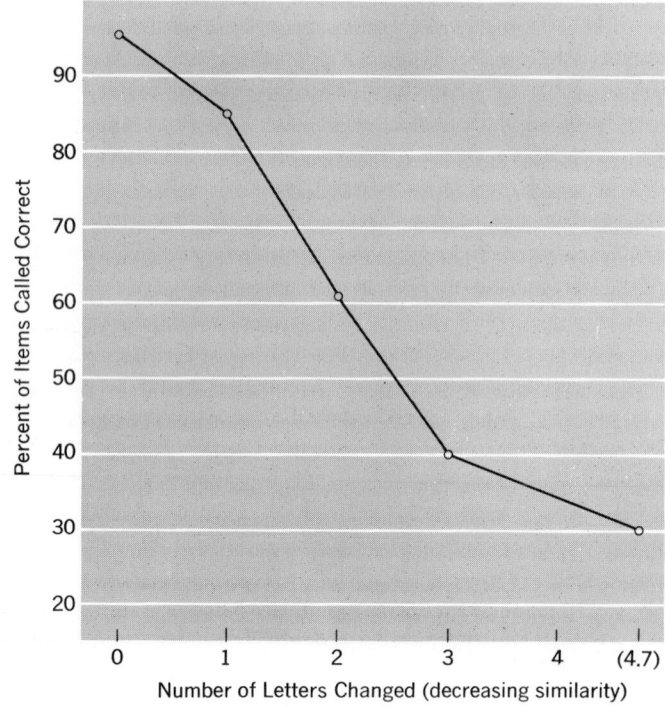

Fig. 12-7. Generalization in recognition memory as a function of formal similarity. Data from Postman (1951).

stimulus-term generalization which is presumed to exist at the end of A-B learning. The stimulus A has a probability of 1.0 of eliciting the response B. As the similarity decreases from identity to complete dissimilarity (A', A'', C), we presume a gradient of response probability corresponding to the gradient of stimulus generalization. A' has a lower probability of eliciting B than does A, A" has a lower probability than does A', and C has zero probability of eliciting B at the end of learning A-B. We have drawn the gradient as a linear one to simplify the exposition.

If there is generalization among stimulus terms as a consequence of variation in formal similarity, we may assume also that there will be a generalization gradient resulting from variation in formal similarity among the response terms. This is pictured in the right panel of Fig. 12-8. Verbally,

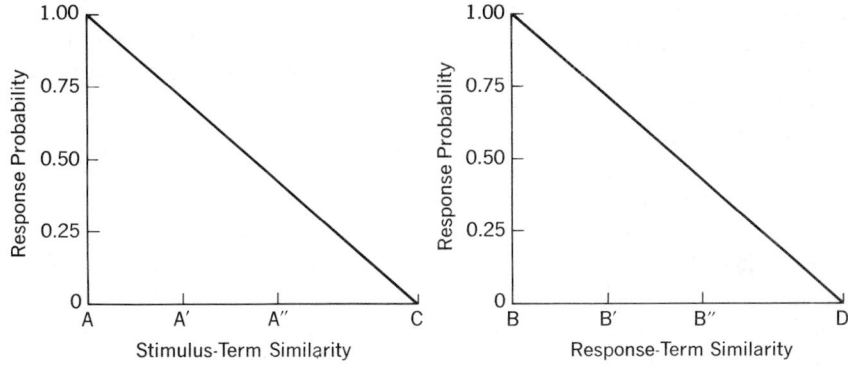

Fig. 12-8. Gradients of stimulus-term generalization and response-term generalization assumed to exist following the learning of the first list in a transfer paradigm. See text for complete explanation.

this generalization represents the probability of B, and response terms similar to it, being evoked by A at the end of first-list learning. Thus, B has a 1.0 probability of being elicited, B' (a response term with high formal similarity to B), a somewhat lower probability, and so on, until we reach D, which has no likelihood of being elicited by A following the learning of A-B.

Next we may relate these gradients to transfer. Consider first the implications of variations in response similarity, remembering that the similarity refers to similarity between the response terms in the first and second list in a transfer situation. Let the paradigm be A-B, A-B' in which the stimuli in the two lists remain the same and the response terms are slightly different. An illustration:

$$A\text{-}B \qquad\qquad A\text{-}B'$$
$$Q\text{-}XUY \qquad\qquad Q\text{-}ZUY$$

A-B having been learned, A has a certain probability (slightly below .75) of eliciting B' immediately at the start of second-list learning. To say this another way, as A-B is learned, an association is also being established between A and B′. Therefore, when S is required to learn A-B′, there is really only a little learning required (a little strengthening of the association) before the response term will be elicited with a probability of 1.0. This situation ought to produce high positive transfer. As we move on down the dimension of response-term similarity, we find the positive effect will be less and less, and when we reach the end of the dimension, we see that the paradigm becomes A-B, A-D, a paradigm we know will produce negative transfer in the usual situation when A-B, C-D is used as the control. If A-B′ produces positive transfer and A-D, negative, we see that at some point on the similarity dimension, the positive effect produced by generalization will be of the same magnitude as the negative effect of associative interference, and the net transfer would be expected to be zero. That is, we recognize that with A-B, A-D, interference occurs in learning A-D because B has just previously been attached to this stimulus. At some point of greater similarity (perhaps B″) the positive effect of response generalization will just counteract the negative or interference effect.

Consider next the variation in stimulus-term similarity. Let the paradigm be A-B, A′-B. The gradient of stimulus generalization indicates that following the learning of A-B, A′ has gained a potential for eliciting B. Thus, when B becomes the response term in the second list, heavy positive transfer should result. Example: XUY - Q followed by ZUY - Q. As stimulus-term similarity between the two lists decreases, we reach the A-B, C-B paradigm which we know may produce some negative transfer because of the backward association. Having learned A-B, there should be no positive effect of stimulus generalization in this paradigm because there is no tendency for C to elicit B.

The two variations we have traced thus far have led us from identity to partial identity (C-B, and A-D) as diagramed earlier in the chapter. We may now see what the situation is as we move from partial identity to complete dissimilarity. Let us start with A-B, C-B and proceed to decrease the similarity between the two response terms. If we assume a gradient of response-term similarity which relates to backward associations, we see that as B becomes less and less similar to the B in the first list (B′, B″, D), there will be a decreasing tendency for the backward association (B to A) to be elicited; and when the second list becomes C-D, we have our control paradigm with zero similarity in all terms (A-B, C-D).

Next, let us start with A-B, A-D and decrease the similarity of the stimulus terms in the two lists (A′, A″, and C). As similarity decreases there will be less tendency for B to be evoked in learning the second list, hence less interference from the forward association developed in learning the first list. At the extreme of this variation we again reach our control paradigm, A-B, C-D.

In summary, we see that we have accounted for the transfer effects discussed earlier in terms of the key paradigms. From C-D to C-B and A-D we have increasing negative transfer until we reach these two points of partial identity; as we go from these points to A-B (complete identity), we have increasing positive effects. Suppose we varied stimulus-term similarity and response-term similarity simultaneously. A paradigm might be A-B, A'-B'. We ask, "Following A-B learning what tendency does A' have of eliciting B'?" We have no precise answer to this question since we have no data on simultaneous variation of stimulus and response similarity, and we could only conjecture how the two sets of probabilities might combine. Clearly we would expect a positive effect; perhaps the amount would be given by multiplying probabilities (roughly $.7 \times .7$), but there is nothing in the theory which specifies this.

The explanation of transfer effects through the use of generalization appears to have considerable validity when formal similarity is manipulated, validity in the sense that available results may be predicted. When we are dealing with meaningful similarity, the theory also has success in handling most available data, but certain types of evidence may deny the existence of sensory generalization. As a consequence, another approach is sometimes taken in order to account for the transfer effects when meaningful similarity is manipulated. Such accounts utilize mediation as the basic mechanism of transfer.

Mediational Theories

Suppose we have an A-B, A'-B paradigm in which the stimulus words are the synonymous adjectives, *icy* and *cold*. The S learns *icy* - Q as a pair in the first list, and *cold* - Q as a pair in the second list. Positive transfer will result. And, as noted above, one could apply generalization theory to account for this. If these items formed an A-B, A-B' paradigm (Q - *icy*, Q - *cold*), positive transfer will also be observed; and this finding, too, could be accommodated within the generalization theory. However, at least two sets of facts argue quite strongly that direct mediational processes are involved.

Suppose that in the first list we have the pair Q - *cradle* and in the second list, Q - *baby*. *Baby* and *cradle* are not similar in meaning in any conventional sense, yet very high positive transfer will occur with such materials (Bastian, 1961; Postman & Stark, 1964). An explanation in terms of generalization is not applicable as long as generalization gradients are related to dimensions of similarity. How, then, can the positive transfer be produced? The answer appears to be mediation. In word-association tests, *baby* is a very common response to *cradle;* therefore, we infer that an associative connection already exists between *cradle* and *baby*. Consequently, in learning the second list, S "gets to" the second list response via the intermediate step of *cradle*. In the first list, the association Q - *cradle* is established; then, in the second list, when Q occurs, *cradle* is elicited, which in turn elicits *baby*. High positive transfer would be expected because there is little or no new learning required in the second step of the mediational chain.

The positive transfer which occurs in the above situation is quite comparable in amount to that which occurs when highly synonymous response terms are used. Could mediation be occurring when highly synonymous adjectives are the response terms? Yes. It is a fact that synonymous words also have high associative connection. Thus, when the pairs are Q - *icy*, Q - *cold*, *icy* and *cold* are already associatively connected so that in learning the transfer list, the mediation runs from Q to *cold* to *icy*. We see, therefore, that positive transfer will occur with highly associated words, whether similar or not, and the mechanism responsible is probably mediation. The fact that the positive effects will be observed with words that are not similar but are associatively related is the first fact that is particularly difficult for generalization theory.

The second difficulty for the generalization theory arises when Ss, following the learning of A-B, A-B', will report with nearly 100 percent agreement that they learned the second list by mediation (Barnes & Underwood, 1959). We cannot by any means always take seriously the reports of S concerning how he learned a given list, but in this case, with nearly perfect agreement among Ss, it seems equally foolish to disregard the reports.

If degree of synonymity, or degree of associative connection between words, is taken as an index of the probability that one word will elicit the other, it is quite possible to run through the various dimensions of "similarity" and show how the transfer effects can be handled in terms of probability that mediation will occur. This is true whether the associative connection is varied between the stimulus terms in the two lists or between the response terms. On the other hand, it is difficult to conceptualize mediation accounting for the transfer effects when formal similarity is varied. At the present time, in order to account for transfer effects, we seem to require two different theories, a generalization theory for formal similarity and a mediation theory for meaningful material.

Studies of mediation per se. Refinements of mediational interpretation of transfer as a function of similarity will, in future years, be aided by studies of mediation as such. This area is engaging the energies of an appreciable number of research workers. We have seen in the previous chapter that in learning a paired associate, S may produce his own simple mediational chain in the act of acquiring the paired associate. If the stimulus term is *dog* and the response, the number 9, S may interpose a single mediational term between *dog* and 9, so that the sequence is *dog* to *cat* to 9. This is to say that in order to produce 9 when *dog* is shown, two already established associations are used: *dog* to *cat* and *cat* to 9. Studies of mediation have taken two forms; one uses only the associations that are formed in the laboratory, and the other uses already established associations. Let us illustrate these two approaches.

A common paradigm for studying mediation is A-B, B-C, A-C. The interest centers in the learning of the third list (A-C). If S puts the associations in the first two lists "to work," he may learn the third list as A to B to C. The control paradigm requires that all other factors are constant except the possibilities for completing the mediational chain in the third list. Thus, a control paradigm might be A-B, X-C, A-C.

The effect of mediation, using the same paradigm and previously established associations, could be studied by assuming that A-B is already in the S's repertoire of associations. Assume A-B is *light - heavy*. In the laboratory S is given *heavy - xoc* as the second list and *light - xoc* as the third, with the presumption that in acquiring the third associate S will mediate from *light* to *heavy* to *xoc*.

Many other mediation paradigms have been used; for example, Horton and Kjeldergaard (1961) report data on eight different paradigms. Essentially, mediational possibilities are present, either via forward or via backward associations, whenever each of the three terms (A, B, and C) occur twice in the three lists. Positive effects in various mediation paradigms have been found, but there have also been many instances of failure to find positive effects. Jenkins (1963) has outlined some of the reasons for such failures and has suggested ways by which the mediational effect may be enhanced. For our purposes, however, it is enough to recognize that any three-stage experiment (characteristic of most mediation experiments) represents a difficult analytical situation when one or more terms change at each stage of the experiment. In effect, these experiments bring into play all of the seven factors discussed earlier in the two-stage transfer paradigm (and perhaps others), but because there are three stages, their effects may be compounded, diminished, or neutralized by the shifting of the various terms.

Furthermore, we cannot always be sure that our control condition is subject to all of the same forces as is the mediation condition, except for the possibilities of mediation on the third list. What might be called a positive effect of mediation might instead be a negative effect in the control condition that is not present in the mediation condition. So, the question is not whether mediation occurs. Clearly it *does* occur and with great effect in two-stage paradigms (e.g., A-B, A-B'). But when we study mediation of the more remote chaining kind, as in several three-stage paradigms, it is difficult with present techniques to identify with finality the particular factor or factors responsible for differences between experimental and control conditions. Yet there is no reason to doubt the occurrence of such mediation; the experimental problem is that of isolating all of the other factors so that the full magnitude of the effect can be gauged. The magnitude may eventually be shown to be much greater than current studies indicate.

OTHER VARIABLES

The study of transfer is so intimately bound to various forms of similarity that we sometimes almost forget that other independent variables may be related to transfer. We will consider briefly some of these other variables.

Degree of learning. This variable refers to degree of learning of the first list or task. There can be no doubt that this is a relevant variable—that transfer will vary as a function of degree of learning—but the influence may differ appreciably as a function of the nature of the transfer paradigm and the particular materials used. Essentially, the analytical problem is to study the influence of degree of learning on all of the subcomponents of transfer and then to relate the values of these subcomponents to an overall effect for a given paradigm using given materials. Very little progress has been made along these lines. However, certain facts and matters of method can be set forth, and these may be considered a series of separate points.

1. The amount of transfer in the A-B, A-D paradigm must necessarily be related to degree of first-list learning. When this paradigm is compared with the A-B, C-D control, we know that in the usual experiment negative transfer may be expected. Necessarily, therefore, there must be some increase in negative transfer as we go from zero learning of A-B to some higher degree of learning. Common sense might say that the higher the degree of learning of A-B, the greater the interference in learning A-D. Available evidence gives no support to this expectation; indeed, there is a little evidence that with extremely high degrees of learning of A-B, there may be a reduction in the negative transfer in learning A-D. It is *as if* S can set aside or keep separate a very strong association and, thereby, the interference is reduced. Possible components in this relationship have been detailed by Mandler (1962). Two studies (Postman, 1962b; Jung, 1962) have shown that after the intial increase in negative transfer as degree of A-B learning increases, there is little further change as degree of learning is increased to a higher level.

In studying degree of first-list learning the usual procedure is to use a different group of Ss for each degree of learning. Another technique has been used occasionally (Spiker & Holton, 1958). Assume that we have 12 pairs in the A-B list and that we give 48 acquisition trials. By arranging the items to be given on each trial, we could present three of the pairs on all 48 trials, three on 36 trials, three on 24 trials, and three on 12 trials. Therefore, by a mixed-list procedure we have four different degrees of A-B learning, each degree represented by three items. Then we proceed to the A-D list and examine the negative transfer on each subset of three pairs, comparing them with three new items (zero degree of first-list learning) which have been introduced into the second list. If LTL and warmup are nonspecific, we see that we do not need a special control condition (A-B, C-D) since the new pairs added to the A-D list provide the required control baseline. If we use this design we must balance across Ss all subsets of items so that each subset will be used equally often for each degree of learning and equally often as the control subset. The mixed-list procedure for studying the effects of degree of first-list learning has not been used frequently, and we do not know what pitfalls might be present in it.

2. Evidence shows that in the A-Br paradigm a direct relationship exists between the degree of first-list learning and the amount of negative transfer (Postman, 1962; Jung, 1962). However, we would be well advised not to accept this as an invariant relationship. Earlier we saw how the transfer in this paradigm ought to be subject to marked changes in magnitude as a function of task variables (intralist similarity, meaningfulness of response terms). Until we know how the transfer of these subcomponents is affected by degree of learning, we cannot be sure that we will always get increasing negative transfer as degree of first-list learning increases for this paradigm.

3. The above cautions will likewise apply to the A-B, C-B paradigm. There is evidence (e.g., Dean & Kausler, 1964) that with this paradigm low degrees of learning are associated with positive transfer (when compared with the C-D control) and higher degrees are associated with negative transfer. According to Dean and Kausler the positive effect with low degrees of learning represents the result of the transfer of response learning whereas with higher degrees of learning this positive effect is overcome by increasing interference from the continually increasing strength of the backward associations.

4. It is likely that degree of first-list learning and amount of positive transfer will be directly related whenever we deal with a paradigm that produces mediation as in A-B, A-B'. In this case we want B to occur to A quickly and consistently in learning the second-list association, and the stronger the A-B association, the more likely this is to occur. There is some evidence to support this expectation (Underwood, 1951).

Anticipation interval. Logically, in paradigms where mediation is responsible for the transfer effects, length of the anticipation interval on the transfer list should be a variable. With a very short anticipation interval, 1 sec. perhaps, it may be difficult to go through the intermediate step to reach the response term within the time allowed. Again, there is some evidence to support this expectation (Runquist & Marshall, 1963; Schulz & Lovelace, 1964). Another phenomenon may be related to the anticipation interval. We have said that when simple mediation occurs in certain of the transfer paradigms, such as A-B, A-B', or A-B, A'-B, positive transfer results. This is generally correct if the observations are made on the early trials in learning the second list. However, it is sometimes observed that on later trials on the transfer list, evidence for interference is obtained (e.g., Postman, 1964b); it is as if the mediator and the word to which the mediator has earlier led become mixed up as to which is which. It may be that this confusion will be greater with a short anticipation interval than with a long anticipation interval.

Finally, we may mention a few other variables that have been studied occasionally with verbal materials: the time interval between the first and second list (e.g., Newton & Wickens, 1956); number of successive lists representing the same paradigm, such as A-B, A-D, where S learns different responses to the same stimuli in successive lists (e.g., Bugelski, 1948; Duncan, 1964); the role of anxiety (e.g., L'Abate, 1962) and of stress on interference paradigms (e.g., Gordon & Berlyne, 1954).

OTHER TASKS

We can take almost any learning task given to man or animal and arrange it so that some form of transfer could be studied. The most common paradigms studied reflect interference relationships. Having trained an animal to make a left turn in a T-maze, we may require him to learn a right turn. Having taught an animal to respond positively to a large square and not to respond to a small square, we could reverse the requirements. Positive effects in learning successive tasks have also been studied with animals. The classic work of Harlow (1949) on the increasing proficiency with which monkeys solve simple discrimination problems, a proficiency which increases over many scores of problems, is an illustration.

With human Ss some of the paradigms of verbal learning may be translated to fit motor tasks; card sorting is a motor task commonly used in the laboratory to demonstrate interference. First S learns to sort a deck of ordinary playing cards into four boxes labeled hearts, diamonds, clubs, and spades. For the second task E changes the positions of the boxes, and S sorts the deck again. As might be expected, S makes many false moves (negative transfer) on the first few trials after the change in the position of the boxes. We would expect that the amount of negative transfer would be directly related to the number of changes in the position of the boxes, and the expectation is verified in a study by Crafts (1935).

Crafts used "Flinch" cards on which the numbers occur in bold type. Nine numbers were used, and each appeared eight times in the deck of 72 cards. Nine boxes, each 4.5 in. square, were placed in tier fashion, and S's task was to sort the cards as rapidly as possible into the appropriately numbered boxes. The response measure was the time required to sort the complete deck, each sorting constituting a trial.

After brief preliminary practice, all Ss were given eight trials; then four groups were matched using the scores on the eight trials as the matching measure. Following the constitution of the four groups, two additional sorting trials were given with the four groups treated as follows:

> Group I: Position of *no* numbers changed
> Group II: Position of 3 numbers changed
> Group III: Position of 6 numbers changed
> Group IV: Position of all 9 numbers changed

The results are shown in Fig. 12-9 where a single performance curve is shown for the first eight trials. On the post-change trials the interference with performance is directly related to the number of changes made. However, it can be seen that the interference or negative transfer must be considered relative negative transfer. Only Group IV did more poorly after the change

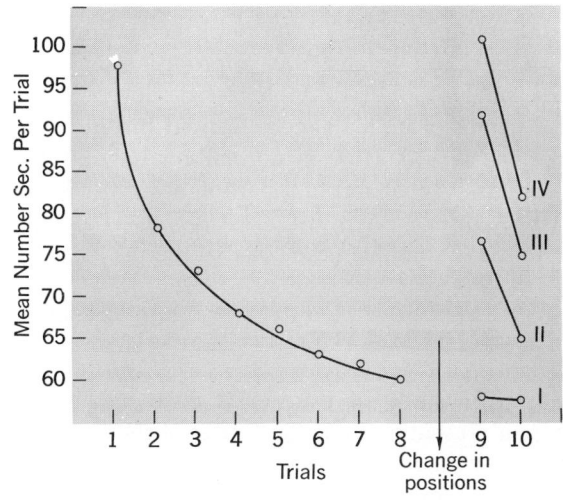

Fig. 12-9. Transfer in card sorting as a function of the number of changes in sorting boxes. Data from Crafts (1935).

than they did on the first trial at the start of the experiment. All other groups show positive transfer when their performance at the start of the experiment is used as a reference point. What we need in such an experiment is a control to correspond to the A-B, C-D control used in verbal-learning experiments as a means of removing LTL and warmup effects. Is it possible to devise such a control for the card-sorting task?

Some of the most severe interference may be observed in the laboratory by giving S a task which requires acts directly opposed to those which through long practice in everyday life have achieved very high strength. Mirror star-tracing, as discussed in an earlier chapter, is one such task. Another, devised by Stroop (1935), may be illustrated. The S is presented with a sheet on which the names of colors are printed in an ink that is a different color from the one signified by the word. Thus, the word red is printed in blue ink; the word blue is printed in yellow ink; the word brown is printed in red ink, perhaps as shown in Fig. 12-10. The task requirement is simple; S must go through the list as rapidly as possible naming the color of the ink of each successive word. Most of the Ss can "feel" the interference. Where does the interference originate? It appears to result from the fact that we have had much experience with words in which the appropriate response is reading the words. Now the task requires us to ignore the words and attend only to the colors of the inks, and this is very difficult to do. An S can practice on this task for many days and still not reach the same speed of naming the colors as he can in naming or reading the words. Actually, not very much analytical work on this task has been published. If one has a set of colored pencils it is quite simple to construct appropriate materials for undertaking some of these analyses. For example, is it relevant that the words name colors? If the names of animals were printed in different colors would the same interference result? How is normal reading behavior influenced by practice on this task? What sort of a paradigm *is* this? It does not seem to be strictly an A-B, A-Br or an A-B, A-C. Is it A-B, C-D in which S has difficulty in attending to the C stimulus (the color of the ink)?

SUMMARY

The study of transfer is concerned with the influence of prior learning on present learning, and most of the contemporary work of an analytical nature with human Ss is being done with verbal material. The work is built around four paradigms, three of which represent key points on a dimension of intertask similarity. The control paradigm, A-B, C-D, represents minimal similarity; A-B, A-D a change to identity of stimuli; and A-B, C-B a change to identity of response terms. A fourth paradigm (A-B, A-Br), one which produces very heavy negative transfer, is used for analytical purposes.

The overall transfer effect observed in these paradigms is broken into subphenomena or subcomponents, several of which were identified: non-associative components which include learning-to-learn and warmup; positive learning components which include transfer of stimulus and response discrimination and of response learning; negative components which result from the interference of forward and backward associations of the first list.

Two explanatory mechanisms, generalization and mediation, were evaluated as explanations for the positive transfer observed in certain paradigms (e.g., A-B, A-B′). It was concluded that generalization may be an appropriate explanatory device for transfer effects resulting from variation in formal similarity but that mediational mechanisms are to be preferred when associated words are used.

The effects of two other variables (degree of learning and length of anticipation interval) were discussed briefly, and transfer in areas other than verbal learning were illustrated.

CHAPTER THIRTEEN

Forgetting

Forgetting is a most exasperating and sometimes even painful phenomenon. We sometimes wonder how forgetting has survived the evolutionary processes, since it appears quite unadaptive. The young man who forgets that certain mushrooms are poisonous will father no children; the child who cannot swim will leave no progeny if he forgets the dangers of playing near water; a life may be lost in war if the meaning of a code signal is forgotten. At the same time, however, it is quite possible that in spite of the sometimes lethal consequences of forgetting, there is a certain adaptive characteristic about it. Perhaps we have the capacity to learn only so much, and, without forgetting, once we have learned to this maximal level we can learn no more. Surely any storage system has limits and to go beyond these limits requires the removal of some of the material already stored (forgetting).

It is an interesting exercise to speculate on the implications if, suddenly, all people no longer forgot. That is, given an unlimited storage system for learning, and given our present laws of learning, what would the consequences be if we never forgot anything of all subsequent learning. We memorize a telephone number today and 10 years from now it remains as vivid and available as it is now. We memorize a passage from Shakespeare in order to pass an examination in an English course, and this passage stands before us 30 years later as clear and stark as it was originally. Once we learn a set of theorems and propositions from a textbook in physics they would be with us always. In time, because we would carry the events of modern history in our heads, such courses might disappear from the school curriculum. Record keeping of all kinds might gradually diminish. At the same time it is possible that a certain amount of chaos might occur in our behavior, for how would we know when a particular response was appropriate at a given moment. We might dial the telephone number of a friend who had long since had it changed; the events of history might become a mishmash of events unless tied specifically to dates orienting us in time. It appears that as a consequence of forgetting occurring over time, there is a downward gradient of response availability extending backward in time; and this gradient gives us temporal orientation and discrimination which allows us to produce the appropriate behavior for the moment, something we might never do adequately if we never forgot. But we are what we are, and included in what we are is the fact that we do forget, so the idle speculations about the state of a world where there is no forgetting may best be left to the cocktail hour.

SOME PRELIMINARIES

Traditionally, the experimental study of forgetting has been closely tied to verbal materials. There is an occasional study of the forgetting of a conditioned response, an occasional study of the forgetting shown by a rat for a maze, and an occasional study of the forgetting of a motor skill, but most of the analytical work on forgetting and most of the theoretical formulations have derived from experiments using verbal materials. It is not unusual to find variables which are known to influence animal learning being "tried out" in human learning experiments. Although the reverse is somewhat more rare, we do find studies using rats (e.g., Gleitman & Jung, 1963) or pigeons (e.g., Kehoe, 1963) or even hedgehogs (Pollard, 1964) which were designed primarily to test theoretical propositions about forgetting which originated from studies using lists of verbal units. It is not a coincidence that both the study of transfer and the study of forgetting have been concentrated heavily in the verbal-learning laboratory, for as we will see, the study of forgetting often results from an extension of a study of transfer, and investigators often measure both in a single experiment.

We have talked about forgetting, but we may have talked with equal validity about retention, for these terms represent reciprocal measures. Forgetting refers to the amount lost, retention to the amount remembered. It has sometimes been said that the choice of one of these two terms by an investigator is diagnostic of a certain aspect of his personality. The pessimist, who refers to the amount of wine in his glass by saying that it is half empty, may use the term *forgetting;* the optimist, who refers to his wine glass as half full, may use the term *retention.* Like many rule-of-thumb techniques for diagnosing personality, this one too is probably faulty. However that may be, in the present chapter we will use both terms. If S learns a list of 10 paired associates to one perfect trial, and if after 24 hr. he is able to produce six of these on a recall test, we say his retention is six items, or 60 percent, and his forgetting is four items, or 40 percent.

The operational definition of forgetting (or retention) is inextricably tied to the passage of time; time is the defining independent variable. If a C Group is given a retention test immediately after learning, and if an E Group is given its test 24-hr. later, and if the performance of the E Group is poorer than that of the C Group, we have defined forgetting. We do not always obtain forgetting by these operations, for we remember in an earlier chapter that *reminiscence* was defined in the same manner except that the performance of the E Group was better than that of the C Group. A number of years ago there were experiments showing evidence for reminiscence for verbal materials over short intervals (e.g., 2 min.), but in more recent years no investigator has been able to produce it consistently, for reasons which thus far have not been determined. Recent evidence indicates a reminiscence effect for certain items within a list, an effect that may not reach its maximal level for a day or a week (Kleinsmith & Kaplan, 1964). However, we will not be concerned with reminiscence in this chapter.

Learning and retention are logically interrelated. In learning a paired associate list by either the anticipation method or by the alternate study and recall method, the so-called learning scores represent the net effect of amount learned and the amount forgotten from trial to trial. In the learning task we usually have a short interval (usually a few seconds) between each trial. Customarily, we speak of studying retention or forgetting whenever the interval between two trials is increased beyond that used to separate the earlier trials. This is a convention, however, and should not lead us to conclude that merely by lengthening the time between two trials we are going to change anything very fundamental about the situation.

Measures of Forgetting

If we extend the above thinking, it can be seen that whenever we lengthen the interval between trials in learning by the anticipation procedure, the first trial after the interval constitutes the recall trial, and the number of correct responses on that trial is used as the *recall measure* of retention. This measure is by far the most widely used index of forgetting, and we will return shortly to certain problems of measurement associated with it.

When Ebbinghaus pioneered the study of forgetting, he commonly used a measure of *relearning* as an index of forgetting. Suppose, for example, that 10 trials were required to learn a task originally to a given criterion of performance. If only five trials are required to relearn the task after a given retention interval, the number of trials saved in relearning is five, or the *savings score* is 50 percent. A more common way of using relearning as a measure of forgetting is to give a constant number of trials following a retention interval or intervals and then determine the difference in number of correct responses during these trials among the various conditions of the experiment. If a recall measure is used from the same data, scores on the recall trial may be eliminated from the relearning measure.

Both the recall measure and the relearning measure require S to produce the response terms. A measure which does not require this production is known as *recognition*. For example, suppose the task is free learning. On a retention test E may place the correct words randomly in a list along with additional words (words which were not in the list) and request S to identify the words which were in the list presented for learning. The recognition measure is a very mercurial one. Most of us have taken multiple-choice tests where the alternative answers were all very similar, and we know how difficult it is to choose the correct alternative in such a case as compared to choosing the correct one where alternatives differ widely. In the same sense, we can manipulate recognition measures a great deal by varying the similarity between the verbal units learned and the added or filler words put in as a part of the recognition test. And, given a constant degree of similarity, the measure should vary as a function of the number of added units, if for no other reason than that guessing probabilities will differ. Because of these problems, the recognition measure is very infrequently used unless it seems necessary for a particular problem. Of course, if we did an experiment in which we measured forgetting by recognition as a function of the length of the retention interval, and if the same retention test is used for all conditions (for all lengths of intervals), there can be no bias. However, the absolute amount of forgetting measured by this procedure has little meaning when compared with another experiment using a different recognition task.

Other measures are sometimes used. For example, a *reconstruction* method might be used following the learning of a serial list. On the retention test S is given the units (he does not have to produce them) and is asked to order them in the manner in which they were ordered during learning. In such a case E would be interested in the retention of particular associations and not in the retention of the items as such. However, we will remember that in an earlier chapter it was noted that the evidence is very confused as to just what the associations are in a serial list. Nevertheless, the reconstruction method may have value in particular situations. In the same sense, an associative matching task might be used for paired associates in which, at recall, S is given both the stimulus and response terms and is asked to pair them as they were paired during learning. We can see that such techinques may be used for certain analytical purposes. For example, assume that we visualize the forgetting process for a paired-associate list as representing both the loss of response terms and a weakening in the strength of the associations between stimulus and response terms. With different groups we might (1) have S produce response terms without regard to whether they are paired with the appropriate stimulus term or not, (2) have S match stimulus and response terms, and (3) have S undergo the usual recall procedure. Would we be able to predict the third measure by summing the losses involved in the first two measures?

The discussion above is merely to remind ourselves once again that we must not become bound by traditional methods. The fact that most of our data on forgetting are based on the recall method should not be taken to mean that we must be tied to this method in subsequent work. The methods must be geared to ideas about phenomena, and if there is a lack of correspondence, the method must go, not the idea.

If we wish to study the retention of a connected passage, such as a paragraph of prose, there are several choices for the response measure. At one extreme we might simply count the number of words correctly recalled; at the other extreme we could score the number of ideas correctly recalled. One of the difficulties with the latter method is that different Es may not agree on what constitutes an idea (Levitt, 1956), hence the absolute retention scores for the work of one E may differ from that of another, even when conditions are the same. Nevertheless, normally we will expect to find positive relationships among any of a variety of methods used to score recall protocols of connected discourse (e.g., King, 1960).

Degree of Learning

At this point we introduce a variable which influences forgetting and do so because of its profound significance for our thinking about the design of experiments for the study of retention. Without presenting any particular data to support the statement, we can say that unless some peculiar circumstances attend the experiment, the greater the number of repetitions of a given association, the more resistant is that association to forgetting. If a paired associate is given correctly twice in the act of learning a list, it will be recalled less well after a specified interval than it would if given correctly 10 times in learning. Or, suppose for one group we carry the learning of a list to the point where S can just reproduce all items correctly on a single trial and then we measure recall of this list after 24 hr. For another group we carry the learning of the list to the same criterion and then add 20 more practice trials before introducing the 24-hr. retention interval. Recall of the latter group will be higher than recall of the former. Carrying the learning trials beyond the point at which S first gets all the items correct is often spoken of as overlearning. Another way to view overlearning is to consider it as starting at a time when we can no longer measure an increase in the performance during learning. When the probability of getting all items correct on a trial reaches and remains constant at 1.0 or slightly below, we say that overlearning is occurring. We note that in these situations we are unable to measure any further increase in associative strength by observing the number of correct responses; however, that a continued increase in the effective associative strength takes place can be inferred from the fact that the rate of forgetting is slower with overlearning than without overlearning.

The relationship between degree of learning and amount retained requires that whenever we are studying the effect of a variable other than degree of learning, we must have a constant degree of learning across all conditions. It will be remembered that we discussed this problem briefly in considering factors influencing extinction, for in studying extinction we are faced with the same problem if level of conditioning and rate of extinction are related. The generalized solution which usually occurs to us for equating degree of learning prior to introduction of the retention interval is to use a criterion of performance, requiring all Ss under all conditions to achieve the same constant level of performance before the retention interval is introduced. We need to examine this solution in some detail.

Common performance criterion. Assume that we are going to study the forgetting of a given task as a function of the length of the retention interval. Different groups of Ss are formed randomly, each group to be given a different retention interval between learning and recall. In learning we carry all Ss in all groups to a common criterion of performance, such as one perfect trial. Because our groups are formed randomly, we expect that the mean number of trials to reach the criterion will not differ for the groups. We must presume that degree of learning is equivalent and, therefore, that the retention scores will not be biased due to differences in degree of learning. As a general principle, we may say that when number of trials to attain a common criterion is roughly equivalent for different groups, we may expect the degree of learning to be equivalent.

For a second case, assume that we are manipulating some variable which influences the rate at which lists are learned, a variable such as meaningfulness of the response terms in a paired-associate list. We pose an important question to ask of an experiment: does level of meaningfulness influence rate of forgetting? The problem is to find an answer which is not biased because of different degrees of learning. It is obvious that we cannot give all groups a constant number of trials prior to the retention interval. Because of the enormous effect of response-term meaningfulness on learning, the degree of learning achieved by the different groups after a constant number of trials would be markedly different; the group having the list with highest meaningfulness would have the highest level of learning, and the group with the list having the lowest level of meaningfulness would have the lowest degree of learning. Retention measurements following this procedure would, potentially, be confounded, being both a function of degree of learning and a function of differences in rate of forgetting as a function of meaningfulness.

Superficially it might seem that the solution to the problem is to carry Ss in all groups to a common criterion of learning. Such a procedure will reduce the differences in degree of learning (as compared with the constant-trials method), but it will not eliminate them. Assume we have two lists, one having very low meaningfulness of the response terms and another having very high meaningfulness. Assume further that there are 12 pairs in the list and that the Ss learning both lists are taken to a common criterion of eight of the 12 responses correctly anticipated on a given trial. Finally, assume that the Ss given the high-meaningfulness list require an average of three trials to achieve the criterion and those given the low-meaningfulness list, 10 trials. The acquisition curves are depicted in Fig. 13-1, with the solid lines indicating the empirical curves. In using the anticipation method of learning, we have

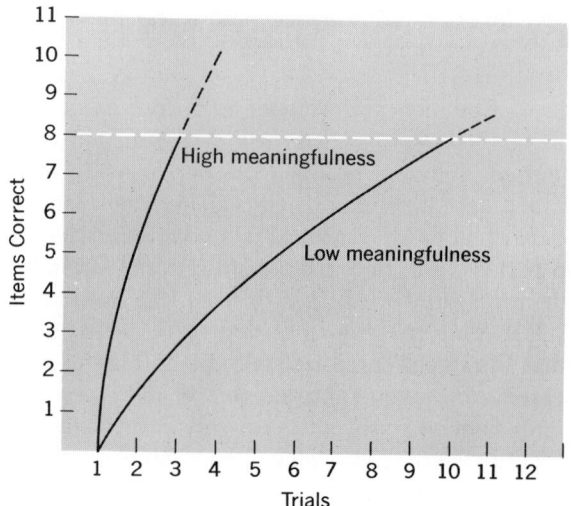

Fig. 13-1. Hypothetical illustration of difficulty in equating degree of learning of materials learned at different speeds to the same criterion.

set the criterion at eight correct responses on a given trial. However, on the trial on which this criterion was achieved, S was also acquiring new associations, and the fact must follow that a greater number of new associations would be acquired for the list of high meaningfulness than for the list of low meaningfulness. This added amount acquired on the final anticipation trial may be estimated by extrapolating the acquisition curve for one trial, as is shown by the dotted lines in Fig. 13-1. It is clear that had there been another learning trial, a trial which would correspond to a recall trial, the degree of learning for the two groups would not have been equivalent but, instead, would have been higher for the list of high meaningfulness than for the list of low meaningfulness. Any differences in the recall scores would, therefore, represent a difference produced by both degree of learning and differences in rate of forgetting as a function of meaningfulness.

Is the extrapolation shown in Fig. 13-1 accurate? If we had two control groups who were given the extra trial, would the performance be accurately estimated by the levels shown at the terminus of the dotted lines? The answer is no; the differences would be still greater. This is because of what is often called the criterion fall. If a criterion of performance is set, such as eight correct responses, the mean performance will *fall* on the trial after the criterion is reached. Why should this be?

We must think of learning performance as being the net effect of a number of processes, some involved in learning and some involved in forgetting from trial to trial. When S first achieves a given level of performance, we must realize that all processes were favorable or "stacked" at that time. Perhaps little forgetting occurred between the previous trial and the trial on which criterion was reached; perhaps the strength of a weak association oscillated just above the recall threshold; perhaps S made a lucky response guess. Assuming some random fluctuation of such processes from trial to trial, we see, on the trial following the attainment of the criterion, that these processes are likely to be less favorable than on the criterion trial. Therefore, unless the amount of new learning is such as to more than counteract these negative or unfavorable processes, performance will fall. The amount of fall to be expected is directly related to the difficulty of the list. If the list is very easy, performance may increase between the criterion trial and the next trial as pictured for the high-meaningfulness list in Fig. 13-1. With the more difficult list, however, we would expect a rather serious fall, as much as 25 percent. If the criterion is eight correct responses, on the next trial the average correct may be as low as six correct responses. So the differences in degree of learning shown in extrapolating the curves in Fig. 13-1 will underestimate the differences in the degree of learning of the two lists. We must conclude that carrying learning to the same criterion does not equate degree of learning when the rate of learning of the lists to be equated differs. Of course, if there is a relatively small difference in rate of learning, there is a corresponding decrease in the differences in degree of learning.

The above discussion indicates that one of the factors involved in producing differences in "true" degree of learning when lists are learned at different rates to the same criterion results from the anticipation method. On the criterion trial, differences in amount of learning will occur and will correspond in magnitude to differences in the rate of list learning up to that point. One way to minimize the effect of this factor is to use alternate study and recall trials, on the assumption that learning will not occur on the recall trials since the correct responses are not shown. But we can say only that we minimize the influence of new learning by using the alternate study and recall method, for, in fact, some changes in performance will occur even though the correct responses are not shown (e.g., Richardson & Gropper, 1964). Of course, the use of the alternate study and recall method does not remove the problem produced by differences in criterion fall. Therefore, while the alternate study-recall method may reduce the seriousness of the problem of differences in degree of learning when lists are learned to the same criterion at different rates, it will not eliminate the problem.

Possible solutions. We have no easy solution to the above problem, but there are solutions, more or less burdensome, which may be applied.

1. We might use control groups which are given one trial beyond the criterion trial. The performance of these groups gives us a base of immediate recall—the amount of recall to be expected *had* the experimental groups (those who will have delayed recall) been given the immediate recall. Then we could determine differences in the slopes of the curves connecting immediate and delayed recall; if these differ, we might conclude that there is a difference in the rate of forgetting independent of degree of learning. Let us illustrate possible outcomes of this procedure.

Assume that we have lists of high and low meaningfulness and that we use a criterion of performance for original learning. Two groups learn the list of high meaningfulness, and two, the list of low meaningfulness. The C Groups are given one trial beyond the criterion trial, and the E Groups recall after 24 hr. We may call the "retention" scores of the C Groups immediate recall, or zero-delay recall, and expect the performance of these two groups to differ. Such a difference is shown for the zero interval for all three panels of Fig. 13-2. Looking at the upper panel, we see that the two curves have the same slope—there is no interaction. The number of items lost over the interval is equivalent for both groups, and we conclude that there is no difference in rate of forgetting. In the middle panel the interaction is apparent; the list associated with highest degree of learning on immediate recall has the poorest 24-hr. recall performance. Clearly, a difference in amount forgotten occurs over and above that which could be attributed to differences in degree of learning.

In the lower panel the interaction is again apparent, but the interpretation is not clear. Either the differences in degree of meaningfulness or the differences in degree of learning, or both, might be involved in the fact that the slope of the retention curve is steeper for the low-meaningfulness list than for the high-meaningfulness list. Such a result, therefore, does not help us very much unless we know precisely the relationship between degree of learning and rate of forgetting for these materials. If we knew this, we could ask whether the difference in the slopes of the curves is greater than could be expected by degree of learning alone. Such a consideration might require us to reevaluate the curves in the upper panel. Since the curve for the list with the lower degree of learning is falling at the same rate as the other, and since according to its degree of learning it would be expected to fall more rapidly, it may mean that there is less forgetting demonstrated by this curve than by the other. Again, there is no way to deny this unless we know the relationship between degree of learning and retention for these materials. At the same time, there is no reason to believe that there will be a sharp difference in rate of forgetting as a function of the relatively small differences in degree of learning which may result from the criterion problem we have

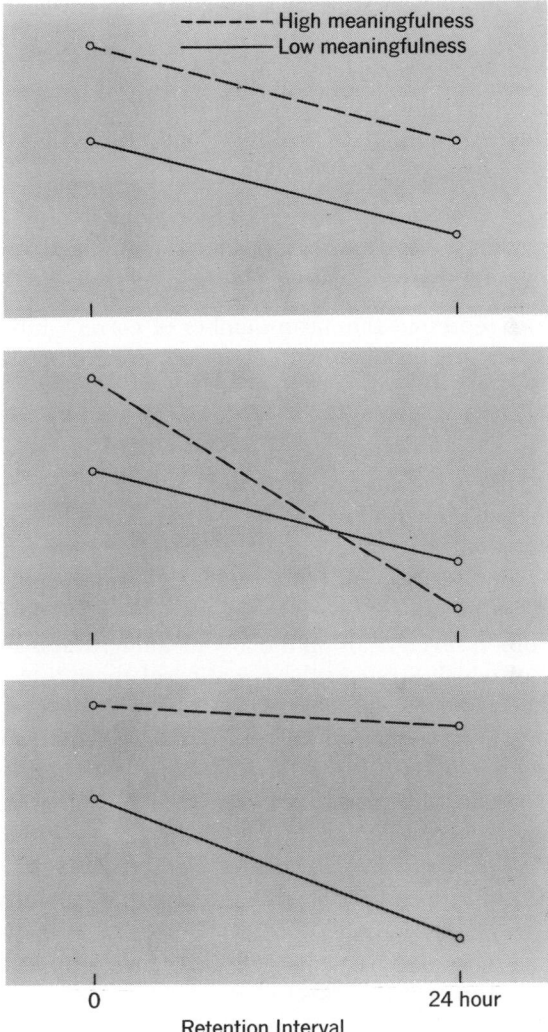

Fig. 13-2. Illustration of possible outcomes of an experiment on forgetting. See text for explanation.

been discussing. Nevertheless, we probably will not feel completely confident that we have demonstrated the effect of a variable on retention under the circumstances we are discussing unless we get marked differences in the slopes of the curves, such as in the middle panel of Fig. 13-2.

2. A more satisfactory procedure for carrying out the above experiment is to use a constant number of trials which, however, differ in number for each list so that it is known that performance on the two lists would be essentially identical had another trial been given. To accomplish this, we must undertake preliminary work with pilot Ss to determine the acquisition curves. We give one group the list of 12 pairs having high meaningfulness, and the other, the list of 12 pairs having low meaningfulness, and then carry the learning for a large number of trials, at least enough so that all Ss in both groups have achieved one perfect recitation. Suppose the mean performance curves for the two lists were as follows:

Trials:	1	2	3	4	5	6	7	8	9	10
High meaningfulness:	2	4	6	8	10	12	12	12 etc.		
Low meaningfulness:	1	2	3	4	5	6	7	8	9	10 etc.

The values represent the mean number of correct anticipations of each successive trial. Our problem is to equate the degree of learning for these lists prior to introducing a retention interval, and we will assume that we wish to take the learning to the level represented by 8 of the 12 responses' being correct on the average. We can see that if we gave three trials on the high-meaningfulness list and seven on the low, mean performance to be expected on the immediately following trials (Trials 4 and 8) would be equivalent for both lists—eight correct responses. Therefore, in the main part of our experiment, we draw two groups of Ss from the same population as that used for the pilot Ss; we give one group three trials on the high-meaningfulness list and the other, seven trials on the low-meaningfulness list. We know that any differences which occur in the retention of these lists cannot be due to differences in degree of learning. This is an ideal method for handling the degree-of-learning problem, but, of course, it requires appreciable work in running the pilot Ss prior to the main part of the experiment.

3. There are additional methods for analyzing in detail the results of experiments performed either by use of the criterion method or by the use of a constant number of trials. These methods may be used to remove any possibility that the differences in retention (if obtained) are due to differences in degree of learning. The amount of space required to present these techniques does not warrant their inclusion here, but they may be found elsewhere (Underwood, 1964).

Let us review. Degree of learning is known to influence the rate of forgetting; if, therefore, we intend to study the influence of some other variable on retention, particularly a variable which produces a marked influence on rate of learning, we must be sure that differences in degree of learning do not prevent us from reaching a conclusion concerning the effect of the variable of interest. We have indicated some of the ways by which we may neutralize degree of learning so that it will not bias our retention measurements.

Degree of learning and retention measures. Suppose we have two groups learn a list of words by free learning (alternate study and recall trials) and then a week later test one group by recall and another group by the recognition method. If the filler, or added, words used on the recognition test are words chosen randomly, hence in no way highly similar to the words in the list learned, the recognition method will give a much higher score than will the recall measure. Such findings have been reported a number of times, and because of them it has often been said that there is less forgetting when measured by recognition than when measured by recall. The findings stand, of course, but we cannot conclude from them that forgetting is slower when measured by recognition than when measured by recall, because once again we may have a confounding produced by differences in degree of learning (Bahrick, 1964). An illustration will lead to the reasoning behind Bahrick's conclusion.

We present a list of 25 words for free learning until a criterion of 15 correct is achieved, after which a retention interval is introduced. A week later we measure half the Ss by recall and half by recognition; we find that by recognition 15 are correct, and by recall 10 are correct. There would appear to be no forgetting when measured by recognition. However, we have no base measurement of degree of learning for recognition. Had we had a recognition test for a C Group immediately after learning, perhaps 20 or more items would have been given correctly, and the number of items lost by both methods of measuring retention would have been roughly comparable. Let us look at this another way. The response strength necessary to elicit a correct recognition is less than the strength required to produce or recall a unit. If, therefore, we want to make degree of learning equivalent, we must measure learning by the methods we are going to use at recall. By a recognition procedure (alternate study and recognition tests) it may take only five trials to reach a given criterion whereas it may take 15 trials to reach the same criterion by alternate study and recall. Only when we measure degree of learning by the method used to measure forgetting will differences in forgetting be meaningful. Bahrick was able to conclude from his work that rate of forgetting was essentially equivalent for recognition and recall when degree of learning was appropriately handled.

We will leave the problems involved in measuring retention and turn to some of the facts of retention and some of the design problems which arise. Our organization may appear to be backward, since we will start with some of the more complex phenomena and work toward the simple. However, the complex phenomena result from operations which are extensions of those used to study transfer, and furthermore, they have historical precedent over simpler phenomena in the evolution of a theory of forgetting. By working from the complex to the simple we will be able to give some of the key historical developments in unfolding an *interference theory* of forgetting.

RETROACTIVE INHIBITION

The general operational definition of retroactive inhibition may be diagramed as follows:

	LEARN TASK X	LEARN TASK Y	RECALL TASK X
C Group	Yes	No	Yes
E Group	Yes	Yes	Yes

If the retention of Task X is poorer for the E Group than for the C Group, retroactive inhibition is said to have occurred. Maximal retroactive inhibition may be produced by using transfer paradigms which produce negative transfer. An E Group is given A-B, A-D and immediately recalls A-B. The C Group learns A-B, rests for the period of time required by the E Group to learn A-D, and then recalls A-B. The amount of retroactive inhibition which can be produced by learning A-D (commonly called the interpolated list) is very large. Under appropriate conditions the loss as measured by recall may be nearly complete, and retroactive inhibition can be shown with nearly any kind of a verbal task, from serial lists to prose material.

Studies on retroactive inhibition number in the hundreds. A little study of the above diagram will demonstrate why; one can see that there are a great many variables which may be manipulated within this general definition. Let us list just a few: degree of learning of Task X; degree of learning of Task Y; length of retention interval; point in the retention interval at which Task Y is inserted; type of task; similarity between the two tasks. In general, we may expect that whenever the habits involved in acquiring the two tasks are somewhat contradictory or conflicting, retroactive inhibition will be observed. But similarity may be varied in the several ways we have discussed in the previous chapter, and it may also be varied at a gross level by having S learn Task X in one environment and Task Y in quite a different environment. This will reduce the amount of retroactive inhibition as compared with that shown if both tasks are learned in the same environment. We will make no attempt to summarize the empirical relationships relating to retroactive inhibition; a relatively recent review of these relationships is available (Slamecka & Ceraso, 1960). At this point, we will give one illustrative study and then examine the implications of retroactive inhibition for theories of forgetting.

Degree of interpolated learning. In a study by Melton and Irwin (1940) the learning material consisted of serial lists of 18 nonsense syllables having an average Glaze association value of about 25 percent. The outlines of the experiment may be diagramed as follows:

CONDITION	ORIGINAL LEARNING	INTERPOLATED LEARNING	REST	RELEARNING
0	5 trials	none	30 min.	two perfect trials
5	5 trials	5 trials	25.5 min.	two perfect trials
10	5 trials	10 trials	22.0 min.	two perfect trials
20	5 trials	20 trials	15.0 min.	two perfect trials
40	5 trials	40 trials	1.0 min.	two perfect trials

The zero condition (first entry) serves as the control. In this condition S was given five trials on the first list (original learning); then after a 30-min. rest he recalled and relearned this list to a criterion of two successive perfect trials. The reason for the 30-min. rest (30-min. retention interval) stems from the fact that in the 40-trial condition, 28 min. were required for the 40 trials on the 18-item list. In order to instruct the S and prepare the memory drum for the interpolated list, 1 min. was needed between the original learning and interpolated learning for all conditions with interpolation. Likewise, 1 min. was required after interpolated learning to handle these mechanical matters prior to relearning. As indicated, with lesser degrees of interpolated learning, there were rest periods between interpolated learning and relearning of such lengths as to make the total retention interval 30 min. for all groups.

We note that there are five conditions. The 24 Ss used in this experiment served twice in all five conditions (two cycles). A form of incomplete between-S counterbalancing was used, and S went through all five conditions once before starting over again. We know that counterbalancing must be incomplete, for with five conditions 120 Ss would be required if all possible orders of the five conditions were used. We may assume that the order of the lists was the same for all Ss, with the order of the conditions randomized. Two lists were needed for each condition except the control condition, and so we may visualize the initial part of the experimental matrix as follows for the first cycle of the experiment.

LISTS	1 & 2	3 & 4	5 & 6	7 & 8	9 & 10
S No. 1	20	5	40	0	10
S No. 2	10	0	5	40	20
S No. 3	0	20	10	5	40

Thus, S No. 1 had as his first condition 20 interpolated learning trials, and these were given with Lists 1 and 2, List 1 being used for the original learning and List 2, for the interpolated learning. On the second day, this S had the condition with 5 interpolated learning trials, on the following day, 40 interpolated learning trials, and so on. When the records for all 24 Ss for the two cycles are combined, each condition will have occurred about equally often at each stage of practice, and each condition will have occurred about equally often with each pair of lists. We would suspect, therefore, that there would be no biasing of any condition due to progressive-error differences or list differences. Of course, it is quite a chore for S to serve in such an experiment since, in addition to serving 10 different days in the experimental conditions, S served initially for 3 days merely for practice in learning. The notion behind giving such practice days is that they will "remove" the steepest portion of the learning-to-learn curve so that changes in performance from day to day attributable to learning-to-learn will be minimized during the experimental days. For reasons which need not be detailed here, this procedure has the effect of decreasing the variability among Ss of the scores for any given condition. However, learning-to-learn was not eliminated by the practice days since performance improved from the first cycle to the second cycle.

The results of this experiment are shown in Fig. 13-3 where the mean correct responses on the first four relearning trials are plotted. The first re-

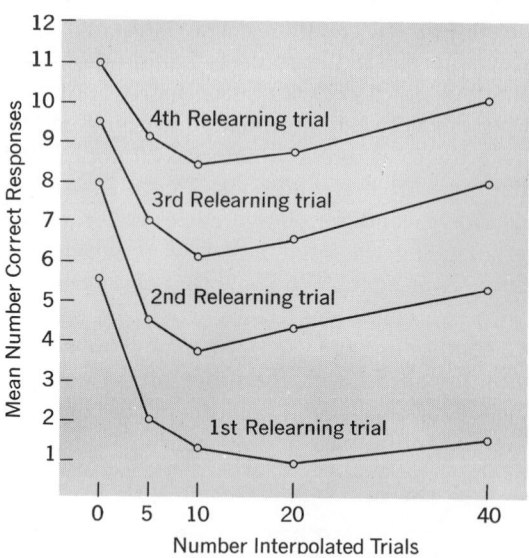

Fig. 13-3. Retroactive inhibition as a function of degree of interpolated learning. Data from Melton and Irwin (1940).

learning trial is the recall trial. These curves do not show retroactive inhibition directly; this would be calculated by subtracting the mean number recalled under each condition from the number recalled under the control condition (zero interpolated learning trials). It can be seen that the amount of retroactive inhibition increases up to 20 interpolated learning trials, with a suggestion that it is slightly less with 40 interpolated trials. The magnitude of the inhibition should be noted. On the recall trial, without interpolated learning, about 5.5 items were correctly anticipated. With five interpolated learning trials, only about two items were given correctly at recall. Furthermore, the inhibitory effect is quite persistent throughout the four relearning trials shown here. This illustrates, then, the general statement made earlier that rather severe forgetting can be produced by interpolated learning in a relatively brief laboratory period. We have attributed this forgetting to interference from conflicting associations. But where, we may ask, are the conflicting associations in this task? The answer is that with lists of nonsense syllables consisting of 18 items, there must necessarily be considerable repetition of letters between the original and interpolated lists so that between sequences of letters in the two lists we have many possibilities for interference from A-B, A-D, from A-B, C-B, and from A-B, A-Br. So, we may assume for the moment that, because of conflicting associations required in the two lists, interference occurs and recall is heavily depressed when there is interpolated learning.

No interpolated learning. We will now consider the forgetting of lists over time when there is no formal interpolated learning. Youtz (1941) performed a study in which Ss served in 30 experimental conditions following six practice days. Each condition consisted of learning a serial list of 12 nonsense syllables of about 25 percent Glaze association value. It would be apparent that the 15 Ss who served in this experiment were handled by a form of incomplete between-S counterbalancing. We will not consider the conditions in detail. For our purposes, it is enough to know that among the conditions there were some in which learning was carried to one perfect recitation of the list; then retention was taken after 10, 20, 40, 60, 120 min., or 24 hr.

The results of this experiment in terms of mean number of items recalled are plotted in Fig. 13-4, where the intervals are placed on a log scale. A straight line has been drawn through the empirical points, although it does not fit very well, and there is no implication that all curves of retention are of this shape. The major point to be made by this graph is the rapid forgetting; after 24 hr. the average S remembers only 1.4 items from the 12-item list.

We have now two sets of facts about forgetting before us. First, from many studies on retroactive inhibition it was known that the insertion of a task between learning and recall of a list greatly depressed the recall of that list. Second, as exemplified in the data of Fig. 13-4, when S learns a single list and then attempts to recall it after 24 hr., there is also a large amount of forgetting measured. The phenomenon of retroactive inhibition was interpreted as being the result of interference from the interpolated learning. Such an interpretation was supported by observations that at the time S attempted to recall the original list, items from the interpolated list (intrusions) would be given. Intrusions may be taken as evidence for the fact that at the time of recall there was response competition which resulted in poorer recall than shown by the control group which had no interpolated learning.

Given this interpretation of retroactive inhibition, and given a desire to maintain consistency in explanations of forgetting, it appeared quite reasonable to apply the retroactive paradigm to the interpretation of the forgetting shown when only a single list was learned. Or, to say this another way, the control condition in a retroactive-inhibition experiment always showed forgetting, too; with interpolated learning the forgetting was simply of greater magnitude. How would we account for the forgetting in the control condition? The apparent answer was to suggest that during the retention interval

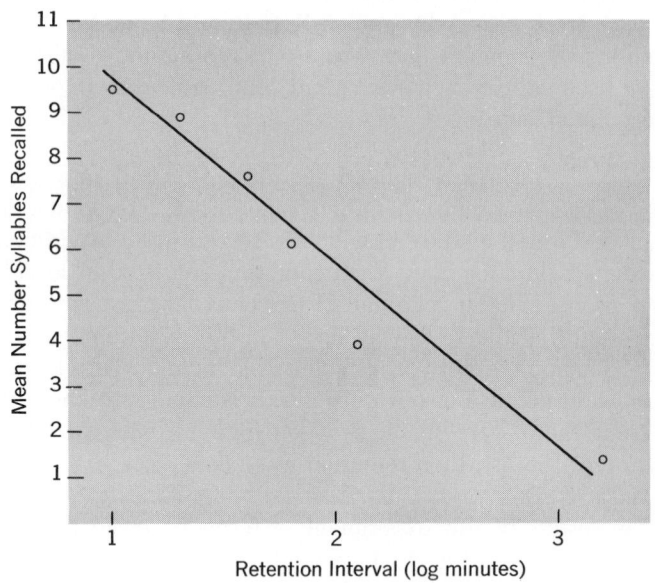

Fig. 13-4. Forgetting as a function of the length of the retention interval (10 min. to 24 hr.). Data from Youtz (1941).

S, while given no formal interpolated learning, was active, was busy, and was often engaged in other learning outside the laboratory if the interval was of such length that he was dismissed during that time from the laboratory (as was the case with the longer intervals in Fig. 13-4). Therefore, this informal activity or learning served somewhat the same role as formal interpolated learning—it resulted in interference at the time of recall. Two additional considerations made such speculations most reasonable.

First, the informal interpolation would be expected to be less similar to the originally learned material than would a formal interpolated list, hence would interfere less. Therefore, forgetting with formal interpolated learning would be expected to be greater than with informal interpolation. If S studied his French lesson during the retention interval, we would expect this activity to produce some interference with the retention of a list of nonsense syllables, but not as much as would a formal interpolation of another list of nonsense syllables. A second fact supporting such theorizing emanated from the so-called sleep studies (e.g., Jenkins & Dallenbach, 1924). It was known that if S learned a list of syllables just before retiring at night, the retention of this list the following morning was appreciably better than if he learned the list in the morning and recalled it in the evening. It was concluded, therefore, that during the daytime retention interval, S learned material or engaged in activities which interfered with the recall of the list learned in the laboratory, but, during sleep, interference from such sources must necessarily be minimal.

In summary, by 1940 a fair assessment of theorizing about forgetting seems to have been as follows: forgetting is produced by interference from the learning of habits which are contrary to the habits previously learned; retroactive inhibition shows this; the retroactive paradigm, therefore, represents the manner in which interference is set up to produce forgetting. Now we may turn to developments since that time, developments which represent refinements in the notions about how interference produces its effect. At the same time we will once more see how closely design problems and theoretical problems are intertwined. Two lines of investigation will be examined as representative of these developments. One deals with *unlearning*, one with *proactive inhibition.*

UNLEARNING

As we have noted, the basic notion of interference as a cause of forgetting stemmed from the facts of retroactive inhibition. The interference, hence the forgetting, so the thinking ran, occurred at the time of recall because of the competition between the responses (those learned originally and those learned in an interpolated task). Certain data in the Melton-Irwin study discussed above, led these writers to suggest another component in the forgetting observed at the time of recall in a retroactive-inhibition study. When there is conflict between associations (as in the A-B, A-D and other interference paradigms), perhaps in the process of acquiring the interpolated associations the original associations are unlearned or weakened. This might be likened to the extinction of a conditioned response; in fact, the words unlearning and extinction are used interchangeably in verbal-learning literature. If unlearning occurred, associations that were unlearned simply would not be available at recall, and an association could not be interfered with at recall if it did not exist. Therefore, it was argued, forgetting observed as a result of the retroactive-inhibition paradigm might be thought of as being the summation of two factors, namely, unlearning and competition of response, the competition occurring because all items may not be unlearned or not unlearned completely.

Some indirect tests of this notion, which need not concern us at the moment, were positive. Then, investigators started to think more directly about unlearning and how to assess its validity. Could the hypothesized unlearning be subject to a more direct experimental test? If, for example, the competition factor were removed in a test of retroactive inhibition, would there still remain forgetting which could be attributed to unlearning or extinction? We have mentioned in a previous chapter how we often, in attempting to answer such questions experimentally, seem to "creep up" on the answer. Techniques are devised which appear fairly satisfactory; then difficulties with them are found, necessitating further refinements until the point is reached where there is fairly general agreement that the technique is adequate for the problem. We noted above that indirect tests of the validity of unlearning were positive. For the more direct tests of the validity, two steps have thus far been taken in the refinement of techniques.

The Briggs study. In his study Briggs (1954) used paired-associate lists consisting of 12 pairs of two-syllable adjectives. Each S learned two successive lists forming an A-B, A-D paradigm. The first list was learned until all items were given correctly on a single trial. In learning the A-D list, subgroups were stopped at various points in the learning and were given tests that have come to be known as modified free-recall tests. The S is instructed as follows:

'The procedure will be changed at this point. I am going to present the first members of the pairs of the two lists that you have been given. As you know, you have learned two responses to each of these stimulus words. For this test, I am not going to show you the response words. Instead, as each stimulus word comes into the window I want you to give the *first* of the two possible responses which come to mind. It is absolutely essential that you give the first of these words which occurs to you. In any event, try to give some response to each stimulus word.'

These recall tests are normally given at quite a slow rate, perhaps 8 to 10 sec. for each stimulus word, in the hopes that some response will be given for each.

In the Briggs study, one group of Ss was stopped and given the recall test after three correct responses had been anticipated on a single interpolated learning trial, another, after six had been correctly anticipated, another, after nine, and a fourth group, after all items were correctly anticipated. The central interest, of course, is in the frequency with which first-list responses are given at the various points in learning the interpolated list. If extinction occurs during interpolated learning, responses from the first list should become fewer and fewer as interpolated learning progresses.

The results are shown in Fig. 13-5. As the degree of learning on A-D increases, the A-B responses become less and less frequent and the A-D responses more and more frequent. It is as if the A-B responses are being unlearned or extinguished. As Briggs pointed out, however, the interpretation is by no means clear. The data need not be interpreted to mean that the associations in the first list have been weakened or extinguished; the data show only that as trials continued on the interpolated list, fewer and fewer

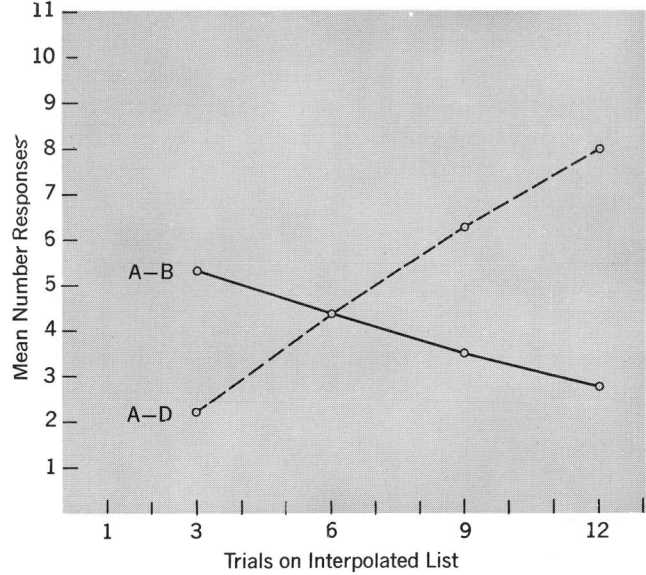

Fig. 13-5. Changes in the frequency of responses given from the first list (A-B) and the second list (A-D) as a function of the point in learning the second list at which recall was requested. Data from Briggs (1954).

first-list responses were given. Was this because the associations were being weakened or only because the second-list, or A-D, associations were becoming stronger? The recall test allowed only one response for each stimulus; if S gave a second-list response, he could not give the first one to the same stimulus. So, again, we are faced with a problem of reciprocal response measures; as one increases, the other must necessarily decrease, or vice versa.

What is causing what? Clearly, this recall test ought to bring out the response which is momentarily stronger, but if this is a second-list response, it does not mean that the first-list response was not available. Still, the results were encouraging for an unlearning notion. When S reached 12 correct responses on the second list, the strength of these associations was objectively equivalent to the strength of the first-list associations except for any forgetting of the first-list associations which may have occurred during the short interval required to learn the second list. Yet the number of responses from the second list was far greater than those from the first. Unlearning of the first list could have been occurring.

A further modification. The next step now becomes quite apparent. To reduce ambiguity in the interpretation, E must request S to give both response terms. If both response terms are requested, and if S is given plenty of time to "dredge up" all he can think of, it might be argued that there is little if any competition of responses such as may occur in traditional, rather rapidly paced recall. If under these circumstances S still cannot produce the first-list responses, it can be taken as fairly convincing evidence that unlearning or extinction of the first-list associations is indeed occurring. The procedure and results may be illustrated by a study performed in the writer's laboratory (Barnes & Underwood, 1959).

The A-B, A-D paradigm was used again. The stimulus terms were nonsense syllables, and the response terms, adjectives, with eight pairs in the lists. The first list was learned to a criterion of one perfect trial. Then independent groups of Ss were stopped at various points (after 1, 5, 10, or 20 trials) in learning the A-D list and given the special recall test. On the recall test, S was given a sheet of paper on which the stimulus terms were listed with two blank spaces under each, and he was instructed to write the responses from both lists in any order he wished. Later he was asked to identify to which list (first or second) each response belonged. The results indicate that if S was able to produce the correct response to the stimulus, he could almost always identify which of the two lists it had been in. Therefore, we will consider only those responses which were correctly paired with the stimulus and correctly identified as to list.

The results are plotted in Fig. 13-6. The frequency with which the first-list, or A-B, responses are produced decreases regularly as the number of trials on the second, or A-D, list increases. It would seem that such data give fairly direct and firm support to the idea that unlearning or extinction does occur with this paradigm. Is competition completely ruled out by this method? Perhaps not. If S thinks of a response from the second list first, perhaps this prevents him in some way from finding the response in his memory for the first list, even though he might be able to had he tried to think of the first-list response first. Perhaps, therefore, we should say that this method minimizes the effect of response competition and that it seems unlikely that all of the loss observed in recall of the first list could be due to competition. Some part of the loss may be attributed to some other factor, and the unlearning factor seems to be indicated. Without giving details, it can be reported that other interference paradigms have also indicated extinction (for example, of backward associations) by use of this recall procedure, and at the present time, most investigators accept the technique as the best available one for studying extinction or unlearning. Furthermore, unlearning has been shown for serial lists and lists acquired by free learn-

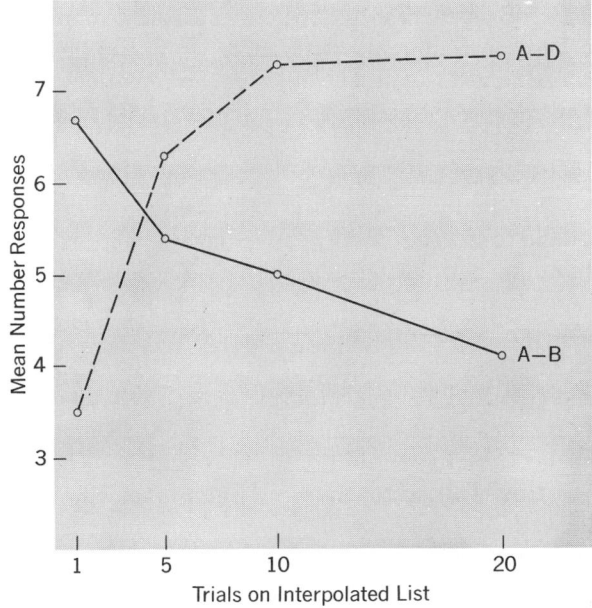

Fig. 13-6. Frequency of responses from the first (A-B) and second lists (A-D) as a function of number of A-D trials when S is asked to recall the responses from both lists. Data from Barnes and Underwood (1959).

ing. There are puzzles remaining, however, the most obvious one being why extinction is not complete. Why are all associations not extinguished?

We conclude that unlearning occurs and may enter into the forgetting that is measured whenever conflicting associations in a retroactive-inhibition paradigm are present. Unlearning, therefore, is the first major refinement in the general theory that forgetting is produced by interference at the time of recall in conformance with the retroactive inhibition paradigm.

PROACTIVE INHIBITION

The Paradigm. The definition of proactive inhibition requires the following general operations:

	LEARN TASK X	LEARN TASK Y	RETENTION INTERVAL	RECALL TASK Y
E GROUP	Yes	Yes	Yes	Yes
C GROUP	No	Yes	Yes	Yes

If the recall (or other measure of retention) is lower for the E Group than for the C Group, proactive inhibition has been demonstrated. If we translate these into the common interference paradigm, we see that the control group has A-B, and A-D, and then, after the retention interval, recalls A-D, whereas the C Group has only A-D and recalls A-D. We may note that these operations would define negative transfer were it not for the fact that the measurements are made after a retention interval.

If proactive inhibition occurs (as it most assuredly does), and if it is to be attributable to interference, then we have a definite counterpart to retroactive inhibition. Retroactive inhibition results from conflicting associations which are learned *after* the learning of the task to be recalled; proactive inhibition is produced by conflicting associations that are learned *prior* to the learning of the task to be recalled. If the task or list we wish to remember is somehow sandwiched *between two* tasks having conflicting associations with it, interference should be maximally severe, and we have what has been called *coactive inhibition* (Koppenaal & O'Hara, 1962).

As was true with retroactive inhibition, we will make no attempt to review the variables which will influence the amount of proactive inhibition. By examining the paradigm, we can see that the factors which influence retroactive inhibition will in general influence proactive inhibition, but the thinking must sometimes be put in reverse. For example, we have seen that degree of interpolated learning influences retroactive inhibition. The corresponding manipulation for proactive inhibition would be the degree of prior learning—the degree of learning of the interfering list. One variable, however, influences the two differentially. As the length of the retention interval increases (the time following learning of the second list), proactive inhibition will increase. Retroactive inhibiton, on the other hand, may remain fairly constant in amount or actually decrease in amount as the retention interval increases. The amount of the forgetting may become equal, after perhaps 24 hr. Later we will return to possible implications of this differential effect of the retention interval.

Some implications of proactive inhibition. One of the most obvious implications of proactive inhibition is that we can no longer think of the retroactive inhibition paradigm as *the* paradigm for the interpretation of forgetting. In the control condition for both paradigms, forgetting is shown. As pointed out earlier, it has been inferred that S learned something during the retention interval which, as in a formal retroactive condition, interfered with recall. Following the same logic, we must now say that the forgetting may be caused also by conflicting habits which S had learned prior to the learning of the control list. Thus, recognition of proactive interference forces us to expand our thinking concerning sources of interference, and we can no longer use the retroactive paradigm as indicative of the manner in which all forgetting occurs. Indeed, we must tolerate the possibility that the forgetting of a given task learned at the moment can be produced by associations learned at any time previously and by associations learned at any time after this moment of learning. The recognition of forgetting produced by proactive interference is the second major refinement in an interference theory of forgetting.

Another implication of proactive inhibition relates to the design of experiments studying retention. Almost exclusively in earlier years, the study of retention was carried out by various forms of between-S counterbalanced designs. We saw earlier in the chapter, for example, how Ss served for a number of days in an experiment (Fig. 13-4) and learned many different lists. We saw also, in the study by Youtz, that forgetting after 24 hr. was very severe—approximately 80 percent of the items were not given at recall. We are now quite sure that this mammoth amount of forgetting was caused by proactive interference from the lists learned previously in the other conditions of the counterbalanced design. If we bring a completely naive S into the laboratory, have him learn a list comparable to those Youtz used, and measure recall after 24 hr., retention will be 80 percent; instead of forgetting 80 percent of the items, S will forget only 20 percent.

Following the original plan of discussion, we have, at this point, completed discussion of what we called the more complex phenomena and are ready to look at somewhat simpler situations. More particularly, our attention will be directed toward a thorough examination of the amount of forgetting shown when no formal interfering task is introduced.

SIMPLE RETENTION

The following situation is basic to our discussion. An S who has never served in an experiment before comes to the laboratory. We give him a list of syllables or words, in paired-associate or serial lists, which we present until he can recite it perfectly. He returns to the laboratory after 24 hr., and as indicated earlier, if he is an average S, he will recall about 80 percent of the responses correctly. If another average S returns after a week, he will recall about 50 percent of the responses correctly. These Ss, therefore, are giving us an index of the amount of forgetting which occurs without introducing a formal interfering task (in a retroactive or proactive sense). One of the central problems in the study of forgetting is trying to account for the forgetting which occurs without the formal interfering task. We will turn to that issue after first examining the implications of these bald and unqualified statements about the amount of forgetting to be expected after 24 hr. and after a week.

Variables

Available data indicate that when the naive S learns a list so that he can recite it just perfectly, his forgetting will be influenced only by the length of the retention interval. No other manipulable variable appears to have any appreciable influence on the forgetting in this situation. Of course, the rate of forgetting will be influenced by the degree of learning of the task, but given a constant degree of learning, the amount of forgetting appears extraordinarily predictable.

It will be remembered that among task variables which influence the rate of learning of a task, meaningfulness and intralist similarity were most potent. Won't lists of high-meaningful items be remembered better than a list of low-meaningful items? Won't a list of common words be retained better than a list of difficult trigrams? Apparently not. If both tasks are taken to the same level of learning, forgetting is about the same. High-similarity lists are not forgotten more rapidly than low-similarity lists. If lists differing widely in difficulty of learning are taken to the same degree of learning, we may expect that after 24 hr., retention of both lists will be about 80 percent correct.

Subjects will differ widely in the rate at which they learn a given task. However, if a slow-learning S and a fast-learning S are taken to the same level of learning, there is no evidence that their recall will differ. Tests over long periods of time have not been made, but for relatively short retention intervals, such as 24 hr., the forgetting of the fast S and the forgetting of the slow S will be about the same. It goes without saying that in all such tests, where rate of learning differs as a function of the variable being manipulated (meaningfulness, intralist similarity, individual differences), certain adjustments in the degree of learning may have to be made to accommodate the fact that acquisition curves approach the criterion of learning at widely different rates.

Perhaps the constancy of the rates of forgetting despite wide differences in task variables, types of task, and individual differences should not be overemphasized, for we do not always find exactly 80 percent retention after 24 hr. Yet, the relative constancy of the forgetting, despite the presence of factors which make for enormous differences in learning, is a rather stark fact. It almost appears as if some factor that is quite independent of any of the variables manipulated, but correlated with time, imposes itself on memory functioning to produce the relatively constant rate of loss. However, one theoretical approach to this problem, to which we now turn, makes no provision for the constancy; rather, it assumes that given the appropriate situation the retention will not remain constant.

Theory

Expansion of interference theory. We have seen how interference in retention can be produced by the retroactive and proactive paradigms. We may examine how interference theory may be expanded to accommodate the forgetting shown by a naive S learning a single list in the laboratory. The expansion requires two steps.

We noted that proactive inhibition increases with time and that retroactive inhibition either remains constant or decreases with time. These facts have suggested that an additional mechanism must be added to refine further the manner in which interference plays its role. We will remember that when associations in successive tasks conflict, unlearning or extinction of the earlier learned association will occur. If we assume that there is *spontaneous recovery* of an extinguished association, the facts associated with length of retention interval and retroactive and proactive inhibition become rather nicely disciplined. This may be seen most clearly if we work around the A-B, A-D paradigm. During the learning of A-D, A-B becomes extinguished, so that maximum retroactive inhibition (recall of A-B) should occur immediately after interpolated learning. But if spontaneous recovery occurs, A-B should gradually become stronger with time, thus minimizing forgetting (for any reason). Retroactive inhibition, therefore, should not increase with the length of the retention interval but may actually decrease. However, if we recall A-D (corresponding to proactive inhibition) at different points in time after learning, its recall should be more and more interfered with by A-B as this association is showing spontaneous recovery. Therefore, proactive inhibition should increase as the length of the retention interval increases.

What about the validity of spontaneous recovery of verbal associations? Validity may be viewed in two ways. If an assumed process or mechanism helps one to order or to understand data, it may be said to have validity in one sense. However, we tend by nature, apparently, to try when possible to obtain empirical validity for such assumed processes by measuring them directly. How would we "get at" spontaneous recovery? The preferred techniques have been those discussed earlier with regard to the study of unlearning or extinction, namely, forms of modified recall taken at various points in time following the learning of A-B, A-D. If the frequency with which A-B is produced increases with time, the spontaneous recovery would be considered empirically validated. We cannot yield space for examining the various experiments and techniques which have been used to assess spontaneous recovery. We may state only that, at the moment, the evidence is contradictory—some positive, in the sense of indicating spontaneous recovery, and some negative. This frustrating state of affairs will probably be clarified in the near future, but for the time being we must assume the validity of spontaneous recovery in the earlier sense; we assume it because it allows us to handle certain facts which could not otherwise be handled by any notions advanced thus far. Therefore, let us assume the validity of spontaneous recovery of extinguished verbal associations and see where it leads us in our quest for an understanding of the forgetting in the single-list experiment.

The second step we take is to assume that whenever S learns a list in a laboratory, there will be some associations in this list which conflict with associations S has learned in the normal course of events. If we require him to learn to associate K to M, other associations, such as O or A to M, which are common sequences in words, will interfere or conflict with the establishment of the K to M. If S is required to learn to respond with *tomato* to the stimulus *dog*, other associates to *dog* (such as *cat* or *animal* or *gone*) may interfere. In turn, these older associates will be unlearned or extinguished during the learning of the list. Over the retention interval, however, these older associates will spontaneously recover and produce interference at recall.

It can be seen that the theory as expanded attempts to account for the forgetting of a single list or a single association by the proactive inhibition which results from associations S learned prior to coming to the laboratory. We would also have to admit that during the retention interval S may learn associations outside the laboratory which will interfere in a retroactive sense with the associations in the list. However, we tend to view this as being a much less likely source than the proactive source. The reasoning is strictly on a probability basis. If the S is 20 years old, we would suspect that during 20 years he has had a greater probability of learning associations which will interfere with those required in the list (proactive interference) than he has of learning such associations during the 24-hr. retention interval (retroactive interference). And, so, without denying that some of the forgetting may be produced by retroactive interference, it appears that most of it would be produced by proactive interference. At the same time, it can be seen that the longer the retention interval, the greater the role which retroactive interference (from associations acquired outside the laboratory) should play.

This, then, is the way interference theory views forgetting at the present time. We have only considered some of the key developments leading to the modern statement of the theory; more detail and nuance can be found elsewhere (Postman, 1961). Whenever we learn a task, interference theory specifies that its retention will be determined primarily by the conflicting associations learned before and after; it will be buffeted and pummeled and may not survive to be recaptured at all. In fact, the question is sometimes raised as to how we ever remember anything. If there is a single answer, it lies in level of learning. When we acquire a task well, when we learn it to a point that it is so strong as to be above the strength of other associations which "seek to destroy it," it will remain long available.

There is also evidence that we can, by appropriate schedules of learning, destroy the conflicting associations or suppress them rather permanently. Consider a study by Keppel (1964). His Ss learned four successive paired-associate lists, each having the same stimuli but different responses. One group of Ss learned all four lists in a single session (massed practice). An-

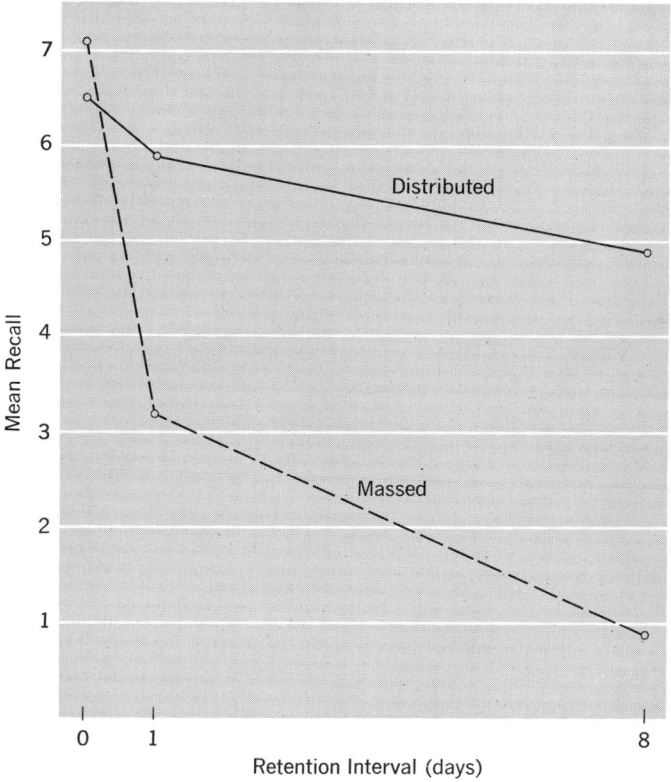

Fig. 13-7. Reduction in proactive interference as a function of massed or distributed trials on the list recalled. Data from Keppel (1964).

other group learned the first three lists in the same manner, but were given a very distributed schedule on the fourth list, namely, two trials a day for four days. The interest was in the recall of the fourth list. What effect did the distribution of learning trials on the fourth list have on its retention—on the proactive interference from the first three lists? Different groups learning the fourth list under massed and under distributed practice were given various retention intervals following the completion of all trials on the fourth list. The recall scores, shown in Fig. 13-7, indicate that the distributed practice markedly reduced the amount of proactive interference.

If forgetting is primarily produced by proactive interference, there are certain rather interesting implications (which thus far have not been given a severe test). Forgetting should increase with age, since as we grow older we presumably will have learned more "things" which could eventually interfere with that which we learn now. We noted earlier that fast and slow learners show almost the same amount of forgetting over short retention intervals. According to the theory, however, we would expect a difference in the long run: the slow learner should show less forgetting than the fast learner. Because a very bright person, in a given period of time, will learn more than a dull person, he should over a period of many years develop a greater number of potentially interfering associations than should a dull person. Therefore, if both learn the same task at the same moment, the bright person should suffer the greater proactive inhibition after a passage of time following learning.

When tested, the expectation may not work out. It is possible that through unknown mechanisms the bright person is more resistant to interference than the dull person—perhaps that is why he is a bright person. We simply do not know much about this at the present time, but there is suggestive evidence. We shall look at one study.

Schoer (1963) used two paired-associate lists of adjectives, each consisting of eight pairs. One list had very high synonymity among all eight stimulus terms and among all eight response terms. The Ss were drawn from two pools of students who were differentiated on scores of a vocabulary test, one pool having high scores, the other, low scores. Two groups from each pool were used, one from each learning the high-similarity list and one from each learning the low-similarity list. All Ss were given 12 anticipation trials; the response measure, therefore, was the mean total correct responses over the 12 trials. These are plotted in Fig. 13-8. On the low-similarity list the two groups did not differ appreciably, but on the high-similarity list the students having low vocabulary scores did much more poorly than those with high vocabulary scores. This suggests the possibility that insofar as vocabulary is a measure of brightness, the bright student may be able to "deal with" interference better than the duller student.

Some discord. If forgetting of a single task is primarily a result of proactive interference from previously learned habits, it would be expected that the amount of forgetting could be changed by varying the degree to which the task to be learned is in conflict with previously learned habits. Such a test requires a knowledge of the habits which S has learned. Our knowledge of these previous habits is somewhat restricted, but it can come from various word-association and letter-association norms as discussed in an earlier chapter. The test, therefore, would be that of comparing the retention of two lists, one in which the required associations conflict strongly

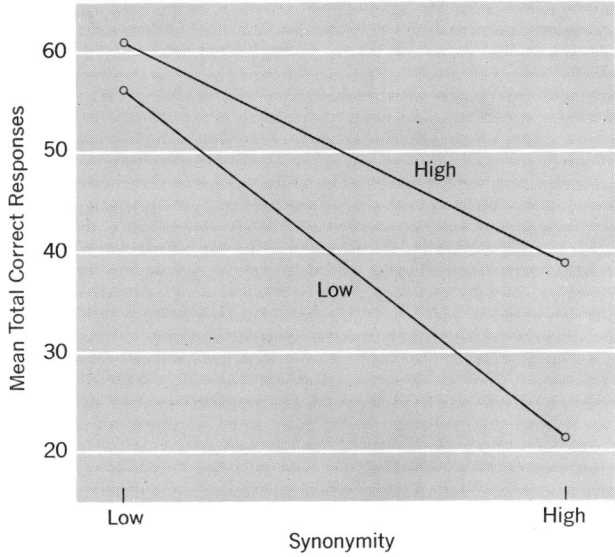

Fig. 13-8. Acquisition of low- and high-similarity lists (degree of synonymity) as a function of high and low vocabulary scores. Data from Schoer (1963).

with associations as indexed by the norms and the other in which the associations apparently do not conflict strongly. We would have to predict the more rapid forgetting of the former list. Several tests have failed to give much support to this expectation. At the present time we are unable to say with any finality whether such failures indicate an inadequacy or incompleteness of the theory or whether the tests are inadequate, but they do throw some discord into our thinking. At the present time we must report that no variables except degree of learning and passage of time have been shown to change appreciably the retention of a list learned by a naive S.

One final comment must be made. We have noted the constancy in the retention of a single list despite differences in material, the Ss, and type of task. One factor which may be involved in this constancy is warmup. We saw in the immediately preceding chapter that warmup will facilitate verbal learning. It is not unreasonable to think that when S returns to the laboratory for a recall test after 24 hr., a nonassociative warmup task might facilitate the recall. In 1948, Irion showed that such a warmup task completely eliminated forgetting in that S actually did a little better on the recall trial than he did on his last learning trial 24 hr. earlier. However, this finding has not been repeatable (e.g., Rockway & Duncan, 1952) even when the conditions appeared to be identical to those used by Irion. This contradiction is not yet understood.

SHORT-TERM MEMORY

The studies of memory which we have considered thus far are often identified as studies of long-term memory, for the retention interval is usually at least minutes and often, hours and days. In contrast are studies of short-term memory in which the retention interval is measured in seconds. Other terms, such as running memory, sequential memory, immediate memory, and memory span are sometimes supplied, although these terms do not all refer to the same techniques. But they identify an area in memory research which has shown great vigor in the past decade. Perhaps a part of this increased activity is due to the advent of computers with their electronic storage systems and the analogies they suggest to the memory-storage system of man. Perhaps it represents a result of the inevitable analytic bent which investigators have and by which they attempt to simplify the gross situations. The acquisition of a list of paired-associates results in a fairly complicated set of habits stored in memory, a set of habits which differ in strength and are held together, if at all, only by the fact that they were acquired at the same point in time with the attendant communalities that this may imply. Certain studies of short-term memory have the advantage of simplicity.

The work on short-term memory has brought with it certain theoretical notions which do not always square with those for long-term memory. One of the easiest ways to visualize forgetting is to think of a decay or a fading of whatever the neurological counterpart is of memory, a fading neural trace, it is sometimes called. This decay theory of forgetting has been moribund for many years but has recently been revived (e.g., Brown, 1958). There is also considerable work being done to test the notion that after learning an association, some time must be allowed for the neural process to consolidate—to form a permanent memory. If, therefore, another activity or other learning material is presented too quickly after the first material, the consolidation of the first will not have been completed, and memory for it will be impaired (retroactive inhibition will be produced). In testing this notion with animal Ss, E gives the S very strong stimulation (e.g., electro-convulsive shock) immediately after S makes a response, and, subsequently, retention of the response is compared with a no-shock control. There is no doubt that some evidence squares quite well with the notion of consolidation (Glickman, 1961). This approach does not deny that interference as dis-cussed earlier in connection with long-term retention is irrelevant, but it does suggest that interference (viewed as resulting from competition of responses) may not alone be enough to account for all forgetting. However, interpretations other than consolidation may be given the electroconvulsive-shock results (e.g., Lewis & Maher, 1965).

What do we mean by short-term retention? Here are some everyday examples which will illustrate some of the problems more or less reflected in the laboratory tasks. Have you ever looked up a number in the telephone directory and then discovered before you had finished dialing that you had forgotten a part of it? Have you ever been given directions by a gas-station attendant (go three stoplights, turn right, continue one block past Elm Street, turn left, and about two blocks further you will find Joe's Place) only to get lost, not because the directions were wrong, but because you forgot them? When an instructor tells you that X=Y and then a minute later asks you what X is equal to, are you always able to tell him? Do you remember how many stoplights, in the above illustration, the gas-station attendant included in his instructions?

In discussing some of the techniques used to study such short-term memory phenomena, we will minimize both the theoretical aspects of the problems and the results. The continuities and discontinuities in theory and fact between short-term and long-term memory have been discussed by Melton (1963) who concludes for the continuity position. Recent reviews of short-term memory studies are also available (Posner, 1963; Postman, 1964).

Single Verbal Units

Assume that E presents to you a single consonant syllable, such as BXK for 2 sec., telling you that he is going to test your memory for it later. Do you think you will remember it 30-sec. later? Most of you would say yes. Peterson and Peterson (1959) were not so sure, and their experiment showed they had good reason for being skeptical. It also introduced a new technique which has, in turn, been copied by many investigators.

Here are the instructions given S:

'Please sit against the back of your chair so that you are comfortable. You will not be shocked during this experiment. In front of you is a little black box. The top or green light is on now. This green light means that we are ready to begin a trial. I will speak some letters and then a number. You are to repeat the number imme-diately after I say it and begin counting backwards by 3's . . . from that number in time with the ticking you hear. I might say, ABC 309. Then you say, 309, 306, 303, etc., until the bottom or red light comes on. When you see this red light come on, stop counting immediately and say the letters that were given at the beginning of the trial. Remember to keep your eyes on the black box at all times. There will be a short rest period and then the green light will come on again and we will start a new trial.' (p. 194)

These *Es* were interested in the retention of the consonant syllables, not in counting backwards. Counting was merely a device to keep S from rehearsing the syllable, and the ticking mentioned in the instructions referred to the ticking of a metronome which paced S in his counting. The consonant syllables were of low association value, and 48 of them were used. There were six conditions in the experiment, the variable being the length of the retention interval, namely, 3, 6, 9, 12, 15, or 18 sec. Each S served in each of these six conditions eight times, thus "using up" all of the 48 syllables. The experimental design, a form of within-S counterbalancing, is quite like the design used in psychophysical experiments. Here is a way one may visualize it. First, the 48 consonant syllables are ordered randomly. Then, the six retention intervals are ordered randomly once, and the order matched with the first six syllables, after which the six retention intervals are randomized again and matched with the syllables 7 through 12, and so on. Since the syllables are ordered randomly, there should be no systematic change in their difficulty as one goes from the first syllable to the last. Since the retention intervals are paired randomly with syllables, there should be no bias regarding particularly easy or difficult syllables being used for a particular retention interval. Finally, since each interval occurs in each successive block of six syllables, there should be no bias due to progressive error. Each S's data should be unbiased; nevertheless, these *Es* used 24 Ss so that there were 192 observations for each retention interval.

The response measure was the percentage of syllables correctly recalled at each retention interval. The results (Fig. 13-9) show that after 18 sec. only 8 percent of the syllables were given correctly, and even after only 3 sec., 79 percent were given correctly. How could 21 percent forgetting occur in 3 seconds? In part, this loss may represent failure to hear the syllable correctly as similar-sounding letters (e.g., V, B, C, D) may have been confused. The *E* took approximately 0.5 sec. to spell the syllable, and such confusion might have been possible. In any event it is quite apparent that forgetting is precipitous.

The orderliness of the data and the simplicity of the procedure are beguiling. Unfortunately, for the study of certain aspects of memory the method has some serious drawbacks. For example, suppose we wished to study retention as a function of meaningfulness of the units, perhaps words versus consonant syllables. If we present both types of units for the same period of time for study (such as 0.5 sec.), the degree of learning will be different, and we are back to the same problem we discussed in connection with long-term retention. Suppose the immediate retention (after 1 or 2 sec.) is 100 percent for both types of material. Under these circumstances we still cannot say the degree of learning is equivalent, for the overlearning may be greater for one than for the other. To solve the problem we need to discover lengths of study intervals, different for each type of material, which will

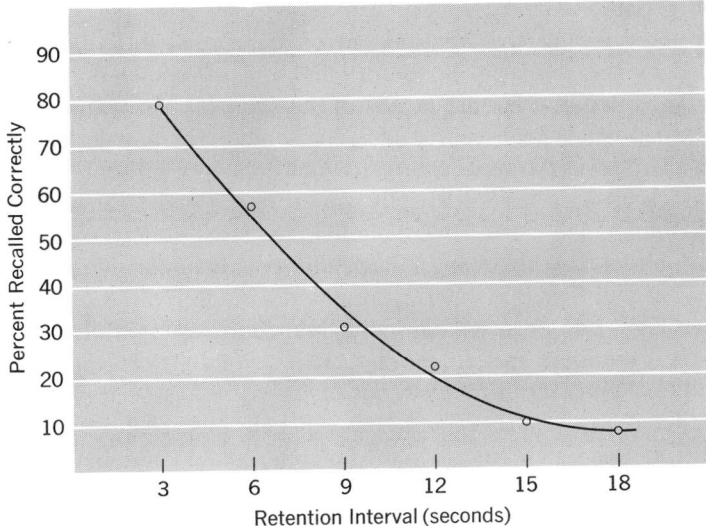

Fig. 13-9. Retention of single consonant syllables as a function of length of the retention interval. Estimated from Peterson and Peterson (1959).

give equal immediate retention at a point clearly below 100 percent, such as 90 percent. If recall percentage is equal at 90 percent on an immediate test, we know that there are not likely to be differences in overlearning for the two types of material and that differences in retention between the materials for longer intervals could clearly be attributed to differences in the materials (in our illustration, to meaningfulness). A more elaborate discussion of this and other problems in such experiments may be found in Keppel (1965).

The above discussion implies that the single-unit method is least likely to be satisfactory when a task variable is to be manipulated because task variables normally influence rate of learning and thereby bring the problem of degree of learning to the fore. However, even if we accept this limitation of the method, there is still "room" for the study of other classes of variables. The efficiency of the single-unit method should not be overlooked. Whereas in long-term retention of lists we normally work with learning periods of many minutes and retention intervals of hours and days, in the single-unit method as devised by Peterson and Peterson we deal with learning periods of a second or two and retention intervals of less than a minute. Furthermore, it is quite feasible to do retroactive inhibition and proactive inhibition studies using the single-unit technique, and the moment this is possible many variables become available for study. Two illustrations will be given concerning one such variable.

We noted earlier that the amount of retroactive inhibition is sharply influenced by the similarity of the original and interpolated lists. We may ask whether this same finding occurs in the short-term retention of a single unit. By spelling, Wickelgrem (1965) presented S a four-letter consonant unit and then during a 4-sec. interval which followed presented eight other letters which were either acoustically similar to the four-letter unit or acoustically dissimilar. More errors were made in the recall following interpolation of similar letters than following interpolation of dissimilar letters.

Bruning and Schappe (1965) presented a single paired associate made up of two CVC nonsense syllables and followed this, in one case, with several six-digit numbers and, in another, with several six-consonant units. On the recall test when the stimulus terms of the paired associate were given, S was instructed to give the response term. Recall intervals up to 16 sec. were used, and in every case recall following interpolated numbers was higher than recall following interpolated consonants. Differences between the items to be recalled and the interpolated items seem to be responsible for the difference in recall.

The single-unit method does not require the use of short retention intervals. For example, Johnson (1964) presented a single paired associate to Ss and for various groups measured its retention up to two weeks, at which time it had fallen to approximately 30 percent. This procedure requires only that Ss be led to believe that they will not be tested for retention.

A modification of the single-unit method consists in presenting more than one verbal unit but requesting the recall of only one *after* all have been presented. For example, Murdock (1964) presented six pairs of words once, and then at recall (which came immediately after presentation) only one stimulus term was presented with S being asked to recall the appropriate response term. Since S did not know which stimulus term was to be presented for the test, he presumably attempted to learn all pairs, and the recall test shows the net effect of learning and forgetting, with the retention interval being automatically varied as a function of the serial position of the item requested at recall.

Running Memory Span

The memory span is the number of units of a specified type which can be repeated correctly (in correct order) immediately after being presented. Digits are often used as the units. Working out the memory span for a given person is like determining an absolute threshold by the method of constant stimuli. The S is presented many series of digits of different lengths, some so short that it is clear he can produce all of the digits correctly and some so long that he will not be able to reproduce them all. Such a range might extend from 4 to 12 digits. The length of a series which S can produce correctly 50 percent of the time is said to be the best estimate of his digit span.

In the running memory span, S is faced with a somewhat different situation. A long series of digits is presented S, and he is under instructions that at a given signal he is to reproduce as many as possible starting with the *last* one given and working backwards. Here is the way one group of investigators viewed such a task:

To an organism repeatedly bombarded with information, the dropping out of items of information (forgetting) is as important as the acquisition and storage of new items of information. Indeed, in many practical situations, as in monitoring a display, the operator is required only to report information of the recent past history of the display. A characteristic feature of many monitoring tasks is, apparently, that the operator is uncertain when he will be interrogated about the display. (Pollack, Johnson, & Knaff, 1959, p. 137)

In the initial discussion in this chapter, we noted that forgetting may have adaptive qualities. In the running memory-span situation this appears to be the case when it is possible for only the more recently presented items to be useful. There is some implication in the above quotation, as well as in the writings of others, that S can in some manner *voluntarily* forget if he chooses to. So far as the present writer knows, there is no evidence that this is possible.

What are some of the variables that might be investigated with running memory span? In the study from which the above quotation was taken, several were included. If S was told ahead of time how long the span of digits would be which he was going to be asked to reproduce, his performance was better than if he did not know this ahead of time. The ability to reproduce a span of a given length gradually decreased as the number of digits given increased before S was asked to report. The more rapidly the digits were presented, the poorer the performance, and finally, performance improved with practice.

Another type of running memory procedure is illustrated by Reid, Lloyd, Brackett, and Hawkins (1961). We may use their sample of words to illustrate the task given S, as follows: Berlin, Willow, Moscow, Dartmouth, Elm, CITY, Golf, Ford, Soccer, TREE. The S was instructed to remember each item he heard (the words were presented by tape) and to recall the items appropriate to a given class when the class name was given. Thus, in the above illustration, when the word CITY occurred, S was to attempt to recall all names of cities that had been presented, and when TREE occurred, he was to give all the names of trees that had been read.

The S was informed that once he had recalled particular words in a given class, he would not be requested to recall them again. Over a series of words there are increases in the number of units to be remembered until recall is asked for, but recall produces a reduction in the number to be remembered. Results of such experiments show clearly that the greater the number of items within a class which are given before recall is requested, the greater the number of errors, but that the moment the recall is taken, performance improves for new items presented in that class. It is as if S can eliminate previous items from his memory once he has recalled them. However, a correlated dimension of time is involved so that in terms of temporal locus new items have a different status from old items in the same class. Indeed, in a study by Yntema and Trask (1963), it was shown that S can quite accurately identify the relative "ages" of words given in a long series. Forgetting does seem to provide us with a temporal dimension for orienting ourselves in time.

Running Recognition

The above types of procedures could be carried out with a recognition measure rather than by requesting S to produce the items, and this is the approach used by Shepard and Teghtsoonian (1961). The S was presented a long series of three-digit numbers, and as each was presented, he had to indicate whether it had or had not occurred earlier in the series. In the series, each number was actually presented twice, but the number of intervening numbers differed for different numbers. As might be expected, the greater the number of intervening numbers between the two occurrences of a given number, the less likely S was to recognize the number as having been presented before.

The present writer has utilized this technique for a somewhat different purpose (Underwood, 1965). We have discussed the possibility that when S is presented words in a learning situation, these words may elicit implicit associative responses. The word *up* may produce an implicit response *down*. If this is happening, certain expectations follow if one uses the recognition procedure devised by Shepard and Teghtsoonian. Suppose a long list of words is read to S and his task is to decide for each word whether or not it has occurred earlier in the list. Now suppose that the tenth word is *up*, and that the one-hundredth word is *down*. If S indicates that *down* occurred earlier in the list, it would be evidence that *up* did elicit *down* implicitly and led S to say that the word had actually been given in the list. A control word was used for each experimental word, a control word being one which was presumed not to have been elicited as an implicit response by any of the previous words. The results were quite positive; more errors were made on the experimental words than on the control words. In the maximum instance, 49 percent of the Ss said a word had occurred earlier in the list when in fact it had not.

SOME CONCLUDING COMMENTS

In presenting the techniques and major phenomena associated with the study of memory, we have followed some of the major developments in one version of an interference theory of forgetting. The theory has considerable versatility, but, at the same time, the phenomena which it can accommodate at the moment may be limited. We have not attempted to elaborate alternative theories, nor have we stated the reservations held by some about the ultimate usefulness of the interference approach. The developments in the interference theory were presented to show how a general theory is refined by laboratory findings extending over many years and in that sense was given as an extended exercise of a type we have not encountered in previous chapters. In the retroactive and proactive paradigms we have powerful tools for manipulating memory, and the interference theory explicitly relies on the findings produced by these paradigms. Because of their power, it is difficult not to believe that they do not have interference counterparts in everyday life. But whether certain phenomena of memory (e.g., repression, distortions in recall, amnesia) will ultimately be accommodated by the theory is a decision for the future.

SUMMARY

In the traditional studies of memory, lists of words are learned, and retention is measured by recall, relearning, recognition, or reconstruction, with recall being the most frequently used measure. Because retention is directly related to degree of learning, it is important to equate for degree of learning for various conditions prior to introducing a retention interval. To accomplish this is sometimes difficult, particularly when a varable is manipulated which influences the rate of acquisition. Solutions to the problem were discussed.

In tracing the development of an interference theory of forgetting, we discussed retroactive and proactive paradigms as the formal means of producing interference experimentally and as the paradigms by which the theory assumes all forgetting occurs. Refinements in the theory, refinements required by discoveries concerning the effect of certain variables on retroactive and proactive inhibition, included unlearning (extinction) and spontaneous recovery of extinguished associations. In the course of examining studies of forgetting, it became apparent that the within-S design will produce a drastically higher estimate of the absolute amount of forgetting than will the random-groups design, and this fact is also predictable from the interference theory.

The interference theory as developed thus far predicts some differences in retention among certain types of lists learned by naive Ss. Very little confirmation of these predictions has been obtained. Except for two variables, degree of learning and length of the retention interval, nothing seems to influence the rate of forgetting of a single list.

Various techniques for studying short-term retention were presented and included memory-span techniques, techniques for studying the retention of a single verbal unit or single pair, running memory span, and running recognition.

CHAPTER FOURTEEN

Problem Solving

Several descriptive terms may be used to identify aspects of the broad range of behavior to be sampled in this chapter, terms such as *thinking, reasoning, concept formation, creativity,* and *originality.* Distinctions may be drawn among them (e.g., Gagne, 1964), but our objectives do not require us to deal with such distinctions. It is sufficient for us to realize that the behavior reflected by these various terms represents the highest capacity of our intellect. The capacity of man to reason, to think, and to create, it is said, provides an enormous gap between man and other animals, and perhaps we can afford a certain smugness about these capacities—until a time when it is discovered that organisms on other planets have capacities that in contrast make ours appear as primitive as those shown by a rat in a Skinner box.

There are two reasons why it is fitting that we conclude with this chapter. First, systematic experimentation represents a continual problem-solving process so that as we study problem solving we are, ostensibly, studying the processes by which theories are formulated, by which experiments are designed, and by which data are interpreted. Surely, therefore, we should find evidence from experiments on problem solving which will help us be better experimentalists. We have examined designs, procedures, and data in detail. Perhaps we should, at the end, back away from the detail and be a little more concerned with the psychology of the experimenter as reflected in the problems he meets when he attempts to solve problems.

The second reason for making this chapter the last stems directly from certain characteristics of problem-solving behavior. We are just beginning to realize fully that many of the subprocesses or subcomponents of problem solving are processes or components about which we know a great deal in isolation; therefore, much of the subject matter in previous chapters is directly relevant when we seek an understanding of problem-solving behavior. Problems are often problems because of *negative transfer* from previous experiences; aspects of *memory* are heavily involved in problem solving. The way we attack problems initially may sometimes be understood in terms of *probability learning. Search processes*, and the various *discriminal capacities* important for search, will loom large in some of the studies. In short, while there may be unique behavioral properties evoked in problem solving, it is becoming more and more apparent that we can with benefit transfer our knowledge from other areas of research. When this transfer is carried out systematically, we may find that the capacity to think, to reason, and to create is not as awesome in its complexity as we have sometimes been led to believe. Men have written sonnets, have created atomic reactors, and have invented languages. Men should also have the creative capacity to discover the composition of the processes by which sonnets are written, reactors created, and language invented.

Research on problem solving has a long but quite undistinguished history, since much of the so-called research could be characterized as consisting of observations made preliminary to experimentation. It is often valuable to make preliminary observations in a new area of research as a means of developing hypotheses about relevant variables. For example, if we wished to inaugurate a research program on the problems involved in the acquisition of a foreign language, we might choose to spend a considerable amount of time initially in a classroom making observations of students as they tried to learn a foreign language. From such observations we would hope to develop some ideas about the components of language learning and what variables might be related to these components. Then we would proceed to the experimental aspects of the program wherein we would attempt to isolate the components and test the influence of variables on them. Until a few years ago the work on problem solving never seemed to go much beyond the observational stage. As late as 1955, Johnson could properly say, "The field is littered with disabled wisdoms cast off by hit-and-run theorists." (p. 1)

The slow progress in the area of problem solving is probably due to a number of reasons, but these may be left to the historian of science to record and evaluate. The fact seems to be that only in quite recent years has the research definitely left the observational stage and launched itself into the analytical stage where the full power of the experimental methods may be brought to bear. We will note that the tasks most frequently being used are relatively simple since they are tasks which allow fairly definitive experimental analysis and, at the same time, make contact with work in other areas which we have already studied. It is perpetually difficult for us to remember that experimentation must necessarily represent an abstraction of real life. Rarely can we deal experimentally with behavior as it occurs naturally in real life since it does not allow the analytical control necessary to discover fundamental cause-effect relationships. If we are going to study processes involved in mastering a foreign language, we would tend to break the entire learning process down into elementary components and not attempt initially to deal in a definitive way with gross acquisition. Furthermore, we might invent our own language for laboratory purposes if such were felt desirable as a means of gaining the necessary government over the variables we wished to control. In the same sense, if we wish to understand the thought processes by which an engineer designs a bridge, we would probably not make the laboratory task the building of bridges. Such a task might not be the appropriate one for the study of the thought processes used in designing bridges.

The research on problem solving has produced an enormous number of different laboratory tasks, so many that to describe adequately even a small portion of them would require far more space than can be allotted. As noted earlier, we shall discuss work which uses relatively simple tasks, not only because these tasks can be readily assembled for laboratory work, but also because the use of such tasks is symptomatic of the current research scene. As usual, we will sample procedures and variables; other sources must be consulted for a more systematic review of the factual base of the field as well as for the diversity present in the conceptual thinking. Some available summary-type articles are Duncan's review (1959) of problem solving, Golann's (1963) on creativity, and Kendler's (1961) on concept formation.

The center headings of this chapter represent variables or processes which are believed to be of fundamental importance in problem solving. As will be seen, these variables are not all at the same level in that some are more inclusive than others. The most fundamental understanding of problem solving will be achieved when we fully comprehend the nature and source of the responses produced by a situation and the variables which govern their production. The chapter as a whole, therefore, is geared toward approaches which may lead to this understanding.

ASSOCIATIVE FREQUENCY

Anagrams

Most of us have attempted to solve anagrams outside of experimental situations since they are sometimes given as puzzles in newspapers and magazines. In recent years the use of anagrams as an experimental task has become widespread, and the outcome of the research has provided a fairly systematic body of knowledge. Somewhat in the same sense that paired associates is a standard task for studying verbal learning, anagrams is becoming a standard task for studying problem solving.

The anagram is a series of letters (e.g., NTKIH) which, when rearranged, make at least one word. There are two versions of the task. In one, S is given the letters and is requested to make as many different words (which may vary in length) as possible within a given interval of time. In the other version, S is instructed to use all letters and to find only a single solution (e.g., THINK). The latter version has been more frequently used than the former in recent years, so we will confine our attention to it.

By way of getting acquainted with anagrams, consider the following two lists. As an initial exercise, alternate between the two columns and try to reach a decision as to which column contains the more difficult anagrams to solve.

LUFX	ERVY
ACMO	TWNA
RMDA	UTSI
LETW	SUHR
JWOL	SATY
UCBH	MGEA
TILS	KALT
DTUE	FDIN
KYIN	ABKN
TAIF	NAHT

As you attempted to solve each anagram, you probably noted that you made implicit responses to yourself; you may have pronounced or tried to pronounce certain rearrangements of the letters to see if they "clicked." It is remotely possible that you did solve an anagram and did not realize it because you failed to recognize the combination of letters as a word. This might be particularly true with some of the anagrams in the left column, although most college students would probably recognize all solutions as words. Unlike certain problems, the anagram task does not emphasize the checking of a solution to see if it works; usually a solution, once obtained, is quickly perceived as being a correct solution. Therefore, the anagram task is primarily a vehicle to study response production.

We should note that you could always solve any anagram, given enough time, provided that you recognized a solution when you arrived at it. With four-letter anagrams, there are only 24 possible orders in which the letters may be arranged, so if you wished you could go through these orders systematically until you found the one that gave a solution. (We believe most of the above 20 anagrams have only a single solution.) With five letters in the anagram, the number of permutations is 120, and although running through all of these possibilities might be somewhat exhausting, it is apparent that solution is always possible by such a procedure. However, it is doubtful that in your attempts to solve the 20 anagrams above, you went about it in this fashion; that is, you probably did not start sifting through your mind for all possible combinations of four letters, nor did you write down the combinations. Other habits of which you may not have been aware may have served to restrict the population of letter combinations which you tried. For example, it is unlikely that you seriously tried to make a word with JW as the first two letters or as the last two letters, or any combination in which these two letters held contiguous positions. Certain language habits which you bring to the situation tend to make some letter combinations more probable than others. This is a point to which we shall return frequently; our response production to a problem situation is seldom random, and we must quickly add, whether or not this lack of randomness in our response production is good or bad for solution depends upon the particular problem situation.

Word frequency and anagram solutions. Perhaps in trying to solve the above two columns of anagrams, you concluded that the left column of anagrams was more difficult as a whole than the right column. If you did, you would be a one-subject confirmation of experimental findings. The left column has anagrams whose solutions represent words of low frequency of use. Thus FLUX, COMA, DRAM, and so on, are much less frequently used words in our speaking and writing than are those in the right column (VERY, WANT, SUIT, and so on). Here is an illustration of how this works out experimentally.

Mayzner and Tresselt (1958) made anagrams of five words from each of four different frequency levels as determined from the Thorndike-Lorge list. These words, from low to high frequency, were as follows: *tango, groin, peony, ghoul,* and *triad; patio, cobra, roach, baton,* and *jaunt; beach, model, clerk, fault,* and *giant; chair, sugar, train, party,* and *labor.* In making anagrams from these words, another variable was introduced, namely, the order of the letters in the anagrams, with one set of easy orders and another set of difficult orders used. Let the order of the letters in the word be symbolized, 12345. An easy order of the anagram would then be 12354. Thus, the word *tango,* when made into an anagram would be *tanog.* Other easy orders used were 23451, 51234, 34512, and 45123. The difficult orders were 14253, 25314, 52413, 31425, and 42513. It is not easy to characterize completely the difference between difficult and easy orders. The easy orders appear to require fewer movements of the letters to achieve solution than do the difficult orders, but this cannot be used as the only rule for constructing easy and difficult anagrams. In any event, as we shall see, the easy and difficult letter orders profoundly influence speed of anagram solutions.

One group of Ss was given the 20 anagrams in the easy orders with each of the five orders being used four times, and a second group was given the anagrams in the difficult orders. Each anagram was presented to S on a 3 by 5-in. card, and the time to solve was recorded. The S was not allowed, however, to use pencil and paper. Presumably the 20 anagrams were randomized for presentation. We will note that as far as the frequency variable is concerned we are dealing with mixed lists, since words at all four frequency levels were given to each S. The letter-order variable (easy versus difficult), on the other hand, was unmixed since one group of 20 Ss was given all difficult orders and another group of the same number was given all easy orders.

The choice of a response measure in problem-solving tasks is sometimes troublesome. What do we do with the records of an S who is unable to solve a problem within a limited period of time? One solution has been to set a specified limit of time and express the results in terms of the number (or percentage) of Ss in each group who did solve. Or, if there are multiple problems, we could set a time limit for each problem and then express each S's score as the number of problems solved. Still another technique is to record solution time and then arbitrarily assign a limiting value for an S who failed to solve. In the present study, a maximum of 4 min. was allowed for solving each anagram, and if the anagram was not solved within that period, E gave S the solution and proceeded to the next anagram. Apparently, a time score of 4 min. was assigned S for the anagram not solved, and as is customary when such arbitrary scores are assigned, medians are used as measures of central tendency. In this study, a median time was determined for each S for the five anagrams within each frequency level, and the mean of the medians used to express the rate of solution for all Ss combined. These values are plotted in Fig. 14-1. It is obvious that frequency of both the words and the letter orders strongly influence rate of anagram solution.

Although the effect of word frequency is apparent in Fig. 14-1, it is also apparent that there is little difference in solution times for the two highest frequency groupings. Whether or not this represents a sampling variation is unclear. Since each frequency level was represented by only five words, it is possible that a larger (or different) sampling of words would have shown a clearer difference between the two highest frequency levels. One might think at first that the appropriate way to choose the words would be to draw them randomly from a specified frequency level. For example, if we decided to use five-letter anagrams. we could separate out all five-letter words at different frequency levels and then draw a specified number randomly from each level. Such a procedure would allow us to assert that the words chosen were representative of the frequency levels, but as discussed in Chapter Eleven, we must choose between representativeness of our materials and purity of the materials with regard to other variables. By purity we mean, of course, that no other variable is covarying with the independent variable whose influence we wish to explore.

Suppose we did draw our sample of words from each frequency level on a random basis; what other variable might covary with frequency? The most obvious one is the number of solutions an anagram may have. Let us assume that the number of different solutions possible to an anagram is directly related to the frequency level of the words drawn at random. If this is true (and it probably is), frequency would have a secondary effect in that the higher the frequency, the more quickly S should find a solution simply because more solutions are possible. Such a finding would be trivial; it would be a mathematical certainty that if S systematically rearranges the

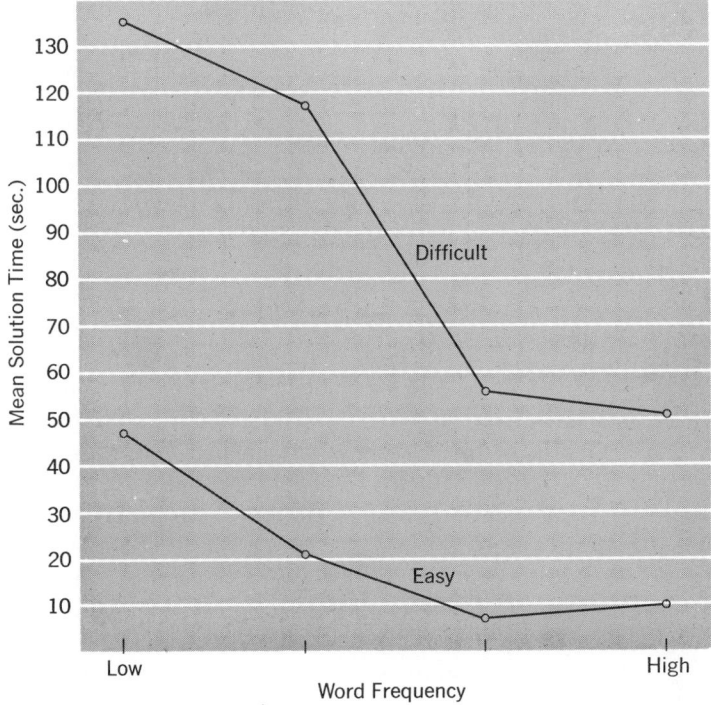

Fig. 14-1. Speed of solving anagrams as a function of word frequency and easy and difficult letter orders. Data from Mayzner and Tresselt (1958).

letters of an anagram, he will more quickly hit upon a solution if there are multiple solutions than if there is a single solution. Because of this, Es normally equate for number of solutions at each level of a task variable when such a variable is being manipulated, and single-solution anagrams have been most commonly used. Presumably the anagrams in the above study were single-solution anagrams. This, however, is not stated, and the present writer has not written out the 120 letter orders for each of the 20 anagrams to determine this for himself.

Perhaps now we may see another line of attack on the problem of representativeness. Perhaps we should determine which five-letter words have a single solution and then draw randomly from them only. Such a procedure would have much to recommend it, but mechanically it is troublesome, for the work involved in determining whether a large number of anagrams have single or multiple solutions would be great. A somewhat more pragmatic approach has sometimes been used; namely, a large group of Ss is given a large number of anagrams, and from the solutions given, a pool of single-solution anagrams is derived.

How does word frequency influence anagram solving? Let us examine a rather ridiculous situation as a means of leading to an answer. I am thinking of a three-letter anagram, and your task is to solve it. Of course, the only avenues open to you are either to ignore the request or to start guessing three-letter words. If you do guess, what will be the nature of your guesses? Very likely you will start emitting very common (high frequency) three-letter words. A great many studies have shown that in a relatively free responding situation, the order of emission of words is directly related to their frequency. Your responses would not be randomly chosen from all three-letter words. In the present situation, some unknown stimulus may cause you to emit the word *cat* initially, and then the associations with *cat* may lead to *dog, rat,* and so on, so that you are responding within the animal category. Nevertheless, within the category your first emissions are likely to be common or high-frequency words—it would be a rare person who would respond with *gnu.* By such responding you may solve the anagram without ever having seen it, particularly if I had chosen the three-letter word freely from my own repertoire, for I should choose a high-frequency word. This tendency to emit words in order of their frequency in a relatively free responding situation has sometimes been described as the "spew" law.

When we transfer this principle to a nonimaginary anagram situation, it seems likely that the initial solution attempts will be high-frequency words restricted to some extent by the particular letters in the anagram. If the solution is, in fact, a low-frequency word, you will have to "run through" many high-frequency words before you reach the appropriate frequency level. Indeed, the failure to solve a low-frequency anagram within a reasonable period of time may result from the difficulty of working against the spew principle; we find it difficult to think of low-frequency words because high-frequency words keep intruding.

The fact is that many problems *are* problems because they require unusual or unique low-frequency responses or infrequently used approaches. The person who is adept at solving parlor puzzles is the one who has learned this lesson well. He knows, and instructs himself, that the obvious approach or the obvious solution attempt is probably inappropriate. It is in somewhat this sense that we have attempted to gear our thinking to problems of experimental design. We do have techniques readily available to handle many problems we meet in designing experiments, and although we should use these if appropriate, we should not be blind about their use. We have continually used the word *thoughtful* to express this caution. If we are going to do a classical psychophysical study using a within-S design, one strong response we have for handling the balancing of progressive error is counterbalancing. But we know we must not automatically use this method, for in certain situations it is not appropriate; randomization of the conditions may be the appropriate method. In testing a hypothesis about learning we should not blindly choose a Skinner box or a paired-associate list; perhaps another approach will provide a more definitive answer to the hypothesis. Over and over again in the history of experimental disciplines, new discoveries are made because E was able to break away from the prevailing modes of thought and prevailing techniques. Comfort in the known often prevents us from knowing the unknown.

Further frequency analysis. A central problem in the study of anagram solving concerns the particular cues to which S responds. What cues produce the hypotheses—the words which are tried? One approach to this problem has been to break the frequency variable down into smaller units. Consider the word *linen*. It can be thought of as a series of two-letter units (*li, in, ne,* and *en*). The frequency with which such two-letter units (bigrams) occur in words is known (e.g., Underwood & Schulz, 1960). Therefore, by summing the successive bigram frequencies we can obtain a total bigram frequency. In the case of *linen* this frequency is very high. For the word *lunch,* the successive bigram totals are relatively small, although the two words do not differ markedly in frequency of use. Is anagram solution a function of summed word bigram frequency?

The anagram itself may be presented to have either high or low summed bigram frequency. For example, *linen* when presented as *nilen* has high bigram frequency and when presented as *lnnie,* low bigram frequency. This variable can, apparently, be manipulated independently of the easy and difficult letter orders as discussed above for the Mayzner-Tresselt experiment. Therefore, a second question which we may ask is whether or not summed anagram bigram frequency influences anagram solution.

The results of several studies designed to answer these two questions are contradictory, for reasons as yet unknown. Dominowski and Duncan (1964) showed an interaction between word bigram frequency and anagram bigram frequency. Best performance occurred when both types of frequency were equivalent (both high or both low), but, relatively, if one frequency was high and one low, performance was poor. Such a finding suggests that low anagram bigram frequencies cause S to produce words with low bigram frequencies, and high anagram bigram frequencies cause him to produce words with high bigram frequencies. It is as if the spew is restricted to a class of words defined by the bigram frequency of the anagrams. Is this possible?

There is some evidence from the rote learning of trigrams that S does adjust his responding to the appropriate level. If a list of very difficult trigrams is used, we know that the letters in sequence in each trigram rarely occur in words (e.g., RZL). When S makes errors in acquiring such trigrams, the letters he puts together are also letters which rarely occur in sequence in words. But if he is learning a list of trigrams which do contain sequences which often go together in words (e.g., FUL), his errors will consist largely of letter sequences which are frequently found in words. It appears that a restriction on the nature of the response attempts will be produced so that these attempts are appropriate for the frequency level of the stimuli.

The above reasoning leads to certain expectations concerning the role of word frequency in anagram solution. In the Mayzner-Tresselt study the lists were mixed lists—each S solved anagrams at different frequency levels. In this case, no restriction on the response attempts due to frequency level should develop; the spew law should hold in the broadest sense. But suppose we gave S an unmixed list of anagrams whose solutions were low-frequency words? It becomes reasonable to expect that spew should become more and more restricted as each anagram is solved (or as E tells S the solution), and when the restriction becomes severe enough, the anagrams leading to low-frequency words may be solved almost as quickly as those leading to high-frequency words. If this is true (and to the writer's knowledge no test of it has been made), we would expect frequency differences to be less with unmixed lists than with mixed.

We have assumed that when we attempt to solve an anagram, we make a series of implicit pronouncing responses to rearranged letters. The response may involve any number of the letters. The above analysis in terms of bigram frequencies assumes that a useful unit of analysis with which E may deal is the bigram. Whether or not this is the most appropriate unit remains to be determined. As a means of making overt the implicit pronouncing responses which are assumed to occur, Mayzner, Tresselt, and Helbock (1964) asked Ss to speak the implicit responses. The anagrams were difficult ones, so that in many cases a long series of responses became available. These overt responses were recorded and subsequently subjected to certain analyses. Here is an initial series of responses recorded for one S to the anagram RTEOPS: *torp, ster, tro, top, stop, pose, serop, pers, te, reports, opest, tempest, pre*. Such a string of responses indicates that no particular size of a unit governed the responses made. Nevertheless, when these Es related the frequency with which particular bigrams were produced (as two letters or as successive bigrams in sequences of more than two letters), they found that the greater the frequency with which a bigram occurs in English words, the more frequently it was given. The frequency with which two letters are associated in the language is reflected in the frequency of solution attempts. The S does not respond randomly.

We may briefly note the role of frequency in another anagram-like task. In this task, S must construct a particular word by guessing the letters. When a correct letter is guessed, its position in the word is specified. As more letters are filled in, S may solve the "anagram"—he may be able to fill in the remaining letters without hesitation. Battig (1957) analyzed the differences in the guessing habits of good and poor performers on this task and found that good performers guessed letters in a manner that corresponded to their frequency of use in words. Poor performers, on the other hand, tended to use alphabetical sequences in their guesses.

Two other comments may be made about anagrams. There is some evidence (e.g., Beilin & Horn, 1962) that if the anagram is presented as a word (the solution being another word), solution is more difficult than if the anagram is presented in usual form as a series of letters which do not make a word. The ideal way to carry out a study on this variable is to use the same letters, presenting them once as a word and once as the usual anagram (to different groups, of course). Obviously, this would mean that the letters must form two words. Can you devise a plan by which this experiment could be carried out?

Investigators have rather uniformly reported that there is little if any practice effect in solving a series of anagrams. This seems a little odd. However, an analysis by Hunter (1959) of the skills involved in solving anagrams led him to the conclusion that these skills are of such nature that they would develop very slowly with practice. On the other hand, is it possible that in solving a series of anagrams in a single session, there might be an increase in interference? Could previous solutions interfere with momentary solution attempts so that the practice effects are counteracted? How would you design an experiment to minimize the effects of such interference?

Concept Recognition

Concept learning has occurred when we are able to make the same response to dissimilar stimuli. When a child has learned the distinction between plants and animals, a great variety of objects elicits the response *animal*, and another great variety elicits the response *plant*. The pure case of concept learning corresponds to the A-B, C-B paradigm as discussed in an earlier chapter, except that both associations are learned simultaneously. Most of our more useful concepts are not based on stimuli which are completely dissimilar (although just what completely dissimilar means is a philosophical problem). Animals are animals because descriptive research has identified certain common properties among them. The similarity in the case of more restricted concepts (e.g., four-footed animals) is obvious. Nevertheless, that two very dissimilar stimuli come to produce the same response represents the end product of concept formation or concept learning. Most laboratory studies do not deal directly with concept learning. Rather, they deal with concept recognition or concept utilization or concept selection. The S brings knowledge of the concept as such to the laboratory, but the situation is so devised that he has to discover which particular concept is appropriate for the situation.

For the moment we will deal with concept recognition based on verbal materials. We are still concerned at this point with the role of associative frequency in the production of responses in problem solving. Because of the manner in which most concept recognition studies are devised, they represent problem-solving situations.

In an earlier chapter we took note of the fact that a word presented to S may produce an implicit associative response. The word *up* may produce the implicit response *down*, and *cat* may elicit *dog*. When verbal materials are used in the study of concept recognition, we are essentially studying the factors which govern implicit responses.

There is an old riddle which is told as follows: "A big Indian and a little Indian stood on a hill. The little Indian is the big Indian's son, but the big Indian is not the little Indian's father. How can this be?" That this is a riddle appears to result from the fact that the description "big Indian" automatically elicits the implicit response "man" or "male" or "chief," and this is probably supported retroactively as an interpretation by the appearance of the word *father* later in the sentence. It is only when we recognize that the implicit response to big Indian is not appropriate that we can solve the riddle.

If we ask how *barrel* and *globe* are related, we will very quickly discover that both elicit the same implicit response, "round." If we ask how *earthworm, closet, freckle,* and *tack* are related, the common implicit response is much less readily elicited. Nevertheless, all of the four objects have been described as "small" in particular contexts. Furthermore, most Ss, given enough time, will eventually arrive at this common response. What appears to happen is that S keeps producing implicit associates to the words, at least to one of them, and checks each against the corresponding implicit responses to all four. The discovery of the commonality among the latter four objects is hindered because other implicit responses are stronger. The first implicit response to *barrel* and to *globe* may be "round"; but the strongest implicit response to *earthworm* is likely to be "wiggle" or "fishing" or "long."

How are *hall, apple, top,* and *family* related? Either in a forward or backward relation, the word "tree" is associated with each of the words. The ability to discover common but very remote associates to words is argued by some to be representative of creative ability, and a test measuring the capacity to discover such remote associates has been constructed (Mednick, 1962). Scores on this test have been shown to relate to rated creative ability shown by graduate students in certain disciplines. The logic of such a test is that those people whose behavior is not bound by strong common responses to situations have the greatest likelihood of discovering new relationships.

Dominance level and response discovery. We may illustrate one method of studying concept recognition with verbal materials by a study from the writer's laboratory (Underwood & Richardson, 1956b). In an earlier study (Underwood & Richardson, 1956a), 153 Ss produced descriptive words to 213 nouns by a word-association procedure. Initially, these Ss were trained to describe objects by what we called "sense-impression" descriptions, these being characteristics given by the perception of the objects. For example, objects may be described as round, small, sharp, or hard. It was necessary to train Ss to produce such descriptions because the dominant associate to many nouns is not of this type. Each noun is then described in terms of the percentage of Ss using each sense-impression word. Thus, to the stimulus *apple,* 67 percent of the Ss responded "round," 19 percent responded "red," and 5 percent, "sweet," with the remaining Ss scattering their responses among several words. These materials are available for constructing tasks for studies of verbal concept recognition. Mayzner and Tresselt (1961) have also made available normative data of this type but used a somewhat different procedure to obtain the norms.

We assume that the greater the frequency with which Ss respond with a given descriptive term to a word, the stronger is that implicit response when S is faced with a concept recognition task. Therefore, when concept recognition requires the use of a strong implicit response, recognition should occur more quickly than if the appropriate recognition response is weak. This seems like an obvious variable, one which we speak of as degree of dominance of the appropriate response. Nevertheless, we may see how it works out in practice.

A list consisted of 24 nouns which had been used in the word-association procedure; therefore, we knew how frequently the various descriptive terms were used for each. The 24 words made up six concepts, with four instances or exemplars of each. The appropriate responses for two of the concepts consisted of high-dominant responses; for another two, the response dominance was medium, and for the last two it was low. The 24 words from one of the lists are shown in Table 14-1. We should note that for the concept name which has low dominance, for example, "soft" as a response to *custard, lips, moss,* and *sheep,* other responses to these words have high dominance. To arrive at the correct recognition (as defined by *E*) of how these objects are related, we presume that S had to "wade through" these strong interfering implicit responses in order to arrive at the low-dominant implicit response.

There were actually three lists used in the experiment, but since all had the same characteristics as the one shown in Table 14-1, they need not concern us. The 24 items were mixed up for presentation, and the task demanded that S produce the appropriate response for each word, the appropriate response being the descriptive word as given in Table 14-1. All Ss were told that four of the words could be described by a single word, four others, by another word, and so on. Therefore, S knew that if he achieved the concept recognition required by E, he would be responding with only six different words. Each word was presented for 4 sec. each, during which time S had to respond and following which he was told "right" or "wrong."

TABLE 14–1

ILLUSTRATION OF A LIST USED TO STUDY THE EFFECT OF DOMINANCE LEVEL ON CONCEPT RECOGNITION. FROM UNDERWOOD AND RICHARDSON (1956b).

HIGH DOMINANCE	MEDIUM DOMINANCE	LOW DOMINANCE
("round")	("white")	("soft")
barrel	bone	custard
doughnut	collar	lips
knob	frost	moss
balloon	lint	sheep
("small")	("smelly")	("big")
village	garlic	camel
minnow	gasoline	forest
crumb	pine	hospital
germ	sulfur	limousine

Three groups were distinguished in terms of their instructions which were presumed to vary the amount of response discovery necessary to master the task. One group was given unrestricted instructions telling them to respond to each word in a free manner, much as in a word-association task. It is clear that Ss in this group had to discover not only the nature of the responses required (sense impressions) but, in addition, the particular sense impressions appropriate to the different words. Another group was given instructions which partially restricted the amount of discovery required. These Ss were told the nature of the descriptive words that were correct and were given illustrations of members of this class (although none of the correct responses was used for this). These Ss, therefore, had to discover only the particular responses required within the class. As a means of further limiting the amount of response discovery required, the Ss in a third group were given cards on which the six correct responses were printed. Therefore, they had only to fit a particular response word to the correct four nouns—response discovery was completely eliminated.

All Ss were given 20 trials, but were instructed to respond on the first trial. The mean numbers of stimuli to which the correct response was given on the first trial are shown in Fig. 14-2. With unrestricted instructions, essentially no responses were given correctly to any of the stimuli, since the dominant responses to these stimuli are not normally sense-impression responses. The role of dominance level is clearly exhibited in the responses of the other two groups, however.

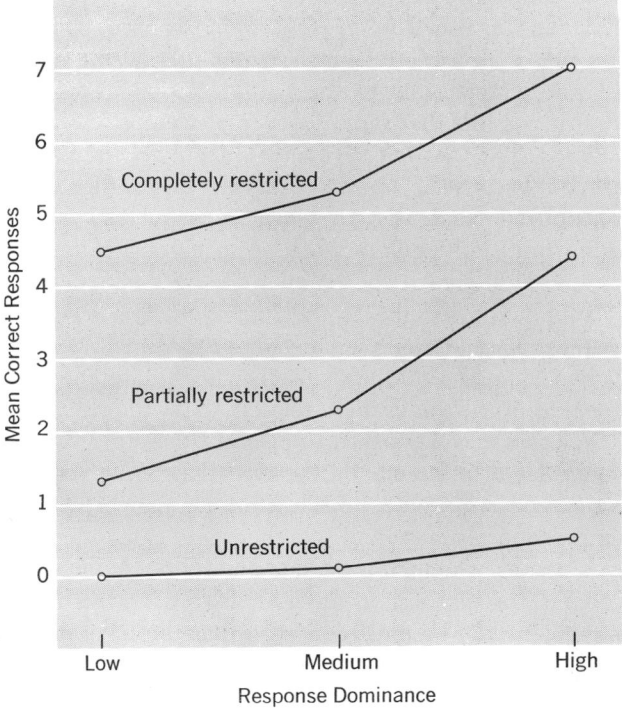

Fig. 14-2. Verbal concept recognition as a function of dominance level and nature of instructions. See text for explanation. Data from Underwood and Richardson (1956b).

Following the first trial the group given the unrestricted instructions rapidly showed a relationship between dominance level and number of correct responses. By studying the nature of the errors made by Ss in this group it was possible to study the learning of the appropriate response class required. After S had first given a correct response (usually a high-dominant response), a rapid increase in the frequency of the sense-impression responses was noted. However, many more erroneous responses within the class were made to the stimuli when a low-dominant response was appropriate than when a medium-dominant response was appropriate, and more were made in the latter than in the instances where a high-dominant response was appropriate. Once Ss had achieved knowledge of the appropriate class of responses, the major difficulty arose out of interference from strongly dominant responses which were incorrect for the stimuli to which a low- and medium-dominant response was required. Not all Ss were able to produce the appropriate response to all four instances of a concept for all concepts within 20 trials. The higher the dominance level, the less frequently this occurred, and this was true for all three types of instructions.

The above procedure, which was used in studying concept recognition, is quite comparable to the methods used in studying rote learning. Indeed, it is possible that some "concepts" were given correctly, not because S discovered that the objects could indeed be described by the common response, but because he associated the response with each of the four stimuli in a concept independently. However, subsequent work by other investigators, using quite different procedures to eliminate the rote-learning possibilities, have also shown the potency of the dominance variable. Coleman (1964) simply showed the Ss the four words related by a common sense impression and asked him to educe what the word was. Kendler and Karasik (1958) had S study eight cards, each with a different noun on it, and told him that four of the nouns were related. After the study period S was given one of the cards and was asked to pick out the other three which had nouns that were related to the one on the card that was given to him. Crouse and Duncan (1963) required Ss to select the nouns which were related by their sense-impression response and sort them into categories. All of these studies produced results which showed that the more frequent (hence we assume the stronger) the response in the normative data, the more quickly the concept is recognized. We must conclude that the level of dominance of a response to a particular problem-solving situation is vitally related to the likelihood of solution.

The study of role of response dominance as discussed above utilizes associates to words which are assumed to have different strengths as inferred from normative frequency studies. When the stimulus word *apple* is described as "round" by 67 percent of the Ss in a normative study and as "red" by 19 percent, it is assumed that for the average S "round" is the more dominant of the two responses. Of course, for some Ss "red" is the more dominant response. In order to study the role of response dominance in a purer form, it is desirable to exercise greater control over the response strengths for each S. To do this, we may start with neutral stimulus terms and build in experimentally two or more associates to each term, with each associate having a known strength. If we followed the plan outlined by Thysell and Schulz (1964), we could use nonsense words (e.g., KALAB, FETOR) and require S to learn sense-impression responses to these originally neutral stimuli. Following such learning we could evaluate the concept-sorting performance as a function of strong and weak appropriate associations and strong and weak interfering associations. Without going into the details of the experiment performed by these investigators, we may report that their results paralleled quite closely those found with the use of normative associations.

SOLUTION FREQUENCY

In this section we will sample results which tell us about behavior exhibited when S solves a series of problems.

Water-Jar Problems

Modern work on this problem dates from Luchins' extensive series of experiments (1942). The water-jar problem, as a single problem, consists in giving S three jars, each of which will hold a specified amount of water. In most experiments these are presented as hypothetical jars or containers, although the same results will hold when S works at a sink with the three jars. Using only the three jars as measuring instruments, S is to arrive at a certain amount of water as specified by E. Thus, if the three jars (when full of water) hold 5, 13, and 2 units, how can one get exactly 1 unit of water? This could be done by filling the 13-unit container first and from it, filling the 5-unit container twice and the 2-unit container once, thus leaving 1 unit in the 13-unit jar. Or, it could be done more simply by filling the 5-unit jar, then filling the 2-unit jar twice, leaving 1 unit.

In the basic experiments conducted by Luchins, nine problems were used. The first was a practice problem used to acquaint S with the procedure, so we will not include it here. The remaining eight problems were as follows:

| | CONTAINERS | | | |
	a	b	c	To Obtain:
Problem No. 2	21	127	3	100
Problem No. 3	14	163	25	99
Problem No. 4	18	43	10	5
Problem No. 5	9	42	6	21
Problem No. 6	20	59	4	31
Problem No. 7	23	49	3	20
Problem No. 8	15	39	3	18
Problem No. 9	28	76	3	25

To obtain the 100 units as requested in Problem No. 2, S would fill the 127-unit container and from it, fill the 21-unit container once and the 3-unit container twice, leaving 100 units in the large container. If these operations are put in algebraic form, the equation reads $b-a-2c=100$. If you will check Problems 3, 4, 5, and 6, you will discover that all of them may be solved by this formula and in no other way. Problems 7 and 8 may also be solved by this equation, but they may in addition be solved in an easier or shorter manner by eliminating the b container entirely. Problem No. 9 can be solved *only* by the short method $(a-c)$.

In a defining experiment by Luchins, two groups of Ss were used. Both groups were given the practice problem after which the C Group was dismissed briefly. The E Group remained and solved, in order, Problems No. 2 through No. 6, and then both groups together were given Problems No. 7 through No. 9. In working Problems No. 2 through No. 6, members of the E Group would normally be allowed enough time to complete each problem since these problems are used to build up a particular solution frequency. The critical comparisons occur on Problems 7, 8, and 9. Diagrammatically, the defining operations are:

	1	2 through 6	7 through 9
	PROBLEMS		
E GROUP	yes	yes	yes
C GROUP	yes	no	yes

Luchins gave these problems to literally hundreds of Ss of varying ages and educational status. The effect of the E Group's working problems 2 through 6 was to cause members of such groups to use the old method, the percentage of Ss using this old method varying from 70 percent to 100 percent. The C Group, on the other hand, rarely used this long method. Thus, the difference in the use of a particular solution between these two groups on Problems 7 and 8, taken in conjunction with the operations noted, defines the phenomenon under investigation. A further extension of the same mechanism is shown on Problem 9—a problem which could not be solved by the formula used on the first six problems. With a restricted amount of time allowed to solve this problem, fewer Ss in the E Group than in the C Group solved it. Apparently, members of the E Group persisted in their attempts to apply the formula which had been quite successful for the earlier problems and so were unable to take quickly a new direction or a new attack on a problem.

Many will recognize that the phenomenon involved is often included under the descriptive term *set*. One way of developing this set, as in the Luchins study, is to allow a series of problems to be solved successfully by a given mode of attack and then testing on a problem for which the mode is inappropriate. As we shall see later, there are other ways by which the scope or range of response attempts may be restricted other than by successful solution frequency. However, when we attempt to manipulate set by manipulating success of a given method of solution, we may predict the effect of certain variables with considerable accuracy by considering the learning which occurs in successful solving as being a form of simple associative learning. For example, the greater the number of problems we give which may be solved by the same method, the greater the magnitude of the set phenomenon (Gardner & Runquist, 1958). Further work using waterjar problems has been summarized by Chown (1959) and Duncan (1959).

Anagrams

Anagrams have also been used to study the effect of successful solutions on subsequent solutions. Four different techniques will be illustrated.

Solution moves. Almost a direct analogue of the water-jar problem was used by Adamson (1959) when he attempted to build up a set for particular letter moves. A series of anagrams in the order 2341 (where 1234 constitutes the word) was presented, and then Ss were tested on anagrams which could not be solved by the formula (moving the last letter of the anagram to the front). Performance on the test anagrams was retarded.

Solution class. Suppose we give S a series of anagrams, all the solutions of which are the names of animals, and then on test trials we give a series (a part of the first series as far as S can tell) in which the solution words are not names of animals. We may expect two things to happen. First, as each successive training word is solved, rate of solution should become faster and faster, because S learns that the appropriate solution is an animal name; thereby, his range of solution attempts is restricted to the appropriate class. Secondly, after S has developed a set for a particular class of words, his performance should be inhibited when the test anagrams are given, for he should continue to search initially for further animal names as solutions. Such expectations are supported (e.g., Maltzman & Morrisett, 1952).

Instructions. If S is told before he starts solving anagrams that the solutions fall within a specified class, he should again immediately restrict the range of solution attempts, and his performance should be facilitated. The instructions should, in effect, produce the same consequence as S's discovering over a series of trials that all solutions fit a class, but they should produce the effect immediately. Indeed, instructions can almost immediately eliminate solution attempts within a class built up by experience of solving within a class or by other instructions. For example, if in a series of anagrams S discovers that all of the solution words are names of animals, and then if he is instructed at a given point that the solution words will no longer be animals, the negative effects of the set induced by solving animal anagrams will be minimal (e.g., Maltzman, Eisman, Brooks, & Smith, 1956).

Associative categories. If the anagram presented is AYHEV and you solve it, the implicit response to the solution word (HEAVY) may be "light." If the next anagram is GTILH, you may "hit upon" the solution more quickly as a consequence of having had the first anagram than if you had had one for which the implicit associative response was not "light." This is the basic notion used by Safren (1962). This investigator had Ss solve groups of six anagrams all of which were associatively related (e.g., *doctor, nurse, health, sick, medicine, cure*), and it was found that the rate of solution increased from an average of 15 sec. for the first anagram to about 5 sec. for the sixth. No test was used to determine if a negative effect would be present on a seventh anagram which was not associatively related, but had this been done, the results would undoubtedly have been much the same as those discussed above.

We will not belabor the procedures and results. Any procedure which results in a restriction in the range of response solutions will facilitate problem solving if the correct response is included within the restricted range, and it will not facilitate, indeed it will probably inhibit, if the correct response is not included. Actually, the evidence indicates that the prolongation of the negative effects of a set are not as great as the above discussion may have implied. A problem or two which will not fit the set solution will usually "break" or extinguish the set.

We have not, in briefly presenting the techniques for inducing sets with anagrams, pointed out the appropriate control conditions. Such controls are, of course, necessary for most procedures. It also seems likely that we could devise many other techniques for restricting the range of response production, for that is the critical aspect of all of the operations involved.

Probability Solutions

In all of the illustrations given above on solution frequency as a determinant of the nature of solution attempts, the "buildup" has been consistent. That is, all of the water-jar problems used in establishing the set had the same solution; all of the anagrams made animal names. In many types of problems, problems which may more closely simulate "real life," different solutions may be possible, and these solutions may have a different likelihood of handling any particular problem. For example, suppose you worked 100 anagrams, 75 of whose solutions were names of towns and 25 of whose solutions were names of animals. What would be your likely initial solution attempt for the one-hundred-first anagram? On a strict probability basis, the chances are 3 to 1 that it would be the name of another town, and very likely, this would be the solution you would try first. This would most likely be true, of course, if the total numbers of town and animal names in your repertoire of words were essentially equivalent and equally available, a condition that is probably not met by towns and animals. But given these conditions, if we were to behave in a manner which might promise greatest probability of immediate success, we would look for a name of a town for the one-hundred-first anagram. Other factors, however, might "throw" our initial attempts toward the animals. If the last 10 anagrams (91 to 100) had been names of towns, we might show the gambler's fallacy and decide that since an animal name has not appeared for some time, it must be about due. In any event, the fact is that we do often deal in probability situations in which different solutions have different likelihoods of handling a particular problem. This may be illustrated with a personal story.

I was preparing for a particularly important conference when I was suddenly attacked by a sore throat, fever, and the customary accompanying general flu-like aches and pains. I went to my physician, told him I had to leave town in four days, and expressed the hope that he could make me reasonably healthy as soon as possible. He took a look at my throat, measured my temperature, and saying that he would have everything taken care of in plenty of time, gave me a prescription for an antibiotic. After 48 hr. and several dollars worth of the drug, the fever remained, the throat was still raw, and "lousy" was the general feeling. I returned to the physician. He seemed puzzled, but patiently examined my symptoms again. Concluding that the particular "bug" involved was stubborn, he prescribed another antibiotic, more potent, more costly than the first, and confidently sent me home to get well. After another 24 hr. and several more dollars spent, I could still detect no improvement. I returned again to the physician and reminded him of his promise. He seemed somewhat hurt by my inability to respond—or, perhaps, my lack of confidence. However, now he became fully fascinated by the problem-solving aspects of the situation. Into the examining room I went again. But this time when he looked at my throat, he exclaimed with joy, "Aha! New symptoms!" I considered this discovery a dubious reason for delight until he explained.

The cause of the trouble was a local infection which in its initial stages of development produced symptoms that were very similar to those for various types of flu, and only on the third visit had unique symptoms appeared. The physician estimated that he saw 98 flu cases to every two cases involving the type of infection I had. He had simply behaved in terms of probability of an event's occurring, and it was not until symptoms appeared which differentiated the two types of infection that the correct diagnosis could be made.

We know from studies covered in previous chapters that we can assimilate differential environmental frequencies with considerable precision. We know this because when we ask Ss to judge relative frequencies of events which have happened, they can do so with rather amazing accuracy. We may expect that an experienced mechanic or electronic repairman will have assimilated certain probabilistic notions about the cause or source of a difficulty when the symptoms indicate that the cause may lie in two or more independent sources. Therefore, in determining the source of a malfunction these notions should influence his problem-solving attempts. They will, but they will also be modified by other factors, and one in particular looms large—the amount of work required to determine the source of the difficulty.

Probability and work. Detambel and Stolurow (1957) studied the effect of amount of work on probabilistic solutions by presenting Ss with a situation in which the source of a malfunction could be in any one of three locations. Each of the three locations was simulated by a small box, all three boxes being identical. However, to determine if the malfunction was in a particular box, S had to remove screws in order to lift off the lid and discover whether this section of the equipment was or was not the source of the difficulty. If it was not the source, OK appeared on the bottom of the inside; if it was the source, this did not appear. The amount of work was varied by varying the number of screws which had to be removed to take off the lid. On a given trial S was faced with three boxes, one malfunctioning and each one having a different number of screws to remove. Over a series of trials the frequency with which the malfunction was discovered to lie in Box A was 50 percent, in Box B, 33 percent, and in Box C, 17 percent. If the amount of work required was equivalent for each box, S would be expected to try Box A first, Box B second, and Box C last after the relative frequencies had been assimilated.

Two groups of Ss were used, the frequency with which the malfunction was found in each box was the same for both groups—50, 33, and 17 percent. However, for one group, the number of screws which had to be removed was 3, 2, and 1 for boxes A, B, and C, respectively, and for the other group the number was 7, 4, and 1. In both cases, the amount of work involved was "against" the probability factor; the box with the smallest number of screws was least likely to be the source of the malfunction, but the amount of work differed for the two groups for Boxes A and B. The Ss were paid for 4 hr. of work but were told that they could leave whenever they had completed the work required, which consisted of 192 trials. It should be noted that on any trial the lids to no more than two boxes had to be removed; if the source of the difficulty was not present in the first two boxes it had to be in the third. However, the Es required S to remove the lid on the third box in such cases and to remove a piece of tape from the bottom of the box which was used to cover the letters OK. In a manner of speaking, S had to repair the malfunction.

The critical response measure is the box examined first on each trial. The percentages for Box A and Box C for Group 3-2-1 is shown in the upper panel of Fig. 14-3, and for Group 7-4-1, in the lower panel. The percentages are for successive blocks of 12 trials. For our purposes, the results for Box B (the box requiring the middle amount of work) need not be considered. We may note that for both groups the box opened first on the initial trials was the box with the smallest number of screws, with the difference between Boxes A and C being greater for Group 7-4-1 than for Group 3-2-1. This seems perfectly reasonable; on the early trials S essentially had to guess in which box the malfunction lay, and the amount of work was the primary determinant of the choice. As trials continued, however, S began to build up an appreciation of the differential probabilities of the location of the malfunction, and there is a corresponding change in the choice of the first box on each trial. A comparison of the two panels shows how the amount

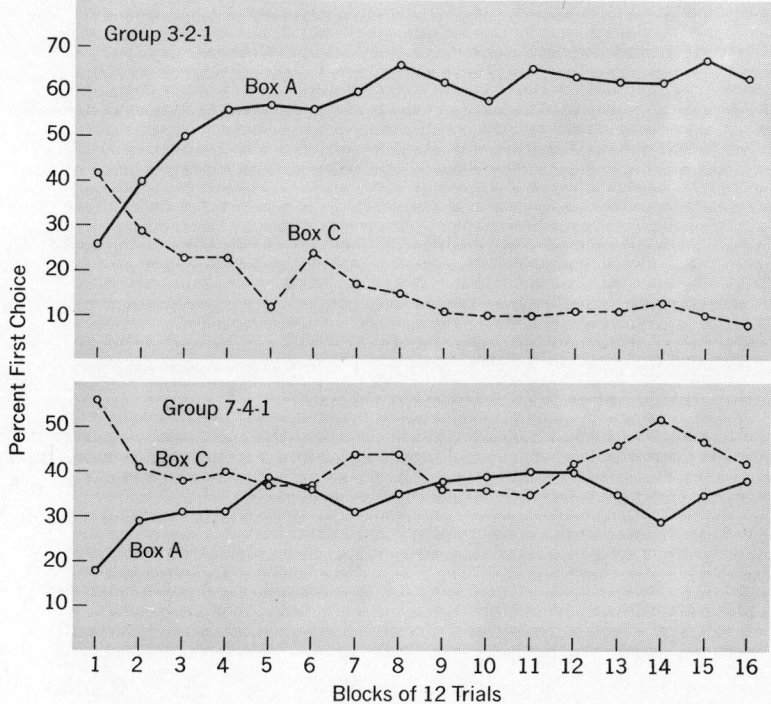

Fig. 14-3. The interaction of probability learning and amount of work in locating the source of malfunctioning. See text for explanation. Data from Detambel and Stolurow (1957).

of work and probability learning interact. When Box A and Box C do not require a great difference in the amount of work, Box A is chosen far more frequently as the first box to open than is Box C (Group 3-2-1), but when the work differential is large (Group 7-4-1), both boxes are opened with about equal frequency on the first try of a trial.

In problem solving or "trouble shooting," as illustrated by the above experiment, we recognize that other factors beyond an appreciation of probabilities will determine the order of solution attempts; and the amount of work required to check on the appropriateness of a solution appears to be one very important factor which modifies behavior based on probability laws. For example, we drive into a garage with our engine "missing." In such cases it may be a very rare occurrence that a sparkplug wire has worked loose; it is much more probable that the source is elsewhere, but the mechanic can very quickly determine if a wire is loose, so this may be his first problem-solving response.

It will be clear that we do not have to have boxes and screws in order to study problem-solving behavior and amount of work to check a solution. We could use any simple probability-learning situation and vary the work in numerous ways, even in so simple a manner as to require S to walk various distances to other rooms to find whether or not his solution was appropriate for a given trial.

Probability matching in concept formation. Let us assume that you are a subject in a concept-formation experiment. The instructions say that you will be given a series of cards and that each card will have two letters and two numbers on it. You are further told that your task is to determine the concept that E is "thinking of." For each card you are to predict whether the concept is contained in the symbols (positive instance) or is not contained in the symbols (negative instance). After the prediction for each card E will tell you whether you are right or wrong. Here are the symbols on the first 12 cards in the deck you are given:

CARD NO.	SYMBOLS	POS. OR NEG.	CARD NO.	SYMBOLS	POS. OR NEG.
1	BA43	Positive	7	AD23	Positive
2	AC24	Negative	8	DB42	Negative
3	DA23	Positive	9	CD34	Negative
4	BC14	Positive	10	BC12	Positive
5	DB31	Positive	11	AB13	Positive
6	CD12	Negative	12	CA41	Positive

Even a series of apparently simple displays such as these afford many possible hypotheses as to the concept that E is calling correct. Looking only at the first card, one might hypothesize at least three possibilities: (1) number of symbols, namely four, irrespective of their nature; (2) the presence of contiguous numbers and letters; (3) contiguous numbers and letters in reverse order. With the appearance of the second card, the first hypothesis is clearly denied or disconfirmed, but the other two remain tenable. However, the third card would force the abandonment of both.

It is rather doubtful that the appropriate concept would be formed after only 12 cards had been presented. But perhaps you did arrive at the correct hypothesis; the correct concept is contained in the symbols if either A or B and either 1 or 3 is present on the same card or if either of the first two letters of the alphabet occurs with an odd number.

The factual point to be made by such an illustration has to do with the probability learning which may occur as a part of concept formation. The probability learning in this case concerns the frequency of positive and negative instances which occur over a long series of trials. In the above illustration, 67 percent of the cards are positive instances, and 33 percent are negative instances. Of course, if S acquires the correct hypothesis, his responses must necessarily reflect these proportions. But recent investigators have demonstrated that S will learn sooner to respond with appropriate probabilities than to instances appropriately (Mandler, Cowan, & Gold, 1964). To say this another way, S's responding frequency (in the above problem) will indicate that for every two cards which he reports as positive instances, he will report one card as a negative instance, but these reports are not correctly matched with the cards. Only as successive trials are given does he pair the appropriate predictions with the appropriate cards—he learns the concept. The initial probability-matching behavior is like a mechanic who looks for trouble in an automobile by considering only the frequency with which various troubles have occurred in the past and ignoring the symptoms for the particular car that is in need of repair at the moment. The full role which such probability matching plays in overall concept acquisition is not clear at present, but there is reason to believe that having learned the probabilities of events in general, S may search more appropriately for particulars which are correlated with these events.

Types of concepts. The above type of concept problem has appeared in many different forms. For some reason a favorite one is the use of geometrical figures with different dimensions or with other characteristics of these figures also varied. Thus, three different types of geometrical figures might be used (squares, circles, triangles), occurring in three sizes (small, medium, large), and in one of three possible colors (red, blue, green). Successive displays might show a large red square (positive), small red circle (negative), large red triangle (positive), and so on, until S discovers or deduces that the correct concept is any large red figure. Thus, only two of the dimensions are relevant, one (type of figure) being irrelevant. Such a concept as "large red" is called a *conjunctive* concept in that it represents the joint presence of two particular values of two dimensions. Another type of concept is called *disjunctive*. In the present illustration, if *either* a large figure or a red figure or both were present on a display, a positive instance would be represented. Thus S would have to treat values on two different dimensions (large and red) as if they were the same.

A number of studies have shown that Ss have more difficulty in forming disjunctive than conjunctive concepts. We appear to be more comfortable with conjunctive concepts. It has been suggested that one of the factors involved in this difference reflects experiential frequency differences of real life. In the normal course of events more of the concepts we form are conjunctive rather than disjunctive. Therefore, on a probability basis, we would attempt to acquire a concept presented to us in the laboratory by attacking it first as if it were a conjunctive concept. If this is true, we might expect to change the probabilities by appropriate laboratory training. Wells (1963) gave Ss four successive concept problems which required disjunctive solutions and then tested them on a problem which allowed the formation of either a conjunctive or disjunctive concept. Following the training, these Ss gave more disjunctive solutions on the test problems than did control Ss.

STIMULUS DOMINANCE

The solution of certain types of problems can be shown to be influenced markedly by the particular biases which S brings to the situation or which are "built in" during an experimental period. The biases to be illustrated show that given an array of stimuli, certain of them, or their attributes, appear to dominate the initial solution attempts in spite of the fact that all have equal objective probabilities of being related to solution. Three approaches will be illustrated.

The Morgan study. Morgan (1944) presented his Ss with a situation which may be schematized as follows:

A	B	C
A	C	B
A	D	C

The letters in a row represent levers, and the Ss were told that when all levers in a row were pressed, a door would open. The problem given S was that of rank ordering the four stimuli (A, B, C, D) for their importance in *causing* the door to open. It will be noted that both A and C occur in each row so that, logically, they should be of equal importance in producing door-opening. Morgan reasoned that if logic only were involved in solution to problems, the Ss would be forced to conclude that neither A nor C could be ranked ahead of the other. The question was, then, whether or not Ss would rank the stimuli anyhow, and if so, what characteristics would determine the ranking.

In the actual experiment, four geometrical forms (circle, square, diamond, rectangle) were used instead of letters, these forms appearing in various sizes and at various positions in the rows. Some forms had lines through them; some did not. Twelve different problems were given, but each was the same as that symbolized above in that two forms were always equivalent logically as causal factors in opening the door.

Out of 246 college students given the problems, only six absolutely refused to rank order the stimuli, rightly insisting that the two factors were equally important in opening the door and how, then, could one rank one ahead of the other. Rankings for the remaining 240 Ss were examined to see if there were population sterotypes concerning the stimuli. Two factors stood out as determining the rankings of the critical two stimuli in each problem, namely, size and position. The larger of the two stimuli was given first rank, other things being equal, and the stimulus that occurred first in the row was preferred (as A might be preferred in the above symbolic illustration of Morgan's situation). It appears that there is something about size and about position which dominate as stimulus attributes and to which S will give more importance as causal factors.

The Wallace study. Wallace (1964) studied the formation of concepts in which the displays consisted of four attributes with three values for each: form (square, circle, triangle), color (red, black, yellow), number of forms (1, 2, 3), and number of border lines on the card presenting a given display (1, 2, 3). On any given display (a card) one value of each of the attributes was present, for example, two red squares with a single border line. To obtain all possible combinations of four three-valued attributes requires 81 cards (3^4).

There were two parts to the experiment. In the first part Wallace explained to Ss the nature of two-attribute concepts in which two of the dimensions are relevant and two, irrelevant. A two-attribute concept would be a blue circle, in which case the number of forms and the number of lines around the border of the card are irrelevant attributes. After it was clear that the Ss knew what was meant by a two-attribute concept, Wallace showed them the full array of 81 cards, asking them to emit as many such concepts as they could. With this array there are 54 possible two-attribute concepts, and Wallace's interest was in the most frequently and most quickly mentioned ones. The results of this procedure showed that color-form attributes were most preferred, and concepts involving number and color were least preferred. Or, to say this another way, color-form attributes appear to present more compelling or dominant attributes than do number-color attributes.

In the second phase of the experiment, Wallace had different groups of Ss attain concepts, in one case where the correct concept was based on high-dominant attributes and in another where it was based on the low-dominant attributes (in which case the high-dominant attributes are irrelevant). We need not be concerned with the method of presenting the stimuli; the basic notion, as in all such studies, was to present S successive cards and give him information as to whether the concept is represented on the card (positive instance) or is not (negative instance). This was continued until S in some manner indicated that he had attained the concept, which he did by correctly identifying a certain number of successive cards as positive or negative instances, or by stating the concept verbally, or both. For our purposes it is enough to report that S required more cards for successfully attaining the concepts based on the combinations of low-dominant attributes than he required in order to attain concepts based on combinations of high-dominant attributes.

The S appears to have certain biases toward certain attributes, and these biases determine initial hypotheses. If these attributes are involved in the correct concept, performance is facilitated; if they are not involved in the correct concept, performance is retarded. This implies an interaction in concept attainment as a function of dominance and relevance. Such an interaction has been shown by Archer (1962), who speaks of the obviousness of the stimulus attributes, but it is apparent that this means much the same as stimulus dominance. The fact is that in forming hypotheses about concepts with materials of the types discussed above, we do not behave like automatic sorting machines in which each combination of attributes has equal opportunity of appearing initially. We are biased sorting machines. However, we should not leave the impression that characteristics of the stimuli will have no influence on our initial hypotheses other than the influence of evoking preference responses. Imai and Garner (1965) have shown that discriminability within an attribute and between attributes also determines initial hypotheses. For example, we might have a strong preference for the size attribute, but if the size differences in a particular problem are very small (hard to discriminate), we can quickly overcome our preference, and other attributes will enter into the hypotheses.

Accepting the fact that we do have preferences or biases for certain stimulus attributes, we may ask how these biases develop. There may be certain perceptual aspects of various stimulus attributes which make them more or less compelling. A color dimension could be inherently more compelling than a length dimension. Nevertheless, the biases we observe in adult Ss may represent the residue of previous learning or previous problem-solving attempts which had reflected differences in the environmental probabilities of the attributes being relevant for learning or problem solving. We do know that we can experimentally produce perceptual biases by appropriate training procedures either in man (Eckstrand & Wickens, 1954) or in animals (Mackintosh, 1965), but this does not necessarily mean that all of the biases observed in problem solving originated in this manner.

A further implication of differential stimulus dominance must be mentioned. Consider the following procedure in which you are the S. You are given a pack of cards to sort into two piles, the two piles to represent different concepts. Half of the cards have large blue circles on them, and the other half, small red rectangles. Suppose your first hypothesis is that color is the relevant attribute; accordingly, on this basis you sort the cards into two piles, reds and blues. Each time you sort a card E tells you you are correct. Suppose you had started sorting on the basis of form (circle versus square) or size (large versus small). Your sorting would have been exactly the same as it was when you sorted by color. Given three attributes, all perfectly correlated, it is impossible to make a mistake. Two of the attributes are said to be redundant as far as the sorting behavior is concerned.

A next step makes the situation a little more complex. The Ss are given cards on which four different attributes or dimensions occur, each attribute having two values, and they are told to discover a particular two-value conjunctive concept. We will assume that three of the attributes are perfectly correlated and that, therefore, two of the three are redundant. More particularly, we will assume that the four attributes are size, color, position, and form and that the latter three are perfectly correlated. Whenever a red figure occurs it is always a square appearing on the left side of the card, and whenever a blue figure occurs it is always a circle appearing on the right side of the card. Size is the irrelevant attribute. Given this situation, with instructions to discover the correct two-value disjunctive concept, different Ss may arrive at the correct solution by different routes. One S, due to his particular biases (stimulus dominance), chooses to test first the hypothesis that red and left are the appropriate values for the concept; the biases of another S lead him to test first red and square as the appropriate values; and still a third S has biases which lead him to test left and square as the appropriate values of the attributes. If the sorting or categorizing performance only is used as the criterion of achievement, all three Ss will achieve equal performance, yet each started out testing different hypotheses. The implication is that the greater the amount of redundancy in concept displays, the more rapid the solution, because different hypotheses may be used to reach the appropriate solution. The expectation works out in practice (e.g., Bourne & Haygood, 1959).

Functional fixedness. One of the few early systematic workers in the area of problem solving was N. R. F. Maier at the University of Michigan. One of the problem situations he developed has been rather widely employed by other investigators and is known as the two-string problem. Two strings are suspended from the ceiling of a room at such a distance apart that S cannot hold on to one and still reach the other, but he is asked to tie the ends of the strings together. A number of objects, such as a pair of pliers, are made available for use in the solution. By tying an object to the end of one string, S can swing this as a pendulum, catching it as he holds on to the other string. In most of the work by subsequent Es, a pictorial method of presenting the problem has been used. Short of giving S some fairly direct hints on the solution, not much can be done to facilitate the solution of this problem (e.g., Duncan, 1961; Maltzman, Belloni, & Fishbein, 1964). However, it has proved a useful device for studying functional fixedness which we class here as a form of stimulus dominance.

In the initial part of an experiment by Adamson and Taylor (1954) Ss were given practice in constructing an electrical circuit from a drawing. Half of the Ss completed the circuit by using a switch, half by using a relay. Following this preliminary work, the Ss were given the two-string problem. Among the objects available, only the switch and the relay were heavy enough to serve as the weight for the pendulum. The question these Es asked was which of the two objects would be used for the solution, the one that had been used in constructing the electrical circuit or the one which had not been used. Earlier work by other investigators (Birch & Rabinowitz, 1951) had shown that in such a situation S will use as a pendulum weight the object which had *not* been used to construct the circuit. If S had used the switch to construct the circuit, he would most likely use the relay as

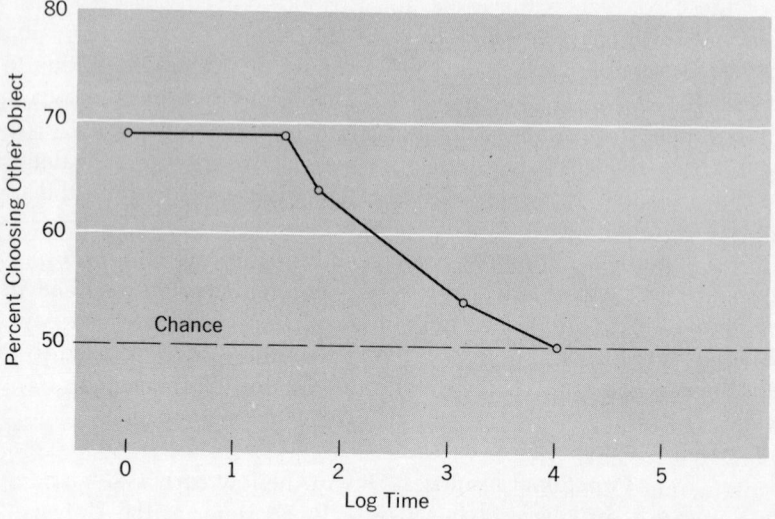

Fig. 14-4. Change in stimulus dominance as a function of time. Data from Adamson and Taylor (1954).

a pendulum; if he had used the relay for the circuit, he would use the switch for the pendulum. It was as if having used the object for one purpose, that purpose remained dominant so that the other, by default, became most frequently used as the pendulum. Adamson and Taylor asked whether this dominance changed as a function of the time between obtaining the experience in building the electrical circuit and the time S was tested on the two-string problem. Five different groups represented five different intervals, namely, 1 min., 30 min., 1 hr., 1 day, and 1 week.

The results are plotted (Fig. 14-4) in terms of the percentage of Ss using as a pendulum the device *not* used (other object) to construct the electrical circuit. Since across all Ss each object was used equally often in constructing the circuit, frequency of use of the other object for the pendulum above 50 percent indicates functional fixedness or the effect of stimulus dominance in not using the object as a pendulum if it had previously been used in the circuit. For the first two time intervals, the values are equivalent (69 percent) indicating that there was a stimulus-dominance effect initially. There is a fall for the three remaining periods so that at one week there is no indication that the use of the objects in the circuits had any effect on the choice of objects for the pendulum. Just why such "forgetting" should occur is not clear, although Adamson and Taylor interpret it as being due, most likely, to a form of retroactive inhibition.

ROLE OF MEMORY

The solution of any problem depends upon the availability of all information pertinent to the solution. Availability does not always mean that solution will be achieved, but it is a prerequisite. There are anecdotes about great thinkers who cram their heads with all facts pertinent to a problem and then trace out various implications of these facts. The use of pencil and paper for recording the relevant facts is a more customary procedure since it guarantees that none of the facts will be overlooked. When we examine a problem-solving situation which has any degree of complexity, we arrive at a conclusion that memory may play a critical role in the solution and is important for two reasons. First, we may not remember all relevant facts in a situation as presented by the stimuli, and second, we may try solutions that we have tried in the past because we forget having tried them. We will examine four approaches to the problem which emphasize these two aspects of memory in varying degrees.

Availability of concept instances. Concept formation studies, particularly those using geometrical forms, often present S with a series of cards or displays (instances), one after the other. Several studies have shown that if S is allowed to keep all previously presented instances in front of him so that he can reinspect them if necessary, he attains the concept more quickly than if all previously presented instances are withdrawn. The illustrative study we will consider evaluates the matter in a less gross fashion.

Bourne, Goldstein, and Link (1964) used six dimensions in presenting their geometrical forms, each dimension having two values. The dimensions were color, size, texture, number, border, and form. For the problem of interest here, three of the dimensions were irrelevant, and S acquired a three-value conjunctive concept based on the other three dimensions. The E presented S one card at a time, and within 15 sec. after each presentation he instructed S to verbalize a guess about the concept. When S had stated the correct concept for four successive cards, the concept was said to have been acquired. The E told S as each card was presented whether it was a positive or a negative instance of the concept. There were six groups of Ss, the conditions for the groups differing only in terms of the number of previous cards, 0, 1, 2, 3, 4, or 5, allowed to remain for S's inspection. With the zero condition, of course, each card was removed after S had stated his guess about the concept. At the other extreme, the 5-card condition, S always had before him not only the card being shown at the moment but also the last five cards shown.

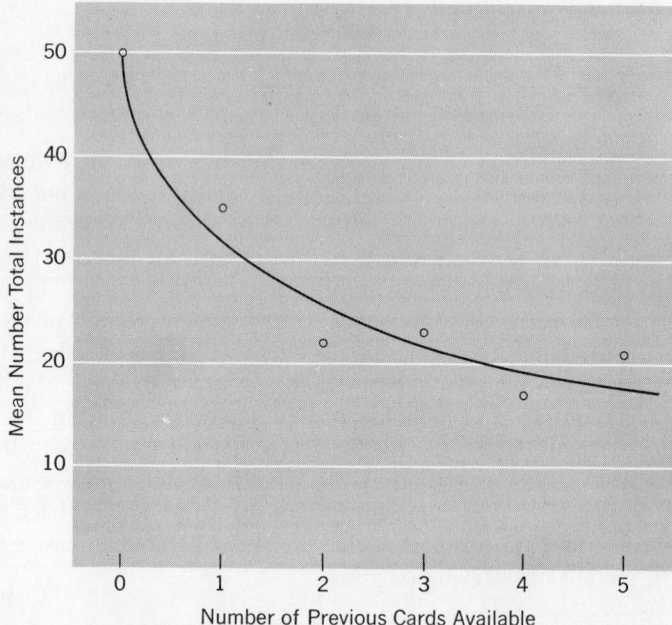

Fig. 14-5. Number of instances to learn concepts as a function of number of previously presented instances available. Estimated from Bourne, Goldstein, and Link (1964).

The mean total instances or cards required to attain the concept is shown in Fig. 14-5. Although the relationship is not linear, as there is an increase in the number of previously presented cards remaining available, there is an increase in the speed of solution. It may be noted that the difference in rate of solution (measured in terms of number of cards) varies from about 50 at one extreme to 20 at the other—a large difference in an absolute sense.

Contiguity of concept instances. As an indirect means of studying the role of memory, the contiguity of concept instances may be varied. For the illustrative experiment we turn to Schulz, Miller, and Radtke (1963), who used the sense-impression responses to stimuli as discussed earlier in the chapter. There were 24 different words in the list. These represented four instances of six different concepts (*round, small, white, smelly, soft, big*). Maximum contiguity of stimuli was obtained by presenting all four instances of a given concept successively, followed by four instances of another concept. Each instance was presented for 4 sec. with S instructed to guess the appropriate sense-impression response. At the other extreme of contiguity, one or more instances of one concept always intervened between presentations of any two instances of another. With medium contiguity, two instances of a given concept always appeared successively with the two other instances separated by one or more instances of another concept. The list of 24 items was presented for 12 trials. The contiguity was manipulated within each list—a mixed list with reference to this variable. That is, the items were so arranged that two of the concepts had high contiguity, two, medium, and two, low. With 36 Ss, 72 concepts would be learned at each level of contiguity since each S was given two at each level. We may consider the results in terms of the number of the 72 concepts which were attained within the 12 trials given, where the attainment of a concept is defined as giving the correct sense impressions to all four instances of a concept on the same trial. These values were 68, 57, and 45, for high, medium, and low contiguity, respectively. Clearly, the higher the contiguity, the more rapid the recognition of the concepts.

How does contiguity work on the memory factor? Assume that two stimuli for the concept "small" are *closet* and *germ*. Assume further that when S sees *closet*, he responds with "dark" and is told he is "wrong." If *germ* follows immediately, and if S responds correctly with "small," he can very likely remember that the preceding stimulus word was *closet* and that he responded incorrectly to it; he can test 'in his mind" whether or not "small" would fit *closet*. On the other hand, if two or three other instances fell between the presentation of *closet* and *germ*, he might not remember what the stimulus word was on which he had been wrong earlier and could not, therefore, test whether "small" would fit it. In short, high contiguity of stimuli to be related reduces the likelihood of interference from intervening stimuli. Recognition that two "things" are related requires that the identical response to both be contiguous. With serial presentation of successive stimuli, high contiguity of related stimuli decreases the role of memory in making the responses to the two stimuli contiguous.

Preparation for thought. D. M. Johnson of Michigan State University has contributed a series of papers dealing with preparation for thought. His analysis emphasizes that there must be a certain acquisition or assimilation of material (a preparation) before S attempts to solve a problem. The material relevant to solution must be examined, synthesized, or processed by S before he turns to the problem as such. In keeping with this analysis, a simple device has been used to measure preparation time and solution time independently. When S is ready for a given problem, he pushes a button which illuminates a card in the left compartment of a two-compartment box. This card presents the problem material, and S, in light of the general instructions, is allowed as much time as necessary to assimilate it or process it as he wishes. When this stage is completed, S presses another button illuminating the right compartment, and the light in the left compartment goes out. On a card in the right compartment is a number of alternative solutions from which S must choose what he believes to be the appropriate solution to the problem that was included in the material presented in the left compartment. By this technique, the material presented in the left compartment must be carried in memory if solution is to be attained.

A specific illustration will show how this works. For a certain class of problems, S is instructed that all the words presented in the left compartment describe a particular object. The words might be *flat, readable, descriptive,* and *gummed,* and the alternatives in the right compartment, *map, book, label, paper,* and *globe.* By appropriate timing devices, E can measure the preparation time independently from solution time and determine what variables influence each stage independently. In one study (Johnson, Lincoln, & Hall, 1961) the number of descriptive words presented in the left compartment was varied from 3 through 11—at the one extreme, only three words were used to describe an object named in the right compartment, and at the other, 11 words were used to describe the object. These Es found that preparation time increased directly as the number of descriptive words increased but that solution time remained constant. In other conditions S was allowed to switch back to the left compartment if he was unable to arrive at a solution. The number of such switchbacks increased somewhat as the number of descriptive words in the left compartment increased, suggesting a failure in memory. Such an increase in switchbacks was more marked as S was given series of numbers of increasing length in the left compartment and had to "solve" the problem by finding a like series of numbers among several series in the right compartment.

Irrelevent dimensions. When a display for studying concept formation is presented to S, the rate of solution is dependent upon the number of irrelevant dimensions involved if the number of relevant dimensions is held constant. More particularly, as the number of irrelevant dimensions increases, time to solve increases. There is nothing magical about this; as the number of irrelevant dimensions increases, the number of possible combinations of dimensions to be tested increases. However, the increase in difficulty of correctly identifying the concept does not increase in the linear manner to be expected if the critical factor is only the number of different hypotheses to be tested as the number of irrelevant dimensions increases. Rather, difficulty increases disproportionately; for example, the difference in the increase in difficulty between three and four irrelevant dimensions is less than the increase between four and five irrelevant dimensions (Archer, Bourne, & Brown, 1955). The function appears to be positively accelerated. The reason for this, as suggested by these investigators, is that S forgets which particular hypotheses he has tested in the past and proceeds to test them again.

We have seen, from various avenues of approach (Dominowski [1965] gives further evidence), that memory factors may loom strong in problem solving. We can, of course, arrange our situations in order to minimize the influence of forgetting. To do so is in accordance with experimental progress to be made in isolating the subprocess involved in overall problem solving.

CONCLUDING COMMENTS

In the first edition of this book, published in 1949, the following statement appeared:

Probably the most telling revelation of the current status of research on thinking is the fact that during the last five years less than a score of truly experimental studies have been published in standard journals.

In preparing the present chapter the writer's worktable and desk were piled high with journals, all containing at least one experimental study on thinking or concept formation or problem solving, and the most frequent were journals published during the last four years. It was not unusual to find a single monthly issue of a journal containing a half dozen experimental reports dealing with the area covered in this chapter. Our sampling of these studies has been limited to those using relatively simple tasks and to those in which the more potent variables were manipulated. We saw that some of the phenomena of problem solving are directly related to the problem-solving efforts of the experimentalist.

We are sometimes led to believe that acts of creation, discovery, or invention are beyond the bounds of study. One who is judged truly creative is sometimes believed to possess skills or traits that are not compounded of the traits and skills which we all possess in varying amounts. Exceptional creativity is said to be a unique trait, and the trait sometimes takes on the attribute of mysticism. However, the roles which accident and trial-and-error play in creative acts cannot be gainsaid, as Campbell (1960) has so forcefully argued. Accidental discoveries and trial-and-error efforts lying behind problem solutions or creative acts are in turn correlated with another dimension, namely, the time spent in trying to solve problems or the time spent trying to make discoveries. Any of the experiments we reported in this chapter may be used to support this proposition. Furthermore, if one studies the biographies of the men of science who have made important discoveries or solved critical problems (e.g., Roe, 1951), one trait possessed by these men stands out above all others—the capacity to work long hours each day, day after day. There is nothing mystical about this trait.

SUMMARY

We have examined one important aspect of problem-solving behavior, an aspect that is prompting most of the contemporary research. Given a problem-solving situation, what is the nature and source of the responses produced by the situation, and what are the variables which govern their production? The chapter was organized around four main factors, factors which taken as a whole provide some answers to the question.

1. Associative frequency is a factor that is important when problems involve words.

2. Solution frequency represents a transfer of methods of solution that were successful in the past but which may impede solution of the problem of the moment.

3. Stimulus dominance is a tendency for the stimuli in a situation to bias our responses in certain directions when the stimuli have equal probabilities of entering into the solution.

4. Memory, which is fallible, allows us to forget relevant facts and to forget that we have attempted certain solutions.

REFERENCES

ABBOTT, D. W., & PRICE, L. E. Stimulus generalization of the conditioned eyelid response to structurally similar nonsense syllables. *J. exp. Psychol.*, 1964, *68*, 368-371.

ADAMS, J. A. A source of decrement in psychomotor performance. *J. exp. Psychol.*, 1955, *49*, 390-394.

ADAMS, J. A. The second facet of forgetting: A review of warm-up decrement. *Psychol. Bull.*, 1961, *58*, 257-273.

ADAMS, J. A., STENSON, H. H., & HUMES, J. M. Monitoring of complex visual displays—II. Effects of visual load and response complexity on human vigilance. *Human Factors*, 1961, *3*, 213-221.

ADAMSON, R. E. Inhibitory set in problem solving as related to reinforcement learning. *J. exp. Psychol.*, 1959, *58*, 280-282.

ADAMSON, R. E., & TAYLOR, D. W. Functional fixedness as related to elapsed time and to set. *J. exp. Psychol.*, 1954, *47*, 122-126.

ALBRIGHT, L. E., BORRESEN, C. R., & MARX, M. H. Reactive inhibition as a function of same-hand and opposite-hand intertrial activity. *J. exp. Psychol.*, 1956, *51*, 353-357.

ALEXANDER, L. T., KEPNER, C. H., & TREGOE, B. B. The effectiveness of knowledge of results in a military system-training program. *J. appl. Psychol.*, 1962, *46*, 202-211.

AMMONS, C. H. Task for the study of perceptual learning and performance variables. *Percept. mot. Skills*, 1955, *5*, 11-14.

AMMONS, R. B. Effects of knowledge of performance: A survey and tentative theoretical formulation. *J. gen. Psychol.*, 1956, *54*, 279-299.

AMSEL, A. The role of frustrative nonreward in non-continuous reward situations. *Psychol. Bull.*, 1958, *55*, 102-119.

AMSEL, A. Frustrative nonreward in partial reinforcement and discrimination learning: Some recent history and a theoretical extension. *Psychol. Rev.*, 1962, *69*, 306-328.

ANDREWES, C. H. The complex epidemiology of respiratory virus infections. *Science*, 1964, *146*, 1274-1277.

ANNETT, J. Learning a pressure under conditions of immediate and delayed knowledge of results. *Quart. J. exp. Psychol.*, 1959, *11*, 3-15.

ARCHER, E. J. Effect of distribution of practice on a component skill of rotary pursuit tracking. *J. exp. Psychol.*, 1958, *56*, 427-436.

ARCHER, E. J. Re-evaluation of the meaningfulness of all possible CVC trigrams. *Psychol. Monogr.*, 1960, *74*, No. 10.

ARCHER, E. J. Concept identification as a function of obviousness of relevant and irrelevant information. *J. exp. Psychol.*, 1962, *63*, 616-620.

ARCHER, E. J., & BOURNE, L. E., JR. Inverted alphabet printing as a function of intertrial rest and sex. *J. exp. Psychol.*, 195 , 52, 322-328.

ARCHER, E. J., BOURNE, L. E., JR., & BROWN, F. G. Concept identification as a function of irrelevant information and instructions. *J. exp. Psychol.*, 1955, 49, 153-164.

ARNOULT, M. D. Stimulus predifferentiation: Some generalizations and hypotheses. *Psychol. Bull.*, 1957, 54, 339-350.

BADDELEY, A. D. Language habits, S-R compatibility, and verbal learning. *Amer. J. Psychol.*, 1964, 77, 463-468.

BAHRICK, H. P. Retention curves: Facts or artifacts? *Psychol. Bull.*, 1964, 61, 188-194.

BAKAN, P. Effect of set and work speed on time estimation. *Percept. mot. Skills*, 1955, 5, 147-148.

BAKAN, P. Extraversion-introversion and improvement in an auditory vigilance task. *Brit. J. Psychol.*, 1959, 50, 325-332.

BAKER, K. E., & DUDEK, F. J. Scaling line-lengths with a modification of the constant-sum method. *Amer. J. Psychol.*, 1957, 70, 81-86.

BARNES, J. M., & UNDERWOOD, B. J. "Fate" of first-list associations in transfer theory. *J. exp. Psychol.*, 1959, 58, 97-105.

BARTLETT, N. R. A comparison of manual reaction times as measured by three sensitive indices. *Psychol. Rec.*, 1963, 13, 51-56.

BASTIAN, J. Associative factors in verbal transfer. *J. exp. Psychol.*, 1961, 62, 70-79.

BATTIG, W. F. Some factors affecting performance on a word-formation problem. *J. exp. Psychol.*, 1957, 54, 96-104.

BATTIG, W. F., & BRACKETT, H. R. Transfer from verbal-discrimination to paired-associate learning: II. Effects of intralist similarity, method, and percentage occurrence of response members. *J. exp. Psychol.*, 1963, 65, 507-514.

BATTIG, W. F., & SPERA, A. J. Rated association values of numbers from 0-100. *J. verb. Learn. verb. Behav.*, 1962, 1, 200-202.

BATTIG, W. G., BROWN, S. C., & SCHILD, M. E. Serial position and sequential associations in serial learning. *J. exp. Psychol.*, 1964, 67, 449-457.

BECK, R. C. On secondary reinforcement and shock termination. *Psychol. Bull.*, 1961, 58, 28-45.

BECK, S. B. Eyelid conditioning as a function of CS intensity, UCS intensity, and Manifest Anxiety scale score. *J. exp. Psychol.*, 1963, 66, 429-438.

BEILIN, H., & HORN, R. Transition probability effects in anagram problem solving. *J. exp. Psychol.*, 1962, 63, 514-518.

BELL, C. R., & PROVINS, K. A. Relation between physiological responses to environmental heat and time judgments. *J. exp. Psychol.*, 1963, 66, 572-579.

BERGUM, B. O., & LEHR, D. J. Vigilance performance as a function of interpolated rest. *J. appl. Psychol.*, 1962, 46, 425-427.

BERGUM, B. O., & LEHR, D. J. Effects of authoritarianism on vigilance performance. *J. appl. Psychol.*, 1963, 47, 75-77.

BERLYNE, D. E. *Conflict, arousal, and curiosity.* New York: McGraw-Hill, 1960.

BERLYNE, D. E., SALAPATEK, P. H., GELMAN, R. S., & ZENER, S. L. Is light increment really rewarding to the rat? *J. comp. physiol. Psychol.*, 1964, 58, 148-151.

BILLS, A. G. Blocking: A new principle of mental fatigue. *Amer. J. Psychol.*, 1931, 43, 230-245.

BILODEAU, E. A., & BILODEAU, I. M. Variation of temporal intervals among critical events in five studies of knowledge of results. *J. exp. Psychol.*, 1958, 55, 603-612.

BILODEAU, E. A., & BILODEAU, I. M. Motor-skills learning. *Annu. Rev. Psychol.*, 1961, 12, 243-280.

BILODEAU, E. A., JONES, M. B., & LEVY, M. C. Long-term memory as a function of retention time and repeated recalling. *J. exp. Psychol.*, 1964, 67, 303-309.

BILODEAU, I. M. Accuracy of a simple positioning response with variation in the number of trials by which knowledge of results is delayed. *Amer. J. Psychol.*, 1956, 69, 434-437.

BILODEAU, I. M., & ROSENQUIST, H. S. Supplementary feedback in rotary-pursuit tracking. *J. exp. Psychol.*, 1964, 68, 53-57.

BINDRA, D., & WAKSBERG, H. Methods and terminology in studies of time estimation. *Psychol. Bull.*, 1956, 53, 155-159.

BIRCH, H. G., & RABINOWITZ, H. S. The negative effect of previous experience on productive thinking. *J. exp. Psychol.*, 1951, 41, 121-125.

BITTERMAN, M. E. Techniques for the study of learning in animals: Analysis and classification. *Psychol. Bull.*, 1962, 59, 81-93.

BOBBITT, J. M. An experimental study of the phenomenon of closure as a threshold function. *J. exp. Psychol.*, 1942, 30, 273-294.

BOLLES, R. C. A psychophysical study of hunger in the rat. *J. exp. Psychol.*, 1962, 63, 387-390.

BONEAU, C. A., & AXELROD, S. Work decrement and reminiscence in pigeon operant responding. *J. exp. Psychol.*, 1962, 64, 352-354.

BORING, E. G. *Sensation and perception in the history of experimental psychology.* New York: Appleton-Century-Crofts, 1942.

BOURNE, L. E., JR., & HAYGOOD, R. C. The role of stimulus redundancy in concept identification. *J. exp. Psychol.*, 1959, 58, 232-238.

BOURNE, L. E., JR., GOLDSTEIN, S., & LINK, W. E. Concept learning as a function of availability of previously presented information. *J. exp. Psychol.*, 1964, 67, 439-448.

BOUSFIELD, W. A., & PUFF, C. R. Clustering as a function of response dominance. *J. exp. Psychol.*, 1964, 67, 76-79.

BOWER, G. H. Drive level and preference between two incentives. *Psychon. Sci.*, 1964, 1, 131-132.

BRIDGER, W. H., & MANDEL, I. J. Abolition of the PRE by instructions in GSR conditioning. *J. exp. Psychol.*, 1965, 69, 476-482.

BRIGGS, G. E. Acquisition, extinction, and recovery functions in retroactive inhibition. *J. exp. Psychol.*, 1954, 47, 285-293.

BROADBENT, D. E. Some effects of noise on visual performance. *Quart. J. exp. Psychol.*, 1954, 6, 1-5.

BROADBENT, D. E. *Perception and communication.* New York: Pergamon Press, 1958.

BROADBENT, D. E., & GREGORY, M. Donders' B- and C-reactions and S-R compatibility. *J. exp. Psychol.*, 1962, 63, 575-578.

BROGDEN, W. J. Contiguous conditioning. *J. exp. Psychol.*, 1962, *64*, 172-176.

BROWN, J. Some tests of the decay theory of immediate memory. *Quart. J. exp. Psychol.*, 1958, *10*, 12-21.

BROWN, J. S., BILODEAU, E. A., & BARON, M. R. Bidirectional gradients in the strength of a generalized voluntary response to stimuli on a visual-spatial dimension. *J. exp. Psychol.*, 1951, *41*, 52-61.

BROWN, J. S., CLARKE, F. R., & STEIN, L. A new technique for studying spatial generalization with voluntary responses. *J. exp. Psychol.*, 1958, 55, 359-362.

BROWN, R. H. Visual sensitivity to differences in velocity. *Psychol. Bull.*, 1961, 58, 89-103.

BRUNING, J. L., & SCHAPPE, R. H. Type of interpolated activity and short-term memory. *Psychol. Rep.*, 1965, *16*, 925-929.

BRUSH, F. R., GOODRICH, K. P., TEGHTSOONIAN, R., & EISMAN, E. H. Dependence of learning (habit) in the runway on deprivation under three levels of sucrose incentive. *Psychol. Rep.*, 1963, *12*, 375-384.

BUGELSKI, B. R. An attempt to reconcile unlearning and reproductive inhibition explanations of proactive inhibition. *J. exp. Psychol.*, 1948, 38, 670-682.

BUGELSKI, B. R. Presentation time, total time, and mediation in paired-associate learning. *J. exp. Psychol.*, 1962, *63*, 409-412.

BUGELSKI, B. R., & RICKWOOD, J. Presentation time, total time, and mediation in paired-associate learning: Self-pacing. *J. exp. Psychol.*, 1963, *65*, 616-617.

CAMPBELL, B. A., & CICALA, G. A. Studies of water deprivation in rats as a function of age. *J. comp. physiol. Psychol.*, 1962, 55, 763-768.

CAMPBELL, B. A., & PICKLEMAN, J. R. The imprinting object as a reinforcing stimulus. *J. comp. physiol. Psychol.*, 1961, *54*, 592-596.

CAMPBELL, D. T. Blind variation and selective retention in creative thought as in other knowledge processes. *Psychol. Rev.*, 1960, *67*, 380-400.

CHOWN, S. M. Rigidity—a flexible concept. *Psychol. Bull.*, 1959, *56*, 195-223.

CHURCH, R. M. The effects of competition on reaction-time and palmar skin conductance. *J. abnorm. soc. Psychol.*, 1962, *65*, 32-40.

CHURCH, R. M. The varied effects of punishment on behavior. *Psychol. Rev.*, 1963, *70*, 369-402.

CHURCH, R. M., & CAMP, D. S. Change in reaction-time as a function of knowledge of results. *Amer. J. Psychol.*, 1965, *78*, 102-106.

CIEUTAT, V. J. Association indices for 446 randomly selected English monosyllables, bisyllables, and trisyllables. *J. verb. Learn. verb. Behav.*, 1963, *2*, 176-185.

CLAUSEN, J. An evaluation of experimental methods of time judgments. *J. exp. Psychol.*, 1950, *40*, 756-761.

COHEN, B. H. An investigation of recoding in free recall. *J. exp. Psychol.*, 1963, *65*, 368-376.

COHEN, J. C., & MUSGRAVE, B. S. Effect of meaningfulness on cue selection in verbal paired-associate learning. *J. exp. Psychol.*, 1964, *68*, 284-291.

COHEN, W. Apparent movement of simple figures in the *Ganzfeld. Percept. mot. Skills*, 1958, *8*, 32.

COLEMAN, E. B. Verbal concept learning as a function of instructions and dominance level. *J. exp. Psychol.*, 1964, *68*, 213-214.

COOK, J. O., & BROWN, J. E. Familiarity and novelty of stimulus and response terms in paired-associate learning. *Psychol. Rep.*, 1963, *12*, 535-545.

COOPER, L. M. Operant behavior as a function of stimulus complexity. *J. comp. physiol. Psychol.*, 1963, *56*, 857-862.

CORCORAN, D. W. J. Doubling the rate of signal presentation in a vigilance task during sleep deprivation. *J. appl. Psychol.*, 1963, *47*, 412-415.

CORNSWEET, T. N. The staircase-method in psychophysics. *Amer. J. Psychol.*, 1962, *75*, 485-491.

CORSO, J. F. A theoretico-historical review of the threshold concept. *Psychol. Bull.*, 1963, *60*, 356-370.

CORSO, J. F., & COHEN, A. Methodological aspects of auditory threshold measurements. *J. exp. Psychol.*, 1958, *55*, 8-12.

COTTON, J. W., JENSEN, G. D., & LEWIS, D. J. Spontaneous recovery interval as a factor in reacquisition of T maze behavior. *J. exp. Psychol.*, 1962, *63*, 555-562.

CRAFTS, L. W. Transfer as related to number of common elements. *J. gen. Psychol.*, 1935, *13*, 147-158.

CRAIK, K. H., & SARBIN, T. R. Effect of covert alterations of clock rate upon time estimations and personal tempo. *Percept. mot. Skills*, 1963, *16*, 597-610.

CROSS, H. A., & BOYER, W. N. Influence of amount of reward in a complex learning situation. *Psychol. Rep.*, 1964, *14*, 427-432.

CROUSE, J. H., & DUNCAN, C. P. Verbal concept sorting as a function of response dominance and sorting method. *J. verb. Learn. verb. Behav.*, 1963, *2*, 480-484.

DALLETT, K. M. Practice effects in free and ordered recall. *J. exp. Psychol.*, 1963, *66*, 65-71.

D'AMATO, M. R., SCHIFF, D., & JAGODA, H. Resistance to extinction after varying amounts of discriminative or nondiscriminative instrumental training. *J. exp. Psychol.*, 1962, *64*, 526-532.

DAVENPORT, J. W. The interaction of magnitude and delay of reinforcement in spatial discrimination. *J. comp. physiol. Psychol.*, 1962, *55*, 267-273.

DAY, R. H. The effects of repeated trials and prolonged fixation on error in the Müller-Lyer figure. *Psychol. Monogr.*, 1962, *76*, No. 14.

DEAN, M. G., & KAUSLER, D. H. Degree of first-list learning and stimulus meaningfulness as related to transfer in the A-B, C-B paradigm. *J. verb. Learn. verb. Behav.*, 1964, *3*, 330-334.

DEBOLD, R. C., MILLER, N. E., & JENSEN, D. D. Effect of strength of drive determined by a new technique for appetitive classical conditioning of rats. *J. comp. physiol. Psychol.*, 1965, *59*, 102-108.

DEESE, J. Influence of inter-item associative strength upon immediate free recall. *Psychol. Rep.*, 1959, *5*, 305-312.

DEESE, J. Frequency of usage and number of words in free recall: The role of association. *Psychol. Rep.*, 1960, *7*, 337-344.

DEMBER, W. N. *Psychology of perception.* New York: Holt, Rinehart and Winston, 1961.

DENENBERG, V. H., & KLINE, N. J. Stimulus intensity *versus* critical periods: A test of two hypotheses concerning infantile stimulation. *Canad. J. Psychol.*, 1964, *18*, 1-5.

DENNER, B., WAPNER, S., McFARLAND, J. H., & WERNER, H. Rhythmic activity and the perception of time. *Amer. J. Psychol.*, 1963, 76, 287-292.

DENNY, M. R., ALLARD, M., HALL, E., & ROKEACH, M. Supplementary report: Delay of knowledge of results, knowledge of task, and intertrial interval. *J. exp. Psychol.*, 1960, 60, 327.

DESIDERATO, O. Generalization of conditioned suppression. *J. comp. physiol. Psychol.*, 1964, 57, 434-437.

DETAMBEL, M. H., & STOLUROW, L. M. Probability and work as determiners of multichoice behavior. *J. exp. Psychol.*, 1957, 53, 73-81.

DEWOLFE, R. K. S., & DUNCAN, C. P. Time estimation as a function of level of behavior of successive tasks. *J. exp. Psychol.*, 1959, 58, 153-158.

DIMOND, S. J. The structural basis of timing. *Psychol. Bull.*, 1964, 62, 348-350.

DODWELL, P. C. Further evidence on learning without performance in a water maze. *Psychon. Sci.*, 1964, 1, 23-24.

DOEHRING, D. G. Accuracy and consistency of time-estimation by four methods of reproduction. *Amer. J. Psychol.*, 1961, 74, 27-35.

DOMINOWSKI, R. L. Role of memory in concept learning. *Psychol. Bull.*, 1965, 63, 271-280.

DOMINOWSKI, R. L., & DUNCAN, C. P. Anagram solving as a function of bigram frequency. *J. verb. Learn. verb. Behav.*, 1964, 3, 321-325.

DRAZIN, D. H. Effects of foreperiod, foreperiod variability, and probability of stimulus occurrence on simple reaction time. *J. exp. Psychol.*, 1961, 62, 43-50.

DUFORT, R. H. The rat's adjustment to 23-, 47-, and 71-hour food-deprivation schedules. *Psychol. Rep.*, 1964, 14, 663-669.

DULANY, D. E., JR., & O'CONNELL, D. C. Does partial reinforcement dissociate verbal rules and the behavior they might be presumed to control? *J. verb. Learn. verb. Behav.*, 1963, 2, 361-372.

DUNCAN, C. P. On the similarity between reactive inhibition and neural satiation. *Amer. J. Psychol.*, 1956, 69, 227-235.

DUNCAN, C. P. Visual and kinesthetic components of reactive inhibition. *Amer. J. Psychol.*, 1957, 70, 616-619.

DUNCAN, C. P. Recent research on human problem solving. *Psychol. Bull.*, 1959, 56, 397-429.

DUNCAN, C. P. Description of learning to learn in human subjects. *Amer. J. Psychol.*, 1960, 73, 108-114.

DUNCAN, C. P. Attempts to influence performance on an insight problem. *Psychol. Rep.*, 1961, 9, 35-42.

DUNCAN, C. P. Learning to learn in response-discovery and in paired-associate lists. *Amer. J. Psychol.*, 1964, 77, 367-379.

DU PREEZ, P. D. The persistence of some effects of handling in infancy on the behavior of the adult rat. *Quart. J. exp. Psychol.*, 1964, 16, 147-155.

DYAL, J. A. Latent extinction as a function of number and duration of pre-extinction exposures. *J. exp. Psychol.*, 1962, 63, 98-104.

EBBINGHAUS, H. *Memory: A contribution to experimental psychology.* Trans. by Ruger, H. A., and Bussenius, Clara E. New York: Teachers College, Columbia Univer., Bureau of Publications, 1913.

EBENHOLTZ, S. M. Serial learning: Position learning and sequential associations. *J. exp. Psychol.*, 1963, *66*, 353-362.

ECKSTRAND, G. A., & WICKENS, D. D. Transfer of perceptual set. *J. exp. Psychol.*, 1954, *47*, 274-278.

EDWARDS, W. Subjective probabilities inferred from decisions. *Psychol. Rev.*, 1962, *69*, 109-135.

EGAN, J. P., GREENBERG, G. Z., & SCHULMAN, A. I. Operating characteristics, signal detectability, and the method of free response. *J. acoust. Soc. Amer.*, 1961, *33*, 993-1007.

EGGER, M. D., & MILLER, N. E. When is a reward reinforcing?: An experimental study of the information hypothesis. *J. comp. physiol. Psychol.*, 1963, *56*, 132-137.

EHRENFREUND, D., & BADIA, P. Response strength as a function of drive level and pre- and postshift incentive magnitude. *J. exp. Psychol.*, 1962, *63*, 468-471.

EISLER, H. Magnitude scales, category scales, and Fechnerian integration. *Psychol. Rev.*, 1963, *70*, 243-253.

EKSTRAND, B., & UNDERWOOD, B. J. Paced versus unpaced recall in free learning. *J. verb. Learn. verb. Behav.*, 1963, *2*, 288-290.

ELLSON, D. G. Quantitative studies of the interaction of simple habits: I. Recovery from specific and generalized effects of extinction. *J. exp. Psychol.*, 1938, *23*, 339-358.

EPSTEIN, W., ROCK, I., & ZUCKERMAN, C. B. Meaning and familiarity in associative learning. *Psychol. Monogr.*, 1960, *74*, No. 4.

ERICKSON, R. L. Relational isolation as a means of producing the von Restorff effect in paired-associate learning. *J. exp. Psychol.*, 1963, *66*, 111-119.

ESTES, W. K. Learning theory and the new "mental chemistry." *Psychol. Rev.*, 1960, *67*, 207-223.

ESTES, W. K. Probability learning. In A. W. Melton (Ed.) *Categories of human learning*. New York: Academic Press, 1964.

EYSENCK, H. J. Reminiscence, drive, and personality theory. *J. abnorm. soc. Psychol.*, 1956, *53*, 328-333.

FALK, J. L., & BINDRA, D. Judgment of time as a function of serial position and stress. *J. exp. Psychol.*, 1954, *47*, 279-282.

FEATHER, B. W. Semantic generalization of classically conditioned responses: A review. *Psychol. Bull.*, 1965, *63*, 425-441.

FERSTER, C. B., & SKINNER, B. F. *Schedules of reinforcement*. New York: Appleton-Century-Crofts, 1957.

FESTINGER, L. Studies in decision: I. Decision-time, relative frequency of judgment and subjective confidence as related to physical stimulus difference. *J. exp. Psychol.*, 1943, *32*, 291-306.

FILLENBAUM, S. Contextual effects in judgment as a function of restrictions in response-language. *Amer. J. Psychol.*, 1963, *76*, 103-109.

FINGER, F. W., & SPELT, D. K. The illustration of the horizontal-vertical illusion. *J. exp. Psychol.*, 1947, *37*, 243-250.

FITTS, P. M. Perceptual-motor skill learning. In A. W. Melton (Ed.), *Categories of human learning*. New York: Academic Press, 1964.

FITTS, P. M., & SWITZER, G. Cognitive aspects of information processing: I. The familiarity of S-R sets and subsets. *J. exp. Psychol.*, 1962, *63*, 321-329.

FITTS, P. M., PETERSON, J. R., & WOLPE, G. Cognitive aspects of information processing: II. Adjustment to stimulus redundancy. *J. exp. Psychol.*, 1963, *65*, 423-432.

FOLEY, P. J., & HUMPHRIES, M. Blocking in serial simple reaction tasks. *Canad. J. Psychol.*, 1962, *16*, 128-137.

FOWLER, H., & TRAPOLD, M. A. Escape performance as a function of delay of reinforcement. *J. exp. Psychol.*, 1962, *63*, 464-467.

FOWLER, H., & WISCHNER, G. J. Discrimination performance as affected by problem difficulty and shock for either the correct or incorrect response. *J. exp. Psychol.*, 1965, *69*, 413-418.

FRAISSE, P. *The psychology of time.* New York: Harper & Row, 1963.

FRAISSE, P., & VAUTREY, P. The influence of age, sex, and specialized training on the vertical-horizontal illusion. *Quart. J. exp. Psychol.*, 1956, *8*, 114-120.

FRANKENHAEUSER, M. *Estimation of time: An experimental study.* Stockholm: Almqvist & Wiksell, 1959.

FRANKMANN, J. P., & ADAMS, J. A. Theories of vigilance. *Psychol. Bull.*, 1962, *59*, 257-272.

FRIEDMAN, H. Wave-length generalization as a function of spacing of test stimuli. *J. exp. Psychol.*, 1963, *65*, 334-338.

FROMER, R. The effect of several shock patterns on the acquisition of the secondary drive of fear. *J. comp. physiol. Psychol.*, 1962, *55*, 142-144.

GAGNÉ, R. M. Problem solving. In A. W. Melton (Ed.), *Categories of human learning.* New York: Academic Press, 1964.

GALANTER, E. The direct measurement of utility and subjective probability. *Amer. J. Psychol.*, 1962, *75*, 208-220.

GALANTER, E., & MESSICK, S. The relation between category and magnitude scales of loudness. *Psychol. Rev.*, 1961, *68*, 363-372.

GARCIA, J., KIMELDORF, D. J., & HUNT, E. L. The use of ionizing radiation as a motivating stimulus. *Psychol. Rev.*, 1961, *68*, 383-395.

GARDNER, R. A., & RUNQUIST, W. N. Acquisition and extinction of problem-solving set. *J. exp. Psychol.*, 1958, *55*, 274-277.

GARDNER, R. W., & LONG, R. I. Errors of the standard and illusion effects with the inverted-T. *Percept. mot. Skills*, 1960, *10*, 47-54. (a)

GARDNER, R. W., & LONG, R. I. Errors of the standard and illusion effects with the L-shaped figures. *Percept. mot. Skills*, 1960, *10*, 107-109. (b)

GARNER, W. R. Context effects and the validity of loudness scales. *J. exp. Psychol.*, 1954, *48*, 218-224.

GARNER, W. R. Half-loudness judgments without prior stimulus context. *J .exp. Psychol.*, 1958, *55*, 482-485.

GARNER, W. R. The development of context effects in half-loudness judgments. *J. exp. Psychol.*, 1959, *58*, 212-219.

GARNER, W. R. *Uncertainty and structure as psychological concepts.* New York: Wiley, 1962.

Gaydos, H. F. Sensitivity in the judgment of size by finger-span. *Amer. J. Psychol.*, 1958, *71*, 557-562.

Gibson, E. J. A systematic application of the concepts of generalization and differentiation to verbal learning. *Psychol. Rev.*, 1940, *47*, 196-229.

Glanzer, M. Grammatical category: A rote learning and word association analysis. *J. verb. Learn. verb. Behav.*, 1962, *1*, 31-41.

Glaze, J. A. The association value of non-sense syllables. *J. genet. Psychol.*, 1928, *35*, 255-269.

Gleitman, H., & Herman, M. M. Replication report: Latent learning in a T maze after shock in one end box. *J. exp. Psychol.*, 1962, *64*, 646.

Gleitman, H., & Jung, L. Retention in rats: The effect of proactive interference. *Science*, 1963, *142*, 1683-1684.

Glickman, S. E. Perseverative neural processes and consolidation of the memory trace. *Psychol. Bull.*, 1961, *58*, 218-233.

Glucksberg, S. The influence of strength of drive on functional fixedness and perceptual recognition. *J. exp. Psychol.*, 1962, *63*, 36-41.

Golann, S. E. Psychological study of creativity. *Psychol. Bull.*, 1963, *60*, 548-565.

Goldiamond, I., & Hawkins, W. F. Vexierversuch: The log relationship between word-frequency and recognition obtained in the absence of stimulus words. *J. exp. Psychol.*, 1958, *56*, 457-463.

Goldstein, H., & Spence, K. W. Performance in differential conditioning as a function of variation in magnitude of reward. *J. exp. Psychol.*, 1963, *65*, 86-93.

Goldstone, S., Boardman, W. K., & Lhamon, W. T. Intersensory comparisons of temporal judgments. *J. exp. Psychol.*, 1959, *57*, 243-248.

Gordon, W. M., & Berlyne, D. E. Drive-level and flexibility in paired-associate nonsense-syllable learning. *Quart. J. exp. Psychol.*, 1954, *6*, 181-185.

Gottsdanker, R., Broadbent, L., & Van Sant, C. Reaction time to single and to first signals. *J. exp. Psychol.*, 1963, *66*, 163-167.

Grant, D. A. Classical and operant conditioning. In A. W. Melton (Ed.), *Categories of human learning*. New York: Academic Press, 1964.

Grant, D. A., & Schneider, D. E. Intensity of the conditioned stimulus and strength of conditioning: I. The conditioned eyelid response to light. *J. exp. Psychol.*, 1948, *38*, 690-696.

Grice, G. R., & Hunter, J. J. Stimulus intensity effects depend upon the type of experimental design. *Psychol. Rev.*, 1964, *71*, 247-256.

Grice, G. R., & Reynolds, B. Effect of varying amounts of rest on conventional and bilateral transfer "reminiscence." *J. exp. Psychol.*, 1952, *44*, 247-252.

Grice, G. R., & Saltz, E. The generalization of an instrumental response to stimuli varying in the size dimension. *J. exp. Psychol.*, 1950, *40*, 702-708.

Guilford, J. P. *Psychometric methods*. New York: McGraw-Hill, 1954.

Hamilton, C. E. The relationship between length of interval separating two learning tasks and performance on the second task. *J. exp. Psychol.*, 1950, *40*, 613-621.

Harcum, E. R. Verbal transfer of overlearned forward and backward associations. *Amer. J. Psychol.*, 1953, *66*, 622-625.

HARLOW, H. F. The formation of learning sets. *Psychol. Rev.*, 1949, *56*, 51-65.

HAVENS, L. L., & FOOTE, W. E. The effect of competition on visual duration threshold and its independence of stimulus frequency. *J. exp. Psychol.*, 1963, *65*, 6-11.

HEBERT, J. A., & KRANTZ, D. L. Transposition: A reevaluation. *Psychol. Bull.*, 1965, *63*, 244-247.

HELSON, H. Adaptation-level as frame of reference for prediction of psychophysical data. *Amer. J. Psychol.*, 1947, *60*, 1-29.

HELSON, H. *Adaptation-level theory.* New York: Harper & Row, 1964.

HELSON, H., & BEVAN, W. An investigation of variables in judgment of relative area. *J. exp. Psychol.*, 1964, *67*, 335-341.

HELSON, H., & STEGER, J. A. On the inhibitory effects of a second stimulus following the primary stimulus to react. *J. exp. Psychol.*, 1962, *64*, 201-205.

HENDERSON, R. L. Remote action potentials at the moment of response in a simple reaction-time situation. *J. exp. Psychol.*, 1952, *44*, 238-241.

HENDRY, D. P., & RASCHE, R. H. Analysis of a new nonnutritive positive reinforcer based on thirst. *J. comp. physiol. Psychol.*, 1961, *54*, 477-483.

HICKS, J. M. Zero-point scaling of social objects as affected by scaling method and context. Unpublished doctoral dissertation, Northwestern Univer., 1962.

HILGARD, E. R. *Theories of learning.* New York: Appleton-Century-Crofts, 1948.

HILL, W. F. Activity as an autonomous drive. *J. comp. physiol. Psychol.*, 1956, *49*, 15-19.

HILL, W. F., & SPEAR, N. E. Choice between magnitudes of reward in a T maze. *J. comp. physiol. Psychol.*, 1963, *56*, 723-726.

HILL, W. F., COTTON, J. W., & CLAYTON, K. N. Effect of reward magnitude, percentage of reinforcement, and training method on acquisition and reversal in a T maze. *J. exp. Psychol.*, 1962, *64*, 81-86.

HOLLAND, H. C. Massed practice and reactive inhibition, reminiscence, and disinhibition in the spiral after-effect. *Brit. J. Psychol.*, 1963, *54*, 261-272.

HOMZIE, M. J., & ROSS, L. E. Runway performance following a reduction in the concentration of a liquid reward. *J. comp. physiol. Psychol.*, 1962, *55*, 1029-1033.

HOROWITZ, L. M. Associative matching and intralist similarity. *Psychol. Rep.*, 1962, *10*, 751-757.

HORTON, D. L., & KJELDERGAARD, P. M. An experimental analysis of associative factors in mediated generalizations. *Psychol. Monogr.*, 1961, *75*, No. 11.

HOVLAND, C. I. Experimental studies in rote-learning theory: III. Distribution of practice with varying speeds of syllable presentation. *J. exp. Psychol.*, 1938, *25*, 622-633.

HOWES, D. H., & SOLOMON, R. L. A note on McGinnies' "Emotionality and perceptual defense." *Psychol. Rev.*, 1950, 57, 229-234.

HOWES, D. H., & SOLOMON, R. L. Visual duration threshold as a function of word-probability. *J. exp. Psychol.*, 1951, *41*, 401-410.

HULL, C. L. *Principles of behavior.* New York: Appleton-Century-Crofts, 1943.

HUMPHRIES, M., & MCINTYRE, J. An attempt to find a locus of temporary work decrement in pursuit rotor performance. *Percept. mot. Skills*, 1963, *17*, 397-398.

HUNT, W. A., & VOLKMANN, J. The anchoring of an affective scale. *Amer. J. Psychol.*, 1937, *49*, 88-92.

HUNTER, I. M. L. The solving of five-letter anagram problems. *Brit. J. Psychol.*, 1959, *50*, 193-206.

IMAI, S., & GARNER, W. R. Discriminability and preference for attributes in free and constrained classification. *J. exp. Psychol.*, 1965, *69*, 596-608.

IRION, A. L. The relation of 'set' to retention. *Psychol. Rev.*, 1948, *55*, 336-341.

JACOBSON, A. L. Learning in flatworms and annelids. *Psychol. Bull.*, 1963, *60*, 74-94.

JAHNKE, J. C., & DUNCAN, C. P. Reminiscence and forgetting in motor learning after extended rest intervals. *J. exp. Psychol.*, 1956, *52*, 273-282.

JARRARD, L. E. The role of visual cues in the performance of ergographic work. *J. exp. Psychol.*, 1960, *60*, 57-63.

JENKINS, H. M. The effect of signal-rate on performance in visual monitoring. *Amer. J. Psychol.*, 1958, *71*, 647-661.

JENKINS, J. G., & DALLENBACH, K. M. Oblivescence during sleep and waking. *Amer. J. Psychol.*, 1924, *35*, 605-612.

JENKINS, J. J. Mediated associations: Paradigms and situations. In C. N. Cofer & B. Musgrave (Eds.), *Verbal behavior and learning*. New York: McGraw-Hill, 1963.

JENKINS, J. J. Stimulus "fractionation" in paired-associate learning. *Psychol. Rep.*, 1963, *13*, 409-410.

JENSEN, A. R. Spelling errors and the serial-position effect. *J. educ. Psychol.*, 1962, *53*, 105-109.

JENSEN, G. D. Preference for bar pressing over "freeloading" as a function of number of rewarded presses. *J. exp. Psychol.*, 1963, *65*, 451-454.

JENSEN, G. D., & COTTON, J. W. Complete generalization to stimuli of different areas in a Grice-type apparatus. *Psychol. Rep.*, 1963, *12*, 647-650.

JOHNSON, D. M. *The psychology of thought and judgment*. New York: Harper & Row, 1955.

JOHNSON, D. M., LINCOLN, R. E., & HALL, E. R. Amount of material and time of preparation for solving problems. *J. Psychol.*, 1961, *51*, 457-471.

JOHNSON, R. C. Meaningfulness of eighty English words. *Psychol. Rep.*, 1961, *9*, 431.

JOHNSON, R. E. Meaningfulness and retention of a single paired associate. *Psychol. Rep.*, 1964, *14*, 951-957.

JOHNSON, W. Language and speech hygiene: An application of general semantics. *Gen. Sem. Monogr.*, 1939, No. 1.

JUNG, J. Transfer of training as a function of degree of first-list learning. *J. verb. Learn. verb. Behav.*, 1962, *1*, 197-199.

JUNG, J. Effects of response meaningfulness (m) on transfer of training under two different paradigms. *J. exp. Psychol.*, 1963, *65*, 377-384.

KALISH, H. I. The relationship between discriminability and generalization: A re-evaluation. *J. exp. Psychol.*, 1958, *55*, 637-644.

KALISH, H. I., & HABER, A. Generalization: I. Generalization gradients from single and multiple stimulus points. II. Generalization of inhibition. *J. exp. Psychol.*, 1963, *65*, 176-181.

KAMENETZKY, J. Contrast and convergence effects in ratings of foods. *J. appl. Psychol.*, 1959, *43*, 47-52.

KAMIN, L. J. Backward conditioning and the conditioned emotional response. *J. comp. physiol. Psychol.*, 1963, *56*, 517-519.

KAMIN, L. J., & SCHAUB, R. E. Effects of conditioned stimulus intensity on the conditioned emotional response. *J. comp. physiol. Psychol.*, 1963, *56*, 502-507.

KAPPAUF, W. E., & PAYNE, M. C. Performance-decrement at an observer-paced task. *Amer. J. Psychol.*, 1959, *72*, 443-446.

KAPPAUF, W. E., & POWE, W. E. Performance decrement at an audio-visual checking task. *J. exp. Psychol.*, 1959, *57*, 49-56.

KARLIN, L. Reaction time as a function of foreperiod duration and variability. *J. exp. Psychol.*, 1959, *58*, 185-191.

KARLIN, L., & MORTIMER, R. G. Effect of verbal, visual, and auditory augmenting cues on learning a complex motor skill. *J. exp. Psychol.*, 1963, *65*, 75-79.

KAUFMAN, H., SMITH, J., & ZEAMAN, D. Tests of the generality of two empirical equations for motor learning. *Percept. mot. Skills.*, 1962, *15*, 91-100.

KAUFMAN, L., & ROCK, I. The moon illusion. I. *Science*, 1962, *136*, 953-961.

KEHOE, J. Effects of prior and interpolated learning on retention in pigeons. *J. exp. Psychol.*, 1963, *65*, 537-545.

KENDLER, H. H., & KARASIK, A. D. Concept formation as a function of competition between response produced cues. *J. exp. Psychol.*, 1958, *55*, 278-283.

KENDLER, T. S. Concept formation. *Annu. Rev. Psychol.*, 1961, *12*, 447-472.

KEPPEL, G. Facilitation in short- and long-term retention of paired associates following distributed practice in learning. *J. verb. Learn. verb. Behav.*, 1964, *3*, 91-111.

KEPPEL, G. Problems of method in the study of short-term memory. *Psychol. Bull.*, 1965, *63*, 1-13.

KEPPEL, G., & SAUFLEY, W. H., JR. Serial position as a stimulus in serial learning. *J. verb. Learn. verb. Behav.*, 1964, *3*, 335-343.

KIENTZLE, M. J. Properties of learning curves under varied distributions of practice. *J. exp. Psychol.*, 1946, *36*, 187-211.

KIMBLE, G. A. Transfer of work inhibition in motor learning. *J. exp. Psychol.*, 1952, *43*, 391-392.

KIMBLE, G. A. *Hilgard and Marquis' conditioning and learning.* New York: Appleton-Century-Crofts, 1961.

KING, D. J. On the accuracy of written recall: A scaling and factor analytic study. *Psychol. Rec.*, 1960, *10*, 113-122.

KINTZ, B. L., DELPRATO, D. J., METTEE, D. R., PERSONS, C. E., & SCHAPPE, R. H. The experimenter effect. *Psychol. Bull.*, 1965, *63*, 223-232.

KLEINSMITH, L. J., & KAPLAN, S. Interaction of arousal and recall interval in nonsense syllable paired-associate learning. *J. exp. Psychol.*, 1964, *67*, 124-126.

KLEMMER, E. T. Time uncertainty in simple reaction time. *J. exp. Psychol.*, 1956, *51*, 179-184.

KLUGMAN, S. F. Retention of affectively toned material by normals and neurotics. *J. abnorm. soc. Psychol.*, 1956, *53*, 321-327.

KOONCE, J. M., CHAMBLISS, D. J., & IRION, A. L. Long-term reminiscence in the pursuit-rotor habit. *J. exp. Psychol.*, 1964, *67*, 498-500.

KOPPENAAL, R. J., & O'HARA, G. N. The combined effect of retroaction and pro-action. *Canad. J. Psychol.*, 1962, *16*, 96-105.

KOTT, M. G. Learning and retention of words of sexual and nonsexual meaning. *J. abnorm. soc. Psychol.*, 1955, *50*, 378-382.

KRAELING, D. Analysis of amount of reward as a variable in learning. *J. comp. physiol. Psychol.*, 1961, *54*, 560-565.

KRANTZ, D. L., & CAMPBELL, D. T. Separating perceptual and linguistic effects of context shifts upon absolute judgments. *J. exp. Psychol.*, 1961, *62*, 35-42.

KRASNER, L. Studies of the conditioning of verbal behavior. *Psychol. Bull.*, 1958, *55*, 148-170.

KRUEGER, W. C. F. The influence of amount limits and time limits upon the rate of work. *J. appl. Psychol.*, 1937, *21*, 113-118.

KÜNNAPAS, T. M. Influence of frame size on apparent length of a line. *J. exp. Psychol.*, 1955, *50*, 168-170.

KÜNNAPAS, T. M. The vertical-horizontal illusion and the visual field. *J. exp. Psychol.*, 1957, *53*, 405-407.

KÜNNAPAS, T. M. Influence of head inclination on the vertical-horizontal illusion. *J. Psychol.*, 1958, *46*, 179-185.

KÜNNAPAS, T. M. The vertical-horizontal illusion in artificial visual fields. *J. Psychol.*, 1959, *47*, 41-48.

L'ABATE, L. Transfer of learning with differences in association value and in mani-fest anxiety. *Amer. J. Psychol.*, 1962, *75*, 251-258.

LABERGE, D. Generalization gradients in a discrimination situation. *J. exp. Psychol.*, 1961, *62*, 88-94.

LANG, P. J., GEER, J., & HNATIOW, M. Semantic generalization of conditioned autonomic responses. *J. exp. Psychol.*, 1963, *65*, 552-558.

LAPPIN, J. S., & ERIKSEN, C. W. Inhibition of a simple visual reaction time by a second stimulus: A failure to replicate. *Psychon. Sci.*, 1964, *1*, 293-294.

LAVERY, J. J. Retention of a skill following training with and without instructions to retain. *Percept. mot. Skills*, 1964, *18*, 275-281.

LAVERY, J. J., & SUDDON, F. H. Retention of simple motor skills as a function of the number of trials by which KR is delayed. *Percept. mot. Skills*, 1962, *15*, 231-237.

LEVITT, E. E. A methodological study of the preparation of connected verbal stimuli for quantitative memory experiments. *J. exp. Psychol.*, 1956, *52*, 33-38.

LEWIS, D. *Quantitative methods in psychology.* New York: McGraw-Hill, 1960.

LEWIS, D. J. Partial reinforcement: A selective review of the literature since 1950. *Psychol. Bull.*, 1960, *57*, 1-28.

LEWIS, D. J., & MAHER, B. A. Neural consolidation and electroconvulsive shock. *Psychol. Rev.*, 1965, *72*, 225-239.

LEWIS, M. Some nondecremental effects of effort. *J. comp. physiol. Psychol.*, 1964, *57*, 367-372.

LIPSITT, L. P., & LOLORDO, V. M. Interactive effect of stress and stimulus general-ization on children's oddity learning. *J. exp. Psychol.*, 1963, *66*, 210-214.

LLOYD, V. V. A comparison of critical fusion frequencies for different areas in the fovea and periphery. *Amer. J. Psychol.*, 1952, *65*, 346-357.

LOGAN, F. A. *Incentive.* New Haven: Yale Univer. Press, 1960.

LOGAN, F. A. Decision making by rats: Delay versus amount of reward. *J. comp. physiol. Psychol.*, 1965, *59*, 1-12.

LONGO, N., KLEMPAY, S., & BITTERMAN, M. E. Classical appetitive conditioning in the pigeon. *Psychon. Sci.*, 1964, *1*, 19-20.

LUCE, D. R. A threshold theory for simple detection experiments. *Psychol. Rev.*, 1963, *70*, 61-79.

LUCHINS, A. S. Mechanization in problem solving. *Psychol. Monogr.*, 1942, *54*, No. 6.

MCALLISTER, W. R., & MCALLISTER, D. E. Postconditioning delay and intensity of shock as factors in the measurement of acquired fear. *J. exp. Psychol.*, 1962, *64*, 110-116.

MCALLISTER, W. R., & MCALLISTER, D. E. Increase over time in the stimulus generalization of acquired fear. *J. exp. Psychol.*, 1963, *65*, 576-582.

MCCORMACK, P. D. Performance in a vigilance task as a function of length of interstimulus interval. *Canad. J. Psychol.*, 1960, *14*, 265-268.

MCCULLERS, J. C. Type of associative interference as a factor in verbal paired-associate learning. *J. verb. Learn. verb. Behav.*, 1965, *4*, 12-16.

MCGARVEY, H. R. Anchoring effects in the absolute judgment of verbal materials. *Arch. Psychol.*, N. Y., 1943, *39*, No. 281.

MCGINNIES, E. Emotionality and perceptual defense. *Psychol. Rev.*, 1949, *56*, 244-251.

MCGUIGAN, F. J. The effect of precision, delay, and schedule of knowledge of results on performance. *J. exp. Psychol.*, 1959, *58*, 79-84.

MCGUIGAN, F. J. The experimenter: A neglected stimulus object. *Psychol. Bull.*, 1963, *60*, 421-428.

MCGUIRE, W. J. A multiprocess model for paired-associate learning. *J. exp. Psychol.*, 1961, *62*, 335-347.

MACKAY, D. M. Psychophysics of perceived intensity: A theoretical basis for Fechner's and Stevens' laws. *Science*, 1963, *139*, 1213-1216.

MCKEACHIE, W. J. Lipstick as a determiner of first impressions of personality: An experiment for the general psychology course. *J. soc. Psychol.*, 1952, *36*, 241-244.

MACKINTOSH, N. J. The effect of attention on the slope of generalization gradients. *Brit. J. Psychol.*, 1965, *56*, 87-94.

MCMAHON, R. R., & GAMES, P. A. Adaptation to cyclic food deprivation in the acquisition of an instrumental running response. *Psychol. Rep.*, 1964, *14*, 755-758.

MADISON, H. L. Experimental extinction as a function of number of reinforcements. *Psychol. Rep.*, 1964, *14*, 647-650.

MALTZMAN, I., & MORRISETT, L., JR. Different strengths of set in the solution of anagrams. *J. exp. Psychol.*, 1952, *44*, 242-246.

MALTZMAN, I., BELLONI, M., & FISHBEIN, M. Experimental studies of associative variables in originality. *Psychol. Monogr.*, 1964, *78*, No. 3.

MALTZMAN, I., EISMAN, E., BROOKS, L. O., & SMITH, W. M. Task instructions for anagrams following different task instructions and training. *J. exp. Psychol.*, 1956, *51*, 418-420.

MANDLER, G. From association to structure. *Psychol. Rev.*, 1962, *69*, 415-427.

MANDLER, G., COWAN, P. A., & GOLD, C. Concept learning and probability matching. *J. exp. Psychol.*, 1964, *67*, 514-522.

MARX, M. H., & KNARR, F. A. Long-term development of reinforcing properties of a stimulus as a function of temporal relationship to food reinforcement. *J. comp. physiol. Psychol.*, 1963, *56*, 546-550.

MAYZNER, M. S., & TRESSELT, M. E. Anagram solution times: A function of letter order and word frequency. *J. exp. Psychol.*, 1958, *56*, 376-379.

MAYZNER, M. S., & TRESSELT, M. E. A comparison of judgmental and associational techniques in developing verbal concept formation materials. *J. Psychol.*, 1961, *51*, 331-342.

MAYZNER, M. S., TRESSELT, M. E., & HELBOCK, H. An exploratory study of mediational responses in anagram problem solving. *J. Psychol.*, 1964, *57*, 263-274.

MECHANIC, A. The responses involved in the rote learning of verbal materials. *J. verb. Learn. verb. Behav.*, 1964, *3*, 30-36.

MEDNICK, S. A. The associative basis of the creative process. *Psychol. Rev.*, 1962, *69*, 220-232.

MEDNICK, S. A., & FREEDMAN, J. L. Stimulus generalization. *Psychol. Bull.*, 1960, *57*, 169-200.

MELTON, A. W. Implications of short-term memory for a general theory of memory. *J. verb. Learn. verb. Behav.*, 1963, *2*, 1-21.

MELTON, A. W., & IRWIN, J. M. The influence of degree of interpolated learning on retroactive inhibition and the overt transfer of specific responses. *Amer. J. Psychol.*, 1940, *53*, 173-203.

MERIKLE, P. M., & BATTIG, W. F. Transfer of training as a function of experimental paradigm and meaningfulness. *J. verb. Learn. verb. Behav.*, 1963, *2*, 485-488.

MEYER, D. R., & MILES, R. C. Intralist-interlist relations in verbal learning. *J. exp. Psychol.*, 1953, *45*, 109-115.

MILLER, G. A. What is information measurement? *Amer. Psychologist*, 1953, *8*, 3-11.

MILLER, N. E. Liberalization of basic S-R concepts: Extensions to conflict behavior, motivation, and social learning. In S. Koch (Ed.), *Psychology: A study of a science*. Vol. 2. New York: McGraw-Hill, 1959.

MINARD, J. G. Response-bias interpretation of "perceptual defense": A selective review and evaluation of recent research. *Psychol. Rev.*, 1965, *72*, 74-88.

MINUCCI, P. K., & CONNORS, M. M. Reaction time under three viewing conditions: Binocular, dominant eye, and nondominant eye. *J. exp. Psychol.*, 1964, *67*, 268-275.

MOLTZ, H. Imprinting: Empirical basis and theoretical significance. *Psychol. Bull.*, 1960, *57*, 291-314.

MOLTZ, H. Imprinting: An epigenetic approach. *Psychol. Rev.*, 1963, *70*, 123-138.

MORGAN, J. J. B. Effect of non-rational factors on inductive reasoning. *J. exp. Psychol.*, 1944, *34*, 159-168.

MORIKAWA, Y. Functions of stimulus and response in paired-associate verbal learning. *Psychologia*, 1959, *2*, 41-56.

MORIN, R. E., & FORRIN, B. Response equivocation and reaction time. *J. exp. Psychol.*, 1963, *66*, 30-66.

MOUNTJOY, P. T. Effects of exposure time and intertrial interval upon decrement to the Müller-Lyer illusion. *J. exp. Psychol.*, 1958, *56*, 97-102.

MOUNTJOY, P. T. Intrasession decrement and intersession recovery to the Müller-Lyer figure. *Percept. mot. Skills*, 1961, *13*, 51-57.

MOUNTJOY, P. T. Effects of self-instruction, information and misinformation upon decrement to the Müller-Lyer figure. *Psychol. Rec.*, 1965, *15*, 7-14.

MOYER, K. E., & KORN, J. H. Effect of UCS intensity on the acquisition and extinction of an avoidance response. *J. exp. Psychol.*, 1964, *67*, 352-359.

MUECHER, H., & UNGEHEUER, H. Meterological influence on reaction time, flicker fusion frequency, job accidents, and use of medical treatment. *Percept. mot. Skills*, 1961, *12*, 163-168.

MUELLER, C., & MCGILL, W. Theories in sensory psychology. In M. H. Marx (Ed.), *Theories in contemporary psychology*. New York: Macmillan, 1963.

MURDOCK, B. B., JR. "Backward" learning in paired associates. *J. exp. Psychol.*, 1956, *51*, 213-215.

MURDOCK, B. B., JR. The immediate retention of unrelated words. *J. exp. Psychol.*, 1960, *60*, 222-234.

MURDOCK, B. B., JR. Proactive inhibition in short term memory. *J. exp. Psychol.*, 1964, *68*, 184-189.

MYERS, J. L. Secondary reinforcement: A review of recent experimentation. *Psychol. Bull.*, 1958, *55*, 284-301.

NAKAMURA, C. Y., & ANDERSON, N. H. Avoidance conditioning in wheel box and shuttle box. *Psychol. Rep.*, 1964, *14*, 327-334.

NEISSER, U. Decision-time without reaction-time: Experiments in visual scanning. *Amer. J. Psychol.*, 1963, *76*, 376-385.

NEWMAN, S. E., & SALTZ, E. Effects of contextual cues on learning from connected discourse. *Amer. J. Psychol.*, 1960, *73*, 587-592.

NEWTON, J. M., & WICKENS, D. D. Retroactive inhibition as a function of temporal position of the interpolated learning. *J. exp. Psychol.*, 1956, *51*, 149-154.

NICKERSON, R. S. Response times for "same"-"different" judgments. *Percept. mot. Skills*, 1965, *20*, 15-18.

NOBLE, C. E. An analysis of meaning. *Psychol. Rev.*, 1952, *59*, 421-430.

NOBLE, C. E. The meaning-familiarity relationship. *Psychol. Rev.*, 1953, *60*, 89-98.

NOBLE, C. E. Measurements of association value (a), rated associations (a'), and scaled meaningfulness (m') for the 2100 CVC combinations of the English alphabet. *Psychol. Rep.*, 1961, *8*, 487-521.

NOBLE, C. E., & PARKER, G. V. C. The Montana scale of meaningfulness (m). *Psychol. Rep.*, 1960, *7*, 325-331.

NOBLE, C. E., STOCKWELL, F. E., & PRYER, M. W. Meaningfulness (m') and association value (a) in paired-associate syllable learning. *Psychol. Rep.*, 1957, *3*, 441-452.

NOHARA, D. M. Variety of responses and reactive inhibition. *Psychon. Sci.*, 1965, *2*, 301-302.

NOVIN, D., & MILLER, N. E. Failure to condition thirst induced by feeding dry food to hungry rats. *J. comp. physiol. Psychol.*, 1962, *55*, 373-374.

Paivio, A. Learning of adjective-noun paired associates as a function of adjective-noun word order and noun abstractness. *Canad. J. Psychol.*, 1963, *17*, 370-379.

Paivio, A. Abstractness, imagery, and meaningfulness in paired-associate learning. *J. verb. Learn. verb. Behav.*, 1965, *4*, 32-38.

Palermo, D. S., & Jenkins, J. J. *Word association norms*. Minneapolis: Univer. of Minnesota Press, 1964.

Parducci, A. An adaptation-level analysis of ordinal effects in judgment. *J. exp. Psychol.*, 1959, *58*, 239-246.

Parducci, A. Range-frequency compromise in judgment. *Psychol. Monogr.*, 1963, *77*, No. 2.

Parducci, A., & Marshall, L. M. Assimilation vs. contrast in the anchoring of perceptual judgments of weights. *J. exp. Psychol.*, 1962, *63*, 426-437.

Paul, C. Effects of overlearning upon single habit reversal in rats. *Psychol. Bull.*, 1965, *63*, 65-72.

Payton, C. R., & Blake, L. Difference limen for perception of the vertical in monkeys. *Percept. mot. Skills*, 1964, *19*, 455-461.

Peryam, D. R., & Haynes, J. G. Prediction of soldiers' food preferences by laboratory methods. *J. appl. Psychol.*, 1957, *41*, 2-6.

Peterson, L. R., & Peterson, M. J. Short-term retention of individual verbal items. *J. exp. Psychol.*, 1959, *58*, 193-198.

Pierce, J. Some sources of artifact in studies of the tachistoscopic perception of words. *J. exp. Psychol.*, 1963, *66*, 363-370.

Pollack, I., Johnson, L. B., & Knaff, P. R. Running memory span. *J. exp. Psychol.*, 1959, *57*, 137-146.

Pollard, J. S. Hedgehogs and the retroaction theory of forgetting. *Psychol. Rep.*, 1964, *15*, 128-130.

Pollock, W. T., & Chapanis, A. The apparent length of a line as a function of its inclination. *Quart. J. exp. Psychol.*, 1952, *4*, 170-178.

Posner, M. I. Immediate memory in sequential tasks. *Psychol. Bull.*, 1963, *60*, 333-349.

Postman, L. The generalization gradient in recognition memory. *J. exp. Psychol.*, 1951, *42*, 231-235.

Postman, L. The present status of interference theory. In C. N. Cofer (Ed.), *Verbal learning and verbal behavior*. New York: McGraw-Hill, 1961.

Postman, L. Rewards and punishments in human learning. In L. Postman (Ed.), *Psychology in the making*. New York: Knopf, 1962. (a)

Postman, L. Transfer of training as a function of experimental paradigm and degree of first-list learning. *J. verb. Learn. verb. Behav.*, 1962, *1*, 109-118 (b).

Postman, L. One-trial learning. In C. N. Cofer & B. S. Musgrave (Eds.), *Verbal behavior and learning*. New York: McGraw-Hill, 1963.

Postman, L. Short-term memory and incidental learning. In A. W. Melton (Ed.), *Categories of human learning*. New York: Academic Press, 1964. (a)

Postman, L. Studies of learning to learn. II. Changes in transfer as a function of practice. *J. verb. Learn. verb. Behav.*, 1964, *3*, 437-447. (b)

Postman, L., & Adams, P. A. Studies in incidental learning: VIII. The effects of contextual determination. *J. exp. Psychol.*, 1960, *59*, 153-164.

POSTMAN, L., & RILEY, D. A. A critique of Kohler's theory of association. *Psychol. Rev.*, 1957, *64*, 61-72.

POSTMAN, L., & SCHWARTZ, M. Studies of learning to learn. I. Transfer as a function of method of practice and class of verbal materials. *J. verb. Learn. verb. Behav.*, 1964, *3*, 37-49.

POSTMAN, L., & STARK, K. Proactive inhibition as a function of the conditions of transfer. *J. verb. Learn. verb. Behav.*, 1964, *3*, 249-259.

POULTON, E. C., & SIMMONDS, D. C. V. Value of standard and very first variable in judgments of reflectance of grays with various ranges of available numbers. *J. exp. Psychol.*, 1963, *65*, 297-304.

PROMISEL, D. M. Visual target location as a function of number and kind of competing signals. *J. appl. Psychol.*, 1961, *45*, 420-427.

PUBOLS, B. H., JR. Incentive magnitude, learning, and performance in animals. *Psychol. Bull.*, 1960, *57*, 89-115.

RAAB, D. H. Effect of stimulus-duration on auditory reaction-time. *Amer. J. Psychol.*, 1962, *75*, 298-310.

RAAB, D. H., FEHRER, E., & HERSHENSON, M. Visual reaction time and the Broca-Sulzer phenomenon. *J. exp. Psychol.*, 1961, *61*, 193-199.

RATNER, S. C. Worms in a straight alley: Acquisition and extinction or phototaxis. *Psychol. Rec.*, 1964, *14*, 31-36.

RECHTSCHAFFEN, A., & MEDNICK, S. The autokinetic word technique. *J. abnorm. soc. Psychol.*, 1955, *51*, 346.

REID, L. S., & FINGER, F. W. The rat's adjustment to 23-hour food-deprivation cycles. *J. comp. physiol. Psychol.*, 1955, *48*, 110-113.

REID, L. S., LLOYD, K. E., BRACKETT, H. R., & HAWKINS, W. F. Short-term retention as a function of average storage load and average load reduction. *J. exp. Psychol.*, 1961, *62*, 518-522.

RENNER, K. E. Delay of reinforcement: A historical review. *Psychol. Bull.*, 1964, *61*, 341-361.

RETHLINGSHAFER, D., & SHERRER, T. I. Supplementary report: Effect of practice on an illusion. *J. exp. Psychol.*, 1961, *62*, 95-96.

REYNOLDS, B., & ADAMS, J. A. Effect of distribution and shift in distribution of practice within a single training session. *J. exp. Psychol.*, 1953, *46*, 137-145.

REYNOLDS, W. F., PAVLIK, W. B., SCHWARTZ, M. M., & BESCH, N. F. Maze learning by secondary reinforcement without discrimination training. *Psychol. Rep.*, 1963, *12*, 775-781.

RICHARDSON, J. Comparison of S-R and R-S learning of paired-associates. *Psychol. Rep.*, 1960, *7*, 225-228.

RICHARDSON, J., & GROPPER, M. Learning during recall trials. *Psychol. Rep.*, 1964, *15*, 551-560.

ROBINSON, E. The effect of degree of knowledge of results on time estimation. *Psychol. Rec.*, 1963, *13*, 355-360.

ROBINSON, E. S. Work of the integrated organism. In C. A. Murchison (Ed.), *A handbook of general experimental psychology*. Worcester, Mass.: Clark Univer. Press, 1934.

ROBINSON, E. S., & BILLS, A. G. Two factors in the work decrement. *J. exp. Psychol.*, 1926, *9*, 415-443.

Rock, I. The role of repetition in associative learning. *Amer. J. Psychol.*, 1957, *70*, 186-193.

Rock, I., & Kaufman, L. The moon illusion, II. *Science*, 1962, *136*, 1023-1031.

Rocklyn, E. H., Hessert, R. B., & Braun, H. W. Calibrated materials for verbal learning with middle- and old-aged subjects. *Amer. J. Psychol.*, 1957, *70*, 628-630.

Rockway, M. R. Bilateral reminiscence in pursuit-rotor learning as a function of amount of first-hand practice and length of rest. *J. exp. Psychol.*, 1953, *46*, 337-344.

Rockway, M. R., & Duncan, C. P. Pre-recall warming-up in verbal retention. *J. exp. Psychol.*, 1952, *43*, 305-312.

Roe, A. A psychological study of eminent biologists. *Psychol. Monogr.*, 1951, *65*, No. 14.

Rohles, F. H., Jr., Grunzke, M. E., & Reynolds, H. H. Chimpanzee performance during the ballistic and orbital Project Mercury flights. *J. comp. physiol. Psychol.*, 1963, *56*, 2-10.

Rosenbaum, G. Stimulus generalization as a function of level of experimentally induced anxiety. *J. exp. Psychol.*, 1953, *45*, 35-43.

Rosenthal, R. On the social psychology of the psychological experiment: The experimenter's hypothesis as unintended determinant of experimental results. *Amer. Scient.*, 1963, *51*, 268-283.

Runquist, W. N., & Marshall, M. A. Transfer, synonymity, and anticipatory interval in paired-associate verbal learning. *Amer. J. Psychol.*, 1963, *76*, 281-286.

Safren, M. A. Associations, sets, and the solution of word problems. *J. exp. Psychol.*, 1962, *64*, 40-45.

Saltz, E., & Newman, S. E. The von Restorff isolation effect: Test of the intralist association assumption. *J. exp. Psychol.*, 1959, *58*, 445-451.

Salzinger, K. Experimental manipulation of verbal behavior: A review. *J. gen. Psychol.*, 1959, *61*, 65-94.

Saufley, W. H., Jr., & Bilodeau, I. M. Protective self-pacing during learning. *J. exp. Psychol.*, 1963, *66*, 596-600.

Saufley, W. H., Jr., & Bilodeau, I. M. Anticipatory rehearsal in reversed printing. *Percept. mot. Skills*, 1964, *18*, 317-320.

Schaeffer, R. W. Learning without running in a Y-maze. *Psychol. Rec.*, 1964, *14*, 95-99.

Schoer, L. Effect of intralist item similarity on paired-associate learning by learners of high and low verbal ability. *J. educ. Psychol.*, 1963, *54*, 249-252.

Schulz, R. W., & Lovelace, E. A. Mediation in verbal paired-associate learning: The role of temporal factors. *Psychon. Sci.*, 1964, *1*, 95-96.

Schulz, R. W., Miller, R. L., & Radtke, R. C. The role of instance contiguity and dominance in concept attainment. *J. verb. Learn. verb. Behav.*, 1963, *1*, 432-435.

Schwartzbaum, J. S., & Wilson, W. A. Taste-discrimination in the monkey. *Amer. J. Psychol.*, 1961, *74*, 403-409.

Segall, M. H., Campbell, D. T., & Herskovits, M. J. Cultural differences in the perception of geometric illusions. *Science*, 1963, *139*, 769-771.

SHEPARD, R. N., & TEGHTSOONIAN, M. Retention of information under conditions approaching a steady state. *J. exp. Psychol.*, 1961, *62*, 302-309.

SHERIF, M., TAUB, D., & HOVLAND, C. I. Assimilation and contrast effects of anchoring stimuli on judgments. *J. exp. Psychol.*, 1958, *55*, 150-155.

SIDMAN, M. *Tactics of scientific research.* New York: Basic Books, 1960.

SIEGEL, S., & WAGNER, A. R. Extended acquisition training and resistance to extinction. *J. exp. Psychol.*, 1963, *66*, 308-310.

SIEGMAN, A. W. Intercorrelation of some measures of time estimation. *Percept. mot. Skills*, 1962, *14*, 381-382.

SIMON, S. H. Differential prediction and postdiction of win-lose events in a spatial-generalization problem. *J. exp. Psychol.*, 1964, *67*, 342-351.

SIPOWICZ, R. R., WARE, J. R., & BAKER, R. A. The effects of reward and knowledge of results on the performance of a simple vigilance task. *J. exp. Psychol.*, 1962, *64*, 58-61.

SLAMECKA, N. J. Choice reaction-time as a function of meaningful similarity. *Amer. J. Psychol.*, 1963, *76*, 274-280.

SLAMECKA, N. J., & CERASO, J. Retroactive and proactive inhibition of verbal learning. *Psychol. Bull.*, 1960, *57*, 449-475.

SMITH, S. L. Color coding and visual search. *J. exp. Psychol.*, 1962, *64*, 434-440.

SOLOMON, R. L. Punishment. *Amer. Psychol.*, 1964, *19*, 239-253.

SOLOMON, R. L., & POSTMAN, L. Frequency of usage as a determinant of recognition threshold for words. *J. exp. Psychol.*, 1952, *43*, 195-201.

SOLOMON, R. L., & TURNER, L. H. Discriminative classical conditioning in dogs paralyzed by curare can later control discriminative avoidance responses in the normal state. *Psychol. Rev.*, 1962, *69*, 202-219.

SOLOMON, R. L., & WYNNE, L. C. Traumatic avoidance learning: The principles of anxiety conservation and partial irreversibility. *Psychol. Rev.*, 1954, *61*, 353-385.

SPEAR, N. E., EKSTRAND, B. R., & UNDERWOOD, B. J. Association by contiguity. *J. exp. Psychol.*, 1964, *67*, 151-161.

SPENCE, J. T., & LAIR, C. V. Associative interference in the paired-associate learning of remitted and nonremitted schizophrenics. *J. abnorm. Psychol.*, 1965, *70*, 119-122.

SPENCE, K. W. *Behavior theory and conditioning.* New Haven: Yale Univer. Press, 1956.

SPENCE, K. W., HOMZIE, M. J., & RUTLEDGE, E. F. Extinction of the human eyelid CR as a function of the discriminability of the change from acquisition to extinction. *J. exp. Psychol.*, 1964, *67*, 545-552.

SPERLING, S. E. Reversal learning and resistance to extinction: A review of the rat literature. *Psychol. Bull.*, 1965, *63*, 281-297.

SPERLING, S. E., & VALLE, F. P. Handling-gentling as a positive secondary reinforcer. *J. exp. Psychol.*, 1964, *67*, 573-576.

SPIELBERGER, C. D., & LEVIN, S. M. What is learned in verbal conditioning? *J. verb. Learn. verb. Behav.*, 1962, *1*, 125-132.

SPIKER, C. C., & HOLTON, R. B. Associative transfer in motor paired-associate learning as a function of amount of first-task practice. *J. exp. Psychol.*, 1958, *56*, 123-132.

STAR, K. H. Reminiscence, drive, and personality theory: Replication. *Percept. mot. Skills*, 1963, *17*, 377-378.

STEVENS, J. C., MACK, J. D., & STEVENS, S. S. Growth of sensation on seven continua as measured by force of handgrip. *J. exp. Psychol.*, 1960, *59*, 60-67.

STEVENS, S. S. The direct estimation of sensory magnitudes—loudness. *Amer. J. Psychol.*, 1956, *69*, 1-25.

STEVENS, S. S. Adaptation-level vs. the relativity of judgment. *Amer. J. Psychol.*, 1958, *71*, 633-647.

STEVENS, S. S. The psychophysics of sensory function. *Amer. Scient.*, 1960, *48*, 226-253.

STEVENS, S. S. To honor Fechner and repeal his law. *Science*, 1961, *133*, 80-86.

STEVENS, S. S. The surprising simplicity of sensory metrics. *Amer. Psychol.*, 1962, *17*, 29-39.

STEVENS, S. S. Concerning the psychophysical law. *Quart. J. exp. Psychol.*, 1964, *16*, 383-385.

STEVENS, S. S., & GALANTER, E. H. Ratio scales and category scales for a dozen perceptual continua. *J. exp. Psychol.*, 1957, *54*, 377-411.

STEVENS, S. S., & GUIRAO, M. Subjective scaling of length and area and the matching of length to loudness and brightness. *J. exp. Psychol.*, 1963, *66*, 177-186.

STEVENS, S. S., & POULTON, E. C. The estimation of loudness by unpracticed observers. *J. exp. Psychol.*, 1956, *51*, 71-78.

STEVENS, S. S., & TULVING, E. Estimations of loudness by a group of untrained observers. *Amer. J. Psychol.*, 1957, *70*, 600-605.

STEVENS, S. S., & VOLKMANN, J. The relation of pitch to frequency: A revised scale. *Amer. J. Psychol.*, 1940, *53*, 329-353.

STOLZ, S. B., & LOTT, D. F. Establishment in rats of a persistent response producing a net loss of reinforcement. *J. comp. physiol. Psychol.*, 1964, *57*, 147-149.

STROOP, J. R. Studies of interference in serial verbal reactions. *J. exp. Psychol.*, 1935, *18*, 643-662.

SUTHERLAND, N. S., MACKINTOSH, N. J., & WOLFE, J. B. Extinction as a function of the order of partial and consistent reinforcement. *J. exp. Psychol.*, 1965, *69*, 56-59.

SUTTON, S., HAKEREM, G., ZUBIN, J., & PORTNOY, M. The effect of shift of sensory modality on serial reaction-time: A comparison of schizophrenics and normals. *Amer. J. Psychol.*, 1961, *74*, 224-232.

SWETS, J. A., TANNER, W. P., JR., & BIRDSALL, T. G. Decision processes in perception. *Psychol. Rev.*, 1961, *68*, 301-340.

TEICHNER, W. H. Recent studies of simple reaction time. *Psychol. Bull.*, 1954, *51*, 128-149.

THEIOS, J. The partial reinforcement effect sustained through blocks of continuous reinforcement. *J. exp. Psychol.*, 1962, *64*, 1-6.

THOMAS, A. R. Some variables affecting latent extinction. *J. exp. Psychol.*, 1958, *56*, 203-212.

THOMAS, D. R., & BISTEY, G. Stimulus generalization as a function of the number and range of generalization test stimuli. *J. exp. Psychol.*, 1964, *68*, 599-602.

THOMAS, D. R., & HISS, R. H. A test of the "units hypothesis" employing wavelength generalization in human subjects. *J. exp. Psychol.*, 1963, *65*, 59-62.

THOR, D. H. Diurnal variability in time estimation. *Percept. mot. Skills,* 1962, *15,* 451-454.

THORNDIKE, E. L., & LORGE, I. *The teacher's word book of 30,000 words.* New York: Columbia Univer. Press, 1944.

THORNTON, G. R. The effect of wearing glasses upon judgments of personality traits of persons seen briefly. *J. appl. Psychol.,* 1944, *28,* 203-207.

THUNE, L. E. The effect of different types of preliminary activities on subsequent learning of paired-associate material. *J. exp. Psychol.,* 1950, *40,* 423-428.

THURSTONE, L. L., & JONES, L. V. Measuring subjective values. In L. L. Thurstone (Ed.), *The measurement of values.* Chicago: Univer. of Chicago Press, 1959.

THYSELL, R. V., & SCHULZ, R. W. Concept-utilization as a function of the strength of relevant and irrelevant associations. *J. verb. Learn. verb. Behav.,* 1964, *3,* 203-208.

TORGERSON, W. S. *Theory and methods of scaling.* New York: Wiley, 1958.

TRAPOLD, M. A., & FOWLER, H. Instrumental escape performance as a function of the intensity of the noxious stimulation. *J. exp. Psychol.,* 1960, *60,* 323-326.

TULVING, E. Subjective organization in free recall of "unrelated" words. *Psychol. Rev.,* 1962, *69,* 344-354. (a)

TULVING, E. The effect of alphabetical subjective organization on memorizing unrelated words. *Canad. J. Psychol.,* 1962, *16,* 185-191. (b)

TUNE, G. S. Response preferences: A review of some relevant literature. *Psychol. Bull.,* 1964, *61,* 286-302.

TURNER, E. D., SANTOS, J. F., & SOLLEY, C. M. Search-discrimination time and task difficulty. *Percept. mot. Skills,* 1962, *15,* 719-724.

TWEDT, H. M., & UNDERWOOD, B. J. Mixed vs. unmixed lists in transfer studies. *J. exp. Psychol.,* 1959, *58,* 111-116.

UMEMOTO, T. Paired-associate learning as a function of similarity: Semantic similarity between stimulus- and response-items. *Amer. J. Psychol.,* 1962, *75,* 85-93.

UMEMOTO, T., & HILGARD, E. R. Paired-associate learning as a function of similarity: Common stimulus and response items within the list. *J. exp. Psychol.,* 1961, *62,* 97-104.

UNDERWOOD, B. J. Associative transfer in verbal learning as a function of response similarity and degree of first-list learning. *J. exp. Psychol.,* 1951, *42,* 44-53.

UNDERWOOD, B. J. *Psychological research.* New York: Appleton-Century-Crofts, 1957.

UNDERWOOD, B. J. Distributed practice on the Tsai-Partington numbers test. *Percept. mot. Skills,* 1961, *12,* 325-326.

UNDERWOOD, B. J. Degree of learning and the measurement of forgetting. *J. verb. Learn. verb. Behav.,* 1964, *3,* 112-129.

UNDERWOOD, B. J. False recognition produced by implicit verbal responses. *J. exp. Psychol.,* 1965, *70,* 122-129.

UNDERWOOD, B. J. Individual and group predictions of item difficulty for free learning. *J. exp. Psychol.,* 1966 (in press).

UNDERWOOD, B. J., & RICHARDSON, J. Some verbal materials for the study of concept formation. *Psychol. Bull.,* 1956, *53,* 84-95. (a)

UNDERWOOD, B. J., & RICHARDSON, J. Verbal concept learning as a function of instructions and dominance level. *J. exp. Psychol.,* 1956, *51,* 229-238. (b)

UNDERWOOD, B. J., & SCHULZ, R. W. *Meaningfulness and verbal learning.* Philadelphia: Lippincott, 1960.

UNDERWOOD, B. J., EKSTRAND, B. R., & KEPPEL, G. Studies of distributed practice: XXIII. Variations in response-term interference. *J. exp. Psychol.*, 1964, *68*, 201-212.

VERPLANCK, W. S. The control of the content of conversation: Reinforcement of statements of opinion. *J. abnorm. soc. Psychol.*, 1955, *51*, 668-676.

VERPLANCK, W. S. The operant conditioning of human motor behavior. *Psychol. Bull.*, 1956, *53*, 70-83.

WAGNER, A. R. Sodium amytal and partially reinforced runway performance. *J. exp. Psychol.*, 1963, *65*, 474-477. (a)

WAGNER, A. R. Conditioned frustration as a learned drive. *J. exp. Psychol.*, 1963, *66*, 142-148. (b)

WALLACE, J. Concept dominance, type of feedback, and intensity of feedback as related to concept attainment. *J. educ. Psychol.*, 1964, *55*, 159-166.

WALLACE, W. P. Review of the historical, empirical, and theoretical status of the von Restorff phenomenon. *Psychol. Bull.*, 1965, *63*, 410-424.

WARD, L. B. Reminiscence and rote learning. *Psychol. Monogr.*, 1937, *49*, No. 4.

WARM, J. S., GREENBERG, L. F., & DUBE, C. S., II. Stimulus and motivational determinants in temporal perception. *J. Psychol.*, 1964, *58*, 243-248.

WARREN, R. M. A basis for judgments of sensory intensity. *Amer. J. Psychol.*, 1958, *71*, 675-687.

WARREN, R. M., SERSEN, E. A., & PORES, E. B. A basis for loudness judgments. *Amer. J. Psychol.*, 1958, *71*, 700-709.

WASSERMAN, H. N. The effect of motivation and amount of pre-rest practice upon inhibitory potential in motor learning. *J. exp. Psychol.*, 1951, *42*, 162-172.

WAUGH, N. C. Free versus serial recall. *J. exp. Psychol.*, 1961, *62*, 496-502.

WELLS, H. Effects of transfer and problem structure in disjunctive concept formation. *J. exp. Psychol.*, 1963, *65*, 63-69.

WERBER, M., & KING, D. J. An investigation of the response mechanism of the size-weight illusions. *J. gen. Psychol.*, 1962, *66*, 85-100.

WHITE, S. H. A note on intensity generalization and prothetic scaling. *Psychol. Rev.*, 1962, *69*, 149-155.

WICKELGREN, W. A. Acoustic similarity and retroactive interference in short-term memory. *J. verb. Learn. verb. Behav.*, 1965, *4*, 53-61.

WICKENS, D. D., & CROSS, H. A. Resistance to extinction as a function of temporal relations during sensory preconditioning. *J. exp. Psychol.*, 1963, *65*, 206-211.

WICKENS, D. D., & WICKENS, C. D. A study of conditioning in the neonate. *J. exp. Psychol.*, 1940, *26*, 94-102.

WICKENS, D. D., SCHRODER, H. M., & SNIDE, J. D. Primary stimulus generalization of the GSR under two conditions. *J. exp. Psychol.*, 1954, *47*, 52-56.

WIENER, E. L. Knowledge of results and signal rate in monitoring: A transfer of training approach. *J. appl. Psychol.*, 1963, *47*, 214-222.

WIKE, E. L., & FARROW, B. J. The effects of magnitude of water reward on selective learning and habit reversal. *J. comp. physiol. Psychol.*, 1962, *55*, 1024-1028.

WILLINGHAM, W. W. Interdependence of successive absolute judgments. *J. appl. Psychol.*, 1958, *42*, 416-418.

WINNICK, W. A., & DORNBUSH, R. L. Role of positional cues in serial rote learning. *J. exp. Psychol.*, 1963, *66*, 419-421.

WITMER, L. R. The association value of three-place consonant syllables. *J. genet. Psychol.*, 1935, *47*, 337-360.

WOODWORTH, R. S., & SCHLOSBERG, H. *Experimental psychology*. New York: Holt, Rinehart and Winston, 1954.

WYERS, E. J., PEEKE, H. V. S., & HERZ, M. J. Partial reinforcement and resistance to extinction in the earthworm. *J. comp. physiol. Psychol.*, 1964, *57*, 113-116.

YATES, A. J., & LASZLO, J. I. Learning and performance of extraverts and introverts on the pursuit rotor. *J. pers. soc. Psychol.*, 1965, *1*, 79-84.

YNTEMA, D. B., & TRASK, F. P. Recall as a search process. *J. verb. Learn. verb. Behav.*, 1963, *2*, 65-74.

YOUNG, R. K. A comparison of two methods of learning serial associations. *Amer. J. Psychol.*, 1959, *72*, 554-559.

YOUNG, R. K. Tests of three hypotheses about the effective stimulus in serial learning. *J. exp. Psychol.*, 1962, *63*, 307-313.

YOUTZ, A. C. An experimental evaluation of Jost's laws. *Psychol. Monogr.*, 1941, *53*, No. 1.

ZAHN, T. P., ROSENTHAL, D., & SHAKOW, D. Effects of irregular preparatory intervals on reaction time in schizophrenia. *J. abnorm. soc. Psychol.*, 1963, *67*, 44-52.

Appendix

1000 Random Sequences of Eight Numbers

1	2	3	4	5	6	7	8	9	10
5	4	8	2	3	4	3	8	2	3
4	7	5	1	4	8	1	7	6	4
7	3	6	6	7	7	2	2	4	5
1	6	3	5	6	3	4	3	8	1
6	2	4	4	8	1	8	1	7	7
3	8	1	7	1	6	5	4	5	2
8	1	2	8	2	5	6	5	3	6
2	5	7	3	5	2	7	6	1	8

11	12	13	14	15	16	17	18	19	20
8	5	5	7	5	8	1	4	2	6
6	8	4	6	4	1	3	7	4	3
1	4	1	4	1	4	8	1	8	4
4	2	3	5	2	7	4	3	6	2
3	6	8	1	8	5	6	5	3	8
5	7	7	3	6	6	2	2	1	7
2	1	6	8	3	2	7	6	5	1
7	3	2	2	7	3	5	8	7	5

21	22	23	24	25	26	27	28	29	30
4	8	1	2	8	6	5	5	6	2
2	2	6	6	3	3	1	1	4	1
6	4	7	1	1	5	3	7	8	4
1	3	4	3	7	2	4	4	7	7
8	7	8	5	6	8	8	2	5	3
7	1	5	4	2	1	6	3	1	6
3	5	2	8	5	4	2	6	3	8
5	6	3	7	4	7	7	8	2	5

31	32	33	34	35	36	37	38	39	40
5	5	7	2	7	6	1	6	3	2
2	6	6	7	8	5	6	7	5	1
7	7	8	6	2	3	4	5	4	8
6	8	3	3	4	1	3	4	8	5
8	1	5	4	6	4	8	8	2	6
4	4	2	1	1	2	2	2	6	4
3	3	1	5	5	8	5	1	1	3
1	2	4	8	3	7	7	3	7	7

41	42	43	44	45	46	47	48	49	50
8	2	2	6	7	1	7	6	1	4
2	3	5	4	4	2	3	1	6	1
5	8	4	3	6	6	6	3	3	5
1	6	6	2	8	5	4	4	4	7
7	5	3	8	5	7	5	5	5	6
4	7	1	5	3	8	1	8	2	3
3	4	7	7	1	3	8	7	8	8
6	1	8	1	2	4	2	2	7	2

51	52	53	54	55	56	57	58	59	60
4	1	1	8	3	7	3	3	7	7
8	6	6	2	2	1	6	8	2	2
1	3	4	3	5	8	4	7	4	8
2	8	2	6	6	2	1	5	1	5
3	4	5	5	4	3	8	2	6	1
7	7	3	1	1	5	5	6	8	4
6	2	8	7	7	6	2	1	3	3
5	5	7	4	8	4	7	4	5	6

61	62	63	64	65	66	67	68	69	70
7	2	2	2	6	1	6	5	6	7
3	3	5	1	3	7	7	4	3	3
5	7	6	5	4	6	3	7	2	1
2	4	1	4	7	3	2	8	1	5
8	6	8	3	8	2	4	2	7	4
1	5	4	6	2	5	8	6	5	8
6	8	3	8	1	8	5	1	8	6
4	1	7	7	5	4	1	3	4	2

71	72	73	74	75	76	77	78	79	80
3	3	4	6	8	2	5	7	6	7
2	6	8	1	7	5	4	8	1	2
5	2	7	4	4	7	7	2	7	3
7	5	3	5	3	4	1	4	8	1
4	7	5	8	1	1	3	6	4	4
6	8	1	7	2	6	6	3	2	6
8	4	6	2	5	8	8	5	5	5
1	1	2	3	6	3	2	1	3	8

81	82	83	84	85	86	87	88	89	90
7	2	8	7	6	8	3	3	5	6
5	8	5	5	1	4	1	8	2	5
8	6	2	8	8	1	6	7	3	2
3	7	1	2	4	7	5	5	1	1
2	1	4	4	3	2	4	2	7	8
4	4	3	1	2	6	8	1	8	4
1	5	7	3	5	3	7	4	4	7
6	3	6	6	7	5	2	6	6	3

91	92	93	94	95	96	97	98	99	100
1	7	3	6	6	3	6	4	2	6
8	6	4	3	1	8	1	5	7	3
5	4	7	4	4	5	5	3	8	2
6	5	2	8	8	4	7	8	3	8
7	2	8	5	3	7	4	7	1	4
3	8	1	2	5	2	2	2	5	7
2	3	6	1	7	1	3	6	6	1
4	1	5	7	2	6	8	1	4	5

101	102	103	104	105	106	107	108	109	110
3	5	2	3	1	6	1	5	3	7
5	2	3	6	6	1	5	8	4	6
7	8	5	2	8	5	7	4	6	3
4	6	7	1	5	3	8	7	7	2
2	3	8	8	3	7	3	1	1	8
6	1	1	7	2	2	4	3	2	1
8	4	6	5	4	4	2	6	5	5
1	7	4	4	7	8	6	2	8	4

111	112	113	114	115	116	117	118	119	120
6	4	6	4	5	4	8	7	1	4
7	5	4	1	3	7	4	3	2	3
8	7	3	2	1	1	3	8	4	7
3	1	1	3	7	8	7	2	3	2
5	8	2	5	6	6	2	6	5	6
2	6	8	7	2	2	1	1	8	1
1	3	5	8	4	3	6	4	7	5
4	2	7	6	8	5	5	5	6	8

121	122	123	124	125	126	127	128	129	130
4	2	8	8	2	6	2	8	8	7
3	3	1	1	3	2	1	2	1	8
8	4	6	4	7	4	3	3	3	6
7	7	5	3	1	3	7	1	6	5
1	1	7	7	5	7	5	5	7	2
2	6	4	6	8	5	6	7	5	3
5	5	2	2	6	8	4	6	2	1
6	8	3	5	4	1	8	4	4	4

131	132	133	134	135	136	137	138	139	140
8	2	6	6	2	6	8	4	4	1
2	4	8	2	7	2	2	8	8	7
3	3	5	4	8	1	4	3	3	2
5	5	2	5	1	5	6	5	7	6
7	6	1	1	5	4	1	2	5	4
4	8	7	8	6	7	3	7	2	3
6	7	3	7	3	3	5	1	1	5
1	1	4	3	4	8	7	6	6	8

141	142	143	144	145	146	147	148	149	150
1	8	8	3	8	6	3	2	3	1
6	4	7	2	4	2	2	5	4	7
2	1	5	5	3	4	1	7	2	2
5	3	1	7	7	8	8	8	6	8
8	6	2	1	6	1	7	3	1	4
7	7	3	4	5	5	4	1	5	3
3	2	4	8	2	3	6	6	8	5
4	5	6	6	1	7	5	4	7	6

151	152	153	154	155	156	157	158	159	160
7	3	5	5	4	6	5	3	3	7
8	2	1	4	2	7	3	6	1	1
4	8	4	8	6	3	2	4	4	4
5	4	7	3	3	4	1	1	8	5
3	1	3	1	8	1	4	7	7	8
1	6	6	7	5	2	6	2	2	2
2	5	2	2	7	5	7	5	5	3
6	7	8	6	1	8	8	8	6	6

161	162	163	164	165	166	167	168	169	170
4	5	7	2	3	7	1	3	4	6
5	2	4	7	5	1	7	5	5	7
8	7	1	8	1	3	4	2	3	2
6	8	3	5	7	2	6	1	1	4
3	1	8	3	2	5	2	8	2	1
2	3	2	1	6	8	8	7	8	8
1	6	5	6	8	6	3	6	6	5
7	4	6	4	4	4	5	4	7	3

171	172	173	174	175	176	177	178	179	180
2	2	6	1	3	7	7	5	1	1
6	7	5	5	1	2	4	8	2	8
7	6	8	2	2	8	3	3	3	2
1	8	1	8	6	4	8	6	6	6
5	5	4	7	4	5	6	2	5	7
4	3	3	3	5	1	1	7	4	5
8	4	7	6	8	3	5	1	8	3
3	1	2	4	7	6	2	4	7	4

181	182	183	184	185	186	187	188	189	190
5	6	4	2	6	6	6	6	5	5
1	8	1	4	8	8	1	8	4	4
6	3	7	1	4	2	4	5	6	3
2	5	6	3	5	4	5	4	3	6
4	4	3	6	7	5	2	3	7	7
7	7	5	7	3	7	3	7	2	8
8	2	2	5	2	3	7	1	1	2
3	1	8	8	1	1	8	2	8	1

191	192	193	194	195	196	197	198	199	200
8	7	4	5	4	8	8	3	6	4
6	6	3	3	5	7	5	7	2	2
7	5	6	2	7	1	2	5	8	7
2	4	2	8	8	2	1	6	3	3
4	8	8	4	2	3	7	8	7	6
5	1	7	1	3	4	6	2	5	1
3	3	5	6	1	6	3	1	4	5
1	2	1	7	6	5	4	4	1	8

201	202	203	204	205	206	207	208	209	210
5	3	2	6	8	7	7	2	2	7
8	1	8	2	3	6	4	7	5	6
2	7	7	5	4	1	3	6	1	2
1	2	4	8	7	2	2	3	6	3
6	5	5	4	6	5	6	8	8	1
7	4	1	7	1	4	8	4	7	4
4	8	3	3	5	8	1	1	3	8
3	6	6	1	2	3	5	5	4	5

211	212	213	214	215	216	217	218	219	220
7	5	1	7	3	5	1	2	1	2
5	3	7	5	1	2	7	1	2	5
1	8	8	8	2	1	6	7	6	8
6	4	6	4	6	7	2	3	5	4
2	2	3	6	7	3	3	6	4	1
4	1	4	2	4	8	8	8	3	7
8	6	5	3	8	4	4	4	8	6
3	7	2	1	5	6	5	5	7	3

221	222	223	224	225	226	227	228	229	230
5	1	3	7	2	6	1	2	6	8
8	3	2	2	4	1	5	3	5	6
2	6	4	6	8	3	3	8	7	7
7	8	5	1	3	2	4	5	1	1
6	4	8	3	7	4	7	7	2	4
1	2	7	4	5	5	8	4	3	2
3	7	6	8	6	7	6	6	4	3
4	5	1	5	1	8	2	1	8	5

231	232	233	234	235	236	237	238	239	240
6	5	8	1	8	1	5	4	7	8
2	4	3	2	5	3	3	5	6	2
8	8	6	5	4	8	2	3	2	5
3	1	5	3	2	2	8	1	5	6
7	3	1	4	3	7	7	2	1	1
4	7	7	7	1	4	1	7	4	3
5	6	2	8	6	5	6	8	8	7
1	2	4	6	7	6	4	6	3	4

	243	244	245	246	247	248	249	250
	8	3	7	7	7	8	2	7
	6	4	5	2	2	4	3	5
6	5	1	6	1	3	2	6	8
1	7	5	4	8	6	7	1	6
8	3	6	8	3	1	3	5	3
4	4	8	3	5	5	1	7	4
5	2	7	2	4	4	5	8	1
7	1	2	1	6	8	6	4	2

251	252	253	254	255	256	257	258	259	260
5	4	3	3	8	5	4	8	1	1
6	5	6	2	7	3	8	4	6	2
7	8	7	8	3	1	6	1	3	4
1	1	2	6	5	4	5	5	8	7
2	3	1	7	4	6	3	7	5	8
3	2	8	5	2	2	1	3	2	6
4	6	5	4	1	8	2	6	4	3
8	7	4	1	6	7	7	2	7	5

261	262	263	264	265	266	267	268	269	270
4	2	7	7	4	6	7	5	7	4
8	5	6	1	2	1	4	3	2	6
2	3	4	8	5	7	6	8	6	3
3	6	1	3	7	8	8	1	5	7
1	8	3	6	3	3	5	4	4	8
7	7	5	5	6	4	3	2	3	1
5	1	2	4	1	5	2	7	1	5
6	4	8	2	8	2	1	6	8	2

271	272	273	274	275	276	277	278	279	280
8	1	3	7	2	8	1	2	8	2
7	7	8	3	6	1	5	1	2	5
4	3	5	5	1	3	4	8	7	1
1	5	4	6	7	4	2	3	3	3
2	2	6	2	8	6	7	4	6	6
3	6	2	8	4	5	8	5	4	4
5	4	7	4	3	7	6	7	5	8
6	8	1	1	5	2	3	6	1	7

281	282	283	284	285	286	287	288	289	290
4	2	8	7	5	3	7	2	7	1
8	6	7	3	2	4	3	1	5	4
2	7	1	4	1	1	5	5	1	2
7	5	2	5	3	7	8	4	2	3
5	1	6	8	7	2	1	3	4	7
3	4	5	1	6	8	2	6	3	8
6	8	4	2	8	5	6	7	8	5
1	3	3	6	4	6	4	8	6	6

291	292	293	294	295	296	297	298	299	300
3	6	1	1	8	3	3	5	1	7
2	3	3	7	5	4	8	7	4	5
7	7	6	6	7	8	6	4	5	2
4	1	2	2	6	5	1	2	3	6
1	8	4	4	2	7	2	3	2	4
6	4	7	5	4	2	7	6	6	1
5	5	5	8	1	6	4	8	8	3
8	2	8	3	3	1	5	1	7	8

301	302	303	304	305	306	307	308	309	310
4	2	7	5	7	7	7	6	8	8
2	8	6	7	4	3	8	8	2	6
6	7	1	1	5	2	3	3	6	5
7	5	3	6	6	1	5	5	5	2
8	1	5	3	8	8	2	7	4	1
3	4	2	8	2	5	1	2	1	7
1	3	4	2	1	6	6	1	7	4
5	6	8	4	3	4	4	4	3	3

311	312	313	314	315	316	317	318	319	320
4	3	5	5	3	5	7	7	6	5
1	6	7	2	6	6	3	4	4	3
2	8	8	3	5	4	4	1	7	1
6	4	2	1	4	1	6	5	3	6
8	7	1	8	7	8	2	2	5	2
3	1	4	6	2	2	8	8	8	4
5	5	3	7	1	7	1	3	1	8
7	2	6	4	8	3	5	6	2	7

321	322	323	324	325	326	327	328	329	330
6	3	7	1	2	4	4	7	4	2
1	6	8	7	1	6	1	1	6	6
3	7	3	6	6	7	5	5	1	5
2	4	2	5	3	2	7	3	5	3
8	5	5	2	5	8	6	8	2	1
7	1	6	8	8	3	3	4	8	4
4	2	4	4	4	5	2	6	3	7
5	8	1	3	7	1	8	2	7	8

331	332	333	334	335	336	337	338	339	340
7	1	6	2	3	5	6	3	3	8
2	6	3	4	2	3	8	5	5	2
4	7	2	7	5	6	3	6	1	3
6	4	5	5	4	2	5	1	6	1
1	5	1	1	7	7	2	4	2	7
5	3	4	8	1	4	1	2	8	6
8	8	8	6	8	1	4	7	4	4
3	2	7	3	6	8	7	8	7	5

341	342	343	344	345	346	347	348	349	350
1	5	6	7	2	1	7	8	8	2
5	2	8	6	5	2	5	4	5	8
7	3	2	8	3	6	1	3	3	4
2	4	3	2	6	5	6	6	2	6
4	6	7	5	7	3	4	7	1	3
8	7	4	4	1	4	8	5	6	1
3	8	1	3	8	7	3	2	4	7
6	1	5	1	4	8	2	1	7	5

351	352	353	354	355	356	357	358	359	360
1	5	8	5	5	5	1	7	3	2
5	1	7	8	3	8	3	3	6	1
7	2	5	4	7	2	6	1	2	6
6	6	2	6	2	4	2	8	5	8
4	4	3	2	1	1	4	2	8	5
2	3	4	3	8	7	8	4	7	4
3	7	1	7	6	6	7	5	4	7
8	8	6	1	4	3	5	6	1	3

361	362	363	364	365	366	367	368	369	370
1	1	4	8	8	1	8	3	3	8
7	6	6	6	4	8	7	5	7	2
3	5	3	2	2	6	2	2	5	6
8	3	2	4	5	2	3	1	6	4
4	7	1	1	3	3	6	8	2	5
5	8	5	7	1	5	5	6	1	3
6	4	7	3	6	4	1	4	4	7
2	2	8	5	7	7	4	7	8	1

371	372	373	374	375	376	377	378	379	380
8	4	5	3	6	5	7	6	8	3
6	7	3	1	5	3	3	4	7	1
3	6	1	5	4	7	5	2	2	8
1	5	6	6	2	6	1	8	1	6
7	1	2	2	3	8	6	1	3	4
5	3	7	4	1	2	8	5	5	5
2	2	8	8	8	1	2	7	6	7
4	8	4	7	7	4	4	3	4	2

381	382	383	384	385	386	387	388	389	390
7	7	8	1	4	8	3	8	5	3
3	6	5	7	5	1	2	3	4	7
2	5	7	5	3	4	8	7	8	4
8	8	6	6	7	7	5	5	7	5
5	3	4	8	2	3	1	4	1	1
1	2	3	2	6	6	7	1	3	2
4	1	1	4	1	5	6	6	2	6
6	4	2	3	8	2	4	2	6	8

391	392	393	394	395	396	397	398	399	400
4	8	5	8	2	3	6	6	6	1
2	5	7	6	5	2	1	1	4	2
3	7	4	3	6	1	5	2	5	5
6	1	1	4	4	8	2	3	8	4
5	6	6	1	8	6	8	8	2	3
1	3	8	7	3	4	3	4	1	8
8	4	2	5	1	7	4	7	7	6
7	2	3	2	7	5	7	5	3	7

401	402	403	404	405	406	407	408	409	410
6	8	1	8	5	2	6	5	3	2
1	6	8	1	6	4	7	8	2	8
4	5	6	5	2	7	2	6	4	4
2	3	5	7	1	1	8	7	7	1
8	7	2	2	7	5	1	2	8	6
5	4	3	4	8	6	4	3	6	7
7	1	7	3	4	8	3	4	1	5
3	2	4	6	3	3	5	1	5	3

411	412	413	414	415	416	417	418	419	420
1	3	4	2	1	2	4	7	7	3
5	6	1	4	7	8	5	3	6	7
3	2	8	8	2	4	1	4	5	1
8	8	5	3	4	1	6	1	4	2
4	1	7	1	5	3	7	2	8	6
6	7	3	5	8	5	2	8	2	4
7	5	6	6	6	7	3	6	3	8
2	4	2	7	3	6	8	5	1	5

421	422	423	424	425	426	427	428	429	430
1	7	5	6	2	5	4	5	6	1
4	2	4	5	3	4	1	3	2	8
7	8	2	2	1	2	8	6	7	4
3	4	6	3	8	1	3	2	5	6
2	6	1	8	4	3	5	8	3	7
5	1	7	4	5	8	7	4	1	5
8	3	8	7	6	6	2	7	4	2
6	5	3	1	7	7	6	1	8	3

431	432	433	434	435	436	437	438	439	440
7	2	7	8	8	2	8	8	2	6
2	8	6	6	5	7	4	5	7	5
8	5	8	7	2	4	5	2	8	4
6	6	5	5	3	6	2	6	6	2
4	1	2	1	1	1	6	3	5	7
1	4	3	2	4	8	3	1	1	8
5	7	1	3	6	3	7	4	3	3
3	3	4	4	7	5	1	7	4	1

441	442	443	444	445	446	447	448	449	450
8	5	1	8	1	3	1	5	5	3
6	1	2	7	7	8	4	8	2	4
1	8	3	2	5	6	6	4	3	1
7	3	7	4	6	1	2	6	1	8
3	6	8	6	2	5	3	7	8	2
4	7	6	5	4	7	8	3	6	7
2	4	5	3	3	4	5	2	7	5
5	2	4	1	8	2	7	1	4	6

451	452	453	454	455	456	457	458	459	460
3	5	1	5	3	8	2	2	2	2
5	6	8	1	8	3	1	6	6	7
6	1	7	6	4	6	3	4	3	4
2	3	2	7	7	1	4	5	8	1
7	4	5	8	6	4	7	3	4	6
4	8	6	2	5	2	5	1	5	8
1	7	3	3	2	7	8	7	1	3
8	2	4	4	1	5	6	8	7	5

461	462	463	464	465	466	467	468	469	470
6	2	1	4	4	5	6	7	1	6
5	5	5	8	5	2	5	3	4	4
7	4	2	7	7	1	3	8	5	8
3	7	3	5	1	8	2	6	7	1
8	6	7	3	3	6	8	5	8	3
2	1	6	1	6	4	7	1	2	2
1	8	8	2	8	3	4	4	3	5
4	3	4	6	2	7	1	2	6	7

471	472	473	474	475	476	477	478	479	480
6	2	6	6	2	6	4	7	3	3
4	1	8	3	3	4	2	8	5	5
2	7	4	2	7	5	3	5	1	4
5	8	1	4	1	2	7	6	8	6
7	3	3	7	4	3	6	1	6	2
8	5	2	8	8	8	1	4	7	1
1	4	7	1	6	7	8	2	2	7
3	6	5	5	5	1	5	3	4	8

481	482	483	484	485	486	487	488	489	490
7	3	2	1	4	2	6	5	7	4
4	2	3	6	8	7	8	8	1	6
3	8	7	8	1	4	5	3	2	1
6	5	6	7	5	1	3	1	8	3
1	4	4	5	7	3	4	7	3	8
5	7	5	3	6	5	7	6	6	7
2	1	8	4	3	6	2	2	4	2
8	6	1	2	2	8	1	4	5	5

491	492	493	494	495	496	497	498	499	500
2	2	2	4	8	7	6	1	6	2
8	6	1	2	5	4	8	2	4	1
3	5	7	5	2	3	1	5	2	4
4	1	6	6	7	8	2	7	8	8
7	4	3	8	3	1	5	4	5	3
6	7	5	7	1	2	7	6	3	6
1	3	8	3	6	5	3	8	1	7
5	8	4	1	4	6	4	3	7	5

501	502	503	504	505	506	507	508	509	510
5	2	5	1	1	7	1	2	3	7
1	7	4	2	7	3	2	7	1	5
4	3	1	7	3	8	6	8	2	4
2	8	6	3	2	4	4	5	5	6
3	1	3	6	5	5	7	1	7	1
8	4	7	5	8	6	5	4	6	3
7	6	2	8	4	1	8	3	8	8
6	5	8	4	6	2	3	6	4	2

511	512	513	514	515	516	517	518	519	520
4	1	5	6	7	7	3	6	1	2
2	6	1	4	2	5	6	2	6	4
5	8	6	2	3	4	8	5	3	3
7	3	7	1	6	2	4	1	8	5
8	2	2	5	1	3	2	3	5	1
3	7	8	8	5	6	1	4	2	7
1	4	4	3	4	1	7	7	7	6
6	5	3	7	8	8	5	8	4	8

521	522	523	524	525	526	527	528	529	530
2	8	4	6	1	7	4	2	4	5
5	6	3	7	6	2	6	7	8	3
7	1	6	4	7	1	1	5	5	2
6	3	7	1	2	5	5	4	3	1
3	5	8	2	5	6	7	6	2	8
8	2	1	3	4	4	8	8	7	7
1	4	2	8	3	8	2	1	1	6
4	7	5	5	8	3	3	3	6	4

531	532	533	534	535	536	537	538	539	540
1	7	6	4	7	3	8	5	3	6
5	5	3	8	5	4	1	7	6	7
8	4	8	1	6	2	7	4	8	2
7	1	1	5	3	8	6	3	4	3
6	8	2	7	1	7	2	8	2	5
2	6	5	2	2	6	5	1	1	4
3	2	7	3	4	1	3	2	5	8
4	3	4	6	8	5	4	6	7	1

541	542	543	544	545	546	547	548	549	550
6	3	6	3	8	4	3	8	4	7
7	5	8	4	2	3	1	1	3	3
5	7	2	2	6	2	4	6	7	4
3	8	3	1	4	7	8	2	2	2
2	6	1	6	5	5	2	7	6	8
1	1	7	8	7	1	5	3	1	1
4	2	4	5	1	8	6	4	5	6
8	4	5	7	3	6	7	5	8	5

551	552	553	554	555	556	557	558	559	560
8	3	8	5	2	7	2	5	8	3
5	5	6	3	5	3	8	4	3	8
3	2	7	7	6	2	6	1	1	5
7	6	4	4	4	1	5	7	5	1
4	1	3	8	3	4	7	2	4	6
6	8	1	2	1	5	4	3	7	4
1	4	2	1	7	8	1	6	6	2
2	7	5	6	8	6	3	8	2	7

561	562	563	564	565	566	567	568	569	570
7	7	7	4	1	3	4	2	1	8
6	8	8	3	6	1	8	4	2	5
8	4	6	1	4	7	1	5	4	2
5	2	5	2	2	6	3	6	3	1
2	6	2	8	8	4	5	7	6	3
3	3	3	7	5	5	2	1	5	6
4	5	1	6	3	8	7	8	7	4
1	1	4	5	7	2	6	3	8	7

571	572	573	574	575	576	577	578	579	580
3	2	8	3	5	4	1	5	1	4
8	7	1	4	3	1	4	6	2	2
6	1	4	1	8	2	3	3	4	3
1	6	5	5	2	3	8	4	5	7
4	5	2	7	7	5	2	7	3	6
5	4	7	8	4	7	5	1	7	1
7	3	6	6	1	6	7	8	6	8
2	8	3	2	6	8	6	2	8	5

581	582	583	584	585	586	587	588	589	590
4	4	1	8	2	1	5	3	6	1
2	1	6	2	7	8	1	5	1	4
6	6	5	4	4	6	3	8	2	2
7	5	8	5	5	7	2	6	7	7
5	7	4	3	6	4	4	4	3	5
3	3	7	6	3	5	6	2	5	8
8	8	2	1	1	3	8	7	4	6
1	2	3	7	8	2	7	1	8	3

591	592	593	594	595	596	597	598	599	600
6	2	4	6	2	7	6	6	8	7
2	1	8	1	3	8	5	4	2	8
3	7	7	3	1	3	3	5	3	3
5	6	3	5	4	1	1	8	5	1
1	5	2	4	8	4	7	3	6	4
7	8	6	7	6	5	4	1	1	6
8	4	1	2	7	2	2	7	4	2
4	3	5	8	5	6	8	2	7	5

601	602	603	604	605	606	607	608	609	610
8	5	6	3	3	3	5	6	5	1
1	6	8	4	4	6	6	4	8	3
7	3	5	8	1	1	2	7	1	8
3	1	4	7	2	4	3	1	7	4
4	8	7	6	6	7	7	5	4	2
5	4	3	2	5	8	8	8	3	5
6	7	1	5	8	2	1	3	6	6
2	2	2	1	7	5	4	2	2	7

611	612	613	614	615	616	617	618	619	620
3	5	1	1	4	5	3	3	6	4
6	7	6	6	8	4	7	6	2	8
1	8	2	3	7	6	4	1	3	2
8	6	5	5	2	1	6	8	5	5
5	3	4	8	3	3	8	7	8	6
7	4	7	7	1	7	1	2	7	3
4	2	8	4	6	8	2	4	4	7
2	1	3	2	5	2	5	5	1	1

621	622	623	624	625	626	627	628	629	630
7	6	8	6	8	6	5	3	3	2
3	4	6	7	3	5	7	2	1	1
4	2	2	4	7	1	2	7	4	7
2	7	3	2	2	2	1	1	7	8
8	5	1	1	6	7	6	4	8	3
1	1	5	3	1	3	8	8	5	4
5	3	7	8	4	8	4	6	2	5
6	8	4	5	5	4	3	5	6	6

631	632	633	634	635	636	637	638	639	640
4	6	6	7	5	1	6	8	6	4
8	7	1	4	4	7	4	5	4	6
2	3	5	6	8	2	5	6	7	8
3	8	7	8	6	4	1	2	1	7
1	1	3	3	7	6	8	4	2	3
7	4	2	5	1	5	7	1	5	5
5	5	8	2	3	3	2	3	3	2
6	2	4	1	2	8	3	7	8	1

641	642	643	644	645	646	647	648	649	650
2	6	8	7	3	2	8	1	5	7
1	7	7	6	4	3	3	7	6	4
7	3	3	2	7	8	5	5	2	1
3	4	5	4	5	1	7	6	3	5
4	8	4	1	1	7	4	2	1	3
8	1	1	8	8	4	6	4	8	8
5	2	2	3	2	6	1	3	7	2
6	5	6	5	6	5	2	8	4	6

651	652	653	654	655	656	657	658	659	660
2	2	2	2	5	4	7	5	3	3
6	7	1	3	4	2	8	2	8	4
8	5	4	5	1	8	1	1	5	7
7	4	3	8	6	7	2	6	4	8
4	8	7	1	7	6	4	3	2	1
1	3	5	4	8	3	5	7	6	5
3	6	8	6	2	1	3	4	7	2
5	1	6	7	3	5	6	8	1	6

661	662	663	664	665	666	667	668	669	670
8	3	3	1	4	6	6	6	1	7
4	2	6	4	1	3	7	7	2	2
7	4	7	5	7	5	3	3	3	8
2	8	4	2	6	7	5	2	4	1
5	6	1	8	8	2	4	4	7	3
3	5	5	3	3	4	2	1	6	6
6	7	2	7	2	1	8	5	5	5
1	1	8	6	5	8	1	8	8	4

671	672	673	674	675	676	677	678	679	680
3	3	1	5	4	2	7	4	4	4
6	2	8	3	5	1	6	1	1	8
7	5	4	1	8	6	5	8	6	3
5	8	3	8	7	7	3	2	8	6
8	7	2	6	6	5	4	3	5	1
1	6	7	7	1	8	8	7	3	2
4	1	5	2	3	4	1	6	7	7
2	4	6	4	2	3	2	5	2	5

681	682	683	684	685	686	687	688	689	690
6	2	6	1	4	4	1	7	8	4
8	3	5	8	3	1	3	1	2	8
1	6	3	2	5	7	7	5	5	7
5	4	7	7	2	2	4	8	1	5
7	8	2	4	6	3	6	4	6	3
2	7	4	3	7	6	8	2	3	2
4	1	8	5	1	5	5	6	7	6
3	5	1	6	8	8	2	3	4	1

691	692	693	694	695	696	697	698	699	700
2	3	4	6	2	1	2	4	5	5
7	7	7	2	4	2	8	3	4	4
1	2	1	5	1	7	5	8	6	7
3	1	6	3	3	8	6	6	7	1
8	6	8	4	7	4	7	1	3	2
4	4	2	8	5	6	3	5	2	6
5	5	5	1	8	5	4	7	8	8
6	8	3	7	6	3	1	2	1	3

701	702	703	704	705	706	707	708	709	710
8	1	8	5	6	4	7	4	1	7
5	3	7	7	8	5	5	6	8	8
4	2	6	2	7	2	4	3	2	6
3	6	3	8	1	6	1	8	3	5
7	4	2	6	4	1	8	7	7	4
1	7	5	1	5	8	2	1	5	1
2	5	4	3	3	7	6	2	6	3
6	8	1	4	2	3	3	5	4	2

711	712	713	714	715	716	717	718	719	720
2	7	1	8	8	4	4	8	1	5
5	2	6	6	2	3	3	4	5	4
6	6	5	5	3	2	2	5	4	6
1	8	7	4	1	5	1	7	2	7
3	3	4	7	4	6	7	6	3	8
7	1	8	1	5	8	6	2	8	1
4	5	2	2	6	7	8	1	7	2
8	4	3	3	7	1	5	3	6	3

721	722	723	724	725	726	727	728	729	730
4	3	2	3	2	8	1	3	8	1
1	7	5	8	1	7	3	1	6	6
3	2	6	4	3	1	8	4	7	2
8	5	1	1	5	5	2	7	4	3
7	1	7	5	4	3	7	8	3	8
6	8	3	7	8	2	6	6	5	5
2	6	4	6	6	4	5	2	2	4
5	4	8	2	7	6	4	5	1	7

731	732	733	734	735	736	737	738	739	740
2	3	1	4	1	6	3	7	7	1
8	6	8	2	8	2	7	1	5	2
3	8	2	7	4	7	8	5	1	6
1	4	4	5	2	5	1	6	6	5
7	5	7	8	7	4	5	3	8	8
4	7	6	1	3	8	2	8	3	7
6	2	5	3	5	3	6	4	2	4
5	1	3	6	6	1	4	2	4	3

741	742	743	744	745	746	747	748	749	750
4	6	6	2	3	2	8	4	4	4
7	3	7	4	6	5	4	6	3	8
1	5	3	3	2	7	1	8	2	2
6	4	2	1	1	8	2	1	8	3
5	1	5	6	8	4	6	3	1	7
3	7	4	5	4	6	5	7	5	6
8	8	8	7	5	3	3	5	6	1
2	2	1	8	7	1	7	2	7	5

751	752	753	754	755	756	757	758	759	760
7	1	6	3	1	2	7	8	4	3
5	5	5	1	7	3	3	6	1	7
1	8	8	2	5	6	6	1	2	5
6	3	3	7	4	7	8	4	7	2
3	6	4	5	3	8	5	7	5	8
8	2	2	8	6	1	1	2	3	4
2	4	1	4	8	5	4	3	6	6
4	7	7	6	2	4	2	5	8	1

761	762	763	764	765	766	767	768	769	770
2	5	5	4	6	2	5	2	4	1
1	1	3	8	8	3	1	6	6	6
5	2	8	3	2	8	7	4	5	5
3	7	6	5	5	5	8	3	1	7
6	6	7	6	3	4	3	1	2	2
4	3	2	7	1	6	4	5	8	8
8	8	4	2	7	7	2	7	3	4
7	4	1	1	4	1	6	8	7	3

771	772	773	774	775	776	777	778	779	780
3	2	1	8	5	2	6	5	6	1
5	1	6	5	8	7	8	6	8	7
1	7	5	4	3	6	7	1	5	5
7	3	3	3	4	5	4	2	7	2
2	5	4	6	7	8	5	3	1	8
4	8	8	1	1	1	2	8	2	4
6	4	7	7	6	3	3	7	3	3
8	6	2	2	2	4	1	4	4	6

781	782	783	784	785	786	787	788	789	790
7	8	3	3	5	7	5	1	3	5
8	2	7	7	8	5	1	5	6	7
1	1	2	4	4	4	7	2	5	3
4	3	5	2	7	2	2	3	1	8
3	5	1	5	2	6	3	7	2	4
5	7	6	8	3	1	8	6	7	6
2	6	8	1	1	3	4	4	8	1
6	4	4	6	6	8	6	8	4	2

791	792	793	794	795	796	797	798	799	800
3	7	5	2	7	8	1	8	8	8
2	3	6	1	4	2	2	4	2	4
5	8	3	4	8	6	6	1	3	6
6	5	8	7	5	3	4	3	5	7
1	1	1	6	1	4	7	6	4	1
8	6	2	8	6	7	8	5	1	2
4	4	4	3	2	1	5	2	6	3
7	2	7	5	3	5	3	7	7	5

801	802	803	804	805	806	807	808	809	810
4	2	8	4	5	7	5	7	2	8
6	7	7	1	8	4	2	8	5	7
8	1	4	7	3	6	8	1	1	1
2	8	2	2	7	8	7	4	3	3
1	4	6	5	6	1	4	6	7	6
3	3	1	6	4	2	3	3	8	4
5	6	5	3	2	5	6	5	6	5
7	5	3	8	1	3	1	2	4	2

811	812	813	814	815	816	817	818	819	820
3	5	5	3	2	5	4	4	4	3
7	8	2	1	6	8	2	1	5	2
6	2	4	4	1	6	7	5	7	8
2	1	6	6	5	4	6	2	8	6
1	4	7	7	8	2	1	6	1	7
5	3	3	2	7	3	8	7	6	1
4	6	1	8	3	7	5	3	2	4
8	7	8	5	4	1	3	8	3	5

821	822	823	824	825	826	827	828	829	830
5	7	3	3	3	3	2	8	2	1
6	6	6	5	5	7	7	5	4	8
8	2	8	2	8	4	3	3	1	3
7	8	1	8	6	5	5	7	6	5
4	1	5	4	1	8	4	1	7	4
2	5	4	6	4	6	1	4	3	6
3	3	7	7	2	1	8	6	8	2
1	4	2	1	7	2	6	2	5	7

831	832	833	834	835	836	837	838	839	840
2	7	6	3	4	2	5	7	7	8
4	8	1	2	3	7	4	4	3	2
1	6	4	1	5	3	6	2	5	3
8	5	3	4	8	5	7	8	1	4
3	3	2	7	2	4	8	3	8	6
6	4	8	5	6	1	3	5	4	5
5	1	5	8	1	8	1	1	6	7
7	2	7	6	7	6	2	6	2	1

841	842	843	844	845	846	847	848	849	850
4	1	1	3	3	7	1	7	2	1
5	3	5	1	1	3	2	1	1	7
8	8	4	8	8	8	8	3	8	6
6	2	6	6	7	4	4	8	7	3
7	7	2	5	6	2	3	5	3	8
3	4	8	2	5	6	7	˙6	5	5
1	5	3	7	4	1	6	4	6	2
2	6	7	4	2	5	5	2	4	4

851	852	853	854	855	856	857	858	859	860
4	5	6	7	3	7	7	6	8	4
1	3	1	1	1	5	2	2	6	5
6	6	8	4	5	8	1	7	4	3
7	8	5	8	4	1	8	4	1	6
3	7	4	3	6	2	5	8	5	2
2	4	2	2	2	4	4	3	3	1
5	1	3	5	7	3	3	1	2	7
8	2	7	6	8	6	6	5	7	8

861	862	863	864	865	866	867	868	869	870
2	2	4	5	5	4	7	6	5	5
3	4	6	3	7	8	5	3	8	1
1	1	1	1	6	3	4	1	6	6
8	6	3	8	2	2	8	2	3	4
7	3	2	7	8	1	2	7	4	7
6	8	8	2	3	5	3	4	7	8
5	7	5	4	4	7	1	8	1	2
4	5	7	6	1	6	6	5	2	3

871	872	873	874	875	876	877	878	879	880
6	7	7	4	6	8	8	2	4	2
8	4	2	5	5	7	2	4	7	5
4	5	6	7	3	6	3	1	8	6
3	6	4	3	1	1	1	3	2	1
5	8	8	6	8	3	4	5	6	7
2	3	3	2	4	4	5	8	1	4
7	2	5	1	7	2	7	6	3	3
1	1	1	8	2	5	6	7	5	8

881	882	883	884	885	886	887	888	889	890
4	5	1	6	1	4	7	1	5	8
6	2	4	5	5	8	6	2	1	5
3	7	5	1	6	5	1	8	8	2
2	3	3	8	8	7	2	6	3	3
8	4	7	4	2	1	5	3	7	6
7	6	8	3	4	6	8	5	4	7
1	1	2	7	3	2	4	7	2	1
5	8	6	2	7	3	3	4	6	4

891	892	893	894	895	896	897	898	899	900
5	5	4	3	4	5	1	4	5	6
2	4	1	7	5	3	8	8	6	4
6	1	7	2	8	4	7	3	7	5
1	3	8	8	1	2	5	1	8	7
8	7	3	6	6	8	6	7	3	2
3	8	6	5	7	7	3	2	2	8
7	6	2	4	3	1	2	5	1	1
4	2	5	1	2	6	4	6	4	3

901	902	903	904	905	906	907	908	909	910
2	1	2	7	2	2	4	1	2	1
5	2	4	3	1	4	6	6	7	4
4	3	1	1	4	6	2	7	1	3
6	8	6	8	7	8	7	5	8	7
1	7	5	5	5	1	3	8	4	8
3	4	8	6	6	7	8	3	6	2
7	6	7	4	3	3	1	4	5	6
8	5	3	2	8	5	5	2	3	5

911	912	913	914	915	916	917	918	919	920
5	7	3	1	5	4	1	5	7	8
3	3	5	6	1	6	8	2	5	7
4	6	2	4	8	2	4	3	2	6
1	5	7	8	7	1	3	7	8	1
6	1	1	2	3	8	7	4	3	2
7	2	8	7	4	5	6	1	1	3
2	8	6	5	6	3	5	6	4	4
8	4	4	3	2	7	2	8	6	5

921	922	923	924	925	926	927	928	929	930
2	8	6	8	6	7	8	7	2	6
8	7	7	3	1	3	1	2	5	8
4	5	4	5	2	8	2	8	7	2
6	4	2	2	7	1	6	5	6	1
1	3	3	6	4	2	5	3	3	3
3	2	5	1	5	5	4	6	8	4
5	1	1	4	8	4	7	4	4	5
7	6	8	7	3	6	3	1	1	7

931	932	933	934	935	936	937	938	939	940
7	4	2	5	7	6	8	6	1	2
2	7	4	8	3	4	2	3	5	6
4	5	3	4	1	8	4	1	8	3
8	1	8	2	5	5	3	5	6	4
3	2	7	7	6	7	7	8	4	8
5	6	6	1	2	3	1	2	2	5
6	8	5	3	4	1	6	7	7	1
1	3	1	6	8	2	5	4	3	7

941	942	943	944	945	946	947	948	949	950
3	8	6	2	8	6	4	3	2	3
5	7	7	3	4	8	6	6	1	1
7	4	8	7	5	4	5	4	6	8
1	5	4	6	6	5	1	2	7	6
6	2	5	1	7	2	3	5	8	5
8	1	3	5	2	1	2	8	5	7
4	3	2	8	1	7	8	7	4	4
2	6	1	4	3	3	7	1	3	2

951	952	953	954	955	956	957	958	959	960
6	7	2	8	5	5	8	4	1	5
1	6	8	7	1	4	5	1	5	2
3	2	3	3	6	1	4	5	2	4
4	5	1	1	8	6	3	3	4	8
8	8	6	5	7	3	6	8	8	7
7	1	7	4	2	7	7	6	6	3
2	3	4	2	4	2	1	7	7	1
5	4	5	6	3	8	2	2	3	6

961	962	963	964	965	966	967	968	969	970
6	1	6	6	3	6	2	3	2	8
3	8	3	4	4	1	7	2	1	1
1	5	1	5	5	8	3	6	7	2
8	4	2	2	7	5	1	5	4	7
7	7	5	7	1	3	8	1	3	5
2	2	4	3	6	4	6	4	6	4
4	6	8	1	8	7	4	8	5	6
5	3	7	8	2	2	5	7	8	3

971	972	973	974	975	976	977	978	979	980
6	7	4	7	7	5	7	4	3	8
2	3	5	1	6	4	1	5	1	4
5	5	7	3	5	3	6	6	6	2
3	2	2	6	3	7	3	3	5	7
1	8	3	2	2	6	2	7	7	3
4	1	1	4	8	2	5	1	4	6
8	6	8	8	4	1	4	2	2	5
7	4	6	5	1	8	8	8	8	1

981	982	983	984	985	986	987	988	989	990
4	2	1	4	3	1	4	6	4	2
8	6	8	5	2	4	3	7	8	8
5	1	4	2	8	6	5	5	6	7
2	7	7	1	6	8	8	3	5	1
6	4	2	8	7	7	2	2	1	5
1	5	6	3	1	2	1	8	3	6
3	8	5	7	4	3	7	4	2	3
7	3	3	6	5	5	6	1	7	4

991	992	993	994	995	996	997	998	999	1000
1	7	1	1	7	2	3	3	4	6
2	2	7	7	8	6	6	8	8	4
4	8	8	3	4	1	7	7	2	5
5	1	2	4	5	4	1	5	5	1
7	4	6	8	3	7	5	2	1	2
6	6	4	6	1	8	4	6	6	8
8	5	3	2	6	5	8	4	7	3
3	3	5	5	2	3	2	1	3	7

AUTHOR INDEX

SUBJECT INDEX